Handbook of
Cross-Cultural Psychology

Handbook of Cross-Cultural Psychology
Second Edition

Edited by John W. Berry, Ype H. Poortinga, Janak Pandey,
Pierre R. Dasen, T. S. Saraswathi, Marshall H. Segall,
and Cigdem Kagitçibasi

VOLUME 1
Theory and Method

VOLUME 2
Basic Processes and Human Development

VOLUME 3
Social Behavior and Applications

性相近　習相遠

**Basic human nature is similar at birth;
Different habits make us seem remote.**

From the *San Zi Jing*

Second Edition

Handbook of
Cross-Cultural Psychology

VOLUME 1
THEORY AND METHOD

Edited by

John W. Berry
Queen's University, Canada

Ype H. Poortinga
Tilburg University, The Netherlands

Janak Pandey
University of Allahabad, India

Allyn and Bacon
Boston • London • Toronto • Sydney • Tokyo • Singapore

Library of Congress Cataloging-in-Publication Data

Handbook of cross-cultural psychology. -- 2nd ed.
      p.   cm.
    Includes bibliographical references and index.
    Contents: v. 1. Theory and method / edited by John W. Berry, Ype
H. Poortinga, Janak Pandey.
    ISBN 0-205-16074-3 (v. 1)
    1. Ethnopsychology.   I. Berry, John W.
GN502.H36   1996
155.82—dc20   96-16261
                                                          C I P

Printed in the United States of America
10   9   8   7   6   5   4   3   2   00   99   98

CONTENTS

VOLUME 1: THEORY AND METHOD
Edited by J. W. Berry, Y. H. Poortinga & J. Pandey

VOLUME 2: BASIC PROCESSES AND HUMAN DEVELOPMENT
Edited by J. W. Berry, P. R. Dasen & T. S. Saraswathi

VOLUME 3: SOCIAL BEHAVIOR AND APPLICATIONS
Edited by J. W. Berry, M. H. Segall & C. Kagitçibasi

FOREWORD

Humans have been interested in how culture influences "naive psychology" (beliefs, customs, ways of life) from the time when they had the leisure to do so, and they have been recording their impressions since Herodotus. The scientific study of the link between culture and psychology started in the 19th century, perhaps with Comte's *Cours de philosophie positive* (6 volumes, 1830 to 1842). Much of the knowledge that had accumulated between the 19th century and the mid-1970s was presented in the first edition of the *Handbook of Cross-Cultural Psychology* (6 volumes, 1980 to 1981).

But science provides an ever-changing panorama. Between 1975 and today some of the ideas about what culture and psychology are have changed. Culture has become a less static, more dynamic, and "constructed" conception. Psychology has finally realized that culture has a major role to play in the way psychology is shaped.

That is so because we humans are all ethnocentric. This is a fundamental reality, reflecting that we all grow up in a specific culture (even when it is cosmopolitan and a mixture of other cultures) and learn to believe that the standards, principles, perspectives, and expectations that we acquire from our culture are *the* way to look at the world. Unexamined assumptions are one of the central aspects of culture. When we construct psychological theories, the more the subject matter deviates from biological and physiological phenomena, the more our culture intrudes in the shaping of the theories that we construct. In social and clinical psychology, for instance, much of what we present as "the truth" reflects our culture. The only way to correct the "false consensus" we perceive as "the truth" is to compare our ideas with the ideas that have been generated in other contexts. This can be done by emphasizing general issues of how culture influences psychological processes, as is done in "cultural psychology." It can also be revealed very sharply when we study different "indigenous psychologies." Much can be learned, in addition, by comparing data from several cultures, as is done in "cross-cultural psychology," and by examining how cultures interact with each other, as is done in "intercultural psychology."

John Berry has wisely included many of these perspectives in the *Second Edition.* He has done this by including more editors and authors from different cultures, traditions, and theoretical perspectives, and by broadening the definition of what is to be included in this edition. Thus, the second edition is broader, with authors who are more diverse in age, culture, and theoretical perspectives, than the first edition.

In this edition there are chapters on indigenous and evolutionary psychologies that were not included in the first edition. The research methods covered in chapters of the *First Edition* have not changed much, so these chapters are "archived" in the *Second Edition;* but two new methodological chapters have been added. Relatively new research areas—the examination of the developmental niche, the construction of identity, individualism and collectivism, intergroup relations, sex and gender issues, aggression, crime, and warfare, cross-cultural training, and health—now have separate chapters.

Some of these topics had a minor presence in 1972, when the first edition was formulated. For instance, the individualism and collectivism theme was not yet a focus of cross-cultural research, but became quite important after the first edition was published. I should have included a chapter on cross-cultural training in the first edition, but I was so concerned that the *Handbook* might include too much material reflecting my own interests that I went too far in holding back such material. It is gratifying that the *Second Edition* corrects this mistake.

The constellation of editors and authors of the *Second Edition* consists of about one-fifth old and four-fifths new writers, of diverse ages and cultures. I am delighted to see that the new generation of cross-cultural psychologists is moving the field forward.

Summer of 1995   *Harry C. Triandis*
                                                     Champaign, Illinois

Harry Triandis is Professor of Psychology at the University of Illinois. His recent books include *Culture and Social Behavior* (1994, New York: McGraw-Hill) and *Individualism and Collectivism* (1995, Boulder, CO: Westview Press). He edited (with W. W. Lambert, J. W. Berry, W. J. Lonner, R. Brislin, A. Heron, & J. Draguns) the first edition of the *Handbook of Cross-Cultural Psychology* (1980–81), and the international volume of the *Second Edition of the Handbook of Industrial and Organizational Psychology* (M. D. Dunnette and L. M. Hough 1990–1994, Palo Alto, CA: Consulting Psychologists). In 1994 he received the Otto Klineberg Award for his work on cultural syndromes, and the American Psychological Association's Award for Distinguished Contributions to the International Advancement of Psychology.

PREFACE

Cross-cultural psychology is the systematic study of relationships between the cultural context of human development and the behaviors that become established in the repertoire of individuals growing up in a particular culture. The field is diverse: some psychologists work intensively within one culture, some work comparatively across cultures, and some work with ethnic groups within culturally plural societies; all are seeking to provide an understanding of these culture-behavior relationships. This inclusive view about the diversity of the field has guided the editing of this second edition of the *Handbook of Cross-Cultural Psychology*.

The field of cross-cultural psychology has greatly evolved and expanded since the publication of the first edition of the *Handbook* in 1980. Under the general editorship of Harry Triandis, the six volumes of the first edition established the field as a wide-ranging but focused and coherent approach to understanding human experience and behavior in cultural context. The fifty-one chapters covered a vast territory, exploring virtually every corner of the discipline of psychology. The focus was consistently on how cultural factors influence psychological development and guide behavioral expression, and the integration was achieved through editorial coordination and collegial exchanges among authors.

Usually, second editions must exhibit both continuity and change. In this edition of the *Handbook,* continuity is represented by similar organization and coverage of materials to those in the first edition. More specifically: the present Volume 1 (Theory and Method) is a sequel to first edition Volumes 1 and 2 (Perspectives, and Methodology); the present Volume 2 (Basic Processes and Human Development) stems from Volumes 3 and 4 (Basic Processes, and Developmental); and the present Volume 3 (Social Behavior and Applications) follows mostly from Volumes 5 and 6 (Social, and Psychopathology). However, in this edition there has been no attempt to replicate the original compendium. Instead, the current editors decided to "archive" many of the earlier chapters, letting them stand as important and comprehensive statements of contemporary knowledge; where appropriate, present chapters refer readers to these earlier treatments. Chapters in the first edition that are considered as "archived" should be consulted by readers who want to have a comprehensive view of the field. These include: in Volume 1, a consideration of psychological universals and of the politics and ethics of cross-cultural research; in Volume 2, presentations of various methods (ethnographic, observational, surveying and interviewing, psychometric assessment, projective testing, experiments, unobtrusive measures, translation and content analysis, and holocultural methods); in Volume 3, surveys of research on motivation; in Volume 4, overviews of Piagetian theory, personality development and games and sports; in Volume 5, examinations of exchange theory, and small group behavior; and in Volume 6, reviews of alienation and depression. The topics of all other chapters in the first edition have, in one way or another, been updated and incorporated in the various chapters in this second edition.

This *Handbook,* in fewer chapters (34), focuses on topics for which there have been important theoretical and empirical advances since the late 1970s. Some chapters are true sequels to earlier ones; authors who are continuing earlier topics were asked to assume that readers have (or can) read the original chapter, and to start their review where the other chapter left off (usually around 1978). Other chapters attend to new topics that were barely evident in 1980; authors of these were asked to develop their material from earlier and more basic sources. The overall results, we hope, is a *Handbook* that can be used alone, or in sequence with the first edition.

The field of cross-cultural psychology has changed considerably over the past two decades. Four changes in particular have been important. One substantial change is in diversification in the concept of *culture* and how it may be related to psychology. Some of this change has followed a move in cultural anthropology away from a view of culture as objectively knowable and describable, providing a relatively stable context for individual human development, to a more interactive and creative relationship between individuals and their sociocultural surroundings. This move in anthropology has led to a parallel shift in cross-cultural psychology, stimulating the emergence of a subfield known as "cultural psychology." This aspect of diversification is represented particularly in Volume 1 by pairs of chapters on Theory and on Method that portray these contrasting perspectives on the concept of culture. A final chapter in Volume 1 attempts to provide an integrative framework within which this recent diversification can be viewed.

There can be no doubt that for many years cross-cultural psychology was done mostly by those in Western, economically and politically powerful nations; the objects of their attention were usually "others." When these others lived elsewhere, they were "tribes," and when they were closer at hand they were "subcultures" or "minorities." Recognizing the ethnocentrism in this arrangement, two other changes have occurred that represent moves away from this position. In the first emergent subfield, cross-cultural psychology has been increasingly carried out with cultural groups that co-reside in culturally plural societies, influencing each other, and being influenced in common by the many institutions that are widely shared in the larger society (e.g., public education, mass media, justice). This new subfield itself has a number of variants, and many terms have been used to describe them: "acculturation psychology," "ethnic psychology," and, in the French language tradition, "psychologie interculturelle." Much of this work has been accomplished by psychologists whose ethnic heritage is within the groups being studied.

In the second emergent subfield there has been increasing interest among the "others" in understanding themselves in their own terms, drawing upon their own culturally-rooted concepts and intellectual traditions. This move has brought about new approaches, known variously as "indigenous psychology," or "ethnopsychology." In these, a single cultural tradition is the locus of interest, and leadership is being provided by psychologists whose cultural backgrounds are also from within the cultural groups being studied, and which cumulatively span an ever-widening range. This search for indigenous origins and outcomes has been advocated both as a valuable activity in its own right, and as an important step towards achieving a more inclusive, panhuman psychology: it is argued that only when the universe of indigenous psychologies has been sampled can a universal psychology be achieved.

A last change has involved a shift away from the search for, and cataloging of, differences in psychological phenomena toward an interest in also identifying similarities. This interest in similarities has been present for many decades but recent developments in human ethology have begun to influence psychology, and are providing a base for this increasing interest in similarities. At the same time, the field has been increasingly clear in its conceptualization of the difference–similarity contrast as a dimension ranging from *relativism* at one pole to *universalism* at the other. All positions on this dimension are represented in this *Handbook*.

Given this diversification, it is no longer possible to give a single definition of key concepts (such as *culture*), to characterize the typical method used (such as the comparative method), or even to provide one definition of the field of cross-cultural psychology that the editors (never mind all the authors) would find to their liking. However, it is possible to identify what does hold the field, and this *Handbook*, together: the field rejects the long-standing exclusion of *culture* by the discipline of psychology; in contrast, it seeks to incorporate cultural aspects of human life as a major factor in behavior. The various ways in which cultural factors are conceptualized and linked to behavior constitutes the diversity of the field. In a sense, this combination of an underlying communality, but with variation in expression, corresponds to the perspective of *universalism*, which makes the assumption that basic psychological processes are shared panhuman characteristics of the species, but that culture provides an opportunity to develop and express these processes in highly variable ways.

In many respects, these changes in the field correspond to the sequence of three methodological orientations to the field outlined in 1969 and later elaborated as three goals of cross-cultural psychology in 1974. As outlined in Chapter 2 in Volume 1, the first goal was to *transport* current hypotheses and conclusions to other cultural contexts in order to *test* their validity. This goal was associated with the *imposed etic* methodological approach, and it has now resulted in a massive amount of data on psychological differences across cultures. For some critics of the field it has also become identified (somewhat erroneously) as the whole of cross-cultural psychology. The second goal was to *explore* new cultural systems to *discover* psychological phenomena not available in the first culture. This goal was associated with the *emic* methodological approach and it can be identified with the moves toward "cultural," "indigenous," and "ethnic" psychologies that we have witnessed over the past decade. The third was to *integrate* psychological knowledge gained from these first two activities, and to *generate* a more panhuman psychology that would be valid for all people. This goal was associated with the *derived etic* methodological approach, and it can be identified with the increased contemporary interest in psychological similarities and the search for a universal psychology. Cross-cultural psychology thus appears to be evolving in a sensible and understandable way.

Cross-cultural psychology is fundamentally concerned with understanding human diversity. As we have just noted, a basic proposition of the field is that cultural factors affect human behavior; it thus follows that cultural factors must also affect the psychology that we do, including the way we conceive of behavior, study it, interpret it, and apply it. In recognition of this cultural impact on psychology, one goal of this second edition of the *Handbook* is to incorporate as much cultural diversity as possible, both by the selection of editors and authors, and by the coverage of the literature. In this endeavor, we have succeeded to some extent: the editors have different cultures of origin, representing Asia, Europe, and North America; their teaching and research experience also include Africa and Oceania (but not South America). Chapter authors include those whose cultural origins are in all continents, representing over twenty mother tongues and with access to psychological literature in all major languages. However, there are evident failures to represent all cultural diversity: research rooted in Western Academic Scientific Psychology (W.A.S.P.), and written in English, overwhelms this *Handbook* as it does any other contemporary psychological work, although hopefully not as much. Moreover, within chapters, there are obvious cultural perspectives taken, and selections made, that result in coverage that falls well short of a pan-cultural treatment. Despite these shortcomings, this *Handbook* represents a serious and honest attempt to engage human diversity where it exists in the psychological literature.

Cross-cultural psychology, while still dominated by Western views and psychologists, is no longer their exclusive preserve. What started as a Western-based attempt to understand the "others" is now a field well-populated by these "others." In part, this has come about by many developing world psychologists having experienced Western psychology (as graduate students, as research collaborators, or as "consumers"), and being both attracted to, and wary of it. The attraction has brought them to the field, while the wariness has brought critical and culturally-rooted alternative perspectives. This process of enrichment by cultural diversification has had a major impact on the field, and continues at an accelerating pace.

The institutions of cross-cultural psychology reflect this growth and diversification. Almost thirty years ago, a meeting of social psychologists concerned with cultural influences took place in Nigeria, and led to the initiation of the *Cross-Cultural Social Psychology Newsletter* (edited by Harry Triandis). A year later (1968) the first of a series of a *Directory of Cross-Cultural Psychological Research* (edited by John Berry) was published in the *International Journal of Psychology* (which was founded in 1966 in part to promote the cross-cultural point of view). Walt Lonner established the *Journal of Cross-Cultural Psychology* in 1970, and John Dawson pulled these various activities and people together in 1972 to found the

International Association for Cross-Cultural Psychology (IACCP). This Association has met every two years in a different country since its inaugural meeting in Hong Kong. In 1984, the French-language Association pour la Recherche Interculturelle (ARIC) was founded, primarily through the efforts of Pierre Dasen. These two associations held a joint meeting in Liège in 1992 in an effort to establish closer ties. Conference proceedings of both associations are a core resource in the field.

Other publications in the field have appeared with increasing frequency. For example, in 1974 Walt Lonner and John Berry initiated the Sage Series on Cross-Cultural Research and Methodology, publishing eighteen volumes on a wide variety of topics in psychology and cognate disciplines; this series has been reconstituted (in 1996) as the Sage Series on Cross-Cultural Psychology. Another series, *Cross-Cultural Psychology Monographs* was established by the IACCP in 1991, under the editorship of Fons van de Vijver and Ype Poortinga. Chapters in the *Annual Review of Psychology* focusing on cross-cultural research have appeared at regular intervals since 1973. In addition to these publications, there has been a virtual explosion of textbooks in the field, some covering all domains in which cross-cultural psychologists are active, and some focusing on specific domains, such as social or developmental psychology.

The three volumes of this *Handbook* attempt to extend these publications in two ways. First, the most recent ideas and information in an area have been incorporated in the chapters; the treatment should thus be the most up-to-date available. Second, the writing has been pitched at a level suitable for graduate students and professionals who have a substantial background in psychology, but not necessarily in cross-cultural psychology. All authors were asked to provide basic definitions and descriptions of their area, and then move on to the main tasks of evaluating and integrating the area.

In Volume 1, theoretical and methodological issues are presented as an initial orientation to the broad features of cross-cultural psychology. In Volumes 2 and 3 the field is reviewed and evaluated in the more or less conventional categories used by general psychology. Readers may prefer to use the *Handbook* by beginning with the chapter that comes closest to their own substantive area, move to cognate areas of interest, and then delve into the broader issues addressed in Volume 1. Whatever your approach to the materials in these volumes, we hope that your understanding of the myriad ways in which culture and behavior can be intertwined will be enriched, and that you will be more convinced than ever about the importance of culture as a factor in the production and display of human diversity.

The process of developing an outline for this *Handbook*, and suggesting appropriate chapter authors, was primarily the responsibility of the team of co-editors. However, we were assisted by an editorial advisory group made up of the Editors of the First Edition of this *Handbook*, including Harry Triandis, Bill Lambert, Walt Lonner, Alastair Heron, Rich Brislin, and Juris Draguns. The task of reviewing drafts of chapters, recommending revisions, and keeping authors on track and on schedule largely fell to my volume co-editors. And, of course, the main work of any writing project has fallen to the chapter authors themselves. Najum Rashid has managed the chapter texts and their numerous revisions with accuracy and diligence. I thank all of them for their efforts, and for their contribution to this *Handbook.*

October, 1995

J. W. Berry
Department of Psychology
Queen's University
Kingston, Ontario
Canada

ABOUT THE EDITORS

John W. Berry

John Berry is a Professor of Psychology at Queen's University, Kingston. He received his B.A. from Sir George Williams University (Montreal) in 1963, and his Ph.D. from the University of Edinburgh in 1966. He has been a lecturer at the University of Sydney for three years, a Fellow of Netherlands Institute for Advanced Study and a visiting Professor at the Université de Nice and the Université de Genève. He is a past Secretary-General, past President and Honorary Fellow of the International Association for Cross-Cultural Psychology, and has been an Associate Editor of the *Journal of Cross-Cultural Psychology* and co-editor of the first edition of this *Handbook.* He is the author or editor of over twenty books in the areas of cross-cultural, social, and cognitive psychology, and is particularly interested in the application of cross-cultural psychology to public policy and programs in the areas of acculturation, multiculturalism, immigration, health, and education.

Ype H. Poortinga

Ype H. Poortinga studied psychology at the Free University in Amsterdam where he obtained his Master's degree (in 1965) and his Ph.D. (in 1971). From 1965–1972 he worked at the National Institute for Personnel Research in Johannesburg. Since then he has been at Tilburg University in The Netherlands, and since 1993 he has held a part-time professorship at the University of Leuven in Belgium. Poortinga's central interest has been in the conditions under which psychological data obtained in different cultural populations can be meaningfully compared. His empirical studies, mainly based on data from Southern Africa, Holland, India and Indonesia, have dealt with information processing, basic personality and social psychological variables. Poortinga has been Secretary-General and President of the International Association for Cross-Cultural Psychology and President of the International Test Commission (ITC), the Dutch Psychological Association (NIP), and the European Federation of Professional Psychologists Associations (EFPPA). His recent publications include two textbooks on cross-cultural psychology written together with John Berry, Pierre Dasen, and Marshall Segall (*Human Behavior in Global Perspective*, 1990; and *Cross-Cultural Psychology: Research and Applications*, 1992).

Janak Pandey

Janak Pandey is a Professor at the Centre of Advanced Study in Psychology, Allahabad University, India. He received his Ph.D. from Kansas State University in 1974. He has been a Fulbright Scholar-in-Residence, Wake-Forest University, visiting Commonwealth Fellow, University of Manitoba, and Assistant Professor, Indian Institute of Technology, Kanpur. He has edited the three-volume set of *Psychology in India: State-of-the-Art* and recently he has co-edited *Asian Contributions to Cross-Cultural Psychology*. He is currently President of the International Association for Cross-Cultural Psychology. He specializes in social and cross-cultural psychology with an emphasis on contemporary issues related to development and change in developing countries.

ABOUT THE CONTRIBUTORS

John Adamopoulos John Adamopoulos is Professor of Psychology at Grand Valley State University, Allendale, Michigan, U.S.A. He grew up in Greece, where he still maintains personal and professional ties. He completed his undergraduate degree in psychology at Yale University, and his graduate training at the University of Illinois, where he received the Ph.D. in 1979. His work has focused on interpersonal structure, the perception of social situations, and the emergence of social meaning systems across cultures and historical periods. He also has interests in theoretical and philosophical psychology, and in the role of culture in psychological explanation. He was editor of the *Cross-Cultural Psychology Bulletin* (1990–1994), and is a consulting editor for the *Journal of Cross-Cultural Psychology*.

Patricia M. Greenfield Patricia Greenfield is a cultural developmental psychologist who received her Ph.D. from Harvard University in 1966 from the Department of Social Relations, an interdisciplinary mix of social psychology, social anthropology, and sociology. Her first cross-cultural fieldwork was carried out in Senegal in 1963–64. Later she became interested in processes by which children are socialized into culture and how cultural tools mediate learning and cognitive processes. More recently, she has extended the cultural–historical approach to psychology to explore the ancestral roots of patterns of development and socialization in minority groups; this exploration has resulted in a book entitled *Cross-Cultural Roots of Minority Child Development*, co-edited with Rodney Cocking. Her article "Language, Tools, and Brain," published in *Behavioral and Brain Sciences*, won the 1992 Behavioral Science Research Prize of the American Association for the Advancement of Science. She is currently Professor of Psychology at UCLA, U.S.A., where she has been since 1974.

Gustav Jahoda Gustav Jahoda is Emeritus Professor of Psychology at the University of Strathclyde, Scotland. Since the 1950s he has carried out cross-cultural field research, mainly in Africa. Following his retirement he has concentrated on theoretical and historical writings, which include *Psychology and Anthropology* and *Crossroads between Culture and Mind*, as well as numerous journal articles. He is a former president and Honorary Fellow of the International Association for Cross-Cultural Psychology, and Membre d'Honneur, Association pour la Recherche Interculturelle.

Heidi Keller Heidi Keller is Professor of Psychology at the University of Osnabrück, Germany. She studied psychology, zoology, and philosophy at the University of Mainz where she obtained her Ph.D. in the Faculty of Biology (1975).

She habitated at the Technical University of Darmstadt in 1984. Her interests in cross-cultural psychology developed out of research on early parent–child interactions. She reanalyzed ethnographic material filmed by I. Eibl-Eibesfeldt, which allowed an integration of cross-cultural socialization patterns with psychobiological thinking and gradually led to the development of an evolutionary orientation.

Bernd Krewer   Bernd Krewer is at the Centre for Environmental Research of the University of the Saarland in Saarbrücken, Germany, the university where he obtained his Ph.D. in 1992. Among his major interests are the history of cross-cultural and cultural psychology, the development of cultural identity, and intercultural communication and training. His publications include *Perspectives de l'interculturel* (edited with Jeanine Blommart) and *Théorie et pratique de l'interculturel*. He is a Vice-President of the Association pour la Recherche Interculturelle since 1991.

Kwok Leung   Kwok Leung earned his Ph.D. from the University of Illinois, Urbana-Champaign, and is Chairman of the Department of Psychology at the Chinese University of Hong Kong. His current research interests include justice, conflict resolution, organizational psychology, social beliefs, and cross-cultural research methodology. He has published widely in social, applied and cross-cultural psychology, and his articles have appeared in such journals as *Journal of Personality and Social Psychology, Journal of Experimental Social Psychology, Journal of Cross-Cultural Psychology, Journal of Applied Psychology, Organizational Behavior and Human Decision Processes,* and *Innovations in Cross-Cultural Psychology* published by Swets and Zeitlinger. He is currently the Associate Editor of *Journal of Cross-Cultural Psychology* and the President-Elect of the Asian Association of Social Psychology.

Walter J. Lonner   Walter J. Lonner is a Professor of Psychology and Director of the Center for Cross-Cultural Research at Western Washington University, Bellingham, Washington, U.S.A. A University of Minnesota Ph.D. (1967), he has been involved with many books in cross-cultural psychology, as author, editor, or contributor. Lonner is Founding Editor of the *Journal of Cross-Cultural Psychology,* and continues to serve as Senior Editor. He is co-editor of two recent books: *Psychology and Culture* (1994) and *Counseling Across Cultures, 4th Ed.* (1996). A Fulbright Scholar (former West Germany, 1984–85), in 1986–88 he served as president of the International Association for Cross-Cultural Psychology, of which he is a charter member. In 1994 the Association made him an Honorary Fellow.

Joan G. Miller   Joan G. Miller is on the faculty in the department of psychology at Yale University, U.S.A. She received her B.A. in psychology from Columbia University and her Ph.D. in human development from the University of Chicago. Her research examines cultural influences on social attribution, interpersonal morality, and motivation, and has been undertaken among adults and children in India and the United States. She is a member of the Human Development and

Aging-I Study Section of the U.S. National Institutes of Health, and has served as an ad hoc reviewer for the National Science Foundation, the National Institute of Mental Health, and for numerous journals. In addition to her many articles and chapters, she is co-author (with Robin L. Harwood and Nydia L. Irizarry) of *Culture and Attachment: Perceptions of the Child in Context.*

Robert L. Munroe   Robert L. Munroe is Research Professor of Anthropology at Pitzer College, U.S.A. Trained in cross-cultural research at Harvard University by John and Beatrice Whiting, his field research has been conducted in New Mexico (San Juan Puebloans), Belize (Black Carib), Kenya (Logoli, Kikuyu), American Samoa, and Nepal (Newars). He has authored more than 90 publications, including (with Ruth H. Munroe) the first textbook on cross-cultural human development, which has been recently reissued by Waveland Press. He has been elected president of the Society for Cross-Cultural Research and of the Society for Psychological Anthropology.

Ruth H. Munroe   Ruth H. Munroe is Research Professor of Psychology at Pitzer College, U.S.A. She received an A.B. from Antioch College and an M.A. and Ed.D from Harvard University, where she was trained in cross-cultural research by John and Beatrice Whiting. Her research was conducted in Africa, Asia, Central and North America, and the Pacific. She coauthored (with Robert L. Munroe) a textbook, *Cross-Cultural Human Development,* and was senior editor of the *Handbook of Cross-Cultural Human Development.* She has served on the editorial boards of five journals, and from 1986 to 1992 was Secretary-General of the International Association for Cross-Cultural Psychology.

D. Sinha   Durganand Sinha was educated at Patna University (India) and Cambridge University. He taught at Patna University and the Indian Institute of Technology (Kharaghur) before joining Allahabad University in 1961 as Professor of Psychology and Head of that department. From 1982 to 1987 he was Director, ANS Institute of Social Studies, Patna. He has been UGC National Lecturer and National Fellow, ICSSR National Fellow, and visiting professor in many institutions, including ETS, Princeton, Jawaharlal Nehru University, M.S. University of Baroda, and University of Hong Kong. He is a Past President and Fellow of the International Association for Cross-Cultural Psychology. His current research interests include psychosocial dimensions of acculturation, deprivation, and poverty, and psychology and national development. He is the author of *Psychology in a Third World Country: The Indian Experience* and coeditor of *Social Values and Development: Asian Perspective* and is currently editing a book with Professor Henry S. R. Kao on Asian perspectives in psychology.

Fons Van de Vijver   Fons van de Vijver earned his Ph.D. from Tilburg University, The Netherlands, where he is lecturer in methodology and cross-cultural psychology. His research interests include methodological aspects of quasi-experimental research, assessment in multicultural settings, and cognitive differences and similarities across cultural groups. He has published papers in the *Journal of Cross-Cultural Psychology, International Journal of Psychology, Applied Psy-*

chological Measurement, Psychophysiology, Journal of Applied Psychology, Journal of Educational Measurement, and *De Psycholoog.* He is editor of the *Bulletin of the International Test Commission,* co-editor of the *Cross-Cultural Psychology Monographs,* and Associate Editor of the *Journal of Cross-Cultural Psychology.* He has co-edited the volume *Journeys into Cross-Cultural Psychology,* published by Swets and Zeitlinger. He is a member of an international committee that has established guidelines for test translations and test adaptations, published in 1996.

INTRODUCTION TO VOLUME 1

This volume provides an overview of theory and methodology in contemporary cross-cultural psychology. As in other rapidly growing fields, major changes can be recorded even over short periods. Some of the developments of recent years have provided challenges that affect the entire subdiscipline. As a consequence, continuity with the first edition of the *Handbook*, published in 1980, is limited. This volume deals with theoretical and methodological approaches from distinctly different perspectives. In addition, there are chapters on two sciences related to cross-cultural psychology: biology and cultural anthropology. There is also a chapter that surveys historical precursors, and one that tries to assess current theoretical and methodological diversification.

Taking the chapters in sequential order, there is first the historical account by Jahoda and Krewer. They trace ideas and distinctions about human diversity that currently dominate the field to early writings, starting with ancient Greek sources and presenting arguments from leading scholars of various periods. They amply demonstrate that contemporary ideas have long roots.

Theories with an emphasis on comparison are the focus of the review by Lonner and Adamopoulos. For them comparison is inherent in the psychological study of culture–behavior relationships. Comparison presumes shared psychological functions and processes, and this forms a basis for universality, thus ensuring the unity of the field. They recapitulate major traditions described in Jahoda's chapter on theory in the first edition of the *Handbook* and present a scheme on a central question in cross-cultural psychology, namely, the conceptual status of the notion of culture. With this scheme in mind they address various theoretical positions in contemporary cross-cultural psychology. In a second chapter on theory Miller deals with approaches that question the notion of the "psychic unity of mankind." This is a major departure from an axiom widely shared by the founders of modern cross-cultural psychology. Miller presents a range of viewpoints including symbolic action theories, cultural theories about the self, and social constructionism, drawing attention to strong points and problems in these various approaches. The third chapter on theory, by Sinha, reviews the progress that has been made in recent years in the formulations of culturally informed research alternatives that derive mainly from non-Western countries ("indigenous psychologies"). Psychology as an applied science has to address quite different issues in various societal contexts. These indigenous psychologies often are a reaction to the culture-centeredness of extant Western theories, but the reader will note that the focus on the question how psychology can play a role in national development does not necessarily lead to a rejection of the ideal of a universal psychology.

The next two chapters each deal with one of the two empirical sciences, biology and cultural anthropology, that are closest to cross-cultural psychology. R. L. Munroe and R. H. Munroe look a the interface of culture and behavior from an anthropological viewpoint, distinguishing between individual level, interpersonal level, and institutional level phenomena. They emphasize the commonalities in psychological functioning that underlie cultural diversity in behavioral manifestations, taking issue with postmodern views that question the status of all knowledge about an objective reality. Keller presents a biological account, more specifically an account steeped in evolutionary psychology. The emphasis is on culture as a property of the human organism that has to be understood within the context of biological evolution, with reproductive success as the central parameter. Keller describes how this framework is used not only at the level of the human species, but also to analyze differences in reproduction strategies between specific socioeconomic groups.

The two chapters that follow are on methodology and present the comparative cross-cultural and the cultural view on how research should be conducted. In many respects the chapter by Van de Vijver and Leung is a summary of a well-established tradition with fairly clear rules about design and analysis. What distinguishes this chapter from a methodology chapter in general psychology is a set of problems that are particularly serious in cross-cultural research, with comparability or equivalence of data as the most central issue. In contrast to this chapter, where the emphasis is more on the justification of one's inferences, the chapter by Greenfield is more concerned with methods for exploration and discovery. A common denominator of the cultural approaches is the rejection of the constraints imposed by the positivistic tradition in science that cross-cultural psychology traditionally tends to share with much of general psychology. Greenfield pleads for methods that allow the researcher to address behavior as an ongoing process, drawing on qualitative research methods. These do not yet compose a well-defined set of prescriptions; they put a premium on insights of the researcher, rather than on psychometric properties of instruments.

In the last chapter Poortinga brings together some of the major concerns addressed in this volume. The chapter does not try to integrate the field; the existing diversity is probably an asset as long as our knowledge in so many respects remains as preliminary and insecure as it is today. Rather various perspectives are juxtaposed, pointing to difficulties as well as to complimentarities and compatibilities.

As will be obvious from these brief remarks, the major theme of this volume is the controversy between cross-cultural and cultural approaches. The definition of the contrast differs between authors, but in all its forms it relates to the well-known epistemological distinction between the human sciences and the natural sciences, perhaps best captured with the German terms of *Geisteswissenschaften* and *Naturwissenschaften*. The cultural orientations tend to be holistic and idiographic, emphasizing the necessity to make unique culture-characteristic patterns of behavior accessible to scientific analysis and leaning towards various forms of phenomenology in methodology. The cross-cultural orientations are more molecular and nomothetic, emphasizing the need to extend existing psychological theories to encompass behavioral phenomena found in other cultures, and relying more on the experimental and psychometric methods of traditional psychology that are geared to establish validity with procedures independent of the particular researcher.

This discussion on the nature of culture–behavior relationships is most clearly present in the two chapters that deal with methodology, one in which Van de Vijver and Leung summarize comparative design and analysis, and another in which Greenfield defines major issues in cultural research methods. A parallel is found in the two theoretical chapters in which Lonner and Adamopoulos review cross-cultural theories and Miller gives an account of perspectives in cultural psychology. However, this major theme extends also to other parts of the volume. It is central in the chapter on the history of cross-cultural psychology by Jahoda and Krewer. In the chapter on indigenous psychologies, Sinha leans towards cultural approaches when showing that perspectives on culture–behavior relationships beyond those developed in the West demand attention. In the discussion of anthropological orientations, R. L. Munroe and R. H. Munroe define the position from which they have written their chapter in terms of the cultural versus cross-cultural contrast, arguing for the existence of psychological similarities underneath the diversity in patterns of human behavior.

A second noticeable point is the fact that there is a chapter titled "Indigenizing psychology." At the time of publication of the first edition of this *Handbook* there would hardly have been enough materials in the literature for a chapter length treatment. Indigenization for a long time has had a marginal presence in cross-cultural psychology and only recently has it acquired a recognizable and respectable position. The ethnocentrism in Western psychology certainly was acknowledged from time to time, but it is only since researchers from non-Western countries started to define their own viewpoints that serious notice has been taken.

A third point bears on the chapter that has least overlap with the others, namely Keller's presentation of biological psychology. In the eyes of many psychologists with a social science orientation this is probably the most controversial account in this volume. The position that Keller takes is close to the orthodoxy of evolutionary psychology. This is a theory that has emerged only fairly recently and is perhaps apt to change in the future. However, the attempts of sociobiology and ethology, especially human ethology, to explain human behavior with principles from evolutionary biology are unlikely to disappear, and no serious student of behavior can afford to ignore these developments.

Compared to the present edition, the first edition of this *Handbook* had several chapters on specific methods, such as field techniques, systematic observation, and the use of the Human Relations Area Files. In view of the more limited space in this edition, a focus on general methodological issues seemed justifiable. There was also a chapter on the politics and ethics of cross-cultural research for which there is no match in the present *Handbook*. The reason for this omission is that in the 70s guidelines for cross-cultural research were a topic of discussion more than in later years. In 1978 a statement on ethics was accepted by the general meeting of the International Association for Cross-Cultural Psychology (IACCP), but since that time there has been no change or revision of this document.

Even for the topics that are treated in this volume the coverage is not meant to be exhaustive; there would have been far too much to report. Still, the text as a whole should give the reader a broad overview of the kinds of reasoning and the kinds of issues that characterize debates on theory and method in cross-cultural psychology today.

A volume like this is the joint product of a number of persons. In particular, we would like to thank the chapter authors for their considerable investment of time and effort in the *Handbook* project. We also like to acknowledge the help of Mr. Rinus Verkooijen of Tilburg University in the preparation of the name index.

November 1995   *Ype H. Poortinga*

Janak Pandey

1

HISTORY OF CROSS-CULTURAL AND CULTURAL PSYCHOLOGY

GUSTAV JAHODA
University of Strathclyde
Scotland

BERND KREWER
University of Saarbrücken
Germany

Contents

Introduction

In treating the history of a relatively young discipline like cross-cultural psychology, one faces the problem of transcending the temporal limits as well as the actual self definition of this subdiscipline of general psychology that was institutionalized during the sixties (cf. Klineberg, 1980; Segall, Dasen, Berry, & Poortinga, 1990). United by the common goal to internationalize at least the empirical base of psychology by exploring the similarities and differences of human psychic organization and functioning all over the globe, cross-cultural psychology has defined itself during the past decades not so much by referring to epistemological, theoretical, or content related features, but rather by pointing to its function as a particular methodological strategy of mainstream psychology (Brislin, 1983): "... cross-cultural psychology is defined primarily by its method. ... Thus, it is our methodology that we must turn to in order to seek our identity as a discipline. ..." (Berry, 1980, p. 1).

Consequently, a historical consideration that would like to avoid restricting itself to the activity of the protagonists of cross-cultural psychology as such, has to refer to predecessors who do not share the methodological and disciplinary presuppositions of scientific mainstream psychology. It is this perspective—one of widening both the scope of the phenomena and the defining criteria—that we share with other historical reflections on the development of cross-cultural psychology (Jahoda, 1990; Segall et al., 1990; Klineberg, 1980). They also looked for their ancestors within the history of the general anthropological discourse on universals and on the diversity of mankind.

On the other hand, the very title of the present chapter reveals that thirty years of comparative cross-cultural research have led to a critical discussion about the initial approach, and to a rediscovery of a more socioculturally oriented tradition in psychology (Boesch, 1991; Cole, 1995; Eckensberger, 1995; Shweder, 1990). This reappraisal, which saw the introduction of the term 'cultural psychology', prompted the current debates on the name of the International Association for Cross-Cultural Psychology (IACCP). The central role of the principle of comparison as the general "name-giving" feature of the association is being called into question (Lonner (1992) and the subsequent discussion). Although 'cultural psychology' is still far from being a unitary theoretical system (Krewer, 1993; Lucariello, 1995; Shweder & Sullivan, 1993), the different approaches developing under this banner have produced a growing awareness that both cross-cultural psychology and general psychology as it is established as a scientific discipline need a widened perspective in order to take the culture-inclusiveness of human psychic development better into account (Dasen, 1993; Eckensberger, 1993; Laboratory of Comparative Human Cognition, 1979; Price-Williams, 1980; Rogoff & Morelli, 1989; Harkness & Super, 1987; Valsiner, 1989).

This widened perspective seems to be more compatible with a historical reconstruction, because it integrates the necessarily broader scope of a culture-related anthropological discourse during different historical periods. Both perspectives—cross-cultural and cultural psychology—in their attempt to analyze, explain, and understand human behavior in different cultures, have to cope with two basic problems; these are ". . . the diversity of human behavior in the world and the link between individual behavior and the cultural context in which it occurs" (Berry, Poortinga, Segall, & Dasen, 1992, p. 1).

Our historical review focuses on this tension between diversity and the search for universals. On the one hand it is concerned with the uniqueness of the relationship between culture and mind and, on the other hand, with the analysis of differences by means of the comparative method. All these perspectives have promoted and nourished anthropological discourse during different historical periods.

Because psychology, as a scientific discipline, is a product of mainly western anthropological reflection and its institutionalization in different disciplines, our attempt to trace the origins of culture-related psychology will be necessarily a somewhat ethnocentric enterprise, dealing with the western search to understand oneself in the mirror of others. Accordingly, we shall start with a brief chronological overview of the anthropological reflection during Antiquity, the Middle Ages, the Renaissance, and the Enlightenment. For each period, we shall focus on three aspects: first, the conceptions of mankind and its diversity; second, the role of other cultures in shaping and underpinning the concept of one's own humanity; and finally the sociohistorical contexts of encounters between different peoples. After this overview of the "prehistory" of relevant ideas, we will turn to the first empirical field studies at the beginning of the 20th century. Then, the main research interests of cross-cultural studies between the two world wars will be summarized, a period marked by scant interest in such studies.

Finally, the onset of cross-cultural psychology, its institutional conditions, and its changing foci of interests will be outlined. As Klineberg (1980) stated in the previous edition of this handbook: "There is no specific date that can be identified with the onset of interest in cross-cultural comparisons" (p. 34). Nevertheless, there is a growing variety of research styles and approaches from the sixties till today. Since Klineberg's review, a number of new topics have developed (cf. dominant value studies, indigenous psychologies, everyday cognition, psychology of acculturation, multicultural management), and cultural psychology—as mentioned above—was also not yet on the map at that time. Thus, in 1980 it was still possible to give a broad survey of major fields of activity in cross-cultural psychology. In the meantime, the range of activities has expanded to such an extent that it is impossible to provide an adequate picture within a brief framework. Accordingly, we shall leave the detailed discussion of more recent research orientations to the respective specialized chapters of the *Handbook* and shall focus more on their historical foundation than on their actual trends.

In a separate section we shall not only point to some enduring methodological debates that have been a prominent feature of the growth of cross-cultural psychology, but also to the relationship between anthropology and psychology. The latter was crucial for the early "culture-and-personality" school and its follower, "psychological anthropology," and also for the emerging cultural psychology.

We shall finish by outlining some recurrent ideas and problems of cross-cultural and cultural reflection on the human mind. These key issues appear as stable elements in changing theoretical and methodological guises: the ethnocentric foundation of theories of mind and culture; the allegedly remarkable sensory acuity and lack of cognitive competence of "savages;" the relationship between language and thought, between environment and the stage of cultural development, between reason and morality, and finally between character (mentality) and culture.

Origins of Ideas about Humanity and Human Diversity

Antiquity and the Middle Ages

Classical Greek and Roman thinking and, even more so, the dominant ideology of the Middle Ages were generally marked by little interest in other peoples. These peoples were mostly interpreted as the complete opposite of one's own order of human existence, which was regarded as the best—or even only—realization of humanity. Accordingly, when taken into account at all, diversity was generally interpreted as distance from the level of "real" human existence.[1] According to the Greek ethnocentric concept of humanity, the best realization of the divine plan were the Greek city-states ("polis"). As the complete opposite to the Greek city dweller, the general image of the "Non-Greek," the "Barbar," was not favorable. The term "bar-bar" was used to imitate foreign languages that the Greeks found incomprehensible and hence interpreted as unintelligible noises, like the twittering of birds as Herodotus described them. But there were also many other negative characteristics attributed to the Barbar, such as being crude, uneducated, unreasonable, lawless, cruel, passionate, immoral, and so forth. Later on, many of these "barbarian characteristics" were to find their continuation in the general image of the savage as the counterpart of the civilized Westerner—an image the traces of which can still be detected in popular stereotypes of our days (Jahoda, 1995). During the Middle Ages this ethnocentric definition of humanity was determined by the dogma of Christian ethnohistory. During that period its canonical worldview had to be accepted against all empirical evidence.

According to Christian monogenist cosmogony, the image of unknown, non-Christian peoples was prestructured by the belief that the distant heathens would be monstrous races living on the border of the empire of God; they were viewed as the degenerated descendants of Noah's condemned son Ham, or as the devil's peoples, Gog and Magog. These images of the monstrous character of foreign peoples was also influenced by a second opposition to the medieval ideal of the civilized knight, namely the pagan savage, the wild man living in the woods, naked, animal-like, and devoid of all social norms. These fabulous images shaped the ethnographic collections of that period, whose main interest was that of uncritically presenting abnormal variants of human diversity. Thus, there is a more than a millenium-old tradition of fabulous, fantastic races in written and drawn constructions of the non-European other. From Plinius the Elder's (23–79

A.D.) *Historia naturalis* to Isodore's *Etymologies* (622/23), Bartholomew's *De Proprietatibus* (13th century), the *Schedel'sche Weltchronik* (1493) and to some extent even later (Lafitau, 1724), one can find examples of the same monstrous creatures: the "Blemmyae" with faces on their chests, the "Cynocephali" with dog heads who communicate by barking, the "Sciopods" with a huge foot that they used as a sunshade while lying on their backs, or the one-eyed Arismaspi.

But besides these similarities there are nevertheless some important differences between the concept of diversity in Antiquity and the Middle Ages. During the Middle Ages the uncritical use of hearsay and tales about monstrous races was embedded in dominant ideology: it was used to support the all-embracing dogma of Christian ethnotheory. Thus, the authority of the Holy Scriptures suppressed and devalued any empirical contradiction of this worldview from the outset.

In opposition to this firmly closed horizon, many classical writings aimed at unraveling the order of things without any prior dogmatic point of reference. Moreover, many classical reports about other regions had to present factual information about lands and peoples for military and administrative purposes resulting from the expansion of the Greek, and later Roman, empires. In that context, the beginnings of some ethnographic descriptions and theoretical reflections on the diversity of mankind can be detected, which remained nearly forgotten till the dawn of the Renaissance.[2]

The most outstanding example of this tradition is the work of Herodotus (460–359 B.C.), often refered to as the father of ethnography and historiography. His collection of information on geography, striking peculiarities, culture (habits), and history was carefully evaluated by cross-checking different sources of information. He was probably also the first author to point explicitly to the universality of the ethnocentric foundations of our judgments of other peoples. As a forerunner of theorizing on general stages of the adaptation of humans to their environment, he distinguished the stages of hunters, nomadism (with cattle-breeding), lower forms of agriculture, and finally civilization (built on higher forms of agriculture and a state-like organization and administration).

During the periods of sophistic and stoic Enlightenment, there was a debate on universal criteria for defining the sameness of mankind, independent of cultural origin. As the predecessor of the idea of psychic unity of mankind during the European Enlightenment, Greek education ("paidea") was introduced by Isokrates (5th century B.C.) and later by Cicero (106–43 B.C.) to distinguish between different degrees of civilization. During the stoic period the notion of "cosmopolitism" was advanced by Zenon (336–264 B.C.) to develop a vision of panhuman civilization.

The idea of environmental determinism, including climate and astrological constellation, as a means of explaining diversity was also widespread among Antiquity's philosophers (Hippocrates, 460–359 B.C.; Ptolemaeus, 2nd century B.C.). But there were also early versions of diffusionalist approaches, tracing back the exchanges between different peoples as a source of cultural development (Herodotus, 460–359 B.C.; Polybios, 201–120 B.C.). Finally, the work of Poseidonus

(135–51 BC) attempted to capture the particularity of peoples by refering to a holistic concept of a dominant psychological feature basic to each people's institutions and habits. He distinguished the "thymos" of northern peoples dominated by emotionality, passion, and courage from the prevailing "logos" of the southern peoples (including Rome and Greece) that is marked by a predominance of reflection, moderation, and control. Apart from his environmentalist stance, his approach resembles the configurationalist ideas of the culture-and-personality school during the first half of our century.

The Renaissance Transition towards Diversity

Between the end of the intellectually dark period of the Middle Ages and the onset of the Enlightenment—basically in the 15th and 16th centuries—there were essential changes in the dominant conceptions of the human being, leading to a new interest in human diversity.[3] The partial cracking of the all-embracing theological shell entailed a new ideology of human self-confidence, highlighting human creative potential, individual responsibility for oneself, and humanistic values such as freedom, equality, and self-realization. The decline of the feudal societal order was pushed forward by the onset of the mercantile and capitalist systems. In philosophy, the comparative look backwards to classical Antiquity presupposed the capacity of "distance-taking," an important condition for localizing "the others" in time and space in order to have a better understanding of one's own position in individual and social life.

Probably the most important factor that increased the awareness of human diversity during the Renaissance was the growing number of contacts with other peoples due to the waves of conquests, discoveries, and mercantile relations with distant countries. Although reports of travellers were still strongly influenced by scholastic images of other peoples, a new interest in realistic accounts of other sociocultural forms of human life came into being. However, these more realistic accounts were greatly influenced by the particular perspectives and goals of travellers, conquerors, and missionaries who, in their turn, shaped the resulting vision of other peoples.

The reports of the conquerors were often relatively factual, describing the indigenous peoples encountered as part of those natural conditions one must take into account to achieve a successful exploitation of material resources. Whether these images were favorable depended heavily on the willingness of these peoples to comply with their invaders: When they resisted, the scholastic images of the savage were recalled; when they were friendly and hospitable, they were described (often with an expression of some surprise) as good-natured, submissive and (stupidly) generous (as a prototypical example, refer to the diary of Columbus (1492/1981).

The missionaries' contact necessarily led to a more intensified and interpersonal concern with other peoples. To convert them to Christian belief, first one had to recognize their humanity, which was officially done by the bull of Pope Paul III in 1537. He declared that the indigenous peoples are "true humans, capable of receiving the Catholic faith and sacraments." As a consequence of their living in indigenous communities, the missionaries developed the first ethnographic and comparative approaches for the analysis of language, customs, and kinship systems (DeLery, Sahagun in the 16th century, Lafitau in the late 17th, but still in the same tradition). Furthermore, they were the promoters of a critical debate on the murderous politics of Europeans in the New World, and the first defenders of the respect for general human rights and for local moral principles. The Dominican monk Bartholome De Las Casas and Montaigne's writings (the latter from an armchair position) are the most striking illustrations of this discourse. Diversity in this context was used to call into question one's own moral standards of behavior and paved the way for the debates on the relativity or universality of moral principles.

Finally, there was another aspect of the Renaissance's reception of human diversity that is worth mentioning: the more popular view of other peoples continued the interest in the curiosities and abnormalities of mankind and kept the monstrous and fabulous creatures of the Middle Ages alive. The popular travel books of that time, such as the famous *Cosmographia* by Sebastian Münster (1544), as well as the first compositions of the so-called "cabinets de curiosité," were expressions of this newly awakened interest in "alien others." In general, the Renaissance's propensity to capture the wonders of the world resulted in the production of various collections, composed of those descriptions of the manifold expressions of nature.

In sum, it is certainly justified to consider the Renaissance concept of humanity and diversity as being at the threshold of a new science of man. One has, however, to point out the half-way character of the period's insights. In spite of the new interest in empirical reports about other peoples, their focus remained mainly descriptive, and interest in collections was still influenced by classical images. Because of this mixed perspective, the Renaissance descriptions of other peoples foreshadowed many stereotypes and hidden assumptions about the nature and character of the non-European humanity, which later became more or less unconscious starting points for empirical studies. But there was - even as far as the great thinkers of that time are concerned—a general acceptance of the belief in the basic unchangeable order of beings and things attributed to the divine plan of creation. Consequently, what was still essentially missing was the idea of exploring the dynamics and the development of this order. As this question had not yet been put, human beings and their diversity were not considered from the perspective of those causal, natural laws determining their progress and decline as natural and cultural beings. This became the central focus of the following Enlightenment period.

The Enlightenment

In spite of the different national foci and temporal culminating points, there were important commonalities in the European Enlightenment period from the 17th to the 19th century, which laid the foundations of our current human scientific disciplines. This shift towards a scientific study of human beings and their various forms of existence was based on a new trust in the human capacity of empirical observation and critical reflection as the "royal road" to knowledge about the material and living worlds. Kant's (1784) slogan in responding to the question what "Enlightenment" means, perfectly illustrates this awakened self-confidence in the human capacity of exploring and understanding himself and his own conditions of life: "Have the courage to make use of your own reason."

The Enlightenment discussion on humanity and its diversity was deeply shaped by the controversy about the double destiny of man as a natural and cultural being. The complete range of man's potential existence modes was conceptualized as a spatial and temporal system ranging from the savage to the civilized state of human life (Duchet, 1971; Gusdorf, 1972). This broad anthropological perspective made some important assumptions necessary, which are still at the center of our methodological debates on cross-cultural comparison. The general "imposed etic" (Berry, 1989) of the Enlightenment philosophers of the 18th century was the presupposition that human beings are endowed with reason. Reason was thought to be the essential feature of the human creature. It constituted the core of two basic assumptions about the unity and equality of mankind which generally characterize the anthropological thinking of that period: the belief in what came later to be referred as the "psychic unity of mankind," and an attempt to grasp the universal history of mankind.

The firm belief in a mental endowment common to all human beings became the base for a comparative consideration of human diversity in different places and different historical periods, as Hume, prototypically for most of the Enlightenment philosophers, put it:

> *It is universally acknowledged, that there is a great uniformity among the actions of men, in all nations and ages, and that human nature still remains the same, in its principles and operations. . . . Mankind are so much the same, in all times and places, that history informs us of nothing new or strange in that particular. Its chief use is only to discover the constant and universal principles in nature."* (Hume, 1784/1894, p. 358).

Thus, the Enlightenment philosophers were mainly driven by the idea of looking for similarities. Diversity was interpreted as constituting different steps on the scale of the universal history of mankind. These developmental stages ranging from savagery to civilization were explained as the result of environmental or societal conditions that promote or hinder the free unfolding of human reason.

Considering the question of how "otherness" was understood, it is interesting to point out that this equating of spatial and temporal distances can be regarded as a characteristic feature of the western "incorporation" of other cultures. By keeping a distant position and excluding a feeling of commonality that is the normal condition of mutual understanding between humans, the cultural other was condemned to remain an object of analysis (Fabian, 1983). The climax of this interpretative scheme of confounding spatial and historical distances was certainly reached by the social evolutionary theorists of the late 19th century (Langness, 1974).

But the 18th century was dominated by the idea of the general progress of mankind, passing through the stages of development of hunting and fishing, pastoralism and animal husbandry, agriculture, and finally commerce and manufacture. The core differences between these stages were, apart from the variant subsistence types, the acquisition of spoken and written language, of the concept of property, and the type of social and political order. As the motor of these changes, reference was made either to external environmental conditions or to an innate internal propensity to improve continously. Furthermore, psychological changes ("new wants") resulting from the respective social and economic orders were considered as potential sources of progress. Thus, the basic dimensions of our actual concept of culture, that are, on the one hand, culture as a system of customs and ritualized behaviors with its respective institutional order and, on the other hand, culture as a shared mentality of a particular group, became of central importance to explain human diversity.

The travellers' reports then available were largely used by the Enlightenment philosophers to fill in their stages of the development of mankind with realistic and empirically founded examples of human variety. In order to reconstruct the progressive development of mankind and to localize the place of their own society within universal history, the Enlightenment philosophers used different images of savage peoples for their argumentation. While generally accepting a certain progress in the past, savage forms of living were mostly considered as immature, deficient stages of human development. This position found its clearest expression through representatives of the optimistic belief in the inevitability of human progress, prototypically incorporated by Condorcet's *Sketch of a Historical Picture of the Progress of the Human Mind* (1794). The first stages describe the "natural human" as dull, incapable of using reason and of establishing a collective social order, imprisoned by the impediments of nature and by mystical beliefs, and fully occupied by daily problems of subsistence.

But there were also more positive descriptions of savage life and mind focusing on the unspoiled character of natural man, his pure character not yet distorted by the constraints of the clerical and aristocratic system. This position was prototypically laid out in Rousseau's *Discours sur l'origine et les fondements de l'inégalité de l'homme* (1755). He considered the "natural peoples" as nearer to the ideal state of the natural man, whom he constructed as a fictional model in order to outline the two fundaments of human progress: self-preservation and compassion, which could only unfold if not hampered by external constraints. Accordingly, he interpreted the stages of civilization and socialization as a process of suppressing and distorting this human potential.

In sum, the Enlightenment reception of reports about savage life oscillated between the extremes of understanding distant forms of life: idealization and rejection. This range, delimited by the noble savage and the uncivilized barbarian, foreshadowed those emotional extremes still existing today when one is confronted with different cultures. They occur either on a scientific, a political, or an interpersonal level, reflecting the range between an ethnocentric and alienated relation to one's own society and the concomitant range between xenophobia and a preference for the exotic with respect to foreign cultures (Erdheim, 1987; Koepping, 1975; Theye, 1985). In addition to a brief sketch of some general features of the Enlightenment discussions about human diversity [4], we shall try to trace back more specific sources of the cultural and cross- cultural point of view during this period. It should be clear from our description so far that the dominant perspective of Enlightenment philosophy was highly compatible with cross-cultural psychology's model of man. Nevertheless, there was a group of thinkers skeptical about a purely natural and universal foundation of human psychic functioning, believing that the human sphere is sui generis. In many respects, these "dissenters" set out the prolegomena of what is now discussed under the banner of cultural psychology.

Predecessors of Cultural Psychology

The protagonists of this rebellion against the Enlightenment (Shweder, 1984) did not establish a consistent school of thought, but shared some important common ideas and conceptions. They were all convinced that humanity and its development could not be adequately understood merely by considering its natural dispositions. For them, human development on the individual as well as on the social plane could only be properly studied by taking into account the fact that the human mind is always shaped by, and embedded in, its sociocultural achievements. Accordingly, human capacities to create collective means of communication and cooperation, especially language, became for them the central criteria for distinguishing between the human and animal orders. Man was not only regarded as a being naturally endowed with reason, but also as a social and emotional creature, because these capacities were essential for mutual understanding and establishing a social order.

Since sociocultural achievements became the major focus of interest, the "dissenters" turned more to the study of particular human groups and their specific forms of social and cultural order. Their work was mostly built on theoretical speculations based on their interpretations of the ethnographic material then available. They made hardly any attempt to carry out empirical studies of their own.

The intricate relationship between the development of mind and culture, which is crucial for sociohistorical approaches, was for the first time explictly stated by Vico (1724). His work was largely ignored by his contemporaries, but today he is often credited with having created the "plot structure" of the sociohistorical perspective (Berlin, 1982; Shotter, 1986). The aim of his *New Science* was to reconstruct the history of human ideas and the principles of social evolution.

Vico interpreted the history of mankind as consisting of repeated cycles of progress and regression between the divine, the heroic and the fully human stage, which occur in what he called "a world of nations." He tried to reconstruct past stages on the basis of what he saw as their predominant modes of symbolic communication, from poetic and metaphoric to rational. Understanding the history of nations was possible, he argued, because history itself had been created by human beings and "its principles are therefore to be found within the modifications of our own human mind" (Vico, 1724/1948, p. 331). Accordingly, the organizing principle of his assumed stages of human development were essentially psychological ones underlying the dominant mode of symbolic communication. He considered the symbolic systems (myths, art, customs, religion and, most importantly, language) as the key to inferring the ways of thinking and feeling of past cultures. This approach later became the "royal road" of "Völkerpsychologie." Thus, he anticipated a central postulate of current adherents to the cultural psychological position: namely, that the human mind is not a constant, but a function of specific socio-historical conditions establishing "context-specific competencies" (Laboratory of Comparative Human Cognition, 1983) or "multiple realities" (Shweder, 1990); and that it has therefore to be studied also by historical and ethnological approaches.

This line of thought was continued by the leading figure of the Romantic rebellion against the mainstream Enlightenment position, Gottfried Herder. He represented the sceptical German reception of Enlightenment philosophy, which was blamed for its dogmatic and arrogant overrating of reason, neglecting all other facets of the human psychic constitution. The general aim of his *Ideas on the philosophy of the history of mankind* (1784–1791) was to outline "the history of human soul in general, in periods and peoples." The concrete realization of this general history was seen as embodied in particular groups or communities, the "Völker" (peoples). They were characterized by a shared language and historical tradition, which was the foundation and, at the same time, the product of the mentality of its members, the "Volksgeist." As a conceptual tool for grasping the particularity of a group's shared mental characteristics, the "Volksgeist" foreshadowed in some respects the concept of the "basic personality structure" of the culture-and-personality school in the first half of the 20th century. In general, Herder's work postulated many principles which were to become central orientations of American cultural anthropology after Boas.

Herder's particularistic stance was accompanied by a positive evaluation of the diversity of human cultures as an important condition for the unfolding of humanity. Consequently, he was an ardent defender of a cultural relativistic position: "Thus, nations change according to place, time and their inner character; each carries within itself the measure of its perfection, incommensurable with others" (Herder, 1784/1969, vol. 4, p. 362).

Language played a prominent role in Herder's vision of the unfolding of human capacities in concrete historico-cultural groups. This idea was elaborated by the work of Wilhelm von Humboldt, who is often credited with having founded the tradition of "Völkerpsychologie." Humboldt's aim was to explore the mentality of peoples by a comparative study of linguistic systems. He interpreted language not only as an indicator of a certain kind of mentality, but as its constitutive factor or even as its synonym: "Language is the outer appearance of the mentality of peoples; their language is their mentality and their mentality is their language; one can hardly overemphasize their identity" (von Humboldt, 1830–35/ 1985, p. 67, translation by the authors). His main idea, that people who share a language develop a similar subjectivity, a "Weltanschauung" (worldview), fore-shadows in essence what later became known as the Sapir-Whorf hypothesis.

The first formal program of Völkerpsychologie was presented in 1860 by Lazarus and Steinthal as an introduction to the first issue of the *Zeitschrift für Völkerpsychologie und Sprachwissenschaft* (Journal of Völkerpsychologie and Philology).[5] Their ambitious goal was to unravel the relationship between basic psychic processes and the mental processes linked to collective life in human societies. They introduced Völkerpsychologie as "the science of the Volksgeist, that is the theory of the elements and laws of the mental life of peoples" (Lazarus & Steinthal, 1860, p. 7). The general task of Völkerpsychologie was divided in two parts: on the one hand, a historical study of mankind as a whole to unravel the general laws governing the change and development of the mind (folk-historical); on the other hand, the study of particular mentalities of different peoples in order to investigate the factors producing specific manifestations of these general laws ("psychological ethnology"). These two basic perspectives somewhat resemble the dual goal of recent cross-cultural psychology, namely the search for similarities and for differences using generalization and differentiation studies respectively (Eckensberger, 1990).

Lazarus and Steinthal's program is not very enlightening as far as methodological approaches are concerned. Hence it is not surprising that their journal between 1860–1890 contained very few empirical studies (Krewer & Jahoda, 1990). Most articles were theoretical speculations, about a third treated philological themes, and a fifth was confined to religion and folklore. If there were any references to specific countries or regions, the articles very rarely dealt with any places outside Europe.

On a theoretical level, the main problem with which Lazarus and Steinthal grappled can still be regarded as a perennial and unsolved one for the cultural sciences. It relates to the double nature of cultural meaning systems as part of individual psychic organization, and as a "superorganic" feature of collective life. In terms of Lazarus and Steinthal's conceptions there was a tension between localizing the Volksgeist in the minds of the individual members of a Volk ("the inner activity common to all individuals"), and simultaneously also in collective phenomena of various kinds. In that respect, their program perfectly parallels an existing controversy concerning the definition and use of the concept of culture in the human sciences (Krewer, 1990; Jahoda, 1984, 1993; Rohner, 1984; Segall, 1984).

The Lazarus and Steinthal proposal was also heavily criticized by Wundt (1888) before he himself began publication of the ten volumes of his Völkerpsychologie in the first decade of the 20th century. In his opinion, Völkerpsychologie should analyze the universal aspect of the development of higher mental processes in their culture-historical contexts. He pleaded for a much more focused and more psychologically oriented Völkerpsychologie. Wundt's own ideas are difficult to summarize because they are scattered throughout his enormous mass of writings.[6] In fact, few of his theoretical reflections are explicitly formulated in the ten volumes on Völkerpsychologie published at the end of his scientific career. The idea of supplementing his individual psychology by

Völkerpsychologie had obviously already emerged at the beginning of his academic work (Graumann, 1980).

Wundt claimed that individual psychology would not be a sufficient theoretical frame to explore the higher mental functions, because these depend upon the collective form of existence of human beings and on the modes of cooperation evolved for this purpose. This basic idea strongly resembles the sociohistorical and symbolic interactionist approaches of our days.

In that perspective, Wundt's Völkerpsychologie was presented as a kind of socio-evolutionary psychology that extended individual development into the sphere of cultural development. But this dependence of individual psychology on Völkerpsychologie was only one side of the coin, because Wundt (1908) also pointed out the fundamental importance of the principles governing individual consciousness for cultural development and the study of collective human achievements: "In so far as Völkerpsychologie can find any psychological laws of independent content, these will always be applications of principles valid for individual psychology. . . . Thus, only the individual psychology and Völkerpsychologie together constitute the whole of psychology." (Wundt, 1908, vol. 3, p. 227-8). This view of the mutual interdependence of individual psychology and Völkerpsychologie is also mirrored in Wundt's units of analysis for exploring the shared collective experiences of cultural groups. In much the same way as language can be regarded as the collective enlargement and structuring of individual cognition, so myths structure collectively individual feelings; and finally customs can be interpreted as the collective shaping of individual volition (Wundt, 1908).

The dialectics between individual and collective psychology in Wundt's approach represents in some way a basic dilemma of psychology having to deal with a subject that is a natural as well as a cultural/historical being. This ancient philosophical controversy about whether psychology is a natural or a cultural science has recently reappeared in the debate between cross-cultural and cultural psychologists (Krewer, 1993).

Given this subtle discussion of the role of a cultural scientific perspective for psychology, it is disappointing to find only a huge collection of ethnographic material and few insights into new theoretical and methodological perspectives for psychology in the ten volumes of Wundt's Völkerpsychologie. Neither Wundt himself, nor any follower, ever tried to realize Wundt's program empirically. In mainstream psychology—contrary to the "grandfather" role attributed to Wundt's work on individual psychology—it was usually ignored and forgotten, and only recently rediscovered in the context of a new wave of interest in culture. One of the reasons for this neglect of Völkerpsychologie was certainly that mainstream psychology generally aimed at establishing itself as a natural scientific discipline, along the lines of the dominant ideology of the Enlightenment.

Cross-Cultural Psychology's Ancestors

As mentioned earlier, the dominant model of man as a natural creature endowed with reason corresponds in many ways to the basic model of cross-cultural psychology. From this perspective, human diversity was conceptualized as a variation on the same theme, and it was this theme that constituted the focus of interest. Evidence of how up-to-date such an approach is can be seen when comparing Poortinga, van de Vijver, Joe, and Van de Koppel's (1987) plea to peel the onion called culture with Geertz's description of the Enlightenment's model of man. "In this conception, man is a composite of "levels," each superimposed upon those beneath it and underpinning those above it. As one analyses man, one peels off layer after layer, . . . Strip off the motley forms of culture and one finds the structural and functional regularities of social organization. . . . Peel off the psychological factors and one is left with the biological foundations—anatomical, physiological, neurological—of the whole edifice of human life" (Geertz, 1970, p. 50/51).

This edifice of human life had to be unravelled by the scientific quest to understand both nature and human nature by assuming a determinism governed by natural laws. It was the attempt to transfer the successful Newtonian model from physics to human affairs that led to a machine-like, mechanical understanding of human beings as prototypically realized in La Mettrie's (1748) *L'homme machine.*

Locke's (1690) *Essay concerning human understanding* laid the foundation of the empiricist conception of the human mind as a product of processing and associating experiences and sensations. In the first book of his Essay, he referred to different reports on distant peoples in order to argue against the assumption of innate ideas put forward by Descartes, who claimed the universality of innate religious beliefs. Among French Enlightenment scholars Locke's "tabula rasa" conception of the human mind was spread by the writings of Condillac who further elaborated the principles of "sensationism." In his *Traité des sensations* (1754) he used a "thought experiment" of a statue originally only endowed with a sense of smell. He then tried to show how all mental processes are built on these basic sensations. These are then compared and associated by means of different modes of attention until the state of complex cognitive operations is achieved. This model of a passive-receptive apparatus led to an increased interest in the malleability of human beings. Thereby sociocultural influences on human development and the limits and possibilities of educational interventions became a major focus of concern. Anticipating the ideas of classical behaviorism, attention turned for instance to the cases of "wild children" (Lane, 1985; Malson, Itard, & Manonni, 1972) in order to empirically investigate a state of nature without the experience of human community and the process of becoming civilized.

Whereas this intellectual climate paved the way for a comparative interest in the conditions of life of other peoples, one had to wait till the end of the 18th century for the first systematic empirical attempts to study human diversity. It was an interdisciplinary group of scientists, called the "Société des Observateurs de l'Homme" (1799–1805), which can be regarded as the first cross-cultural scientific association. Its wide-ranging theoretical and empirical work has been rediscovered and is accessible in different languages (Copans & Jasmin, 1994; Jahoda, 1992; Moravia, 1977; Stocking, 1968). The "Observateurs" consisted of a group of outstanding contemporary scientists from different disciplines. Their ambitious common goal was dedicated to the "physical, moral and intellectual aspects of the science of man" as the Société's founder, Louis-François Jauffret, declared in his introductory *Mémoires*. They were united by the conviction that unsubstantiated theories had to be replaced by empirical observation. Jauffret's introduction formulated the broad anthropological scope of the "Observateurs de l'Homme": their interest encompassed the study of comparative anatomy; the analysis of the relationship between external conditions and the development of the human being; the exploration of different customs, habits, and forms of collective life; and finally the different forms of moral (in our terms, psychological) expressions and their relationship to the physiological constitution (a question attributed in our days to psychosomatic approaches).

In order to realize these aspirations, the empirical and comparative study of human diversity became the "royal methodological road," at home and abroad. Accordingly, at home interest shifted towards representatives of other ethnic groups, whose physiological and moral characteristics were studied. In that context, the above-mentioned cases of wild children became a preferred object of observation and discussion of the Société, because they represented in a sense a real-life version of Condillac's statue, a version that develops psychologically by processing and associating new sensory input. The famous case of Victor of Aveyron served for many years as an object of empirical studies for the physician Itard and the psychiatrist Pinel, who were engaged in an early form of what we today call the nature–nurture controversy to explain the mental retardation of Victor. In order to investigate human diversity abroad, the Société's members participated in the preparation of expeditions to systematically observe varieties of the human condition. In this context, the first versions of field manuals for empirical cross-cultural observations were developed. Dégérando's *Considérations sur les diverses méthodes à suivre dans l'observation des peuples sauvages,* which was written as a guide for the anthropological observations during Baudin's expedition to Australia (1800-1804), foreshadowed in many respects current reflections on the goals and methods of ethnographic fieldwork. It was a plea for a positivist approach to human diversity, explicitly warning of the ethnocentric pitfalls related to the observation of other peoples and the potential distortions by the presence of participant observers. Dégérando's detailed collection of domains of inquiry and observations almost reads like a first draft of a table of contents of a handbook in cross-cultural psychology: he proposed, among other things, an analysis of the savage's sensations (perception), , association of ideas, foresight, reflection (cognitive processes and language), opinions and judgement (belief systems, morals and conventions), attention and reflective needs (emotion and motivation, the cognitive part being integrated!), imbecility (psychopathology) and the moral education of children (developmental niche). For each domain (selected according to Condillac's sensationist theory) several important questions were defined and various hints concerning methodological strategies were offered. Because of the unfortunate external circumstances of the voyage, this field manual could not be put into effect during Baudin's expedition. Nevertheless, the member of the Société who participated in the enterprise and represented the sciences of men, François Peron, was the first to test a cross-cultural differential hypothesis using experimental methods. As far as empirical studies of other peoples are concerned, another member of the "Observateurs" has to be mentioned, namely Volney. He used his firsthand information about the life of the North-American Indians to argue against the armchair theories then prevailing about these peoples. His account of indigenous social organization and mentality can be interpreted as a forerunner of the later culture-and-personality approaches (Mauviel, 1988).

Due to political changes and a general shift in the intellectual climate, these early predecessors of empirical cross-cultural studies of human diversity were forgotten for more than a century. The 19th-century conception of the variety of human forms of life was marked by two important changes of perspective, diverting dominant interest away from what we understand as cross-cultural psychology's major goals.

First, there was a strong orientation towards a biological explanation of differences between human groups as distinct "races" having separate origins (Banton, 1987). This emphasis on differences rather than similarities arose in part from efforts at empirical classification (of the living world in general and humans in particular), based initially on the "Great chain of beings." The great taxonomists of the 18th century, like Buffon, Linnaeus, or Blumenbach still defended the idea of the unity of all human forms. But the craniological approaches, which became dominant from the first half of the 19th century onward, attributed the supposed mental inferiority of savages to genetically determined anatomical features. Such ideas are not altogether extinct even at the end of the second millenium (Rushton, 1995).

Second, belief in the general progress of mankind was replaced by two main alternative views. One was that of the above-mentioned race theorists who claimed that each race had a separate origin (polygenism). The other view granted a common origin, but one that was located in the far distant past and claimed that an irreversible diversification had taken place. The latter idea, although not necessitated by Darwinian theory, was not incompatible with it; and polygenists made use of it for their purpose. In such biologically oriented discourse, cultural variations were treated as secondary manifestation of inferiority due to race differences. While race theories were dominant, others like Pritchard in Britain, or Waitz and Bastian in Germany, opposed them and maintained the Enlightenment tradition of psychic unity. A related strand of thought was philological, concerned with the evolution of languages. From mid-19th century onward this became fused with the socio-evolutionary theories of Comte, Spencer, Tylor, and Frazer. Although they were partly influenced by ideas about race, the major thrust of their argument was that climatic and socioeconomic factors, operating over a long time span on a basically uniform human psyche, had produced the existing cultural variations; savages were merely less advanced along the evolutionary path. The social evolutionists prepared the ground for empirical studies, which began during the latter part of the 19th century. This concludes the prehistory, and the second part will deal with outstanding figures and some more recent trends.

Early Pioneers

Edward Burnet Tylor (1832–1917)

Tylor, often regarded as the father of anthropology, framed the famous definition of *culture*:

> Culture or Civilization, taken in its widest ethnographic sense, is that complex whole which includes knowledge, belief, art, morals, law, custom, and any other capabilities and habits acquired by man as a member of society. The condition of culture among the various societies of mankind, in so far as it is capable of being investigated on general principles, is a subject apt for the study of laws of human thought and action. (1871/1958, p. 1).

Note the phrase "laws of human thought," implying that these are universal, and so he also regarded the linear progressive development, at differing rates, of all human groups. In the absence of historical information social evolutionists believed that this sequence could be reconstructed by the "comparative method," which entailed looking at the features of contemporary peoples at varying stages of development and thereby teasing out uniform causes. Tylor (1889) proposed a quantitative approach to this problem in a paper read at a meeting in 1888. His aim was to investigate "the development of institutions" by systematic cross-tabulation, in order to demonstrate clusters of customs that must have been the result of general causes, essentially psychological in character. Also present at the meeting was Galton, who pointed that some of the "adhesions" (read "correlations") may be the result of geographical propinquity and consequent borrowing; this is still known as "Galton's problem" (cf. Naroll, 1973). The comparative method was later applied by Hobhouse, Wheeler, and Ginsberg (1930) in what they sub-titled "an essay in correlation." The idea was subsequently taken up by the American anthropologist G. P. Murdock who created a massive database of all world cultures known as the "Human Relations Area Files" (HRAF). The HRAF has become an important tool for "hologeistic" research, testing hypotheses across a wide range of cultures.

By then, of course, the method had long become entirely divorced from the social evolutionism from which it had originated. The demise of the theory was largely due to the influence of the German-born American anthropologist Franz Boas (1858–1942) to whom we shall return.

Francis Galton (1822–1911)

Galton, a cousin of Charles Darwin, was the originator of the study of psychological differences between individuals and groups. In his *Hereditary genius* (1869/1914) he devised a scheme for the "classification of men according to their natural gifts," under which he included both "general power" and "special aptitudes." He devised a scale ranging from A (very low) to G (very high), and in the latter part of the book attempted an assessment of "the comparative worth of different races" on that basis. For this purpose he made certain simplifying assumptions about the distribution of abilities within races. On this basis he rated the ancient Greeks some two grades above contemporary Anglo-Saxons, and the "Lowland Scotch and English North country men . . . a fraction of a grade superior to that of the ordinary English . . ." (1914, p. 328). The African Negroes he ranked two grades below the English, and the Australian Aborigines one grade below Negroes. This sketchy summary might convey the impression that his ratings were arbitrary and merely a function of the racial prejudice so common at the time. Prejudice probably played some part, but Galton also considered a variety of factors, as may be illustrated in relation to Negroes. He began by stating that "If the negro race in America had been affected by no social disabilities, a comparison of their achievements with those of the whites in their several branches of intellectual effort, having regard to the total number of their respective populations, would give the necessary information. As matters stand, we must be content with much rougher data." (1914, pp. 326/7). He then went on to say that there were some outstandingly able Negroes, and many others well above the average of Whites. On the other hand he adduced several supposed reasons why the bulk of Negroes should be considered well below that average; for instance he cited the then generally accepted view that a high proportion of Negroes are half-witted. Galton himself had travelled extensively in Africa, making careful observations. He made use of those in his studies of what he called the "visualising faculty," by which he meant what we now call "space perception": "Among the races that are thus gifted are the commonly despised, but, as I confidently maintain from personal experience, the much underrated Bushmen of South Africa." (Galton 1883/1928, p. 70). Similarly, he attributed to Eskimos the ability "to see vast tracts of country mapped out in their heads" (p. 72). These observations have since been confirmed by more recent work in cross-cultural psychology (cf. Berry, 1966). Galton was also interested in problems of what we would call "acculturation" of "savages" to civilized life and issued a questionnaire on the topic (cf. Jahoda, 1980), though no results were ever published.

William Halse Rivers (1864–1922)

Rivers was an experimental psychologist at Cambridge when he was invited by the anthropologist Alfred C. Haddon to take part in the Cambridge Anthropological Expedition to the Torres Straits (New Guinea) in 1898. Rivers in turn recruited two other psychologists, William McDougall and C. S. Myers, but his was the major contribution. At the time Rivers was still under the influence of social evolutionary theory, especially Herbert Spencer's version which held that "primitives" expend most of their mental energy on perception and therefore have not developed the higher cognitive processes. Accordingly, the research program, on which Rivers consulted Galton, concentrated on sensory functioning. It covered a remarkably wide range, including many measures of sensory acuity (visual, auditory, and tactile), designed to test the century-old belief that "savages" were closer to animals in possessing a much higher degree of sensory acuity than Europeans. Among other topics were colorvision, color blindness, color nomenclature, sensitivity to pain, discrimination of weights, and motor skills.

It is neither possible nor necessary to say much about the findings, with a few exceptions. What is of major concern in the present context is the methodological sophistication displayed by Rivers and his colleagues, in what must be remembered was the first systematic effort to study "primitives" by psychological methods. All their methods had either been adapted or specially devised for the particular circumstances. Communication was initially in "pidgin English," but they gradually acquired relevant vernacular terms. They were well aware of the need to "sell" their work and "the natives were told that some people had said that the black man could see and hear etc., better than the white man, and that we had come to find out how clever they were. . . ." (Rivers, 1901, p. 3). Men received a reward of a stick of tobacco for a morning's work, children sweets; moreover, medical services were provided for the inhabitants. Even though motivated to do their best, attention would flag when the procedure was lengthy, and pauses were introduced to reduce the effects of fatigue. An increase in "mean variation" (the precursor of standard deviation) over a session was taken as an index of decreasing attention. To control for this, repeated testing was done at different times of the day. On the whole Rivers was confident of the reliability of his measures: "In fact, I believe that the results are in some cases even more consistent than those made by civilized people, and especially by students of psychology. The latter, when asked to make a given measurement, are very apt to begin to speculate about what they are asked to do and allow their knowledge to influence their judgements" (Rivers, 1901, p. 6). It should be mentioned here that Titchener (1916) in a critical article questioned not merely many of Rivers' conclusions as unsubstantiated, but expressed doubts as to whether it is possible in principle to conduct valid experimental research in the field. Essentially he argued that such research cannot be replicated, since no two field situations are alike. His was probably the first attempt at a radical critique of cross-cultural methods. Returning to Rivers, he was faced with the problem of ascertaining ages, often still encountered. He used a variety of devices for rank-ordering, since people usually knew relative ages. He was also well aware that differential familiarity with materials affects the outcome of comparisons, and for this reason introduced practice sessions. Thus he commented that Murray Islanders, as compared with adults from Aberdeen, benefited more rapidly from practice in pitch discrimination.

Rivers displayed considerable ingenuity in devising new approaches. For instance, for the purpose of assessing color preferences he organized discussion groups, checking this (with what are now called "unobtrusive methods") by noting the colors of the cloths worn. A similar approach was used for color nomenclature, where he sought to link an alleged defective sensitivity to blue to the nature of color names. This is one of the areas intensively studied more recently. The other is that of visual illusions, where it had been thought that "savages," being stupid, would be more readily deceived. By showing that Europeans are more susceptible to certain types of illusions, Rivers not only disposed of that notion, but provided the inspiration for the extensive work of Segall, Campbell, and Herskovits (1966) .

Rivers' studies were followed up by taking advantage of the presence at the 1904 St. Louis Fair of "primitives" from several parts of the world. F. G. Bruner

(1908) produced a lengthy and detailed report concluding that the hearing of whites, contrary to prevaling beliefs, is superior to that of "primitives." Woodworth (1910), who had also tested people on various sense modalities, disagreed, confirming in most respects Rivers' results. Unlike Rivers, Woodworth never published the details of his procedures (Hayslip, 1973).

Richard Thurnwald (1869–1954)

Seemingly unaware at the time of Rivers' studies, the German ethnologist Richard Thurnwald was engaged on fieldwork in Melanesia between 1906 and 1909. Although not a trained psychologist, he was interested in what he called "ethnic psychology" and carried out a number of small-scale studies as a kind of sideline to his main ethnographic work. Unburdened by the preconceptions of social–evolutionary theory, he decided on some pilot investigations of what we would call cognitive functioning (Thurnwald, 1913). His aim was to bring together ethnology and psychology, and he may thus be regarded as a precursor of what was much later to become psychological anthropology. For that purpose he reckoned that psychophysical studies of sensory processes were unimportant compared with an understanding of differences in higher mental functioning. His approach was ingenious, and in some respects remarkably in advance of his time. For instance, he was the first to employ the method of serial reproduction later associated with Bartlett (cf. Jahoda, 1989). Although much less well known outside his native Germany than Rivers, his contribution was far from negligible and deserves to be better remembered.

Frederic C. Bartlett (1886–1969)

Bartlett was a student of Rivers, which explains the direction of his interests that first found expression in his *Psychology and primitive culture* (1923). In it he argued against the still prevailing ethnocentrism, but it was essentially a rather general and speculative work without empirical data. A decade later he became more directly involved, as he explained in his classic work *Remembering:* "A visit to Africa gave me the opportunity to carry out some first-hand observation on social recall in the relatively little studied group of Swazi natives. Whatever else this part of the work may amount to, I think it may fairly be claimed to point to a type of field investigation for the psychologist which has been strangely neglected, but which might readily yield results, not only of theoretical, but also of great practical importance and value" (1932, p. vi). These were prophetic words, ignored at the time. The book contains the first empirical studies of cultural influences on memory, carried out in both field and laboratory.

An Example: Psychological Research in Africa

A survey of worldwide psychological research during the first half of the 20th century would be a mammoth undertaking that is well beyond our means. However, the existence of excellent bibliographies focusing on Africa makes it possible to roughly outline the major lines of work in that continent. Of the three main sources available, Andor (1966) lacks an unambiguous classification of articles, Irvine, Sanders, and Klingelhofer (1970) do not cover years prior to 1950, and therefore the work of Hoorweg and Marais (1969) has been used.

Out of a total of some sixty studies reported for the period up to 1949, more than half were concerned with either IQ-testing as such or discussions (often with few if any data) of African learning ability; a single important exception is dealt with more fully below. About one-third of the studies concern the performance of African children at school. The remainder is largely clinical, though if one counts contributions made by psychiatrists (which have been excluded) the proportion would be higher. Experimental studies are conspicuous by their absence, unless one includes work by Thouless (1933) on perception, done with African students in Britain, or a study by an anthropologist originally trained in psychology (Nadel, 1937).

Generally, it will be seen that apart from IQ-testing the total amount of cross-cultural work over half a century was practically neglible, and that in spite of the fact that psychologists were active in the European countries with colonial possessions in Africa. The reasons for this indifference are probably twofold: psychologists other than those concerned with individual and group differences were at the time, even more than now, convinced that theirs was a universalist science; and then there was the simple fact that few, if any, psychologists had any opportunity for a career in Africa. The one important exception, referred to above, was South Africa where professional psychology existed. One educational psychologist, affiliated with the National Bureau for Educational and Social Research, wrote a report in which he claimed that African children in early adolescence are some four or five years inferior in educability, as judged by IQ tests, than European children. A powerful refutation of this absurd claim was published in a book by Biesheuvel (1943), who subsequently became one of the most distinguished occupational and cross-cultural psychologists. The early post-war years remained rather fallow, but thereafter began a surge that is evident from Table 1–1, covering the decade of the 1950s.

TABLE 1–1 Psychology in Africa 1950–1959: Numbers of publications (of a total of 187) dealing with various topics

Occupational	36
IQ tests and similar ("learning ability")	34
Clinical	26
Social	21
Developmental	18
Experimental	14
Educational	13
Personality/Motivation	11
Projective techniques	10
Effects of malnutrition	3

It will seen that some three times more was done during that decade than during the whole of the preceding half century. Moreover, the range of topics became greatly widened, a change for which several factors were responsible. The dominance of occupational psychology reflects the intense activity of the National Institute of Personnel Research in South Africa and to a lesser extent that of institutions like the Institut Français de l'Afrique Noire (IFAN). The category "IQ tests and similar" now covers a much greater proportion of occupational ability testing, and clinical work by psychologists also increased, notably in the francophone territories. There was also a great surge in nonapplied research, due in considerable part to the founding of new universities to which psychologists (initially in very small numbers) came to be recruited. Lastly, a trickle of researchers from outside Africa began, notably from the United States where there had been a long tradition of black–white comparisons. Although it is of course not suggested that this African example is representative of the world output of cross-cultural research, it is probably typical of a period of increasingly rapid expansion. It should also be noted that until the 1970s, when the number of black African psychologists had begun to increase, the bulk of research in Africa had been undertaken by expatriates or South African whites.

Psychology in India and Latin America[7]

In these countries, unlike the situation in Africa, indigenous psychologists existed and were active during the postwar years. While they sometimes collaborated with (mainly North American) colleagues, independent contributions became increasingly common. Similarly, while at the outset "transplanted" western psychology was dominant and much of the work was imitative and consisted of replications, this also began to change toward the end of the period considered here.

In India much of the early work was prompted by doubts as to whether the findings of "borrowed" psychology were valid under the very different sociocultural conditions of the Indian subcontinent. This concerned studies in a variety of spheres such as reaction time, perception, and moral judgments—very different from the African research conducted by expatriates with its strong emphasis on intelligence testing. Much of the work dealt with applied fields such as problems of morale and effective supervision in industrial organizations (Bose, 1955, 1958; Ganguli, 1954, 1961) and factors affecting job satisfaction (Sinha, 1958). Many of these studies were not directly comparative, but others were, such as Sinha (1963) on manifest anxiety and Minturn and Lambert (1964) on child-rearing practices. Generally, aspects of child development became a salient topic during the 1960s (Verma et al., 1969; Muralidharan, 1971), but Piagetian studies came later. Lastly, special mention should be made of a pioneering study by Sinha (1969) of motivation among a rural population, which anticipated the "cultural psychology" approach. From the 1970s onward cross-cultural psychology blossomed into a vigorous area of research activity (Mitra, 1972; Pareek, 1981; Pandey, 1988; see also Sinha chapter in this volume).

Latin America has a long tradition in psychology, and as early as 1920 a psychologist in Lima used the Binet–Simon Test with Peruvian children. After the translation of Freud's work in 1923 the influence of psychoanalysis became important, as reflected, for instance, in studies of black Brasilians (Ardila, 1982, 1994). Such scattered early studies were not comparative, and the impetus for the beginnings of cross-cultural studies stemmed from the foundation in 1951 in Mexico of the Inter-American Society of Psychology. By the time of the third congress of the Society, which took place in Austin, Texas, the general tenor of the contributions had a pronounced cross-cultural flavor (Gilbert, 1956). In successive congresses this tendency became progressively more marked, and a distinctive new approach focusing on the concept of "sociocultural premises" was introduced by Diaz-Guerrero (1963, 1964). The presidential address of the eleventh congress was entitled "Cross-cultural studies in psychology," which epitomized the overall theme (Natalicio, Hereford, & Natalicio, 1967). Lastly, special mention should be made of one of the most comprehensive comparative (Mexican versus US) studies ever undertaken, which employed a longitudinal overlapping design with a sample of children aged between 7 and 18 years, which started with work by Diaz-Guerrero (1964) and was later published as a book (Holtzman, Diaz-Guerrero, & Swartz, 1975). As evidenced, from the 1950s onward a lively concern with cross-cultural issues developed in Latin America, which has also been documented by Ardila (1968, 1982).

The Institutionalization of Cross-Cultural Psychology

The 1960s saw a continuing expansion at an accelerated rate, reflected in the growth of publication outlets: the *Journal of Social Psychology* published many early cross-cultural studies; the *International Journal of Psychology*, largely devoted to cross-cultural and cross-national topics, first appeared in 1966, to be followed in 1970 by the *Journal of Cross-Cultural Psychology*. Enough material was by then available for the publication of a series of books of readings, the first and least well known among these being a collection of translations from French sources (Wickert, 1967). Under the aegis of the International Biological Programme several cross-cultural psychologists under the editorship of Biesheuvel (1969) were invited to contribute to a manual concerned with "practical knowledge of cross-cultural testing and its problems." This showed a recognition of special cross-cultural expertise by a prestigious international body. The International Association for Cross-Cultural Psychology was established in 1972 with Jerome Bruner as the president. A year later the *Annual Review of Psychology* for the first time included a chapter on "psychology and culture" (Triandis, Malpass, & Davidson, 1973). In terms of publication outlets and an institutional basis, cross-cultural psychology had "arrived" by the mid-1970s. In 1984 it was formally established also in the francophone scientific community by the foundation of ARIC ("Association pour la recherche interculturelle").

However, as far as university curricula are concerned, the acceptance of the relevance of culture for psychology has been exceedingly slow and patchy; the gains achieved by the mid-90s have not been negligible, but neither have they been very substantial. There are several reasons for this reluctance, and possibly the major one is the threat posed by cross-cultural psychology to the supposed universality of psychological "laws" based on studies in western industrial countries. Surveying the overall trends in cross-cultural psychology from Rivers to the present, certain features stand out. While Rivers followed well-controlled experimental procedures, this approach fell largely into abeyance for some sixty years. Most of the work during that period tended to be loosely descriptive, without any guiding theory or hypotheses. It was either oriented toward practical problems in the colonial setting, or chiefly concerned to demonstrate "differences" (read "deficiencies") between non-western peoples and Europeans. This was usually done by comparing either performances or responses on some kind of scale by Europeans and non-Europeans, and often adducing a more or less ad hoc (and often "racial") interpretation of the differences found.

One notable exception was the work of Luria in Uzbekistan during the early 1930s. Its theoretical basis was the Russian socio-historical school of Vygotsky, which in turn goes back to Marx and Hegel, though in addition Vygotsky drew his inspiration from Janet, Lévy-Bruhl, and Wundt. Unlike the then prevailing preoccupation with intelligence testing, Luria was concerned with modes of cognitive functioning, especially syllogistic reasoning and its relationship to formal schooling. Since its results were at the time regarded as politically unsound, it was not published for more than a generation until the political climate had changed (Luria, 1976). The Vygotskyan socio-historical theory inspired Michael Cole, who was largely responsible for introducing it into the West. Trained as an experimental psychologist, his early work in West Africa was conducted basically along the lines of cross-cultural psychology. However, as he himself explained (Cole, 1978), he began to have doubts about the assumptions underlying much of cross-cultural psychology and some loss of faith in conventional experimentation in that field. The theories of Vygotsky and Luria led him to a fundamental rethinking of the nature of "culture" and its relation to the human mind, and also of the ways in which these issues could be investigated. Hence he moved from "cross-cultural" to what is now known as "cultural" psychology, but his position is in some respects very different from that adopted later by Shweder (1990).

Returning to the main line of cross-cultural psychology, this did not take off again until after the Second World War. The most outstanding turn towards more rigorous research was the effort by Segall, Campbell, and Herskovits (1966) to provide explanations for the old findings by Rivers concerning visual illusions. Their hypothesis that ecological factors were responsible was largely confirmed, and from then onward and for more than two decades ecological theorizing remained prominent. Unlike their interpretation of a direct effect of ecology on perceptual processes, later studies saw ecology as determining modes of subsistence, which in turn tended to shape culture or at least set certain constraints on it. For a period psychological differentiation became a key concept linking ecology with culture and individual development; but eventually in a large-scale critical project (Berry et al., 1986) it failed to come up to its initial promise. Roughly the same period also saw a burgeoning interest in the cross-cultural testing of Piagetian theory, whose origins will be examined in more detail in the following section. Moreover, the cross-cultural study of infant and child development also came to be pursued in alternative theoretical contexts (e.g., Vygotsky and attachment theory), all of which yielded valuable fresh insights. As far as social psychology is concerned, much attention has lately been devoted to acculturation studies, and cultural differences in individual and group behaviour have been analyzed in terms of "individualism-collectivism." The latter, it should be noted, is essentially a descriptive concept, the question as to why cultures come to be located in particular segments of this dimension being so far left open. Other topics displaying more continuity over several decades have been perception, memory, and other cognitive processes.

The Beginnings of Piagetian Studies

In his earliest writings Piaget, influenced by Lévy-Bruhl, put a great deal of emphasis on what we would now call socio-cultural factors. For instance, he argued (Piaget, 1928) that "primitive mentality" is less socialized than our own. There followed a phase when this stance appears to have been largely abandoned, the theory being presented as though it had been a purely psychobiological one. Perhaps this impression is misleading, but what is certain is that most publications of that period scarcely contain any mention of possible cultural variations. During the 1950s Piaget took part in discussions on child development (Tanner & Inhelder, 1960) attended also by Margaret Mead. It is likely that her persuasive arguments made some impact. At any rate, his own contribution, while still under the heading of "psychobiological development" was marked by a distinct change of tone:

> As regards the cultural and social aspect, we may recall how Margaret Mead, who proposed repeating in New Guinea certain of our intelligence tests (conservation, spatial relations, etc.) was in agreement with the theory according to which the stages of reactions to these tests might be the same as regards the order of succession, but might be very different as regards average ages or even the non-attainment of higher levels. And this implies that social factors are constantly interacting with other factors . . . all this is self- evident (Tanner & Inhelder, 1960, p. 5).

In fact Margaret Mead's (1932) work with Manus children of the Admiralty Islands had been a pioneering study of animism. Her radically negative conclusions were, however, generally not supported in numerous subsequent replications inspired by Piaget. Early ones include Dennis (1943) with Zuni and Hopi children, and Jahoda (1958) with Ga, Ewe, and Fante ones in Ghana. In 1959 an unpublished Ph.D. thesis by D. M. G. Hyde at the University of London dealt with the development of the concept of number among children in Aden. This was followed by Price-William's (1961) work on concepts of conservation of quantity with Tiv children in Nigeria, and Goodnow's (1962) Piagetian study with Hong Kong Chinese children. A few years later Piaget (1966) gave his full blessing to such efforts, going so far as to concede that his theory must remain "conjectural" as long as it has not been verified cross-culturally. Thereafter followed an almost exponential expansion of cross-cultural Piagetian studies across the globe, largely confirming a uniform sequence of stages though not their chronology in terms of age (Dasen, 1972). In order to explain such developmental differences, research turned to the analysis of factors influencing cognitive performance in different cultures. These included ecological settings, the kinds of objects present in the children's environments, and the pattern of everyday activities (Dasen & Heron, 1981). These lines of research meshed with the socio-historical approach, which focused on the functional relationship between situational demands and cognitive competencies, stressing context-specificity in structuring cognitive development (Laboratory of Comparative Human Cognition, 1983).

While cognitive development has been by far the most important topic of cross-cultural research, mention should also be made of Kohlberg whose (1958) thesis on "moral thinking" was based on Piaget's (1932) classical work on moral judgment. Kohlberg postulated a more elaborate series of stages of "moral reasoning" which he regarded as universal. The outcome of numerous cross-cultural tests of this claim remains ambiguous. One the one hand, the existence and invariant sequence of most of Kohlberg's stages could be demonstrated in many cultures and the often presumed western bias of his morality concept (e.g., Simpson, 1974) could not be firmly established. On the other hand, cross-cultural research revealed that Kohlberg's key choice of the justice principle is not as comprehensive as theoretically assumed: there are other ethical principles like filiation, cosmic orientation, or collective happiness (Eckensberger 1993; Eckensberger & Zimba in this *Handbook*; Edwards, 1981, 1986; Snarey, 1985).

Some Methodological Debates

The simple comparisons of (usually) a European with a non-European group on some measures have been radically challenged by Campbell and Naroll (1961), on the grounds that any comparison of two natural groups can in practice seldom be adequately interpreted. The context in which they developed their discussion was Malinowski's critique of Oedipal theory, a perennial topic of debate. Since there are innumerable differences of various kinds between Trobriand and Vienna, many of these could provide alternative explanations that could not be ruled out; hence in such pairwise comparisons "other things" cannot assumed to be equal, and therefore the significance of such results remains obscure. The minimum requirement is "triangulation," making it possible to show that certain relationships remain constant across three of more cultures.

Subsequently, one way in which the comparison of two natural groups can be rendered meaningful has been demonstrated by Rosch Heider (1972) in the context of color focality. The hypothesis was that focal colors would be better re-called than non-focal ones, irrespective of cultural background or color lexicon. There are, of course, vast differences between the Dani and Americans, including a sharp contrast in color vocabulary (Dani have only two terms). It is thus not surprising that in absolute terms American subjects recalled far more colors than Dani subjects; but *relatively* better recall of focal colors was found in both sets of subjects.

Another issue, dealt with more fully in later chapters of this volume, con-cerns the logical status of "culture" from a methodological point of view. An early approach was that of Strodtbeck (1964), who proposed that "culture" could be regarded as an experimental "treatment" for individual subjects. Perhaps the investigator has reason to believe that some kind of experience may affect indi-viduals in a particular way; he may then search for a culture which can serve as a natural experiment to test this idea (cf. Berry, 1966). But Segall (1984) dismissed "culture" as an intolerably vague entity and proposed substituting sets of vari-ables. He agreed with LeVine's (1970) suggestion that one should start with de-pendent variables: "first find a puzzle, then try to find the variables that solve it" (p. 129). But how do you find a worthwhile puzzle? This clearly depends on prior research having been done. It would be useful in this connection to distinguish between "hypothesis-generating" and "hypothesis-testing" research.

These kinds of discussions clearly indicate that the ideal-type cross-cultural psychology takes natural science as its model. The avowed object is to discover the causes of such cultural differences as may be encountered, and to tease out the universal psychological features underlying such surface differences. These aims are grounded in the posivist philosophy whose origins, together with that of its alternative, have already been sketched. This alternative has in recent years re-emerged under the banner of "cultural psychology." In its ideal-type version this implies a complete rejection of the natural science model in favor of the status of a Geisteswissenschaft, a humane discipline.

The Rise and Decline of the Culture-and-Personality School

In a seminal paper Boas (1896) attacked the basic assumption of social evolution-ary theory, in particular the supposed uniformity of progressive development taken to be the outcome of the same psychic disposition responding to similar environmental contingencies. Boas argued that apparently similar cultural phe-nomena could have been produced by quite different historical, environmental, and psychological influences. The methodological consequence was that one should abandon global theorizing, concentrating instead on particular local cul-tures. This emphasis on historical and environmental factors also led him to criti-cize interpretations in terms of race (Boas, 1911). Among his students were Edward Sapir, Ruth Benedict and Margaret Mead, who each in their own way extended and reinterpreted Boas' environmental determinism. Unlike Tylor, who always referred to "culture" in the singular, they were concerned with particular cultures; and under the influence of Gestalt psychology they saw them as specifically patterned and integrated. This suggested a parallel between the organization of a culture and that of a personality, an analogy carried furthest by Benedict (1934) who stated that culture is "personality writ large"; accordingly, she also used a typology derived from Jung to characterize cultures. Mead began as a psychology "Major" and in many of her field trips carried a psychological toolbox with her. Her early book on Samoa (1928) has the subtitle *A psychological study of primitive youth for Western civilisation* (revealing incidentally the axe she had to grind), and in an appendix the tests she used are listed. Her initial unbridled environmentalism, moderated later, led her to claim that human behavior is almost infinitely malleable.

The predominance of the "configurational" approach to culture and personality declined when Ralph Linton replaced Boas at Columbia University (Department of Anthropology) and ran seminars on the topic with Abram Kardiner, a neo-Freudian psychoanalyst. Their aim was to move from broad generalities to identifying the actual processes linking culture, ecology, and personality. They proposed a causal chain going from ecology to "primary institutions" (types of subsistence, households, and child training) to what they named "basic personality structure" (shared motivations and neuroses, etc.) to "secondary institutions" (religion, mythology, and other projective elements). While Kardiner directed the enterprise from Columbia, the anthropologists went into the field and collected data (which included Porteus Maze tests, children's drawings, and notably Rorschach protocols) to be subsequently analyzed (Kardiner et al., 1939, 1945). This model held out the promise of being able to unravel the dynamic interactions between subsistence, child training, and shared psychological characteristics. Unfortunately the model suffered from many weaknesses. As Melford Spiro once wrote, its juxtaposition of culture and personality was "a false dichotomy."

When the assumption of common "basic personality structure" was not merely incapable of being demonstrated empirically, but came to be questioned theoretically, Cora DuBois (1944/1961) suggested a shift to the notion of "modal personality." This implies that each culture has a personality type that occurs with the greatest relative frequency, which seems more plausible. Strict ascertainment of "modal personality" is, however, complicated by the shortcomings of personality measures and the practical difficulty of achieving representativeness in larger populations. One of the most interesting and sophisticated examples of this kind of approach was of LeVine (1966), who concentrated on levels of achievement motivation in three major Nigerian groups, namely Hausa, Ibo, and Yoruba. He postulated the following causal chain: status mobility system—parental values (concept of ideal successful man)—child rearing practices—frequencies of certain personality variables. His predicted decreasing order of nAch (Ibo, Yoruba and Hausa) was confirmed, a fact which embroiled him in controversy with the advent of the Biafran war. While the original culture-and-personality school faded away in the post-war period, the concern with the relationship between child training and personality persisted. Outstanding contributors in this sphere were John and Beatrice Whiting, who moved from initial use of the Human Relations

Area Files to an extensive program of systematic observations. An overview not only of their work, but that of most prominent others in that field can be found in Spindler (1978).

Relations between Psychology and Psychological Anthropology

As far as academic psychology is concerned, the relationship has been almost exclusively an asymmetric one. Most anthropologists have always recognized their need for a psychology (cf. Jahoda, 1982). Amateur as well as later professional ethnographers were expected to provide information about the psychological characteristics of the peoples they visited. As soon as psychological tools became available, anthropologists began to use them in the field. In the Hall of Pacific Peoples of the American Museum of Natural History, dedicated to Margaret Mead, her collection of psychological testing materials is displayed. Yet all this was before there was any "psychological anthropology" as such. The first use of that expression dates back to mid-19th century, when the notorious racist (and, incidentally, uncle of Rivers) James Hunt uttered these prophetic words in his retiring adress to the Anthropological Society of London: "After a time, I think it will be found that the study of physical anthropology will be followed by researches in psychological anthropology." (Hunt, 1867, p. lxviii) Two years later Owen Pike commented that "without psychology there is no anthropology" (1870, p. xi). But it was not until 1961, when Hsu edited what appears to have been the first book with the title "psychological anthropology," that a new specialization was so named. Initially it was in fact a re naming of the culture-and-personality tradition, that had fallen into some disrepute. The need for such a special field had been been recognized in 1931 by Malinowski, who had written: "Between the spheres of psychology and anthropology, there is today a No-man's-land. Whether or not this will ever be claimed a special branch of science, it must for the present be filled by workers in both fields making excursions towards the other's province. Nor should the serious worker in either field ignore or resent such excursions, for they may have much of value for him in indicating new lines of research" (Malinowski, 1931, p. xi).

Although Malinowski was based at the London School of Economics, his views were far from typical of British anthropology. From the 1930s until about the 1960s this was dominated by the Durkheimian ideology of Radcliffe-Brown, whose social–structural approach, contrasted with the cultural style of American anthropology, denied any relevance of psychology. One later British anthropologist remarked on the "phobic reaction to psychology and psychoanalysis of Radcliffe-Brown and his followers" (Lewis 1977, p. 2).

Similarly, early in the century French anthropology was predominantly physical. The distinguished psychologist Henri Piéron wrote an article in 1909 with the title *L'anthropologie psychologique* that invited French anthropologists to take advantage of what psychology then had to offer; there seems to have been no response. The same was true in Britain of a paper by Sir Frederic Bartlett (1937) on *Psychological methods and anthropological problems.* The differences in American and European attitudes to psychology are probably to be accounted for by the enormous influence on American anthropology of Franz Boas, who from the early stages of his career onwards had a lively interest in the subject. During the later post-war period anthropological opinion in France and Britain changed. Radcliffe-Brown's dominance faded, and in France Lévi-Strauss echoed Owen Pike when he said "l'ethnologie est d'abord une psychologie." (Ethnology is first of all a psychology).

Returning to psychological anthropology, this has undergone substantial changes of direction during the past two decades or so. Originally it had remained fairly closely tied to its inheritance from the personality-and-culture school, with its psychoanalytic theories and projective techniques. The reason was that the academic theories of the period had little to offer towards an understanding of what Kluckhohn called "human nature in the raw," the behavior of people in their sociocultural contexts, their meanings and values which concern anthropologists. The coming of the "cognitive revolution" and the progress in developmental psychology changed all that, and they eagerly (perhaps sometimes excessively so) seized upon conceptual tools which, together with others from linguistics and biology, they came to regard as valuable and relevant. A convergence occurred whereby anthropologists from America and Europe, irrespective of whether or not they adopted the label "psychological," seized upon the new ideas. This may exemplied by a recent book on cognitive aspects of religious symbolism (Boyer, 1993): three, including the editor, are British; and the others are French, American, and Canadian. This cross-national rapprochement between anthropology and psychology unfortunately remains very one-sided. In a recent survey of developments in psychological anthropology (Schwartz, White, & Lutz, 1992) several of the contributors note regretfully that their acceptance of modern psychology has not been reciprocated. Few psychological texts cite any anthropological work, and though the contributors fail to mention it, this also applies largely to texts in cross-cultural psychology.

Continuing Foci of (Cross-) Cultural Interest from the Past Until Today

Our brief sketch of the history of cultural and cross-cultural psychology should have revealed recurring methodological approaches and theoretical ideas. Whether this may be considered the result of the universal psychic structure of the human beings involved in theory building (as Vico would have argued), or whether caused by the historical transmission of basic ideas, are moot issues. In any case, there is a lesson to be learned: being more familiar with the work of our historical ancestors not only helps to give a clearer awareness of our own hidden assumptions, but may also reduce the danger of a periodic re-invention of the wheel. Thus, to conclude, we would like to summarize some of these continuing themes of (cross)-cultural theory building and research.

The Cultural Bias of Human Self-Understanding

What is actually discussed under the title of the "emic-etic" problem, or the challenge of establishing equivalent forms of concepts and methods for cross-cultural analysis, has a long history in different guises. Ethnocentric distortions could be purely taxonomic, totally ignoring the status as a human being of the cultural other; or they could be evolutionary, considering otherness as an immature form of our actual existence; or they appear in our empirical approaches by measuring, observing, and conceptualizing the other through our lenses. Thus, in spite of their very different forms, all historical approaches to the analysis of human diversity seem to entail the inevitability of cultural reference points in attempts at human self-understanding.

Perception and Cognition

Until the end of the 19th century it was believed, on the basis of anecdotal evidence, that the sensory acuity of "savages" greatly exceeded that of Europeans. This notion was linked to the supposedly greater "animality" of savages. For a long time this remained merely part of the conventional wisdom, until Cuvier's "new biology" seemed to provide it with a scientific foundation. Some observers began to question this view during the latter part of the 19th century, and one of Rivers' chief aims in the course of the Cambridge expedition to the Torres Straits was to settle the issue. Rivers demonstrated the falsity of the belief and also carried out studies of illusion susceptibility, putting forward a hypothesis to explain the differences. After a lapse of about half a century this was taken up in the now classical work of Segall et al. (1966), which marked the start of modern cross-cultural studies of perceptual function.

The supposedly greater "animality" of "savages" also long entailed the view that they were ignorant and stupid, lacking in reason. This notion came to be modified by many of the thinkers of the Enlightenment, who saw in the savages the infancy of humanity, destined to continuous upward progress. They distinguished ignorance from stupidity: according to them, savages were ignorant in the sense that they had not yet achieved art and science, but they were not stupid. The possession of reason was regarded as an inherent characteristic of all humans, who differed only in the extent to which they were able to apply reason effectively. This view, which corresponds essentially to our own, largely came to be abandoned during the 19th century. Biological racism implied the permanent inferiority of the "lower races." The contrast can be nicely illustrated by a comparison: both Ferguson in mid-18th century, and Lubbock some hundred years later, gave similar accounts of the practical skills of savages. While the former sought thereby to show that they were far from stupid, the latter used it to exemplify their low levels of functioning. The social evolutionist Herbert Spencer argued that "primitives" were so preoccupied with perception that they had little mental energy left for reflection. This was a view Rivers had accepted at the time of the Cambridge expedition, who therefore made no attempt to assess higher mental functioning, confining himself to sensory processes. Early in the 20th century Lévy-Bruhl put forward his (often misunderstood) thesis that the modes of thought of primitives were fundamentally different from those of westerners, though he did not suggest that they were stupid. In somewhat different form, the kinds of problems raised by him still remain central to many contemporary studies of cognition across cultures.

Language and Thought

The relationship between language and thought was extensively debated by 18th century philosophers, including such figures as Vico, Condillac, Maupertius, Monboddo, and Reid. Several of them pointed to the close connection between the language and the character or "spirit" of a people, especially Herder who regarded language as the embodiment of the Volksgeist, and Leibnitz. Wilhelm von Humboldt put forward a view that was fairly close to the Sapir-Whorf hypothesis, and toward the end of the 19th century Müller rather extravagantly argued for the identity of language and thought. Wundt regarded language as the product of higher cognitive processes, while Piaget (like Tylor before him) viewed such processes as to some extent separate from language. The relationship of language to culture and thought continues to be a prominent theme in psychological anthropology and to a lesser degree in cross-cultural psychology.

Reason and Morality

The notion that reason and morality go together is a very ancient one: reason is a necessary precondition for being able to make moral judgments. "Savages" were regarded as being devoid of both. The conjunction is implicit in the title of Chapter V of Darwin's *The Descent of Man:* "On the development of the intellectual and moral faculties during primeval and civilized times." Although this link had long been taken for granted, it was not until the work of Piaget and its elaboration by Kohlberg that the processes underlying it had been systematically examined. Since then cultural influences on "moral reasoning" have been extensively studied.

Character and Personality

The idea of "national character" is an ancient one. In the 18th century Montesquieu discussed it, and Hume wrote a celebrated essay on it. Herder put forward the concept of the "Volksgeist," which foreshadowed Shweder's version of contemporary cultural psychology. The determinants of national character were extensively discussed by Murray (1808), who took a remarkably modern view: "But I think it evident that the characteristic qualities . . . are wholly unconnected with those external marks by which races are distinguished. . . . Mind is a more flexible substance, and yields more readily to the influence of altered circumstances." (p. 151). Nineteenth century travellers and missionaries reported regularly on the character of the peoples they had visited, though their accounts were usually rather simplistic and stereotypical. This may have been the reason why Galton (1877) proposed a more systematic approach. Interestingly, he suggested that since writers of fiction and plays are expert at depicting character, anthropologists should elaborate a typology derived from literature; and could form the basis for future more exact measurement.

Around the turn of the century a number of books were published in France on the "psychologie des peuples" that usually contained character sketches. These may be regarded as the precursors of more recent writings on national character, but not of the culture-and-personality school which had other sources. It was Wundt's Völkerpsychologie which prompted Freud to write Totem and Taboo, thereby inspiring the anthropologist Roheim to conduct psychoanalytically oriented field studies. Another impetus came from Boas who encouraged his students, notably Benedict and Mead, to examine "the way in which personality reacts to culture" (Boas, 1928, p. xiv). Subsequently Kardiner, a neo-Freudian, drew on both traditions in formulating his own approach which is most closely associated with the label of "culture and personality." The decline of that school was paralleled by an increasing resort to the Human Relations Area Files and the rise of what became known as "psychological anthropology."

There has been a resurgence of interest in aspects of the relationship between culture and personality, chiefly focusing on two domains. One is that of cultural variations in concepts of self and personhood, and the consequences in terms of psychological functioning of such variant "cultural selves" (Markus & Kitayama, 1991; Marsella, DeVos & Hsu, 1985; Miller, 1994, in this handbook; Smith & Bond, 1993). The other concerns cultural options of identity management in the process of acculturation (Camilleri et al., 1990; Camilleri & Malewska-Peyre in this handbook; Liebkind, 1992).

Eco-Systems and Mind

Differences between peoples have long been attributed to environmental factors. Originally climate was regarded as the main determinant, but from the 18th century onward the emphasis shifted to modes of subsistence. During the 19th century Waitz used environmental arguments and coined the now well-worn phrase of the "psychic unity of mankind" in opposing the biological racists (cf. Jahoda, 1995). Marx stressed the effects of material conditions of life on mental functioning. His modern successors were Vygotsky and Luria, and they in turn inspired Cole's version of cultural psychology (Cole, 1990). In a somewhat different style an ecological approach to anthropology developed, which was subsequently taken up in cross-cultural psychology, notably by Berry (1966, 1994).

Conclusion: Continuity and Novelty

The preceding brief sketch illustrates the continuity of some dominant themes over long periods of time. Against such similarity of broad themes, which often fails to be adequately recognized, must be set the substantial changes that have taken place. Most of the earlier discussions, while often shrewd and insightful, remained in essence speculative and the evidence at best anecdotal. The advent of empirical studies has entailed the posing of more precise questions to which the answers had to be sought. New and powerful methods have been elaborated that make it possible to go beyond the establishment of links between disparate phenomena, by specifying the processes which constitute these links. This has resulted in the opening up of new fields that had previously barely been touched upon.

An interesting example is that of childhood. All the old writers took it for granted not only that "the child is the father of the man," but that children grow up to become members of a particular culture (as we would call it now). However, it never seems to have occurred to them that this was in any way problematic. Another sphere which had to await modern research is that of social behavior. Customs and beliefs were certainly described, sometimes in insightful ways, but few broader generalizations were attempted. Not surprisingly, in periods when Europeans regarded most others peoples as savages or barbarians devoid of reason, no one thought of the possibility of "indigenous psychologies." The current interest in these is a product of our very different intellectual climate. Yet this climate no doubt also imposes constraints on our own constructs, constraints that will become obvious only to future generations.

Endnotes

1. For detailed information about the predecessors of anthropology during Antiquity and the Middle Ages see Baldry, (1965); Friedman, (1981); Hodgen, (1964); Müller, (1972).

2. It remains to be mentioned that the Arab tradition of ethno- and historiographic description was well advanced as compared with European work of the Middle Ages (Voget, 1975). But as the Arabs were strongly influenced by the anthropological theorizing of classical Antiquity during this period, it is not surprising that they also shared the beliefs in monstrous races and unfavorable images of Blacks (Al-Azmeh, 1992).

3. For a detailed description of the Renaissance's conception of humanity see Garin (1990) and Rowe (1965). A rich documentation of the Renaissance's image of other peoples and an analysis of the reports of outstanding conquerors and missionaries is offered by Bitterli (1991), Dickason (1984), Greenblatt (1990), Schmitt (1984), and Todorov (1985).

4. For more detailed information on the history of Anthropology see Bitterli (1991), Duchet (1971), Harris (1968), Jahoda (1992), Krewer (1992), Mühlmann (1986), Slotkin (1965), Stocking (1968, 1987), Voget (1975).

5. Lazarus (1851) already published the basic ideas about ten years earlier.

6. For a detailed analysis see Jahoda (1992), Oelze (1991), Schneider (1991).

7. We are greatly indebted to Professors Rogelio Diaz-Guerrero and Durganand Sinha, leading figures of cross-cultural research, who gave us the benefit of their unrivalled experience. We have freely borrowed from the accounts they very kindly made available.

References

Al-Azmeh, A. (1992). Barbarians in Arab eyes. *Past & Present, 134*, 3–18.

Andor, L. E. (1966). *Aptitudes and abilities of the Black man in sub-Saharan Africa 1784–1963.* Johannesburg: NIPR.

Ardila, R. (1968). Psychology in Latin America. *American Psychologist, 23*, 567–574.

Ardila, R. (1982). Psychology in Latin America today. *Annual Review of Psychology, 33*, 103–122.

Ardila, R. (1994). Psychology in Latin America. In R. J. Corsini (Ed.), *Encyclopedia of psychology.* (2nd ed., Vol. 3). New York: Wiley.

Baldry, H. C. (1965). *The unity of mankind in Greek thought.* Cambridge: Cambridge University Press.

Banton, M. (1987). *Racial theories.* Cambridge: Cambridge University Press.

Bartlett, F. C. (1923). *Psychology and primitive culture.* Cambridge: Cambridge University Press.

Bartlett, F. C. (1932). *Remembering.* Cambridge: Cambridge University Press.

Bartlett, F. C. (1937). Psychological methods and anthropological problems. *Africa, 10*, 410–419.

Benedict, R. [1934] (1946). *Patterns of culture.* New York: Mentor.

Berlin, J. (1982). *Wider das Geläufige.* Aufsätze zur Ideengeschichte. Frankfurt: Europäische Verlagsanstalt.

Berry, J. W. (1966). Temne and Eskimo perceptual skills. *International Journal of Psychology, 1*, 207–229.

Berry, J. W. (1980). Introduction to Methodology. In H. C. Triandis & J. W. Berry (Eds.), *Handbook of cross-cultural psychology*, (Vol. 2, pp. 1–28). Boston: Allyn and Bacon.

Berry, J. W. (1989). Imposed etics—emics—derived etics: the operationalization of a compelling idea. *International Journal of Psychology, 24*, 721–735.

Berry, J. W. (1994). An ecological perspective on cultural and ethnic psychology. In E. Trickett, R. Watts & D. Birman (Eds.), *Human diversity* (pp. 115–141). San Francisco: Jossey-Bass.

Berry, J. W., Poortinga; Y. H., Segall, M. H. &

Dasen, P. R. (1992). *Cross-cultural psychology: Research and applications.* Cambridge: Cambridge University Press.

Berry, J. W., Van de Koppel, J. M. H., Sénéchal, C., Annis, R. C., Bahuchet, S., Cavalli-Sforza, L. L. & Witkin, H. A. (1986). *On the edge of the forest: Cultural adaptation and cognitive development in central Africa.* Lisse: Swets & Zeitlinger.

Biesheuvel, S. (1943). *African intelligence.* Johannesburg: South African Institute of Race Relations.

Biesheuvel, S. (Ed.). (1969). *Methods for the measurement of psychological performance.* International Biological Programme, No. 10. Oxford: Blackwell Scientific Publications.

Bitterli, U. (1991). *Die Wilden und die Zivilisierten.* München: Beck.

Boas, F. (1896). The limitations of the comparative method of anthropology. *Science, IV.*

Boas, F. [1911] (1939). *The mind of primitive man.* New York: Macmillan.

Boas, F. (1928). Foreword to Margaret Mead: *Coming of age in Samoa.* New York: William Morrow.

Boesch, E. E. (1991). *Symbolic action theory and cultural psychology.* Berlin: Springer.

Bose, S. K. (1955). Employee morale and supervision. *Indian Journal of Psychology, 27*, 117–125.

Bose, S. K. (1958). Industrial motivation for higher production. *Indian Journal of Psychology, 33*, 237–247.

Boyer, P. (Ed.). (1993). *Cognitive Aspects of religious symbolism.* Cambridge: Cambridge University Press.

Brislin, R. W. (1983). Cross-cultural research in psychology. *Annual Review of Psychology, 34*, 363–400.

Bruner, F. G. (1908). The hearing of primitive peoples. *Archives of Psychology, 11*, 1–113.

Camilleri, C., Kastersztein, J., Lipiansky, E. M., Malewska-Peyre, H., Taboada-Leonetti, I. & Vasquez, A. (1990). *Stratégies identitaires.* Paris: PUF.

Campbell, D. T. & Naroll, R. (1972). The mutual methodological relevance of anthropology and psychology. In F. L. K. Hsu, (Ed), *Psychologial Anthropology* (pp. 435–468). Cambridge: Schenkman.

Cole, M. (1978). Ethnographic psychology of cognition—so far. In G. D. Spindler (Ed.), *The making of psychological anthropology* (pp. 614–631). Berkeley: University of Califoria Press.

Cole, M. (1990). Cultural psychology: A once and future discipline? In: J. J. Berman (Ed.), *Cross-cultural perspectives* (pp. 273–335). Lincoln: University of Nebraska Press.

Cole, M. (1995). Culture and cognition development: From cross-cultural research to creating systems of cultural mediation. *Culture & psychology* (Vol. 1, No. 1), 25–54.

Columbus, C. [1492] (1981). *Bordbuch.* Frankfurt: insel.

Condorcet, M.J. (1794/1966). *Esquisse d'un tableau historique des pogrès de l'esprit humain.* Paris: Editions Sociales.

Copans, J. & Jamin, J. (1994). *Aux origines de l'anthropologie françaises.* Paris: Editions Jean-Michel Place.

Dasen, P. R. (1972). Cross-cultural Piagetian research: a summary. *Journal of Cross-Cultural Psychology, 7*, 75–85.

Dasen, P. R. (1993). L'ethnocentrisme de la psychologie. In M. Rey-von Allmen (Ed.), *Psychologie clinique et interrogations culturelles.* Paris: L'Harmattan.

Dasen, P. R. & Heron, A. (1981). Cross-cultural tests of Piaget's theory. In H. C. Triandis & A. Heron (Eds.), *Handbook of cross-cultural psychology* (Vol. 4, pp. 295–341). Boston: Allyn and Bacon.

Dennis, W. (1943). Animism and related tendencies in Hopi children. *Journal of Abnormal and Social Psychology, 38,* 21–37.

Diaz-Guerrero, R. (1963). Sociocultural premises, attitudes and cross-cultural research. *Annuario de Psicologia, 2,* 31–45.

Diaz-Guerrero, R. (1964). Personality development of Mexican schoolchildren. *Anuario de Psicologia, 3,* 99–109.

Dickason, O. P. (1984). *The myths of the savage.* Edmonton: University of Alberta.

DuBois, C. [1941] (1961). *The people of Alor* (2 vols). New York: Harper & Row.

Duchet, M. (1971). *Anthropologie et histoire au siécle des lumières.* Paris: Maspero.

Eckensberger, L. H. (1990). On the necessity of the culture concept in psychology. In F. J. R. van de Vijver & G. J. M. Hutschemaekers (Eds.), *The investigation of culture* (pp. 153–183). Tilburg: University Press.

Eckensberger, L. H. (1993). Moralische Urteile als handlungsleitende soziale Regelsysteme im Spiegel der kulturvergleichenden Forschung. In A. Thomas (Ed.), *Kulturvergleichende Psychologie* (pp. 259–295). Göttingen: Hogrefe.

Eckensberger, L. H. (1995). Action or activity: Two different roads toward an integration of culture into psychology. *Culture & Psychology, 1, 67–80.*

Edwards, C. P. (1981). The comparative study of the development of moral judgment and reasoning. In: R. H. Munroe, R. L. Munroe & B. B. Whiting (Eds), *Handbook of cross-cultural human development.* New York: Garland Press.

Edwards, C. P. (1986). Cross-cultural research on Kohlberg's stages: the basis for consensus. In S. Modgil & C. Modgil (Eds.), *Lawrence Kohlberg: consensus and controversy* (pp. 419–430). London: Falmer Press.

Erdheim, M. (1987). Zur Ethnopsychoanalyse von Exotismus und Xenophobie. In *Exotische Welten. Europäische Phantasien* (pp. 48–53). Institut für Auslandsbeziehungen, Württembergischer Kunstverein, Edition Cantz.

Fabian, J. (1983). *Time and the other.* New York: Columbia University Press.

Friedman, J. B. (1981). *The monstrous races in medieval art and thought.* Cambridge, MA: Harvard University Press.

Galton, F. (1877). *Address to the anthropology section of the British association for the advancement of sciences Plymouth.* London: Clowes.

Galton, F. [1869] (1914). *Hereditary genius.* London: Macmillan.

Galton, F. [1883] (1928). *Inquiries into human faculty and its development.* London: Dent.

Ganguli, H. C. (1954). An inquiry into incentives for workers in an engineering factory. *Indian Journal of Social Work, 15,* 30–40.

Galton, F. [1883] (1928). *Inquiries into human faculty and its development.* London: Dent.

Ganguli, H. C. (1954). An inquiry into incentives for workers in an engineering factory. *Indian Journal of Social Work, 15,* 30–40.

Ganguli, H. C. (1961). *Industrial productivity and motivation*. Bombay: Asia Publishing House.

Garin, E. (1990). (Ed.). *Der Mensch der Renaissance*. Frankfurt: Campus.

Geertz, C. (1970). The impact of the concept of culture on the concept of man. In E. Hammer & W. Simmons (Eds.), *Man makes sense* (pp. 46–65). Boston: Brown & Company.

Gilbert, G. M. (1956). *Psychological approaches to intergroup and international understanding*. Austin, Texas: Hogg Foundation for Mental Health, University of Texas.

Goodnow, J. J. (1962). A test of milieu effects with some of Piaget's tasks. *Psychological Monographs, 76 (36)*, Whole No. 555.

Graumann, C.-F. (1980). Experiment, Statistik, Geschichte. *Psychologische Rundschau, 31*, 73–78.

Greenblatt, S. (1990). *Wunderbare Besitztümer*. Berlin: Wagenbach.

Gusdorf, G. (1972). *Dieu, la nature, l'homme au siécle des Lumières*. Paris: Payot.

Harkness, S. & Super, C. M. (1987). The use of cross-cultural research in child development. In G. J. Whitehurst & R. Vasta (Eds.), *Annals of child development* (Vol. 4), 209–244.

Harris, M. (1968). *The rise of anthropological theory*. London: Routledge & Keagan Paul.

Hayslip, B. (1973). Psychology at the world's fair of 1904: a methodological account. Unpubl. seminar paper. *Archives of the history of American psychology*. Akron, Ohio.

Herder, J. G. [1784] (1985). *Ideen zur Philosophie der Geschichte der Menschheit*. Wiesbaden: Fourier.

Hobhouse, L. T., Wheeler, G. C. & Ginsberg, M. (1930). *The material culture and social institutions of the simpler peoples*. London: Chapman & Hall.

Hodgen, H. T. (1964). *Early anthropology in the sixteenth and seventeenth centuries*. Philadelphia, PA: University of Pennsylvania Press.

Holtzman, W. H., Diaz-Guerrero, R., & Swartz, J. D. (1975). *Personality development in two cultures*. Austin: University of Texas Press.

Hoorweg, J. C. & Marais, H. C. (1969). *Psychology in Africa, a bibliography*. Leyden: Afrika-Studiecentrum.

Hsu, F. L. K. (1961) (Ed.). *Psychologial anthropology*. Homewood: Dorsey Press.

Hume, D. [1784] (1894). *Essays literary, moral and political*. London: Routeledge.

Hunt, J. (1867). Retiring address. *Anthropological Review*, V.

Irvine, S. H., Sanders, J. T. & Klingelhofer, E. L. (1970). *Human Behaviour in Africa*. Mimeo. Althouse College of Education, Ontario, Canada.

Jahoda, G. (1958). Child animism I: A critical survey of cross-cultural research; child animism II: A study in West Africa. *The Journal of Social Psychology, 47*, 197–212 and 213–222.

Jahoda, G. (1980). Cross-cultural comparisons. In M. H. Bornstein, (Ed.), *Comparative methods in psychology* (pp. 105–148. Hillsdale, NJ: Erlbaum.

Jahoda, G. (1982). *Psychology and anthropology*. London: Academic Press.

Jahoda, G. (1984). Do we need a concept of culture? *Journal of Cross-Cultural Psychology, 15*, 139–151.

Jahoda, G. (1989). Zum Ursprung der "Serial reproduction"—Methode. *Psychologie und Geschichte, 1*, 46–48.

Jahoda, G. (1990). Our forgotten ancestors. In J. Berman (Ed.), *Cross-cultural perspectives* (pp. 1–40). Nebraska Symposium on Motivation, 1989. Lincoln: University of Nebraska Press.

Jahoda, G. (1992). *Crossroads between culture and mind*. Cambridge, MA.: Harvard University Press.

Jahoda, G. (1993). The colour of a chameleon: perspectives on concepts of "culture." *Cultural Dynamics, 6*: 277–287.

Jahoda, G. (1995). The ancestry of a model. *Culture and Psychology, 1*, 11–24.

Kant, E. (1787/1989). Was ist Aufklärung? In E. Bahr (Ed.), *Was ist Aufklärung? Thesen und defintionen* (pp. 9–17). Stuttgart: Reclam.

Kardiner, A. (1939). *The individual and his society.* New York: Columbia University Press.

Kardiner, A. (1945). *The psychological frontiers of society.* New York: Columbia University Press.

Klineberg, O. (1980). Historical perspectives: cross-cultural psychology before 1960. In H. C. Triandis & W. W. Lambert (Eds.), *Handbook of cross-cultural psychology* (Vol. 1, pp. 1–14). Boston: Allyn and Bacon.

Koepping, K.-P. (1975). From the dilemma of the ethnographer to the idea of humanitas. *Occasional Papers in Anthropology, 4,* 124–136.

Kohlberg, L. (1958). *The development of modes of moral thinking and choice in the years ten to sixteen.* Unpublished doctoral dissertation, University of Chicago.

Krewer, B. (1990). Psyche and culture. Can a culture-free psychology take into account the essential features of the species "Homo Sapiens"? *The Quarterly Newletter of the Laboratory of Comparative Human Cognition* (Vol. 12, 1), 24–37.

Krewer, B. (1992). *Kulturelle Identität und menschliche Selbsterforschung.* Saarbrücken: Breitenbach.

Krewer, B. (1993). Théorie d'action et psychologie culturelle. *Revue Suisse de Psychologie, 52,* 82–92.

Krewer, B. & Jahoda, G. (1990). On the Scope of Lazarus and Steinthal's "Völkerpsychologie" as reflected in the "Zeitschrift für Völkerpsychologie und Sprachwissenschaft" (1860–1890). *The Quarterly Newletter of the Laboratory of Comparative Human Cognition* (Vol. 12, 1), 4–12.

Laboratory of Comparative Human Cognition (1979). What's cultural about cross-cultural psychology? *Annual Review of Psychology, 30,* 145–172.

Laboratory of Comparative Human Cognition (1983). Culture and cognitive development. In: P. H. Mussen & W. Kessen (Eds.), *Handbook of child psychology* (Vol. I: pp. 295–356). New York: Wiley.

Lafitau, P. F. (1724). *Moeurs des sauvages américains comparées aux moeurs des premiers temps.* Paris.

Lane, H. (1985). *Das wilde Kind von Aveyron.* Frankfurt: Ullstein.

Langness, L. L. (1974). *The study of culture.* San Francisco: Chandler & Sharp.

Lazarus, M. (1851). Über den Begriff und die Möglichkeit einer Völkerpsychologie. *Zeitschrift für Literatur, Kunst und Öffentlichkeitsleben,* 1, 112–126.

Lazarus, M. & Steinthal, H. (Eds.). (1860). Einleitende Gedanken über Völkerpsychologie als Einladung in einer Zeitschrift für Völkerpsychologie und Sprachwissenschaft. *Zeitschrift für Völkerpsychologie und Sprachwissenschaft, 1,* 1–73.

LeVine, R. A. (1966). *Dreams and deeds: Achievement motivation in Nigeria.* Chicago: University of Chicago Press.

LeVine, R. A. (1970). Cross-cultural study in child psychology. In P. H. Mussen (Ed.), *Carmichael's manual of child psychology* (Vol. 2, pp. 559–612). New York: Wiley.

Lewis, I. M. (1977). *Ecstatic religion.* Harmondsworth: Penguin.

Liebkind, C. (1992). Ethnic identity—challenging the boundaries of social psychology. In G. M. Breakwell (Ed.), *Social psychology of identity and the self concept,* (pp. 147–185). London: Surrey Univ. Press.

Lonner, W. J. (1992). Does the association need a name change? *Cross-Cultural Psychology Bulletin* (Vol. 26, No. 3), 1.

Lucariello, J. (1995). Mind, culture, person: Elements in a cultural psychology. *Human Development, 38,* 2–18.

Luria, A. R. (1976). *Cognitive development: Its cultural and social foundations* (M. Cole, Ed.). Cambridge, MA: Harvard University Press.

Malinowski, B. (1931). *Introduction to C. R. Aldrich: The primitive mind and modern civilization.* (Reprinted 1969). New York: AMS Press.

Malson, L., Itard, J. & Manonni, O. (1972). *Die wilden Kinder.* Frankfurt: Suhrkamp.

Markus, H. & Kitayama, S. (1991). Culture and the self: implications for cognition, motivation and emotion. *Psychological Review, 98,* 224–253.

Marsella, A. J., DeVos, G. & Hsu, F. L. K. (1985). (Eds.). *Culture and self: Asian and Western perspectives.* London: Tavistock Publications.

Mauviel, M. (1988). Volney précurseur de l'anthropologie psychologique? In J. Roussel (Ed.), *L'heritage des lumières: Volney et les idéologues* (pp. 319–334). Angers: Presses de l'Université.

Mead, M. (1928). *Coming of age in Samoa.* New York: William Morrow.

Mead, M. (1932). An investigation of the thought of primitive children, with special reference to animism. *Journal of the Royal Anthropological Institute, 62,* 173–90.

Miller, J. G. (1994). Cultural psychology: bridging disciplinary boundaries in understanding the cultural grounding of self. In P. K. Bock (Ed.), *Psychological anthropology* (pp. 139–170). London: Praeger.

Minturn, L. & Lambert, W. W. (1964). *Mothers in six cultures.* New York: John Wiley.

Mitra, S. K. (Ed.). (1972). *A Survey of research in psychology.* Bombay: Popular Prakashan.

Moravia, S. (1977). Philosophie und anthropologie in der Aufklärung. *Beobachtende Vernunft.* Frankfurt: Ullstein.

Mühlmann, W. E. (1986). *Geschichte der Anthropologie.* Wiesbaden: Aula, 4. Auflage.

Müller, K. E. (1972). *Geschichte der antiken Ethnographie und der ethnologischen Theoriebildung.* Wiesbaden: Steiner.

Murlidharan, R. (1971). *Developmental norms of Indian childen two years to five years.* Project Report. New Delhi: NCERT.

Murray, H. (1808). *Enquiries, historical and moral, respecting the character of nations and the progress of society.* Edinburgh: Anderson.

Nadel, S. F. (1937). A field experiment in racial psychology. *British Journal of Psychology, 28,* 195–211.

Naroll, R. (1973). Galton's problem. In R. Naroll and R. Cohen (Eds.), *A handbook of method in cultural anthropology* (pp. 974–989). New York: Columbia University Press.

Natalicio, L. S., Hereford, C.F . & Natalicio, D. S. (1967). La contribucion de las ciencias psicologicas y del comportamiento al desarollo social y economico de los Pueblos. *Proceedings of the XI Interamerican Congress of Psychology* (Vol. 1). Mexico: Universidad Nacional Autonoma de Mexico.

Oelze, B. *Wilhelm Wundt. Die Konzeption der Völkerpsychologie.* Münster: Waxmann.

Pandey, J. (Ed.). (1988). *Psychology in India: State of the art.* New Delhi: Sage.

Pareek, U. (Ed.). (1981). *A survey of research in psychology.* Bombay: Popular Prakashan.

Piaget, J. (1928). Logique génétique et sociologie. *Revue Philosophique, 105,* 165–205.

Piaget, J. (1932). *Le jugement moral chez l'enfant.* Paris: Alcan.

Piaget, J. (1966). Nécessité et signification des recherches comparatives en psychologie génétique. *International Journal of Psychology, 1,* 3–13.

Piéron, H. (1909). L'anthropologie psychologique. *Revue de l'Ecole d'Anthropologie de Paris, 19,* 113–127.

Pike, L. O. (1870). On the method of anthropological research. *Anthropological Review, VIII,* iii–xiii.

Poortinga, Y. H., Vijver, F. J. R. van de, Joe, R. C. & Vande Koppel, J. M. H. (1987). Peeling the onion called culture: A Synopsis. In C. Kagitcibasi (Ed.), *Growth and progress in cross-cultural psychology* (pp. 22–34). Amsterdam: Swets & Zeitlinger.

Price-Williams, D. R. (1961). A study concerning concepts of conservation of quantities among primitive children. *Acta Psychologica, 18,* 297–305.

Price-Williams, D. R. (1980). Toward the idea of cultural psychology. *Journal of Cross-Cultural Psychology, 11,* 75–88.

Rivers, W. H. R. (1901). Part 1, Introduction and vision. In A. C. Haddon (Ed.), *Reports of the Cambridge anthropological expedition to Torres Straits* (Vol. 2). Cambridge: Cambridge University Press.

Rogoff, B. & Morelli, G. (1989). Perspectives on children's development from cultural psychology. *American Psychologist, 2,* 343–348.

Rohner, R. (1984). Toward a conception of culture for cross-cultural psychology. *Journal of Cross-Cultural Psychology, 15,* 111–138.

Rosch Heider, E. (1972) Universals in color naming and memory. *Journal of Experimental Psychology, 93,* 10–20.

Rousseau, J.-J. [1755] (1981). Abhandlung über den Ursprung und die Grundlagen der Ungleichheit unter den Menschen. In H. Ritter (Ed.), *J.-J. Rousseau Schriften*. Frankfurt: Ullstein.

Rowe, J. H. (1965). The Renaissance foundations of anthropology. *American Anthropologist, 67*, 1–20.

Rushton, J. P. (1995). *Race, evolution and behavior*. New Brunswick, NJ: Transaction Publishers.

Schmitt, E. (1984). (Ed.), *Die großen Entdeckungen. Dokumente zur Geschichte der europäischen Expansion*. Vol. 2. München: Beck.

Schneider, C.M. (1991). *Wilhelm Wundts Völkerpsychologie*. Bonn: Bouvier.

Schwartz, T., White, G. M. & Lutz, C. A. (Eds.) (1992). New directions in psychological anthropology. Cambridge: Cambridge University Press.

Segall, M. H. (1984). More than we need to know about culture, but are afraid not to ask. *Journal of Cross-Cultural Psychology, 15*, 153–162.

Segall, M. H., Campbell, D. T. & Herskovits, M. J. (1966). *The influence of culture on visual perception*. Indianapolis: Bobbs-Merrill.

Segall, M. H., Dasen, P. R., Berry, J. W. & Poortinga, Y. H. (1990). *Human behaviour in global perspective*. New York: Pergamon Press.

Shotter, J. (1986). A sense of place. Vico and the social production of social identities. *British Journal of Social Psychology, 25*, 199–211.

Shweder, R. A. (1984). Anthropology's romantic rebellion against the enlightenment, or there's more to thinking than reason and evidence. In R. Shweder & R. LeVine (Eds.), *Culture theory* (pp. 27–66). Cambridge, MA: University Press.

Shweder, R. A. (1990). Cultural Psychology: What is it? In J. W. Stigler, R. A. Shweder & G. Herdt (Eds), *Cultural psychology: Essays on comparative human development* (pp. 1–43). Cambridge, MA: Cambridge University Press.

Shweder, R. A. & Sullivan, M. A. (1993). Cultural psychology, who needs it? *Annual Review of Psychology, 44*(4), 497–523.

Simpson, E. L. (1974). Moral development research—a case study of scientific cultural bias. *Human Development, 17*, 81–106.

Sinha, D. (1958). Job satisfaction in office and manual workers. *Indian Journal of Social Work, 19*, 39–46.

Sinha, D. (1963). Manifest anxiety in an Indian sample. *Journal of Psychology. 69*, 261–265.

Sinha, D. (1969). *Motivation of rural population in a developing country*. Bombay: Allied Publishers.

Slotkin, J. S. (1965). *Readings in early anthropology*. New York: Wenner-Gren Foundation for Anthropological Research.

Smith, P. B. & Bond, M. H. (1993). *Social psychology across cultures*. Hertfordshire: Harvester Wheatsheaf.

Snarey, J. R. (1985). Cross-cultural universality of social-moral development. A critical review of Kohlbergian research. *Psychological Bulletin, 97*, 202–232.

Spindler, G. D. (Ed.). (1978). *The Making of psychological anthropology*. Berkeley: University of California Press.

Stocking, G. W. (1968). *Race, culture, and evolution*. New York: Free Press.

Stocking, G. W. (1987). *Victorian anthropology*. New York: Free Press.

Strodtbeck, F. L. (1964). Considerations of meta-method in cross-cultural studies. *American Anthropologist, 66*, 223–229.

Tanner, J. M. & Inhelder, B. (1960). *Discussions on child development* (Vol. 4). London: Tavistock.

Theye, T. (1985). *Wir und die Wilden*. Hamburg: Rororo.

Thouless, R. H. (1933). A racial difference in perception. *Journal of Social Psychology, 4*, 330–339.

Thurnwald, R. (1913). Ethno-psychologische Studie an Südseevölkern. *Beihefte zur Zeitschrift für angewandte Psychologie und psychologische Sammelforschung, 6*. Leipzig: Barth.

Titchener, E. B. (1916). On ethnological tests of sensation and perception. *Proceedings of the American Philosophical Society, 55*, 204–236.

Todorov, T. (1985). *Die Eroberung Amerikas—Das Problem des Anderen*. Frankfurt: Suhrkamp.

Triandis, H. C. Malpass, R. S. & Davidson, A. R. (1973). Psychology and culture. *Annual Review of Psychology, 24*, 355–378.

Tylor, E. B. [1871] (1958). *The origins of culture*. New York: Harper and Row.

Tylor, E. B. (1889). On the method of investigating the development of institutions. *Journal of the Royal Anthropological Institute of Great Britain and Ireland, 18,* 245–72.

Valsiner, J. (1989). *Human development and culture.* Toronto: Lexington Books.

Verma, A., Poffenberger, T., Pathak, P., Shah, J. M. & Shah, H. B. (1969). Motor and Mental Growth of Baroda Babies. *Research Report No. 3.,* Dept. of Child Development, M. S. University, Baroda.

Vico, G. [1724] (1948). *The new science.* New York: Cornell University Press.

Voget, F. W. (1975). *A history of ethnology.* New York: Holt, Rinehart & Winston.

Von Humboldt, A. (1830–1835/1985). Über die Verschiedenheit des menschlichen Sprachbaues und ihren Einfluß auf die geistige Entwicklung des Menschengeschlechts. In M. Riedel (Ed.), *Geschichte der Philosophie in Text und Darstellung* (Vol. 7, pp. 66–100). Stuttgart: Reclam.

Wickert, F. R. (1967). *Readings in French African psychology.* Michigan: African Studies Center, Michigan State University.

Woodworth, R. S. (1910). Racial differences in mental traits. *Science, 31,* 171–186

Wundt, W. (1888). Über Ziele und Wege der Völkerpsychologie. *Philosophische Studien,* IV.

Wundt, W. (1908). *Logik.* Logik der Geisteswissenschaften (Vol. 3). Stuttgart: Enke.

2

CULTURE AS ANTECEDENT TO BEHAVIOR

WALTER J. LONNER
Western Washington University
United States

JOHN ADAMOPOULOS
Grand Valley State University
United States

Contents

Introduction

We present in this chapter the central underlying theoretical frameworks, assumptions, and unique characteristics, as well as criticisms, of the cross-cultural comparative approach in psychology. Also included are overviews of several current perspectives in cross-cultural psychology that have been described by their progenitors and practitioners as frameworks, models, theories, paradigms, or heuristic devices. Whatever they are called, all of them suggest specific orientations and methodologies designed to help explain interrelationships, at the level of the individual, between some aspect of culture and some psychological process or phenomenon. This general survey should bring the reader up to date on current thinking in cross-cultural psychology with respect to the various theoretical guidelines used by psychological researchers asking questions about the effect(s) that culture exerts on human behavior.

Historical Approaches

Our first task is to update Gustav Jahoda's chapter that appeared in the first edition of the *Handbook of Cross-Cultural Psychology* (Jahoda, 1980). Entitled "Theoretical and Systematic Approaches in Cross-Cultural Psychology," Jahoda summarized the main characteristics of the leading frameworks, theories, and models that had guided a generation of psychologists who attempted to make sense out of the complex relationships between culture, as an antecedent of thought and action, and human behavior. Jahoda organized his chapter around seven perspectives which, in the late 1970s when he reviewed the literature, were popular and influential in cross-cultural psychology. The following brief review of and commentary on Jahoda's chapter provides a background against which most of the more recent perspectives in cross-cultural psychology might be compared and contrasted.

When Jahoda began his review about 18 years ago he had the daunting task of finding threads of cross-cultural research activity that had been running through various disciplines for several decades. Because there were few books in the area and a scarcity of extensive and reliable organizations or networks of cross-cultural researchers to use as guides, Jahoda assumed the role of both synthesizer and critic. The perspectives Jahoda selected were culture and personality, achievement motivation, subjective culture, psychometric approaches, psychological differentiation, Piagetian genetic psychology, and experimental anthropology. This chapter includes a brief summary of what Jahoda identified as major theoretical and systematic approaches, with historical insights to help us understand and explain current perspectives.

Culture and Personality

The venerable "culture and personality" school was dominated for many years (1920–1945 in particular) by anthropologists, and especially by those who primarily employed psychoanalytic theories and techniques in attempts to understand behavior in specific cultures (Piker, 1994). The basic idea was (and still is) that one's personality and one's culture are inextricably intertwined—not that one *exactly* defines the other, but that a powerful way to appreciate the characteristic mode of the behavior of other people is to understand the role their culture plays in influencing their behavior, a link with which it would be impossible to disagree. How and when and why this happens, however, is what makes the cultural sciences different from one another. Books by Hsu (1972) and Kaplan (1961) contain a good representation of the type of research done by anthropologists in the days when studies of culture and personality were dominant. Classic books by Kardiner (1939; 1945) were cited by Jahoda as examples of earlier thought and work by those who studied relationships between one's culture and one's characteristic mode of thought and behavior. The core of Kardiner's theory of basic personality is that *primary institutions* (such as kinship and socialization) form the *basic personality structure* of a society (Piker, 1994), which in turn leads to *secondary institutions* such as religion, art, and folklore.

The single most important development by scholars in the culture and personality area, in terms of its influence on cross-cultural psychology, was the research program developed by the cultural anthropologists John and Beatrice Whiting, Irving Child, and many of their colleagues and students. The most well-known research effort carried out by these researchers was the Six Cultures Project (e.g., Whiting & Whiting, 1975). The Whitings and their team sought to uncover causal connections between cultural phenomena and the behavior of members of cultures they studied. Accordingly, the primary focus was on the socialization of children and how child rearing practices varied as a function of family type (nuclear—extended) and type of economy (simple—complex). Thus the Whitings believed that any culture, with its specific environment and historical background, can be understood as a "maintenance system" that is antecedent to child-training practices that match the specific needs of each culture. These practices, in turn, lead to the development of certain personality "types," observable in a culture's "projective system," which in the psychoanalytic tradition includes such things as music, art, recreation, play behavior, crime and suicide rates, and so on.

The work of the Whitings and their colleagues resulted in one of the first attempts to develop a model explaining the various relationships between culture and the development of human personality. The model has been influential in generating hypotheses about connections between the individual and the society in which he or she has been socialized; it also influenced the development of more recent models in cross-cultural psychology—for example, the ecocultural model (discussed later in this chapter).

The Six Cultures Project has had continued significance on and importance for the development of cross-cultural psychology. For example, researchers who use systematic observation in naturalistic settings can thank those early efforts in developing such methods, for these techniques and procedures were a central part of data-gathering strategies used by the Whitings and their colleagues

(Longabaugh, 1980; Weick, 1985; Munroe & Munroe, 1994a, b). Also, the currently popular idea of the "developmental niche" proposed by Super and Harkness (1986, 1994; Volume 2, this *Handbook*) is a direct descendent of the Six Cultures Project.

Achievement Motivation

Followers of Henry Murray's neo-Freudian theory of personality, which was influential from the 1930s through the 1970s, made noteworthy contributions to the understanding of personality in Western societies. A major reason for this influence was the many creative ways that David McClelland attempted to establish connections between the need to achieve, one of Murray's psychogenic ("learned") needs, and various societal- and individual-level characteristics. McClelland focused especially on how aggregate levels of individual achievement motivation can be used to help explain a society's economic development (McClelland, 1961). Significantly influencing his research strategy was the line of sociological thinking supporting Max Weber's thesis that the Protestant work ethic was of utmost importance in the development of modern capitalism (Weber, 1904) .

McClelland's approach in studying achievement motivation is an extension of the culture and personality school. This is so for two primary reasons. First, like other scholars, he attempted to explain diverse cultural approaches to child rearing. Second, a host of background factors—high achievement standards imbued by the family (especially the mother), low dominance by father, certain religious values, and a temperate climate, to name a few, were thought by McClelland and his colleagues to be involved in shaping a child's level of motivation. These factors were treated as "causative" variables. They caused children to compete for internalized standards of excellence, which in turn influenced a culture's rate of economic growth. Of course, the path of causality can be stated differently: A country's rate of economic growth and other indicators of achievement, and indeed a host of other ways that a country might be understood, can be traced to specific child-rearing practices and other background factors that might be seen as predictor variables.

Another reason why the study of achievement motivation is similar to the culture-and-personality approach lies in the idea of "projective systems"—that is, a person's motives or a society's motives can be understood by the ways in which a person's characteristic thought patterns, fantasies, and other products and artifacts are manifested in everyday behavior. Murray developed the Thematic Apperception Test to assess human motives, and that projective test became a mainstay in McClelland's research. Two books dealing with the achievement motive look at the "big picture" both contemporaneously and historically (McClelland, Atkinson, Clark, & Lowell, 1953; McClelland, 1961). A third book describes a large project that was designed to increase or to exploit need achievement in several cultures where achievement motivation has been, by standard Western definitions, rather low (McClelland & Winter, 1969).

Subjective Culture

All people have unique and characteristic ways of viewing the human-made parts of their societies. This has been called their *subjective culture*. Research on subjective culture can be traced to the work of the late psycholinguist Charles Osgood and his colleagues (Osgood, 1964; Osgood, May, & Miron, 1975). Osgood used the idea of subjective culture in a psycholinguistic sense. Thus studies of lexicons in various cultures, through the use of the "semantic differential technique" to measure affective meaning, led to a comparative base permitting the identification of both universals and cultural specifics in the connotative, or metaphorical, meaning that humans give to their world(s). Osgood carried out a rich and creative program of research throughout the 1950s, 1960s, and 1970s. His work inspired many throughout psychology.

The psychologist who extended Osgood's research most visibly and energetically, albeit not in the psycholinguistic sense, was Harry Triandis. His book, *The Analysis of Subjective Culture,* written in collaboration with several colleagues in other countries, was among the first clearly cross-cultural psychological books to be published in the "modern" era of cross-cultural psychology (Triandis, 1972). The analysis of subjective culture involved searching for an understanding of how people from different societies perceive their respective social worlds. In his attempts to assess how people in assorted cultures "cut up the pie of experience" and otherwise view the human-made part of the environment, Triandis developed techniques to measure roles, attitudes, stereotypes, norms, beliefs, and values, all human activities that are central to the field of social psychology that he has represented for many years. Like the Six Cultures Project and McClelland's studies of achievement motivation, Triandis also developed a theoretical model of subjective culture, which postulated an array of psychological antecedents and behavioral consequents. Other approaches to comprehending various subjective cultures can be seen in Triandis's more recent efforts to deal with intercultural variations in terms of "cultural syndromes," which are characterized by concepts such as cultural complexity, cultural "tightness" and "looseness," and mainly individualism—collectivism (see Triandis, 1994, 1995). Studies of subjective culture have made their greatest impact by helping to stimulate the growth and development of culture-training programs (e.g., Brislin, Cushner, Cherrie, & Yong, 1986; Cushner & Brislin, 1996; Landis & Bhagat, 1996).

Psychometric Approaches

In selecting this category of research efforts that comprised a meandering, eclectic, yet distinctive thread running through the earlier years in cross-cultural psychology, Jahoda (1980) primarily sought to throw "new light on an old and still controversial problem, namely the intellectual abilities of people of different cultures" (p. 96). More specifically, in his review Jahoda focused on attempts to analyze the cognitive skills prevalent in different societies by examining the structure of mental abilities. The domain of psychometrics has been at once energetic, popular, and controversial in cross-cultural psychology. Several influential books in the field—which more often than not were edited books resulting from various measurement-oriented conferences—had as a common denominator a desire to understand culture and its relationship to cognition, intelligence, and other dimensions of human performance (Cronbach & Drenth, 1972; Berry & Dasen, 1974; Irvine & Berry, 1983). More recent books continue the tradition of exploring ways in which culture and cognition interact (e.g., Altarriba, 1993).

If the approach known as psychometrics is used in a more generic sense, which means the broad field of psychological testing, then this fourth of the seven frameworks that Jahoda summarized can boast by far the largest number of publications in the domain of cross-cultural psychology. The approach used in this domain is rather simple and straightforward: Select a test, scale, or device (or construct one) that is designed to measure a personality or cognitive dimension, translate it or otherwise modify it for cross-cultural comparative use, and employ it in attempts to discern similarities and/or differences across cultures. A large percentage of published cross-cultural research has relied on more or less traditional psychological testing to gather data that researchers assume will help them understand interactions between culture and behavior.

In the domain of personality measurement, there is a rather deep reservoir of literature that addresses a question of critical interest to clinicians and others who deal with culturally and ethnically diverse clientele: How does one measure the various dimensions of personality and pathology so that the measurements make sense cross-culturally? The cross-cultural study of affective disorders, especially depression, has received considerable attention (Kleinman & Good, 1985; Marsella, Hirschfeld, & Katz, 1987). Likewise, anxiety has been studied extensively across cultures (Spielberger, 1989; Spielberger & Diaz-Guerrero, 1976). There have also been many attempts, using psychometric procedures, to study a variety of other pathological or clinical conditions across cultures. For instance, the Minnesota Multiphasic Personality Inventory, the most widely used paper-and-pencil measure of personality and pathology in the world, is extensively used by many in the clinical wing of psychology (Butcher & Graham, 1994). The current availability of 115 translations of the MMPI and/or MMPI/2, which have spread across at least 65 countries, attests to its popularity as a measure of important human characteristics. Dana (1993) and Lonner and Ibrahim (1996) review the cross-cultural use of psychological tests in clinical and other applied areas.

Psychological Differentiation

The late Herman A. Witkin developed a theory of psychological differentiation that posited individual differences in many domains of psychological functioning such as perception, spatial abilities, psychopathology, child-rearing, and interpersonal behavior (Witkin, Dyk, Faterson, Goodenough, & Karp, 1962).

Using differentiation theory, numerous attempts were made to account for much human behavior depending upon where one fell on a "cognitive style" continuum anchored on one end by a "field dependent" and on the other end by a "field independent" mode of thinking, perceiving, and behaving. From the late 1960s through the early 1980s, Witkin's theory figured strongly in hundreds of research projects, many of them cross-cultural (Witkin & Berry, 1975; Berry, 1976; Witkin & Goodenough, 1981), and was an important element in Dawson's biosocial psychology (Dawson, 1971). Indeed, it was the transporting and testing of components of differentiation theory in other cultural and ethnic groups that breathed new life into research on cognitive style. To a large extent, the development of John Berry's ecocultural model (discussed later in this chapter) can be traced to his collaboration with Witkin, and a few years earlier, his work with John Dawson. Shortly after Witkin passed away in 1979, there was a noticeable drop in publications that used his ideas.

Piagetian Genetic Psychology

The field of developmental psychology has had an understandably strong influence on cross-cultural psychology (Best & Ruther, 1994). The dominant theory in the developmental domain of psychological research has been Piaget's genetic epistemology. Jahoda observed that this work ". . . constitutes what is perhaps the most comprehensive and substantial body of knowledge in psychology at present" (1980, p. 108). Note that he said in *psychology* and not just cross-cultural psychology, where its impact has also been substantial. Piaget's approach is a "natural" for cross-cultural extensions (which Piaget, 1966/1974, himself encouraged; cf. Jahoda & Krewer, this volume), because it concerns relationships involving stages and rates of cognitive development and a host of factors that might influence cognitive growth. This is so even though it assumes universality based on the fundamental biological foundation of human experience. Space constraints prevent going into Piagetian psychology in any detail, because the contributions have been so numerous, rich, and varied. There are excellent sources to consult (Dasen, 1972; Dasen, 1977; Segall, Dasen, Berry, & Poortinga, 1990; Mishra's chapter in Volume 2 of this *Handbook*), in addition to Jahoda's summary.

Experimental (Cognitive) Anthropology

The publication of *The Cultural Context of Learning and Thinking* (Cole, Gay, Glick, & Sharp, 1971) some 25 years ago can be taken as the starting point of an approach that in several important ways has been at variance with some basic tenets of cross-cultural psychology. Led primarily by Michael Cole, researchers who follow this general approach have avoided traditional and standard cross-cultural testing and comparisons. Instead, they have placed a premium on exploring and understanding the specific context in which learning and thinking take place. As Jahoda noted, Cole and his colleagues emphasized the concept of the "psychic unity of humankind." The ideas of the Russian psychologist Vygotsky have particularly influenced their research. Skeptical about the reductionism and assumptions involved in traditional cross-cultural psychological research, the agenda of these researchers often has been to show that psychological processes are common across the human species (e.g., Scribner & Cole, 1981). They have argued that an understanding of psychological processes is best done as a result of detailed experimentation in specific cultural settings. To these researchers, "context" is not only paramount in influencing human behavior; behavior can *only* be conceptualized as embedded in specific sociocultural contexts. In this sense Cole and his associates have had a major impact on the development of cultural psychology. Thus, despite the fact that this culture-centered research has often been placed under the banner of cross-cultural psychology (e.g., Cole, 1989) it is perhaps more accurate to situate it under cultural psychology (see following) or cognitive anthropology (Bock, 1988; Miller, this volume). This approach was appropriately identified by Jahoda as one of the leading paradigms in the study of culture and human behavior. It continues to be influential, especially in the developmental area (Cole & Cole, 1993). Given the current interest in constructivism (Neimeyer, 1993), the approaches favored by cultural psychologists will continue to address many important questions regarding the nature of human thought processes and their cultural antecedents.

An Interim Commentary

When Jahoda started to work on his 1980 chapter, cross-cultural psychology as we know it today was barely more than a decade old. The International Association for Cross-Cultural Psychology, for instance, was just in its sixth year. As mentioned earlier, Jahoda had the challenging task of sifting through the publications produced by an entire generation of researchers who had shown at least some interest in the interface between culture and behavior. To a large extent, this generation had been extending to other cultures the different paradigms or theories that were developed in "mainstream" psychology. While this theory-extension and hypothesis-testing process continues to be a major purpose of cross-cultural psychology (Poortinga & Malpass, 1986; Malpass & Poortinga, 1986; Berry, Poortinga, Segall, & Dasen, 1992), at the time of Jahoda's review there were only a few models that attracted much attention. These were already mentioned as the "psychocultural model" used in the Six Cultures Project, McClelland's achievement motivation research, and Triandis's ideas regarding the network of interrelationships in studies of subjective culture. Through collaboration with Witkin involving extensions of differentiation theory as well as his own research, Berry began developing his ecocultural model (see following discussion). We have seen research in two of the seven approaches summarized by Jahoda to fall off sharply after the death of Witkin in 1979 and after McClelland's interests turned elsewhere. Subjective culture survives primarily as a way to train people for intercultural encounters—though it has informed much of the recent work on cultural syndromes. Psychometric approaches are likely to be part of research efforts as long as psychologists see a need to measure such things as cognitive abilities and achievements, personality, and the generous range of psychological constructs that embraces all facets of human behavior. Piagetian approaches, still dominant in part of cross-cultural developmental research, will no doubt continue for a long time to come, as will the pragmatic and empirical approaches of Cole and his colleagues. The records of all these approaches can speak for themselves. Collectively, they account for a significant percentage of cross-cultural psychological research.

Having reviewed the past, we now turn primarily to developments and progress since Jahoda's chapter. To appreciate the role played by cross-cultural psychology within the broad domain of psychology, one must become familiar with the basic, underlying characteristics of this particular type of inquiry. One should also be familiar with the several other perspectives in the social and behavioral sciences in which culture is prominently featured. What follows is a brief overview of the main components of these different ways to invoke culture as both a cause and consequence of human behavior.

Perspectives on Culture as Antecedent

There are four more or less psychological perspectives whose adherents focus on human culture as the paramount factor that shapes and influences thought and behavior. These orientations are cross-cultural psychology, cultural psychology, psychological anthropology, and indigenous psychology. All of them have made important contributions, and we assume that each will continue to maintain its own identity, but with considerable cross-over into the epistemological and methodological preferences taken by the other three. In this chapter we shall review the major features of cross-cultural psychology as well as some of its problems. Aspects of cultural psychology (Miller), indigenous psychology (Sinha), and anthropological approaches (Munroe & Munroe) are detailed in other chapters in this volume.

Cross-Cultural Psychology: Major Features and Goals

While it is difficult to define cross-cultural psychology to the complete satisfaction of all who identify with it, the various definitions that have appeared during the last quarter century contain many commonalities. Consider the following, which are amalgamations (not direct quotes) of assorted definitions found in the literature:

- It is interested in the nature and scope of human diversity at the level of the individual, and in reasons underlying such diversity; it is also interested in documenting psychological universals.
- The basic power of the cross-cultural method is that it capitalizes on extending the range of variation so that the widest possible range of settings where human behavior occurs might be incorporated into research designs.
- It assumes that one's culture is a major, if not the major, factor contributing to individual differences in behavior.

- It involves comparisons, either explicitly or implicitly, of behavior as it occurs in two or more cultural settings; if comparisons are made they must be based on equivalent methods of measurement.
- It is ultimately interested in the development of a psychology that will be much more "universal" in its scope and application than is the case at present.

Taking these commonalities together, we can see that cross-cultural psychology has much in common with so-called "mainstream" psychology. Both, after all, are interested in the study of individual differences and the sources of those differences; both (but to greatly varying degrees) recognize the important role played by the environment or context in shaping behavior; both use natural science methodologies and are typically guided by some current theory (or specific hypothesis derived from an extant theory); and both are interested in a psychology that includes broad topical coverage. Mainstream psychology, however, has been both culture-bound and culture-blind—a situation that was the main impetus in the development of cross-cultural psychology. At the scientific as well as practical level, the major difference between cross-cultural psychology and mainstream psychology is that in the former's process of extending the range of variation as far as possible, researchers are confronted with differences in behavior patterns that fit neither Western "common-sense" notions about behavior nor their formal and almost entirely Western theories. When pursuing cross-cultural investigations, a number of methodological problems enter the picture and must be resolved. Among the more important of these problems are those that involve a) the rationale used in the selection of cultures or ethnicities for the purpose of testing the limits of some theory, and b) the solution of problems associated with measures or procedures used during the study so that any comparisons made or conclusions drawn are based on equivalent data (cf. Van de Vijver & Leung, this volume). It follows from the above that the results of any particular study will be seriously, perhaps fatally, flawed if it can be shown that either in the selection of cultures or the measures used in a particular study the researchers did not pay adequate attention to the unique methodological, conceptual, and even logistical challenges that are always involved in sophisticated cross-cultural psychological research. More will be said later of these challenges.

A comprehensive definition of cross-cultural psychology is the one given by Berry et al. (1992, p. 2):

> *Cross-cultural psychology is the study of similarities and differences in individual psychological functioning in various cultural and ethnic groups; of the relationships between psychological variables and sociocultural, ecological, and biological variables; and of current changes in these variables.*

The same authors summarize what they consider to be the major goals of cross-cultural psychology:

1. Testing the limits of psychological theory by extending to other cultures a particular theory and/or the hypotheses that may be generated from it in order

to determine how generalizeable the theory might be. This has been called the "transport and test" function. That is, a theory is transported to other cultures and tested in those contexts.

2. The exploration and discovery goal that includes examining variations of behavior not present in one's own culture and seeking explanations for such variations. In other words, failures to generalize (the first goal) should be explored in an effort to discover interesting variations of behavior that may then be "folded back" into the theory that guided the research in the first place.

3. The integration function, wherein the findings generated in pursuit of the first two goals can be combined in efforts to help develop a more universal psychology. In addition to the first goal of testing the generality of findings, several advantages of cross-cultural studies have been identified. For instance, cultures provide natural experiments.

Because cultures are not "manipulations" or clever laboratory replicas of real-world circumstances, the cross-cultural researcher can exploit this fact and do research in genuine settings. Also, cultures can serve the important function of unconfounding variables. In the past, many studies have been troubled because two or more variables have been confounded. The classic example of confounded variables involved Malinowski's (1927) research in the Trobriand Islands, an example that has served for years as a conceptual and methodological teething ring for budding cross-cultural psychologists. Using orthodox Freudian theory, Malinowski investigated the generality of Freud's "Oedipal" situation—the idea that a young boy is jealous of his father because they are competing for the affection of the same woman, who happens to be both the boy's mother and the father's lover. At least that is the way it was alleged to have been in Freud's Vienna. The Trobriand society provided anthropologist Malinowski with an alternative view; there Oedipal-like reactions were found for mother's elder brother, who happens to be the main disciplinarian of a boy in that society. The Viennese boys' "unresolved Oedipal conflict" could be seen as a reaction not to father-as-mother's lover but to father-as-disciplinarian. These two variables were unconfounded. It turned out that the Freudian Oedipal problem did not transport well to the Trobriands because it was the uncle that the boy feared and not his father.

Other advantages of cross-cultural psychology are 1) to study culture change and the effects it has on people, and 2) to aid in the reduction of ethnocentrism by the application of cross-cultural studies, an advantage high on the list of many cross-cultural social psychologists (Triandis, 1994). The more we know about human variations in behavior, and the reasons for those variations, the more enlightened and "worldly" we become (or the fewer reasons we have to believe that we are the center of all human activity, which is the essence of ethnocentrism). Yet another benefit of cross-cultural research is to use the accumulated results of research in culture-training programs (Brislin & Yoshida, 1994a, b). Most of the materials used by psychologists and educators who train people to work and live elsewhere are based on empirical cross-cultural research. For instance, Ptak, Cooper, and Brislin (1995) report that a survey of 94 professional culture trainers revealed that they wish they would have had a better knowledge of Hofstede's (1980, 1991) work-related values when they were introducing their trainees to cultural variations in attitudes, beliefs, expectations, and values.

Kenneth Berrien (1970) exhorted cross-cultural psychologists to develop a "super-ego" in designing, conducting, and interpreting their research, and George Miller (1969) thought that psychologists should learn to "give their discipline away" as a means of promoting human welfare. In the spirit of their recommendations, we should learn to "give cross-cultural psychology away" in the context of applications to real-world problems of an applied nature such as represented by the above.

Psychology as it has developed and has been practiced in the psychologically dominant Western world is a relatively young branch of science. Its youth has meant that there has been insufficient time and international interest for it to have matured. Yet it is believed by most cross-cultural psychologists that it is possible, and indeed highly desirable, to develop a psychology that tries to establish what is universal and generalizeable in the tremendous cultural diversity of human behavior patterns. In principle, most cross-cultural psychologists believe that there are indeed general laws of human behavior, and that their discovery and documentation can only be realized if the goals of cross-cultural psychology are pursued.

Cultural Psychology: A Contrasting View

We now turn to an ongoing dialogue focusing on a central question in those aspects of psychology that assign culture a prominent role as an antecedent to behavior. The dialogue involves two juxtaposed yet remarkably similar perspectives: cultural psychology (see Miller's chapter, this volume) and cross-cultural psychology, both of which share a number of concerns while at the same time differing in several important ways with regard to conceptions of culture-behavior relationships as well as methods of inquiry.

In cross-cultural psychological research a hypothesis is tested by extending the range of variation (including other cultures or ethnic groups) according to the independent variable of interest (some aspect of the sociocultural or ecological context). Participants in the study are chosen by using appropriate sampling procedures, and one or more measures of the dependent variables are administered. Then the data are analyzed and interpreted.

While most cross-cultural psychological research is not as tidy as this scheme, the strategy it suggests has received considerable attention in terms of what to do and what not to do (e.g., Berry et al., 1992; Lonner & Berry, 1986; Van de Vijver & Leung, in preparation; cf. also Van de Vijver & Leung, this volume). It can be and has been quite useful in helping to develop a better understanding of basic human processes, capacities, social interactions, and virtually all psychological topics. It also shows, as noted earlier, that cross-cultural psychological research is normally not very different from so-called mainstream and essentially experimental and reductionistic research.

The above approach, however, may not be adequate for the study of all forms of human behavior that vary across cultures. This is where epistemology enters the picture. As Jahoda (1994) observes, in cross-cultural psychological research "the independent variables do not usually exert their effects in a simple and direct manner of the stimulus-response type; rather . . . they are mediated in a complex and as yet still inadequately understood manner by such processes as socialization and the experiences of interaction with others." Jahoda continues by noting that these processes "take place within an overarching cultural framework, and to ignore this is to be guilty of gross oversimplification."

This is also where a number of subtle concerns regarding methods of inquiry and various procedural details enter the picture. For example, as Jahoda points out above, the status of culture as an independent variable has to be questioned. In classic experimentation, the researcher can "control" the nature and magnitude of the independent variable. In cross-cultural research, such control can, at best, only be approximated. Furthermore, key independent variables may operate differently in different societies. For instance, what is called the "independent variable" in a particular study may have a substantially different meaning in society A than it does in other societies; it may, in fact, have different meanings in all societies. How cross-cultural psychologists handle methodological problems such as the non-equivalence of samples, unintended differences in the meaning of stimuli, and cultural effects of researcher-subject interactions often involve complex matters (Van de Vijver & Leung, in preparation; Van de Vijver & Leung, this volume). Here we focus on the question of how and to what extent culture is to be understood by psychologists and, therefore, the role that culture should play in the field of psychology.

In what is frequently offered as a sharp contrast to research methods typically used by cross-cultural psychologists, cultural psychologists deal with culture and methodologies used to study it in somewhat different ways. Another citation of Jahoda can serve to define cultural psychology and to describe the contrast with the cross-cultural approach. Jahoda asserts that ". . . culture and mind interpenetrate each other, so that all behavior is inescapably cultural. It is therefore futile to try and decontextualize behavior in an attempt to get at universal invariants [a task he believes is assumed by cross-cultural psychologists], for humans without culture are inconceivable" Jahoda (1992). Jahoda has, however, written that he thinks the two approaches are complementary, ". . . since both in their different ways seek to understand human behavior in context" (p. xi). He also believes that there is no sharp boundary between the two. The osmotic nature of this boundary can be seen in another definition of cultural psychology:

> [It] *seeks to discover systematic relationships between cultural and behavioral variables, asking whether individuals growing up in culture A tend to develop that culture's psychological qualities. The hallmark of cultural psychology is the attempt to understand individual psychological functioning in the cultural context in which it developed" (Berry, 1994, p. 120).*

The above definition was given in the context of making distinctions between the goals of cultural psychology and ethnic psychology, the latter being yet another way to approach variations in the cognitions, attitudes, and behaviors of individuals who have undergone the acculturation process as members of a group who have joined, for one reason or another, a larger and dominant nation-state.

Ernest Boesch, a cultural psychologist who uses his complex and probing Symbolic Action Theory (Boesch, 1991) to explain behavior-in-context, was asked to comment on the differences between cultural and cross-cultural psychology. He argues (personal communication) that they are different "actions" carried out in similar fields—that is, in cultures foreign to the researcher. The typical cross-cultural psychologist, as Boesch sees it, is not primarily interested in a specific culture. In a paper detailing the "seven flaws of cross-cultural psychology," Boesch (unpublished manuscript) asserts that most cross-cultural psychologists are interested in a problem of general psychology; "culture" is taken as a "treatment," or an "independent variable." Cross-cultural psychologists desire to understand reasons behind cultural variation in general in an effort to help build a more universally acceptable psychology. Boesch believes that, by contrast, cultural psychologists desire to know the "fabric" of a specific culture; that is, to them culture is the primary focus. The questions asked by cross-cultural psychology tend to be restricted to specific interactions of variables, while cultural psychology focuses on "constellations."

What are constellations? The cultural psychologist would be interested in the forms of behavior within one specific culture and how these relate to other forms of behavior within that culture. In other words, he or she would be concerned with a detailed within-culture analysis of various constellations of interrelationships. Cultural psychologists would therefore have more in common with the typical anthropological method of "deep cultural immersion." They would be less interested in the pursuit of universals, and they would emphasize that standard psychological experimentation falls short in the quest to fathom the essential core of a particular society (cf. Miller, this volume; Greenfield, this volume).

The issue of comparativism also can be raised. Cultural psychologists tend to denounce the usually explicit comparative nature of cross-cultural psychological research, but comparativism in cultural psychology is present, even if only implicit. For instance, Shweder and Sullivan (1993) have said that "cultural psychology is, first of all, a designation for the comparative study of the way culture and psyche make each other up" (p. 488). They also describe other goals of cultural psychology. These include a reconsideration of "methods and procedures for studying mental states and psychological processes across languages and cultures." That goal has been central to cross-cultural psychology, and has been driven by another feature of cultural psychology about which cross-cultural psychological methodologists have expressed considerable concern: that "performance differences among human populations may arise from the partial translatability or limited commensurability of stimulus sitations and materials" (Shweder & Sullivan, 1993, p. 489). The cumulative record of methodological books and treatises in cross-cultural psychology shows that these concerns have been central, for many years, in research on cognition and other basic processes (e.g., Brislin, Lonner, & Thorndike, 1973; Berry & Dasen, 1974; Berry, 1980; Lonner & Berry, 1986; Berry et al., 1992) as well as in more applied areas (e.g., Brislin, 1989; Lonner & Ibrahim, 1996).

Many cross-cultural psychologists, including ourselves, would disagree with the assertion that they are more interested in the results of "treatments" than they are in the "fabric" or "core" of culture, that they are not interested in insights derived from "deep cultural immersion," and so on. Cole, a cultural psychologist, acknowledges this. In a chapter footnote, he says that he did "not want to give the impression that the views identified here are the only way to conceive of cultural psychology. For example, Berry (as cited by Cole, 1989, p. 282) defines cultural psychology as 'an analogous term to social, industrial, developmental (etc.) psychology. That is, it identifies an area of study which seeks to discover systematic relationships among cultural and behavioral variables'."

Psychological Anthropology

The field of psychological anthropology can claim as its pioneers some of the more influential thinkers in anthroplogy (Bock, 1994). While most psychologists probably are not very familiar with their impressive intellectual legacy, a generation or two of anthropologists were strongly influenced by the works of such giants as Abraham Kardiner, Ralph Linton, Bronislaw Malinowski, Franz Boas, Margaret Mead, Ruth Benedict, and Edward Sapir. A contemporary spokesperson for this academic orientation, Robert Paul, says that in a "narrow" sense "the specialty [of psychological anthropology] within anthropology... seeks to look at that partial range of phenomena to which psychological methods and questions are particularly appropriate, just as economic anthropology is a specialty focused on those parts of socio-cultural reality to which economic activity can be applied" (Paul, 1994, p. 100). He goes on to say that in a broader sense the phrase ". . . designates an approach to anthropology as a whole which, in contrast to other approaches, accepts the view that individual human beings are in a strong sense autonomous agents endowed with certain specifiable capacities and subject to certain specifiable limits, who are able to set goals, and plan to follow strategies in pursuit of those goals" (p. 100).

Asserting that all anthropology is psychological and that all psychology is cultural, Bock (1988) identified four major schools and approaches of psychological anthropology:

- Psychoanalytic anthropology (orthodox and neo-Freudian)
- Culture and personality (e.g., basic and modal personality, national character)
- Social structure and personality (e.g., materialism and interactionism)
- Cognitive anthropology (e.g., primitive mentality, development, and ethnosemantics)

Of the above categories, only the latter includes names of individuals and their approaches with whom contemporary cross-cultural psychologists have considerable familiarity. Among them are Piaget, Witkin, Cole, and Price-Williams.

Borrowing notation from LeVine (1982), Bock (1988, pp. 101- 102) summarized the ways in which different approaches have characterized the relationship between culture and personality:

> *Culture (C) may be viewed as caused by psychological states, motives, or complexes (P → C); or the two may be considered virtually identical (P = C). In some approaches, personality is considered to be completely determined by cultural or social-structural conditions (C → P). In others, personality is viewed as mediating between different parts of a culture, integrating its customs and institutions (C$_1$ → P → C$_2$). Finally, in one view, personality systems interact with sociocultural systems, and relative stablility is attained only when psychological needs and social demands are 'congruent' (P ↔ C).*

The edited book by Suarez-Orozco, Spindler, and Spindler (1994) contains several chapters that are representative of what psychological anthropologists do. In their preface to the book, the editors say that

> *This phenomenological, existential conception of the relation between human minds, environment, and culture is not new and indeed has been a preoccupation of intellectuals of various persuasians for centuries, probably in some form since the first stirrings of human consciousness. But while the rest of anthropology seems bogged down in the extreme relativism of cultural diversity, psychological anthropology minds the processes of minding and of human agency, and tends to the maintenance of sanity (as well as its breakdown) as humans impose their 'realities' on what is 'out there' (p. vii).*

What is meant by the term "minding," and how does it differ from "mind"? It refers to commonalities in the "processing of thought, emotion, perception, and the dynamics of the psyche, such as transference, counter-transference, projection, and reaction formation, derived from the psychoanlytic model" (p. 4). As mentioned above, the writings of Freud, Piaget and others are prominent in the works of psychological anthropologists; considering especially the intricacies and complexities of psychoanalytic theory, one can readily see that Freudian-oriented psychological anthropologists would hardly be at a loss to explain the dynamics of a particular culture. The Six Cultures Project, mentioned earlier, is a good example of the kinds of research that psychological anthropologists do. In our opinion the reader of this chapter should become familiar with this particular anthropological subfield. We think that it has substantial similarities with "cultural psychology"; we also think that cross-cultural psychology owes a debt to this field for the insights it has provided regarding the nature of the human mind, and for its methodological operations, which almost always involve long-term forays into the field. We further believe that it is incumbent upon the cross-cultural psychologist to understand the mutual methodological relevance of anthropology and psychology (Campbell, 1961) along with the historical and epistemological similarities, continuities, and differences involving psychology and culture (Jahoda, 1990, 1992; Jahoda & Krewer, this volume).

Indigenous Psychologies

Partially because of disappointment with the Western domination of psychology, and partially because of a concomitant belief that the Western-trained psychologist cannot really fathom with equal and deep understanding all other cultures, a growing interest in indigenous psychologies has recently emerged. Kim and Berry (1993, p. 2) define indigenous psychologies (plural is appropriate because ostensibly any group of people for whom the indigenous label applies can develop its own psychology) as "the scientific study of human behavior (or the mind) that is native, that is not transported from other regions, and that is designed for its people."

There are many psychologists who, while usually also identifying with cross-cultural psychology, are proponents of the growing phenomenon of the "indigenization" of psychology (see, for example, Durganand Sinha's chapter in this volume). Consider Diaz-Guerrero's (1993) assertion that one cannot fully understand the psychology of the Mexican unless and until one has a complete understanding of the "socio-historico cultural premises" that have shaped Mexico and its numerous peoples. It seems to us only logical that for a "psychology" to be completely indigenous it would have to be so culture-bound, so relative, and so heavily "emic" that the only understanding an outsider could hope for is to view it from afar, making no attempts to "reduce" it to common denominators for comparative purposes. The latter process would involve "etics," or some sort of reductionistic or categorization process that was not initiated by the developers of various indigenous approaches. However, both Enriquez (1993) and Berry and Kim (1993) suggest a way to chart the future by moving ahead with a "cross-indigenous" approach to forge a "universal" psychology—that is, to carry out an etic process.

In fairness to their analysis, however, it should be noted that in their opinion the development of a "universal" psychology is one of the goals of the indigenous psychology approach. While it may be helpful and interesting to discover threads of continuity and commonality among indigenous psychologists, one wonders why indigenous psychologies would have to be scrutinized and analyzed for this purpose. On the surface, it may seem somewhat contradictory to encourage the development of indigenous and unique psychologies on the one hand, and on the other hand to endorse the development of a strategy to examine them for commonalities! It can be argued, however, that a universal psychology might emerge only after indigenous psychologies are examined and their common elements identified. Here, potentially, we have the "ideal" situation: Indigenous psychologies that have been forged in, by, and for specific societies, but that also have been examined for common elements—elements that could well serve either as bases for meaningful comparisons or as ways to help understand other societies.

Conceptualizations of Culture as Antecedent

As noted earlier in this chapter, a wide variety of primarily social psychological topics and the hypotheses they have generated continue to dominate the literature in cross-cultural psychology (Öngel & Smith, 1994). No single social psychological theme or theory, however, such as attribution theory or studies of leadership, has dominated the publication landscape during the last 15 years. On the other hand, within this same period several somewhat unrelated tributaries of research activity have been noteworthy as they are flowing into the main effluent of cross-cultural literature. We turn our attention to brief summaries of these streams of ongoing activity.

The overwhelming majority of the cross-cultural approaches to culture and psychology (e.g., Berry et al. 1992; Triandis, 1994), as well as many of the alternative perspectives (e.g., Shweder, 1990), assume explicitly that culture—however defined—is an antecedent to human thought and behavior. For example, Berry et al. (1992) have proposed that the major orientations in cross-cultural psychology tend to assume cultural explanations for psychological and behavioral differences among groups of people. A second, potentially quite different, approach that attempts to describe culture in terms of the constraints that "limit," rather than "determine," a group's behavioral repertoire also assigns antecedent status to culture (Poortinga, 1990). Finally, as described earlier, cultural psychology, an orientation that claims to be quite antithetical to cross-cultural psychology, makes similar assumptions. Shweder (1990, p. 1) states, for example, that "cultural traditions . . . regulate . . . the human psyche, resulting . . . in ethnic divergences in mind, self, and emotion." It is difficult to see how the language used in this case to describe a "new" discipline differs fundamentally from that used by comparative researchers. At some level, it appears that nearly all social scientists in this field acknowledge that culture can play a crucial role in shaping virtually any aspect of human behavior.

This basic and widespread acknowledgment and agreement among researchers notwithstanding, there are significantly different ways in which a theoretically complex construction like "culture" can be conceptualized as an antecedent of other human phenomena. Unfortunately, the various orientations that give primacy to interactions between psychology and culture have not engaged in adequate debate on just what kind of an antecedent of human experience "culture" is (or ought to be). This may stem, at least in part, from the often adversarial positions historically taken by the relevant social and behavioral sciences (i.e., psychology, anthropology, and sociology) with regard to the ontological status of the construct. More important perhaps is the absence of competing comprehensive theoretical frameworks that provide alternative interpretations of the relationship between culture and the many varieties of human experience. Indeed, it may be argued that cross-cultural psychology is richer in data and "findings" than in major theoretical paradigms.

The above statement may appear rather surprising, considering the healthy flourishing of cultural and psychological research in recent years. However, it is important to keep in mind that much of this work is not theory-driven, but, rather, data-oriented—a situation that is more characteristic of cross-cultural psychology than it is of cultural psychology. It would not be unfair to state that, as we would expect on historical grounds, clever methodology and somewhat orphaned though sometimes creative hypotheses have once again outpaced theory-building.

It is critical, therefore, that we pose the question as explicitly as possible: "In which way(s) is culture treated as an antecedent variable in modern psychological theories and models?" Or, put in a somewhat different way, "What are some of the major ways in which the rather nebulous construct 'culture' can be conceptualized as an antecedent variable?" While reviews of definitions and conceptions of culture might be instructive (e.g., Soudijn, Hutschemaekers, & Van de Vijver, 1990; Lonner, 1994), nothing can replace systematic empirical attempts to explain the slippery phenomenon.

Figure 2–1 presents a classification of different types of conceptions of culture as it relates to theory that can be generated by considering two major issues: (1.) What role does the construct "culture" play in a particular theory? How important is "culture" in determining the primary phenomena of interest? Is "culture" of immediate interest, or is it considered a "third" variable? (2.) Does the theory or model assume that "culture" has a direct effect or an indirect effect on the dependent variable(s) measured?

As shown in Figure 2–1, those theoretical models that assign primary importance to "culture" and, at the same time, view its influence on the dependent variable(s) of interest as direct (i.e., see culture as a direct antecedent of some other human phenomenon) inevitably treat culture in a straightforward manner operationally as the *independent* variable in the same sense that it is used in the experimental tradition. Theoretical models that assign an equal importance to culture but view its influence on the dependent variable(s) of interest as indirect

		Role of Culture in Theoretical Framework	
		Primary	Secondary
Assumed Influence of Culture on Dependent Variable(s)	Direct	Culture Independent Variable	Culture Mediator
	Indirect	Culture Context	Culture Moderator

FIGURE 2–1   **Four perspectives on culture as antecedent of thought and action**

(i.e., consider that there may be a number of other, more proximal, influences underlying mental and behavioral events) may be thought of as looking at culture as a *contextual* variable or set of variables. Here more emphasis is placed on analysis of relationships, although culture is still treated conceptually as an independent variable. In such cases culture becomes the overarching explanatory frame for a vast number of phenomena, including gender differences, sub-cultural and ethnic differences, and sociohistorical changes.

The situation becomes even more complicated when culture is viewed as an *intervening* antecedent variable of secondary (or indirect) importance. The theoretical assumption here typically is that there are systems of variables that should be thought of as the most significant or primary determinants of human thought and behavior. For example, a particular theoretical orientation may assume that personality traits are the primary determinants of behavioral consistency. Contextual, sociocultural, or situational variables would not necessarily be ruled out within such an orientation, but their role would clearly be considered indirect. Such an orientation would assume, for instance, that a pattern of conformity behavior exhibited by an individual was caused by underlying dispositions (i.e., an individual who is a member of a specific culture might score low on a scale measuring how "dominant" he or she is). The impact of legitimate authority on conformity behavior might be recognized, but not emphasized within this framework.

The two types of perspectives that emerge in this latter analysis of social environment/culture-behavior relationships parallel conceptually the well-known distinction between mediator and moderator variables (e.g., Baron & Kenny, 1986).

Mediator variables typically are used as explanatory constructs to account for the relationship between a psychological (predictor) and a performance (criterion) variable (Baron & Kenny, 1986). Consider a theoretical model that attempts to explain individual differences in degree of conformity to ingroup expectations. The model may propose, for example, that a personality trait (e.g., idiocentrism versus allocentrism; Triandis, Leung, Villareal, & Clack, 1985) predicts conformity quite well. Of course, it is quite possible that a third variable (or set of variables)—"culture"—may account completely for the performance variable (conformity). "Culture" in this case may be conceptualized as a set of norms, beliefs, or values (Triandis, 1990) which are at least partially related to and determined by the psychological variable of interest (idiocentrism/allocentrism) and, in turn, affect conformity. Once the relationship between such a mediator and the performance variable is taken into account, the link between the psychological and the performance variables may be at best minimal. In the specific example, normative, culturally-based beliefs about one's relationship with his/her ingroup may completely account for the observed individual difference without any need to rely on assumptions about an underlying personality trait. In a related example, Eagly and Wood (1991) have shown that sex-differentiated beliefs about the effects of aggressive behavior and expectations about the likelihood of engaging in such behavior predicted obtained sex differences in aggression. Clearly, culture can be an enormously important construct in this context.

Moderator variables "control" and potentially alter the strength or direction of the relationship between an independent variable and a dependent variable. Thus, moderator variables often manifest themselves through an interaction with the primary predictor or independent variable of interest. Consider, for example, the description by Whiting and Child (1953) of the relationship between age of weaning and anxiety later in life. In Western cultures, this relationship typically follows a monotonically increasing function that ranges between one and six months. However, in non-Western cultures, in which weaning occurs much later, the relationship between the two variables manifests a negative slope. In this case culture moderates the relationship between a social (independent) and a psychological variable.

Another, more recent, example, of a moderating variable is found in the analysis of sex differences. Eagly and Wood (1991) have reported that a number of contextual variables (e.g., social settings, the presence or absence of an audience during social interaction, the interpersonal or task orientation of an activity) appear to moderate the relationship between the sex of the actor and his/her behavior. Presumably, in all of these cases the contextual variable interacts with the sex of the actor (or group) and either attenuates or enhances performance.

The remainder of this section will consider a number of the more significant theoretical models and frameworks in cross-cultural psychology in the context of the scheme presented above and in Figure 2–1. The aim of this analysis is to provide a critique that may lead to insights not only regarding the theories themselves, but also the overall interpretive dynamic of the discipline.

Contemporary Theoretical Perspectives

So far in this chapter we have (1) summarized seven research traditions that Jahoda (1980) documented as popular and significant guides in cross-cultural research through the late 1970s, and (2) given overviews of current and overlapping orientations which focus on culture as antecedent to behavior. We turn now to a question that is important for both contemporary contemplation and future considerations: What have been the leading paradigms or frameworks in cross-cultural psychology since Jahoda's review, and what do they portend for cross-cultural psychological research in the coming years?

Several contemporary perspectives are noteworthy, and perhaps the first to be mentioned is the ecocultural model. Others include individualism–collectivism, research on cultural variations in the construal of self, utilitarian and exchange theories, values, and evolutionary approaches. We shall comment briefly on these latter areas, especially with respect to the ways that they can be construed as antecedent to behavior.

The Ecocultural Framework

The ecocultural framework, which is often associated with John Berry, is designed to accommodate a considerable range of topics that might concern those who identify with cultural psychology, just as it has been instrumental in guiding numerous studies and experiments in comparative traditions of cross-cultural psychology.

The basic idea underlying the development of this framework is fairly simple and immediately understandable: all psychological phenomena are essentially viewed as adaptations to specific cultural and ecological contexts. While Jahoda (1995) correctly points out that speculations and theories regarding cultural and ecological influences on behavior (human and otherwise) have been around for centuries, Berry's model is an improvement over earlier models, as he pointed out in a rejoinder to Jahoda (Berry, 1995). It may be viewed as a synthesis of features of various earlier models, but one that has grown out of ongoing cross-cultural psychological research. One should also remember that Berry's ecocultural framework is not a theory. It is a heuristic device, the use of which may help researchers develop hypotheses about specific interrelationships between culture/ethnicity, ecology, and behavior.

The rudiments of the framework can be seen in Berry's (1966) study in which he hypothesized and tested relationships between ecological conditions and visual perception. That study, which included samples of individuals from sedentary agriculturalists (the Temne) and nomadic Inuit (Eskimos), was expanded over the years and included samples of individuals from a sizeable number of other cultures (see Berry et al., 1992, for details). The framework postulates *probabilistic relationships* between ecological and sociocultural settings and a person's behavior. That is, the behavior of a person from a specific setting can be expected to fall within a certain range of variation. This approach requires full use of the idea of "interactionism" or, to use Bandura's social learning theory term, "reciprocal determinism." The idea behind reciprocal determinism is that there is a continual three-way interaction between situation, person, and behavior. Situation (environmental) variables constitute the setting in which a person behaves, person variables determine how a situation is understood and analyzed, and behavior provides both feedback concerning how the person analyzes the situation and modifies the environment (Bandura, 1986). Theoretical precursors to these ideas include Barker's (1968) ecological psychology and Lewin's Field Theory or topological psychology (Lewin, 1935) as well as Rotter's (1981, 1982) social learning views. Lewin's formula, $P = f(LS)$—the Person is a function of his Life Space—alternately expressed as $B = f(P, E)$—Behavior is a function of the interaction between the Person and the Environment—is an austere version of what Berry started to develop some thirty years later. The common element is that of environmental adaptation. And, as pointed out earlier in this chapter, the "psychocultural model" developed by the Whitings and their colleagues is probably the closest to the nature and intent of Berry's ecocultural model. These related frameworks suggest strong dynamic relationships between different parts of a complex equation: when any part of the equation changes, all other parts can be expected to change as well. These delicate, context-dependent interactions appear to come close to what the cultural psychologist would call constellations. The major components of the ecocultural framework are shown in Figure 2–2.

While the reader is referred to more complete explanations of the framework and how it has guided different research projects (Berry, 1994; Berry et al., 1992),

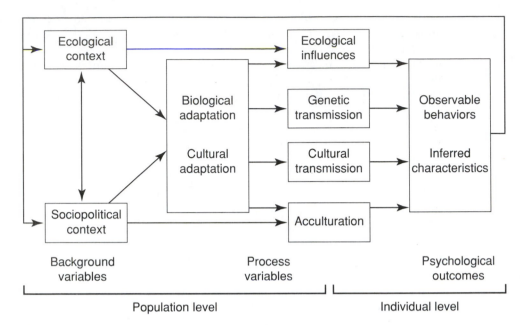

FIGURE 2–2   **The ecocultural framework**

Source: Berry et al. (1992).

some of its major characteristics are presented here. The model distinguishes between population-level and individual-level of analysis. As explained in Berry et al. (1992, p. 11), "The flow of the figure is from left to right, with population-level variables conceived of as influencing the individual outcomes . . . we wish to account for individual and group differences in psychological characteristics as a function of population-level factors." The proponents of this framework go on to explain that "the ecological context is the setting in which human organisms and the physical environment interact," and that the "central feature of this ecological context is economic activity, in which non-industrial cultural groups are rated with respect to their degree of reliance on five kinds of economic activity: hunting, gathering, fishing, pastoralism, and agriculture" (p. 13). It is also important to note that both cultural and biological factors contribute to psychological outcomes.

The ecocultural framework has been referred to extensively, by Berry as well as by others who view the relationship between psychology and culture to be potentially complex and highly interactive. Examples of research that has been done utilizing the framework are in the area of cognition (Berry & Bennett, 1989; Berry, Irvine, & Hunt, 1988; Dasen, 1975) and psychological factors associated with acculturation (Berry, 1990; Berry & Sam, Vol. 3 of this *Handbook*).

"Culture" clearly plays a very important and complex role in the ecocultural framework. Various types of cultural variables appear at both the population and individual levels. At the population level, culture is generally treated as an independent variable that leads to particular cultural adaptations to the ecology (e.g., inventions, social institutions, etc.). However, culture is also treated at this level as a mediator that can account for the relationship between cultural adaptations and individual behavior (Segall et al., 1990). At the individual level of analysis, the ecocultural framework appears to treat certain aspects of culture (e.g., cultural adaptations) as independent variables that determine the outcome of psychological processes and individual behaviors.

Such complexity in the conceptualization of the function of cultural variables is an obvious strength of the framework in that it maximizes the range of human phenomena to which it can be applied. At the same time, however, the complexity of this framework makes it quite difficult to generate a concise and unambiguous definition of culture within its context. While not necessarily a deficiency, this difficulty may limit the contributions of the framework to the epistemological debate in the area of psychology and culture.

Individualism–Collectivism

The constructs of individualism and collectivism have a long history in the social sciences. Their precursors played a significant role in much of the work of Parsons and Shils (1951) on the dynamics of human action, and were introduced in a societal context as *Gesellschaft* and *Gemeinschaft,* respectively, by Tönnies (1964). Tonnies used the term *Gemeinschaft* to refer to traditional agricultural communities where solidarity and trust was important, and *Gesellschaft* to refer to industrial urban settings populated by unrelated, competitive strangers. In anthropology, Hsu (1983), among others, has emphasized these ideas as primary and defining characteristics of the Western and Eastern worlds.

Hofstede's (1980) research on cross-cultural differences in work values appears to have provided the most significant stimulus for the emergence of individualism and collectivism as important psychological constructs. For the first time, systematic analyses of individual responses from a number of different societies provided support for the theoretical importance of the constructs in a way that was more widely acceptable to the methodological demands of psychologists.

So much discussion, speculation and research has been done in this area that Kagitçibasi (1994) identified the 1980s as the decade of individualism–collectivism. This trend continues with no signs of abating (Kim, Triandis, Kagitçibasi, Choi, & Yoon, 1994; Triandis, 1995; Kagitçibasi, Vol. 3, this *Handbook*).

Bakan (1966) contended that all human beings have two "senses": a sense of agency (selfness, unique identity, autonomy, individuality, and pleasure seeking) and a sense of communion (selflessness, belongingness, group solidarity, sharing, and emotional dependence). Similar constructs have been discussed in analyses of social behavior (Triandis, 1990, 1993, 1994), morality (Miller, Bersoff, & Harwood, 1990; Shweder & Bourne, 1982), cultural patterns (Hsu, 1983), cognitive differentiation (Witkin & Berry, 1975; Witkin & Goodenough, 1981), and the construal of the self (Markus & Kitayama, 1991; Triandis, 1989). "Mainstream psychology" has been rather slow in incorporating individualism and collectivism in its theoretical repertoire, though occasional attempts have been made in recent years (e.g., Hogan, 1975; Sampson, 1977; Smith, 1978; Waterman, 1981). There are a number of reasons for this, not the least of which is a lack of systematic analyses of hypotheses derived from the two constructs. In addition, the overwhelming dominance of the "Western" perspective in psychology — including even cross-cultural psychology—has trivialized the importance of studying alternative views of human nature (e.g., Triandis, 1990; Sinha, this volume).

As far as the theoretical status of individualism and collectivism is concerned, the almost meteoric rise to prominence of the two constructs has been accompanied by "growing pains" (e.g., Triandis, 1990). The problems have been of both a methodological (e.g., low measurement reliabilities) and a theoretical nature, though the present discussion will focus on the latter.

There is considerable ambivalence in the cross-cultural literature regarding the appropriate level of analysis for the constructs. Specifically, following the initial development of the cultural constructs, Triandis et al. (1985) proposed a set of psychological constructs—idiocentrism and allocentrism—to parallel individualism and collectivism. This distinction, though unusual and inspired in its attempt to bridge individual and communal tendencies, generates some difficult questions regarding proper interpretive and analytic levels for cross-cultural psychology—questions that are increasingly the focus of an important debate in the field.

Triandis (1990) clearly assigns primacy to culture in one of his early analyses of individualism and collectivism. He writes, "The effect of cultural complexity [one of the major determinants of individualism] is to create separation, distinction, and different life-styles. Then the individual is confronted with conflicting norms and worldviews" (p. 44). This appears to be a classic example of "culture-as-an-independent-variable." Culture is conceptualized as a major cause of individual dispositions, and variations in human behavior are interpreted on the basis of cultural differences.

Other work appears to shift the causal emphasis from the global, cultural level to the individual level. For example, as mentioned earlier, Triandis et al. (1985) developed a model in which psychological, rather than cultural, constructs were described as immediate determinants of individual behavior. Specifically, allocentrism and idiocentrism were conceptualized as stable personality dispositions that affect individual action and judgment. "Culture" is then described as a theoretical concept determined by the preponderance of individual dispositions, or "sampling" of individualist versus collectivist elements within a particular group (Triandis, 1989). Individualism and collectivism are thus defined as "syndromes" (Triandis, 1993, 1994), or profiles that come as close to defining "culture" as is possible within this framework. At the same time, "culture" is also implicitly afforded some causal properties over individual behavior (Triandis et al., 1985).

While theoretically consistent, this second approach appears to rest upon a different assumption about the relationship between culture and behavior. Culture acquires a secondary, or perhaps distal, status as a causal construct, and as such internal, intra-individual determinants of behavior are viewed as proximal causal mechanisms. This is a fairly common position within Western psychology, and is theoretically and methodologically very seductive in its directness and accessibility to (quasi-) experimental analysis.

This model of individualism and collectivism implicitly treats culture as a mediator variable (cf. Figure 2–1). Specifically, it defines culture in terms of the preponderance of individual tendencies, and at the same time assigns some causal properties to culture (e.g., collectivist cultures provide support that protects individuals from mental illness; Triandis et al., 1985).

It is noteworthy that Hofstede's (1980) original account of individualism and collectivism also appears to treat these cultural syndromes as mediator variables. Hofstede's approach is conceptually similar to the work of Osgood, which was used extensively nearly a generation ago to investigate "semantic space" (Osgood et al., 1975). Using the semantic differential technique, Osgood and his colleagues claimed to have found three robust, universal dimensions of metaphorical meaning: Evaluation, Potency, and Activity (often referred to as EPA).

The essential similarity between Hofstede and Osgood is that both developed ways to categorize certain aspects of human behavior, but that neither claimed to have found the *only* way to understand behavior in their respective domains. In other words, just as the factors of EPA do not account for *all* of the variability in metaphorical meaning, the dimensions Hofstede identified do not account for all variability in human values.

An enduring problem in cross-cultural psychology, in fact, concerns how many human values there are, what values do in terms of predicting or explaining behavior, and how they should be used in any psychological orientation that attempts to explain cultural variations in behavior. A group calling itself the Chinese Culture Connection (1987) demonstrated that Hofstede's values, while not necessarily totally culture-bound, may miss important aspects of certain societies. For instance, these researchers found a value orientation, which they called Confucian Work-Dynamism, that is important in many Asian societies but perhaps of less relevance in everyday interaction in Western societies (see Hui & Luk, Volume 3 of this *Handbook*).

What exactly is the role of culture in this research on work-related values? Hofstede (1980, 1991) proposed that psychological relationships like person–organization fit, organizational assessments of individual merit, and individual compliance with organizational demands, among others, are all "affected" by the prevalence of individualistic or collectivist norms in society. Of course, a number of other cultural dimensions ("power distance," "masculinity-femininity," and "uncertainty avoidance") are also considered significant components of social processes, but the mediating function of individualism and collectivism is often clearly implied in explaining relationships among psychological and/or behavioral variables.

The Construal of the Self

The distinction that has been made between the independent and interdependent construal of the self (Markus & Kitayama, 1991) has received a good deal of attention in recent years (cf., Kagitcibasi, Volume 3 of this *Handbook*) because it appears to account for many cross-cultural differences in interpersonal and motivational processes, and in the experience of emotion. Markus and Kitayama proposed that construals of self, to which they refer as "mediators," are essential components of the self-system. Their analysis of the self-system, however, appears to relegate culture not only to a secondary but also to an indirect role in a causal analysis of human behavior (i.e., a moderator function in terms of Figure 2–1). For example, the self-system is conceptualized in their theoretical analysis as a "regulator" of important interpersonal processes (e.g., social comparison and social interaction). Though not entirely clear in their analysis, it appears that culture influences the emergence of particular types of self-systems in society and thus can potentially alter important psychological processes. Such an assumption places culture squarely in the "moderator" category because it defines culture's function as one of altering the manner in which psychological variables affect social behavior.

An example may help clarify this conceptual analysis. Consider the basic assumption underlying social comparison processes: all people "need" to evaluate their abilities, and in the absence of objective criteria for such an evaluation they rely on comparing themselves to similar others. At this point there is no major or explicit role for culture. In the perspective advocated by Markus and Kitayama (1991, p. 230), the self-system is thought to "regulate" such a process. We assume this means that the self-system interacts with, and guides the process of information-seeking about personal abilities. In other words, the self-system, which is shaped by a cultural emphasis on individual autonomy or interdependence, functions like a moderator variable.

Finally, it should be pointed out that the self-construal approach subtly places much greater emphasis on the notion that self-systems, regardless of their form or type, have important influences on our social lives, rather than that culture, which gives self-systems their form, is an important determinant of our lives in a more direct sense. We suggest that greater attention be paid to these implicit assumptions, especially considering that most of the empirical support for the general importance of the self-system in psychological functioning has originated within the context of the Western experimental tradition.

Utilitarian and Exchange Theories

As yet not very cohesive, there exists in cross-cultural psychology an even broader perspective that makes utilitarian assumptions about human nature, and, on the basis of these assumptions, generates related interpretations of diverse psychological phenomena. Most theoretical models classified in this category assume that human cognitive and behavioral activity is functional and has utility at either the personal or the collective level. Malpass (1990), long an advocate of such a perspective, has shown that subjective expected utility models of decision making, attitude–behavior models, theories of achievement motivation, optimal foraging, and face recognition, as well as signal-detection theory, all lend themselves to utilitarian analysis.

Models of attitude and behavior, main staples of social psychology (e.g., Ajzen & Fishbein, 1980) in the United States, have been used with some success cross-culturally. For example, Triandis (1980) proposed that social behavior is a function not only of prior habits, but also of self-instructions (intentions) to act in specific ways in particular social situations. Such self-instructions are determined by sociocultural norms about appropriate behavior, expectations about possible consequences of performing the behavior, and affective reactions. Thus, the utility of the behavior in the social as well as in the personal domain is a fundamental component of the decision to perform it.

Culture may, but does not have to, play a substantial role in such models. Proximal determinants of interpersonal behavior are primarily subjective states (attitudes) and individual cognitions about the world. Knowledge of these states is enough to allow prediction of individual behavior. However, culture is assumed to act as a moderator variable influencing the relationship between attitudinal variables and behavior by making certain norms and expectations more plausible than others.

A different type of utilitarian model is based on the assumption that all human social behavior involves the exchange of resources. One of the cross-cultural pioneers in this area, Uriel Foa, developed a body of research suggesting that most human interactions aim to exchange one or more of a small number of resource categories: (a) love; (b) status; (c) information; (d) money; (e) goods; and (f) services (Foa & Foa, 1974). This simple, yet quite elegant theoretical framework introduced the importance of meaning to early formulations of exchange theory (see Hinde, 1993), and thus made this approach particularly suitable to the needs of cross-cultural researchers. Unfortunately, the framework did not receive the attention it deserved, though in recent years a number of psychologists around the world have begun to pay attention to its fundamental assumptions (e.g., Foa, Converse, Tornblom, & Foa, 1993).

Adamopoulos (1984, 1988, 1991) adopted certain aspects of Foa and Foa's (1974) resource framework in an attempt to explain the emergence of interpersonal dimensions like affiliation, dominance, subordination, and intimacy. All these dimensions are generally considered psychological universals (Lonner, 1980). Adamopoulos argued that a number of constraints characteristic of all human interaction (e.g., whether a resource being exchanged is material or abstract; whether a resource is being given or denied; whether the specific relation between actor and target is crucial to the exchange or not) determine a process of differentiation of social behavior, which ultimately leads to uniquely determined interpersonal structures.

There is often a deceptive simplicity and descriptive power associated with these models that can easily hide the difficulty in developing proper testing procedures. In addition, the role of culture is not always clearly explicated or under-stood. However, in most instances culture—and more generally the ecosystem—are thought to regulate the frequency with which individuals in a particular com-munity are exposed to, and therefore have the opportunity to sample, specific resources, or are subjected to specific constraints. Thus, once again, these ap-proaches appear to emphasize the moderating role of culture in theoretical ac-counts of human behavior.

In the last few years, a related framework has received much attention. Fiske (1990, 1992) has proposed that all interpersonal interaction is brought about by individual participation in four "elemental" forms of social relationships: com-munal sharing, authority ranking, equality matching, and market pricing. Briefly, communal sharing refers to the sharing of pooled resources within a group; au-thority ranking involves the operation of a power norm, where superiors control resources but are also responsible for the well-being of subordinates; equality matching refers to the equal sharing of resources among persons of equal status; finally, market pricing describes resource exchange based on profit expectations and market demands.

Fiske (1990) has provided extensive anthropological and socio-psychological evidence in support of his model. This evidence is rather impressive, but its most attractive feature is its simplicity. Fiske argues that the four forms are "funda-mental" and that they can capture most of the significant variance in social situ-ations. However, we suggest that these four "fundamental" structures may be reducible to combinations of just two major dimensions of social interaction: (a) affiliation (association) versus disaffiliation (dissociation); and (b) independence (dominance) versus interdependence. Equality matching then can be understood as the label of the affiliation-independence quadrant, communal sharing describes interactions falling in the affiliation-interdependence quadrant, authority rank-ing is a label for the disaffiliation-interdependence quadrant, and, finally, market pricing summarizes the nature of the disaffiliation-independence quadrant. The four structures, however, fail to capture many other important dimensions of our social life (e.g., intimacy), which are believed to be independent of the two un-derlying dimensions in the theory proposed by Fiske.

What is the role of culture in such a theory? As with other utilitarian analy-ses, Fiske's (1990) model assigns to culture an important, but not necessarily a causal role. Specifically, culture is thought to guide the implementation of the four universal forms in a person's life. Within a particular social domain, any of the four structures may be the determinant of individual behavior. However, cul-ture plays a significant role in shaping its specific manifestation. Thus, once again culture appears to be viewed as an important moderator variable (or system) in the explanation of human behavior.

Values

Cultural scientists in the various academic disciplines have shared an interest for many years in defining, describing, and measuring human values, and in trying to determine to what extent values might be coterminous with superordinate constructs such as culture or society. Many have argued that culture can be defined as a group of people who share a core set of values and beliefs that they want to pass on to the next generation. If this transmission of values is the essence of culture, then it is important to know what the nature of human values is, why they exist, and why it is important for people to hand them down to their offspring.

There have been many attempts to make sense out of the interaction between values and culture (e.g., Zavalloni, 1980; Smith & Schwartz, Volume 3 of this *Handbook*). The most recent singular effort to tackle the problem of values and culture has been led by Shalom Schwartz (1992; 1994; Schwartz & Bilsky, 1990), while the most influential approach in this area since 1980 has been Hofstede's research on work-related values (Hofstede, 1980; 1991).

Schwartz (1992) has proposed an elaborate theoretical complex which is based on the assumption that values are belief structures about goals that can guide human social behavior in a variety of situations. These belief structures are organized in a hierarchical fashion that reflects the emergence of generalized motivational types (e.g., self-direction, security, power, achievement, etc.), which in turn reflect underlying, universal individual and group needs. For example, the biological needs of organisms, the need for group welfare, and rules for predictable social exchange are all fundamental requirements for human existence, and, therefore, are thought to underlie the motivational categorization of human values (Schwartz & Bilsky, 1990).

An impressive array of cross-cultural data from more than 40 societies has led to a number of refinements and elaborations of this theory. Most are beyond the scope of this chapter. It is important to note that this framework, unlike most in cross-cultural psychology, incorporates content-based, structural, and dynamic elements. For example, it does not stop at describing the specific content of value categories, but defines structural relationships among the categories based on expectations of conflict or compatibility among them (e.g., values like autonomy and obedience are antagonistic; values like obedience and social order are compatible; Schwartz, 1992). In this sense, this work is an important theoretical development in the tradition of constructing universal accounts of human experience that are sensitive to cultural variation (e.g., Osgood et al., 1975; Triandis, 1972).

Like most theories that attempt to define the *origin* of psychological structure, however, Schwartz's theory of values may suffer from a certain degree of conceptual indeterminacy. For instance, the underlying notion that basic, universal requirements for human survival may lead to the emergence (and hence the theoretical derivation) of motivational types of values is compatible with a number of psychological models. Adamopoulos and Smith (1990) have independently proposed the emergence of remarkably similar psychological structures beginning with different assumptions about basic human needs (i.e., focusing almost exclusively on fundamental constraints of social life, rather than on basic biological constraints). It is important to point out that this is not a problem unique to this particular theory. Rather, it is a weakness inherent in most structural theories in which the explanation of the emergence of structure is exogenous to the core of the theory. It behooves cross-cultural psychologists working in the general area of human values to develop structures and methodologies that will allow for more rigorous testing of such fundamental theoretical assumptions.

What exactly is the role of culture in this theory of human values? Schwartz (1992), to his credit, appears to be more explicit than most cross-cultural psychologists on this issue. He suggests that culture, manifested through specific values held by individuals of a society, functions as a moderator of the relationship between experience and social behavior. Unfortunately, the only way such a function can be detected is when the empirical procedures employed fail to detect universal values. This leads to a rather disturbing circularity: If values are culture-based moderators of the relationship between social experience and social behavior, then they must interact with experience to generate unique, rather than universal, response patterns in different cultures. But how do we know that they are culture-based moderators? Because empirical analyses yield no universal patterns. At the same time, this approach is an improvement over many models and frameworks that are currently popular.

In addition to the problem of circularity, there are concerns about using what Berry (1996) has called the "Jack Horner" strategy in cross-cultural research. This strategy, perhaps still fairly common but considered too simplistic, involves three steps: 1) collecting data from (usually) large samples of convenience in several societies, 2) calculating some statistical outcomes, such as scores or indexes for all individuals in the samples, and 3) invoking interpretations that are usually post hoc, rather than being based on a priori hypotheses that have been clearly stated.

Evolutionary Approaches

The emergent field of evolutionary psychology (Barkow, Cosmides, & Tooby, 1992) has significant implications for cross-cultural psychology (cf. Keller, this volume) and evolutionary psychological anthropology (Barkow, 1994). Within that context, Buss (1989, 1994a, b) employed a theory of sexual strategies to study one of the more pervasive of all human behaviors: mate preferences. The basic idea is that, far from being arbitrary or culture-bound, mate preferences are guided by certain enduring characteristics that men want in women, that women want in men, and over which neither has much control. In other words, these strategies, claims Buss, result in more similarities attributable to biological commonalities than to factors that reside in culture. He and numerous colleagues in many societies have used paper-and-pencil techniques to gather data.

One of the instruments used was a questionnaire designed many years ago for use with United States college samples to measure 18 characteristics desired in a mate. Four of the items in the scale consisted of "target variables": good financial prospect, good looks, chastity (no sexual intercourse before marriage), and ambition and industriousness. The second instrument was a ranking scale; participants were required to rank 13 characteristics of mates, including the target variables "good earning capacity" and "physically attractive." Other variables that received attention include age differences preferred between self and spouse. Painting the results with a broad and uncritical brush, the results of this research show that males have a greater tendency to look for mates who are good looking and chaste, and that females have a somewhat higher preference for mates who are ambitious and industrious as well as being good financial prospects. Males tend to want somewhat younger women as mates, and women prefer somewhat older men. All of these tendencies have been interpreted along evolutionary and adaptive lines, such as males preferring good looking and younger females because both are "signals" of fecundity, and females preferring ambitious and economically successful males to provide security for both themselves and their children.

The studies that Buss and his colleagues have carried out have led to many interesting and thought-provoking results. Cross-cultural data banks such as those provided in this research are valuable. However, in addition to the favorable reception it has received by many, there are numerous arguments and alternative explanations that this line of research has stimulated. These concerns are both methodological and epistemological (see the Open Peer Commentary section that accompanies Buss (1989)).

Despite his commitment to and emphasis on evolutionary explanation, much of the research on mate selection that Buss has reported (cf. Buss et al., 1990) has revealed strong cross-cultural differences. In fact, although it has not yet been attempted systematically, it is quite plausible that also acculturation processes and related phenomena involving sociocultural change may explain some of the results. In view of the proportion of variance unaccounted for so far, such factors may even turn out to be more powerful explanations than those supplied by evolutionary psychology.

A significant question regarding this approach is the role that it assigns to culture. By default, the interest and focus of evolutionary psychologists do not lie on cultural explanations. It would be expected, then, that the role of culture in discussing human behavior would be straightforward in this context. Indeed, Buss et al. (1990) appear to assume that culture may have a direct causal effect on behavior, just as any other independent variable (e.g., sex) might have. That effect may be moderated by individual-level variation, but the assumption seems to be that there exists a cause–effect relationship between culture and behavior.

Summary

The above analyses, to the extent that they reflect the implicit or explicit assumptions about the role of culture of individual investigators, suggest that frameworks and theoretical perspectives that are often thought to be similar may vary considerably in their understanding and treatment of the role of culture. The explicit statement of these variations may be an important first step in the construction of major theoretical frameworks in cross-cultural psychology.

The approaches reviewed in this section seem to relegate culture to the status of a "third" variable. Ultimately, however, they all hold the possibility that culture can account completely for the relationship between individual dispositions and individual behavior at some deep level of analysis. Of course, given the present state of knowledge, it would be both pretentious and overinclusive to maintain that either an "individualistic" or a "collectivist" culture, or a culture that emphasizes an "independent" as opposed to an "interdependent" construal of the self, can account for all thought and behavior of its citizens. The methodologies necessary to test explicitly the mediating or moderating role of culture (e.g., Baron & Kenny, 1986) are often not easily attainable in cross-cultural psychology. A beginning has been made, however, with the ever-increasing nomological networks that are utilized in the development of some of these theoretical perspectives (e.g., Singelis, Triandis, Bhawuk & Gelfand, 1995).

Conclusions

In this chapter we have attempted an extensive—though not comprehensive—review and critique of many of the dominant frameworks and models used in the study of psychology and culture. There is no doubt that the field is intellectually active and imbued with a sense of excitement, is vigorous and growing, is striving for methodological sophistication, and is very "relevant" in the context of global geopolitical relations. What is less clear is the ability of the field to make lasting theoretical contributions to the understanding of humanity. There is no single, comprehensive theory that informs the work of even a majority of researchers.

To be sure, we have described many frameworks, models, and shopping lists of important variables in the preceding pages. Some of them are quite insightful, and hold promise for future developments. However, these theoretical constructions are much better at *describing* research data than at *predicting* them. And therein lies the danger: they are often so broad in the range of human experience they attempt to capture that they can explain most patterns of obtained data with relative ease, but with little ability to discriminate among competing explanations for specific phenomena.

Even more important, there seems to be little agreement on the appropriate definition of culture, and particularly on the ontological status of the construct. There are 200 or more definitions of "culture" in the literature of the social sciences (Lonner, 1994), not one of which has been embraced by a substantial number of social scientists. We suggest that the inability of cross-cultural researchers to define culture consistently may have led to the frequent treatment of culture in research, almost by default, as a moderator variable. Such an approach may have profound implications for the future of cross-cultural psychology. As we explained earlier, the treatment of culture as a moderator variable (or set of variables) assigns to it a control function: it may alter the relationship between antecedents (e.g., "person" variables) and consequences (e.g., performance outcomes). In some ways, it can be argued that this treatment relegates culture to secondary status as a theoretical variable, and deprives it of strong explanatory power. Thus, cause-effect relationships are quite frequently presented in terms of the effects of typical psychological variables (e.g., "attitudes," "values"), moderated by "culture," on social behavior, personality development, and the like.

Regardless of its theoretical status, when dealing with culture as a moderator variable one provides arguments for those "mainstream" psychologists who have traditionally challenged the necessity of including culture in psychological theory. After all, the essential theoretical variables remain the same, and culture simply adds refinement. Seen from this angle, one may legitimately wonder whether or not cross-cultural psychology is working against itself by relying so heavily on such a treatment of culture. In addition, we must consider the possibility that all these approaches are in subtle but powerful ways influenced by Western conceptions of agency, and by the notion that human behavior is generated mainly by internal, psychological variables—an argument forcefully brought forward by those emphasizing cultural and indigenous approaches.

Our analysis suggests that it is mainly the approaches using the ecocultural framework or the individualism–collectivism constructs that bestow upon culture a more powerful explanatory function—though frequently an indirect one—as a mediating variable. They leave open the possibility that cultural context consists of or generates processes that account for the relationship between a wide range of intra- or interpersonal antecedent conditions and behavioral outcomes. This may explain in part the popularity that these approaches have enjoyed in recent years, and points to the significance of explicitly stating the status of culture in psychological theory.

Are these two major criticisms that we have outlined (i.e., the inability to define culture consistently, and the general lack of more precise theoretical statements) necessarily bad for the field? We do not think so. Cross-cultural psychology may be thought of as being at an intermediate stage of maturity, between naive empiricism and opportunistic research on the one hand, and theoretically-grounded and theory-driven science on the other. The former characterized much of cross-cultural research not too long ago, as Doob (1973) has so eloquently noted. The latter may well be an ideal state that much of modern psychology—indeed, of modern science—has not reached (Stam, 1991), despite occasional pretensions to the contrary. This leaves cross-cultural psychology poised for intellectual growth and may portend exciting developments for the not-too-distant future.

In general, what we observe in our analysis, above all, is an invigorated attempt to reintroduce some form of contextualism in a psychology that has long ignored the importance of the environment, broadly defined, as a constitutive component of human behavior. It is not clear that most current cross-cultural approaches, which seem to assign secondary status to the role of culture in psychological explanation, will be successful in this quest, but it is very encouraging to see that after a slow start cross-cultural psychology has found a voice that is heard beyond the borders of its own provinces.

References

Adamopoulos, J. (1984). The differentiation of social behavior: Toward an explanation of universal interpersonal structures. *Journal of Cross-Cultural Psychology, 15,* 487–508.

Adamopoulos, J. (1988). Interpersonal behavior: Cross-cultural and historical perspectives. In M. H. Bond (Ed.), *The cross-cultural challenge to social psychology* (pp. 196–207). Thousand Oaks, CA: Sage.

Adamopoulos, J. (1991). The emergence of interpersonal behavior: Diachronic and cross-cultural processes in the evolution of intimacy. In S. Ting-Toomey & F. Korzenny (Eds.), *International and intercultural communication annual (Vol. 15,* pp. 155–170). Thousand Oaks, CA: Sage.

Adamopoulos, J. & Smith, C. M. (1990). *The emergence of individualism and collectivism as cultural patterns of interpersonal behavior.* Paper presented-at Conference on Individualism and Collectivism: Psychocultural Perspectives from East and West. Seoul, Korea.

Ajzen, I. & Fishbein, M. (1980). *Understanding attitudes and predicting social behavior.* Englewood Cliffs, NJ: Prentice-Hall.

Altarriba, J. (Ed.). (1993). *Cognition and culture: A cross-cultural approach to cognitive psychology.* Amsterdam: North Holland.

Bakan, D. (1966). *The duality of human existence.* Chicago: Rand McNally.

Bandura, A. (1986). *Social foundation of thought and action: A social cognitive theory.* Englewood Cliffs, NJ: Prentice-Hall.

Barker, R. G. (1968). *Ecological psychology.* Stanford, CA: Stanford University Press.

Barkow, J. H. (1994). Evolutionary psychological anthropology. In P. K. Bock (Ed.), *Psychological anthropology* (pp. 121–137). Westport, CT: Praeger.

Barkow, J. H., Cosmides, L., & Tooby, J. (Eds.). (1992). *The adapted mind: Evolutionary psychology and the generation of culture.* New York: Oxford University Press.

Baron, R. M. & Kenny, D. A. (1986). The moderator-mediator variable distinction in social psychological research: Conceptual, strategic, and statistical considerations. *Journal of Personality and Social Psychology, 51,* 1173–1182.

Berrien, F. K. (1970). A super-ego for cross-cultural research. *International Journal of Psychology, 5,* 1–9.

Berry, J. W. (1966). Temne and Eskimo perceptual skills. *International Journal of Psychology, 1,* 207–229.

Berry, J. W. (1976). *Human ecology and cognitive style: Comparative studies in cultural and psychological adaptation.* New York: Sage/Halsted.

Berry, J. W. (1980). Introduction to methodology. In H. C. Triandis & J. W. Berry (Eds.), *Handbook of cross-cultural psychology: Vol. 2, Methodology* (pp. 1–28). Boston: Allyn and Bacon.

Berry, J. W. (1990). Psychology of acculturation. In J. J. Berman (Ed.), *Nebraska Symposium on Motivation 1989: Cross-cultural perspectives* (pp. 201–234). Lincoln, NE: University of Nebraska Press.

Berry, J. W. (1994). An ecological perspective on cultural and ethnic psychology. In E. J. Trickett, R. J. Watts, & D. Birman (Eds.), *Human diversity: Perspectives on people in context* (pp. 115–141). San Francisco: Jossey-Bass.

Berry, J. W. (1995). The descendants of a model: Commentary on Jahoda. *Cultural Psychology, 1,* 373–380.

Berry, J. W. (1996). New approaches to the study of intercultural and international organization psychology. In C. Earley & M. Erez (Eds.), *Frontiers of industrial and organizational psychology.* San Francisco: Jossey-Bass.

Berry, J. W. & Bennett, J. (1989). Syllabic literacy and cognitive performance among the Cree. *International Journal of Psychology, 24,* 429–450.

Berry, J. W., & Dasen, P. R. (Eds). (1974). *Culture and cognition.* London: Methuen.

Berry, J. W. & Kim, U. (1993). The way ahead: From indigenous psychologies to a universal psychology. In U. Kim & J. W. Berry (Eds.), *Indigenous psychologies: Research and experience in cultural context* (pp. 277–280). Newbury Park, CA: Sage.

Berry, J. W., Irvine, S. H., & Hunt, E. B. (Eds.). (1988). *Indigenous cognition: Functioning in cultural context.* Dordrecht: Nijhoff.

Berry, J. W., Poortinga, Y. H., Segall, M. H., & Dasen, P. R. (1992). *Cross-cultural psychology: Research and applications.* Cambridge: Cambridge University Press.

Best, D. L. & Ruther, N.M. (1994). Cross-cultural themes in developmental psychology: An examination of texts, handbooks, and reviews. *Journal of Cross-Cultural Psychology, 25,* 54–77.

Bock, P. K. (1988). *Rethinking psychological anthropology: Continuity and change in the study of human action.* New York: W. H. Freeman.

Bock, P. K. (Ed.). (1994). *Psychological anthropology.* Westport, CT: Praeger.

Boesch, E. E. (unpublished manuscript). The seven flaws of cross-cultural psychology: The story of a conversion.

Boesch, E. E. (1991). *Symbolic action theory and cultural psychology.* Berlin: Springer-Verlag.

Brislin, R. W. (1989). *Applied cross-cultural psychology.* Newbury Park, CA: Sage Publications.

Brislin, R. W. (1993). *Understanding culture's influence on behavior.* Fortworth, TX: Harcourt Brace Jovanovich.

Brislin, R. W., Cushner, C., Cherrie, C., & Yong, M. (1986). *Intercultural interactions: A practical guide.* Newbury Park, CA: Sage.

Brislin, R. W., Lonner, W. J., & Thorndike, R. M. (1973). *Cross-cultural research methods.* New York: Wiley.

Brislin, R. W. & Yoshida, T. (Eds.). (1994a). *Improving intercultural interactions: Modules for cross- cultural training programs.* Thousand Oaks, CA: Sage.

Brislin, R. W. & Yoshida, T. (Eds.). (1994b). *Intercultural communication training: An introduction.* Thousand Oaks, CA: Sage.

Buss, D. M. (1989). Sex differences in human mate preferences: Evolutionary hypotheses tested in 37 cultures. *Behavioral and Brain Sciences, 12,* 1–49.

Buss, D. M. et al. (1990). International preferences in selecting mates. *Journal of Cross-Cultural Psychology, 21,* 5–47.

Buss, D. M. (1994a). Mate preferences in 37 cultures. In W. J. Lonner & R. S. Malpass (Eds.), *Psychology and culture,* (pp. 197–201). Boston: Allyn and Bacon.

Buss, D. M. (1994b). *Sexual strategies: The evolution of human mating.* New York: Basic Books.

Butcher, J. N. & Graham, J. R. (1994). A new standard for personality assessment and research in counseling settings. *Measurement and Evaluation in Counseling and Development, 27,* 131–150.

Campbell, D. T. (1961). The mutual methodological relevance of anthropology and psychology. In F. Hsu (Ed.), *Psychological anthropology* (pp. 333–352). Homewood, IL: Dorsey Press.

Chinese Culture Connection (1987). Chinese values and the search for culture-free dimensions of culture. *Journal of Cross-Cultural Psychology, 18,* 143–164.

Cole, M. (1989). Cultural psychology: A once and future discipline. In J. J. Berman (Ed.), *Cross-cultural perspectives: Nebraska Symposium on Motivation* (pp. 279–335). Lincoln: University of Nebraska Press.

Cole, M. & Cole, S. (1993). *The development of children* (2nd ed.). New York: Scientific American Books.

Cole, M., Gay, J., Glick, J., & Sharp, D. (1971). *The cultural context of learning and thinking.* New York: Basic Books.

Cronbach, L. J. & Drenth, P. J. D. (1972). *Mental tests and cultural adaptation.* The Hague: Mouton.

Cushner, K. & Brislin, R. W. (1996). *Intercultural interactions: A practical guide* (2nd ed.). Thousand Oaks, CA.: Sage.

Dana, R. H. (1993). *Multicultural assessment perspectives for professional psychology.* Boston: Allyn and Bacon.

Dasen, P. R. (1972). Cross-cultural Piagetian research: A summary. *Journal of Cross-Cultural Psychology, 7,* 75–85.

Dasen, P. R. (1975). Concrete operational development in three cultures. *Journal of Cross-Cultural Psychology, 6,* 156–172.

Dasen, P. R. (Ed.). (1977). *Piagetian psychology: Cross-cultural contributions.* New York: Gardner.

Dawson, J. L. M. (1971). Theory and research in cross-cultural psychology. *Bulletin of the British Psychological Society, 24,* 291–306.

Diaz-Guerrero, R. (1993). Mexican ethnopsychology. In U. Kim and J. W. Berry (Eds.), *Indigenous psychologies: Research and experience in cultural context* (pp. 44–55). Newbury Park, CA: Sage.

Doob, L. W. (1973). Foreword. In R. W. Brislin, W. J. Lonner, & R. M. Thorndike, *Cross-cultural research methods*. New York: Wiley-Interscience.

Eagly, A. H. & Wood, W. (1991). Explaining sex differences in social behavior: A meta-analytic perspective. *Personality and Social Psychology Bulletin, 17*, 306–315.

Enriquez, V. (1993). Developing a Filipino psychology. In U. Kim & J. W. Berry (Eds.), *Indigenous psychologies* (pp. 152–169). Newbury Park, Sage.

Fiske, A. P. (1990). *Structures of social life: The four elementary forms of human relations*. New York: Free Press.

Fiske, A. P. (1992). The four elementary forms of sociality: A framework for a unified theory of human relations. *Psychological Review, 99*, 689–723.

Foa, U. G. & Foa, E. B. (1974). *Societal structures of the mind*. Springfield, IL: Charles C. Thomas.

Foa, U. G., Converse, J., Jr., Tornblom, K. Y., & Foa, E. B. (1993). (Eds.), *Resource theory: Explorations and applications*. San Diego: Academic Press.

Hinde, R. A. (1993). Epilogue. In U. G. Foa, J. Converse, Jr., K. Y. Tornblom, & E. B. Foa (Eds.), *Resource theory: Explorations and applications* (pp. 271–274). San Diego: Academic Press.

Hofstede, G. (1980). *Culture's consequences: International differences in work-related values*. Newbury Park, CA: Sage.

Hofstede, G. (1991). *Cultures and organizations*. London: McGraw-Hill.

Hogan, R. (1975). Theoretical egocentrism and the problem of compliance. *American Psychologist, 30*, 533–540.

Hsu, F. L. K. (Ed.). (1972). *Psychological anthropology*. Cambridge, MA: Schenkman.

Hsu, F. L. K. (1983). *Rugged individualism reconsidered*. Knoxville: University of Tennessee Press.

Irvine, S. H. & Berry, J. W. (Eds.). (1983). *Human assessment and cultural factors*. New York: Plenum.

Jahoda, G. (1980). Theoretical and systematic approaches in cross-cultural psychology. In H. C.Triandis & W. W. Lambert (Eds.), *Handbook of cross-cultural psychology: (Vol. 1. pp. 69–141)*. Boston: Allyn and Bacon.

Jahoda, G. (1990). Our forgotten ancestors. In J. J. Berman (Ed.), *Cross-cultural perspectives* (pp. 1–40). Lincoln: University of Nebraska Press.

Jahoda, G. (1992). Foreword. In Berry, J. W., Poortinga, Y. H., Segall, M. H., & Dasen, P. R., *Cross-cultural psychology: Research and applications*. Cambridge: Cambridge University Press.

Jahoda, G. (1992). *Crossroads between culture and mind*. Hemel Hempstead. Harvester Wheatsheaf.

Jahoda, G. (1993). The colour of a chameleon: Perspectives on concepts of culture. *Cultural Dynamics, 6*, 277–287.

Jahoda, G. (1995). The ancestry of a model. *Cultural Psychology, 1*, 11–24.

Kagitçibasi, C. (1994). A critical appraisal of individualism and collectivism: Toward a new formulation. In U. Kim, H.C. Triandis, C. Kagitabasi, S. C. Choi, & G. Yoon (Eds.), *Individualism and collectivism: Theory, method, and applications* (52–65). Newbury Park, CA: Sage.

Kaplan, B. (Ed.). (1961). *Studying personality cross-culturally*. Evanston, IL: Row Peterson.

Kardiner, A. (1939). *The individual and his society*. New York: Columbia University Press.

Kardiner, A. (1945). *The psychological frontiers of society*. New York: Columbia University Press.

Kim, U. & Berry, J .W. (1993). *Indigenous psychologies*. Thousand Oaks, CA: Sage.

Kim, U., Triandis, H. C., Kagitçibasi, C., Choi, S.-C., & Yoon, G. (Eds.). (1994). *Individualism and collectivism: Theory, method, and applications*. Thousand Oaks, CA: Sage.

Kleinman, A. & Good, B. (Eds.). (1985). *Culture and depression: Studies on the anthropology and cross-cultural psychiatry of affective disorder*. Berkeley: University of California Press.

Landis, D. & Bhagat, R. (Eds.) (1996). *Handbook of intercultural training* (2nd ed.). Newbury Park, CA: Sage.

LeVine, R. A. (1982). *Culture, behavior, and personality* (2nd ed.). Chicago: Aldine.

Lewin, K. (1935). *A dynamic theory of personality.* New York: McGraw-Hill.

Longabaugh, R. (1980). The systematic observation of behavior in naturalistic settings. In H. C. Triandis & J. W. Berry (Eds.), *Handbook of cross-cultural psychology (Vol. 2,* pp. 57–126). Boston: Allyn and Bacon.

Lonner, W. J. (1980). The search for psychological universals. In H. C. Triandis & W. W. Lambert, (Eds.), *Handbook of cross-cultural psychology (Vol. 1,* pp. 143–204). Boston: Allyn and Bacon.

Lonner, W. J. (1994). Culture and human diversity. In E. J. Trickett, R. J. Watts, & D. Birman (Eds.), *Human diversity: Perspectives on people in context* (pp. 230–243). San Francisco: Jossey-Bass.

Lonner, W. J. & Berry, J. W. (Eds.). (1986). *Field methods in cross-cultural research.* Newbury Park, CA.: Sage.

Lonner, W. J. & Ibrahim, F.A. (1996). Assessment and appraisal in cross-cultural counseling. In P. P. Pedersen, J. G. Draguns, W. J. Lonner, & J. E. Trimble (Eds.), *Counseling across cultures (4th ed.,* pp. 293–322). Newbury Park, CA: Sage.

Malinowski, B. (1927). *Sex and repression in savage society.* London: Kegan Paul.

Malpass, R. S. (1990). An excursion into utilitarian analysis. *Behavior Science Research, 24,* 1–15.

Malpass, R. S. & Poortinga, Y. H. (1986). Strategies for design and analysis. In W. J. Lonner & J. W. Berry (Eds.), *Field methods in cross-cultural research* (pp. 47–83). Newbury Park, CA: Sage.

Markus, H. R. & Kitayama, S. (1991). Culture and the self: Implications for cognition, emotion, and motivation. *Psychological Review, 98,* 224-253.

Marsella, A. J., Hirschfeld, R. M. A., & Katz, M. M. (Eds.). (1987). *The measurement of depression.* New York: Guilford Press.

McClelland, D. C. (1961). *The achieving society.* Princeton: Van Nostrand.

McClelland, D. C. & Winter, D. G. (1969). *Motivating economic achievement.* New York: Free Press.

McClelland, D. C., Atkinson, J. W., Clark, R. A., & Lowell, E. L. (1953). *The achievement motive.* New York: Appleton-Century-Crofts.

Miller, G. A. (1969). Psychology as a means of promoting human welfare. *American Psychologist, 24,* 1063–1075.

Miller, J. G., Bersoff, D. M., & Harwood, R. (1990). Perceptions of social responsibilities in India and the United States: Moral imperatives or personal decisions? *Journal of Personality and Social Psychology., 58,* 33–47.

Munroe, R. H. & Munroe, R. L. (1994a). Behavior across cultures: Results from observation studies. In W. J. Lonner & R. S. Malpass (Eds.), *Psychology and culture* (pp. 107–111). Boston: Allyn and Bacon.

Munroe, R. H. & Munroe, R. L. (1994b). Field observations of behavior as a cross-cultural method. In P. K. Bock (Ed.), *Psychological anthropology* (pp. 255–277). Westport, CT: Praeger.

Neimeyer, G. J. (Ed.). (1993). *Constructivist assessment: A casebook.* Thousand Oaks, CA: Sage.

Öngel, A. & Smith, P. B. (1994). Who are we and where are we going? JCCP approaches its 100th issue. *Journal of Cross-Cultural Psychology, 25,* 25–53.

Osgood, C. E. (1964). Semantic differential technique in the comparative study of cultures. *American Anthropologist, 66,* 171-200.

Osgood, C. E., May, W. H., & Miron, M. S. (1975). *Cross-cultural universals of affective meaning.* Urbana, IL: University of Illinois Press.

Parsons, T. & Shils, E. A. (1951). *Toward a general theory of action.* Cambridge, MA: Harvard University Press.

Paul, R. A. (1994). My approach to psychological anthropology. In M. M. Suarez-Orozco, G. Spindler, & L. Spindler (Eds.), *The making of psychological anthropology II* (pp. 80–102). Fort Worth, TX: Harcourt Brace.

Piaget, J. (1966). Néccesité et signification de recherches comparatives en psychologie génétique. *International Journal of Psychology, 1,* 3–13. Reprinted in J. W. Berry & P. R. Dasen (Eds.) (1974), *Culture and cognition.* London: Methuen.

Piker, S. (1994). Classical culture and personality. In P. K. Bock (Ed.), *Psychological anthropology* (pp. 1–17). Westport, CT: Praeger.

Poortinga, Y. H. (1990). Towards a conceptualization of culture for psychology. *Cross-Cultural Psychology Bulletin, 24*(3), 2–10.

Poortinga, Y. H. & Malpass, R. S. (1986). Making inferences from cross-cultural data. In W. J. Lonner & J. W. Berry (Eds). *Field methods in cross-cultural research* (pp. 17–46). Newbury Park, CA: Sage.

Ptak, C. L., Cooper, J., & Brislin, R. W. (1995), Cross-cultural training programs: Advice and insights from experienced trainers. *International Journal of Intercultural Relations, 19,* 425–453.

Rotter, J. B. (1981). The psychological situation in social learning theory. In D. Magnusson (Ed.), *Toward a psychology of situations: An interactional perspective* (pp. 169–178). Hillsdale, NJ: Erlbaum.

Rotter, J. B. (1982). Social learning theory. In N. T. Feather (Ed.), *Expectations and actions: Expectancy-value models in psychology.* Hillsdale, NJ: Erlbaum.

Sampson, E. E. (1977). Psychology and the American ideal. *Journal of Personality and Social Psychology, 35,* 767–782.

Schwartz, S. H. (1992). Universals in the content and structure of values: Theoretical advances and empirical tests in 20 countries. In M. P. Zanna (Ed.), *Advances in experimental social psychology* (Vol. 25, pp. 1–65). San Diego: Academic Press.

Schwartz, S. H. (1994). Beyond individualism/collectivism: New cultural dimensions of values. In U. Kim, H. C. Triandis, C. Kagitçibasi, S. Choi, & G. Yoon (Eds.), *Individualism and collectivism: Theory, method, and applications* (pp. 85–119). Newbury Park, CA: Sage.

Schwartz, S. H. & Bilsky, W. (1990). Toward a universal psychological structure of human values. *Journal of Personality and Social Psychology, 53,* 878–891.

Scribner, S. & Cole, M. (1981). *The psychology of literacy.* Cambridge: Harvard University Press.

Segall, M.H., Dasen, P.R., Berry, J.W., & Poortinga, Y.H. (1990). *Human behavior in global perspective: An introduction to cross-cultural psychology.* New York: Pergamon/Allyn and Bacon.

Shweder, R. A. (1990). Cultural psychology: What is it? In J. W. Stigler, R. A. Shweder, & G. Herdt (Eds.), *Cultural psychology: Essays on comparative human development* (pp. 1–43). Cambridge: Cambridge University Press.

Shweder, R. A. & Bourne, R. A. (1982). Does the concept of the person vary cross-culturally? In A. J. Marsella & G. M. White (Eds.), *Cultural conceptions of mental health and therapy* (pp. 97–137). London: Reidel.

Shweder, R. A. & Sullivan, M. A. (1993). Cultural psychology: Who needs it? *Annual Review of Psychology, 44,* 497–523.

Singelis, T. M., Triandis, H. C., Bhawuk, D. S., & Gelfand, M. (1995). Horizontal and vertical dimensions of individualism and collectivism: A theoretical and measurement refinement. *Cross-Cultural Research, 29,* 240–275.

Smith, M. B. (1978). Perspectives on selfhood. *American Psychologist, 33,* 1053–1063.

Soudijn, K. A., Hutschemaekers, G. J. M., & Van de Vijver, F. J. R. (1990). Culture conceptualisations. In F. J. R. Van de Vijver & G. J. M. Hutschemaekers (Eds.), *The investigation of culture: Towards a cultural psychology* (pp. 19–39). Tilburg: Tilburg University Press.

Spielberger, C. D. (1989). *State-Trait Anxiety Inventory: A comprehensive bibliography.* Palo Alto, CA: Consulting Psychologists Press.

Spielberger, C. D. & Diaz-Guerrero, R. (Eds.). (1976). *Cross-cultural anxiety* (Vol. 1). Washington DC: Hemisphere.

Stam, H. J. (1991). Theory and psychology: The re-emergence of theory in psychology. *Theory and Psychology, 1,* 5–11.

Suarez-Orozco, M. M., Spindler, G., & Spindler, L. (Eds.). (1994). *The making of psychological anthropology II.* Fort Worth, TX: Harcourt-Brace.

Super, C. M. & Harkness, S. (1986). The developmental niche: A conceptualization at the interface of child and culture. *International Journal of Behavioral Development, 9,* 545–569.

Super, C. M. & Harkness, S. (1994). The developmental niche. In W. J. Lonner & R. S. Malpass (Eds.), *Psychology and culture* (pp. 95–99). Boston: Allyn and Bacon.

Tönnies, F. (1964). *Community and society.* East Lansing: Michigan State University Press.

Triandis, H.C. (1972). *The analysis of subjective culture.* New York: Wiley.

Triandis, H. C. (1980). Values, attitudes, and interpersonal behavior. In H. E. Howe & M. M. Page (Eds.), *Nebraska Symposium on Motivation, 1979* (pp. 195–260). Lincoln, NE: University of Nebraska Press.

Triandis, H. C. (1989). The self and social behavior in differing cultural contexts. *Psychological Review, 96,* 506–520.

Triandis, H. C. (1990). Cross-cultural studies of individualism and collectivism. In J. Berman (Ed.), *Nebraska symposium on motivation, 1989* (pp. 41–133). Lincoln, NE: University of Nebraska Press.

Triandis, H. C. (1993). Collectivism and individualism as cultural syndromes. *Cross-Cultural Research, 27,* 155–180.

Triandis, H. C. (1994). *Culture and social behavior.* New York: McGraw-Hill.

Triandis, H. C. (1995). *Individualism and collectivism.* Greeley, CO: Westview Press.

Triandis, H. C., Leung, K., Villareal, M. J., & Clack, F. L. (1985). Allocentric versus idiocentric tendencies: Convergent and discriminant validation. *Journal of Research in Personality, 19,* 395–415.

Van de Vijver, F. J. R., & Leung, K. (in preparation). *Methodology for cross-cultural research.* Thousand Oaks, CA: Sage.

Waterman, A. S. (1981). Individualism and interdependence. *American Psychologist, 36,* 762–773.

Weber, M. (1904). *The protestant ethic and the spirit of capitalism.* New York: Scribner.

Weick, K. E. (1985). Systematic observational methods. In G. Lindzey & E. Aronson (Eds.), *The handbook of social psychology* (3rd ed., Vol. 1, pp. 567–634). New York: Random House.

Whiting, J. W. M. & Child, I. L. (1953). *Child training and personality.* New Haven: Yale University Press.

Whiting, B. B. & Whiting, J. W. M. (1975). *Children of six cultures: A psycho-cultural analysis.* Cambridge, MA: Harvard University Press.

Witkin, H. A. & Berry, J. W. (1975). Psychological differentiation in cross-cultural perspective. *Journal of Cross-Cultural Psychology, 6,* 4–87.

Witkin, H. A. & Goodenough, D. (1981). *Cognitive styles: Essence and origins.* (Psychological Monographs, 51). New York: International Universities Press.

Witkin, H. A., Dyk, R. B., Faterson, H. F., Goodenough, D. R., & Karp, S. (1962). *Psychological differentiation.* New York: Wiley.

Zavalloni, M. (1980). Values. In H. C. Triandis & R. W. Brislin (Eds.). *Handbook of cross-cultural psychology (Vol. 5,* pp. 73–120). Boston: Allyn and Bacon.

3

THEORETICAL ISSUES IN CULTURAL PSYCHOLOGY

JOAN G. MILLER
Yale University
United States

Contents

Introduction

For most of the twentieth century, cultural considerations have been accorded a relatively peripheral role in psychological theory (Jahoda, 1990, 1993a). With the dominance of natural science models of explanation, psychology has tended to focus on the identification of laws of behavior that are invariant across time and historical context. This stance has remained relatively unchallenged during most of this period, both within and outside the discipline. The extensive body of research undertaken within cross-cultural psychology, as reported, for example, in the first edition of this Handbook, built upon rather than challenged this mainstream psychological stance - accepting the assumptions of the discipline that psychological processes are fundamentally unaffected by content or context as well as its commitment to the identification of psychological universals. Within certain early anthropological and sociological work, psychological phenomena were approached merely as facets of cultural knowledge, with little or no reference to individual subjectivity and behavior (e.g., D'Andrade, 1976; Tyler, 1969). In addition, questions of cultural learning or of the reproduction of cultural systems were treated in deterministic ways that assumed an isomorphism between cultural meanings and individual motivation (e.g., Durkheim, 1961; Parsons, 1961; Radcliffe-Brown, 1965). Only relatively recently have theorists begun to take into account that language involves action and reality creation, rather than merely reference (e.g., Austin, 1962; Searle, 1969), and to approach language learning as based on processes of cultural communication, negotiation, and meaning creation, rather than solely of code acquisition (Ochs, 1988; Schieffelin & Ochs, 1986).

Even more recently, perspectives have emerged or, it may be argued, re-emerged (Cole, 1990; Jahoda, 1990, 1993a; Jahoda & Krewer, this volume) that accord cultural considerations a more central role in psychological theory. In these approaches, psychological processes and structures are seen as patterned, in part, by cultural meanings and practices, just as such meanings and practices have significance only with reference to particular communities of intentional agents. This stance does not result in the denial of universal aspects of psychology, but rather in a view that psychological structures and processes may vary fundamentally in different cultural contexts. While not invariably leading to a rejection of the use of empirical methodologies, the recent approaches are challenging conventional psychological perspectives. These challenges concern the understanding of psychological phenomena in the context of everyday practices, attention to natural language categories and patterns of discourse, and recognition of the need for a perspective that makes more explicit the impact of the observer on the knowledge generation process and the systems of power and domination that inform everyday cultural practices, including those of social science. Thus, for example, consideration is given to respects in which the framing of research questions as well as the use of particular methodologies may privilege the perspectives of certain subgroups in a population more than those of other subgroups.

The purpose of this present chapter is to identify some of the problems that must be addressed in developing cultural approaches to psychology that embody these premises and to evaluate the strengths and limitations of some of the major current theoretical perspectives in this area. Attention will center both on approaches that fall within cultural psychology as well as on approaches within social constructionism. Arguments will be made that these recent cultural perspectives hold the promise of contributing new theoretical and methodological insights to psychology, with this promise most likely to be fulfilled by drawing on a variety of theoretical and methodological orientations developed in these traditions.

The approaches to psychology under consideration in this chapter are diverse in character. As noted, they include perspectives in the tradition that has been identified as cultural psychology (e.g., Bruner, 1990; Cole, 1990, 1995; Price-Williams, 1980; Shweder, 1990; Shweder & Sullivan, 1990; 1993; Wertsch, 1995a, 1995b). This tradition may be considered to have the characteristics of a merging continuum (J. G. Miller, 1994a), with investigators within the tradition sharing most but not all of their theoretical and methodological commitments. What distinguishes an approach as being within this tradition is not whether it involves single as compared with multi-cultural analyses or even what type of methodological stance it assumes: An approach may involve cross-cultural comparisons and empirical methods and still be in the tradition of cultural psychology (e.g., Markus & Kitayama, 1991), or it may involve analysis of a single culture through interpretive ethnographic techniques and be in the tradition of cross-cultural psychology (e.g., Spiro, 1982). Rather, the characteristics which distinguish cultural psychology from cross-cultural psychology are the theoretical presuppositions held.

The dominant stance within cultural psychology is to view culture and psychology as mutually constitutive phenomena, i.e., as phenomena which make up each other or are integral to each other. In such a view, it is assumed that culture and individual behavior cannot be understood in isolation yet are also not reducible to each other. Such a stance contrasts with the tendency particularly in early work in cross-cultural psychology, for culture and psychology to be understood as discrete phenomena, with culture conceptualized as an independent variable that impacts on the dependent variable of individual behavior (Eckensberger, 1990a).

In addition to considering perspectives within the tradition of cultural psychology, this chapter will focus on social constructionist approaches (e.g., Buss, 1975; Edwards & Potter, 1992; Gergen, 1982, 1991, 1994; Harré, 1984, 1986; Potter & Wetherell, 1987; Shotter, 1993; Shotter & Gergen, 1989). While closely related to cultural psychology, these approaches differ from the former tradition in treating psychological processes exclusively as cultural phenomena.

In this chapter, attention will be given to ways in which various approaches address the problem areas listed in Table 3–1. One problem concerns representing the complexity of culture. Included here is the need to take into account: (a) the multiple functions of cultural meanings; (b) the differentiated and dynamic nature of culture; and (c) the relationship of culture to ecological and socio-political factors. Another problem area concerns understanding the interdependence

TABLE 3–1 Problems for cultural approaches to psychology

I.   Representing the complexity of culture
    A.   Multiple functions of cultural meanings
    B.   Differentiated and dynamic nature of culture
    C.   Relationship to ecological and sociopolitical factors

II. Understanding the interdependence of culture and the self
    A.   Multifaceted and culturally grounded nature of self
    B.   Psychologically relevant theories of culture
    C.   Agent and culture as active influences on psychological processes.

III. Formulating successful explanations
    A.   Explanatory force
    B.   Methodological adequacy

of culture and the self. Included here is the need: (a) to recognize the multi-faceted and culturally grounded nature of self; (b) to formulate psychologically relevant theories of culture; and (c) to portray both the agent and the culture as active influences on psychological processes. A final problem area concerns formulating successful explanations. Included here is the need to achieve explanatory force and to meet standards of methodological adequacy. In the following discussion, mention is made of the relevance of these problem areas to specific perspectives in cultural psychology and in social constructionism. An in-depth theoretical examination of the problem areas is undertaken in the third section of the chapter, which considers directions for future research.

Overview of Select Cultural Approaches

The substantive approaches in cultural psychology and social constructionism under consideration in this section are grouped into subsections that reflect commonalities in their origins and foci of concern. The first subsection concerns symbolic action theory and sociocultural approaches, perspectives that have tended to center primarily on issues of cognition and learning. The second subsection concerns cultural approaches in the traditions of developmental psychology, social psychology, sociolinguistics, cognitive anthropology, and psychological anthropology that have tended to center on issues of self and social development. Finally, the third subsection concerns approaches in the tradition of social constructionism that have centered on the self and on issues in the philosophy of science.

In describing the varied perspectives, brief mention is made of their origins, assumptions, and of illustrative findings. Because of space limitations, no attempt is made to provide an in-depth and comprehensive overview or critique of each viewpoint, nor is the account inclusive enough to encompass all of the varied approaches in cultural psychology and social constructionism.

Symbolic Action Theory and Sociocultural Approaches

The perspective of *symbolic action theory* (Boesch, 1987, 1991; Eckensberger, 1990a, 1990b, 1995; Eckensberger & Meacham, 1984) offers a dynamic and theoretically rich way of understanding the mutual constitution of culture and self or, as Boesch phrases it, questions of "how from individual experience collective structures will be formed and how these, in turn, will act on individual experiences" (Boesch, 1991, p. 10). Eclectic and integrative in nature, action theory builds on diverse theoretical roots, including Piagetian constructionism, Janet's dynamic theory, field theory, and ecological perspectives. Among the key explanatory constructs from this perspective are those of individual agency and of action. Agents are conceptualized as being future-oriented, self-reflective, responsible, and as potentially conscious of the goals of their activities, with intentional action conceptualized as the dynamic link between individuals and situations.

Eckensberger and Meacham (1984) illustrate ways in which action and agency are understood from an action theory perspective in the example of a person using an ax to chop down a tree. From the perspective of symbolic action theory, the behavior is understood as fulfilling a future goal of the person, such as that of building a house, with the agent seen as having consciously selected an ax among other possible means that might have been employed to achieve this goal. It is assumed that, whereas agents may not be consciously attending to all facets of their decisions at any point in time, they may bring the factors that influenced their decisions into awareness when their attention is directed to these factors. They are also responsible for both the intended and unintended consequences of their behaviors (e.g., inadvertently destroying a bird's nest that was in the tree). From this perspective, actions are seen as having a temporal structure, as involving affective processes, and as energetic in the sense of involving mobilization of effort.

To date, the perspective of symbolic action theory has been applied most frequently as an analytic tool in addressing certain unanswered questions raised from cognitive developmental viewpoints. For example, Boesch (1984) has documented respects in which an action theory perspective challenges the Piagetian assumption that the development of cognition and of affect emerge separately. Rather, processes are identified through which affective development serves to motivate cognitive development. In another example, providing an action-theoretic analysis of Kohlbergian theory, Eckensberger (1981) maintains that only three rather than six qualitatively distinct stages of moral development can be identified, with postconventional levels of thought encompassing both justice and caring concerns.

Regarding the problem areas for cultural psychology identified earlier, a strength of symbolic action theory is that it takes into account multiple functions of cultural meanings as well as differentiated forms in which these meanings are embodied. Attention is paid to the extent to which cultural practices and artifacts may be symbolic and not merely instrumental in nature and may have shared affective connotations. Thus, for example, the meaning of a tree is recognized to differ in the case in which it is decorated as a symbol of Christmas as contrasted to being made into part of a floor.

Action theory stresses the importance of understanding the relationship be-
·tween culture and material conditions. It is assumed that all experience is cultur-
ally-mediated or, as Boesch points out, "nature is not antipode to culture but
rather is, as we experience it, already culture" (Boesch, 1991, p. 21). However, it
is also recognized as necessary to bridge the gap between materialism and ideal-
ism and to take into account simultaneously the roles of both causality and indeterminacy in the context of human action (Eckensberger, 1995). Thus, aspects of
the ecology and of the social structure are understood from this perspective as
representing objective constraints that impact on behavior. An action theory perspective acknowledges the need to embody both an active view of the agent and
of the culture. Action is portrayed as taking place in a cultural environment that
is assimilated by the individual and transformative of individual psychology at
the same time that individuals through their collective actions are understood as
transforming culture. Development is also recognized to occur in multiple directions, with cultures and individuals changing in ways that may be pathological
or maladaptive rather than invariably progressive.

One critique that may be directed at action theory concerns the adequacy of
its views on self. It may be argued, for example, that the theory does not fully
encompass recent insights from empirical work in cognitive and developmental
psychology. Such research underscores the influence on behavior of motives that
may not even be potentially accessible to consciousness (Sigel, 1984) and calls
into question the stage-like character of cognitive processes assumed in cognitive
developmental theory (Gelman & Baillargeon, 1983). Concerns may also be raised
about the extent to which the theory of self assumed in action theory is premised
on certain culturally-bound assumptions. Thus, for example, it may be argued
that the emphasis on individual control and responsibility for conduct that is
assumed in action theory is reflective, at least in part, of modern Western notions
of self and may be less applicable in other cultures.

Finally, some additional concerns might be raised about whether the claims
of action theory lead to empirically testable propositions or whether they remain
merely analytical devices that fit any situation. As Eckensberger and Meacham
themselves commented on the perspective over ten years ago, ". . . it remains an
open question at this point whether action theory is merely a descriptive tool,
flawed with the problems of eclecticism, or whether action theory has the potential to be a truly integrative paradigm for psychology" (Eckensberger & Meacham,
1984, p. 172).

In turn, the label of *sociocultural approaches* is applied here to a diverse range
of perspectives that have their roots in the tradition of Soviet psychology, as reflected in the work of Vygotsky (1978, 1981a, 1981b), Leontiev (1979a, 1979b),
Luria (1979, 1981), and Bakhtin (1986), as well as in Marxist traditions, as reflected, for example, in the work of Bourdieu (1977), Giddens (1979), and Sahlins
(1976b). These various perspectives include a diversity of distinct viewpoints (e.g.,
Cole, 1988, 1990; Rogoff, 1990, 1995; Valsiner, 1988, 1989, Van de Veer & Valsiner,
1988; Wertsch, 1979, 1991), such as those of situated learning (Lave & Wenger,
1991) and of distributed cognition (Salomon, 1993).

Some of the central assumptions shared across this set of perspectives concern the roles of cultural mediation, history, and of concrete practical activity in psychological functioning (Cole, 1988, 1990; Laboratory of Comparative Human Cognition, 1983; Wertsch, del Rio & Alvarez, 1995). From the viewpoint of sociocultural approaches, human behavior is seen as dependent on cultural tools or on other mediational means, with language recognized to be among the most central of these cultural supports. The psychological functioning of members of each generation is viewed as modified by existing cultural artifacts and practices while at the same time members of successive generations contribute to the modification of these artifacts and practices (Cole & Engestrom, 1993). Embodying a broad lens, sociocultural approaches focus on understanding human activity at phylogenetic, historical, ontogenetic and microgenetic levels, with cultural practices viewed in terms of their place in larger socio-political contexts.

One of the striking theoretical shifts in research from a sociocultural perspective is the move away from a focus on psychological processes as internal to individuals to a focus on their embodiment in the context of social interactions and engagement with cultural tools (Gauvain, 1995; Lave, 1988, 1993; Rogoff, 1990; Rogoff, Mistry, Gonku & Mosier, 1993). As Cole and Engestrom argue, from this perspective "mind" is seen as residing neither under the skin nor in cultural artifacts but rather as representing an "emergent quality in the continuous interactions between subjects, artifacts and the world of objects" (Cole & Engestrom, 1995, p. 21). Whereas this perspective does not deny the existence of individual subjectivity, the fundamental unit of analysis becomes the "person in activity" (Rogoff, in press) rather than either the individual or the culture. Consideration of a few representative examples of the vast body of empirical research conducted in this tradition illustrate some of the important empirical findings and new conceptual understandings emerging from the perspective.

Sociocultural research has demonstrated, for example, that interaction with cultural tools and participation in everyday cultural practices leads to powerful domain-specific changes in thought. Thus, Stigler (1984) has shown that Chinese abacus experts are more successful in solving math problems and employ more complex cognitive processing strategies in their solution than do individuals who have no experience in use of the abacus. In other research, Scribner (1984) has demonstrated that contrasting mathematical skills are developed through role-specific experiences in a dairy plant, with workers' strategies for arithmetic solution reflecting the particular constraints associated with their jobs in the plant. In another example of research in everyday work environments, Saxe (1991) has documented the impressive arithmetic competencies displayed by Brazilian street children when engaged in candy selling.

Sociocultural studies also offer new solutions to some classic theoretical problems in cognitive development. For example, in research on the teaching of reading, Cole addresses the well-known "paradox of development"—that is, the problem of explaining how individuals acquire a more powerful structure if they do not already possess that structure (Cole, 1995). It is demonstrated that a range of mediational means are available in the culture that support reading and thus that many of the structures entailed in the achievement of reading may be seen to exist between persons before they appear as individual competencies. Research in the sociocultural tradition also offers new ways of understanding cognitive transfer and internalization (Cole & Griffin, 1980; Lave, Murtaugh & de la Rocha, 1984; Lave & Wenger, 1991). Evidence is presented to suggest that the problem of cognitive transfer "dissolves" when behavior is understood in the context of practices, rather than as an individual acquisition. As Rogoff comments:

> *The question of relating activities to each other is a recasting of the classic question of transfer or generalization. It differs in that the focus is on determining how activities relate to each other and how people move from one activity to another, rather than on how mental objects are transferred (as if they existed in isolation in the head) or how physical similarities in the materials elicit transfer (as if the materials carry meaning outside of their use) (Rogoff, in press).*

Likewise, the concept of internalization is considered a less important vehicle for the reproduction of culture than is activity in relation to contexts of practice.

Among the key strengths of research in the sociocultural tradition are the development of psychologically relevant theories of culture and the examination of ways in which cultural activities relate to aspects of the ecological setting and to socio-political conditions (e.g., Gauvain,1995; Penuel & Wertsch, 1995; Serpell, 1993). Sociocultural research is providing new theoretical ways of understanding everyday cognitive competencies and of improving practice, particularly in educational settings (e.g. Engestrom, 1993; McDermott, 1993).

It would be valuable to direct greater attention to the area of development of a view of the person as an active agent (Rogoff, 1992). Theoretically, the perspective recognizes the role of individual agency and views cultural systems as subject to transformation through participation in cultural practices. However, in empirical research conducted in this tradition most attention has been directed to understanding the processes through which individuals become competent in the knowledge and skills of their communities, with much less attention directed to understanding respects in which individuals develop novel responses or resistance to cultural expectations (Goodnow, 1990).

In future sociocultural research, greater weight could also be given to the multiple functions of cultural meanings and to more multifaceted views of self. Sociocultural research has focused heavily on the instrumental aspects of cultural activities, while paying much less attention to their symbolic meanings and to ways in which these latter meanings may affect individuals' participation in cultural practices. Criticizing early research in the Vygotskian tradition as involving "a kind of data reduction that systematically ignored information about issues such as emotion, power, and authority," Wertsch and Rupert (1993, p. 228), for example, illustrate the importance of attending to issues of status and identity in analyses of the use of mediational means. As they demonstrate in a case analysis of parent-child conversation, patterns of interchange reflect not only cognitive goals but also desires to gain prestige, authority and legitimacy through invocation of specific cultural symbols.

Cultural Approaches to the Self

The label of *"psychological/self"* is being coined to designate perspectives that have relatively close links to work in developmental or social psychology, addressing theoretical issues elaborated in these fields. Heterogeneous in nature, the perspectives grouped here have roots in psychological anthropology (e.g., Harkness & Super, 1983, 1985; LeVine, 1990; LeVine et al., 1994), developmental sociolinguistics (e.g., Heath, 1983; P. J. Miller, 1982; Ochs, 1988; Schieffelin & Ochs, 1986), and in research on social cognition and social development (e.g., Markus & Kitayama, 1991). The boundary between the present perspectives and those grouped here under the category of "anthropological/self" perspectives is somewhat arbitrary, with work in psychological anthropology and in sociolinguistics represented in each category.

Common to the present set of psychological/self perspectives is a focus on the importance of cultural meanings in psychological functioning, the role of cultural communication in the origin of ideas, and the need for relativistic views on psychological diversity. The argument is made that cultural meanings, as expressed in cultural symbols and as embodied in cultural practices, form an essential source of patterning of human psychology. As Bruner comments in defending his conviction that "the central concept of human psychology is *meaning* and the processes and transactions involved in the construction of meanings":

> *This conviction is based upon two connected arguments. The first is that to understand man you must understand how his experiences and his acts are shaped by his intentional states, and the second is that the form of these intentional states is realized only through participation in the symbolic systems of the culture (Bruner, 1990, p. 33).*

From the present perspective, it is recognized that whereas there are many rational bases for cultural meanings and practices, these cultural forms also reflect presuppositions that are non-rational in the sense of being beyond reason and evidence (Shweder, 1984, 1991). It follows from this insight that cultural communication is essential in the development of understanding. Language is approached as a tool for creating, maintaining, and communicating social and psychological realities, rather than merely as a representational system (Ochs, 1988). Children are also understood to be developing culturally-based views of the self and of society as they learn language (Ochs & Schieffelin, 1984).

The view of cultural meanings and practices as based, in part, on non-rational presuppositions calls into question the possibility of fully rank-ordering alternative cultural forms on the basis of relative adequacy (Shweder, 1993). Rather, such a stance leads to a relativistic view of cultural diversity as reflecting alternative yet equally adequate modes of understanding or forms of life. As Greenfield argues in applying such a perspective to an understanding of minority child development, this type of perspective goes beyond either the developmentalism of a "deficit" model or the functionalism of a "coping" model to a "diversity" model "in which learning differences are viewed as rooted in historic cultural values that need not be assimilated out of existence . . ." (Greenfield, 1994, p. 26). In a diversity model, there is no expectation that cultural meanings and practices will necessarily converge over time, because they are not assumed to be inadequate and thus in need of change, and also are not assumed to be fully explained by reference to socioeconomic status and modernization.

One contribution of research in the present psychological/self tradition has been to elaborate theoretical frameworks for understanding child development that take into account both the symbolic and utilitarian aspects of cultural practices. Such a stance is captured, for example, in LeVine's notion of a "cultural rationale" or of an explanation for a cultural practice that makes sense against the backdrop of some arbitrary cultural assumption (LeVine, 1984, p. 79). Illustrating such a stance in the Nyakyusa practice of segregating adult generations into separate villages, he observes that whereas such a practice is functional in reducing inconvenience associated with the intergenerational avoidance taboos, the taboos themselves are premised on cultural assumptions that appear to be arbitrary. As another example of a framework for integrating ecological and symbolic aspects of context, Harkness and Super (1983) show that the contexts for child development may be seen to form a "developmental niche." Embodied in culturally variable ways, such a niche includes: (a) the physical and social settings in which the child develops; (b) culturally regulated systems of child care; and (c) the culturally informed beliefs and values that inform the ways in which parents and others structure environments and respond to children (Super & Harkness, Volume 2 of this Handbook). Experiences in contrasting niches, their research reveals, lead to the development of qualitatively distinct views of self and expectations of social relationships (Harkness & Super, 1985, Harkness et al., 1996, in press).

An additional major contribution of research in the present tradition is in forwarding culturally diverse theories of psychological functioning, including emotion (Kitayama & Markus, 1994; Shweder, 1994), self (Markus & Kitayama, 1991), morality (Miller, 1994b; Shweder, Much, Mahapatra & Park, in press), and mental health (Good, 1994; Kleinman, 1980; LeVine, 1990). It has been argued, for example, that emotions represent complex intentional states that can be decomposed into distinct components, such as their antecedents, implications for self appraisal, somatic and affective phenomenology, social appraisal, self management, and so forth (Russell, 1991; Frijda, 1986; Mesquita, Frijda & Scherer, Volume 2 of this *Handbook*; Shweder, 1994). These components are shown to be filled in and combined in culturally variable ways. In another example, research conducted among Americans from New Haven and Hindus from Mysore has provided evidence for the existence of culturally diverse interpersonal moralities and challenged the assumed universalism of the morality of caring framework proposed by Gilligan (J.G. Miller & Bersoff, 1992; J. G. Miller, 1994b).

In terms of the problems for cultural psychology noted earlier, strengths of the present psychological perspectives are that they take into account the multiple functions of cultural meanings and develop culturally grounded theories of self and psychological functioning. Work from the present perspective is providing some of the most compelling evidence for the need to recognize the existence of qualitatively distinct psychological processes. The developmental focus of work in the present psychological tradition also has enhanced its success in embodying an active view of both the agent and of the culture. Thus, for example, cross-cultural research has provided evidence to suggest that children's understandings may differ from those of adults in ways that cannot be explained merely by reference to enculturation (J. G. Miller, 1986; Shweder & LeVine, 1976). Equally, empirical studies have documented that within particular cultural populations, there exists both contextual variation and individual differences in beliefs and attitudes (e.g., Cousins, 1989; Heine & Lehman, 1995; Morris & Peng, 1994). Findings of this type reveal that even though individual understandings are influenced by cultural meanings, they do not mirror these meanings in a deterministic way.

One criticism of some of the work in this tradition, particularly research comparative in nature, is that it has failed to include a differentiated view of culture. Meanings have at times been portrayed at global levels of generality, associated with the individualism/collectivism distinction, or with whole cultural populations—a stance that fails to take into account the considerable within culture heterogeneity in meanings as well as the contested character of many of these meanings. In addition, relatively little attention has been paid to issues of power and politics as they impact on the nature of cultural practices and on access to cultural resources.

Although increasing, to date the concern with developing psychologically relevant theories of culture has been limited within this tradition. This relative neglect reflects, in part, the focus of the present type of work on cultural meanings that are broad in nature (e.g., conceptions of self as an autonomous agent) and expressed in a variety of cultural forms. In contrast, then, to cases in which the content of what is learned is more circumscribed, if not also more concrete (e.g., a child learning to eat in a culturally appropriate way), it may be more difficult to trace a link between experiences with specific cultural symbols or practices and specific shifts in experiences of self. Arguably this neglect also arises, at least in part, from the heavy reliance in some work in this tradition on quantitative methodologies that are not well suited to the analysis of cultural practices.

In turn, the label of *"anthropological/self"* perspectives has been coined to designate approaches within the traditions of cognitive and psychological anthropology (e.g., D'Andrade & Strauss, 1992; Holland & Quinn, 1987; Schwartz, White & Lutz, 1992). These perspectives share the concern of approaches discussed previously with formulating culturally grounded psychological theory. However, whereas the previous approaches arose most directly as cultural critiques of theories in mainstream psychology, the present perspectives arose most directly as critiques of the treatment of psychological considerations in cognitive and sociocultural anthropology.

Early work in cognitive anthropology assumed that cultural knowledge is organized in terms of taxonomic structures and that this knowledge can be tapped through assessment of individual cognitive representations (e.g., Tyler, 1969). The reproduction of cultural systems was treated as non-problematic and complete, and relatively little interest was shown in processes of cultural learning. In the more recent anthropological viewpoints under consideration, culture is approached in less monolithic terms. It is maintained that cultural meanings should be understood as potentially conflicting and as generally loosely organized (Holland & Quinn, 1987). Rejecting the sociocultural determinism characterizing early work in cognitive anthropology, it is assumed that cultural learning represents a cognitively complex and active process, characterized by both innovation and resistance (D'Andrade, 1984, 1992; Strauss, 1992a). Work in this recent tradition shares with social constructionist viewpoints (e.g. Edwards & Potter, 1992; Gergen, 1994; Potter & Wetherell, 1987) a focus on practices, social interaction, and experience with cultural tools. However, it differs from constructionist theory in its assumption that it is essential also to understand individual cognitive representations and that processes of internalization are entailed in culture learning. As Strauss argues:

> If our cultural–ideological milieu were unchanging, unambiguous, and internally consistent, there would be no need to study how social messages are appropriated by individual minds. Yet as we now recognize, conflicting messages, ambiguity, and change are found in all societies, even "traditional" ones. . . . These complications in the public world of social facts make it clear that it is not enough to know what *information people are exposed to; we also have to study* how *they internalize that information.* . . . *This point needs to be stressed because, paradoxically, at present the very analysts who are most likely to stress ambiguity, contestation, and multiple voices in social life are also most likely to be persuaded (e.g., by Foucault 1977) that we need to "decenter" discourse and behavior away from the individual actor. (Strauss, 1992a, p. 8, 11).*

Research from the recent anthropological perspectives is contributing to an understanding of the socially distributed nature of cultural knowledge and to the processes through which cultural knowledge obtains motivational force for individuals. For example, research by Strauss (1992b) documents that cultural schemas differ in their perceived objectivity and resultant influence on behavior. In particular, it is shown that whereas working class American men endorse the American cultural model of "success" as a consciously held value, it is the "breadwinner" cultural model that most directly impacts on their actions. This latter model is not consciously understood by the men to be an aspect of culture but rather is perceived to be a part of reality that is outside of culture. In another example of work in this tradition, Holland (1992) provides evidence that it is in the context of application that individuals begin to identify with and to internalize cultural schemata. Treating the cultural schema of "romance" as a domain of expertise, it is shown that internalization of this cultural model co-develops along with expertise in the practice of romance.

The anthropological perspectives under consideration are also contributing to an understanding of ways in which psychological processes are culturally constituted. In one example of such an effort, D'Andrade calls attention to respects in which motivation is based on cultural schemas that become organized into individual goal hierarchies (D'Andrade, 1992). It is maintained that parallel distributed processing (PDP) models provide a way of understanding how these schema are learned, with PDP models able to explain how behavior may appear to be rule-governed without the individual having ever been taught explicitly encoded rules (e.g., Rummelhart, McClelland & the PDP Research Group, 1986).

Other work in this broad tradition highlights the need to understand emotions in terms of their social meanings and pragmatic consequences (Lutz & White, 1986). It is shown that emotions can be understood, at least in part, as means for addressing moral problems and for mediating interpersonal relationships (White, 1990, 1994, 1995). For example, reflecting the asocial cultural view of the person, in modern Western cultures, emotions tend to be treated as internal feeling states that may at times be disruptive to interpersonal relationships. Within such cultures, there is a tendency to make use of psychotherapy or other individualistic solutions to socio-moral problems. In contrast, in assuming a more social view of self, small-scale traditional cultures tend to treat emotions in more relational terms, with collective rather than individualistic strategies formulated for ameliorating socio-moral conflicts.

In terms of strengths, research in this tradition is distinguished in its efforts to formulate psychologically relevant theories of culture. The work calls attention to the manner in which the same cultural symbol may come to have contrasting significance for individuals depending on whether it is communicated through direct inculcation or other relatively explicit means, or through means that are more transparent to members of the culture. Studies conducted in this tradition also succeed in embodying an active view of the agent, in their concern with individual differences in psychological functioning.

A limitation of certain research in this tradition is a reliance on mainstream psychological theories of self that may not be sufficiently culturally sensitive. Work in this tradition has drawn not only on PDP models of learning, as noted, but also on other select psychological theories, such as psychoanalysis, Gilligan's morality of caring framework, and Festinger's cognitive dissonance theory (e.g., Derne, 1992; Ewing, 1992). This effort to bridge disciplinary boundaries and to integrate psychological theory with anthropological work on culture theory represents a strength. However, in this effort, insufficient attention may have been paid to respects in which the assumptions of these psychological theories may be culturally bound or otherwise fail to take into account the role of cultural meanings in mediating cognition and behavior (J. G. Miller, 1994a).

Social Constructionism

Considered in this section are approaches within social constructionism (e.g., Edwards & Potter, 1992; Gergen, 1982, 1991, 1994; Harré, 1986; Potter & Wetherell, 1987; Sampson, 1993; Semin & Gergen, 1990; Shotter, 1993). A tradition that includes many diverse approaches, social constructionism has roots in such areas as the sociology of knowledge, Marxist ideological critiques, sociocultural theory and research, literary rhetorical analyses, ethnomethodological studies, and feminism. It is closely linked to and may be considered part of postmodernism.

A core assumption of social constructionism is a view of discourse as prior to and constitutive of the world. The assumption is made not only that experience can only be known in terms of observer–dependent categories, but that psychological processes must be understood as products of discourse that are constituted in interaction. As Shotter characterizes social constructionism:

> *Common to all the versions of it known to me is the central assumption that— instead of the study of the inner dynamics of the individual psyche (romanticism and subjectivism) or the already determined characteristics of the external world (modernism and objectivism), the two polarities in terms of which we have thought about ourselves in recent times (Taylor, 1989; Gergen, 1991)—it is the contingent flow of continuous interaction between human beings which becomes the central focus of concern: a self-other dimension of interaction (Shotter, 1993, p. 12).*

The perspective of social constructionism is neutral as to the existence of an observer-independent world of experience, that is, neither assuming nor denying the existence of such a world. However, it is assumed that because such a world cannot be known in ways that are independent of cultural meanings and practices, it is only these meanings and practices and not this ultimately unknowable reality that should be treated as the subject matter of psychological inquiry.

Social constructionism maintains a more radical position on the place of culture in psychology than do the other cultural viewpoints discussed in this chapter. Whereas these other approaches assume that experience is, in part, culturally constituted and always known in observer–dependent terms, they do not share the view that psychological experiences represent only cultural performances. As Edwards notes, in contrasting discursive perspectives with those of cultural psychology:

> *Where discursive and cultural psychology come together is in the recognition given to the primacy of representation (discourse, mediation, etc.), and its locus in situated social practices rather than abstracted mental models. In discursive psychology we also recognize that culture should not be treated as a causal variable, but that carries through to not treating 'mind' as a dependent one. It involves rejecting a* product *and* process *psychology of mental development, where mind is viewed as an objective developmental outcome, in favor of a discursive–constructive notion of mind as a participants' category (Edwards, 1995, pp. 63–64).*

Illustrating ways in which psychological processes are understood as cultural activities, Gergen notes, for example, that from a social constructionist perspective: "to hold an attitude is to occupy a particular position in a conversation (Potter

& Wetherell, 1987), to possess an identity is to play a part in a relational configuration (Davies & Harré, 1990), to have an emotion is to perform appropriately in a relational scenario (Gergen & Gergen, 1988), and to possess a memory is to act according to socially negotiated rules (Middleton & Edwards, 1990) (Gergen, 1992, p. 14).

From a social constructionist perspective, the scientific enterprise is seen as no less a product of discourse than is psychological functioning. Called into question is the privileged position of scientific knowledge relative to lay knowledge, and the greater authority of the scientist relative to the layperson. Emphasis is placed on cultivating a self-critical perspective on the part of investigators, who should seek both to increase their awareness of the biases that they contribute to their studies, as well as to enter into research relationships that are more egalitarian and dialogic in nature than those typical of the mainstream empirical tradition of psychology. With the abandonment of the goal of contributing privileged knowledge to society, the goal of science becomes that of furthering responsible social action.

Treating cultural meanings and practices as in continuous transformation and flux, social constructionist viewpoints question the possibility of distinguishing between communities on the basis of their cultural beliefs and practices. Gergen, for example, argues that, with the mutual interpenetration of cultures brought about through expanded communication, it is no longer possible to identify enduring cultural traditions:

> We are not speaking here of the blending of all, the emergence of monoculture, but rapid and continuous transformations in cultural forms, as they are subject to multiple influences and in their altered state become the impetus for change in other locales. . . . If there is a continuous blending, appropriation, dissolution, and the like, how are we to draw distinctions among cultural processes? (Gergen, as interviewed in Gulerce, 1995, p. 149–150).

Culture from this perspective then is characterized as fundamentally "pastiche-like" in character, both when considered at the level of meanings and at the level of practices.

Work in social constructionism has led to the re-conceptualization in discursive terms of an extensive range of phenomena, such as, for example, conceptions of the child (Gergen, Gloger-Tippelt & Berkowitz, 1990), emotions (Greenwood, 1994; Harré, 1986), identity (Shotter & Gergen, 1989), moral judgments (Robinson, 1992), and psychotherapy (Sass, 1992). This type of work not only has provided new relational ways of understanding these phenomena but has offered cultural critiques of practices in these domains. For example, social constructionist work on psychotherapy is making apparent the extent to which this practice is structured in ways that enhance therapists' power, control, and authority over clients (McNamee & Gergen, 1992). Contributing to the sociology of knowledge, social constructivist approaches also offer insight into the philosophical, cultural, and applied concerns that have impacted on the history of psychology (Gergen, 1994).

In terms of the problems for cultural approaches noted earlier, strengths of social constructionist viewpoints are in developing psychologically relevant theories of culture and in representing the complexity of culture. In the attention paid to language as a form of action and of communal participation, social constructionist approaches present a dynamic portrayal of the processes through which cultural practices impact on behavior. Sensitive to the non-rational and affective aspects of cultural meanings, social constructionist perspectives also succeed in offering a powerful challenge to the representational views of knowledge that have dominated work in mainstream psychology. Such approaches equally are distinguished in their attention to oppression, discrimination, racism and other socio-political processes that structure institutions and practices.

In terms of limitations, social constructionist work may be criticized for giving insufficient weight to the individual as agent or actor and for maintaining a view of culture that is so differentiated as to have little or no explanatory force. With the rejection of the notion of the psychological self, it becomes difficult in social constructionism to account for individual opposition to cultural practices. As Morawski, for example, charges, "the active subject is lost, or at least subjectivity comes to be flattened and mechanical, leaving no simple way to explain resistance, rebellion or subversion" (Morawski, 1994, p. 162). It may be argued that whereas the sensitivity shown to cultural heterogeneity, fluidity, and interchange in social constructivist work is important, it is an overstatement to assume that no sources of regularity may be located that distinguish between cultural traditions or practices (Jahoda, 1986a, 1986b; yet see Gergen, 1986). Such a position also may be criticized for leading investigators to overlook the extent to which their own analyses are culturally grounded. Thus, for example, as Jahoda (1986a) has charged, in certain cases little recognition is given to the extent to which observed patterns may be culturally-specific or to the extent to which various social constructionist accounts of persons as autonomous and self-directing may themselves be premised on certain Western individualistic cultural assumptions. More broadly, critics have charged that the dual stance of both questioning the reality of the self and the possibility of distinguishing between groups on cultural grounds ironically impedes rather than enhances an appreciation of diversity. As Butler argues in questioning the implications of this type of postmodern turn in giving voice to feminist concerns:

> If it is not a female subject who provides the normative model for a feminist politics, then what does? . . . What constitutes the "who," the subject, for whom feminism seeks emancipation? If there is no subject, who is left to emancipate? (Butler, 1990, p. 327).

Finally, questions might be raised about the explanatory force achieved in social constructivist accounts. The perspective rejects not only the conventional standards of methodological adequacy employed in empirical psychology, but also those employed in ethnographic or other qualitative research. Whereas this stance is motivated by a conviction that all methodological standards ultimately have an arbitrary cultural grounding, it leads investigators at times to offer accounts that have only an anecdotal or illustrative rather than systematic quality, and that may suffer then in their persuasiveness.

Problems in Cultural Approaches to Psychology

This section covers extended theoretical discussion of the specific problems for cultural psychology and for social constructionism identified earlier. The analysis is intended as a conceptual tool that may be useful in guiding future theoretical work in these traditions. It is assumed that not all of the problems identified will be accepted as important within social constructionist approaches. In particular, some of the considerations regarding the understanding of the cultural grounding of psychological processes and regarding the formulation of successful explanations may not be regarded as valid by certain social constructionist theorists who reject the need for a concept of psychology and/or for standards of explanatory adequacy.

The Complexity of Culture

The concept of culture that has dominated the tradition of cross-cultural psychology has historically been eclectic and functionalistic in nature (Kroeber & Kluckhohn, 1952/1963; Soudijn, Hutschemaekers & Van de Vijver, 1990). The eclecticism may be seen, for example, in Herskovits' definition of culture as "the man-made part of the human environment" (Herskovits, 1948, p. 7)—an approach to culture which, Triandis (1980) observes, fits most of the work in cross-cultural psychology, as described in the previous edition of this *Handbook*. The functional character of this approach to culture is evident in the assumption that culture is causally related to ecological and social structural constraints. Thus, for example, in the area of culture and personality, explanatory frameworks have been formulated that trace a causal path from the physical ecology and associated social structure, through patterns of socialization and personality development, to expressive aspects of culture (e.g., LeVine, 1973; Whiting & Child, 1953; Whiting & Whiting, 1975). Similarly, work on the cultural construct of individualism/collectivism has linked the emergence of these cultural orientations to contrasting environmental conditions, such as population pressures, affluence, mobility, economic structure, and so forth (e.g., Hofstede, 1980; Triandis, 1989, 1993).

One limitation of a functional view of culture is that, in an important sense, it renders the concept of culture superfluous. To the extent that culture is understood as bearing a one-to-one relationship to environmental and social structural constraints, it contributes no explanatory force. Rather, it becomes sufficient merely to take into account these objective constraints, because no independent effects are assumed to be attributable to cultural meaning systems (Segall, 1983). Reflecting an awareness of this need for clarification of the concept of culture, Jahoda concluded his chapter on cross-cultural psychology in the previous edition of this *Handbook* with the comment that "further theoretical advance in cross-cultural psychology will probably depend to a considerable extent on a more rigorous analysis and operationalization of the concept of `culture' " (Jahoda, 1980, p. 131; see also Jahoda, 1993b).

In contrast to the dominant approaches to culture in cross-cultural psychology, a semiotic approach to culture—focused on meaning—tends to be emphasized in cultural psychology and in social constructionism. As exemplified in Geertz's (1973) classic definition of culture as "an historically transmitted pattern of meanings embodied in symbols" (Geertz, 1973, p. 89), culture is treated from this perspective as an intersubjective reality through which worlds are known, created, and experienced. By considering culture as a symbolic system that is embodied in artifacts and practices, those aspects are emphasized that bear an open or indeterminate relationship to objective constraints—whether given in the structure of experience or in biological propensities of the organism (Bruner, 1990; LeVine, 1984; Sahlins, 1976a; Schneider, 1976).

One of the central problems for a semiotic view of culture involves taking into account the *multiple functions of cultural meanings*. As a representational system, cultural meanings include information about the structure of experience and encompass what is generally considered as shared knowledge, whether of a formal or an informal kind (D'Andrade, 1984). In turn, as a directive system, culture includes rules or norms for conduct. The representational and regulative aspects of culture have typically been subject to most attention within psychology, because of their recognized importance for adaptation and because of their tangible character in making reference to observable patterns of behavior.

It is important to recognize the constitutive aspects of culture as well. In these aspects, culture serves to create or to define intentional realities, that depend on social agreement for their existence (Schneider, 1968, 1976; Searle, 1969; Taylor, 1979). Reference to empirical reality is neither necessary nor sufficient for the existence of culturally constituted entities. Thus, for example, the cultural category of "unicorn" is understood to be fictive in character and to make no such reference.

The presence of culturally constituted categories, it may be noted, is widely acknowledged within psychology, with recognition given to the role such categories play in defining certain social practices and roles, such as the practice of marriage and the role of bride (Turiel, 1983). What is less widely recognized, however, is the pervasiveness of culturally constituted entities. Thus, even primary categories of epistemological knowledge, such as conceptions of mind and of the natural and social order, depend on conventional cultural definitions (e.g., Heelas & Lock, 1981; Marsella, DeVos & Hsu, 1985). Challenging the assumption made in mainstream psychology that the objects of psychological inquiry are "natural" structures, processes and states that can be inductively studied without reference to categories of cultural knowledge, the present perspective implies that the objects of psychological inquiry are, in part, culturally constituted entities that depend on cultural definitions and practices for their existence (Morawski, 1994).

It is important to consider that cultural meanings include shared affective associations that also cannot be explained merely in terms of their link to the particular contexts or events in which they were originally invoked. As Geertz (1973) observes, this evocative dimension tends to pervade all aspects of culture, including the intellectual domains of math and science.

In recognizing the multiple functions of cultural meanings, the present view underscores the complexity of the cultural learning process. Whether a young child, immigrant, or anthropologist, the cultural novice cannot discern cultural meanings merely by observation but, through cultural communication, must be made aware of the values, beliefs, and premises that inform cultural practices. As Shweder points out:

> . . . the nonrational suppositions, ideas about worth, and classifications of a people (a cousin is a person not to marry; a pig is an animal not to eat; a mother's sister's husband is an "uncle"; members of a family eat together at the same time and food gets distributed equally) are not derivable from reason or direct experience with nature—one must, somehow, be "let in" on the secret, one must, somehow, receive the "frame" of understanding from others (Shweder, 1984, p. 49).

Such cultural learning depends critically on gaining access to the natural language concepts applied by members of the culture in making sense of their experiences (Geertz, 1984).

The present considerations also imply that the use of cultural symbols and tools cannot be approached merely in terms of considerations of utility but also needs affectively grounded cultural definitions that may link, for example, prestige or degradation to certain cultural symbols. The affective aspects of cultural meanings lead them to be motivationally engaging. As Goodnow points out, cultural knowledge carries with it implications for social identity that impact on processes of cultural learning:

> If I had to choose one process that is essential to consider for the acquisition of cognitive values and that should be considered for any domain, it would probably be the linking of areas of knowledge and skill to social identity . . . the acquisition of knowledge or skill proceeds differently in areas where there are strong cultural values about the way one should think than it does in more neutral areas (Goodnow, 1990, pp. 282–283).

Finally, attention to the constitutive dimensions of cultural meanings also highlights their non-rational character. Constitutive presuppositions may be seen to be arbitrary in the sense that they do not arise from and thus may not be contradicted by empirical evidence or by logical standards of disproof (Shweder, 1984, 1991). They differ from the affective or evocative dimensions of cultural meanings in that they serve to define social realities. To the extent, then, that cultural meanings and practices are based on alternative presuppositions of this type, a certain incommensurability results. In particular, in such cases it may not be possible to comparatively evaluate the alternative cultural meanings and practices in terms of their fit with experience or rational grounding.

Taking into account the *differentiated and dynamic nature of culture* represents an additional challenge for cultural approaches to psychology. Attention must be paid to the heterogeneity of cultural meanings and practices across contexts as well as within populations. Equally, it is important to recognize that cultural meanings and practices shift in complex ways over historical time.

A view of culture as totally integrated, such as presented in Benedict's early portrayal of Japanese culture (Benedict, 1946), is widely recognized to be an oversimplification. Cultural meanings and practices are not fully consistent, and may even be conflicting (Shweder, 1979a). Illustrating this type of event, it has been shown that individuals participate in cultural activities that have contradictory meanings. For example, Zinacantecos families of Chiapas, Mexico have been observed to utilize both Shamans and Western doctors, even though the latter practice goes against Zinacanteco religious norms (Cancian, 1975). Similarly, survey research conducted among Americans has shown that individuals maintain contradictory cultural beliefs and values (McClosky & Brill, 1983). Thus, a value commitment that tends to be endorsed in the abstract (e.g., "I believe in free speech for all no matter what their views might be") may frequently be disavowed when applied to concrete behaviors (e.g., "A community should allow the American Nazi party to use its town hall to hold a public meeting").

Attention must also be paid to the heterogeneity of cultural meanings and practices at the level of subgroups within populations. Whereas cultural knowledge is to some extent shared, the degree of this sharedness varies. Particular subgroups, because of their expertise and/or power, may have differential access to specific cultural messages or have a differential influence on their formation. Equally, the level of sharedness may differ depending on the level of analysis, with families or work groups, for example, maintaining systems of meaning and associated practices that may not be maintained within larger population groupings, such as at the level of a city, nation, or other geographical region.

However, whereas it is critically important to attend to variation in meanings and practices both within and between cultural populations, this stance should not lead to the conclusion that cultural meanings and practices are so diverse and unintegrated that it is impossible to characterize them in terms of meaningful thematic tendencies. As Geertz comments:

> *It's possible to overthematize, and it's possible to underthematize . . . the elements of culture are not like a pile of sand and not like a spider's web. It's more like an octopus, a rather badly integrated creature—what passes for a brain keeps it together, more or less, in one ungainly whole (Geertz, 1973).*

This recognition that there is at least some internal consistency to cultural meanings and practices implies that it is possible to draw meaningful contrasts between different cultural communities, a stance that would be precluded in the absence of identifiable themes. At the same time, awareness of the heterogeneity of cultural meanings and practices implies that such contrasts need to be drawn in ways that acknowledge rather than obscure or overlook sources of diversity and conflict in cultural meanings.

As part of a dynamic view of culture, recognition must also be given to the open-ended and multi-directional nature of processes of cultural change. The present semiotic view of culture implies that processes of cultural change cannot be assumed to conform to the patterns predicted within modernization viewpoints (e.g., Hallpike, 1979; Inkeles & Smith, 1974). In particular, it cannot be assumed that particular meanings and practices follow inevitably from technological development, or that cultural change is necessarily unidirectional and progressive (Yang, 1988). Rather, the present viewpoint highlights the need to recognize the indeterminate elements in cultural transformations, with certain shifts in cultural meanings and practices understood as resulting, at least in part, from contingent historical processes, rather than from predictable functional relationships. It also highlights the importance of acknowledging that cultural change may be multi- directional or cyclical in nature, with cultural meanings and practices gaining and losing prominence in ways that do not necessarily represent advances but rather may be non-directional or even regressive in nature (Kessen, 1984, 1990; Shweder, 1993).

A further challenge for cultural approaches to psychology is to address the *relationship of culture to ecological and sociopolitical factors.* As noted, the present semiotic view of culture assumes that cultural meanings and practices do not arise as causal concomitants of structures given either in the physical or social environment. It is thus assumed that the same social structural arrangements and ecological conditions may be associated with different cultural meanings and practices and that cultural meanings and practices are not exclusively functional in character. However, the present approach to culture is incomplete without consideration of material conditions that impact on psychological functioning in ways that are culturally mediated.

The ecological setting, considered both in terms of a physical setting and in terms of social structural and political aspects, may be seen to present certain adaptive requirements as well as certain resources for meeting these requirements. These types of factors, it may be noted, have been studied extensively by Berry and his colleagues in an approach that focuses on the functional interrelationships between ecological and cultural factors (Berry, Poortinga, Segall & Dasen, 1992). Whereas ecological requirements and resources do not fully determine cultural meanings or practices, they may impact on the patterning of cultural forms, or, in extreme cases, may even overwhelm such forms (Scheper-Hughes, 1990; Heath, 1990). It thus becomes important in cultural approaches to psychology to take these constraints into account, not as factors that are assumed to provide a "deeper" explanation of cultural meanings and practices, but as sources of regularity in human behavior that afford a range of modes of behavioral adaptation. Thus, for example, cultural activities need to be understood in relation to materialistic causal influences, such as the systems of power, hierarchy, and control characteristic of political systems.

Importantly, the present semiotic view of culture stands not only to be enriched by consideration of materialistic influences on cultural forms and psychological outcomes but also can serve to complete such materialistic accounts. Thus, evidence illustrates that socioeconomic status does not have the same impact on psychological functioning in all cases but rather may have effects that are culturally mediated. For example, it has been demonstrated that whereas maternal views of attachment are affected by socioeconomic status among both American and Puerto Rican mothers, the nature of this impact differs in ways that reflect the meanings systems and practices emphasized in each cultural community (Harwood, Miller & Lucca, 1995).

The Interdependence of Culture and the Self

Arguably, the most central problem for cultural psychology concerns understanding the interdependence of culture and the self.[1] It is this problem that motivated the label of cultural psychology, with its connotations of culture and of psychology as integral rather than separable units. To address this broad problem, at least three interrelated issues must be considered:

   1.   One issue concerns the need to formulate theories of psychology that treat psychological functioning as complex and multi-faceted yet also as culturally grounded and as, at least potentially, culturally variable. Addressing this issue requires building on the insights of mainstream psychological theory and research, while also raising questions about the cross-cultural applicability of some of its theoretical assumptions and findings.
   2.   A second issue concerns the need to understand the processes through which culture impacts on individual subjectivity and behavior. Addressing this issue raises questions about the ways in which individuals appropriate meanings from cultural symbols and practices.
   3.   Finally, a third issue, which bridges these two, is how to develop theories that, while recognizing the formative impact of culture on psychological functioning, define the person as an agent and take into account individual variation in psychological functioning. Addressing this issue raises questions about whether it is possible to bridge the gap between the organismic and mechanistic traditions in psychology and of ways in which perspectives in cultural psychology differ from constructivist (e.g., Piaget, 1968, 1970) and learning theory approaches (e.g., Bandura, 1977).

   In regard to the need to formulate *multi-faceted and culturally grounded views of self*, the status of the self represents one of the most debated issues in the perspectives represented in cultural psychology and in social constructionism. As discussed earlier in the chapter, social constructionist perspectives reject the need for a concept of self or for other psychological concepts, with this rejection representing one of the central tenets that distinguishes social constructionist approaches from those within the domain of cultural psychology.
   Within cultural perspectives that retain the notion of individual psychology, it is important to embody a multifaceted view of behavior. Acting persons must be understood in complex terms as performing cognitively, as experiencing emo-

tions, as having identity needs, and as maintaining a sense of morality and of other social cognitive understandings (Goodnow, 1990; Shweder, 1995). Behavior must also be understood within the context of the family and other social collectives, with as unit of analysis the dyad or larger social unit rather than only the solitary agent (D. T. Miller & Prentice, 1994). Equally, it is important to focus on explaining actions, interpretations of experience, and the relationship between them, with this relationship treated as open.

Importantly, cultural psychology should be grounded on findings from recent mainstream psychological research, which challenge earlier theories of psychological functioning. Although it is beyond the scope of the present paper to delineate these insights, certain illustrative examples may be mentioned. For example, any notion of personality forwarded from a cultural psychology perspective needs to take into account challenges to global stage and structural models that show behavior to be more contextually specific and less longitudinally stable than previously assumed (Mischel, 1968, 1973; Mischel & Peake, 1982). Similarly, any views of cognition forwarded from a cultural psychology perspective must be informed by empirical challenges to stage models, which demonstrate the limited behavioral generality of cognition and the dependence of modes of reasoning on the content under consideration (e.g., Gelman & Baillargeon, 1983; Wason & Johnson-Laird, 1972). In still another example, work in cultural psychology needs to be sensitive to the shortcomings of human information processing as well as to the limited access that individuals have to their cognitive processes (Nisbett & Ross, 1980). Such considerations must be taken into account in order to avoid adopting one-sided models of the agent as either exclusively rational or exclusively irrational. In addition, they have methodological implications in affecting the interpretations placed on self-report information, such as those employed in talking diary methodologies (e.g., Quinn, 1992). In sum, a minimal requirement for work in cultural psychology is to build on an awareness of the insights of recent psychological theory and empirical research.

A distinctive challenge for cultural psychology, however, is to develop psychological theories that are less parochial and more culturally grounded than many presently existing. This does not imply that there is in all cases a need to create new theories or that no universals can be identified. As theorists have pointed out (Pepitone, 1978; Pepitone & Triandis, 1987), it appears that some universals can be identified that are linked to biologically based propensities of the human organism or to features of the ecology. However, even in the case of such universals, they frequently appear to require completion by attention to cultural meanings and practices. Thus, in a well-known example, the universal semantic primitives identified by Osgood and his colleagues (Osgood, May & Miron, 1975)—with their documentation of common affective associations to divergent concepts (e.g., linking bird and woman as concepts which are universally seen as low in potency)—do not explain the psychologically significant and behaviorally consequential differences associated with the divergent concepts, differences which can only be explained by taking into account cultural meanings and practices. In other instances, the universals that have been identified have the status of open constraints that are developed in culturally diverse ways, such as in the case of early capacities for discriminating sounds (Werker, 1989) as well as of various other biologically based perceptual and linguistic capacities documented to be present in infants. Still, in other cases, such as in Chomsky's grammatical model (Chomsky, 1968) or in Fiske's model of social relationships (Fiske, 1991, 1992), universals have the status of ideal types that only become evident in culturally patterned forms, such as when individuals come to speak specific languages and to function in particular social settings characterized by varied culturally based conceptions of self.

In addition to completing various biologically based explanations of psychological phenomena, cultural considerations may be expected to enter into all psychological explanations that are premised on a view of individuals as intentional agents, whose interpretations of experience have a formative impact on their psychological functioning. Notably, with the cognitive revolution in psychology, theories that are premised on a view of agents as imposing meaning on their experiences have grown to such an extent that some commentators have even suggested that it becomes impossible to distinguish between competing approaches on this basis (Markus & Zajonc, 1985). As Flavell comments:

> *One sees a variety of models postulating such patently "structural" cognitive structures as sentence and story grammars, schemata, frames, scripts, prototypes, implicit or naive theories, production systems, systematic judgmental and inferential biases, executive processes, organized strategies, knowledge structures, expertise, and semantic networks. . . . Virtually everyone nowadays agrees with Piaget that we assimilate input to our existing knowledge structures rather than merely copy it—that our learning, comprehension, and other cognitive activities are heavily constructive or "top down" in nature (Flavell, 1982, p. 4).*

The present considerations imply that cultural considerations must be taken into account to understand these cognitively-mediated phenomena or, as Bruner puts it, "to recapture. . . . the originating impulse of the Cognitive Revolution" (Bruner, 1990, p. 35). More broadly, they lend support to claims that psychology is and has always been cultural, even if it is not fully recognized as such (Bock, 1988; Harris, 1991; J. G. Miller, 1994a; Schwartz, 1992), and that experience in a cultural environment is necessary for the emergence of most psychological propensities. As Geertz argues for this "incompleteness" hypothesis:

> *. . . there is no such thing as a human nature independent of culture. Men without culture ... would be unworkable monstrosities with very few useful instincts, fewer recognizable sentiments, and no intellect: mental basket cases. . . . symbols are thus not mere expressions, instrumentalities, or correlates of our biological, psychological, and social existence: they are prerequisites of it (Geertz, 1973, p. 49).*

To understand the cultural grounding of psychological phenomena, attention must be paid to the ways in which cultural meanings impact on the content of cognitive representations as well as on the interpretations given to ecological and social structural constraints. Perhaps even more fundamentally, it is critical to identify respects in which cultural meanings and practices are constitutive of psychological structures and processes and thus qualitatively impact on their forms. To give an example from the area of emotion, consideration must be given not only to ways in which cultural conceptions of the self influence individuals' construals and expressions of emotion, but also to ways in which these cultural conceptions and associated practices impact on whether and in what forms emotions are even experienced. Thus, ethnographic research has shown that certain affective maladies that have been identified among European-Americans, such as anxiety and panic disorders, do not appear to be present among Asian and Latin cultural populations, and that marked cultural differences exist in the incidence of psychologization versus somatization as responses to personal and social problems (Good, 1994; Jenkins, 1994; Kleinman, 1986).

In regard to the need to formulate *psychologically relevant theories of culture*, it may be recalled that within the cultural approaches to psychology under consideration, culture is conceptualized as a semiotic system that is, in part, constitutive of reality and that represents a source of patterning of the self. Cole (1995) draws attention to this formative impact of culture by drawing an analogy between the term as applied in biology and in the social sciences. He suggests that just as a tissue culture represents a medium in which cells proliferate, a human culture represents a medium, consisting of ideational messages and their material embodiments, that is integral to human development.

A challenge for cultural approaches to psychology is to understand the nature of this cultural medium and the ways in which it interfaces with individual subjectivity (Glick, 1991; Cole, 1995; Wertsch, 1995a). Thus, it becomes important not only to characterize the varied material forms in which cultural meanings are expressed, but to understand the processes through which individuals become engaged with these forms. Among the dimensions that must be considered in such analyses are the degree of formality, deliberateness and transparency of cultural tools, practices, and artifacts. As reflected in the anthropological distinction between "great" and "little" cultural traditions (Redfield, 1956, p. 70), cultural meanings are seen as expressed in both formal vehicles, such as philosophical, religious, and legal texts, as well as in more informal aspects of culture, such as in the lay media and in everyday routines and rituals (Keyes, 1983; Markus & Kitayama, 1994a, 1994c). Attention must be paid to respects in which differential status, if not also differential cognitive accessibility, may be related to the formality of cultural sources (Goodnow, 1990). Equally, it must be recognized that messages may be transformed through the interchange that occurs between formal versus informal cultural forms. Thus, for example, it has been demonstrated that expert information about parenting is systematically altered as it is communicated to American parents through such vehicles as parenting magazines (Young, 1990) and the everyday educational practices of pediatricians (Harkness & Super, 1996; Harkness, Super & Keefer, 1992).

It also must be recognized that the deliberateness of cultural messages varies. It is important then to attend both to values and beliefs that are overtly acknowledged and even consciously promoted, as well as to ones that are unrecognized or disavowed within the culture. As Dumont (1970) illustrates, whereas modern Western cultures overtly promote egalitarian values and disparage hierarchy, hierarchical values are tacitly promoted and, in many cases, are even more influential in structuring practices. It also must be recognized that cultural practices frequently enter into designs other than those for which they were intended—a phenomenon which Wertsch (1995b) characterizes as cultural "spin-off." As illustrated in Olson's historical account of the development of the Greek alphabet, in some of these cases, the cultural tools may even be appropriated for uses for which they are not well suited:

> [It] is now recognized that the development of the alphabet, like the development of the syllabary, was a rather straightforward consequence of applying a script which was suitable for one language, to a second language for which it was not [designed], namely, of applying a script for a Semitic language in which vocalic differences were relatively insignificant, to a Greek language in which they were highly significant (Olson, 1995).

The present considerations imply that attention must be paid not only to the ideal potentials or affordances of cultural tools and artifacts, but to the ways in which such tools and artifacts are appropriated for use within specific cultural communities.

Finally, an additional consideration is the need to take into account transparent as well as non-transparent cultural media. Transparent media are associated with facets of cultural knowledge that are relatively accessible to the members of a culture. Included here, for example, are cultural texts that are linked to explicit cultural values or to deliberate institutional arrangements. Thus, the ideas of the Bhagavad Gita embody a range of relatively transparent cultural messages that are communicated in readings of it and in its many enactments through everyday dance and drama performances in local Hindu Indian communities. It is also important to recognize, however, that many cultural forms are transparent, with their messages not consciously accessible as either declarative or procedural knowledge. Included here, for example, are everyday cultural routines, such as sleeping arrangements, with their communication and instantiation of views of the self as autonomous versus interdependent agents (Morelli, Rogoff, Oppenheim & Goldsmith, 1992; Rogoff, in press; Shweder, Jensen & Goldstein, 1994), and the wide variety of everyday cultural tools that structure experience, such as the canonical forms of narrative employed in a non-self conscious way in storytelling (Feldman, Bruner, Kalmar & Renderer, 1993). As theorists have noted, among the most pervasive and influential of these transparent cultural media are the many structuring devices of language, such as its indexical expressions (Ochs, 1990; Wertsch, 1989, 1995a).

Ironically, it may be argued that cultural media, being in many cases relatively invisible or transparent, has contributed to the downplaying of cultural influences on psychological functioning both by laypersons and by many psychological investigators (J. G. Miller, 1996). One of the key challenges for cultural psychology is to contribute to making culture, as a medium for human development, more visible. In this way the processes through which cultural meanings are created, communicated, and transformed as well as through which they pattern psychological functioning may be better understood.

In regard to treating both the *agent and culture as active influences on psychological processes*, it is important to maintain an active view of the individual. The individual must be portrayed as an enculturated being whose subjectivity and motivation is, in part, culturally constituted, yet also as an agent who is capable of resisting, modifying, and reflecting on cultural meanings and practices (J.G. Miller & Bersoff, 1995).

Within cognitive developmental and related traditions (e.g., Piaget, 1968, 1970; Turiel, 1983), the assumption has been made that processes of cultural learning do not allow for a sense of agency. An interactionist position is posited in which individuals are seen as constructing understandings of experience based on deductive or inductive processing of information to which they have been exposed. From this perspective, development is assumed to be dependent on social interaction, a universal characteristic of human environments, that is viewed as providing individuals with experiences on which they may construct cognitive understandings. In contrast, development is regarded as unaffected by culture-specific forms of enculturation, such as language learning, interaction with cultural tools, exposure to cultural beliefs, or participation in formal schooling and other cultural practices. This downplaying of cultural influences derives, in large part, from the assumption that culture learning represents a passive activity, in which individuals merely absorb the messages of their culture (Piaget, 1966).

Although cognitive developmental and related viewpoints are linked to the organismic tradition in psychology and are associated with an agentic as contrasted with a mechanistic view of self, the argument can be made that their type of constructivist stance actually precludes a sense of agency (J. G. Miller, 1996). In particular, there appears to be little or no room for individual agency in a system that portrays persons as all conforming to the same universal set of understandings, assumed to be given in the structure of reality.

In contrast, it may be argued that viewpoints within cultural psychology give greater weight to human agency, at least on a collective level. From a cultural psychology perspective, the direction of development is assumed to be contingent on cultural meanings and practices as well as on historical circumstances (Kessen, 1990; J. G. Miller, 1984, 1988; Shweder & Bourne, 1984); development is not given in a universal structure either of reality or of the human mind. Such approaches then assume that there may be multiple veridical understandings of experience and multiple adaptive forms of psychological functioning rather than one universal set of understandings or adaptive developmental outcomes.

However, whereas this type of cultural sense of agency is critically important in transcending the "pristine processor" and "naturalist" stance of cognitive developmental approaches and related viewpoints (Harris, 1991; Schwartz, 1981; Markus & Kitayama, 1994b), it is not sufficient. To avoid the sociocultural determinism of portraying cultural meanings as received in the identical form in which they are communicated, approaches within cultural psychology must also embody a sense of individual agency (D'Andrade, 1984). One way to achieve this goal is to pay greater attention to developmental and individual differences in psychological functioning.

Although children must be always considered to be members of a culture, and their experiences even in utero, in part culturally patterned, they also represent cultural novices in the sense of entering specific prestructured communities of meanings and practices that impact on their sense of self.

Without presupposing that there is such an entity as a precultural or acultural being, it can be assumed that there are certain early constructions of experience that distinguish in many cases young children's understandings from those of older children and adults. This early childhood subjectivity includes culturally-specific as well as universal elements and emerges from a range of sources (Shweder & LeVine, 1976). For example, certain concepts are more spontaneous than others in the sense that they are less dependent on specialized forms of enculturation. Thus, simple narrative scripts might be expected to be part of children's early interpretations of their experiences in many if not in all cultures (J. G. Miller, 1986), whereas probabilistic modes of reasoning would not be (Nisbett & Ross, 1980; Nisbett, 1993). It also is likely that certain innate propensities are most evident early in development, before they have undergone differential amplification or downplaying through processes of enculturation. As Werker (1989) has shown, whereas young children appear capable of discriminating a wide range of sounds in the first year of life, this capacity is lost through the process of learning their native tongue. Equally, experiences of childhood may make certain modes of understanding more relevant than others (Hamlyn, 1971). It must be recognized that young children do not merely adopt understandings and modes of response that constitute adult endpoints in a given culture, but they develop outlooks that are not communicated in the culture or that may even be in conflict with those that are emphasized in the culture (Goodnow, 1990).

Therefore, it seems clear that individual differences in psychological functioning also represent a critical domain to examine in developing agentic views of the person. Such an examination would entail taking into account personality or motivational differences between persons as well as respects in which unique autobiographical experiences and personal constructions affect the cultural patterning of self (e.g., Markus & Kitayama, 1994b; Valsiner & Lawrence, Volume 2 of this *Handbook*). Attention must also be paid to ways in which broad cultural meanings and practices are transformed as they are instantiated in smaller cultural or social structural units, such as specific families, school or community groups or even in groups distinguished by socioeconomic status (e.g., Costanzo, 1991).

Finally, a focus on expert/novice differences in particular domains of practice provides another important vehicle for exploring individual agency within cultural approaches. Involving many similar issues in understanding age-related variation in psychological functioning, the study of the processes involved in developing competence in specific cultural activities can highlight ways in which individuals become integrated into new cultural practices and ways in which their prior experiences and knowledge impact on their emerging expertise, both in facilitative and inhibitory senses. Importantly, it also provides a dynamic means of investigating cultural change, by emphasizing ways in which individuals collectively transform cultural practices as they create and participate in them.

Explanation

The interdisciplinary character of the questions under consideration in cultural psychology and social constructionism leads to complexity in the efforts to formulate successful explanations. These traditions maintain the goal of drawing on the strengths of their many roots while avoiding the perceived pitfalls of these past approaches (Bock, 1994). As Shweder comments in relation to cultural psychology:

> *Cultural psychology tries to synthesize, or at least combine, some of the virtues of general psychology, cross-cultural psychology, psychological anthropology, and ethnopsychology while seeking to disencumber itself of their vices (Shweder, 1990, p. 17).*

Complexity is also entailed because work in these traditions embodies the self-reflexivity, awareness of the limitations of positivism, and skepticism regarding the possibilities of knowledge associated with postmodernism.

In this section consideration will focus on theoretical and methodological problems entailed in formulating explanations in cultural approaches to psychology. The importance of avoiding certain pitfalls associated with past theoretical approaches will be shown. Arguments will also be made for the need to build on the existing diversity of the field, and to avoid privileging single explanatory agendas to the exclusion of other agendas.

In terms of *achieving explanatory force*, consideration must be given to the goals of explanation. In this regard, the goals of cross-cultural psychology include testing the generality of psychological theories in diverse cultural contexts as well as identifying variation in psychological functioning not accounted for in existing psychological theories (Berry & Dasen, 1974). In turn, its ultimate aim is to "generate a more nearly universal psychology" based on an integration of what has been learned in pursuing the first two aims (Berry et al., 1992, p. 3).

It may be noted that, in this concern with uncovering culture-specific variation in psychological processes, overlap exists in the goals of cross-cultural psychology and of cultural psychology (Segall, 1993). What appears most distinctive about their aims is the commitment to a universal psychology. Whereas the possibility of identifying panhuman characteristics, or the postulate of psychic unity, is not denied within cultural psychology, it is questioned whether a focus on such universals is theoretically productive. Thus, it is assumed that the panhuman characteristics that can be identified are likely to be so abstract that they have little explanatory force in accounting for specific psychological phenomena of interest. Articulating this type of stance, Jahoda notes that the doctrine of psychic unity was embraced by cross-cultural psychologists at the turn of the nineteenth century, in counterpoint to then current racial interpretations of behavioral diversity, and may no longer be informative in light of current understandings:

> *Attempts to identify the existence of psychological universals, such as Lonner's (1980), have not been very fruitful. Furthermore, the implication of uniformity runs counter to our newly acquired insights that cultural influences can have important psychological effects. . . . Hence there appear to be good grounds for arguing that at the present time, when "race" has ceased to be theoretically relevant, the notion of "psychic unity" has also outlived its usefulness (Jahoda, 1993a, pp. 191–2).*

Within cultural psychology, there is recognized to be a need for explanations that assume a universal form, as well as for explanations that are local in character. However, explanations that make reference to pan human characteristics are not then treated as more fundamental than are local explanations.

Universal explanations in cultural approaches to psychology may be proposed to account for various component processes involved in specific cultural activities. Such constructs as "scaffolding," "joint problem solving," and "guided participation" represent examples of general explanatory constructs (Greenfield, 1984; Rogoff, 1990; Rogoff & Lave, 1984). In other cases, universal explanatory constructs may refer to abstract components of psychological processes that empirically exist only as instantiated in culturally specific forms. The system of universal semantic primitives developed recently by Wierzbicka (1992, 1994) to explain emotional states represents an example of the latter type of explanatory scheme.

In formulating these types of general explanations it is important to avoid problems of ethnocentrism, reductionism and of non-falsifiability. Universal explanatory constructs need to be formulated in ways that do not distort the perspectives of particular cultural groups—a stance which, it may be argued, has occurred in many cases in mainstream psychology when theories that have been developed on Western cultural populations are applied without modification to divergent cultural populations (see critique in Misra & Gergen, 1993). Equally, it is critical not to assume a reductive stance in which behavioral phenomena of interest are treated as being fully determined by universal properties of non-cultural origin (Bendix, 1970; Sahlins, 1976b; Shweder, 1979b). The stance of treating culture as variable content that fills in culture-free structures or processes—a position termed "absolutism" by Berry et al. (1992)—is problematic because it fails to take into account the extent to which culture represents a source of patterning of psychological structures and processes (Miller & Bersoff, 1994). Finally, it is critical that general constructs be formulated with enough specificity that they may be called into question by empirical evidence rather than formulated in such a global way that they explain every situation. Thus, for example, a construct such as "scaffolding" must be described in a way that makes it possible to recognize situations in which such a process is not occurring, or in which it is occurring in ways that are defective or lead to maladaptive outcomes.

In turn, explanations in cultural approaches to psychology may also be formulated that are culturally specific in nature, meaning that they characterize psychological functioning only within particular cultural groups or within particular cultural contexts or points in historical time. Such local explanations directly embody the monistic assumption of cultural psychology that views psychology and culture as mutually constitutive. Theories identifying culturally specific emotions (e.g., Kitayama & Markus, 1994), moral codes (e.g., J. G. Miller, 1994b; Shweder, Mahapahtra & Miller, 1990)), modes of personality development (e.g., Roland, 1988; Rosenberger, 1992), and attributional processes (e.g., Markus & Kitayama, 1991) represent examples of this type of explanatory construct.

Local explanations of these specific types must be formulated in ways that take into account indigenous cultural meanings and practices and that are sensitive to the specific historical and sociopolitical contexts that may impact on particular behaviors of interest (see chapter by Sinha, this volume). At the same time, an appropriate level of analysis needs to be chosen to avoid proliferation of theories that may have limited explanatory force. It cannot be assumed that, with their sensitivity to nuances of culture, more differentiated or local levels are invariably the preferred levels of explanation—for example, a theory that characterizes culturally-unique emotional states among the Ilongots of the Philippines (Rosaldo, 1984). Equally, it cannot be assumed that more generalized or global levels of explanation are inherently preferable, such as a theory that characterizes types of emotional states found generally in cultures emphasizing interdependent cultural views of the self (e.g., Markus & Kitayama, 1994b). Rather, the choice of an appropriate level of generality depends on the theoretical questions under consideration.

More generally, it may be argued that it is important, as a collective endeavor, for approaches in cultural psychology as well as in social constructionism to adopt pragmatic rather than either essentialist or encyclopedic views of explanation (White, 1963). There is no one type of explanation or explanatory construct that is preferred in all cases in some absolute sense. Neither is there a simple way in which explanatory constructs and approaches may be additively combined to provide explanations that are more adequate by virtue of being more complete. Rather, the adequacy of explanations depends on their success in answering the particular theoretical question under consideration (Wertsch, 1995a).[2]

In terms of *methodological adequacy*, a concern with agency and with meaning may be expected to be a feature of methodological procedures adopted in cultural psychology, if not also in social constructionism. This concern reflects a recognition of the active role of individuals in contributing meaning to experience, and thus of the need to take into account that constructions of experience may be idiosyncratic to the individual while also reflecting cultural meanings. The concern with agency and with meaning also needs to be self-directed, with investigators sensitive to the biases that they contribute to their investigations as well as to the limitations inherent in all modes of scientific inquiry.

In addition, it is important for methodological approaches in cultural psychology and social constructionism to be eclectic by drawing on multiple disciplinary and research traditions (J. G. Miller, 1994a). The same pragmatic stance applied at a theoretical level in formulating constructs obtains at a methodological level. The stance that all methodological approaches must employ interpretive techniques that make use of indigenous language distinctions is just as one-sided as the stance that all approaches must be comparative or experimental in nature. It must be recognized that methodological strategies bring with them their own characteristic strengths and weaknesses, and that decisions about their relative utility or adequacy can only be answered in relation to the questions under consideration (Campbell & Naroll, 1972).

Future Directions

The present overview of cultural psychology and social constructionist approaches has highlighted the dynamic character of these emerging fields. It has been seen that the perspectives in these traditions are characterized by broad, although not complete, agreement on the conceptual problems that need to be addressed. Theoretically innovative in nature, this work has a self-reflective quality, as investigators struggle to articulate new ways of understanding the mutual constitution of culture and the self and to contribute to the creation of the emerging traditions of cultural psychology and, in the case particularly of social constructionist approaches, of postmodernism.

In future work in this area, diverse types of relationships need to be cultivated between the specific approaches represented. In certain cases perspectives that share many of their basic conceptual presuppositions pose different answers to the same theoretical problems. In such instances, it would be expected that direct interchange can valuably be undertaken between the viewpoints. For example, in working to formulate culturally grounded theories of self, anthropological/self perspectives may be enhanced by drawing on theories of self formulated within psychological/self perspectives that appear to be less parochial. In turn, certain psychological/self perspectives stand to be enriched by incorporating some of the focus on interaction and on social practices emphasized in work from anthropological/self perspectives.

In other cases, perspectives that share basic assumptions direct their attention to contrasting issues. In such cases, the relationships between the perspectives must be recognized as complementary, with each viewpoint providing certain insights that are not apparent from the other viewpoint. This type of complementary situation may be seen to arise in cases in which perspectives are applied in addressing diverse issues. For example, with the exception of action theory that focuses on a wide range of content areas, most approaches in cultural psychology and in social constructionism have centered primarily on either cognition or on the self and not on both. With this intellectual division of labor, there is a need to integrate findings from multiple perspectives in order to gain a comprehensive understanding of the cultural grounding of psychological processes.

Complementary situations also arise in cases in which perspectives that share many of their basic tenets focus on contrasting aspects of the same problems because of their interest in speaking to different issues and/or audiences. For example, much of the interest in cultural variation in self linked to the broad individualism/collectivism distinction within work from a psychological/self perspective, arises from an interest in speaking to mainstream psychological investigators who start from a view of psychological processes as universal and for whom evidence of cross-cultural variability in psychological functioning is unexpected. In contrast, much of the interest in exploring individual variation in the motivational force of local cultural schemata, within work from an anthropological/self perspective, arises from a concern with speaking to anthropological investigators who, while taking the existence of cultural variation in the self for granted, question the need for attention to psychological considerations in understanding culture.

Finally, cases exist in which approaches focus on the same questions but maintain markedly divergent conceptual assumptions. In such instances, a certain incommensurability occurs as findings from one approach are interpreted in markedly different terms from the perspective of the other approach. In this type of case, a simple interchange between the divergent viewpoints is not possible and findings are not directly complementary across viewpoints. In such cases, however, it still may be expected that valuable shifts in understandings can take place through the process of dialogue. For example, whereas both social constructionist approaches and sociocultural approaches focus on understanding processes of interaction in the context of everyday social practices, they draw contrasting conclusions about the psychological implications of their observations. However, each perspective stands to be enriched through ongoing debates that are occurring between them—even if no position of uniformity results as an end product of such argumentation.

More generally, it may be argued that it is important to avoid a position that privileges one particular theoretical approach or mode of understanding as the sole direction to be taken in future research, dismissing other approaches as providing little or no insight. Rather, the present considerations highlight the importance of extending the relativistic perspective that cultural approaches apply to understanding diverse cultural traditions and practices to the field as a whole. Emphasis needs to be placed on cultivating an appreciation of the strengths and weaknesses of the varied conceptual and disciplinary traditions within cultural psychology and social constructionism as well as within cross-cultural psychology. Theoretical and methodological heterogeneity may be expected to be a permanent feature of cultural approaches to psychology and not merely a reflection of temporary growing pains. Such heterogeneity not only represents a strength of cultural approaches to psychology but constitutes a feature that is required to provide answers to the complex problems motivating work in this field.

Endnotes

1. The use of the term "self" rather than "person" reflects the concern with understanding the individual as a knowing agent who is capable of volition and reflection, rather than as an entity that is incapable of self-awareness (Hallowell, 1955).

2. This type of argument has been made, for example, by Berry (1989) in underscoring the respective strengths of both single culture approaches, that rely on concepts formulated by an observer.

References

Austin, J. L. (1962). *How to do things with words.* Oxford: Clarendon Press.

Bakhtin, M. M. (1986). *Speech genres and other late essays.* (C. Emerson & M. Holquist, Eds., V. W. McGee, Trans.) Austin: University of Texas Press.

Bandura, A. (1977). *Social learning theory.* Englewood Cliffs, NJ: Prentice-Hall.

Bendix, R. (1970). The pitfalls of personality reductionism: Compliant behavior and individual personality. In N. J. Smelser & W. T. Smelser (Eds.), *Personality and Social Systems* (2nd ed., pp. 100–113). New York: Wiley.

Benedict, R. (1946). *The chrysanthemum and the sword.* Boston: Houghton Mifflin.

Berry, J. W. (1989). Imposed etics-emics-derived etics: The operationalization of a compelling idea. *International Journal of Psychology, 24,* 721–735.

Berry, J. W. & Dasen, P. R. (Eds.). (1974). *Culture and cognition: Readings in cross-cultural psychology.* London: Methuen.

Berry, J. W., Poortinga, Y. H., Segall, M. H. & Dasen, P. R. (1992). *Cross-cultural psychology: Research and applications.* Cambridge: Cambridge University Press.

Bock, P. K. (1988). *Rethinking psychological anthropology: Continuity and change in the study of human action.* New York: Freeman.

Bock, P. K. (1994). Conclusions: Toward the twenty-first century. In P. K. Bock (Ed.), *Handbook of psychological anthropology* (pp. 379–82). Westport, CT: Greenwood Press.

Boesch, E. E. (1987). Cultural psychology in action-theoretical perspective. In C. Kagitçibasi (Ed.), *Growth and progress in cultural psychology* (pp. 41–51). Berlin: Springer.

Boesch, E. E. (1991). *Symbolic action theory and cultural psychology.* Berlin: Springer.

Bourdieu, P. (1977). *Outline of a theory of practice* (R. Nice, Trans.). Cambridge: Cambridge University Press.

Bruner, J. (1990). *Acts of meaning.* Cambridge, MA: Harvard University Press.

Buss, A. R. (1975). The emerging field of the sociology of psychological knowledge. *American Psychologist, 30,* 988–1002.

Butler, J. (1990). Gender trouble, feminist theory and psychoanalytic discourse. In L. Nicholson (Ed.), *Feminism/Postmodernism* (pp. 324–340). London: Routledge & Kegan Paul.

Campbell, D. T. & Naroll, R. (1972). The mutual methodological relevance of anthropology and psychology. In F. L. Hsu (Ed.), *Psychological anthropology* (pp. 435–468). Cambridge: Schenkmane Publishing Co.

Cancian, F. (1975). *What are norms?* Cambridge: Cambridge University Press.

Chomsky, N. (1968). *Language and mind.* New York: Harcourt Brace Jovanovich.

Cole, M. (1988). Cross-cultural research in the sociohistorical tradition. *Human Development, 31,* 137–157.

Cole, M. (1990). Cultural psychology: A once and future discipline? In R. A. Dienstbier & J. Berman (Eds.), *Nebraska Symposium on Motivation* (pp. 279–335). Lincoln, NE: University of Nebraska Press.

Cole, M. (1995). Culture and cognitive development: From cross-cultural research to creating systems of cultural mediation. *Culture and Psychology, 1,* 25–54.

Cole, M., & Engestrom, Y. (1993). A cultural-historical approach to distributed cognition. In

G. Salomon (Ed.), *Distributed cognitions: Psychological and educational considerations* (pp. 1–46). Cambridge: Cambridge University Press.

Cole, M. & Engestrom, Y. (1995). "Mind, culture, person: Elements in a cultural psychology": Comment. *Human Development, 38,* 19–24.

Cole, M., & Griffin, P. (1980). Cultural amplifiers reconsidered. In D.R. Olson (Ed.), *The social foundations of language and thought* (pp. 343–364). New York: Norton.

Costanzo, P. R. (1991). Morals, mothers, and memories: The social context of developing social cognition. In R. Cohen & A. W. Siegel (Eds.), *Context and development* (pp. 91–132). Hillsdale, NJ: Erlbaum.

Cousins, S. D. (1989). Culture and self-perception in Japan and the United States. *Journal of Personality and Social Psychology, 56,* 124–131.

D'Andrade, R.G. (1976). A propositional analysis of U.S. American beliefs about illness. In K. H. Basso & H. A. Selby (Eds.), *Meaning in anthropology* (pp. 155–180). Albuquerque, NM: University of New Mexico Press.

D'Andrade, R. G. (1984). Cultural meaning systems. In R. A. Shweder & R. A. LeVine (Eds.), *Culture theory: Essays on mind, self, and emotion* (pp. 88–119). New York: Cambridge University Press.

D'Andrade, R. G. (1992). Schemas and motivation. In R. G. D'Andrade & C. Strauss (Eds.), *Human motives and cultural models* (pp. 23–44). Cambridge: Cambridge University Press.

D'Andrade. R. G., & Strauss, C. (Eds.). (1992). *Human motives and cultural models.* Cambridge: Cambridge University Press.

Davies, B., & Harré, R. (1990). Positioning: The discursive production of selves. *Journal for the Theory of Social Behavior, 20,* 43–63.

Derne, S. (1992). Beyond institutional and impulsive conceptions of self: Family structure and the socially anchored real self. *Ethos, 20,* 259–288.

Dumont, L. (1970). *Homo hierarchicus: An essay on the caste system.* Chicago: University of Chicago Press.

Durkheim, E. (1961). *Moral education: A study in the theory and application of the sociology of education.* (E. K. Wilson and H. Schnurer, Trans., E. K. Wilson, Ed.). New York: Free Press.

Eckensberger, L. H. (1981). On a structural model of the development of stages of moral development. In L. Oppenheimer (Ed.), *Action theoretical approaches to (developmental) psychology.* Report No. 81.

Eckensberger, L. H. (1990a). On the necessity of the culture concept in psychology: A view from cross-cultural psychology. In F. J. van de Vijver & J. Hutschemaekers (Eds.), *The investigation of culture: Current issues in cultural psychology* (pp. 153–183). The Netherlands: Tilburg University Press.

Eckensberger, L. H. (1990b). From cross-cultural to cultural psychology. *Quarterly Newsletter of the Laboratory of Comparative Human Cognition, 1,* 37–52.

Eckensberger, L. H. (1995). Activity or action: Two different roads towards an integration of culture into psychology? *Culture and Psychology, 1,* 67–80.

Eckensberger, L. H., & Meacham, J. A. (Eds.). (1984). Action theory, control and motivation: A symposium. *Human Development, 27,* 163–210.

Edwards, D. (1995). A commentary on discursive and cultural psychology. *Culture and Psychology, 1,* 55–66.

Edwards, D., & Potter, J. (1992). *Discursive psychology.* London: Sage.

Engestrom, Y. (1993). Developmental studies of work as a testbench of activity theory: The case of primary care medical practice. In S. Chaiklin & J. Lave (Eds.), *Understanding practice: Perspectives on activity and context* (pp. 64–103). Cambridge: Cambridge University Press.

Ewing, K. P. (1992). Is psychoanalysis relevant for anthropology? In T. Schwartz, G. M. White, & C. A. Lutz (Eds.), *New directions in psychological anthropology* (pp.251–268). Cambridge: Cambridge University Press.

Feldman, C., Bruner, J., Kalmar, D., & Renderer, B. (1993). Plot, plight and dramatism: Interpretation at three ages. *Human Development, 36,* 327–342.

Fiske, A. P. (1991). *Structures of social life: The four elementary forms of human relations.* New York: Free Press.

Fiske, A. P. (1992). Four elementary forms of sociality: Framework for a unified theory of social relations. *Psychological Review, 99,* 689–723.

Flavell, J. H. (1982). Structures, stages, and sequences in cognitive development. In W. A. Collins (Ed.), *Minnesota Symposia on Child Psychology (Vol. 15,* pp.1–28). Hillsdale, NJ: Erlbaum.

Foucault, M. (1977). *Discipline and punish: The birth of the prison.* (A. Sheridan, Trans.). New York: Random House.

Frijda, N. H. (1986). *The emotions.* Cambridge: Cambridge University Press.

Gauvain, M. (1995). Thinking in niches: Sociocultural influences on cognitive development. *Human Development, 38,* 25–45.

Geertz, C. (1973). *The interpretation of cultures.* New York: Basic Books.

Geertz, C. (1984). "From the native's point of view": On the nature of anthropological understanding. In R. A. Shweder & R. A. LeVine (Eds.), *Culture theory: Essays on mind, self, and emotion.* (pp.123–136). New York: Cambridge University Press.

Gelman, R., & Baillargeon, R. (1983). A review of some Piagetian concepts. In J. H. Flavell & E. M. Markman (Eds.), *Cognitive development: Vol. 3 of P. Mussen (Ed.), Manual of child psychology* (pp. 167–230). New York: Wiley.

Gergen, K. J. (1982). *Toward transformation in social knowledge.* (R. F. Kidd, Ed.). New York: Springer.

Gergen, K. J. (1986). Interpreting the texts of nature and culture: A reply to Jahoda. *European Journal of Social Psychology, 16,* 31–37.

Gergen, K. J. (1991). *The saturated self.* New York: Basic Books.

Gergen, K. J. (1992). Psychology in the postmodern era. *The General Psychologist, 28,* 10-15.

Gergen, K. J. (1994). *Realities and relationships: Soundings in social construction.* Cambridge, MA: Harvard University Press.

Gergen, K. J., & Gergen, M. M. (1988). Narrative and the self as relationship. In L. Berkowitz (Ed.), *Advances in experimental social psychology (Vol. 21,* pp. 17–56). New York: Academic Press.

Gergen, K. J., Gloger-Tippelt, G., & Berkowitz, P. (1990). The cultural construction of the developing child. In G. R. Semin & K. J. Gergen

(Eds.), *Everyday understanding: Social and scientific implications* (pp. 108–129). Newbury Park, CA: Sage.

Giddens, A. (1979). *Central problems in social theory.* Los Angeles: University of California Press.

Glick, J. (1991). Postmodern psychology: Cultural psychology and apprenticeship. *Cognitive Development, 6,* 343–353.

Good, B. J. (1994). *Medicine, rationality, and experience: An anthropological perspective.* New York: Cambridge University Press.

Goodnow, J. J. (1990). The socialization of cognition: What's involved? In J. W. Stigler, R. A. Shweder, & G. Herdt (Eds.), *Cultural psychology: Essays on comparative human development* (pp. 259–286). New York: Cambridge University Press.

Greenfield, P. M. (1994). Independence and interdependence as developmental scripts: Implications for theory, research, and practice. In P. M. Greenfield & R. R. Cocking (Eds.), *Cross-cultural roots of minority child development* (pp. 1–40). Hillsdale, NJ: Erlbaum.

Greenwood, J. D. (1994). *Realism, identity and emotion.* London: Sage.

Gulerce, A. (1995). Culture and self in postmodern psychology: Dialogue in trouble? (An interview with K. J. Gergen). *Culture and Psychology, 1,* 147–159.

Hallowell, A. I. (1955). The self and its behavioral environment. In A. I. Hallowell, *Culture and experience* (pp. 75–110). Philadelphia: University of Pennsylvania Press.

Hallpike, C. R. (1979). *The foundations of primitive thought.* New York: Oxford University Press.

Hamlyn, D. W. (1971). Epistemology and conceptual development. In W. Mischel (Ed.), *Cognitive development and epistemology* (pp. 3–24). New York: Academic Press.

Harkness, S., & Super, C. M. (1983). The cultural construction of child development: A framework for the socialization of affect. *Ethos, 11,* 221–231.

Harkness, S., & Super, C. M. (1985). Child-environment interactions in the socialization of affect. In M. Lewis & C. Saarni (Eds.), *The socialization of emotions* (pp. 21–36). New York: Plenum.

Harkness, S., & Super, C. M. (1996). Ask the doctor: The negotiation of cultural models in

American parent-pediatrician discourse. In S. Harkness & C. M Super (Eds.), *Parents' cultural belief systems: Their origins, expressions, and consequences* (pp. 289–310). New York: Guilford Press.

Harkness, S., & Super, C. M. (in press). Parental ethnotheories in action. In E. Sigel (Ed.), *Parental belief systems: The psychological consequences for children and families* (2nd ed.). Hillsdale, NJ: Erlbaum.

Harkness, S., Super, C. M., & Keefer, C. H. (1992). Learning to be an American parent: How cultural models gain directive form. In R. D'Andrade & C. Strauss (Eds.), *Human motives and cultural models* (pp. 163–178). Cambridge: Cambridge University Press.

Harré, R. (1984). *Personal being: A theory for individual psychology.* Cambridge, MA: Harvard University Press.

Harré, R. (Ed.). (1986). *The social construction of emotions.* New York: Basil Blackwell.

Harris, P. L. (1991). Uneasy union and neglected children: Cultural psychology and its prospects. *Current Anthropology, 32,* 82–89.

Harwood, R. H., Miller, J. G. & Lucca, N. (1995). *Culture and attachment: Perceptions of the child in context.* Series on Culture and Human Development, S. Harkness & C. Super (Series Eds.). New York: Guilford Press.

Heath, S. B. (1983). *Ways with words: Language, life and work in communities and classrooms.* Cambridge: Cambridge University Press.

Heath, S. B. (1990). The children of Trackton's children: Spoken and written language in social change. In J. W. Stigler, R. A. Shweder, & G. Herdt (Eds.), *Cultural psychology: Essays on comparative human development* (pp. 496–519). New York: Cambridge University Press.

Heelas, P., & Lock, A. (Eds.). (1981). *Indigenous psychologies: The anthropology of the self.* London: Academic Press.

Heine, S. J., & Lehman, D. R. (1995). Cultural variation in unrealistic optimism: Does the west feel more invulnerable than the east? *Journal of Personality and Social Psychology, 68,* 595–607.

Herskovits, M. J. (1948). *Man and his works.* New York: Knopf.

Hofstede, G. (1980). *Culture's consequences.* Beverly Hills, CA: Sage.

Holland, D. (1992). How cultural systems become desire: A case study of American romance. In R. D'Andrade & C. Strauss (Eds.), *Human motives and cultural models* (pp. 61–89). Cambridge: Cambridge University Press.

Holland, D., & Quinn, N. (Eds.). (1987). *Cultural models in language and thought.* New York: Cambridge University Press.

Inkeles, A., & Smith, D.H. (1974). *Becoming modern: Individual change in six developing countries.* Cambridge, MA: Harvard University Press.

Jahoda, G. (1980). Theoretical and systematic approaches in cross-cultural psychology. In H. Triandis & W. Lambert (Eds.), *Handbook of cross-cultural psychology* (Vol. 1, pp. 69–141). Boston: Allyn and Bacon.

Jahoda, G. (1986a). Language games, or As you like it: A reply to Gergen. *European Journal of Social Psychology, 16,* 39–42.

Jahoda, G. (1986b). Nature, culture and social psychology. *European Journal of Social Psychology, 16,* 17–30.

Jahoda, G. (1990). Our forgotten ancestors. In J. J. Berman (Ed.), *Nebraska Symposium on Motivation: Vol. 37. Cultural perspectives* (pp.1–40). Lincoln, NE: University of Nebraska Press.

Jahoda, G. (1993a). *Crossroads between culture and mind: Continuities and change in theories of human nature.* Cambridge, MA: Harvard University Press.

Jahoda, G. (1993b). The colour of a chameleon: Perspectives on concepts of 'culture'. *Cultural Dynamics, 6,* 277–287.

Jenkins, J. H. (1994). Culture, emotion, and psychopathology. In S. Kitayama & H. R. Markus (Eds.), *Emotion and culture: Empirical studies of mutual influence* (pp. 307–335). Washington, DC: American Psychological Association.

Kessen, W. (1984). Introduction: The end of the age of development. In R. Sternberg (Ed.), *Mechanisms of cognitive development* (pp.1–17). New York: W. H. Freeman.

Kessen, W. (1990). *The rise and fall of development.* Worcester, MA: Clark University Press.

Keyes, C. F. (1983). Introduction: Popular ideas of karma. In C. F. Keyes & E. V. Daniel (Eds.), *Karma* (pp. 1–24). Berkeley, CA: University of California Press.

Kitayama, S., & Markus, H.R. (Eds.). (1994). *Emotion and culture: Empirical studies of mutual influence.* Washington, DC: American Psychological Association.

Kleinman, A. (1980). *Patients and healers in the context of culture: An exploration of the borderland between anthropology, medicine and psychiatry.* Berkeley, CA: University of California Press.

Kleinman, A. (1986). *Social origins of distress and disease: Depression, neurasthenia, and pain in modern China.* New Haven, CT: Yale University Press.

Kroeber, A. L., & Kluckhohn, C. (1952/1963). *Culture: A critical review of concepts and definitions.* Cambridge, MA: Harvard University Press.

Laboratory of Comparative Human Cognition. (1983). Culture and cognitive development. In W. Kessen & P. H. Mussen (Eds.), *Handbook of child psychology: History, theory and method* (pp. 295–356). New York: Wiley.

Lave, J. (1988). *Cognition in practice: Mind, mathematics, and culture in everyday life.* Cambridge: Cambridge University Press.

Lave, J. (1993). The practice of learning. In S. Chaiklin & J. Lave (Eds.), *Understanding practice: Perspectives on activity and context* (pp. 3–32). Cambridge: Cambridge University Press.

Lave, J., Murtaugh, M., & de la Rocha, O. (1984). The dialectic of arithmetic in grocery shopping. In B. Rogoff & J. Lave (Eds.), *Everyday cognition: Its development in social context* (pp. 67–94). Cambridge, MA: Harvard University Press.

Lave, J., & Wenger, E. (1991). *Situated learning: Legitimate peripheral participation.* Cambridge: Cambridge University Press.

Leontiev, A. N. (1979a). The problem of activity in psychology. In J. V. Wertsch (Ed.), *The concept of activity in Soviet psychology* (pp. 37–71). Armonk, NY: M. E. Sharpe.

Leontiev, A.N. (1979b). Sign and activity. In J. V. Wertsch (Ed.), *The concept of activity in Soviet psychology* (pp. 241–255). Armonk, NY: M. E. Sharpe.

LeVine, R. A. (1973). *Culture, behavior, and personality.* Chicago: Aldine.

LeVine, R. A. (1984). Properties of culture: An ethnographic view. In R. A. Shweder & R. A. LeVine (Eds.), *Culture theory: Essays on mind, self, and emotion* (pp.67–87). New York: Cambridge University Press.

LeVine, R. A. (1990). Infant environments in psychoanalysis: A cross cultural view. In J. W. Stigler, R. A. Shweder, & G. Herdt (Eds.), *Cultural psychology: Essays on comparative human development* (pp. 454–474). New York: Cambridge University Press.

LeVine, R. A., Dixon, S., LeVine, S., Richman, A., Leiderman, P. H., Keefer, C., & Brazelton, T. B. (1994). *Child care and culture: Lessons from Africa.* Cambridge: Cambridge University Press.

Lonner, W. J. (1980). The search for psychological universals. In H. C. Triandis & W. W. Lambert (Eds.), *Handbook of Cross-Cultural Psychology* (Vol 1, pp. 143–204). Boston: Allyn and Bacon.

Luria, A. R. (1979). *The making of mind: A personal account of Soviet psychology.* (M. Cole & S. Cole, Eds.). Cambridge, MA: Harvard University Press.

Luria A. R. (1981). *Language and cognition.* (J. V. Wertsch, Ed., Trans.). New York: Wiley.

Lutz, C., & White, G. M. (1986). The anthropology of emotions. *Annual Review of Anthropology, 15,* 405–436.

Markus, H., & Kitayama, S. (1991). Culture and the self: Implications for cognition, emotion and motivation. *Psychological Review, 98,* 224–253.

Markus, H. R., & Kitayama, S. (1994a). A collective fear of the collective: Implications for selves and theories of selves. *Personality and Social Psychology Bulletin, 20,* 568–579.

Markus, H. R., & Kitayama, S. (1994b). The cultural construction of self and emotion: Implications for social behavior. In S. Kitayama and H. R. Markus (Eds.), *Emotion and culture: Empirical studies of mutual influence* (pp. 89–130). Washington, DC: American Psychological Association.

Markus, H. R., & Kitayama, S. (1994c). The cultural shaping of emotion: A conceptual framework. In S. Kitayama & H. R. Markus (Eds.), *Emotion and culture: Empirical studies of mutual influence* (pp. 241–284). Washington, DC: American Psychological Association.

Markus, H., & Zajonc, R. B. (1985). The cognitive

perspective in social psychology. In G. Lindzey & E. Aronson (Eds.), *Handbook of social psychology* (3rd ed., Vol. 1, pp. 137–230). New York: Random House.

Marsella, A. J., DeVos, G., & Hsu, F. L. (Eds.). (1985). *Culture and self: Asian and Western perspectives.* New York: Tavistock.

McClosky,H., & Brill, A. (1983). *Dimensions of tolerance: What Americans believe about civil liberties.* New York: Sage.

McDermott, R. P. (1993). The acquisition of a child by a learning disability. In S. Chaiklin & J. Lave (Eds.), *Understanding practice: Perspectives on activity and context* (pp. 269–305). Cambridge: Cambridge University Press.

McNamee, A., & Gergen, K. J. (1992). *Therapy as social construction.* Newbury Park, CA: Sage.

Middleton, D., & Edwards, D. (Eds.). (1990). *Collective remembering.* London: Sage.

Miller, D. T., & Prentice, D. A. (1994). The self and the collective [Special issue]. *Personality and Social Psychology Bulletin, 20.*

Miller, J. G. (1984). Culture and the development of everyday social explanation. *Journal of Personality and Social Psychology, 46,* 961–978.

Miller, J. G. (1986). Early cross-cultural commonalities in social explanation. *Developmental Psychology, 22,* 514–520.

Miller, J. G. (1988). Bridging the content-structure dichotomy: Culture and the self. In M. H. Bond, *The cross cultural challenge to social psychology* (pp. 266–281). Newbury Park, CA: Sage.

Miller, J. G. (1994a). Cultural psychology: Bridging disciplinary boundaries in understanding the cultural grounding of self. In P. K. Bock (Ed.), *Handbook of psychological anthropology* (pp. 139–170). Westport, CT: Greenwood Press.

Miller, J. G. (1994b). Cultural diversity in the morality of caring: Individually oriented versus duty-based interpersonal moral codes. *Cross-Cultural Research, 28,* 3-39.

Miller, J. G. (1996). A cultural psychology perspective on intelligence. In R. J. Sternberg & E. L. Grigorenko (Eds.), *Intelligence, heredity, and environment* (pp. 269–302). Cambridge: Cambridge University Press.

Miller, J. G., & Bersoff, D. M. (1992). Culture and moral judgment: How are conflicts between justice and interpersonal responsibilities resolved? *Journal of Personality and Social Psychology, 62,* 541–554.

Miller, J. G., & Bersoff, D. M. (1994). Cultural influences on the moral status of reciprocity and the discounting of endogenous motivation. *Personality and Social Psychology Bulletin, 20,* 592–602.

Miller, J. G., & Bersoff, D. M. (1995). Development in the context of everyday family relationships: Culture, interpersonal morality, and adaption. In M. Killen & D. Hart (Eds.), *Morality in everyday life: A developmental perspective* (pp. 259–282). Cambridge: Cambridge University Press.

Miller, P. J. (1982). *Amy, Wendy and Beth: Learning language in south Baltimore.* Austin: University of Texas Press.

Mischel, W. (1968). *Personality and assessment.* New York: Wiley.

Mischel, W. (1973). Towards a cognitive social learning reconceptualization of personality. *Psychological Review, 80,* 252–283.

Mischel, W., & Peake, P. K. (1982). Beyond déja vu in the search for cross-situational consistency. *Psychological Review, 89,* 730–755.

Misra, G., & Gergen, K. J. (1993). On the place of culture in psychological science. *International Journal of Psychology, 28,* 225–243.

Morawski, J. G. (1994). *Practicing feminisms, reconstructing psychology: Notes on a liminal science.* Ann Arbor: University of Michigan Press.

Morelli, G. A., Rogoff, B., Oppenheim, D., & Goldsmith, D. (1992). Cultural variation in infants' sleeping arrangements: Questions of independence. *Developmental Psychology, 28,* 604–613.

Morris, M. W. & Peng, K. (1994). Culture and cause: American and Chinese attributions for social and physical events. *Journal of Personality & Social Psychology, 67,* 949–971.

Nisbett, R. E. (Ed.). (1993). *Rules for reasoning.* Hillsdale, NJ: Erlbaum.

Nisbett, R. E., & Ross, L. (1980). *Human inference: Strategies and shortcomings of social judgment.* Englewood Cliffs, NJ: Prentice-Hall.

Ochs, E. (1988). *Culture and language development: Language acquisition and language socialization in a Samoan village.* Cambridge: Cambridge University Press.

Ochs, E. (1990). Indexicality and socialization. In J. W. Stigler, R. A. Shweder, & G. Herdt (Eds.), *Cultural psychology: Essays on comparative human development* (pp. 287–308). New York: Cambridge University Press.

Ochs, E., & Schieffelin, B. B. (1984). Language acquisition and socialization: Three developmental stories and their implications. In R. A. Shweder & R. A. LeVine (Eds.), *Culture theory: Essays on mind, self, and emotion* (pp. 276–320). New York: Cambridge University Press.

Olson, D. (1995). Writing and the mind. In J. V. Wertsch, P. del Rio, & A. Alvarez (Eds.), *Sociocultural studies of mind* (pp. 95–123). New York: Oxford University Press.

Osgood, C. E., May, W. H., & Miron, M. S. (1975). *Cross-cultural universals of affective meaning.* Urbana: University of Illinois Press.

Parsons, T. (1961). *Social structure and the development of personality: Studying personality cross-culturally.* (B. Kaplan, Ed.). Evanston, IL: Row, Peterson.

Penuel, W. R., & Werstch, J. V. (1995). Vygotsky and identity formation: A sociocultural approach. Unpublished manuscript.

Pepitone, A. (1978). Toward a normative and comparative biocultural social psychology. *Journal of Personality and Social Psychology, 34,* 641–653.

Pepitone, A., & Triandis, H. C. (1987). On the universality of social psychological theories. *Journal of Cross-Cultural Psychology, 18,* 471–499.

Piaget, J. (1966). Need and significance of cross-cultural studies in genetic psychology. *International Journal of Psychology, 1,* 3–13.

Piaget, J. (1968). *Six psychological studies.* (A. Tenzer, Trans.). New York: Vintage Books.

Piaget, J. (1970). Piaget's theory. In P. H. Mussen (Ed.), *Carmichael's manual of child psychology,* Vol. 1. New York: Wiley.

Potter, J., & Wetherell, M. (1987). *Discourse and social psychology: Beyond attitudes and behaviour.* London: Sage.

Price-Williams, D. (1980). Toward the idea of a cultural psychology: A superordinate theme for study. *Journal of Cross Cultural Psychology, 11,* 75–88.

Quinn, N. (1992). The motivational force of self-understanding: Evidence from wives' inner conflicts. In R. D'Andrade & C. Strauss (Eds.), *Human motives and cultural models* (pp. 90–126). Cambridge: Cambridge University Press.

Radcliffe-Brown, A.R. (1965). *Structure and function in primitive society: Essays and addresses.* New York: Free Press.

Redfield, R. (1956). *Peasant society and culture: An anthropological approach to civilization.* Chicago: University of Chicago Press.

Robinson, D. N. (Ed.). (1992). *Social discourse and moral judgement.* New York: Academic Press.

Rogoff, B. (1990). *Apprenticeship in thinking: Cognitive development in social context.* New York: Oxford University Press.

Rogoff, B. (1992). Three ways to relate person and culture: Thoughts sparked by Valsiner's review of *Apprenticeship in thinking. Human Development, 35,* 316–320.

Rogoff, B. (1995). Observing sociocultural activity on three planes: Participatory appropriation, guided participation, apprenticeship. In J. V. Wertsch, P. del Rio, & A. Alvarez (Eds.), *Sociocultural studies of mind.* New York: Cambridge University Press.

Rogoff, B. (in press). Developmental transitions in children's participation in sociocultural activities. In A. Sameroff & M. Haith (Eds.), *Reason and responsibility: The passage through childhood.* Chicago: University of Chicago Press.

Rogoff, B., & Lave, J. (Eds.). (1984). *Everyday cognition: Its development in social context.* Cambridge, MA: Harvard University Press.

Rogoff, B., Mistry, J., Gonku, A., & Mosier, C. (1993). Guided participation in cultural activity by toddlers and caregivers. *Monographs of the Society for Research in Child Development, 58* (No. 7, Serial no. 236).

Roland, A. (1988). *In search of self in India and Japan: Toward a cross-cultural psychology.* Princeton, NJ: Princeton University Press.

Rosaldo, M. Z. (1984). Toward an anthropology of self and feeling. In R. A. Shweder & R. A. LeVine (Eds.), *Culture theory: Essays on mind, self, and emotion* (pp. 137–157). New York: Cambridge University Press.

Rosenberger, N. R. (Ed.). (1992). *Japanese sense of self.* London: Cambridge University Press.

Rummelhart, D., McClelland, J. & the PDP Research Group (1986). *Parallel distributed processing, Vol I: Foundations.* Cambridge, MA: MIT Press.

Russell, J. A. (1991). Culture and the categorization of emotions. *Psychological Bulletin, 110,* 426-450.

Sahlins, M. (1976a). *The use and abuse of biology: An anthropological critique of sociobiology.* Ann Arbor: University of Michigan Press.

Sahlins, M. (1976b). *Culture and practical reason.* Chicago: University of Chicago Press.

Salomon, G. (Ed.). (1993). *Distributed cognitions: Psychological and educational considerations.* Cambridge: Cambridge University Press.

Sampson, E. E. (1993). *Celebrating the other: A dialogic account of human nature.* London: Harvester Wheatsheaf.

Sass, L. A. (1992). The epic of disbelief: The postmodernist turn in contemporary psychoanalysis. In S. Kvale (Ed.), *Psychology and postmodernism* (pp.166–182). London: Sage.

Saxe, G. B. (1991). *Culture and cognitive development: Studies in mathematical understanding.* Hillsdale, NJ: Erlbaum.

Scheper-Hughes, S. (1990). Mother love and child death in northeast Brazil. In J. W. Stigler, R. A. Shweder, & G. Herdt (Eds.), *Cultural psychology: Essays on comparative human development* (pp. 542–565). New York: Cambridge University Press.

Schieffelin, B. B., & Ochs, E. (Eds.). (1986). *Language socialization across cultures.* Cambridge: Cambridge University Press.

Schneider, D. (1968). *American kinship: A cultural account.* Englewood Cliffs, NJ: Prentice-Hall.

Schneider, D. (1976). Notes toward a theory of culture. In K. Basso & H. Selby (Eds.), *Meaning in anthropology* (pp. 197–220). Albuquerque, NM: University of New Mexico Press.

Schwartz, T. (1981). The acquisition of culture. *Ethos, 9,* 4–17.

Schwartz, T. (1992). Anthropology and psychology: An unrequited relationship. In T. Schwartz, G. M. White, & C. Lutz (Eds.), *New directions in psychological anthropology* (pp. 324–349). New York: Cambridge University Press.

Schwartz, T., White, G. M., & Lutz, C. (Eds.). (1992). *New directions in psychological anthropology.* New York: Cambridge University Press.

Scribner, S. (1984). Studying working intelligence. In B. Rogoff & J. Lave (Eds.), *Everyday cognition: Its development in social context* (pp. 9–40). Cambridge, MA: Harvard University Press.

Searle, J. R. (1969). *Speech acts: An essay in the philosophy of language.* Cambridge: Cambridge University Press.

Segall, M. H. (1983). On the search for the independent variable in cross-cultural psychology. In S. H. Irvine & J. W. Berry (Eds.), *Human assessment and cultural factors* (pp. 127–138). New York: Plenum.

Segall, M. H. (1993). Cultural psychology: Reactions to some claims and assertions of dubious validity. *Cross-Cultural Psychology Bulletin, 27,* 2–4.

Semin, G. R., & Gergen K. J. (Eds.). (1990). *Everyday understanding: Social and scientific implications.* London: Sage.

Serpell, R. (1993). *The significance of schooling: Life-journeys in an African society.* Cambridge: Cambridge University Press.

Shotter, J. (1993). *Cultural politics of everyday life: Social constructionism, rhetoric and knowing of the third kind.* Buckingham, England: Open University Press.

Shotter, J., & Gergen, K. J. (Eds.). (1989). *Texts of identity.* London: Sage.

Shweder, R. A. (1979a). Rethinking culture and personality theory. Part I: A critical examination of two classical postulates. *Ethos, 7,* 255–279.

Shweder, R. A. (1979b). Rethinking culture and personality theory. Part II: A critical examination of two more classical postulates. *Ethos, 7,* 279–311.

Shweder, R. A. (1984). Anthropology's romantic rebellion against the enlightenment, or there's more to thinking than reason and evidence. In R. A. Shweder & R. A. Levine (Eds.), *Culture theory: Essays on mind, self, and emotion* (pp. 27–66). New York: Cambridge University Press.

Shweder, R.A. (1990). Cultural psychology—what is it? In J. W. Stigler, R. A. Shweder, & G. Herdt (Eds.), *Cultural psychology: Essays on comparative human development* (pp. 1–43). New York: Cambridge University Press.

Shweder, R. A. (1991). Post-Nietzschean anthropology: The idea of multiple objective worlds. In R. A. Shweder, *Thinking through cultures: Expeditions in cultural psychology* (pp. 27–72). Cambridge, MA: Harvard University Press.

Shweder, R. A. (1993). "Why do men barbecue?" and other postmodern ironies of growing up in the decade of ethnicity. *Daedalus, 122,* 279–310.

Shweder, R. A. (1994). "You're not sick, you're just in love ": Emotion as an interpretive system. In P. Ekman & R. J. Davidson (Eds.), *The nature of emotion: Fundamental questions.* New York: Oxford University Press.

Shweder, R. A. (1995). The confessions of a methodological individualist. *Culture and Psychology, 1*(1), 115–122.

Shweder, R. A., & Bourne, E. J. (1984). Does the concept of the person vary cross-culturally? In R. A. Shweder & R. A. Levine (Eds.), *Culture theory: Essays on mind, self, and emotion* (pp. 158–199). New York: Cambridge University Press.

Shweder, R. A., Jensen, L., & Goldstein, W. (1994). "Who sleeps by whom" revisited: A method for extracting the moral goods implicit in practice. In J. Goodnow, P. Miller & F. Kessel (Eds.), *Contextualizing development.* San Francisco: Jossey-Bass.

Shweder, R. A., & LeVine, R. A. (1976). Dream concepts of Hausa children: A critique of the "doctrine of invariant sequence" in cognitive development. In T. Schwartz (Ed.), *Socialization as cultural communication: Development of a theme in the work of Margaret Mead.* Berkeley, CA: University of California Press.

Shweder, R. A., Mahapatra, M., & Miller J. G. (1990). Culture and moral development. In J. W. Stigler, R. A. Shweder, & G. Herdt (Eds.), *Cultural psychology: Essays on comparative human development* (pp. 130–204). New York: Cambridge University Press.

Shweder, R. A., Much, N. C., Mahapatra, M. & Park, L. (In press). The "big three" of morality (autonomy, community, divinity), and the "big three" explanations of suffering. In A. Brandt & P. Rozin (Eds.), *Morality and health.* Stanford, CA: Stanford University Press.

Shweder, R. A., & Sullivan, M. A. (1990). The semiotic subject of cultural psychology. In L.

A. Pervin (Ed.), *Handbook of personality theory & research.* New York: Guilford Press.

Shweder, R. A., & Sullivan, M. A. (1993). Cultural psychology: Who needs it? *Annual Review of Psychology, 44,* 497–527.

Sigel, I. E. (1984). Reflections on action theory and distancing theory. *Human Development, 27,* 188–210.

Soudijn, K. A., Hutschemaekers, G. J., & Van de Vijver, F. J. R. (1990). Culture conceptualisations. In F. J. R. van de Vijver & G. J. Hutschemaekers (Eds.), *The investigation of culture: Current issues in cultural psychology* (pp. 19–29). The Netherlands: Tilburg University Press.

Spiro, M. E. (1982). *Oedipus in the Trobriands.* Chicago: University of Chicago Press.

Stigler, J. W. (1984). "Mental abacus": The effect of abacus training on Chinese children's mental calculation. *Cognitive Psychology, 16,* 145–176.

Strauss, C. (1992a). Models and motives. In R. D'Andrade & C. Strauss (Eds.), *Human motives and cultural models* (pp. 1–20). Cambridge: Cambridge University Press.

Strauss, C. (1992b). What makes Tony run? Schemas as motives reconsidered. In R. D'Andrade & C. Strauss (Eds.), *Human motives and cultural models* (pp. 191–224). Cambridge: Cambridge University Press.

Taylor, C. (1979). Interpretation and the science of man. In P. Rabinow & W. Sullivan (Eds.), *Interpretive social science: A reader* (pp.25–71). Berkeley, CA: University of California Press.

Taylor, C. (1989). *Sources of the self: The making of the modern identity.* Cambridge, MA: Harvard University Press.

Triandis, H. C. (1980). Introduction to handbook of cross-cultural psychology. In H. C. Triandis & W. W. Lambert (Eds.), *Handbook of Cross-Cultural Psychology (Vol 1,* pp. 1– 14). Boston: Allyn and Bacon.

Triandis, H. C. (1989). The self and social behavior in differing cultural contexts. *Psychological Review, 96,* 506–520.

Triandis, H. C. (1993). Collectivism and individualism as cultural syndromes. *Cross-Cultural Research, 27,* 155–180.

Turiel, E. (1983). *The development of social knowledge: Morality and convention.* New York: Cambridge University Press.

Tyler, S. A. (Ed.). (1969). *Cognitive anthropology: Readings*. New York: Holt, Rinehart and Winston.

Valsiner, J. (Ed.). (1988). *Child development within culturally structured environments: Social co-construction and environmental guidance in development* (Vol. 2). Norwood, NJ: Ablex.

Valsiner, J. (Ed.). (1989). *Child development in cultural context*. Toronto: Hogrefe and Huber.

Van de Veer, R., & Valsiner, J. (1988). Lev Vygotsky and Pierre Janet: On the origin of the concept of sociogenesis. *Developmental Review, 8,* 52–65.

Vygotsky, L. S. (1978). *Mind in society: The development of higher psychological processes*. (M. Cole, V. John-Steiner, S. Scribner, & E. Souberman, Eds.). Cambridge, MA: Harvard University Press.

Vygotsky, L. S. (1981a). The genesis of higher mental functions. In J. V. Wertsch (Ed.), *The concept of activity in Soviet psychology* (pp.144–188). Armonk, NY: M. E. Sharpe.

Vygotsky, L. S. (1981b). The instrumental method in psychology. In J. V. Wertsch (Ed.), *The concept of activity in Soviet psychology* (pp. 134-143). Armonk, NY: M. E. Sharpe.

Wason, P. C., & Johnson-Laird, P. N. (1972). *Psychology of reasoning: Structure and content*. Cambridge, MA: Harvard University Press.

Werker, J. (1989). Becoming a native listener. *American Scientist, 77,* 54–59.

Wertsch, J. V. (Ed.). (1979). *The concept of activity in Soviet psychology*. Armonk, NY: M.E. Sharpe.

Wertsch, J. V. (1985). *Vygotsky and the social formation of mind*. Cambridge, MA: Harvard University Press.

Wertsch, J. V. (1991). *Voices of the mind: A sociocultural approach to mediated action*. Cambridge, MA: Harvard University Press.

Wertsch, J. V. (1995a). Sociocultural research in the copyright age. *Culture and Psychology, 1,* 81–102.

Wertsch, J. V (1995b). Introduction. In J. V. Wertsch, P. del Rio, & A. Alvarez (Eds.), *Sociocultural studies of mind*. New York: Cambridge University Press.

Wertsch, J. V., & Rupert, L. J. (1993). The authority of cultural tools in a sociocultural approach to mediated agency. *Cognition and Instruction, 11,* 227–239.

Wertsch, J. V., del Rio, P. & Alvarez, A. (Eds.). (1995). *Sociocultural studies of mind*. New York: Cambridge University Press.

White, G. M. (1990). Moral discourse and the rhetoric of emotions. In C.A. Lutz & L. Abu-Lughod (Eds.), *Language and the politics of emotion* (pp. 46–68). Cambridge: Cambridge University Press.

White, G. M. (1994). Affecting culture: Emotion and morality in everyday life. In S. Kitayama & H. R. Markus (Eds.), *Emotion and Culture: Empirical studies of mutual influence* (pp. 219–240). Washington, DC: American Psychological association.

White, G. M. (1995). Emotions inside out: The anthropology of affect. In M. Lewis & J. Haviland (Eds.), *The handbook of emotions*. New York: Guilford Publications.

White, M. (1963). The logic of historical narration. In S. Hook (Ed.), *Philosophy and History: A symposium* (pp. 3–31). New York: N.Y.U. Press.

Whiting, J. W., & Child, I. L. (1953). *Child training and personality*. New Haven, CT: Yale University Press.

Whiting, B. B., & Whiting, J. W. (1975). *Children of six cultures: A psycho-cultural analysis*. Cambridge, MA: Harvard University Press.

Wierzbicka, A. (1992). Talking about emotions: Semantics, culture and cognition. *Cognition and Emotion, 6,* 285–319.

Wierzbicka, A. (1994). Emotion, language, and cultural scripts. In S. Kitayama & H. R. Markus (Eds.), *Emotion and culture: Empirical studies of mutual influence* (pp. 133–196). Washington, DC: American Psychological Association.

Yang, K. (1988). Will societal modernization eventually eliminate cross-cultural psychological differences? In M. H. Bond (Ed.), *The cross-cultural challenge to social psychology* (pp. 67–85). Newbury Park, CA: Sage.

Young, K. T. (1990). American conceptions of infant development from 1955 to 1984: What the experts are telling parents. *Child Development, 61,* 17–28.

4

INDIGENIZING PSYCHOLOGY

D. SINHA
University of Allahabad, India

Contents

Introduction

In this chapter, indigenization of psychology is discussed as a facet of worldwide concern for making knowledge culturally appropriate. Culture-bound and culture-blind tendencies of mainstream psychology constitute the principal reason for this process. Various forms of indigenization are described, as they are unfolding in different regions, particularly of the developing world. The character and extent of indigenization in some countries is described, and some pitfalls and prospects are outlined. It is concluded that the indigenous approach has two concerns: that of embedding psychology in specific cultural context, and of establishing the universality of its empirical base and principles. In the latter case, indigenization is considered to be vital step towards a universal psychology.

Social scientists generally agree that the concepts and categories of science, and its tools for the perception of reality, are mediated by social forces, culture, and tradition. As Y. Singh (1986) has observed, "social conditioning of knowledge is revealed by the extent to which the concepts, methods and priority areas of research have the imprint of history and the social forces operative in society" (p. ix).

This perspective has led to an approach to knowledge that can be termed "indigenous." This approach places particular emphasis on culture-specific factors in human functioning—the researcher wants to know what is native, or rooted in specific societies or cultures. The Vygotskian emphasis on the embeddedness of learning and development in the cultural context offers a rationale for an indigenous approach in psychology. Luria's (1971, p. 262) observation on cognitive activities as "social phenomena in origin, and as processes formed during the course of mastery of general human experience" provides a similar argument for indigenizing psychology.

The concern for indigenization of knowledge is worldwide; it is not confined to a few countries or regions of the world, or only to psychology and the social sciences. In the former colonial countries that were under the intellectual domination of the West, there is a strong trend towards *decolonization* of knowledge, or in the words of Bhattacharya (1954) "*swaraj* or '*self-rule*' in ideas." Yamasoka (1968) from Japan remarked that "We Asian scholars have done little more than import the several social sciences directly from the West, and use them to prepare and deliver our lectures, but we have failed to give birth to creative theories designed for, and derived from, Asian realities" (p. 4). Speaking about the need of Pacific nations, Samy (1978) from Fiji asserted that "We need, amongst other things, a relevant social science with *appropriate* analytical tools, in order to articulate and transform the 'Pacific way' into a reality in this rapidly changing and shrinking world" (p. 30). Similar reflections can be discerned in the intellectual movement for Islamizing knowledge in Pakistan (Al Faruqi, 1982) and in other parts of the Islamic world, in the "Sinicization" of social and behavioral science research in China (Yang, 1982), in the teaching of Vedic mathematics in India, and in the popularity of treatises on physical and positive sciences of ancient Hindus (Seal, 1958). In many developing countries, there is growing scepticism, sometimes even

outright opposition, to accepting western scientific and technological developments. Instead, there is a plea for "appropriate" technology. There is an upsurge
in the popularity of traditional/indigenous medicines and techniques, such as
Ayurvedic and *Unani* systems in India, acupuncture and Chinese medicine and
herbal and Tibetan medicine. All this is indicative of the growing scepticism about
the Western system, and the search for "appropriate" remedies indigenously.

Definition: Indigenous Psychology and Indigenization

There is some confusion about the meaning of the expressions *indigenous psychology* and *indigenization*. Though frequently used, these terms do not occur
in most psychology dictionaries. According to the concise Oxford dictionary
of current English (Sykes, 1976), "indigenous" (in reference to flora and fauna)
means "produced naturally in a region; belonging naturally to the soil." Extending the biological meaning to the sphere of epistemology, it would refer
to those elements of knowledge that have been generated in a country or a
culture, and that have developed therein, as opposed to those that are imported or brought from elsewhere. In Webster's dictionary (Merriam-Webster,
1976) "indigenous" is characterized by two basic features: it is native and not
transplanted from outside, and it is *of* and designed *for* the natives (usually
non-European people). Extending these aspects to psychology, Kim (1990) defines indigenous psychology as "a psychological knowledge that is native,
that is not transplanted from another region, and that is designed for its people"
(p. 145). Or, to follow Enriquez (1990), indigenous psychology is a system of
psychological thought and practice that is rooted in a particular cultural tradition. Heelas (1981) regards it as distinct from *specialist* psychology that has
grown out of scientific experiments. It is rooted in "the cultural views, theories, conjectures, classifications, assumptions and metaphors—together with
notions embedded in social institutions—which bear on psychological topics"
(p. 3). In other words, "Indigenous psychology attempts to develop a
behavioural science that matches the sociocultural realities of one's own society" (Berry, Poortinga, Segall & Dasen, 1992, p. 381).

In these definitions of indigenous psychology, four underlying threads are to
be noted. First, psychological knowledge is not to be externally imposed; rather
the cultural tradition should give rise to it. Second, true psychology lies not in
artificially (experimentally contrived) induced behavior, but in daily, mundane
activities of people. Third, behavior is to be understood and interpreted not in
terms of imported categories and foreign theories (i.e., imposed etics), but in
terms of indigenous and local frames of reference and culturally derived categories (Berry et al., 1992, p. 380–381). Fourth, indigenous psychology embodies psychological knowledge that is relevant and is designed for its people. In other
words, it reflects the sociocultural reality of its society. Indigenous psychology is
also "appropriate" psychology, or as Azuma (1984) puts it, it is a route to "appropriate" psychology.

The last point refers to a point that has been emphasized by Adair (1989b) who speaks about a blending of foreign models, theories, and methods with indigenous ones to make them culturally appropriate. According to (Adair, 1992b) "an indigenous psychology gradually develops from blending of an imported discipline with increasing attention to unique elements within that culture." In this definition, less emphasis is placed upon the culturally-derived categories as such. It is the *blend* of the exogenous with the unique elements of the recipient culture that is vital. Thus, indigenous psychology is regarded as an outcome that results from the interaction between two systems of psychological knowledge. Or, as D. Sinha (1965) has put it in the Indian context, it is "an integration of modern psychology with Indian thought" (p. 6). This, as we will see, is regarded as a process of *indigenization*, and is implied in the definition advanced by Berry et al. (1992).

If indigenous psychology is taken in a narrow sense, it would imply that its constituents belong entirely to a culture that has not been contaminated or influenced by outside elements. But if nature is said to abhor a vacuum, it is very much so in cultural functioning. With global contacts and communication, such cultural isolation is rare. Influences emanating from various regions and cultures invariably interact with the local culture; this is the phenomenon of *acculturation* (see chapter by Berry & Sam, this *Handbook*). Therefore, indigenization can be said to refer to the transformations that the transplanted or borrowed external elements undergo so that they suit the characteristics of the region or the culture (D. Sinha, 1993, p. 34). According to Adair (1992a) also, "indigenization is the process of taking development from elsewhere (such as U.S. psychology) and introducing modifications to make it fit the new culture" (p. 62). This contrasts with endogenous development that is entirely from within. Because the borrowed elements in psychology in most countries were from the United States, which has a predominant place in modern psychology, Adair (1992a) adds that "most would agree that an indigenous psychology should resemble the North American discipline, although its variables and theories will reflect the local culture" (p. 62).

Puhan and Sahoo (1991) have considered indigenization as coextensive with a process of assimilation and gradual adaptation. Enriquez (1987, p. 276) refers to it in the Filipino setting as the *contextualization* of psychology. A definition by Adair, Puhan, and Vohra (1993) emphasizes this aspect of the process of indigenization, which "emanates from, adequately represents, and reflects back on the culture in which behaviour is studied, rather than a discipline that is imported from, and primarily addresses Developed World models" (p. 150).

In the growing volume of publications in this area, both indigenous psychology and indigenization are frequently used interchangeably. The former refers to psychology that is generated and develops in a particular culture and utilizes its collective creations, constructs, and categories. The latter refers to a process of the transformation of the imported elements of modern psychology to make them appropriate to the sociocultural setting. The two aspects can be designated respectively as *internal indigenization* and *indigenization of the exogenous*—a distinction that corresponds with Enriquez's (1987) "indigenization from within" and "indigenization from without." Thus indigenization is an ongoing process rather than a finished product; it is gradual and comes about in stages (D. Sinha, 1986).

Kim and Berry (1993, p. 3-4) have discussed six fundamental assumptions and research strategies that are shared in the indigenous psychology approach. First, this approach emphasizes understanding rooted in ecological, cultural and historical context. It attempts to document, organize, and interpret the understanding people have about themselves and their world, and examines how individuals and groups interact within their own context. Second, it is not a study of "strange," bizarre, and the "exotic" people in far away places. While this misconception is quite common, indigenous psychology only affirms the need for each culture to develop its own understanding. Third, the approach accepts that within any society or culture there can be a variety of perspectives not shared by all groups. In fact, in many societies, especially those belonging to the developing world, the existence of parallel systems of psychological knowledge that may have little interaction with each other is recognized (Moghaddam, 1993; D. Sinha, 1993). Fourth, the approach does not affirm or preclude the use of a particular method. It is a misconception that, as a reaction to modern scientific psychology, indigenous approaches are opposed to scientific methods. Rather, much is being done to discover and forge appropriate methods for investigating a phenomenon of interest. There is no denial of experimental and scientific methods. The approach only asserts that scientists cannot and should not be bound by a particular method. Fifth, the approach does not assume the inherent superiority of one particular perspective over another on a priori grounds. On the contrary, it asserts the existence of *alternative* perspectives and orientations for studying psychological phenomena. Finally, one of the main goals of the indigenous psychology approach is the discovery of universal facts and principles. There is a widespread misunderstanding that it is committed to cultural relativism and denies the existence of universal psychological principles. This issue will be discussed in a subsequent section. For the present, note that the approach challenges only the existence of psychological universals that are simply *assumed* on a priori grounds, rather than established through cross-cultural and cross-indigenous comparisons.

Theoretical Rationale

Historical Background

Indigenous approaches in psychology can be linked to the ancient Indian wisdom of regarding the reality of humankind as inextricably interwoven with the sociocultural milieu. To understand and judge human behavior and conduct, it was considered essential to place them in the context of *desh* (place), *kala* (time) and *patra* (person/individual). In other words, behaviour and conduct had to be viewed in their proper cultural context. This orientation prevails to a considerable extent even today among Indian people and many others on the Asian continent. In the European tradition, the need for historical and cultural analysis can similarly be been traced back to ancient times. These historical roots are discussed at length by Jahoda and Krewer (this volume).

With the vast post-World War II expansion in psychology, especially in the United States, psychology became equated with the research and publications of that country. Berry et al. (1992, p. 381) observe that this literature took "the role and status of *the* psychology." But it is best characterized as psychology of, by, and for the United States and not as a universal psychology (Kim & Berry, 1993, pp. 5-6). The fact that psychology had its roots in positivistic and mechanistic traditions, and had developed in a specific situation was ignored. Though the data on which theories and principles were based had been obtained from a special population and reflected the issues and concerns of that country, they were used to explain behavior not only of societies that shared largely the same characteristics, but of other peoples irrespective of differences in culture, traditions, and history. With the growth of cross-cultural psychology and the accumulation of data that demonstrated the influence of culture on social and even on cognitive processes so far regarded as universal, the need for studying these in context came to be recognized. Though cross-cultural psychology served as an impetus to indigenous psychology, it was not entirely its outgrowth. As D. Sinha (1989) observes, "Indigenous psychology in many cases predates cross-cultural, but the latter in certain ways has tended to revive and generate the process of indigenization, which in turn has enriched the former. The two are complementary to each other" (p. 26). To an important extent, it has developed as a reaction to or rejection of dominance of Western psychology (D. Sinha, 1981) and has assumed almost the shape of a "movement" in many erstwhile colonial and developing countries.

Thus, the first and probably foremost factor in indigenizing psychology is the reaction against the ethnocentric tendencies of mainstream psychology, and its culture-bound and culture-blind character. Many scholars, including Americans themselves, have dubbed modern psychology as a "Euro-American product" (Campbell, 1968) and as an "indigenous psychology of the West" (Rudmin, 1987, p. 1) and are aware of its "monocultural" nature (Kennedy, Scheirer, & Rogers, 1984). The validity and generalizability of its findings and theories to other cultures have been seriously questioned (e.g., Diaz-Guerrero, 1993; Ho, 1993; D. Sinha, 1993). There is a focus on issues and problems of the United States and American society. Ardila (1993) has stated that "psychology takes into consideration problems relevant for Anglo-Saxon culture, not for other cultures" (p. 171). In addition, it is felt that American psychologists may fail to appreciate phenomena found outside of the United States. As Azuma (1984) observes, "when a psychologist looks at a non-Western culture through Western glasses, he may fail to notice important aspects of the non-Western culture since the schema for recognizing them are not provided by his science" (p. 49).

Another factor that reflects the ethnocentric character of mainstream psychology is the neglect of scientific contributions made by researchers in other countries. American authors rarely refer to publications outside of the United

States even though these are in English. The two-volume third edition of the *Handbook of Social Psychology* (Lindzey & Aronson, 1985) is an example. In thousands of studies cited, it contains hardly a dozen references to Indian scholars and then only to studies published in American and British journals, mostly by expatriates. Moreover, there is a somewhat patronizing tone when Jones (1985, p. 63) states that "Festinger was clearly impressed by the Indian rumour studies of two of Bartlett's students (D. Sinha, 1952; Prasad, 1950) in developing his theory of cognitive dissonance." One does not find many references to studies conducted even by European scholars, or to studies published in oriental language journals.

Indigenous sources in other countries contain valuable materials about the nature of human behavior, and of personality, social, and interpersonal interactions. However, they were hardly regarded as "scientific" in the strict sense of the term. Thus, when modern psychology was transplanted to the developing countries, it was imported as a "ready-made intellectual package" (Nandy, 1974, p. 71) and swept away indigenous knowledge. There was an uncritical acceptance of psychological theories, concepts and techniques developed and used in the West.

Mohanty (1988) has made a content-analysis of the articles published during 1984 and 1985 in one of the important journals in psychology in India, namely, *Psychological Studies*. In 86 percent of the cases, the main source was an American journal or dissertation; in 8 percent it was a European or Japanese international journal; and for 6 percent no definite source could be determined. As far as originality of the research idea was concerned 84 percent of the articles were replications or near-replications of studies by overseas (almost always American) colleagues. In another analysis, approximately three-fourths of the cited references were found to be non-Indian (Adair, 1989a). This subservience sometimes went to the ridiculous length of conceptualizing social phenomena in American terms. For example, in India caste was conceptualized as if it were race, communalism as anti-semitism, and the untouchables as American blacks (Nandy, 1974, p. 8).

The same has been true for psychological measurement instruments. Referring to the psychological tests used in developing countries, Diaz-Guerrero (1977a) observed that such borrowing has done little to stimulate the development of local instruments that would reflect sociocultural characteristics of the country and not be blind to cultural peculiarities and personality dynamics.

The "foreignness" of studies divorced psychology both from traditional systems that could have provided strong cultural roots, and from the issues and problems of the country that could have imparted vigor and vitality to them. Further, some basic foundations of modern psychology have had a restrictive influence. The positivistic and mechanistic bias and the emulation of a natural sciences model, though assets in some ways, have acted as a shackle for further development. Instead of adapting existing methods or developing new ones, which match the diverse and highly complex subject matter of human behavior, the modern psychologist, in a way, tended to force every problem into a set scheme, and to ignore those that did not appear to be amenable to experimental design (D. Sinha, 1965, p. 270). This attitude of negation toward highly complex processes because it was difficult to simplify the stimuli, isolate the response, and exercise strict "control," still lingers in modern "scientific" psychology. Moreover, the basic orientation of psychology as it has developed in the West is microcosmic. It places disproportionate emphasis on narrow aspects of behavior so that larger societal issues and structural and systemic variables are ignored. The basic unit of analysis is the individual and this leads to an individualistic orientation (Koch & Leary, 1985). Psychology is concentrated almost entirely on personal characteristics of individual actors in social processes rather than on complex sociostructural factors.

Growing disillusionment with the foreign roots of psychology, the realization of the non-applicability of its concepts and tools of research in radically different sociocultural contexts, its "irrelevance to vital issues facing the country and failure to make a thrust in the national life" (Pareek, 1980a, p. ix) were signs of growing crisis in psychology in many developing countries. Scholars began to articulate the need for contextualization and what Enriquez (1987, 1994) has called "de-colonization" of the psyche and "cultural empowerment." Attempts were made to develop approaches that were "relevant" and rooted in the sociocultural soil of a country.

Types of Indigenization

Kumar (1979, pp. 104-105) has distinguished three types of indigenization: *structural, substantive,* and *theoretical.* Structural indigenization refers to the institutional and organizational capabilities of a nation for the production and diffusion of knowledge that is relevant. One rarely finds a department of psychology in a country with the professed and explicit goal of focusing research on topics or issues of wide social and national concern and developing a psychology based on culturally-derived constructs and categories. There are some exceptions (for example, in the Philippines), but the number of such institutions and departments is small. With concern for indigenization getting stronger, especially among psychologists in non-Western countries, such capabilities are expected to develop gradually.

Substantive indigenization can be also termed content-indigenization. It argues that the main thrust of psychology should be on its own society, people, and problems. In Canada, indigenization consisted in a greater emphasis in research on "social and applied" content derived from the context of the country (Berry, 1974; Berry & Wilde, 1972) and in India, it is evidenced in the need to put psychology in the arena of social change and national development (D. Sinha, 1966) and make it problem-oriented (D. Sinha, 1983, 1984; Pareek, 1980a). As Pareek (1980b) points out, "new developments have shown that psychology has to share with other social sciences the task of contributing to the solution of national problems both in terms of conceptual and intervention insights" (p. vii).

Theoretical indigenization takes place when scientists are involved in constructing distinctive conceptual frameworks and metatheories which reflect their worldviews, social and cultural experiences, and perceived goals (Kumar, 1979,

p. 105). Because concepts and theories are products of a culture, they are difficult to transfer from one culture to another. Therefore, the main form that indigenization has taken in psychology is the re-examination and modification of the theoretical frameworks and models borrowed from the West, and the adaptation of culturally-derived categories for understanding and explaining psychological realities. Progress in this direction, however, has been slow and psychologists in most non-Western countries have paid little attention to developing their own theories that can serve as alternatives to those implanted from the West.

To these three types of indigenization, a fourth one, namely, "indigenization of methods" can be added, which will be discussed in a subsequent subsection.

Levels of Indigenization

As suggested by Berry et al. (1992), Western psychological research tends to be ethnocentric at the levels of (1) selection of items and stimuli in a test, (2) choice of instruments and procedures, (3) definition of theoretical concepts, and (4) choice of topics for research. Indigenization of psychology, therefore, is taking place at all these four levels. For the sake of convenience, we would put the last two under the broad heading of "conceptual indigenization" and the first two under "indigenization of methods." Both categories are discussed briefly.

The Western orientation among psychologists from non-Western countries has produced two outcomes. First, they followed current fashions and focused on topics that were popular but not necessarily of relevance to their country. Thus, the first step in indigenizing psychology was to pursue problem-oriented research (D. Sinha, 1986, 1993) and address problems related to the development of one's country. This change in orientation automatically led to the "phase of indigenization" in the 70s that has become more articulate since the 80s. It was marked by questioning the appropriateness of Western theories and models and doubts about the efficacy of tools for data collection developed in the West. An effort was made to modify Western theories to make them appropriate to the social milieu and also develop culturally-based theories and constructs for understanding local social realities.

Conceptual indigenization has taken two main forms: explanatory and paradigmatic. First, culture has been utilized as a source providing psychological explanation and for understanding of phenomena; and second, for deriving constructs that set the pattern of the study to be conducted.

Morality and moral judgement among Indians and Chinese are cases in point. While the Piagetian–Kohlbergian model that emphasizes individual rights, responsibility, and autonomy is popular among psychologists in the West, entirely different criteria reflecting a code of social duties derived from the cultures themselves have been utilized in non-Western societies (Miller, Bersoff & Harwood, 1990). Shweder, Mahapatra, and Miller (1990) have proposed the existence of "alternative post conventional moralities" based upon specific religio-philosophical conceptions of *dharma* (natural law), justice, acceptance of social responsibilities towards persons, and social duties rather than upon factors of individualism, autonomy, secularism, and social contract that characterize Western social functioning. Similarly with respect to Chinese society, an indigenous model rooted in traditional precepts of Confucius and others has been developed (Ma, 1988, 1989). This is discussed at some length in the subsection dealing with China.

Paradigmatic indigenization constitutes the next step. It is manifested in two forms. In the first, Western theories and models are modified to correspond with social reality ("indigenization of the exogenous"). For example, analyzing Indonesian culture, Hofstede (1988) argued that its assumptions, and those of McGregor's theory, were not in consonance. Taking Indonesian culture into account, Hofstede reconceptualized McGregor's model in which Theory X and Theory Y were not mutually exclusive opposites, but complementary.

The second form consists of the discovery of cultural categories and constructs utilized for designing psychological studies ("indigenization from within"). "Indigenization from within" is reflected in the explorations by psychologists in many developing countries of ancient religio-philosophical treatises and traditional folk culture for constructs and models that can be utilized for designing psychological investigations. In China, there is a spurt of interest in the psychological thoughts of ancient and medieval Chinese scholars (Yan, 1987, 1988; Shuh & Gao, 1983). Similar is the case of India where ancient treatises and systems of philosophy have been explored for psychological constructs (Akhilananda, 1948; Safaya, 1976). These researches highlight alternative constructs and models, and indicate their potential for designing psychological studies. D. Sinha (1990) has utilized the ancient Indian medical treatises, the *Bhagwatgita* and Sankhya philosophy for developing an Indian model for coping and psychological well-being rooted in the notion of man's symbiotic relationship with the environment. The model emphasizes harmony with environment rather than control and exploitation (as it is in the West).

Systematic experimental investigation has been conducted on a construct derived from *Bhagwatgita*, that is to say, *niskamakarma* (non-attachment or work without attachment to its outcome) by Pande and Naidu (1986, 1992) who have identified an orientation to work that is different from the western practice of setting a goal and obsession with attaining it. The alternative model suggested is of "effort orientation," that is, performing work as best as one can without being overly concerned with its outcome. They have operationalized the concept of "non-attachment," developed and standardized a scale for measuring it, and analyzed its correlates.

Indigenization of methods is the process of transformation in instruments to make them suitable for the specific characteristics of a population. As has been observed already, methods of data collection are "ethnocentric" with regard to the nature of items and stimuli used and in the choice of instruments and procedures. Doubts have often been raised about the use of Western tests, especially with unsophisticated populations from the developing countries, because of different cultural background, education, and test sophistication. Therefore, development of "appropriate" measures is considered essential.

The first and most common step in indigenizing assessment procedures has been the "adaptation" of foreign tests and the construction of tests in local languages largely modeled on Western measures (Adair, 1992a). Test items are modified or replaced by ones that are considered suitable for the local situation. "Back translation" is utilized as a check on the meaning. Despite these efforts, many tests have continued to be "Western" and adaptation has generally meant making superficial changes in borrowed foreign tests.

Another strategy for indigenization of methods is to keep constant the original conceptualization of the measure, but to utilize materials and activities prevalent in the community thereby making the measure "appropriate." Utilizing available materials and activities such as sorting of grains or rural games for measuring level of aspiration provides an example of a culturally appropriate instrument suitable for use on preliterate rural and tribal populations (D. Sinha, 1969). While such indigenizing of procedure has considerable potential, it does not solve the problem of the culture-based nature of the constructs underlying the test.

A more radical approach to the indigenization of methods is reflected in Ho (1988) and Enriquez (1990). These authors have been highly sceptical about modern psychological procedures that have been modeled almost entirely on physical sciences. Ho asserts that "it would make much better methodological sense to take advantage of indigenous techniques and approaches to data gathering available in the culture, and thus avoid many of the problems arising from over-reliance on foreign measures and devices (such as psychological tests) which has plagued research" (p. 57). The common practice in Filipino culture of making informal inquiries or *pagtatanungtanong* (groping or asking around) has been suggested as a useful technique for data gathering (Pe-Pua, 1990). It is unobtrusive and nonreactive, and has the advantage of being a natural kind of social interaction among the people. A similar suggestion has been made by Mataragnon (1988) for *pakikiramdan*, which relates to social intercourse.

It would be premature to assess the utility of these indigenous methods. They constitute good instances of indigenizing of psychological assessment procedures, and of a broadening of the methodological repertoire of psychology that Kelman (1972) recommended more than two decades ago.

Indigenization of Psychology in the Developing World

In this section, indigenization of psychology in different regions of the world is described, mainly in the developing world. Due to limitations of space, discussion is confined to some countries and a few fields of psychology. The selection has been somewhat arbitrary. The main consideration has been that those selected display an appreciable level of indigenization and throw light on the process involved in it. The trend to indigenize psychology is more pronounced in erstwhile colonies and developing countries of Africa, Asia, and Latin America than elsewhere. However, it is important to note that the process also has been underway in Europe and Canada.

"Europeanization" has been a significant feature of the development of social psychology in Europe. Emphasizing the culture-bound character of contemporary social psychology (Berry, 1978; Bond, 1988; Jaspars, 1986; Jahoda, 1979, 1986). Moscovici (1972, p. 19) observed that because its themes of research and the context of its theories related only to U.S. society, its generalizations become questionable in other cultural contexts. He contends that "in Europe, we must turn towards our own reality, towards our own maxims from which we must derive our 'scientific' consequences" (p. 19). . . . "Social psychology that we ought to create must have an origin in our own reality" (p. 23).

In Canada, the inappropriateness of importing American socio-psychological concepts has been pointed out, and it is contended that the solution lies in creating indigenous social psychologies (Berry, 1974). The major impetus towards it can be discerned as early as 1955 in the analysis of psychology in Canadian universities and colleges made by MacLeod (1955). Taking account of the multiculturalism and special features of Canadian society, scholars have endeavored to create a psychology that reflected the local reality (Berry, 1974, 1984, 1993). Though they strongly subscribe to the long-term goal of universal psychology (Berry, 1978), they are very much alive to the local societal issues and to the need to develop a psychology in the Canadian context with a distinct orientation and emphasis (Berry, 1974, 1983).

The process of indigenization is less evident in those fields of psychology that are concerned with biological and physiological aspects of behavior in which culture-specific variables play a very minor role. In fields like ergonomics and physiological psychology, the universal validity of theories and principles is seldom questioned and a need for a cultural perspective is rarely felt. However, even in certain aspects of perception and cognition, characteristic habits of information processing are inculcated by culture (see the chapter by Mishra, this *Handbook*) and emphasis on cultural variables and indigenization is considered necessary. As the degree of complexity of behavior increases, the indigenous approach appears fruitful if the goal of universality of psychological principles is to be attained rather than merely assumed.

Africa

When asked about African psychology, Durojaiye (1993, p. 211) was emphatic in asserting that he did "not know of any African psychological processes that are distinct from those found elsewhere in the world" (p. 211). In the very same paper, however, he states that "indigenous psychology is characterized by a search into the cultural and traditional practices and identifying psychological principles that underlie these practices" (p. 211).

In the indigenization of psychology on the vast African continent three main developments can be recognized. First, as elsewhere in the developing world, modern psychology in Africa during the colonial period was almost entirely dependent on the West for ideas, theories, and personnel who were either foreign scholars, Africans trained in British, French, and American universities, or in the few departments of psychology that overwhelmingly subscribed to the Western ethos and interests. Serious doubts arose about the appropriateness of theories, models, and tests borrowed from the West. The initial impetus to indigenizing psychology was to relate psychology to the national need as a "provider of competent teachers, research workers and supplier of services" (Heron, 1975, p. 16). It became essential that those engaged in the task of personnel selection were aware of the African realities and modified the tests and procedures to suit the nature of population that were not exposed to modernizing influences. The work of Biesheuvel and his colleagues in South Africa provides an early example of numerous creative attempts to construct assessment instruments suitable for indigenous African populations (e.g., Biesheuvel, 1954; Reuning & Wortley, 1973). In their treatment of the history of cross-cultural psychology Jahoda and Krewer (this volume) make some comments on the development of psychology in Africa.

In the 90s, the principal goal of most psychologists and psychological associations in Africa comprises involvement in the solution of societal problems. Durojaiye (1987, pp. 34-35) observes that "There is a serious effort to make psychology an indigenous discipline useful to national development." There is a strong urge among psychologists working in African countries to link psychological research to the process of social change and the needs of the African community. Mundy-Castle (1993) has analyzed the psychological effects of rapid modernization and provides an African conceptual and theoretical perspective. The shift in the approach not only requires newer constructs derived from the sociocultural context, but as Van Vlaenderen (1993, p. 93) adds, "a new methodology, new research techniques, and a new type of relationship between the researcher and other participants in the research effort."

The second significant development has been what Durojaiye (1993, p. 214) calls the "search for meaning in indigenous psychology" in Africa. Foreign psychologists, such as Jahoda in Ghana and Ombredane in Francophone Africa, sought to unravel indigenous psychology in Africa. Two areas of work in this respect stand out: The first is the interest in folk medicine and folk practices for mental health, and the other is the indigenous concept of intelligence. There has been increasing interest in traditional healing and psychiatric practices (Ogedengbe, 1993; Peltzer, 1987). Many kinds of trance and possessions have been identified that are used for psychotherapeutic purposes. They appear bizzare and are often dismissed as superstitions from an outsider's point of view. But many psychologists and anthropologists have tried to understand them in local terms and study them scientifically. This open-minded approach provides evidence that they are being accepted into Western medical thought as supplementary to other psychotherapeutic practices (Jilek, 1988).

The conceptualization and understanding of intelligence in different African societies began with a study conducted in Niger. The indigenous concept of *lakkal* (translated as "intelligence" in English) had at least two dimensions: the first concerned aptitude and know-how (corresponding to our conventional concept of intelligence) and the other social competence (Ombredane, 1954). Similarly, among the Baganda (in Uganda), Wober (1974) observed that the term *obugezi* referred equally to wisdom and social skills. Intelligence was associated with "slow, careful, active, straightforward and sane." The Chewa of Zambia defined intelligence as "cooperation" and "obedience" (Serpell, 1977). Exploring the concept of *n'glouelé* among the Baoulé in Cote d'Ivoire, Dasen et al. (1985) observed that intelligence was conceived not only as having a social dimension, but that the cognitive dimension was subordinated to it. The concept possessed components like "a willingness to help," carry out the task well, and in a responsible manner; in short, it described a person who does the chores without being told. As Mundy-Castle (1974) hypothesized, indigenous concepts of intelligence in Africa possess both a social and a cognitive/technological dimension in which the latter is subordinated to the former.

A significant step has been the work of Nsamenang (1992) who stresses the need for human development research in context. The main thrust of his approach is that bioecological constraints on development are complemented by a particular society's "cultural formulas and mechanisms for canalizing development in some but not other directions." The framework enables contextualization of child rearing and human development in West Africa so that they can be understood and appreciated in their own terms.

To provide the proper context, Nsamenang (1992, Chapter 4) presents an account of an indigenous African worldview that constitutes a different frame of reference from that in contemporary developmental psychology. A social ontogenetic dimension constitutes its most salient component. The life cycle is partitioned into three basic dimensions of personhood: *spiritual selfhood* beginning at conception and ending with naming, *social selfhood* from naming until death, and *ancestral selfhood* that follows biological death (pp. 144–148). Social selfhood in turn is subdivided into seven socio-ontogenetic stages, each of which is characterized by a distinctive developmental task, defined within the framework of culture's primarily socio-affective, developmental agenda. The stages of the life cycle in social ontogeny corresponding approximately to the conventional developmental stages are given in Table 4–1.

TABLE 4–1   Ontogeny: West African view of life stages

Socio-ontogenic stages	Conventional development stages
Spiritual self-hood	Prenatal stage
Period of the newborn	Neonatal stage
Social priming	Infancy
Social apprenticing	Childhood
Social entrée	Puberty
Social induction/internment	Adolescence
Adulthood	Adulthood
Old age/death	Senescence/death
Ancestral self-hood	?

Source: After Nsamenang, 1992, p. 148.

This characterization of ontogeny as a cumulative process of integration within the community and the clan has close resemblance to the developmental stages with their corresponding rituals and norm of activities in the Indian traditional system. On the other hand, its theoretical focus differs sharply from the more individualistic accounts of developmental stages proposed by Freud, Erikson, and Piaget in the West. As Serpell (1994, pp. 18–19) in his review of Nsamenang's book comments, "its resonance with cultural preoccupations expressed by parents in many African societies, where social responsibility is valued above personal autonomy and intellectual alacrity, suggests that it will be well received in the emerging field of African psychology."

Further, Nsamenang's account of socialization and child care in West Africa is different from what is observed in Western developmental psychology. As contrasted with the West, respect for seniority and obedience to elders and superiors is one of the keys to decoding West African behavior. Bonds and deference in the West African peer culture and the caring roles of older siblings are other salient aspects of socialization that emphasizes notions of locus of authority, seniority, and filial service (Nsamenang, 1992, p. 148).

The total African context shapes the pattern of socialization and human development in Africa of which the modern methods of isolating particular behaviors from the full range of contextual constraints can provide only a distorted picture. Therefore, the remedy that is proposed is methodological. Rather than the psychological tradition of hypothesis-testing using pre-structured instruments to measure planned samples of behavior, Nsamenang argues for an ethnographic approach that is open-ended, personally involved, and improvising. Emphasis on indigenization is prominent in the assertion that "researchers in West Africa should think of how best to 'assign' 21st century goals to indigenous structure, rather than replace them" (p. 124).

Latin America

Indigenous roots of psychology in Latin America, as in other parts of the world, are inextricably embedded in the development of language, magic, religion, and philosophy (Diaz-Guerrero, 1994, p. 717). But, as in other developing countries, modern psychology developed under the influence of foreign powers, first of Spain and Portugal and later of the United States. Psychology remained alien and largely removed from the realities of the region. Recently, there has been a close interaction between Western philosophical and scientific traditions and cultural heritage and local needs. With this, the process of indigenization has started.

Ardila (1982) contends that there is no such thing as "Latin American psychology" in the sense of a psychology circumscribed by continental, regional or national boundaries. He feels that a more appropriate expression would be "Psychology *in* Latin America." But in a recent paper (Ardila, 1993), he talks of "Latin American psychology" and poses the question whether it can be integrated with world psychology. Again, the main characteristic is the emphasis on practical aspects. This is especially the case with developments in Cuba, Venezuela, and Mexico.

In Cuba, psychology is tied to medical care and an emphasis on prevention, health being regarded as a social phenomenon and a right of every citizen (Averasturi, 1980). In Venezuela, psychological knowledge is used extensively in political image building, and organizing political campaigns (Salazar, 1984). Psychology received a strong impetus with the emergence in 1979 of the national program for the development of intelligence. In Mexico, apart from usual areas of application, the discipline has extended itself to action research, participatory research, and educational and social program evaluation in rural communities (Diaz-Guerrero, 1993).

Ethnopsychology as developed in Mexico reflects a significant trend in indigenizing psychology. It drives from fascination with the psychology of the Mexican (Diaz-Guerrero, 1993). As early as 1901, Chavez analyzed the distinctive character traits of the Mestizo, the Indian, and the Criollo. Quantitative efforts started in the late 40s, and since the 60s, Diaz-Guerrero and his colleagues have been working consistently on the development of Mexican ethnopsychology. It is contended that human behaviors will never be understood unless account is taken of historical, biological, individual and social psychological, economic, political, social, and cultural anthropological variables (Diaz-Guerrero, 1977b, p. 938). Ethnopsychology postulates the existence of specific human ecosystems and begins their systematic explorations through the measurement and determination of individual and group differences in verbal expressions and dimensions discovered specifically for a given culture. Through systematic procedures, historico-sociocultural premises (HSCP) are established that constitute culturally significant statements defined operationally as those held by a majority of people (Diaz-Guerrero, 1982, 1993). Drawing from a large number of HSCPs applied to different types of populations, factor scales were extracted (Diaz-Guerrero, 1982). A well-known example is an active–passive dimension of coping style called *Filosofia de Vida* (Views of Life). It is postulated that HSCPs represent traditional Mexican beliefs and modes of coping, and embody a significant aspect of the Mexican culture. Following a similar strategy, Diaz-Loving (1994) and his associates have developed a multidimensional self-concept inventory, and an authoritarianism scale based on Mexican cultural characteristics. As Diaz-Guerrero (1977b) concludes, there is a basis to speak about sociocultural psychologies, such as a Mexican psychology. Emphasizing the need for sociocultural/indigenous psychology, what is challenged is not the scientific character of the mainstream psychology, but its universality.

China and Chinese-Speaking Countries

In China and the Chinese-speaking regions especially of Hong Kong and Taiwan, the indigenous approach is reflected in five ways. First, special interest has been generated in the psychological thought of ancient philosophers and social thinkers. China has a rich heritage of psychological knowledge especially in the writings of Confucius (551–479 B.C.), Mencius (468–312 B.C.), Xun Zi (295–236 B.C.), and Gao Zi (about 300 B.C.). They deal extensively with the nature of man, and contain elaborate discussions on norms of social functioning and interpersonal interactions. As in most non-Western countries, early modern psychology was entirely an imported product (Ching, 1984, p. 57), initially linked to European and American psychology and later in the People's Republic of China to Marxist principles and Soviet psychology. More recently psychology in China has been influenced by its own tradition arising from ancient civilization and culture, the Western modern thought, and the contemporary political structure (Petzold, 1987). Indigenization in contemporary China displays the interactional operation of these various influences.

Second, "imported" psychology did not grow in answer to specific needs of Chinese society, but was applied to the needs of new Western-based educational and industrial programmes (Petzold, 1987, pp. 223–224). During the turmoil of the Cultural Revolution (1966–1976), it was denounced as a "luxury" science, a "bourgeois pseudoscience," and metaphysical nonsense and was completely liquidated as a scientific discipline. After the Cultural Revolution, psychology was revived and rehabilitated, and closely tied with national aspirations (Ching, 1984, p. 61). It was called upon to work for the cause of the Four Modernizations—in industry, agriculture, science and technology, and defense (Ching, 1984; Xu, 1979). As Jing (1994, p. 672) points out, the policy of reform and openness to the outside world pushed Chinese psychology into a new era. Wang (1980) has outlined the goal for the turn of the century. Among other things, he emphasized two aspects: its uniqueness in basic theory and methodology, being guided exclusively by dialectical materialism; and its typically Chinese character, fully revealing and elevating those rich psychological thoughts in Chinese history, and fully reflecting the true spirit of Chinese people on their march to the four modernizations in the era of socialism (Lee & Petzold, 1987, p. 118). Thus, the linkage of the discipline to the overall requirements of national development and growing interest in the rich cultural heritage has provided the main impetus for indigenizing psychology in China.

Third, the indigenous approach is evidenced in developmental psychology, which constitutes one of the main areas of study in China. Though Western influences, particularly that of Piaget, are strong, studies increasingly display the imprint of features of Chinese reality. Chinese, as an ideographic language with its unique writing and structure, has attracted attention in attempts to understand its acquisition, and its impact on developmental and thought processes (Jing, 1994, p. 671). Moral development is also of special interest to Chinese psychologists. Though the Kohlberg model is popular, it has been drastically revised by including the notion of the "golden mean" (behaving in the way the majority of people do in society) and "good will" (the virtue of complying with nature). The Chinese model emphasizes Ch'ing (human affection or sentiment) more than Li (reason, or rationality), and the Confucian values of jen (love, human-heartedness, benevolence, and sympathy), filial piety, group solidarity, collectivism and humanity (Ma, 1988, 1989, p. 172). This is a reconceptualization of what constitutes moral development, particularly at the highest level of post-conventional morality (Berry et al., 1992, p. 33).

Socialization has been analyzed and studied in terms of Confucian notions, (Ho, 1981). It also shows how a research topic and approach to it are conditioned by national policies and programs. Socialization of the "only child," with both paternal and maternal grandparents alongside the parents constituting the family surround, raises special interest. These developmental problems are peculiar to society in contemporary China as a consequence of the policy of the "one child" family.

Fourth, China has a large number of indigenous health and other practices that have attracted the attention not only of the Chinese psychologists but also of other professions. Utilizing modern scientific techniques, phenomena such as acupuncture, *qigong* (Dorcus & Wang, in press), and calligraphy (Kao & Goan, 1990; Kao & Robinson, 1990) have been investigated, not only for their validity but also for their therapeutic effects. Though based on conceptualizations about the nature of universe and energy, and human metabolic functioning that are very different from those in modern science, they are being integrated with other measures to enhance not only mental but general health. Petzold (1986) observes that although scientific concern and international contacts are more developed today, one could conclude that Chinese psychologists are concerned with following up indigenous developments, and that "dependence of Chinese psychology on Western psychology does not occur because of the strong reference to Chinese sources. This might indicate the development towards an indigenous Chinese psychology" (p. 65).

The fifth manifestation of indigenization in Chinese-speaking populations is in the area of social psychology. In fact, there is a movement that shares many aspects with other Asian countries, providing an alternative to Western ideas. As Ho (1988, p. 55) observes, social psychology with an Asian identity is rooted in certain conceptions of human nature, the goal and meaning of life, and the relationship between man and other human beings, the family, society, nature, the cosmos, and the divine. It has a strong "relational orientation" (Ho, 1993) which is different from the conception of man as a segregated autonomous being underlying the western conceptions. Hsu (1963) has highlighted certain essential features of Chinese culture which mold thinking and conceptualization in social psychology. He characterizes the Chinese world as "situation-centred" with ties "that permanently unite closely related human beings in family and clan. Within this basic human constellation the individual is conditioned to seek mutual dependence" (Hsu, 1963, p. 1). On the other hand, in the individual-centered world of the West, the ties are temporary and an individual's basic orientation to life and environment is one of self-reliance. Again, Hsu (1985) holds that "the meaning of being human is found in interpersonal relationships" (p. 27) in which the individual is seen in terms of a larger whole. In the central Chinese concept of *ren* or *jen* (person), the place of the individual is in the web of interpersonal relationships. In fact, to emphasize this interrelatedness, Hsu (1971) advises forgetting the term personality (p. 27), and to employ instead the concept of "psychosocial homeostasis." Traditional Chinese concepts that have been commonly utilized in understanding social behavior are *quanxi* (interrelatedness), "filial piety" (Yang,

1988; Yang & Bond, 1990; Yang & Yeh, 1991), *yin* (principal cause) and *yuan* (subsidiary cause) (Yang & Ho, 1988), and righteousness or justice (Chiu, 1989, 1991). *Yin* and *yuan* are traditionally considered to be the basis on which interpersonal relationships are formed and dissolved. This predominantly social perspective with two main components of group-orientation and other-orientation (Yang & Ho, 1988), is reflected in "a predisposition towards such behaviour patterns as social conformity, non-offensive strategy, submission to social expectations, and worry about external opinions in an attempt to achieve one or more of the purposes of reward attainment, harmony maintenance, impression management, face protection, social acceptance, and avoidance of punishment, embarrassment, conflict, rejection, ridicule and retaliation in a social situation" (p. 159).

India

In India the trend to indigenize psychology was discernible soon after Independence in 1947. It developed through gradual stages and was articulated especially since the 1980s (D. Sinha, 1986). First, the rich heritage of psychological knowledge enshrined in religious and philosophical treatises, and in folklore and folk practices, which had been long ignored by Indian psychologists, is now being studied and their relevance to contemporary life is being examined. To this extent, there is integration of scientific psychology with Indian thought.

Second, both indigenization from *without* and from *within* can be discerned. Initially, indigenization consisted mostly of transformations of Western theories and models to match the Indian sociocultural reality. Traditional Indian concepts of the development of self (D. Sinha & Naidu, 1994), personality (Beena, 1990; Paranjpe, 1988), and stress (Palsane, 1987; Palsane, Bhavsar, Goswami & Evans, 1986) are becoming part of the conceptual repertoire of psychologists. Mostly parallels with western theories of personality have been drawn. But there have also begun to emerge new paradigms for understanding personality and designing investigations.

Third, emphasis on problem-oriented research has led to concern for contemporary societal issues and their investigation from a psychological perspective. Increasingly, Indian psychologists are displaying interest in studying problems arising from national development and rapid socioeconomic transformations. Societal issues like poverty, social inequality, agro-economic development, unemployment, intergroup relations, and fertility behavior are popular topics.

As a consequence contextualization of research has become necessary. Further, because understanding and study of societal issues necessitates a broader perspective, there is a strong trend towards interdisciplinary research and a more macroscopic perspective than is normally the case in mainstream psychology. There is also a movement away from laboratory studies to studies in natural, rural, and tribal settings. With unsophisticated and semiliterate populations becoming the focus of study, the need for appropriate techniques of data collection is being felt increasingly. But indigenization of methods has not gone far enough. Unlike their Filipino counterparts (cf. later section), Indian researchers have confined themselves by and large to the level of "adaptive indigenization" and have not displayed much innovation. They have seldom utilized indigenous approaches and culturally available techniques to avoid problems arising out of over-dependence on foreign measures and procedures for data collection. However, the concern for indigenization of methods is very much there.

The indigenous approach is much in evidence in the fields of developmental psychology, psychotherapy, and social psychology. Early developmental psychology in India tended to study the child out of sociocultural context. Nevertheless the beginning of a cultural perspective and indigenization have been in existence for a long time. Since the famous "Six Cultures Study" (Whiting & Whiting, 1975), "psychocultural analysis" of child development has become a favorite tool. The ecocultural (Berry, 1976) and ecological (Bronfenbrenner, 1977) frameworks have further emphasized this perspective. The notion of "developmental niche" proposed by Super and Harkness (1986; see chapter in this *Handbook*), apart from integrating the biological and cultural approaches, has given a particular impetus to indigenization. Not only has the cultural context been an essential component, but these authors put special emphasis on culturally determined rearing and educational practices, and on the parental beliefs and values held about the development of children (parental ethnotheories).

Adopting a largely psychoanalytic and Eriksonian stance, but at the same time keeping within the realm of Indian cultural heritage, Kakar (1979) describes the interplay between the universal processes of development and the specific forces of Indian social reality surrounding the growing child, such as the religious ideals, historical traditions, and social institutions that are unique to the Indian scene.

The ancient Indian Ayurvedic theory of childhood development consists of five periods: (1) the prenatal period *(garbha)* (2) *ksheerda* (0 to 6 months) when the infant lives on milk, (3) *ksheerannada* (6 months to two years), the period when weaning takes place, (4) *bala* (2 to 5 years), and (5) *kumara* (5 to 16 years). According to Indian tradition, major rituals of childhood take place at ages that mark the transition from one period to another. These rituals and folk practices constitute the context of psychological development and identity formation, and provide elaborate guidelines for the education and rearing of Indian children.

Studies on moral development have indicated how an indigenous model was necessary to explain findings that were not consistent with those obtained in the West. When Saraswathi, Saksena, and Sundaresan (1977) obtained results that did not conform to Kohlberg's theory, they did not question its cross-cultural validity. However, indigenization trends are now visible: when Indians are observed to score lower on Kohlberg's moral dilemma test, the theory is examined and reformulated in the context of Indian sociocultural reality (Miller, Bersoff & Harwood, 1990; Shweder, Mahapatra & Miller, 1990). A purely cultural explanation of moral judgment has been advanced, as noted earlier.

Psychotherapists in India have also attempted to integrate indigenous concepts into the practice of psychotherapy. There has been an upsurge of interest all over the world in yoga, meditation, *asana* (body posture), and other traditional

Indian healing and mental care practices (Kakar, 1982; Kapur, 1979). Here again, instead of just eulogizing them simply because they are ancient and part of Indian cultural tradition, many scholars have begun to analyse these phenomena using sophisticated physiological and psychological techniques and to integrate them with modern health practices. For example, Neki (1975) has used *sahaja* (balance, harmony) as an ideal of mental health. It is conceptualized both as a process and a state characterized by spontaneity and equilibrium bringing about harmony within oneself as well as of the self with the environment, and culminating in illumination. It signifies heightened consciousness, deep awareness, and keen sensibility. The affective experiences associated with *sahaja* include an experience of inner harmony in which one directly perceives one's inner rhythmicity.

Interest in Islamic practices related to health has also been growing. A good example is the *tasawwuf* therapy of the mystics *(Sufis)* in which the focus is on the state called *ahwal* reported by a seeker of God (*salik* or *murid*) to his mentor (*murshid, sheikh* or *pir*). This focus is quite similar to that addressed by mental health professionals. Within the *sufi* practice, treatment is conducted in the context of the pursuit of gnosis under the guidance of a spiritual mentor (for details, see Ajmal, 1986).

Kakar (1984) has emphasized a *relational model* as being more congruent to Indian healing traditions. Among the techniques of counseling based on this model, he highlights the role of *darshan*. It contains a re-experiencing of the mutual relationship between the mother and the infant. The *darshan* is the deepening of the bond with the *guru*, and the brief but regular fulfilment of this basic human need for affirmation is charged with therapeutic power.

In India many folk healing traditions exist. Kakar (1982) has described at length the healing practices of a *pir* (wise elder), a tribal healer and other *shamans*, mystics, and *ayurveda* practitioners, as well as of healing rituals in temples. Contrasts regarding the nature and goal of Indian and Western therapeutic procedures clearly stand out. In the indigenous healing rituals, there is the element of the religious that is missing in the Western therapeutic procedures where the "sacred" and the "profane" are kept separate, with the latter dominating entirely the realms of medicine and psychotherapy. Then again, there is the involvement and integration of the entire family, relatives, and even the community in the healing process, whereas psychotherapy in the West, until recently, has remained almost entirely an individual affair. Western psychotherapy places a high value on the limitless respect for the individual and brings about a cure through the development of new cognitions in the client. On the other hand, the underlying values in the Indian traditional healing rituals "stress that faith and surrender to a power beyond the individual are better than individual effort and struggle, that the source of human strength lies in a harmonious integration with one's group, in the individual's affirmation of the community's values and its given order, in his obedience to the community's goods and in his cherishing of its traditions" (Kakar, 1982, p. 88). Instead of summarily dismissing these traditional healing practices as unscientific and bizarre, an effort has been made to understand them in their own terms and at the same time explain them by bringing out idioms of Freud and Western psychology generally.

Turning to the area of social psychology, Indian social psychologists share to a large extent the relational orientation of their Chinese and Japanese counterparts. In the West, the individual is regarded as an autonomous and segregated being, a degree of duality is implied as epitomized in the expression "man *and* society" or "man *in* society." The model according to Indian tradition is "man-society"; a kind of symbiotic relationship between the two is posited where one cannot be separated from the other (D. Sinha, 1981). The individual's identity is conceived not so much in terms of his/her personal qualities and achievements, but in the context of his/her family, caste, place, institutions, and a whole web of interpersonal roles and relationships. It is in this perspective that social behavior is analyzed and interpreted. Thus, lower need for achievement scores in Indian samples is explained not in terms of the absence of the Protestant work ethic, but as differences in work culture and socialization. The sociocultural context and relational view of the individual are thus brought into the picture (Misra & Gergen, 1993, p. 236). Studies (Agarwal & Misra, 1986; Singhal & Misra, 1989) have demonstrated that unlike in the West, familial and social concerns like "being a good person," "well-being of others," and fulfilling one's duties and helping others are predominant parts of the achievement goals of Indian people. A relational orientation is also evidenced in the conceptualization of the nurturant task leader (J. B. P. Sinha, 1980), which will be discussed in a later section.

Japan

In Japan indigenization is evidenced in strong interest in indigenous psychotherapeutic techniques, indigenous approaches to management, the study of Japanese values in child rearing and socialization, and in social psychology. Particular mention must be made of the systematic work of Koji Sato in Zen Buddhism and oriental psychology, and his establishment of the journal *Psychologia*, which has become a vehicle of local psychological research. However, as Hoshino and Umemoto (1987) report on Japanese psychology, it reflects the status of Western (particularly American) psychology in Japan. Apart from a few exceptions, such as work done in Kyoto, indigenous Japanese psychology is mainly handled by anthropologists, philosophers, and humanists.

Of special interest are the Japanese indigenous approaches to psychotherapy. *Morita* therapy is rooted in the Japanese core cultural value of *amae*. It is greatly influenced by Buddhist-based treatment for various kinds of neuroses. Its chief characteristics include isolated bed rest and guided work therapy (Reynolds, 1981). The therapeutic process reflects *amae* (a term that in general means "need for dependency"), which is thought to be highly valued in Japanese life and interpersonal relationships. It implies the "wish to be loved" or "dependency need," and aims at acquiescence to whatever circumstance one happens to be in (Doi, 1978, p. 215). Its centrality in the life of a Japanese reflects a basic psychological difference with the Western world. The goal of *Morita* therapy, as Pedersen (1981) points out, is to have the patient accept the realities of one's life (i.e., "to take in") rather than attempt to bring reality into line with one's needs and desires.

Another indigenous procedure popular in Japan is *Naikan* therapy. It relies on a kind of introspection to discover and realize personal and authentic guilt for being ungrateful and troublesome to others, and is aimed at establishing a positive attitude towards individuals who have extended themselves on behalf of the client in the past. That is, its goal is to have the client discover both guilt and gratitude, which brings about a profound change in self image and interpersonal attitude (Murase, 1982, p. 317). Here, in a boldly moralistic manner, the burden of blame is put on the client rather than on others. At the root of *Naikan* lies another key concept for the understanding of Japanese personality structure, namely, *sunao*. Though it has a variety of meanings, it implies being docile or obedient, accepting (rather than being assertive), open minded, free from antagonism and rivalry, and maintaining harmony in relation to others. On the personal plane, it refers to being relaxed, flexible, gentle, and free from frustrations and conflicts. *Sunao* constitutes an assembly of values that include being at peace with oneself and one's surroundings.

In the area of social psychology, the two concepts of *attribute* and *frame* (Nakane, 1970) are relevant. The former refers to an individual's qualities acquired not only by birth but also through personal achievement, and the latter refers to an institution, locality, or a particular relationship that binds a set of individuals into a group. Individuals are classified on the basis of frame rather than attributes. Overriding importance is attached to one's institutional affiliations which provide a strong sense of group consciousness, identification, and loyalty. Moreover, social sensitivity is considered the chief characteristic of the Japanese ethos (Lebra, 1976); consequently they are extremely concerned about social interactions and relationships.

Pakistan and the Muslim World

In Pakistan, the process of indigenization has been encouraged by the concern of psychologists about their role in the formulation and execution of a plan of national development and economic transformation (Moghni, 1987, p. 31). Moreover, the general awakening in the Muslim world and the call for Islamization of knowledge has formed a strong impetus towards indigenization. Interest in traditional indigenous health practices and psychological elements of Sufism has developed. Zaman (1991, p. 227) refers to integrating "the Europeanate and indigenous dogma and practices relating to mental health and mental illness, and the role of biology, culture, society, and social psychology in the definition." Ajmal (1986) has analyzed Muslim contributions to psychotherapy.

In other Islamic countries psychology as a discipline is not well developed. A book by Badri (1979), which has made considerable impact in the Muslim world, describes the dilemma of Muslim psychologists. Discussing the union of psychology with Islam, he concludes that although there is nothing intrinsically unacceptable about psychology, the discipline must be adapted before it can be utilized within the context of Islamic values. Arab psychologists have displayed special interest in analyzing the Islamic model of change and investigating the relationship between the Islamic work ethic and organizational development (Ali, 1992). It is contended that this work ethic does not stand for a life of denial, as it is sometimes erroneously said, but for life fulfillment, and holds business motives in the highest regard. According to Prophet's preachings, hard work causes sins to be absolved and that "no one eats better food than he who eats out of his work." It serves as an alternative to the Protestant work ethic, and has inspired many studies especially in the field of organizational behavior. Ali and Azim (1994) have identified cultural attributes in the Arab world and indicated their implications for organizational development. They conclude that Islamic cultural values, if correctly identified and understood, can facilitate organizational changes and development.

The Philippines

Of the countries in Asia, the trend to indigenizing psychology is strongest and most articulate in the Philippines. Enriquez (1982), one of its most vocal and creative proponents, has written about "decolonizing the Filipino psyche," and the "contextualization of psychology in the Philippines" (p. 276). A plea for *Sikolohiyang Pilipino* (Enriquez, 1982) was made, and has been loudly articulated in two of Enriquez's most recent publications (1992, 1994).

Enriquez (1993, pp. 154–155) points out that against the colonial background of Filipino psychology, a movement to develop indigenous psychology has evolved that emphasizes four dominant themes: identity and national consciousness, and the indigenous conception and definition of the psyche as a focus of social psychological research; social awareness and involvement in social issues and problems; national and ethnic cultures and languages, including the study of traditional psychology; and application of indigenous psychology in health practices, agriculture, art, mass media, religion and the study of behavior and abilities found applicable to the Philippine setting.

It represents three primary areas of protest. First, it is a movement for a "liberated psychology," for "reawakening" and decolonization of the Filipino psyche. Second, it aims at developing industrial psychology appropriate for the Philippines; this is conceptualized as a *livelihood/economic psychology* focussing not on the privileged and the elite, but on the needs of the disadvantaged and underprivileged. Lastly, it is a movement against a psychology used for the exploitation of the masses *(sikolohiyang mapagpalaya)*. In short, as Rood (1985) points out, the three interrelated goals of *sikolohiyang Filipino* are the development of indigenous psychological concepts, the utilization of indigenous research methods, and the creation of more authentic and appropriate social scientific psychology.

Concepts relevant to understanding Filpino culture and behavior have been identified, including *hiya* (shame), *pakikisama* (yielding to the leader or the majority), *utang na loob* (gratitude), *amor proprio* (sensitivity to personal affront), and *bayanihan* (togetherness in common effort). Underlying all these is *kapwa* (unity of self and others), which is considered the core value. Analysis of Filipino language has identified eight different levels of interrelatedness, or human interactions, ranging from "the relatively uninvolved civility in *pakikitungo* to the total sense of identification in *pakikiisa*" (Enriquez, 1978). These concepts are utilized not only for explaining and interpreting the behavior of the Pilipinos, but also for designing psychological studies, that is, for explanatory and paradigmatic indigenization.

Filipino researchers have also taken radical steps in the direction of indigenization of methods. They are highly sceptical about modern psychological procedures rooted in a positivistic tradition. Apart from basing psychological investigations on culturally derived constructs, development and application of local and culturally meaningful innovative methods are important steps towards indigenization. Suggestions have been made for utilizing common practices in Filipino culture, like *pagtatanung-tanong* or "asking around and groping" and *Piling-piling Huwebes,* which is a combination of a survey and a focussed discussion (Enriquez, 1994). Further, it has been suggested to utilize *pakikiramdan* (sensitivity to social intercourse)—which is one of the core concepts of Filipino culture, for studying interpersonal interaction.

It is too early to assess the full utility of these indigenous approaches and techniques as a source of gathering psychological data. They constitute methods that are calculated to avoid the problems arising out of over-reliance on foreign procedures and devices. In this respect, Filipino psychologists have taken a significant step in broadening the methodological repertoire for psychology.

Turkey

In Turkey, European and American influences initially played significant roles in the establishment of psychology departments and in the conceptualization of research interests (Acar & Sahin, 1990). New trends were visible in the studies of Mumtaz Turhan and Muzaffar Sherif even as early as the 1930s. They linked psychology to national and societal issues like migration of the rural population, impact of technology, and cultural change. In fact, commenting on today's situation, Acar and Sahin (1990, p. 241) refer to "indigenization efforts especially in studies related to migration, family, gender and socialization issues, besides other approaches that emphasize the determining of power of economic relations, the interaction among cultural and economic relations and the explanation by international processes." At the present time, as Kagitçibasi (1994) points out, Turkish psychologists are actively involved in research problems of direct relevance to social development issues. The integration of problem-oriented research with scientific soundness and theoretical sophistication is felt to be essential.

Indigenization in Work Organization and Management

We have seen many overlapping interests in the countries dealt with so far. This has been true especially in the areas of social psychology and psychotherapy. A topic for which this holds even stronger, and which in the contemporary world almost by its very nature has an international flavor, is organizational psychology. Overwhelmed by the rapid industrial development of the West, the developing countries have typically adopted Western technology, structures, and systems of management. Underlying this has been the belief that the patterns of effective organization and management are universal, conditioned mainly by the demands of modern technology. Organization theorists in the West (and following them their counterparts in other regions of the world) have advocated the use of a single set of management techniques for *all* employees *all over* the world. This is true even of the humanistic approaches to management, such as participative management and job enrichment advocated by Likert (1961), McGregor (1960), and Herzberg (1966). On the psychological plane, McClelland and Winter (1969) have emphasized the inculcation of a need for achievement among entrepreneurs for heightening economic activities, and Triandis (1971) has identified a "syndrome of characteristics" that is considered vital for the full utilization of modern technology. These principles and practices have turned into "organizational fads" (Kanungo, 1980). But as Kanungo and Jaeger (1990, p. 1) have observed, "uncritical transfer of management theories and techniques based on Western ideologies and value systems has in many ways contributed to organizational inefficiency and ineffectiveness in the developing country context."

Of late, increasing numbers of behavioral scientists are questioning the universal applicability of single management techniques such as participation, incentive systems, job enrichment, and so on. Studies have demonstrated their limited applicability, while cultural embeddedness of industrial organizations has been emphasized (J. B. P. Sinha, 1993b).

The phenomenal economic success of Japan, and more recently of the four "Asian Tigers," have exploded the myth not only of the superiority, but also of the universality of Western management. These countries have adopted development strategies that utilize sociocultural features of their own society for overall organizational and managerial effectiveness.

The indigenous perspective has two outcomes. First, there is a search for alternative paradigms. As experiences in Japan and among the "Asian Tigers" have demonstrated, alternative patterns of organizations and management that have taken into account the cultural realities are more effective than the implanted Western practices (see Kao, Sinha, & Ng, 1994). Secondly, a new perspective in management training has been advanced. Because it is not possible to discuss these in detail, only a brief outline is given. (See also chapter by Hui and Luk, this *Handbook*).

Organizational and management practices in Japan, Hong Kong, Korea, Singapore, and Taiwan share many of the features of American practices. But they have integrated local basic values and behavior patterns with Western principles, and evolved styles of management and patterns of organization that are unique in many ways. They provide excellent examples of the process of indigenization in that the culture-specific contemporary is integrated with the modern technological requirements. As Fujisawa, the cofounder of Honda Motor Company is reported to have remarked, "Japanese and American management is 95 percent the same, and different in all important respects" (quoted in Adler,

Dokfor, & Redding, 1989). Japanese managers and workers are said to have a sense of identity with their work groups, an ethic of cooperativeness, a high dependence on the larger entity, a strong sensitivity to status, and an active respect for each individual as a person (see Adler et al., 1989). Three underlying factors at the heart of Japanese management are: a long-range planning horizon, commitment to lifetime employment, and collective responsibility—all rooted in Japanese culture (Keys & Miller, 1984). Individuals in Japanese corporations are evaluated on the basis of their contribution to the team rather than how far they can push ahead of their colleagues (Moghaddam, Taylor & Wright, 1993). Further, American managers are more "segmented" while the Japanese are both segmented and "holistic" (Ouchi, 1981). Another feature is the central importance of the group in the decision-making process. Grouping implies not simply "affiliation," but a sense of interrelatedness among all natural elements that results in strong cohesion.

Chinese management shares many of the characteristics with the Japanese and is embedded in the Confucian traditional ethos; it is paternalistic and rooted in normative values of trust, subtlety, and loyalty. The Chinese work organization is also characterized by personalism and particularism of economic relationships. Derived from the agrarian past, some of the cherished values in Chinese management are paternalistic authority, loyalty, familial cohesion and mutual dependence (Yang, 1988), altruism, rules of seniority, and respect for wisdom of the elders (Chao, 1990, p. 585).

The participative style of management generally found effective in the West is conditioned by certain sociocultural factors. An alternative model has been proposed that incorporates features of both autocratic and democratic leaderships and is felt to be congruent with dominant Indian cultural values (J. B. P. Sinha, 1980). It suggests an indigenous style of management in which the leader cares for subordinates, shows affection, takes personal interest in their well-being, and above all is committed to their growth. The leader is committed to the group goal and is task-oriented. Subordinates who meet his expectations are reinforced by nurturance. As they develop and grow in confidence and handle their work, the dependency is reduced, and in time, the superior gives more work responsibility. In the course of time, he replaces his paternalistic style and the relationship becomes more participative. Nurturant task leadership as an indigenous management style is considered more appropriate in developing countries (J. B. P. Sinha, 1993a).

Chakraborty's (1987, 1991, 1993) work provides an example of indigenization in management training. A new perspective is being advanced by referring to religio-philosophical literature on the Indian view of an effective person (Chakraborty, 1987; N. K. Singh, 1990). In Western approaches to training, the emphasis has been on acquiring skills, knowledge, and motivation to develop systems and organize resources (both men and material) in order to realize targets set by the organization as well as to develop themselves by being integrated into the organization. The emphasis, in essence, has been on managing and organizing others. On the other hand, the emphasis in Indian thinking is on the "purity" of the individual's mind. The individual is considered the central force and work is a duty meant for self-purification. The aim of training is to develop managers who, instead of being analytic and technical, should function in a synthetic and spiritual way. For the purpose, Chakraborty (1987, 1991) advocates yoga and meditation as the techniques for experiential training. The core of the training programme is *chittashuddhi* (purification of mind/heart) by providing in modules materials derived from Hindu and Buddhist philosophers and the writings of Sri Aurobindo. The approach has been tried in some industrial organizations, and the "feedback" received from the participants was positive. Despite the evidence, the approach is still open to further examination. Its effectiveness in stress management is more conclusive than in other areas of manager's functioning. The approach exemplifies indigenization in the field of management by seeking to blend traditional management practices with modern ones in order to attain more effectively the goals of work organizations.

Scope and Prospects of Indigenization

It is too early to make an appraisal of the impact of indigenization on the development of psychology. But some prospects, both negative and positive, are already visible.

An Empirical Study of Indigenization

Theoretical analyses of indigenization have been made by many psychologists. As discussed in earlier sections, these have consisted mainly of analyses of the concept, the constituents of the process, and the prospects. Efforts to quantify indigenization and to make a cross-cultural comparison of the extent to which it is realized have been rare. In this respect, studies conducted by Adair and his colleagues mark a definite advance.

Indigenization was operationalized as the extent to which the concepts, problems, hypotheses, methods, and tests emanate from, adequately represent, and reflect back upon the cultural context in which behavior is observed (Adair, 1992a; Adair, Puhan & Vohra, 1993, p. 149). It was pointed out that indigenization can be measured by change in content, methods, problem development, hypotheses, and interpretations of published research results (Adair, 1992a, p. 63). Using these indicators, comparisons of the extent of indigenization in Bangladesh, Canada, and India were made by content-analyzing papers published in some journals over a period of time. Cultural sensitivity was maximum in Canadian publications while reference to social problems was highest in studies in Bangladesh and India. In the latter countries there was a substantial increase in references to cultural variables in recent years, but indigenous cultural elements had not become the main focus of study. Indigenization of methods was weak, with continued heavy dependence on tests and measuring devices borrowed from the West. The general conclusion that emerged from the studies was that there has "been some slight movement towards an indigenous discipline" (Adair, Puhan & Vohra, 1993, p. 149).

The chief merit of these studies is that the analysis of indigenization has been concretized and put on a quantitative plane. With indicators and criteria identified, the procedure opens the way for empirical studies of indigenization. But the procedure does not seem sensitive enough to identify the diverse ways in which the process is unfolding in various cultural contexts. The criteria utilized appear too simple, and any analysis entirely based on them is likely to miss the subtleties and nuances of a very complex and varied process.

Pitfalls of Indigenization

There are certain pitfalls inherent in the process of indigenization, which if not guarded against may lead to cultural chauvinism and anti-scientific tendencies that are likely to be dysfunctional to the development of the discipline.

A spurious manifestation of the process, is "cosmetic indigenization" (D. Sinha, 1993). It involves making casual references to certain concepts and formulations from local cultural sources while dealing with a "modern" psychological problem. This is meant more for enhancing appearance rather than for better understanding of the phenomenon.

It has been observed that indigenization has almost assumed the form of a movement. In many countries, "a broader set of investigators have begun to jump on to the bandwagon" (Adair, 1992b). For these second-stage promoters, indigenization has become a slogan. There is not only confusion about what constitutes an indigenous psychology, but also uncertainty about how to make one's own research more indigenous (Adair, 1992b). Sometimes, as Naidu (1990) points out, there is more talk than action, and confusion about its approach and the direction that psychology should take.

Berry (1986) has suggested a model for conceptualizing intercultural relations, which is useful in understanding the dynamics of the processes of indigenization. According to the model, the outcome is governed by reactions of people to two different but interacting systems of knowledge—in the present case, the traditional/indigenous and the modern/Western psychology. As a reaction against the domination of imported Western psychology, the process of indigenization (to follow Berry's model) consisted of reacting positively to one's own system and negatively to the imported one. This is exactly what has happened in many cases. The inadequacies of the positivistic and mechanistic orientations of modern scientific psychology in understanding complex phenomena such as human personality, mental health, and so on have been highlighted, and the psychological knowledge enshrined in traditional and cultural sources were eulogized uncritically. The outcome has been a kind of "revivalism" in psychology. The proponents refer to the superficiality of modern psychology and expose the weaknesses of scientific values without suggesting a satisfactory alternative. At the same time, they talk glibly about all kinds of esoteric phenomena like transmigration of the soul, rebirth, and supernatural powers. They extract from ancient sources speculative views about phenomena whose only claim to validity is their ancient origin.

Another danger that emanates from indigenization is parochialism in knowledge, built on a kind of Western vs non-Western dichotomy. In their zeal to emphasize the distinctive characteristics of psychology in their country, many scholars give the impression that the two systems are irreconcilable and they make a plea for psychology confined to local areas. Such parochialism is ill conceived. Though a scientific enterprise is conditioned by historical and sociocultural factors, there is no question of knowledge being circumscribed by national and regional boundaries. Science, which seeks truth, cannot be compartmentalized by national or continental limits (D. Sinha, 1992, p. 42). What has been objected to is the uncritical dependence on the Western system for concepts, models and theories, and viewing non-Western cultures and psychological functioning through the lens of Western norms. The goal of indigenization is not parochialism in psychology, but the development of "appropriate" psychology. Since indigenization is essentially a cultural approach, it sometimes tends to generate a kind of "radical cultural relativism" (Berry, 1972) in understanding and studying reality. In its extreme form, it does not encourage comparison between cultures. The emphasis seems to be more on *cultural* than on *cross-cultural* understanding. As a consequence, it is likely to lead to a proliferation of psychologies, with every population, every locality, and every village having its own psychology. This kind of cultural relativism and parochialism has not much to commend it, and in the last analysis is inimical to the development of the discipline.

A related manifestation of indigenization, which has gained popularity, is "cultural parallelism." Here, different systems are not dichotomized but parallels are highlighted between concepts, ideas, and formulations contained in traditional systems and those propounded by modern psychology. To provide an example from India, many treatises have been produced that give analyses and conceptualizations of perception, personality, dreams, and so forth, as they are found in ancient writings. Similarities with formulations made by psychologists in the West are pointed out. But little effort is made to bring together and integrate the two approaches. Such efforts seem to take for granted that two distinct systems of psychology coexist, and imply that no interface or interaction is necessary. Though the main purpose of the studies like those of Akhilananda (1948) and Paranjpe (1984) is the "meeting of the East and the West," they seem to take for granted that the Indian and the Western systems, because of vital differences in approach and method of study, cannot be reconciled. However, indigenization by its very definition does not imply cultural duality of knowledge, but essentially endeavors to bring about an interface of the two to their mutual advantage.

Prospects and Potential

In spite of the dangers involved, indigenization has opened a new vista in the development of psychology. In terms of Berry's (1986) model, it is a position in which scholars entertain positive views towards their own traditional system as well as towards the one that has been imported. Though critical of each other, various aspects of both systems are valued. An interface between the two is sought to produce an organic integration. The process has been termed as "assimilative synthesis" of the two systems of knowledge in which what is valuable is retained and old knowledge is re-stated in new forms adapted to the present needs (D. Sinha, 1992, p. 44). It enables the maintenance of the cultural identity of one's own system as well as a movement to become an integral part of the larger framework.

The process can be viewed as a "battle for consciousness" (Gopal, 1989, p. 61), a challenge to western intellectual domination, and a search for restoring the identity of people who had lost it. It would be oversimplification to regard indigenization as an ethnocentric denial of the West, or as a clash between tradition and modernity. It is not an approach to embrace the past and to hold on to it at all cost; nor are western ideas rejected simply because they are foreign and therefore bad.

Indigenization and Universal Psychology

Indigenization has two concerns: the need for roots in a specific cultural setting and the establishment of universal psychology. This dual aspect is not always appreciated. Some overenthusiastic proponents of indigenous psychology take the extreme position of radical cultural relativism that precludes intercultural comparisons. On the other extreme, others overanxious about maintaining the intellectual dominance of (Western) mainstream psychology look to indigenous developments with a high degree of scepticism and suspicion. The misplaced apprehension is amply reflected in the remark of the then APA President during a symposium on "Unity of Psychology." At the International Congress of Applied Psychology in Kyoto in 1990 that all was well within the discipline, except possibly, for the threat from the indigenous psychology movement (see Adair, 1992b, p. 2).

The most common criticism of indigenization, as Berry et al. (1992, p. 384) observe, is that there will be a proliferation of psychologies. On the one hand, it is erroneous to think that indigenous psychology ignores the achievements of Western psychology, or, for that matter, any significant development in psychology in any part of the world. On the other hand, the culture-bound (and frequently culture-blind) character of modern psychology has made it necessary to take into account other viewpoints and perspectives in the study of human behavior. This does not preclude the eventual development of a universal psychology. Like cross-cultural psychology, indigenous psychology aims at better understanding of human functioning, which it feels is not possible without analyzing human behaviors in their cultural contexts. The ultimate goal of indigenous psychology is the development of a universal psychology that incorporates all indigenous (including Western) psychologies (Berry & Kim, 1993); it only asserts that panhuman psychological principles and theories cannot be taken for granted or assumed merely because they are developed in the West. What indigenous psychology does is to assert clearly and unambiguously that the road to universal psychology is through the development of indigenous psychologies. Challenging the principles and theories of mainstream psychology is not destructive in its orientation. Indigenization is a necessary step towards the establishment of true universals in psychology which are *proved*, rather than merely *assumed*.

Because the indigenous perspectives are critical of the monocultural nature of mainstream psychology, an erroneous impression is often produced that it holds a particularistic and radical cultural relativistic stance. One of the strongest proponents of indigenous psychology, Enriquez (1993) not only points to "global psychology" as its goal, but suggests a model for attaining it through a "cross-indigenous approach": "Different cultures of the world are tapped as sources of cultural knowledge. The resulting pool may then be called cross-cultural knowledge. More aptly, it is cross-indigenous knowledge, to distinguish it from the kind of cross-cultural knowledge derived from an application of the psychology of industrialized countries to data gathered from the Third World" (p. 154). As Kim and Berry (1993, p. 11) have concluded, "From systematic studies of indigenous psychologies across different cultures, it is possible to look for general principles and universals. . . . With the cross-indigenous approach, not only can universal regularities be discovered, but the total range of a phenomenon investigated is increased."

Thus, indigenous psychologies widen the database for the development of a universal psychology. As we know, the main purpose of cross-cultural psychology is the establishment of panhuman verities in psychology. But, as Enriquez (1993, p. 154) observes, "cross-cultural psychology will remain a promise as long as indigenous psychologies are untapped because of language and cultural barriers." Discussing the interdependence of cross-cultural psychology and indigenous psychology, D. Sinha (1989, p. 26) asserts that while indigenous psychology predates cross-cultural psychology, the latter in certain ways has tended to revive and generate the process of indigenization, which in turn has enriched cross-cultural psychology.

This points to the function that indigenous psychologies provide: alternative perspectives and approaches for studying and analyzing psychological phenomena. By approaching them from a different cultural perspective, it shows the phenomena in a new light, and thereby challenges whatever the prevailing perspective of the discipline may be. Such controversies are essential for the progress of any science and prevent it from becoming rigid and lapsing into dogmas. In this context, it is to be noted that though Boring (1929, p. 90) found challenges and controversies personally abhorrent, he came reluctantly to the conclusion that scientific truth, like justice, must come about by controversy. Therefore, there is a need for an alternative perspective, another forum independent from the one that prevails currently in modern psychology, that cannot be brushed aside. Alternative perspectives and new paradigms are essential for the healthy growth of any science. The same is true of psychology. In this respect, indigenous psychologies represent a crucial step in the development of psychology.

References

Acar, G. & Sahin, D. (1990). Psychology in Turkey. *Psychology and Developing Societies, 1990,
2,* 241–256.

Adair, J. G. (1989a). Indigenous developments in
Indian psychology: A quantitative assessment. Paper presented at the Annual Meeting of the Canadian Psychological Association, Halifax, Nova Scotia.

Adair, J. G. (1989b). Development of the discipline
and its contribution to social development in
developing countries. Paper presented at the
Inter-American Congress of Psychology,
Buenos Aires, Argentina.

Adair, J. G. (1992a). Empirical studies of
indigenization and development of the discipline in developing countries. In S.
Iwawaki, Y. Kashima & K. Leung (Eds.), *Innovations in cross-cultural psychology* (pp. 62–
74). Amsterdam: Swets & Zeitlinger.

Adair, J. G. (1992b). The indigenous psychology
bandwagon: Cautions and considerations.
Paper presented at the 4th Asian Regional
IACCP Conference, Kathmandu, Nepal.

Adair, J. G., Puhan, B. N. & Vohra, N. (1993).
Indigenization of psychology: Empirical assessment of progress in Indian research. *International Journal of Psychology, 28,* 149–169.

Adler, N. J., Doktor, R. & Redding, S. G. (1989).
From the Atlantic to the Pacific century:
Cross-cultural management reviewed. In A.
B. Chimezie & Y. Osigweh (Eds.), *Organiza-
tional science abroad* (pp. 27–54). New York:
Plenum.

Agarwal, R. & Misra, G. (1986). A factor analytic
study of achievement goals and means: An
Indian view. *International Journal of Psychology, 21,* 717–731.

Ajmal, M. (1986). Muslim contributions to psychotherapy and other essays. *Psychological
Research Monograph 5,* Islamabad: National
Institute of Psychology, Quaid-i-Azam University.

Akhilananda, S. (1948). *Hindu psychology,* London:
George Allen & Unwin.

Al Faruqi, I. R. (1982). Islamization of knowledge:
General principles and work plan. International Institute of Islamic Thought, Washington DC.

Ali, A. J.(1992). Islamic work ethic in Arabia. *Journal of Psychology, 126,* 507–519.

Ali, A. J. & Azim, A. (1994). Islamic work ethic
and organizational development. Paper pre-
sented at the symposium on "Organizational
Development: Religio-Spiritual and Socio-
Cultural Perspectives," 23rd International
Congress of Applied Psychology, Madrid,
Spain, July 17–22.

Ardila, R. (1982). Psychology in Latin America
today. *Annual Review of Psychology, 33,* 103–
122.

Ardila, R. (1993). Latin American psychology and
world psychology: Is integration possible?
In U. Kim & J. W. Berry (Eds.), *Indigenous
psychologies: Research and experience in cultural
context* (pp. 170–176). Newbury Park, CA:
Sage.

Averasturi, L. G. (1980). Psychology and health
care in Cuba. *American Psychologist, 35,* 1090–
1095.

Azuma, H. (1984). Psychology in a non-Western
country. *International Journal of Psychology, 19,*
45–56.

Badri, M. B. (1979). *The dilemma of Muslim Psychologists.* London: M.W.H. London
Publishers.

Beena, C. (1990). *Personality typologies: A comparison of western and ancient Indian approaches.*
New Delhi: Commonwealth Publishers.

Berry, J. W. (1972). Radical cultural relativism and
the concept of intelligence. In L. J. Cronbach
& P. J. D. Drenth (Eds), *Mental tests and cultural adaptation* (pp. 77–88). The Hague:
Mouton.

Berry, J. W. (1974). Canadian psychology: Some
social and applied emphases. *Canadian Psychologist, 15,* 132–139.

Berry, J. W. (1976). *Human ecology and cognitive
style: Comparative studies in cultural and psychological adaptation.* New York: Sage/
Halsted.

Berry, J. W. (1978). Social psychology: Comparative, societal and universal. *Canadian Psychological Review, 19,* 93–104.

Berry, J. W. (1983). The sociogenesis of social sciences: An analysis of cultural relativity of
social psychology. In B. Bain (Ed.), *The*

sociogenesis of language and human conduct (pp. 449–458). New York: Plenum Press.

Berry, J. W. (1984). Multiculturalism in Canada: A social psychological analysis. *Canadian Journal of Behavioural Science, 16,* 353–370.

Berry, J. W. (1986). Multiculturalism and psychology in plural societies. In L. H. Ekstrand (Ed.), *Ethnic minorities and immigrants in cross-cultural perspective* (pp. 35–51). Lisse: Swets and Zeitlinger.

Berry, J. W. (1993). Psychology in and of Canada: One small step towards a universal psychology. In U. Kim & J. W. Berry (Eds.), *Indigenous psychologies: Research and experience in cultural context* (pp. 260–276). Newbury Park, CA: Sage.

Berry, J. W. & Kim, U. (1993). The way ahead: From indigenous psychologies to a universal psychology. In U. Kim & J.W. Berry (Eds). *Indigenous psychologies: Research and experience in cultural context,* (pp 277–280). Newbury Park, CA: Sage

Berry, J. W., Poortinga, Y. H., Segall, M. H. & Dasen, P. R. (1992). *Cross-cultural psychology: Research and application.* Cambridge: Cambridge University Press.

Berry, J. W. & Wilde, G. J. S. (Eds.). (1972). *Social psychology: The Canadian context.* Toronto: McClelland and Stewart.

Bhattacharya, K. C. (1954). *Swaraj in ideas. Viswa Bharati Journal, 20,* 103–114.

Biesheuvel, S. (1954). The measurement of occupational aptitudes in a multi-racial society. *Occupational Psychology, 28,* 189–196.

Bond, M. H. (Ed.). (1988). *The cross-cultural challenge to social psychology.* Newbury Park, CA: Sage.

Boring, E. G. (1929). The psychology of controversy. *Psychological Review, 36,* 97–121.

Bronfenbrenner, U. (1977). Towards an experimental ecology of human development. *American Psychologist, 32,* 513–531.

Campbell, D. T. (1968). A comparative multinational opinion sample exchange. *Journal of Social Issues, 24,* 245–256.

Chakraborty, S. K. (1987). *Managerial effectiveness and quality of work life: Indian insight.* New Delhi: Tata McGraw-Hill.

Chakraborty, S. K. (1991). *Management by values: Towards cultural consequence.* Delhi: Oxford University Press.

Chakraborty, S. K. (1993). *Management transformation by values: A corporate pilgrimage.* New Delhi: Sage.

Chao, Y. T. (1990). Culture and work organization: The Chinese case. *International Journal of Psychology, 25,* 583–592.

Ching, C. C. (1984). Psychology and the four modernizations in China. *International Journal of Psychology, 19,* 57–63.

Chiu, C. (1989). The notion of justice and pattern of justice behaviour in Chinese culture. Unpublished Master essay. Hong Kong University, Hong Kong.

Chiu, C. (1991). Righteousness: The notion of justice in Chinese societies (in Chinese). In C. F. Yang & H. S. R. Kao (Eds.), *Chinese people and Chinese society* (pp. 261–285). Taipei: Yuen Liao.

Dasen, P. R., Dembele, B., Ettien, K., Kabran, K., Kamagate, D., Kaffi, D. A. & N'Guessan, A. (1985). N'glouele, l'intelligence chez les Baoulé [N'glouele, intelligence among the Baoule]. *Archives de Psychologie, 53,* 293–324.

Diaz-Guerrero, R. (1977a). Editorial response. *IACCP Newsletter, 11,* 4–6.

Diaz-Guerrero, R. (1977b). A Mexican psychology. *American Psychologist, 32,* 934–944.

Diaz-Guerrero, R. (1982). Psychology of the historic sociocultural premise. *Spanish Language Psychology, 2,* 382–410.

Diaz-Guerrero, R. (1993). Mexican ethnopsychology. In U. Kim & J. W. Berry (Eds.), *Indigenous psychologies: Research and experience in cultural context,* (pp. 44–55). Newbury Park, CA: Sage.

Diaz-Guerrero, R. (1994). Origin and development of psychology in Latin America. *International Journal of Psychology, 29,* 717–727.

Diaz-Loving, R. (1994). Indigenous personality traits in developing countries: Serendipity vs. active search and confirmation. Paper presented during the symposium on "Indigenous Psychologies: Several National Perspectives," 23rd International Congress of Applied Psychology, Madrid, Spain, July 17-22.

Doi, L. T. (1978). *Amae:* A key concept for understanding Japanese personality structure. In R. J. Corsini (Ed.), *Readings in current personality theories* (pp. 213–219). Ithaca: Peacock Publishers.

Dorcus, A. & Wang, T. S. (in press). Chinese Qigong research. In H. S. R. Kao & D. Sinha (Eds.), *Asian perspectives in psychology*, Delhi: Sage.

Durojaiye, M. O. (1987). Black Africa. In A. R. Gilgen and C. K. Gilgen (Eds.), *International handbook of psychology* (pp. 24–36). New York: Greenwood Press.

Durojaiye, M. O. (1993). Indigenous psychology in Africa: The search for meaning. In U. Kim & J. W. Berry (Eds.), *Indigenous psychologies: Research and experience in cultural context* (pp. 211–220). Newbury Park, CA: Sage.

Enriquez, V. G. (1978). *Kapwa:* A core concept in Filipino social psychology. *Philippine Social Sciences and Humanities Review, 42,* 100–108.

Enriquez, V.G. (1982). *Towards Filipino Psychology: Essays and Studies on Language and Culture.* Quezon City: Psychological Research & Training House.

Enriquez, V. G. (1987). Decolonizing the Filipino psyche: Impetus for the development of psychology in the Philippines. In G. H. Blowers & A. H. Turtle (Eds.), *Psychology moving East* (pp. 265–287). Boulder: Westview Press.

Enriquez, V. G. (Ed.). (1990). *Indigenous psychologies.* Quezon City: Psychology Research & Training House.

Enriquez, V. G. (1992). *From Colonial to liberation psychology: The Philippine experience,* (1st ed.). Manila: De la Salle University Press.

Enriquez, V. G. (1993). Developing a Filipino psychology. In U. Kim & J. W. Berry (Eds.), *Indigenous psychologies: Research and experience in cultural context* (pp. 152–169). Newbury Park, CA: Sage.

Enriquez, V. G. (1994). *Pagbabangong-Dangal: Indigenous Psychology and Cultural Empowerment.* Quezon City: Akademya ng Kultura at Sikolohiyang Pilipino.

Gopal, S. (1989). *Radhakrishnan: A biography.* Delhi: Oxford University Press.

Heelas, P. (1981). Introduction: Indigenous psychologies. In P. Heelas & A. Lock (Eds.), *Indigenous psychologies: The anthropology of the self.* London: Academic Press.

Heron, A. (1975). Psychology and national development: The Zambian experience. In J. W. Berry & W. J. Lonner (Eds.), *Applied cross-cultural psychology* (pp. 13–17). Amsterdam: Swets & Zeitlinger.

Herzberg, F. (1966). *Work and the nature of man.* Cleveland: World Publishing.

Ho, D.Y. F. (1981). Traditional pattern of socialization in Chinese society. *Acta Psychologica Taiwanica, 23,* 81–95.

Ho, D. Y. F. (1988). Asian psychology: A dialogue in indigenization and beyond. In A. C. Paranjpe, D. Y. F. Ho, & R. W. Rieber (Eds.), *Asian contributions to psychology* (pp. 53–77). New York: Praeger.

Ho, D. Y. F. (1993). Relational orientation in Asian social psychology. In U. Kim & J. W. Berry (Eds.), *Indigenous psychologies: Research and experience in cultural context* (pp. 240–259). Newbury Park, CA: Sage.

Hofstede, G. (1988). McGregor in Southeast Asia? In D. Sinha & H. S. R. Kao (Eds.), *Social values and development: Asian perspectives,* (pp. 304–314). Delhi: Sage.

Hoshino, A. & Umemoto, T. (1987). Japanese psychology: Historical review and recent trends. In G. Blowers & A. Turtle (Eds.), *Psychology moving East: The status of western psychology in Asia and Oceania* (pp. 183–196). Boulder: Westview Press.

Hsu, F. L. K. (1963). *Clan, Caste and Club.* New York: van Nostrand.

Hsu, F. L. K. (1971). Psychosocial homeostasis and *jen:* Conceptual tools for advancing psychological anthropology. *American Anthropologist, 73,* 23–44.

Hsu, F. L. K. (1985). The self in cross-cultural perspective. In A. J. Marsella, G. DeVos & F. L. K. Hsu (Eds.), *Culture and self: Asian and western perspectives* (pp. 24–55). London: Tavistock.

Jahoda, G. (1979). A cross-cultural perspective on experimental social psychology. *Personality and Social Psychology Bulletin, 5,* 142–148.

Jahoda, G. (1986). Nature, culture and social psychology. *European Journal of Social Psychology, 16,* 17–30.

Jaspars, J. (1986). Forum and focus: A personal view of European social psychology. *European Journal of Social Psychology, 16,* 3–15.

Jilek, W. (1988). *Indian healing: Shamanic ceremo-*

nialism in the Pacific Northwest. Vancouver: Hancock House.

Jing, Q. (1994). Development of psychology in China. *International Journal of Psychology, 29,* 667–675.

Jones, E. E. (1985). Major developments in social psychology during the past five decades. In G. Lindsay & E. Aronson (Eds.), *Handbook of social psychology* (3rd ed.) (pp. 47–107). New York: Random House.

Kagitçibasi, C. (1994). Psychology in Turkey. *International Journal of Psychology, 29,* 729–738.

Kakar, S. (1979). *Indian childhood: Cultural ideals and social reality.* Delhi: Oxford University Press.

Kakar, S. (1982). *Shamans, mystics and doctors: A psychological enquiry into India and its healing traditions.* Bombay: Oxford University Press.

Kakar, S. (1984). Psychological counselling: Is there an Asian model? Proceedings of the 5th Biennial Conference-Workshop of the Association of Psychological and Educational Counsellors of Asia, Bangalore.

Kanungo, R. (1980). *Biculturalism and management.* Toronto: Butterworth.

Kanungo, R. N. & Jaeger, A. M. (1990). Introduction: The need for indigenous management in developing countries. In A. M. Jaeger & R. N. Kanungo (Eds.), *Management in developing countries* (pp. 1–19). London: Routledge.

Kao, H. S. R. & Goan, C. H. (1990). The therapeutic effect of Chinese calligraphy. In Chinese University of Hong Kong Extra-Mural Department (Ed.), *Stress: Causes and remedies* (pp. 59–64). Hong Kong: Commercial Press.

Kao, H. S. R. & Robinson, L. (1990). Chinese calligraphy and stress reduction. In Chinese University of Hong Kong Extra-Mural Department (Ed.), *Stress: Causes and remedies* (pp. 51–58). Hong Kong: Commercial Press.

Kao, H. S. R., Sinha, D. & Ng, S. H. (Eds.). (1994). *Effective organizations and social values.* New Delhi: Sage.

Kapur, R. L. (1979). The role of traditional healers in mental care in rural India. *Social Science & Medicine, 136,* 27–33.

Kelman, H. C. (1972). Roles of behavioural scientist in policy oriented research. In G. V. Coelho & G. V. Rubinstein (Eds.), *Social*

change and human behaviour. Bethesda, MD: NIMH.

Kennedy, S., Scheirer, J. & Rogers, A. (1984). The price of success: Our monocultural science. *American Psychologist, 39,* 996–997.

Keys, J. B. & Miller, T. R. (1984). The Japanese management theory jungle. *Academy of Management Review, 9,* 342–353.

Kim, U. (1990). Indigenous psychology: Science and applications. In R. Brislin (Ed.), *Applied cross-cultural psychology* (pp. 142–160). Newbury Park, CA: Sage.

Kim, U. & Berry, J. W. (1993). Introduction. In U. Kim & J. W. Berry (Eds.), *Indigenous psychologies: Research and experience in cultural context* (pp. 1–29). Newbury Park, CA: Sage.

Koch, S. & Leary, D. E. (1985). Introduction. In S. Koch & D. E. Leary (Eds.), *A century of psychology as science.* New York: McGraw-Hill.

Kumar, K. (1979). Indigenization and transnational cooperation in social sciences. In K. Kumar (Ed.), *Bonds without knowledge.* Honolulu: East-West Cultural Learning Institute.

Lebra, T. S. (1976). *Japanese patterns of behaviour.* Honolulu: University of Hawaii Press.

Lee, H. W. & Petzold, M. (1987). Psychology in the Republic of China. In G. H. Blowers & A. M. Turtle (Ed.), *Psychology moving East* (pp. 105–125). Boulder: Westview Press.

Likert, R. (1961). *New pattern of management.* New York: McGraw-Hill.

Lindzey, G. & Aronson, E. (Eds.). (1985). *The handbook of social psychology.* New York: Random House.

Luria, A. R. (1971). Towards the problem of historical nature of psychological processes. *Internatioal Journal of Psychology, 6,* 259–272.

Ma, H. K. (1988). The Chinese perspective on the moral judgement development. *International Journal of Psychology, 23,* 201–227.

Ma, H. K. (1989). Moral orientation and moral judgements in adolescents in Hong Kong, Mainland China and England. *Journal of Cross-Cultural Psychology, 20,* 152–177.

Macleod, R. B. (1955). *Psychology in Canadian universities and colleges.* Ottawa: Social Science Research Council.

Mataragnon, R. H. (1988). *Pakikiramdan* in Filipino social interaction: A study of subtlety and sensitivity. In A. C. Paranjpe, D. Y. F. Ho & R. W. Rieber (Eds.), *Asian contributions to psychology* (pp. 251–261). New York: Praeger.

McClelland, D. C. & Winter, D. G. (1969). *Motivating economic development.* New York: Free Press.

McGregor, D. (1960). *The human side of enterprise.* New York: Harper.

Merriam-Webster, G. C. (1976). *Webster's third new international dictionary.* Chicago: Encyclopedia Britannica.

Miller, J. G., Bersoff, D. M. & Harwood, R. L. (1990). Perceptions of social responsibilities in India and the United States: Moral imperatives or personal decisions. *Journal of Personality and Social Psychology, 58,* 33–47.

Misra, G. & Gergen, K. J. (1993). On the place of culture in social sciences. *International Journal of Psychology, 28,* 225–243.

Moghaddam, F. M. (1993). Traditional and modern psychologies in competing cultural systems: Lessons from Iran, 1978-1981. In U. Kim & J. W. Berry (Eds.), *Indigenous psychologies: Research and experience in cultural context* (pp. 118–132). Newbury Park, CA: Sage.

Moghaddam, F. M., Taylor, D. M. & Wright, S. C. (1993). *Social psychology in cross-cultural perspective.* New York: Freeman.

Moghni, S. M. (1987). Development of modern psychology in Pakistan. In G. H. Blowers & A. M. Turtle (Eds.), *Psychology moving East* (pp. 23–38). Boulder: Westview Press.

Mohanty, A. (1988). Beyond the horizon of Indian psychology. The Yankee doodler. In F. M. Sahoo (Ed.), *Psychology in Indian context* (pp. 1–8). Agra: National Psychological Corporation.

Moscovici, S. (1972). Society and theory in social psychology. In J. Israel & H. Tajfel (Eds.), *The context of social psychology* (pp. 17–68). London: Academic Press.

Mundy-Castle, A. C. (1974). Social and technological intelligence in Western and non-Western cultures. *Universitas* (University of Ghana, Lagos), *4,* 46–52.

Mundy-Castle, A. C. (1993). Human behaviour and national development: Conceptual and theoretical perspectives. *Ife Psychologia, 1,* 1–16.

Murase, T. (1982). *Sunao:* A central value of Japanese psychotherapy. In A. J. Marsella & G. White (Eds.), *Cultural conceptions of mental health and therapy* (pp. 317–329). Dordrecht: Reidel.

Naidu, R. K. (1990). Academic self-respect vs pseudo universalism: The travails of an Indian psychology teacher. *Indian Journal of Social Science, 3,* 569–574.

Nakane, C. (1970). *Japanese society.* Berkeley: University of California Press.

Nandy, A. (1974). The non-paradigmatic crisis in psychology: Reflections on the recipient culture of science. *Indian Journal of Psychology, 49,* 1–20.

Neki, J. S. (1975). *Sahaja:* An Indian ideal of mental health. *Psychiatry, 36,* 1–11.

Nsamenang, A. Bame. (1992). *Human development in cultural context: A Third World perspective.* Newbury Park, CA: Sage.

Ogedengbe, R. O. (1993). Some contributions of the traditional psychiatrists toward mental health in Nigeria. *Ife Psychologia, 1,* 17–31.

Ombredane, A. (1954). L'exploration de la mentalité des Noirs congolais. *Memoires de l'Institut Royal Colonial Belge, 37,* 1–243.

Ouchi, W. G. (1981). *Theory Z: How American business can meet the Japanese challenge.* Reading: Addison-Wesley.

Palsane, M. N. (1987). Yoga as psychotherapy. In M. L. Gharote & M. Lockhart (Eds.), *The art of survival.* London: Unwin.

Palsane, M. N., Bhavsar, S. N., Goswami, R. P. & Evans, G. W. (1986). The concept of stress in the Indian tradition. *Journal of Indian Psychology, 5,* 1–12.

Pande, N. & Naidu, R. K. (1986). Effort and outcome orientations as moderators of stress-strain relationship. *Psychological Studies, 32,* 207–214.

Pande, N. & Naidu, R. K. (1992). *Anasakti* and health: A study of non-attachment. *Psychology and Developing Societies, 4,* 89–104.

Paranjpe, A. C. (1984). *Theoretical psychology: The meeting of East and West.* New York: Plenum.

Paranjpe, A. C. (1988). A personality theory according to Vedanta. In A. C. Paranjpe, D. Y. F. Ho & R. W. Rieber (Eds.), *Asian contributions to psychology* (pp. 185–213). New York: Praeger.

Pareek, U. (1980a). Preface. In U. Pareek (Ed.), *A survey of research in psychology, 1971-1976,* Part I. Bombay: Popular Prakashan.

Pareek, U. (1980b). *A survey of research in psychology, 1971-1976.* Part I. Bombay: Popular Prakashan.

Pedersen, P. (1981). Alternative futures for cross-cultural counselling and psychotherapy. In A. Marsella & P. Pedersen (Eds.), *Cross-cultural counselling and psychotherapy* (pp. 22–58). New York: Pergamon.

Peltzer, K. (1987). *Some contributions to traditional healing practices towards psycho-social health care in Malawi.* Eschborn bei Frankfurt am Main: Fachbuchhandlung für Psychologie Verlagsabteilung.

Pe-Pua, R. (1990). *Pagatatanong-tanong:* A method for cross-cultural research. In V. G. Enriquez (Ed.), *Indigenous psychology: A book of readings,* (pp. 231–243). Quezon City: Psychology Research and Training House.

Petzold, M. (1986). Psychology in the People's Republic of China—A historical overview and quantitative analysis. *Psychologia, 29,* 57–65.

Petzold, M. (1987). The social history of Chinese psychology. In M. G. Ash & W. R. Woodward (Eds.), *Psychology in twentieth-century thought and society* (pp. 213–231). Cambridge: Cambridge University Press.

Prasad, J. (1950). A comparative study of rumours and reports of earthquakes. *British Journal of Psychology, 41,* 129–144.

Puhan, B. N. & Sahoo, F. M. (1991). Indigenization of psychological studies: Research agenda. *Indian Journal of Current Psychological Research, 6.* 101–107.

Reuning, H. & Wortley, W. (1973). Psychological studies of the Bushmen. *Psychologia Africana,* (Monograph Supplement No. 7).

Reynolds, D. K. (1981). Morita psychotherapy. In R. J. Corsini (Ed.), *Handbook of innovative psychotherapies* (pp. 489–501). New York: John Wiley.

Rood, S. (1985). Language and Philippine social science. In A. Aganon & S. M. Assumpta David, (Eds.), *New directions in indigenous psychology* (pp. 76–90). Quezon City: National Book Store.

Rudmin, F. (1987). Should the IACCP expand its mandate? Three specific proposals. *Cross-Cultural Psychology Bulletin, 21,* 1–2.

Safaya, R. (1976). *Hindu psychology.* New Delhi: Munshiram Manoharlal Publishers.

Salazar, J. M. (1984). The use and impact of psychology in Venezuela: Two examples. *International Journal of Psychology, 19,* 113–122.

Samy, J. (1978). Development and research for whom? Towards a critique of economism in the Pacific, and session on theory and methods. In A. Mamak & G. McCall (Eds.), *Paradise postponed: Essays on research and development in the South Pacific.* Rushcutters Bay, NSW: Pergamon Press.

Saraswathi, T. S., Saksena, K. & Sundaresan, J. (1977). Development of moral judgement of Indian children between ages eight to twelve years. In Y. H. Poortinga (Ed.), *Basic problems in cross-cultural psychology* (pp. 168–177). Lisse: Swets & Zeitlinger.

Seal, B. N. (1958). *Positive science of the ancient Hindus.* Delhi: Motilal Banarsi Das.

Serpell, R. (1977). Estimates of intelligence in a rural community in Eastern Zambia. In F. M. Okatcha (Ed.), *Modern psychology and cultural adaptation* (pp. 179–216). Nairobi: Swahili Language Consultants and Publishers.

Serpell, R. (1994). An African ontogeny of selfhood (book review). *Cross-Cultural Psychology Bulletin, 28,* 17–20.

Shweder, R. A., Mahapatra, M. & Miller, J. G. (1990). Cultural and moral development. In J. Stigler, R. A. Shweder & G. Herdt (Eds.), *Cultural psychology: Essays in comparative human development* (pp. 130–204). New York: Cambridge University Press.

Shuh, P. & Gao, J. (Eds.). (1983). *A history of Chinese psychology.* Beijing: People's Education Press.

Singh, N. K. (1990). *The dialogue with Yeti: Insight on man and organization.* New Delhi: Foundation for Organizational Research and Education.

Singh, Y. (1986). *Indian sociology: Social conditioning and emerging concerns.* New Delhi: Vistaar Publications.

Singhal, K. & Misra, G. (1989). Variations in achievement cognitions: Role of ecology, age and gender. *International Journal of Intercultural Relations, 13,* 93–107.

Sinha, D. (1952). Behaviour in a catastrophic situation: A psychological study of reports and rumors. *British Journal of Psychology, 43,* 200–209.

Sinha, D. (1965). Integration of modern psychology with Indian thought. In A. J. Sutchi & M. A. Vick (Eds.), *Readings in humanistic psychology* (pp. 265–279). New York: Free Press.

Sinha, D. (1966). Psychology in the arena of social change. Presidential address to the Section of Psychology and Educational Sciences, 53rd. Indian Science Congress, Chandigarh, January.

Sinha, D. (1969). *Indian villages in transition: A motivational analysis.* Delhi: Associated Publishing House.

Sinha, D. (1981). Social psychology in India: A historical perspective. In J. Pandey (Ed.), *Perspectives on experimental social psychology in India* (pp. 3–17). New Delhi: Concept.

Sinha, D. (1983). Applied social psychology and the problems of national development. In F. Blackler (Ed.), *Social psychology and developing countries* (pp. 7–20). Chichester: John Wiley.

Sinha, D. (1984). Psychology in the context of third world development. *International Journal of Psychology, 19,* 17–29.

Sinha, D. (1986). *Psychology in a Third World country: The Indian experience.* New Delhi: Sage.

Sinha, D. (1989). Cross-cultural psychology and the process of indigenization: A second view from the Third World. In D. M. Keats, D. Munro & L. Mann (Eds.), *Heterogeneity in cross-cultural psychology* (pp. 24–40). Lisse: Swets & Zeitlinger.

Sinha, D. (1990). Concept of psychological well-being: Western and Indian perspectives. *NIMHANS Journal, 8,* 1–11.

Sinha, D. (1992). Appropriate indigenous psychology in India. In S. Iwawaki, Y. Kashima & K. Leung (Eds.), *Innovations in cross-cultural psychology* (pp. 38–48). Lisse: Swets & Zeitlinger.

Sinha, D. (1993). Indigenization of psychology in India and its relevance. In U. Kim & J. W. Berry (Eds.), *Indigenous psychologies: Research and experience in cultural context* (pp. 30–43). Newbury Park, CA: Sage.

Sinha, D. & Naidu, R. K. (1994). Multilayered hierarchial structure of self and not-self: The Indian perspective. In A-M. Bouvy, F. J. R. van de Vijver, P. Boski & P. Schmitz (Eds.), *Journey into cross-cultural psychology* (pp. 41–49). Lisse: Swets & Zeitlinger.

Sinha, J. B. P. (1980). *The nurturant task leader.* New Delhi: Concept Publishing Company.

Sinha, J. B. P. (1993a). A model of effective leadership style in India. In A. M. Jaeger & R. N. Kanungo (Eds.), *Management in developing countries* (pp. 252–263). London: Routledge.

Sinha, J. B. P. (1993b). Cultural embeddedness and developmental role in industrial organizations in India. In M. V. Dunnette (Ed.), *Handbook of industrial and organizational psychology,* (Vol. 4, pp. 727–764). Palo Alto, CA: Consulting Psychologists Press.

Super, C. M. & Harkness, S. (1986). The developmental niche: A conceptualization at the interface of child and culture. *International Journal of Behavioural Development, 9,* 545–569.

Sykes, J. B. (1976). *The concise Oxford dictionary of current English,* sixth edition. Delhi: Oxford University Press.

Triandis, H. C. (1971). Some psychological dimensions of modernization. *Proceedings of the 17th. International Congress of Applied Psychology* (Vol. 2, pp. 57–65). Brussels: Editat.

Van Vlaenderen, H. (1993). Psychological research in the process of social change: A contribution to community development. *Psychology and Developing Societies, 5,* 95–110.

Wang, J-S. (1980). On the modernization of psychology in China: Fundamental theoretical viewpoint and methodology. *Acta Psychologica Sinica, 12,* 30–36 (in Chinese). English translation: *FBIS-REPORT Joint Publications Research Service,* No. 76133, 103–114.

Whiting, B. B. & Whiting, J. W. (1975). *Children of six cultures: A psychocultural analysis.* Cambridge, MA: Harvard University Press.

Wober, M. (1974). Towards an understanding of the Kiganda concept of intelligence. In J. W. Berry & P. R. Dasen (Eds.), *Culture and cognition* (pp. 261–280). London: Methuen.

Xu, Lain-cang (Hsu Lien-tsang). (1979). Psychology in the service of four modernizations. *Acta Psychologica Sinica, 11,* 22–28 (In Chinese).

Yamasoka, K. (1968). Introduction. In *Relevance of the social sciences in contemporary Asia*. Tokyo: World Student Christian Federation.

Yan, K. T. (1987). *Psychological thought of Chinese scholars in T'ang and Sung dynasties*. Ch'ang-Sha, China: Hu-nan People's Publishing Co. (In Chinese).

Yan, K. T. (1988). *Psychological thoughts of Chinese scholars in Ming and Ch'ing dynasties*. Ch'ang-Sha, China: Hu-nan People's Publishing Co. (In Chinese).

Yang, C-F. (1988). Familism and development: An examination of the role of family in contemporary China Mainland, Hong Kong and Taiwan. In D. Sinha & H. S. R. Kao (Eds.), *Social values and development: Asian perspectives* (pp. 93–123). New Delhi: Sage.

Yang, K. S. (1982). Sinicization of psychological research in Chinese societies: Directions and issues. In K. S. Yang & C.I. Wen (Eds.), *The Sinicization of social and behavioural science research in China* (pp. 153–187). Taipei, Taiwan: Institute of Ethology, Academia Sinica (In Chinese).

Yang, K. S. (1988). Chinese filial piety: A conceptual analysis. In K. S. Yang (Ed.), *The psychology of the Chinese people: An indigenous perspective* (pp. 39–73). Taipei, Taiwan: Kuei-Kuan Publishing Co. (In Chinese).

Yang, K. S. & Bond, M. H. (1990). Exploring implicit personality theories with indigenous or imported constructs: The Chinese case. *Journal of Personality and Social Psychology, 58,* 1087–1095.

Yang, K. S. & Ho, D. Y. F. (1988). The role of the *yuan* in Chinese social life: A conceptual and empirical analysis. In A. C. Paranjpe, D. Y. F. Ho & R. W. Rieber (Eds.), *Asian contributions to psychology* (pp. 263–281). New York: Praeger.

Yang, K. S. & Yeh, K. H. (1991). Psychological studies on Chinese filial piety: Concepts, methods and findings. In H. S. R. Kao & C. F. Yang (Eds.), *Chinese people, Chinese mind: Traditional perspectives* (pp. 193–260). Taipei, Taiwan: Yuan-Liu Publishing Co. (In Chinese).

Zaman, R. M. (1991). Clinical psychology in Pakistan. *Psychology and Developing Societies, 3,* 221–234.

5

A COMPARATIVE ANTHROPOLOGICAL PERSPECTIVE

ROBERT L. MUNROE
Pitzer College
United States

RUTH H. MUNROE
Pitzer College
United States

> *. . . the work of comparison, which is always planned but*
> *rarely undertaken.*
> —*Dan Sperber,* On Anthropological Knowledge.

Contents

Introduction

The defining characteristic of cultural anthropology is its emphasis on the study of human groups *in situ*. This thrust means that anthropology differs modally from psychology in its concern with qualitative field research, with the explication of natural situations rather than with study under controlled conditions. Anthropology's concomitant focus on supra-individual phenomena, specifically cultural systems or sociohistorical traditions rather than individuals, has frequently prompted comments that psychology is irrelevant to the goals of the field, though anthropology's use of concepts involving beliefs, motives, emotions, and values belies such a position (D'Andrade, 1994; Jahoda, 1982). As we shall see in this chapter, the complementary perspectives furnished by these distinctive approaches in the two disciplines have helped forge an enlarged understanding in cross-cultural psychological research.

The anthropological subdiscipline most closely related to cross-cultural psychology is psychological anthropology. Its most advanced area of inquiry, the anthropological study of cognition, has been masterfully reviewed by D'Andrade (1995a; cf. also Casson, 1994; Frake, 1994; Romney, 1994). Besides cognition, other common interests of psychological anthropology and cross-cultural psychology include topics such as emotion, the self, discourse, altered states of consciousness, and child socialization and development. Psychological anthropology also embraces topics and techniques not usually emphasized in today's cross-cultural psychology, e.g., primatology, political terror, myth, the arts, dreams, intepretation of TAT cards, psychoanalytic interviewing, and ethnographies as "experiments." Edited volumes by Bock (1994) and by Suárez-Orozco, G. Spindler, and L. Spindler (1994) set forth the details of these disparate pursuits.

Despite anthropology's substantive focus on culture, many definitions of the concept have been employed, as seen in Kroeber and Kluckhohn's (1952) compendium in which 164 were listed. The most significant recent change in the concept within anthropology has been the "interiorization" of culture. As D'Andrade (1984) put it, "When I was a graduate student, one imagined people *in* a culture; ten years later culture was all in their heads. The thing went from something out there and very large to something that got placed inside" (p. 7). Thus culture, though remaining at a supra-individual level, now is viewed by many in anthropology as "a conceptual structure or system of ideas" (Geertz, 1984, p. 8). It is understood that not all aspects of such a structure or system could be articulated by the members of a society (D'Andrade, 1995a). Within cross-cultural psychology, the concept of culture is currently employed in two primary ways, in one as a matter of identifying contexts, in the other as an antecedent variable. These differences from anthropological usage are due to cross-cultural psychologists' interest not in the systems as such but in individual behavior, either as a function of the cultural framework within which it occurs or as a response to a specific (antecedent) element of that framework (cf. various chapters of this volume). The contrasts also illustrate how the concept of culture may be differentially conceptualized depending upon the goals of the inquiry.

Many anthropologists would maintain that attempts at comparison are premature and must wait until some future time while fieldwork-based case studies are pursued (Lindholm, 1982). Nonetheless, a flourishing anthropological subdiscipline, comprised of both field research (Johnson, 1991; R. L. Munroe & R. H. Munroe, 1991; B. B. Whiting & Edwards, 1988) and archival studies (C. R. Ember & Levinson, 1991; Schlegel, 1994), has established the viability of comparative anthropology, and much of it is based directly upon the field data gathered by ethnographers. In the meantime, as recent years have witnessed the transformation of tribal societies, field anthropology has increasingly turned to the study of cities (Breitborde & Glasser, 1990; Sanjek, 1990) and of groups within the urban-industrial world, e.g., ethnic minorities within plural societies (Roosens, 1989), nonconventional families (Weisner, Bausano, & Kornfein, 1983), streetchildren (see Aptekar and Stöcklin chapter, this *Handbook*), and practitioners ranging from physicists (Traweek, 1988) to witches (Luhrmann, 1994). Ultimately, the cumulating knowledge from these investigations will provide a new basis for future comparative accounts.

In the first edition of this *Handbook* (R. L. Munroe & R. H. Munroe, 1980), we argued that universals, generalizations, and similarities across cultures could be expected due to our single-species heritage and the necessity of adapting to environmental constraints (R. L. Munroe & R. H. Munroe, 1980). Although our theme was nomothetic, it was balanced by recognition of interest in holistic and contextual accounts, which meant corresponding idiographic concerns. In several respects, such a dual focus has been of long standing, with roots in the division between those who advocate *Naturwissenschaften* (natural sciences) versus *Geisteswissenschaften* (humanities and social studies) as approaches to the understanding of human behavior (Jahoda, 1992; Jahoda & Krewer, this volume). The current debate between positivism and postmodernism continues to reflect several of these issues. We shall briefly address some of the main arguments and offer our own position.

There is a strong form of postmodernist critique that abjures every type of objective knowledge from science to history, argues that no basis exists for knowledge-claims, posits that no rationale can be invoked for choosing between conflicting interpretations, and holds that "there are no adequate means for representing [external reality]" (Rosenau, 1992, p. 110). This postmodernist position would ask us to abandon the entire knowledge-gaining enterprise in which we are engaged, and indeed to approach a form of nihilism. Alternatively, postmodernists may ask us, as many in anthropology now do, to adopt a *critical stance that impugns traditional anthropology for its complicity in relations of* domination and points us instead toward becoming "alarmists and shock troopers" (Scheper-Hughes, 1995, p. 417) and "principled moralists" (see the analysis by D'Andrade, 1995b, of this movement, and chapter by Miller, this volume).

Another element of the postmodern outlook, both more familiar and less extreme than those cited above, is a stress on diversity and uniqueness, and a desire to try to understand in "particular detail, with . . . specificity" (Nelson, 1987, p. 217, cited in Rosenau, 1992, p. 8; Abu-Lughod, 1991). A constructivist expression of this outlook can be seen in cultural psychology, which has grown up, according to Shweder and Sullivan (1993), in an atmosphere "valuing processes and constraints that are local, variable, context-dependent, [and] contingent" (p. 500). Shweder is an anthropologist, but a similar stance is increasingly found in psychology. For instance, in a discussion of emotion, Campos (1994) has written, "Culture is important . . . for illustrating human variation and how such variations come about" (p. 14). The variability celebrated by constructivists appeals, for example, to "group difference psychology" (Shweder & Sullivan, 1993, p. 517), or to apparent differences of meaning in the Strange Situation for infants in different cultures (Campos, 1994; cf. the chapter by Keller in this *Handbook*), or to the proposition that "human developmental trajectories may be virtually infinite in their variegation" (Gergen, 1980, p. 37). The "unit" of difference depends on the constructivist's interests: For the anthropologist, it is cultures, or features of them, that differ; for the "minority"-oriented social scientist, it is the ethnic or racial group; and for the Western psychologist, it is individuals.

"Diversity" is the watchword of social scientists concerned with challenging the so-called white European male hegemony, thus the distinctive mixing of advocacy and research that mark the human sciences in those disciplines oriented toward "minority" issues. (As Spiro, 1993, characterizes this approach, "All scholarship is politics by other means.") It is to the advantage of these individuals to deny the validity of generalizations (for example, by meeting the "kernel of truth" element in stereotypes with numerous cases of counter-instances), or to conceptualize our worlds of experience and behavior as always (and only) socially constructed, and therefore to view that behavior as being "fundamentally open-ended" (Gergen, 1980, p. 35). Sometimes the denial of regularities leads not to a "difference" position but to its opposite, as with statements that adoptive and biological children are fundamentally alike, that later-borns and firstborns share more than they fail to share, or that women and men "really" differ only in biological sex, every other "extension" being purely cultural (for the latter, cf. Bem, 1993). In either case, the rhetoric of constructivism takes on a skeptical, rejecting, or dismissive tone.

Consistent with the constructivist position, there are anthropologists who argue that most social–scientific categories, being Western-derived, are culture-bound and thus inapplicable cross-culturally (cf. Schneider, 1984). When Quine (1960) presented his now-famous *gavagai* example to illustrate the indeterminacy of translation, his philosophical point was that we cannot "know" for certain across cultures. It is worth recalling, however, that Quine admitted the actuality of translation for full bilingual speakers. Likewise, science's analytical categories can be said often to "work" despite epistemological uncertainties (cf. the "descriptive epistemology" of Donald Campbell, 1988). Thus, it seems to us that the cross-cultural usefulness of any construct must be evaluated in a pragmatic way, and not rejected on the grounds that it reflects Western categories of thought, or that it *may* be inapplicable in non-Western cultural settings.

Although the variability emphasized by constructivists certainly will be characteristic of any set of phenomena, consideration of that aspect alone produces a one-sided and misleading view, in fact a half-truth. All classes of phenomena, whether concepts, processes, or covariations among factors, whether within cultures or across cultures, will also display central tendencies, not simply a rectangular distribution of equally likely and unique variates. By "classes" we refer not to haphazard collections of objects but to phenomena that fall together into some analytical category. We assume that the members of a class, taken in sufficient numbers, will both aggregate to some degree and disperse to some degree—and constructivism, at the cost of failing to acknowledge the regularities, has been almost obsessed with the differences. To state the matter in other terms, constructivism has been concerned with the unexplained portion of the variance, even endeavoring to enlarge the unexplained variance by means of devices such as reflexivity, reinterpretation, and deconstruction.

At the same time, to pursue the statistical metaphor, positivists have characteristically overemphasized the central tendencies while playing down the dispersion. They have learned over the past three decades, however, that their categories are less fixed than they had thought, the relationships less robust than expected, and the regularities more limited in extension and in temporal reference than hoped. To us, these considerations suggest that, just as with constructivism, the one-sidedness of the positivist orientation has limited its effectiveness. But for all its overclaiming and shortcomings, the positivist program can also point to some success in the behavioral sciences. And if in this chapter we again emphasize the "anchoring" rather than the variability, it is not because we believe that one is more important than the other in any ultimate sense, but because the defining quest of science is to find general explanations. In this search we hold, with Romney (1994), that "the general universal regularities will only be found by focussing upon similarities rather than differences" (p. 256; cf. also D. E. Brown, 1991). We tend to agree as well with Hull's (1988) characterization of the scientific enterprise, overstated though his assessment of its success may be: "Science *is* one of the major ways that people in Western and Westernized societies today establish their beliefs, but it is neither the only way nor merely the way that they do so. What science has in its favor is that it beats all other ways hollow" (p. 26).

In the discussion that follows, three levels of behavioral and sociocultural topics have been identified—the individual, the interpersonal, and the institutional.[1] Although many of these topics could be discussed at more than one level, and all of them carry psychological implications, we have chosen to undertake coverage at the lowest level at which a phenomenon commonly appears. Thus sex-typing, though manifested at every level, is discussed in the first section, on individual-level variables. This hierarchical division is consistent with psychology's dominant interest in individual behavior.

Our treatment will not be exhaustive; more detailed coverage of a number of the topics that we touch upon can be found in other chapters of this *Handbook*. Additionally, in some instances we report cultural practices which, to the best of our knowledge, have become extinct since the time they were recorded in the ethnographic literature. (Any such practice is noted herein by means of an asterisk. It is standard anthropological practice to refer to such customs in the present tense.) These customs are of more than antiquarian interest, often indicating as they do the "strong treatments" (Ellsworth, 1977) to which peoples of the world are capable of subjecting themselves, treatments that for ethical reasons we cannot experimentally impose on subjects.

Individual-Level Variables

Biological Needs

The variables considered in this section, grounded in basic physiological functions, can generally be expected to have demonstrable survival value and to display a more compact range of expression than other variables. The limits are due to our shared biological heritage and to the interaction of biology with environmental constraints: Despite all claims that culture has allowed human beings to penetrate to the far reaches of the earth, no culture-group has lived at altitudes approaching those of the higher mountains of the world, and none has been self-sustaining on the continent of Antarctica. Approximately half the world's population lives in a single region, the temperate-forest zone, which indicates that even though human beings have established themselves in all of the earth's main environmental zones, they are less likely to thrive under marginal conditions. Furthermore, the 10° C (50° F) winter temperature isotherm sharply delineates types of infant care practices (type of clothing worn, and whether infants are in their mothers' beds and held next to their bodies during daylight), and in premodern times it acted as an effective constraint on peoples' migration and expansion (J. W. M. Whiting, Sodergren, & Stigler, 1982).

Frustration of the biological needs of hunger, thirst, elimination, sleep, or sex, even if temporary, can breed both severe discomfort for the individual and potential conflict for the group. It is perhaps for these reasons that every society channels the needs, controlling and shaping them during the period of socialization and defining their appropriate modes, times, or places of expression in adulthood. Natural rhythmicity appears to constrain the cultural patterning of these needs—the cycle of gratification is always twenty-four hours or less, except for sex. Ingestion and sleep are always culturally defined as appropriately occurring at least once each day; elimination seems to be patterned this way behaviorally, but seldom with explicit cultural expectations.[2]

These body functions are probably tied to the circadian system and its regulation of many physiological and bodily biochemical functions including body temperature, blood sugar, cell division, and adrenal activity (Halberg, 1960). Recent research on the treatment of sleep disorders by light therapy, that is, the resetting of the circadian system by means of bright artificial light (Nowak, 1994), carries promising cross-cultural potential. Sleep disorders often affect shift workers and others whose internal clocks are not being set by proper exposure to sunlight. One can posit, then, that under natural conditions, peoples in areas of the world with high coefficients of daily sunlight might exhibit fewer symptoms of sleep disorder than those in other areas. Also, the use of light therapy for depression points to another possibility (Wetterberg, 1994): A low incidence of depression has often been reported for traditional societies, which are disproportionately located in high-sunlight tropical and subtropical areas (Marsella, 1980; Wittkower, 1969). We already know that seasonal depressions during winter months show higher prevalence rates in the northern latitudes of a temperate-climate nation like the United States (Rosen et al., 1990). The suggestive connection between depression, sleep disorders, and circadian rhythms might be profitably investigated on a worldwide basis.

For some segments of many populations, fasting and sleeplessness are frequently observed for periods of several days under ritual conditions, especially those preparatory to status changes, e.g., transition to adulthood, marriage, pregnancy, childbirth, and during mourning, but such restrictions do not apply to the society as a whole. Sexual activity, both more controlled and more variable than any other need, is sometimes denied overt expression altogether among special classes of individuals, e.g., celibate priests, specially chosen virgins among the Inca* of Peru (Rowe, 1946), or celibate transvestites among the Subanun of the Philippines (Christie, 1909). Among the Grand Valley Dani of Irian Jaya, Indonesia (West New Guinea), there is a five-year period of postpartum sexual abstinence, which is invariably observed, with no alternative sexual outlets and no accompanying unhappiness or stress, and which is supported without strong sanctions or powerful explanations (Heider, 1976).[3] An unusual example of within-society variability occurs among the Sambia of Papua New Guinea, where boys are involved in homoerotic contacts first as insertees and later as inserters until after marriage and fatherhood, at which time they begin exclusively heterosexual activities (Herdt, 1987).

Other biological needs have received only spare treatment. Breathing seems seldom subject to control in any society (Ford, 1939; Sapir, 1951), although yoga has effectively demonstrated the possibility of reducing oxygen intake to one-third of normal for brief periods (e.g., Prowitt & Daly, 1972). The avoidance of pain is much less widespread than one might conjecture, and ascetic and masochistic elements form part of many ceremonies and rituals, especially initiation rites. The possibility of strong differences in the actual experience of pain is suggested by an experimental study of Nepalese hill dwellers, who displayed much higher pain thresholds to electrical stimulation than did a sample of Westerners (Clark & Clark, 1980). A similarly high tolerance for pain had been obtained by the Torres Strait Expedition at the turn of the century (Haddon, 1901, 1903).

Maintenance of body temperature would seem to require clothing and shelter of some sort in all except tropical climates, but in subantarctic South America (summer mean temperature around 10° C with snow common, winter mean temperature near the freezing point), the Ona* sleep in the open with rude wind shelters (Cooper, 1946a) and the Yahgan* wear only shoulder and breast capes, often going naked (Cooper, 1946b). (Darwin observed naked Yahgan sweating profusely on the edge of a campfire while well-clad Europeans huddled near the fire in an attempt to warm themselves.) It can be pointed out, however, that individuals in these two societies do not scant both clothing and shelter: The Ona, with little shelter, cover themselves with long capes and mocassins, and the Yahgan, with little clothing, build huts and make fires within.

It is not difficult to establish that anatomical and physiological features of humankind together with environmental pressures have been the chief elements affecting the range of expression of the variables considered here. Occasionally observers will point to somewhat arbitrary customs in this domain, e.g., central heating being activated in the Moscow area on October 1 no matter what the weather, or the Chinese regularly wearing winter underwear until the month of May. Let us note, though, that these are institutionalized responses which are modally adaptive, and that central heating is not being *de*activated in Moscow on October 1, nor are the Chinese doffing their winter underwear at that time. As to the obviously high plasticity of sexual expression, the minimum reported above for the Dani, with their five-year postpartum sex taboo, is counterbalanced to some extent for married Dani males by the fact that 47 percent of them have multiple wives (Heider, 1976). (Due to Heider's focus on males, little is known about the sexual needs and outlets of Dani women.) Overall, while the variability with respect to biological needs is far from trivial, the nodes are striking and substantial. Further details on this topic can be found in the authors' discussion in the first edition of the *Handbook.*

Perception and Cognition

The evidence is strong that in the realm of *perception* there is an essential panhuman unity, and that most differences among cultures amount to only a "fine tuning" (Annis & Frost, 1973). Fundamental perceptual competencies such as object constancy, depth perception, and intersensory integration, which seem to be shared by humans with many other species, are probably the normal outcome of neurophysiological characteristics and common environmental experiences. Furthermore, in almost all cultures the vocabularies for visual and auditory experiences are more elaborate than those for the other senses. Thus the preoccupation of scientists with audio-visual perception may be due not to a Western bias but to an interest built upon our special primate capacities in these sensory modalities.

Cross-cultural support for the idea of a natural "perceptual salience" and resulting focal categories is available from the study of cultural color-naming systems (Berlin & Kay, 1969; Kay, Berlin, & Merrifield, 1991), plant and animal categorization (Berlin, 1992), geometric forms (Rosch, 1973), and phonetic distinctive features (Jakobson, Fant, Gunnar, & Halle, 1963). The evidence is strongest for color terminology: "Consistency and reaction times for applying color terms show that all the 11 basic color terms [white, black, red, yellow, green, blue, brown, purple, pink, orange, grey] form a separate class and are probably all associated with universal physiological processes" (Abramov & Gordon, 1994, p. 469; cf. M. H. Bornstein, 1973; Boynton & Olson, 1990; and Russell, Deregowski, & Kinnear, this *Handbook*). Developmentally, at least for English, the words used by the child in the one-word stage refer more frequently to entities than relations, and the names refer to whole objects and not parts or attributes of objects. In all of the above, language may be following "the human perceptual system in naming units that have the unity described by gestalt principles" (Greenfield & Smith, 1976, p. 223).

Differences in *cognitive performance* across cultures are widespread, with modern and urban–industrial peoples consistently outperforming individuals in traditional societies on a wide variety of tests, including Piagetian tasks (Dasen & Heron, 1981), logical reasoning (Scribner, 1979), level of moral reasoning (Edwards, 1981; Snarey, 1985), and memory (Wagner, 1981). In favor of the idea that these differences are real and meaningful are the following considerations: (a.) Under conditions of convergence in learning environments, e.g., formal education, urbanization, and industrialization, traditional peoples perform more like modern groups (Rogoff, 1981; H. W. Stevenson, 1982); (b.) *Within* the ranks of traditional societies, superior performance, such as a higher level of spatial ability or more rapid development of specific Piagetian conservation concepts, is associated with ecocultural demands that appear to favor the cognitive skills we do find highly developed (Berry, 1976; Dasen, 1975); (c.) *Within* the ranks of urban–industrial societies, superior performance, such as the better mathematics skills of Japanese vis-à-vis American schoolchildren (H. W. Stevenson & Stigler, 1992), is associated with recent high levels of accomplishment in the economic sphere.

In assessing cognition, cross-cultural psychologists have typically deployed Western-derived instruments. Some observers argue that the many methodological problems found in cross-cultural testing, such as unfamiliarity of test materials and cultural inappropriateness of test demands, render comparative performances difficult to interpret (Cole & Means, 1981), or that the performances are best understood as an index of test-taking skill in the urban–industrial mode. Kagitçibasi (1995) asserts, however, that many researchers are reluctant to use comparative standards because they want to avoid ethnocentric value judgments. Her position, as a psychologist in a developing country, is that so-called middle-class parental orientations have been found "beneficial to children's development in general and for their cognitive development and school performance in particular" (Kagitçibasi, 1995, p. 299). She states further that in traditional societies, superior cognitive performance, as judged by cross-culturally valid criteria, is precisely the means to social mobility. While acknowledging the importance of cultural sensitivity, Kagitçibasi believes that withholding judgment about poor performance in nonindustrial societies amounts to a relativistic double standard.

Results from numerous studies support Kagitçibasi's (1995) argument that "school-related cognitive achievement criteria" (p. 299) can be used to construct valid comparative standards of cognitive performance. To cite one major example, Berry's (1976, 1990) extensive research showed that education was positively related to performance on the Embedded Figures Test in virtually all his samples worldwide. Within plural societies as well, tested differences have come to be seen as meaningful: "It is now generally recognized that within a society intergroup differences in test scores often are a reflection of a real state of affairs" (Berry, Poortinga, Segall, & Dasen, 1992, p. 313).

Yet to assume that "school-like skills" (Kagitçibasi, 1995, p. 299) inescapably promote a generalized cognitive development is to go beyond current evidence. Certainly the well-known Vai (Liberia) case presents a challenge to this view. The careful work of Scribner and Cole (1981) found that on a battery of cognitive tests, persons literate in the Vai script (but without formal schooling) did not exhibit an overall cognitive performance superior to Vai nonliterates. Reading and writing, the central skills associated with schooling, failed to provide general cognitive enhancement, and the effects of literacy were instead restricted to specific test performances reflecting particular elements of the Vai script. When Berry and Bennett (1989) essayed a replication of Scribner and Cole among the Cree (Canada), they also found that the non-schooled syllabic script used there tended to improve not overall cognitive performance but only mental operations important in using the script. These findings run counter to the contention that literacy has served everywhere to transform and modernize society, to spur developments in technology, science, and art, and to raise the level of intellectual functioning (Goody & Watt, 1968).

The Vai and Cree studies, in separating out the effects of literacy from those of other cultural features, suggest the significant contribution of specific sociohistorical factors to the generation of cognitive skills. Approaches of this sort presume that if we are to understand cognitive performance and its development, we must carefully analyze the details of the sociocultural context (Cole, 1990; Gauvain, 1995; Rogoff, 1990). Consistent with such an idea, recent studies have turned to the interpretation of "everyday cognition," in which *culturally relevant* cognition is the focus (cf. Schliemann, Carraher & Cecci, Volume 3 of this *Handbook;* also Chapter 9 in Segall, Dasen, Berry, & Poortinga, 1990). These studies do not undermine previous cross-cultural generalizations about cognitive functioning, but in melding psychological experimentation and anthropological observation (Cole, 1982), they move us toward explication of the acquisition and workings of human thought processes under diverse cultural circumstances.

Language [4]

Human languages are *species-specific* (Dale, 1972). Remarkable accomplishments in language learning by chimpanzees (Greenfield & Savage-Rumbaugh, 1990) and even by an African Grey parrot (Pepperberg, 1990) have not obscured the fundamental points that (a.) human languages are unique in structural complexity, and (b.) human beings are apparently unique in their ability continually to produce new utterances. Probably, as many observers have suggested, language has a significant biological component (Jackendoff, 1994; Lenneberg, 1967; Pinker, 1994). Nevertheless, normal environmental input appears necessary for proper language development, and a severe stunting may occur when human beings undergo extreme isolation and social deprivation in the early years (for a recent case, cf. Rymer, 1993).

Human languages are *species-uniform* (Dale, 1972); that is, all languages are highly complex and apparently communicatively equivalent, and there is no range of superiority of expression. Furthermore, numerous linguistic universals can be identified, e.g., subjects and predicates, classes of nouns, verbs, pronouns, and persons (addresser, addressee, and impersonal), as well as a means of giving commands, expressing negation, and asking questions (Greenberg, 1966; cf. also Talmy, 1987). At the most general level, every language has rules for building sounds (phonology), for building words (morphology), and for building sentences (syntax). The constraints on sounds (imposed by mouth, tongue, and throat) were described more than a half-century ago by Pike (1943), who has recently pointed out that in subsequent work with almost a thousand languages, only a tiny number of exceptions have been discovered; Pike lists three (quoted in Kaye, 1994). A syntactical regularity is word order, with all languages having a dominant or preferred order for nominal subject, verb, and nominal object. In English it is subject–verb–object (SVO), as in "John throws the ball." Although there are six logically possible types of word order (SVO, SOV, VSO, VOS, OSV, and OVS), and three of them occur commonly in the languages of the world, "the [specific] dominant order is almost always one in which the subject precedes the object" (Greenberg, 1966, p. 77). (For a case in which the dominant order holds for adults but is not the basic order for young children, see Chapter 6 in Ochs, 1988, on Samoan.)

According to data from several societies (Slobin, 1972), children everywhere go through a one-word stage lasting from about twelve months of age up to eighteen or twenty-four months. A two-word stage has regularly followed the single-word period. (For the polysynthetic language of the Greenland Eskimo [Inuit], children attain not a two-word but a two-*morpheme* stage, according to Fortescue & Lennert Olsen, 1992.) During this time the utterances of the child reflect what Piaget called *sensorimotor* intelligence, that is, descriptions of the child's here-and-now transactions with people and objects (R. Brown, 1973; Slobin, 1973). Two-word utterances do not include highly abstract concepts such as hypothetical events, causality, number, and the past and future, but they do carry semantic functions like predication, modification, and negation (R. Brown, 1973). The expressions gradually expand beyond two words, and by the age of about four the child has mastered the basic grammatical operations of its particular language. Interestingly, however, errors increase at this age because improved grammatical competence has also increased the child's range of options (Slobin, 1992).

These similarities in language acquisition emerge despite large cultural differences in peoples' attempts to teach language. Kaluli adults (in Papua New Guinea) give children carefully controlled and explicit instruction in language forms and conversational skills while Samoan adults, believing that early utterances are meaningless, do not formally train very young children in language use (Ochs & Schieffelin, 1983). The similarities also appear even though in some cultures, young children are decidedly nonverbal; during fieldwork among the Luo of Kenya, for instance, Blount (1969) was able to collect fewer than 200 spontaneous utterances from a total of six children. And the similarities are present despite the fact that during learning, the linguistic structures of particular languages pose different kinds of problems for children, leading to relative facility or difficulty in acquisition of certain subsystems (Slobin, 1982).

The strength of the generalizations that can be made for grammar is great enough that Joseph Greenberg, the leading comparative linguist of our time, has expressed himself as follows about the occasional "violation" of regularities:

> *A rule that's peculiar is called peculiar because it occurs in very few languages of the world. And it's found only in a few languages because it can only arise from certain specific situations, and what's more, when it does come into existence, it's historically unstable . . . you have to understand the historical processes that produce this strange rule . . . it can only arise in a few situations and it can't last very long. (quoted in Newman, 1991, p. 463)*

One of the most powerful generalizations discovered about language is that all known writing systems encode spoken language—"Writing is speech put in visible form" (Coe, 1992, p. 13). This may seem a truism, but for a century after the discovery of the Mayan ruins, almost none of the written records (except for calendars) could be read; the leading scholars argued that Mayan writing conveyed ideas directly, independently of the spoken language, and was thus impenetrable to us today. Ultimately, a Soviet scholar, isolated from Mayanists, showed that Mayan writing was based on the same principles as scripts in other parts of the world, and initiated the breakthrough in translation of the ancient language (Knorosov, 1952). As Coe (1992) points out, earlier application of the comparative method could have saved generations of Mayanists from the fatal assumption of Mayan "uniqueness."

Some generalizations about semantic systems can be made. For example, there are the regularities in affective meaning found by Osgood and associates in thirty communities (universally, "brightness" is more positively evaluated than "darkness") (Osgood, May, & Miron, 1975), or the far greater than chance appearance of figurative labels for body parts ("child of the eye" for the pupil of the eye, "mother of the hand" for the thumb) (C. H. Brown & Witkowski, 1981). Also, a large-scale comparative study of world languages indicates that the basis for the evolution of grammars lies in some irreducible notions which carry semantic substance, for example, movement, existence, or social status, and that this common semantic substratum is responsible for the widespread "grammaticization" paths found in diverse language phyla (Bybee, Perkins, & Pagliuca, 1994).

Despite these advances, the regularities in semantics cannot match those found in systems of phonology, morphology, syntax, and writing. It is often remarked that while anthropologists learn to speak exotic languages, they never fully master the complexities of meaning in those alien tongues. Even for native speakers of a language, problems such as a low degree of "terminologization" in sets of related words pose difficulties—consider the eight English terms *bound, hop, jump, leap, prance, skip, spring,* and *vault,* which U.S. graduate-level students cannot reliably match with dictionary definitions (Weinreich, 1966). Given problems of this sort, in which entire lexical fields can possess components of low criteriality, major advances in the comparative understanding of semantics are likely to be slow in coming.

But this is not to adopt the pessimistic stance of many constructivists who, aiming at "complete understanding of a phenomenon" (Poortinga & Van de Vijver, 1994), insist that meaning must be fully determined before we can achieve *any* valid interpretation (Sampson, 1994). If interpretations are "totally contingent on time, place, and person" (D'Andrade, 1986, p. 26) because human beings, "uniquely," impose systems of meaning on their activities, then a higher-order phenomenon, the semantic system, is completely overriding all else. Such an assertion, we submit, would be refuted by a great deal of what is discussed in this *Handbook*.

Sex-Typing

Margaret Mead once made a dramatic anthropological claim about variation in sex-typing. Her assertion, cited approvingly by innumerable textbooks ever since (Minderhout, 1986), was that all the logical contrasts to Western sex-typing could be found in three New Guinea societies: Among the Arapesh, both men and women were "gentle" and "unaggressive" (Mead, 1935, p. 161); among the Mundugumor, both men and women were "ruthless, aggressive . . . the Mundugumor ideal is the violent aggressive man married to the violent aggressive woman"; among the Tchambuli, "the woman [is] the dominant, impersonal, managing partner, the man the less responsible and the emotionally dependent person" (Mead, 1935, p. 279).

The facts seem to be very much otherwise. Among the "gentle" Arapesh, an independent observer has described the *obligation* of a young man to commit homicide in order to attain adult status (Tuzin, 1977); and another has expressed doubt that the personality types of the two sexes are the same, and cites the Arapesh's own proverb: "Men's hearts are different; women's hearts are different" (Fortune, 1939, p. 36). Among the "violent aggressive" Mundugumor, as Daly and Wilson (1988) have pointed out, although the men were "avid polygynists, raiding neighboring tribes for wives, and for heads" (p. 151), the women did not raid for husbands or for heads. Women's aggressive impulses were expressed by "fishing and eating better than men, or serving dishes tastier than their co-wives to a common husband" (Mead, 1955, p. 98). As for the sex-reversed Tchambuli, the men—not the women—were the warriors, the slaying of one's first enemy was important for a young man, and it was the husbands who could beat wives, not vice versa. Furthermore, a follow-up visit to the Tchambuli (Gewertz, 1981) found no evidence of the female dominance that Mead had insisted upon. We must conclude that Mead's "demonstration" was a myth.

The aggression of New Guinea males is found among men elsewhere, and in no society are the women the central warriors, or, for that matter, the central killers. Daly and Wilson (1988) state: *"The difference between the sexes is immense, and it is universal.* There is no known human society in which the level of lethal violence among women even begins to approach that among men" (p. 146). Moreover, the sex difference in aggression begins early: Among young children observed in everyday settings in ten societies, the boys were more aggressive than the girls in eight cases, no differences were found in two, and in none were the girls more aggressive (R. H. Munroe & R. L. Munroe, 1994a). Such differences are comparable to those found among the higher primates (Wrangham, 1995), and, as Daly and Wilson (1988) make clear, they are not a story concocted by "the dark forces of ethnocentrism and sexism" (p. 150). The same sense is conveyed by the findings of Williams and Best (1982; cf. also Best & Williams, volume 3 of this *Handbook*) in their 30-nation study of sex stereotypes and by the discussion on aggression (see chapter by Segall, Ember & Ember, Volume 3 of this *Handbook*).

The differentiation between the sexes is further borne out by women's involvement in the care of children (Weisner & Gallimore, 1977). By far the strongest case of father care of infants in the ethnographic literature is reported by Hewlett (1991) for the Aka Pygmies of the Western Congo Basin; there, fathers are found no farther than an arm's length from their babies for half the day, and, in the Aka's forest–camp setting, are within view of the baby 88 percent of the time. Yet even among the Aka, the father's level of caretaking, as elsewhere in the world, does not match that of the mother. In *all* cultures, females are the main caretakers of infants and young children.

A robust set of sex differences has been found by Buss (1989, 1994a) concerning mate preferences in a world sample of 37 societies (and a total of more than 10,000 individuals). For all subsamples, men both preferred and married women who were younger than themselves, and they also valued good looks or attractiveness more highly than did women. Buss found that females, on the other hand, in 36 of the 37 subsamples "valued [the concept] 'good financial prospect' in a potential mate more highly than males did" (Buss, 1989, p. 5), and the sole nonsignificant case was nevertheless in the predicted direction (cf. also J. M. Bailey, Gaulin, Agyei, & Gladue, 1994; Sprecher, Sullivan, & Hatfield, 1994). These findings accord with expectations from evolutionary theory, which predicts that human *females*, as the sex that is investing more heavily in offspring (e.g., gamete size, gestation, breastfeeding), will carefully seek mates with ample resources, that is, men who can help children survive and thrive; and that human *males* will place a premium on a potential mate's age and physical appearance, interpreted as a signal of fertility and good reproductive capacity (Buss, 1994b). The link between physical appearance and reproductive capacity has not been investigated cross-culturally, where it is known that the characteristics defining attractiveness are variable. Even within a single society, such as the United States, concepts of feminine beauty have exhibited marked variation through time (Banner, 1983).

E. E. Maccoby (1990a, 1990b) has drawn attention to what she terms children's early and "spontaneous adoption of sex-appropriate behavior," including self-segregation by sex, and the rougher play and greater environmental exploration of boys than girls. Maccoby's (1990a) reading of the literature leads her to conclude that sex-typing by self-selection "is a very powerful process, perhaps the most powerful one" (p. 6). Given these early tendencies, the other regularities described above, and the parallels with our near primate relatives (McGrew, 1992), it seems likely that some sex differences are innately determined. But whether innately different or not, the two genders, as Schlegel (1989) observes, "are firmly grounded in the biological reality of sex difference" (pp. 266–267). And the biological sex differences in turn are firmly grounded in requisites of human reproduction, the basis for existence. It is then reasonable to hypothesize that in every sociocultural system, behavioral sex differences will arise early, will be salient, and will be laden with significance.

The enormous plasticity in various aspects of sex-typing cannot be gainsaid, but neither can the irreducible distinctions outlined here. In the face of all this, some (feminist) constructivists, by attending to variability and not the central tendencies, have arrived at questionable conclusions—to wit, that sex differences are arbitrary social constructions (Bem, 1993), that they are entirely the products of stereotypes and roles (Basow, 1992), and, even more strongly, that whether men are basically different from women depends upon whether society wants them to be or not (Hyde, 1991). With respect to the latter assertion, it seems that Hyde either believes the above differences not to be "basic," or believes them to be completely reversible—with females committing homicide at far greater rates than males in all culture-groups, and so on—were each "society" so to decide. One certainly must agree with Hyde (1991) that feminism is a different paradigm from psychology as it is usually practiced. Additionally, as J. M. Bailey et al. (1994) have stated concerning mating psychology, "It is ironic that sex differences so large have been scientifically ignored until recently, when so much energy has been expended examining relatively small sex differences" (p. 1087; cf. also Eagly, 1995).

The evidence presented in this section supports the idea that cross-cultural variability is limited by biopsychological constraints. Perceptually, the capacities and skills of human beings everywhere are comparable enough that the term "panhuman unity" seems applicable. In the domain of cognition, there are, as noted, important cultural differences, but the statement undoubtedly holds that normal individuals in all cultures can "remember, generalize, form concepts, operate with abstractions, and reason logically" (Scribner & Cole, 1973, p. 553). For language, we have pointed out just a few of the many cross-cultural regularities in phonology, grammar, and writing systems. Sex-typing in all known cultures displays a bias toward male aggression and female caretaking of infants and children, and, for those cultures where the investigation has been carried out, a strong sex difference in mating patterns. All these uniformities resonate with those we have seen for the expression of biological needs. While emphasizing universality we have also drawn attention to the impressive cultural diversity in most of the above areas.

Interpersonal-Level Variables

The lives of human beings in all societies center on their relationships with others, and these associations are weighted with powerful emotional responses both positive and negative. That is true of the topics to be considered in this section, namely, reciprocity, group polarization, status, solidarity, and ethnocentrism. Reciprocity and group polarization, though conceptually unrelated, are discussed together below because they appear to be subject to the same types of sociocultural constraints. Status, solidarity, and ethnocentrism are more likely to occur in highly regular ways and to be only minimally affected by sociocultural conditions. Aside from the topic of reciprocity, psychologists have investigated these topics more than anthropologists, who have usually emphasized the study of kinship and other structural features in social relations (see subsection on social–organizational institutions).

Reciprocity and Group Polarization

Anthropologists and sociologists have long stressed the importance of a principle of reciprocity in social behavior (Gouldner, 1960; Mauss, 1924/1954; Sahlins, 1972). The concept reached its apogee in Lévi-Strauss's (1969) argument that the reciprocal transfer of messages (language), goods (economics), and women (social organization) is underlain by a universal urge to engage in exchanges, thereby creating interdependencies. Such patterns of reciprocity, however, appear to be characteristic only of hunting–gathering and simple horticultural systems. At a slightly more complex level, that is, among subsistence societies possessing political hierarchies, the exchange of goods and services involves not direct reciprocity but the accumulation of resources for subsequent redistribution. And at the highest level of complexity, in urban–industrial societies, very many transactions are undertaken in terms of market exchanges (C. R. Ember & M. Ember, 1993), which are nested within social class systems, that is, conditions fostering objective inequalities. The idea, then, that a norm of reciprocity is "no less universal and important an element of culture than the incest taboo" (Gouldner, 1960, p. 171) does not seem to hold up beyond the level of the least complex socioeconomic systems. Such a principle, however, may be valid *within* though not *across* social levels in complex systems, as exchange and equity research indicates (R. Brown, 1986). If so, it would then resemble statements about relationships among intimates, and thus be more or less equivalent to the solidarity norm, discussed in the next section.

Another social tendency that may covary with cultural complexity is the intensification of opinion under conditions of face-to-face contact, a process termed *group polarization*. When group members share common attitudes, repeated attitude expression magnifies their initial inclinations (Brauer, Judd, & Gliner, 1995). The effect has been shown experimentally in France (Moscovici & Zavalloni, 1969) and in the United States (Lamm & Myers, 1978). We suggest that this process is likely to be strongly operative under the natural conditions typically found in small-scale societies, where enforced intimacy and lifelong contact are experienced by all society members. This should be an ideal context for the appearance of the group polarization effect; and should such an intensifying process occur, some of the seemingly extreme social forms these cultural groups adopt could be accounted for. Goldschmidt (1966) states the issue in these terms: "People are more alike than cultures . . . for instance, the average Zuñi and average Kwakiutl behave a good deal more alike than the normative patterns of the two cultures are alike" (p. 134). The "Apollonian" and "megalomanic" characteristics attributed to Zuñi and Kwakiutl culture, respectively (Benedict, 1934), then might reflect an interactionally generated difference that had only minor grounding in individual tendencies. But the implication of our suggestion is that average Zuñi and Kwakiutl individuals, by virtue of membership in small-scale societies, would exhibit a stronger group-polarization effect in experimental settings than would most individuals from urban-industrial societies. The general hypothesis is that the group polarization process will covary with cultural complexity, exhibiting the strongest effects in small-scale societies and the weakest among urban–industrial groups. Research of this sort remains undone even though it does not appear to present major methodological difficulties.

Thus, according to the view we propose, the similarities in reciprocity and group polarization are, first, that both have a high probability of frequent and perhaps universal occurrence in small-scale societies; second, that they would appear less frequently in complex sociocultural systems; and third, that their natural occurrence in complex systems would be primarily under conditions of close relationships among individuals of the same social level.

Status and Solidarity

Human societies and many animal societies display both status relationships (differential access to privileges, dominance hierarchies) and solidarity relationships (mutual liking, high rates of interaction with some individuals and not others) (R. Brown, 1965). In human societies, not only do these dimensions of relationship apparently always occur, but they are manifested in numerous facets of life. White's (1980) study of A'ara (Solomon Islands) emotion words yielded a pattern that fit well the dimensions of power and solidarity. In interaction-process analysis there is the "power" factor on the one hand and the "love" factor on the other (Leary, 1957). In small-group interaction, there is the familiar instrumental–expressive distinction, which is also found—though not without ambiguity—in male–female relationships or role enactments (R. Brown, 1986; Spence, Deaux, & Helmreich, 1985). Moreover, something similar to these two dimensions appears in sociopolitical roles (F. G. Bailey, 1972), and in the potency and evaluative factors of the semantic differential (Osgood, May, & Miron, 1975).

Degrees of status and solidarity tend to be manifested in congruent ways. For example, the maintenance of physical distance is used both to display deference to those of high status and low solidarity (nonintimacy) to those of brief or remote acquaintance. In accordance with this principle, R. Brown (1965) has formulated an "invariant norm of address," which Kroger and colleagues have documented for Chinese, Greek, and Korean social usage (Kroger, Cheng, & Leong, 1979; Kroger, Wood, & Beam, 1984; Kroger, Wood, & Kim, 1984). The relationship is that "the forms of address used by the superior [member] of an unequal dyad are also the forms reciprocally used between intimate equals, while the forms used by the inferior of an unequal dyad are also the forms reciprocally used between distant equals" (Kroger, Wood, & Beam, 1984, p. 261). Thus one would typically address a boss (superordinate) and a stranger (distant) with more formal terms (e.g., title plus last name), and an employee (subordinate) and a friend (close) with more informal terms (e.g., first name). Although the norms are thought to be universal, the specific role relationships embraced by the superiority/inferiority and intimacy/distance dimensions differ by culture. The Chinese, for instance, consider the wife of the younger brother to be subordinate in relation to the self, but the Greeks do not so categorize a younger brother's wife (Kroger, Wood, & Kim, 1984). R. Brown (1965) hypothesized that the general norm may be based on the fact that if individuals of differing status are to move toward greater intimacy, the move must come from the individual of higher status. In other words, the positive association of high status markers and high solidarity markers protects those of high status from unwanted advances from below and protects those of low status from painful rebuffs from above.

Recent research on gender and social dominance is consistent with a status–solidarity interpretation. In one study, males displayed a higher level of *social dominance orientation* (SDO) than females across a wide range of cultural and ethnic groups (Sidanius, Pratto, & Bobo, 1994). The construct of SDO expresses preference for superordinate in-group status, a view of social relations as inherently zero-sum, and a preference for hierarchical relationships between social groups, all factors which cross-culturally are strongly associated with the male role (C. R. Ember & M. Ember, 1993). In another investigation, SDO was negatively correlated with communality, empathy, and altruism, and positively related to seeking of specific hierarchy-enhancing professional roles, and to belief in particular ideologies that support group-based hierarchy (Pratto, Sidanius, Stallworth, & Malle, 1994). In other work, Moskowitz (1990) found for a Western sample that males gave accurate self-reports about dominance whereas females were most accurate in self- assessments of friendliness. This latter research would seem to lend itself well to cross-cultural study.

Regarding *the maintenance of status and solidarity,* P. Brown and Levinson (1987) have illustrated, with rich data from three languages, the ways in which "politeness" systems allow individuals to maintain and ratify their public self-images. In the Brown–Levinson theory, politeness is called for when a speaker wishes to express anything that will threaten the listener's "face." The assumption is that many social acts—criticisms, complaints, offers, requests—are intrinsically threatening to face and thus require "softening." For a small request, for example, the speaker uses language that stresses in-group membership and social similarity (as in the inclusive pronominal of "Let's have another cookie then"). For a somewhat larger request, the speaker uses formal politeness (hedges, apologies for intrusion). And for a request that perhaps should not be made, the speaker uses indirect expressions. P. Brown and Levinson (1987) also point out that honorifics ("direct grammatical encodings of relative social status between participants," p. 179) especially co-occur with the use of requests.

In several Pacific societies where egalitarian relations prevail, it is noteworthy that confrontation and coercion are avoided by means of oblique and indirect speech when situations of potential conflict arise (Brenneis & Myers, 1984). The absence of formal hierarchy dictates that autonomous actors negotiate, through discourse, acceptable interpretations of their social relationship. The "indirection" of public political talk allows for multiple interpretations, thus sustaining the appearance of autonomy for the individual actors in these cases where no defined relations of subordination or superordination are present.

The politeness principle and the egalitarian-society research help us to understand the "micro" social processes by which systems of status and solidarity are reproduced. Yet, as R. Brown (1988) pointed out for the politeness findings, and as is true for the results on egalitarian political orders, the research has not involved experimentation or knowledgeable use of quantitative methods. Further, P. Brown and Levinson (1987) note that notions of politeness vary culturally (e.g., it is impolite to ask where someone is going in Tamil), and threats to face cannot be assessed properly without detailed cultural knowledge; the same of course would be true of the details of social relationships in egalitarian societies. Or again, the egalitarianism results are limited to investigations of Pacific societies, and the politeness data are detailed for only English, South Indian Tamil, and Tzeltal, with examples drawn from Malagasy, Japanese, and other languages. Nevertheless, the findings from both these sets of research offer the enticing possibility of "the reduction of 'ritual' to principles of rational action" (P. Brown & Levinson, 1987, p. 3).

Ethnocentrism

Human beings display what may be a built-in propensity to favor the in-group. In Tajfel's (1981) *minimal-group* paradigm, distinctions arise immediately whenever humans are divided into groups, even on a random basis. Thus we apparently have a natural ethnocentrism "in the sense of in-group preference, favoritism, and over-valuation" (R. Brown, 1986, p. 584). The results found in the minimal-group experiment are said by Brown to be based on universal and primordial motives of the individual. But even more fundamental mechanisms may be contributing to the effect. In animal species at many phylogenetic levels, adaptive behavior requires that individuals be reliably distinguished and identified, and two of the mechanisms that promote recognition are early patterns of association and phenotype matching (Fletcher & Michener, 1987). A predisposition to trust and favor those in one's own social groups and to fear strangers (Seligman & Hager, 1972) could well be based on such deepseated patterns, as could the early development of attachment, separation anxiety, and stranger anxiety among human infants (Ainsworth, 1985; van IJzendoorn & Kroonenberg, 1988). These processes may help to account for the strong tendencies found in minimal-group experiments. Consistent with this interpretation is the recurrent finding reported from Malpass's (1990) research on the "cross-race effect," namely, that people "have greater difficulty recognizing [by face] individuals from other groups, compared with own-group individuals" (p. 10). Given phenotype matching and its implications, it may be expectable that members of groups dissimilar to the self are categorized by broad features, thus establishing only their non-membership in one's own group. Fellow group members, that is, those with whom one regularly interacts, command close attention and the learning of a variety of distinctive features (cf. Medin, 1989).

The minimal-group effect is highly robust (Tajfel, 1981), and it appears to possess a sufficient number of real-world manifestations, as in ethnic and nationalistic strife (cf. Horowitz, 1985; Shaw & Wong, 1989) and warfare (cf. Segall, Ember & Ember, Volume 3 of this *Handbook*). Additionally, a 30-society study of intergroup attitudes in East Africa reported that: (a.) Culture-groups (e.g., the Kikuyu) expressed the most liking for those other culture-groups (e.g., the Kamba) that were culturally similar, geographically close, and well known to them; (b.) high-status culture-groups (e.g., the Baganda, Chagga, and Kikuyu) were respected, but were rated as being high *or* low in attractiveness depending upon their similarity to the culture-group making the evaluation; (c.) as the strongest finding, all culture-groups rated themselves both more favorably and as being higher in status than did other culture-groups, and all groups but one rated themselves the highest on desirable traits (Brewer & Campbell, 1976).

Segall and colleagues have argued that "the pervasiveness of ethnocentrism is best explained as a consequence of socialization" (Segall, Dasen, Berry, & Poortinga, 1990, p. 343), and that the expression of the phenomenon is subject to institutionalized control. The assumption is that under the right circumstances, we could "depart" from ethnocentrism and cultural parochialism. It is true that under carefully specified conditions, elements of the minimal-group effect can be dampened: If group membership is not salient (Turner, 1978), or if the dimension of comparison is unimportant (Mummendey & Schreiber, 1984), then subjects do not favor in-group over out-group members. But in a myriad of actual circumstances of group relations, group membership *is* salient, and the dimensions of comparison *are* important. Even if we could create an institutional arrangement in which ethnocentric attitudes and behaviors were absent, such a system would not have the inertial stability possessed by many other sociobehavioral systems. Every new social grouping would be an occasion for the potential regeneration of in-group favoritism and out-group devaluation, and these behaviors would tend to emerge unless there were endless monitoring of all by all, including the constant surveillance by adults of children, who in their peer groups would create these attitudes effortlessly. The conclusion, then, is that a fundamental phenomenon like ethnocentrism will spontaneously appear in the behavior of culture-groups unless a general climate of tolerance is strongly embedded, and unless institutional arrangements countering ethnocentric tendencies operate without cease—an unlikely condition.

Notwithstanding the ubiquitous tendencies toward ethnocentrism indicated above, relationships between natural groups can and do vary from peaceful co-existence to severe conflict. Within a single intergroup relationship, that of

Hindu–Muslim, the contact dates back more than a thousand years, but it has been marked by growing violence between the two ethnic groups during recent years. DeRidder and associates (in DeRidder & Tripathi, 1992) investigated norm violations and norms of redress among members of different ethnic groups and organizations in India and the Netherlands. Using self-report measures, they created inventories of norm violations for each sample (autochthonous Dutchmen and Turkish immigrants, Hindus and Muslims, Indian managers and workers, and Dutch supervisors and subordinates), and scales for own group identification, intergroup attitudes, perceived power, and fraternal relative deprivation. The main results may be phrased as follows: When two groups have coexisted for some time, norm violations by members of one group trigger negatively biased attributions. Within the victim group there will be retaliatory and escalator tendencies, which will be strong if the victim group members judge their own group's power to be superior. Although the victim group will retaliate with an equally serious norm violation, norms of redress also come into play and initiate de-escalating behavior. We can see that norms exist not only for group relations, but that there are further norms prescribing how one group should react to another group's norm violation. Thus, "tendencies towards escalation are restrained, the balance of power existing before the incident(s) took place is preserved, and a future co-existence between the two groups is, at least temporarily, guaranteed" (DeRidder, Schruijer, & Tripathi, 1992a, p. 182).

The findings indicate that the position of groups vis-à-vis one another (e.g., majority–minority status) is an important factor influencing the attribution process, and that the specific social context of a given intergroup relationship must be taken into account. As with the research on politeness theory and egalitarian-society discourse, norm-violation theory requires extension into a larger number of cross-cultural settings. Nevertheless, the findings thus far support the expectation of DeRidder, Schruijer, and Tripathi (1992b) that "the effects of . . . group contrast factors on reactions to norm violations . . . and norms of redress [will be] similar across different cultures" (p. 37).

In this section, we have attended primarily to regularities in the ways that social features such as status/solidarity and ethnocentrism are expressed. Anthropologists often point to factors such as the shifting boundaries of nation–states as evidence that social orders are "precipitates of historically located, on-going social interactions" (Segal, 1988, p. 317). While valid with respect to the extent and the limits of a phenomenon like ethnocentrism, the point is relevant to the peripheral aspects and not the focal elements of the regularity. The in-group, typically encompassing long-term members of an individual's network of associations, is usually highly stable at its core, and it is here that the favoritism would be manifested most powerfully vis-à-vis the out-group. Extensions of the in-group in terms of ethnicity, nationality, religion, and so on would necessarily involve fluctuating boundaries for ethnocentrism in real-world situations, just as the minimal-group effect can be easily manipulated experimentally with artificially created groups.

Institutional-Level Variables

The present interest is in how major societal institutions reveal the operation of psychological factors. The regularities discussed in the preceding sections would lead us to expect comparable outcomes at the institutional level. Because a full-scale investigation of this question would be immense in scope, we shall attempt to draw parallels for a few selected topics. Murdock's (1945) well-known list of 73 "universals," which to his knowledge occur in every culture known to history or ethnography, reflects capacities and constraining factors similar to those already described, for example, perceptual constants, language competence, and abstracting abilities. But beyond this obvious truth, it is possible to tie many of the items to specific, underlying biopsychological and social invariants—*age-grading* to maturation, *cleanliness training* to hygienic needs, *greetings* to the expression of status and solidarity, *housing* to the maintenance of body temperature, *mourning* to affective capacities, and so on. The list has held up remarkably well in the years since it was first compiled. One possible exception, the question of universality of the *family,* has been a source of much debate (Fallers & Levy, 1959). Further, *firemaking* is a trait apparently not possessed by the Bolivian Siriono*, who carry fires with them from place to place and maintain that they once could make fires but subsequently lost the skill (Holmberg, 1950/1969). The particular group of Mbuti Pygmies studied by Turnbull (1962) was also without knowledge of firemaking. Lonner (1980), in his chapter on universals in the first edition of this *Handbook,* presents a helpful classification of Murdock's categories.

Another impressive regularity lies in the parallel trajectories achieved by the high cultures of the past (Adams, 1966). The most important cases—because the most nearly independent—are the civilizations of the so-named Old World and New World. In both hemispheres, animals were domesticated, wild plants were brought under cultivation, pottery was invented, fibers and wools were woven into cloth, and metal-working began, first in gold and copper, then in bronze (Kidder, 1940). Systems of writing were independently evolved. In nonmaterial spheres the parallels also hold: Craft and occupational specialties emerged, priesthoods appeared, and political states rose. The significance of the New World is that it represents, in Harris's (1968, p. 682) term, "a second Earth," a set of conditions close to those of the Old World. The resulting parallelisms in development can be taken as further evidence for the general operation of stable biopsychological and social factors. Earlier origin and spread of these patterns in the Old World is probably traceable in part to climatic and geographic factors, including the west–east axis of Eurasia across a band of temperate latitudes (see preceding discussion on biological needs) (Diamond, 1994).

Sociocultural evolution is regular enough in its cumulative nature for strong Guttman-scale characteristics to be detectable on a worldwide basis (C. R. Ember & Levinson, 1991). For example, societies that have full-time governmental and magico–religious specialists also possess class or caste systems. The existence of political and religious specialists—legitimized representatives of higher-level control and reward systems—presupposes the existence of economic surplus and an unequal distribution of such resources, that is, class/caste structures.

The following discussion of specific institutions will follow a conventional tripartite classification into techno–enviro–economic (relation of man to nature) social–organizational (relation of man to man), and magico–religious (relation of man to the expressive world) (Harris, 1968).

Techno–Economic Institutions

This area is closely involved with both the satisfaction of biological needs and adaptation to the givens of the environment. It is probably the significance of these two kinds of "constant press" that has led numerous anthropological theorists to set up chains of association among types of institutions and to place techno–economic institutions as the first elements, and social–organizational and ideational institutions as dependent elements (Goldschmidt, 1965; Harris, 1968). Even more fundamentally, regularities in the archaeological record have suggested to many that the source-variable for cultural evolution in the techno–economic sphere is population pressure. Introduced by Boserup's (1965) thesis that human population pressure stimulates agricultural innovation, the hypothesis has been applied at several levels (Cohen, 1977; Pryor, 1986).

The strongest claim, made by Rosenberg (1990), is that "it is possible to argue that the simple tendency to population growth . . . suffices to explain not just the origins of agriculture, but the bulk of the intensificatory and expansionist cultural innovations that dot the prehistoric record" (p. 411). The argument that selective advantages accrue in response to population pressure can be seen as equivalent to the evolutionary–ecological principle that heightened population density favors competitive ability (Mueller, 1988; R.L. Munroe, 1992; Pianka, 1978).

This principle runs counter to the Malthusian perspective, which in essence foresees negative outcomes from increasing population. And some hold that the incessant increase—with more than 250,000 individuals now added daily to the world's population—marks *the* underlying problem for the future of humankind (Ehrlich, 1995; Tobias, 1994; Triandis, 1993). Most of the psychological research along these lines has been concerned not with population density *per se*, but rather with the concept of insufficient personal space, or crowding, and it has yielded ambiguous results. (For comment on this issue, see Brown, Werner, & Altman, volume 3 of this *Handbook*.) But investigation into the psychological aspects of population density itself would seem to be important for both its scientific and its humanitarian implications.

Predictability, control, and *efficiency* are all concepts more applicable to the techno–economic sphere than to other institutions. Issues in this area frequently carry their own logics of solution, and the many observed commonalities are to be expected, that is, simultaneous inventions in Western history such as the telescope, the steamboat, the telephone, and the phonograph (Kroeber, 1948). Again, transformations of form tend to occur according to a principle of efficiency; one does not find societies moving from industrial economies to foraging, or from steel axes to stone axes, or from grinding of grain at a power mill to grinding with simple hand-held tools. Trends of this sort indicate that techno–economic institutions may be analyzed in terms of a generalized hedonic model borrowed from the individual level. Two caveats must be entered, however. First, the concept of efficiency does not imply that people are making decisions that take long-term effects into account. We once believed that pre-modern peoples lived in harmony with nature, leaving it unmarked, but this idea is now seen as a "pristine myth" (cf. Butzer, 1993). Efficient changes are not necessarily heedful of ultimate consequences. Second, although an unwillingness to adopt a new techno–economic system does occur (e.g., in technical aid programs), the point is that when one techno–economic system (or part of a system) is given up for another, the trend is unidirectional, that is toward greater efficiency, and reversals are very few.

Social–Organizational Institutions

Without any doubt, the most important social groups are organized in terms of kin relations. Levinson and Malone (1980) estimate that approximately 30 percent of all ethnographic information in the Human Relations Area Files deals with kinship. Any claims that kinship relations are "arbitrary" (Sahlins, 1976) or that "there is no such thing as kinship" (Schneider, 1984, p. vii) must provoke wonderment in the face of the following: (a.) There exists everywhere a core familial grouping consisting of a woman and her dependent children, and this grouping clearly is based to some extent in biology (Wilson, 1983); (b.) Also everywhere, "reproduction is legitimate only if a social father is linked to mother and child in the reproductive unit" (Hendrix, 1993, p. 213); (c.) In all types of kinship systems, half or more of the individuals who are culturally defined as kin-related (to any given ego) are also genetically related (to that ego); that is, in systems of bilateral descent, cultural and biological kinship tend to coincide completely, but even in unilineal-descent systems, the overlap between cultural and biological kinship is 50 percent.

The apparent roots of kinship in biological relatedness probably help account for the pervasive association of kinship with favored and privileged treatment— or "prescriptive altruism," as Fortes (1969) characterized it. Certainly the principle from evolutionary biology must be taken seriously that, *ceteris paribus*, an individual's helping of others will be proportional to the degree of biological relatedness to those others. Thus it could hardly be "arbitrary" that, worldwide, the relationships among *primary relatives* (those belonging to the same nuclear family) are characterized by "a high degree of reciprocal cooperation, loyalty, solidarity, and affection" (Murdock, 1949, p. 93); and that such relationships are stronger for one's primary relatives as a whole than for one's secondary, tertiary, or other relatives. A system that espoused strong affective ties among, say, tertiary relatives and weak ties among primary relatives would run counter to all we expect, and indeed no system like this appears to exist. In addition, the greater meaningfulness of close kin than distant kin is reflected in an almost inviolable way in terminology: Terminological distinctions among close kin—that is, among people who are likely to be important to one—either equal or exceed the number of distinctions made among more distant relatives in 339 of 340 societies (D'Andrade, 1971).

Although the details of kinship organization vary greatly, Murdock's (1959) survey of 447 societies representing all areas of the world and all levels of culture found only five major types of kinship systems. In Murdock's (1959) view, the small number of types is due to the fact that "only a certain limited number of combinations of rules of descent, residence patterns, forms of family organization, and methods of classifying kinsmen constitute configurations whose elements are genuinely consistent with each other" (p. 135). "Consistency" may be interpreted to mean that the systems do not often require individuals to display highly incompatible behavioral tendencies, or to disperse affective ties equally among all persons near and far, or to operate with uneconomic cognitive categories. (In the first edition of this *Handbook*, we discussed the behavioral compatibility implied by rules of residence and of descent.)

As an example of *cognitive economy*, the technique of componential analysis, which is a kind of descriptive semantics, has shown successfully that a small number of discriminant features (such as sex, generation, and lineality) can be used to "generate" the kin terms used in any language (Lounsbury, 1969). In English, for instance, "father" can be defined as "lineal-male-of-first-ascending-generation." The results of such analyses have matched well the relationships among kinsmen as determined by other methods, and can furthermore be said to have a high degree of "psychological reality" (Romney & D'Andrade, 1964; Weller & Romney, 1990). As a second example of cognitive economy, the terms used for siblings in all societies are again based on a small number of criteria (such as sex of speaker, sex of relative, and older versus younger relative age), and the discovery has been made that the criteria used to generate a given term are almost always either *conjunctive* or *relational*, but hardly ever *disjunctive* (Nerlove & Romney, 1967). (A kin term is conjunctive if it is defined by a shared characteristic, say, *both* the relative's being male *and* the speaker's being male. A term is relational if it is, as the term indicates, defined by a relationship, say, the seniority—that is, status of being older—of the speaker. A term is disjunctive if it is defined by a discrepant characteristic, say, *either* the relative's being male *or* the speaker's being male.) In the 245 cases of sibling terminology examined by Nerlove and Romney (1967), there were only five cases of disjunctive systems of sibling terminology.

As well as upholding the idea that cognitive economy is prevalent in kinship usages, the findings on sibling terminology constitute a natural case of support for earlier Western experimental work demonstrating the greater ease of learning of conjunctive and relational concepts over disjunctive concepts (Bruner, Goodnow, & Austin, 1956). When Murdock (1949) asserted, almost a half-century ago, that the regularities discovered in human social organization were approaching those for natural-science knowledge, he was premature; but the above findings of Romney, D'Andrade, and their colleagues (cf. Romney, 1994) have begun to justify this bold statement.

Our earlier point concerning the legitimation of reproduction is worth pursuing. The linkage of the mother/child unit to a social father has been noted by prominent kinship specialists, including Goodenough (1970), who states that we always find associated with the mother–child group "socially recognized sexual unions in which women are eligible to bear and from which women and especially men derive rights in children and thus establish parent–child relationships" (p. 97). Hendrix (1993) goes even further, arguing that this principle of legitimacy underlies other purported family universals, including marriage, incest taboos, and exogamy, and that all of these "assume the prior existence of the social father" (p. 213).

One reason for the significance of socially recognized fatherhood may be the impact of father absence on the psychological development of boys (M. R. Stevenson & Black, 1988). The apparent effects range from inappropriate sex-typing choices (Biller, 1993) through intellectual-performance deficits (Shinn, 1978) to institutional modes of expression (R. L. Munroe, R. H. Munroe, & J. W. M. Whiting, 1981). An observational study (R. L. Munroe & R. H. Munroe, 1992) compared father-absent with father-present boys (3- to 9-year-olds) in four cultures—in American Samoa, Belize, Kenya, and Nepal—and found, in each sample, that father-absent boys looked more than children from father-present families at the males in their social environments, as if in attempted compensation for the lack of a father figure. (There were no comparable effects of father absence for girls.) When the mothers in these societies were interviewed about the early lives of their children, they too seemed to be compensating for father absence: Their reports for early father presence in the home were at such high levels as to be dubious (R. L. Munroe, R. H. Munroe, Suppe, & Muhm, 1993). That these mothers would revise upward the actual degree of adult male presence appears to constitute additional evidence for the importance of the legitimacy principle. On a global scale, there has been an increase in father absence (Mencher & Okongwu, 1993) due to migratory wage labor in traditional societies and to high rates of marital dissolution in the Western world, and the study of its psychological effects should continue to offer a major subject for comparative investigation.

Anthropologists study many other structural groupings, though the psychological concomitants remain largely unexplored cross-culturally. Among the associations that might be looked into, some of which have parallels in industrial nations, are secret societies, informal but stable work groups, mutual-aid societies, bachelor associations, and age-sets (individuals of the same age and sex forming a formal cohort for life) (C. R. Ember & M. Ember, 1993).

Magico–Religious Institutions

In the first edition of this *Handbook* we addressed the diametrically opposed positions taken by investigators on several issues in the study of magico–religious phenomena, for example, magic and religion as rational versus nonrational phenomena; as radical versus conserving versus reactive phenomena; as determined by childhood experience versus adult experience; and as causal factors versus dependent phenomena. We pointed out that the positions on these issues were not necessarily incompatible, but that no satisfactory synthesis existed which could effectively account for the myriad of findings. Such an assessment remains valid.

A cultural–evolutionary typology proposed by Wallace (1966), dividing religions into four major types, is of interest because many psychological variables are related to sociocultural complexity [5] (C. R. Ember & Levinson, 1991; Triandis, 1980), and Wallace's typology offers a way to describe increasing complexity in the realm of religion. The types: *shamanic* (containing only shamanistic and individualistic cult institutions), *communal* (containing groups of laymen responsible for performance of rituals important to various social groups), *Olympian* (containing a variety of ecclesiastical institutions, in which there is a professional clergy), and *monotheistic* (containing a monotheistic ecclesiastical cult institution). The varieties of institutions form a Guttman-type scale, so that, for example, in societies with communal institutions there will also be shamanistic and individualistic cult institutions, but not vice versa.

Among the "great" religious traditions, Slobodkin (1992) has detected a cyclical process in which the simple elements of a preexisting religion are made complex, and the more complex elements either simplified or dropped. For instance, he asserts that Judaism, against a backdrop of polytheism, minimized theology and generated great legal complexity; that Christianity then minimized the legalisms while complicating the theology; and that Islam subsequently reversed the process. Likewise, in his view, a comparable sequence occurred in the East as Buddhism and Jainism reversed the Hindu emphasis on theological complexity. This pattern implies schema changes that involved many thousands of individuals, and that only worked themselves out over hundreds of years, in somewhat the same way that pronouns of address in several European languages underwent systematic changes that took centuries (R. Brown, 1965).

Notwithstanding long-term processes like those outlined above, it has often been observed that supernaturalistic beliefs and practices tend to persist even while substantial sociocultural change is occurring. Some examples are the notorious strength of witchcraft beliefs in traditional societies despite modernization, and the stability of death customs in traditional societies despite Christian missionization (for the latter, cf. Rosenblatt, Walsh, & Jackson, 1976). Numerous urban Native Americans now living in Los Angeles have maintained a tradition of taking their adolescents into the California wilderness for vision-quest or questlike experiences, and some Native American culture-groups in California continue to seclude women during their menstrual periods. (In these latter instances, issues of maintenance or redefinition of identity probably also play a role.)

Nor are such occurrences limited to the members of traditional societies. In the so-called secularized modern world, there are, for example, the revival of long-banned religious customs in the former Soviet Union, and a renaissance of ceremonial practices in American prison populations, the observances ranging from Christianity and Judaism to voodoo (Glionna, 1995). In England several thousand people—witches, druids, Egyptian priests, shamans—participate in magical subcultures on a regular basis, raising the question, as Luhrmann (1994) phrases it, of "how to explain apparently irrational beliefs held by apparently rational [and highly educated] people" (p. 62).

In seeking to account for these and comparable phenomena, we assume that the deepseated affective component of magico–religious experience offers an important clue (cf. theorists as disparate as Durkheim, 1915, Freud, 1918, and Geertz, 1966). Related to this point, we want to invoke the core elements of Zajonc's *mere-exposure effect* (1968), which indicates that attitudes toward a stimulus are enhanced given only repeated, unreinforced exposure and nothing more. Investigations following up Zajonc's finding (now demonstrated in more than 200 published experiments) have discovered that the mere-exposure effect is amplified if stimuli, rather than being consciously perceived, are perceived without awareness (R. F. Bornstein & D'Agostino, 1992). The fact that the relationship is particularly strong after subliminal exposure is attributed by R. F. Bornstein and D'Agostino (1992) to what they call "perceptual fluency" regarding stimuli. (They argue that conscious awareness induces a correction process that partially offsets positive affect toward the stimuli.) The feelings and attitudes surrounding supernaturalistic phenomena are typically absorbed in the early years, and childhood experience, with its informal, often untutored learning, ought to provide frequent, and commonly "unaware," exposure to these phenomena. We therefore suggest that the processes involved in the mere-exposure effect, already applied to the understanding of stereotypes, social perceptions, and environmental preferences (R. F. Bornstein & D'Agostino, 1992), may be usefully investigated in relation to persistence in magic and religion.

The centrality of affect in magico-religious experience can also be seen in altered states of consciousness (ASCs), which occur cross-culturally on a widespread basis. According to one survey, either *trance* or *possession* states, or both, were institutionalized in 90 percent of the cultures in a large world sample (Bourguignon & Evascu, 1977; cf. also Bourguignon, 1994). Societal case studies of ASCs, and their relationship both to psychopathology and therapeutic functions, are presented in Colleen Ward's (1989) edited volume on the topic. But she points out the vast differences in purpose and function of drug-induced ASCs in Peruvian healing rituals and on American university campuses, and cogently notes that "the already substantial problems inherent in undertaking mainstream research on states of consciousness . . . rise dramatically with the extension of scientific inquiry to the cross-cultural domain" (Ward, 1989, p. 11). Approaching the topic from the perspective of the neurosciences, Laughlin, McManus, and d'Aquili (1992) attempt to show how ASCs such as dreams, ecstasies, shamanic experience, and ritual can be understood as means of expanding humanity's experiential scope, and hold that anthropologists must themselves become involved in more of these "possible cognized environments" if they are to comprehend the full range of human experience.

We have discussed a series of regularities at the institutional level that can be plausibly interpreted as underlain by fundamental biopsychological factors. In efforts to understand such phenomena as parallelisms in cultural evolution, responses to population pressure, and efficiency as a motivational force in techno–economic changes, evolutionary–psychological concepts like adaptation and optimality appear useful. In the analysis of kinship, the notion of cognitive efficiency and the neo-Darwinian concept of kin selection seem helpful. And in trying to account for persistence in magico–religious institutions, we have proposed that psychological elements associated with Zajonc's (1968) mere-exposure effect could be operative. For some of the relationships, solid and convincing support has already been found, while for others the connections are no more than tentative. But in all cases, suggestive research undertakings are discernible.

Conclusion

As we have seen, robust generalizations can be made concerning the great majority of topics considered in this chapter. The impressive regularities and central tendencies are of course constrained by boundary conditions and balanced by exceptional cases and the fact of the inescapable uniqueness of all sociocultural groups. Even prior to movements like postmodernism and constructivism, the natural-history orientation of anthropology channeled it toward playing the role of devil's advocate (Brenneis, 1990) and "taking issue with the extent to which [our colleagues in other fields] generalize their findings and theories" (p. 170); whereas, in contrast, the emphasis of cross-cultural psychology has been precisely on the generalizations and the regularities. Each of these approaches has had its drawbacks. The characteristic methods of cultural anthropology have included a reliance on verbal–descriptive data, and a scanting of questions involving operationism, measurement, and validity. Cross-cultural psychology has typically employed structured test situations with standard instructions and predefined response modalities, which have reduced the cultural appropriateness of its methods.

But the strengths of the two fields are significant and clear. Anthropologists' descriptive accounts of the shared ideas and beliefs of peoples, of their "collective representations," constitute a contribution distinctive from that of any of the other social and behavioral sciences (Jahoda, 1982). This documentation, carried out during the exotic-fieldwork phase of anthropology, lasted long enough and was extensive enough that we have been able to assess with some confidence the overall distribution and features of most cultural elements. The record of much of that fieldwork can be found in the Human Relations Area Files (HRAF) (Barry, 1980; C. R. Ember & M. Ember, 1988), the archive consisting of reproduction of the original texts on some 350 societies, with the information distributed into more than 700 topical categories. HRAF is currently in the process of extending its coverage to ethnic minorities within the United States. In addition, a series of more than 100 codes on various cultural practices for over 850 societies has been collated and published as the *Ethnographic Atlas* (Murdock, 1967). Both of these repositories stand as invaluable resources for the psychologist planning cross-cultural research.

While the HRAF collection allows the building of a sample of pre-industrial societies (e.g., Murdock & White, 1969), cross-national samples have been selected on a rather haphazard basis. A corrective has been offered, however, with the contribution of Georgas and Berry (1995), who have constructed a taxonomy of 121 nation-states arranged into clusters according to indicators in ecology, education, economics, mass communications, population, and religion.

Cross-cultural psychology's continuing concern with enhancing methodological rigor can be seen in discussions of translation issues (Brislin, 1986), design and analysis (Malpass & Poortinga, 1986), assessment of aptitudes, personality, and social behavior (Lonner & Berry, 1986), and recently introduced instrumentation. For the latter, there are, for example, electrical stimulation in the detection of pain thresholds (Clark & Clark, 1980), thermal and oxygen probes for assessing infants' microenvironments (Tronick, Thomas, & Daltabuit, 1994), and EEG readings, thermographic scanners, and autonomic nervous system responses for emotion (Levenson, Ekman, Heider, & Friesen, 1992).

The most promising development, however, has been the prospect of a *rapprochement* between the fields. Methodologically, anthropologists have begun to undertake the use of sophisticated instrumentation, for instance, the application of measures of cardiovascular reactivity and salivary cortisol for gauging internal responses to social stimuli (Flinn & England, 1991). Members of both disciplines have made efforts to establish reliable techniques for systematic behavioral observations (Bochner, 1986; A. Johnson & O. R. Johnson, 1987; Longabaugh, 1980; R. H. Munroe & R. L. Munroe, 1994b; B. B. Whiting & Edwards, 1988). And as anthropologists have turned more frequently to better defined, more circumscribed and more controlled forms of research, cross-cultural psychologists have begun to enlarge their units of analysis, such as in the study of everyday cognition (cf. Greenfield, this volume and Schliemann, Carraher & Cecci, Volume 3 of this *Handbook*).

One major lack in both fields has been the dearth of direct measurement of the independent, or "cultural," variable. Typically culture-groups are sorted on the basis of some classificatory principle (modern versus traditional, carpentered versus noncarpentered), and actual measurements are confined to the dependent variable. It might appear that massive data collection would be required to justify cultural classifications, but the significant contributions of Romney and Weller (Romney, Weller, & Batchelder, 1986; Romney & Weller, 1984; Weller, 1987; Weller & Romney, 1988) have demonstrated that precise statements about the cultural level often can be generated with small numbers of subjects, as few as four to six in many instances. Their procedure is a variant of reliability theory, with the important differences that data are coded *as given* by subjects (rather than as correct or incorrect), and that we are considering a universe of subjects rather than of items. Subjects provide responses to a series of questions, and one is able from these data not only to estimate how much each individual knows but also to arrive at a composite picture of what it is that, collectively, the subjects do "know." In this way one arrives at a set of cultural statements. Trying to construct full ethnographies via "consensus theory" would be tremendously ambitious; but for any given study, we wish to obtain only a selected few of such systematically produced statements, which can then be treated as cultural scores. As Weller and Romney (1988) phrase it, "Consensus theory allows us . . . to reconstruct the correct answers with about as much assurance as if we had the actual answers" (pp. 73–74).

Ideally, however, cross-cultural psychology would not treat cultures, even with well-constructed "scores," as categorical variables. Instead, the aim would be to link the scores of individuals, on a set of hypothetical independent "cultural variables," with some particular outcome variable. Such a treatment was elaborated by Sears (1961) as a means of investigating psychological processes cross-culturally (cf. also Berry & Dasen, 1974; Berry & Kim, 1993; Malpass & Poortinga, 1986; Poortinga & Malpass, 1986; Segall, 1983). As an example, one might hypothesize that parental beliefs in benevolent or malevolent supernatural beings would influence those parents' views on the goodness of children and on the need for punishment (cf. Lambert, Triandis, & Wolf, 1959). These elements of "culture," then, could be isolated through consensus theory and, at the same time, individual parent "scores" on belief in supernatural beings could be constructed. Through interviews and observations, individual scores on the dependent variables—beliefs and practices regarding children's goodness and the use of punishment—would allow both a within- and an across-culture search for the linkage. (Note that differences between quantitative comparison and structural, qualitative, relationships, as discussed by Van de Vijver and Leung's chapter in this volume, may reduce the likelihood of such pancultural findings.) As Sears pointed out, it is unnecessary that either variable have precisely the same components in different cultures since one is attempting to replicate a relationship for variables that are *conceptually* equivalent. Only a few instances of even adumbrated attempts at this approach can be cited (e.g., Diaz-Guerrero, 1993), probably due in large part to the commitment of time and other resources that would be required for a full-scale program. But the model would make possible cultural comparisons using ecologically valid measures and, in this ideal form, could establish the most robust regularities.

In the selection of dependent variables, the comparative, process-seeking approach may have hindered cross-cultural psychologists. This can be seen in: (a.) the selection of variables more important to Western psychological theory than to either the concerns of psychologists in other cultures or the possible construction of culture-distinctive "separate psychologies" (Kim & Berry, 1993), and; (b.) the ignoring of cultural differences that may be psychologically significant but not directly measurable verbally, that is, individual behaviors that do not appear to be under some codified cultural control yet still have distinctly different central tendencies and ranges for various cultural, subcultural, and ethnic groups. Among these are behaviors such as body stance, patterns of speaking, gaze, holding, touching, and maintenance of interpersonal distance (cf. Hall, 1966). While some behaviors of this sort are being explored (for instance, allowable emotional display—cf. Brenneis, in press) more systematic investigation might be profitable in learning just when and how such patterns are learned and distributed within and between cultures.

The above suggestions for further research remind us that the variability stressed by constructivists must be appreciated and embraced to the extent that we want to explore all the manifestations of human behavior in cross-cultural settings. Nevertheless, our emphasis on "generality" in this chapter is in keeping with the goals of cross-cultural psychology (Poortinga & van de Vijver, 1994). Altogether, it constitutes an ambitious project, one made more daunting by the recognition that, in Donald Campbell's (1988) humbling phrase, "we are cousins to the amoeba, and have received no direct revelations not shared with it" (p. 442). But we believe the findings discussed in this chapter and in the remainder of the *Handbook* indicate that a fair beginning has been made.

Acknowledgments

We are grateful for the helpful reading and commentary on various versions of this chapter by Donald Brenneis, Carmella Moore, and Daniel Segal. We thank also A. J. Gonzalez, of Pitzer College, and Jill Huntley, of Claremont Graduate School, who ably assisted with checking of citations and references.

Endnotes

1. The term "institutional" refers to the broad aspects of formal societal organizations—the techno-economic, social, and ideational—and should be distinguished from "institutionalized," or rule-governed, behavior. The individual, interpersonal, and institutional phenomena we consider herein all deal with institutionalized behavior, which represents anthropology's special domain, the sociocultural.

2. We take this opportunity to acknowledge an error in the first edition of the *Handbook*, in which we stated inaccurately that the Black Carib (Belize) term *mama au* was the name for a fart.

3. Unusual or intuitively unlikely ethnographic reports must be evaluated with conflicting factors in mind. One is the natural skepticism we feel when confronted with possible realities that diverge greatly from our own. This response is all the more likely when the practices in question belong to a now-extinct cultural situation. Such skepticism can prevent us from accepting the factuality of anything outside our own experiences. Nevertheless, we are right to be wary because anthropological fieldwork is typically carried out in a relatively informal, nonsystematic style, and

can be placed among the least rigorous of methodological strategies. Beyond this, any claim of an absent phenomenon also must grapple with the epistemologically insoluble problem of "proving the negative."

4. Issues of language in relation to cognition, termed the "linguistic relativity hypothesis" (or "Whorfian hypothesis"), have been discussed by Lucy (1992). While penetratingly dissecting the available empirical research, Lucy points out its overall paucity. As he notes, the hypothesis challenges fundamental assumptions in the behavioral sciences, and this may be the primary reason the topic generates so much controversy. On the other hand, reviews of the evidence would prompt many to conclude, with Talmy (1995), that language and other cognitive systems are "largely independent of each other" (p. 109).

5. Complexity, defined in terms of factors like settlement size, occupational specialization, and social stratification, is associated with child training techniques, treatment of the aged, relative status of men versus women, sexual restrictiveness, family type, and expressive culture (art, dance style, games) (C. R. Ember & Levinson, 1991).

References

Abramov, I., & Gordon, J. (1994). Color appearance: On seeing red—or yellow, or green, or blue. *Annual Review of Psychology, 45,* 451–485.

Abu-Lughod, L. (1991.) Writing against culture. In R. G. Fox (Ed.), *Recapturing anthropology* (pp. 37–62). Santa Fe, NM: School of American Research Press.

Adams, R. M. (1966). *The evolution of early society.* Chicago: Aldine.

Ainsworth, M. D. S. (1985). Patterns of infant-mother attachments: Antecedents and effects on development. *Bulletin of the New York Academy of Medicine, 61,* 771–791.

Annis, R. C., & Frost, B. (1973). Human visual ecology and orientation anisotropies in acuity. *Science, 182,* 729–731.

Bailey, F. G. (1972). Conceptual systems in the study of politics. In R. Antoun & I. Harik (Eds.), *Rural politics and social change in the Middle East* (pp. 21–44). Bloomington: Indiana University Press.

Bailey, J. M., Gaulin, S., Agyei, Y., & Gladue, B. A. (1994). Effects of gender and sexual orientation on evolutionarily relevant aspects of human mating psychology. *Journal of Personality and Social Psychology, 66,* 1081–1093.

Barry, H. III. (1980). Description and uses of the Human Relations Area Files. In H. C. Triandis & J. W. Berry (Eds.), *Handbook of cross-cultural psychology* (Vol. 2) (pp. 445–478). Boston: Allyn and Bacon.

Basow, S. A. (1992). *Gender: Stereotypes and roles* (3rd ed.). Pacific Grove, CA: Brooks/Cole.

Bem, S. L. (1993). *The lenses of gender: Transforming the debate on sexual inequality.* New Haven, CT: Yale University Press.

Benedict, R. (1934). *Patterns of culture.* Boston: Houghton Mifflin.

Berlin, B. (1992). *Ethnobiological classification: Principles of categorization of plants and animals in traditional societies.* Princeton, NJ: Princeton University Press.

Berlin, B., & Kay, P. (1969). *Basic color terms.* Berkeley: University of California Press.

Berry, J. W. (1976). *Human ecology and cognitive style.* New York: Sage/Halsted/Wiley.

Berry, J. W. (1990). Cultural variations in cognitive style. In S. Wapner (Ed.), *Bio-psycho-social factors in cognitive style* (pp. 289–308). Hillsdale, NJ: Erlbaum.

Berry, J. W., & Bennett, J. (1989). Syllabic literacy and cognitive performance among the Cree. *International Journal of Psychology, 24,* 429–450.

Berry, J. W., & Dasen, P. R. (1974). Introduction: History and method in the cross-cultural study of cognition. In J. W. Berry & P. R. Dasen (Eds.), *Culture and cognition* (pp. 1–20). London: Methuen.

Berry, J. W., & Kim, U. (1993). The way ahead: From indigenous psychologies to a universal psychology. In U. Kim and J. W. Berry (Eds.), *Indigenous psychologies,* (pp. 277–280). Newbury Park, CA: Sage.

Berry, J. W., Poortinga, Y. H., Segall, M. H., & Dasen, P. R. (1992). *Cross-cultural psychology.* Cambridge: Cambridge University Press.

Biller, H. B. *Fathers and families.* (1993). Westport, CT: Auburn House.

Blount, B. G. (1969). Acquisition of language by Luo children. Unpublished doctoral dissertation, University of California, Berkeley.

Bochner, S. (1986). Observational methods. In W. J. Lonner & J. W. Berry (Eds.), *Field methods in cross-cultural research,* (pp. 165–201). Newbury Park, CA: Sage.

Bock, P. K. (Ed.). (1994). *Handbook of psychological anthropology.* Westport, CT: Greenwood.

Bornstein, M. H. (1973). Color vision and color naming: A psychophysiological hypothesis of cultural differences. *Psychological Bulletin, 80,* 257–285.

Bornstein, R. F., & D'Agostino, P. R. (1992). Stimulus recognition and the mere exposure effect. *Journal of Personality and Social Psychology, 63,* 545–552.

Boserup, E. (1965). *The conditions of agricultural growth.* Chicago: Aldine.

Bourguignon, E. (1994). Trance and meditation. In P. K. Bock (Ed.), *Handbook of psychological anthropology* (pp. 297-313). Westport, CT: Greenwood.

Bourguignon, E., & Evascu, T. (1977). Altered states of consciousness within a general evolutionary perspective: A holocultural analysis. *Behavior Science Research, 12,* 199–216.

Boynton, R. M., & Olson, C. X. (1990). Salience of basic chromatic color terms confirmed by three measures. *Vision Research, 30,* 1311–1317.

Brauer, M., Judd, C. M., & Gliner, M. D. (1995). The effects of repeated expressions on attitude polarization during group discussions. *Journal of Personality and Social Psychology, 68,* 1014–1029.

Breitborde, L. B., & Glasser, I. (1990). *Urban anthropology for the 1990s.* Washington DC: Society for Urban Anthropology.

Brenneis, D. L. (1990). Musical imaginations: Comparative perspectives on musical creativity. In M. A. Runco & R. S. Albert (Eds.), *Theories of creativity* (pp. 170–189). Newbury Park, CA: Sage.

Brenneis, D. L. (In press). "Caught in the web of words": Performing theory in a Fiji Indian community. In J. A. Russell (Ed.), *Everyday conceptions of emotions.* Dordrecht, Holland: Kluwer.

Brenneis, D. L., & Myers, F. R. (Eds.). (1984). *Dangerous words.* New York: New York University Press.

Brewer, M. B., & Campbell, D. T. (1976). *Ethnocentrism and intergroup attitudes.* New York: Wiley.

Brislin, R. W. (1986). The wording and translation of research instruments. In W. J. Lonner & J. W. Berry (Eds.), *Field methods in cross-cultural research* (pp. 137–164). Newbury Park, CA: Sage.

Brown, C. H., & Witkowski, S. R. (1981). Figurative language in a universalist perspective. *American Ethnologist, 8,* 596–615.

Brown, D. E. (1991). *Human universals.* New York: McGraw-Hill.

Brown, P., & Levinson, S. C. (1987). *Politeness.* Cambridge: Cambridge University Press.

Brown, R. (1965). *Social psychology.* New York: Free Press.

Brown, R. (1973). *A first language.* Cambridge, MA: Harvard University Press.

Brown, R. (1986). *Social psychology: The second edition.* New York: Free Press.

Brown, R. (1988). More than P's and Q's [Review of the book *Politeness*]. *Contemporary Psychology, 33,* 749–750.

Bruner, J. S., Goodnow, J. J., & Austin, G. A. (1956). *A study of thinking.* New York: Wiley.

Buss, D. M. (1989). Sex differences in human mate preferences: Evolutionary hypotheses tested in 37 cultures. *Behavioral and Brain Sciences, 12,* 1–49.

Buss, D. M. (1994a). *The evolution of desire.* New York: Basic Books.

Buss, D. M. (1994b). Mate preferences in 37 cultures. In W. J. Lonner & R. Malpass (Eds.), *Psychology and culture* (pp. 197–201). Boston: Allyn and Bacon.

Butzer, K. W. (1993). No Eden in the New World. *Nature, 362,* 15–17.

Bybee, J., Perkins, R., & Pagliuca, W. (1994). *The evolution of grammar.* Chicago: University of Chicago Press.

Campbell, D. T. (1988). Descriptive epistemology: Psychological, sociological, and evolutionary. In E. S. Overman (Ed.), *Methodology and epistemology for social science: Selected papers, Donald T. Campbell* (pp. 435–486). Chicago: University of Chicago Press.

Campos, J. (1994, Spring). The new functionalism in emotion. *SRCD Newsletter,* pp. 1, 7, 9–11, 14.

Casson, R. W. (1994). Cognitive anthropology. In P. K. Bock (Ed.), *Handbook of psychological anthropology* (pp. 61–96). Westport, CT: Greenwood.

Christie, E. B. (1909). *The Subanuns of Sindangan Bay.* The Bureau of Science Divisions of Ethnology (Vol. 6, Part 1). Manila: Division of Bureau of Printing.

Clark, W. C., & Clark, S. B. (1980). Pain responses in Nepalese porters. *Science, 209,* 410–411.

Coe, Michael D. (1992). *Breaking the Maya code.* New York: Thames and Hudson.

Cohen, M. N. (1977). *The food crisis in prehistory.* New Haven, CT: Yale University Press.

Cole, M. (1982). Foreword. Foreword to the book *No five fingers are alike,* by J. C. Berland. Cambridge, MA: Harvard University Press.

Cole, M. (1990). Cultural psychology: A once and future discipline? In J. J. Berman (Ed.), *Nebraska symposium on motivation, 1989* (pp. 279–335). Lincoln: Univesity of Nebraska Press.

Cole, M., & Means, B. (1981). *Comparative studies of how people think*. Cambridge, MA: Harvard University Press.

Cooper, J. M. (1946a). The Ona. In J. H. Steward (Ed.), *Handbook of South American Indians* (Vol. 1, pp. 107–125). Washington, DC: U.S. Government Printing Office.

Cooper, J. M. (1946b). The Yahgan. In J. H. Steward (Ed.), *Handbook of South American Indians* (Vol. 1, pp. 81–106). Washington, DC: U.S. Government Printing Office.

Dale, P. S. (1972). *Language development*. Hinsdale, IL: Dryden Press.

Daly, M., & Wilson, M. (1988). *Homicide*. New York: Aldine de Gruyter.

D'Andrade, R. G. (1971). Procedures for predicting kinship terminologies from features of social organization. In P. Kay (Ed.), *Explorations in mathematical anthropology* (pp. 60–76). Cambridge, MA: MIT Press.

D'Andrade, R. G. (1984). Comment, in Preview: A colloquy of culture theorists. In R. A. Shweder & R. A. LeVine (Eds.), *Culture theory* (pp. 1–24). Cambridge: Cambridge University Press.

D'Andrade, R. G. (1986). Three scientific world views and the covering law model. In D. W. Fiske & R. A. Shweder (Eds.), *Metatheory in social science* (pp. 19–41). Chicago: University of Chicago Press.

D'Andrade, R. G. (1994). Introduction: John Whiting and anthropology. In E. H. Chasdi (Ed.), *Culture and human development: The selected papers of John Whiting* (pp. 1– 14). Cambridge: Cambridge University Press.

D'Andrade, R. G. (1995a). *The development of cognitive anthropology*. Cambridge: Cambridge University Press.

D'Andrade, R. G. (1995b). Moral models in anthropology. *Current Anthropology, 36,* 399–408.

Dasen, P. R. (1975). Concrete operational development in three cultures. *Journal of Cross-Cultural Psychology, 6,* 156–172.

Dasen, P. R., & Heron, A. (1981). Cross-cultural tests of Piaget's theory. In H. C. Triandis & A. Heron (Eds.), *Handbook of cross-cultural psychology* (Vol. 4, pp. 295–341). Boston: Allyn and Bacon.

DeRidder, R., Schruijer, S. G. L., & Tripathi, R. C.

(1992a). Norm violation and intergroup relations: Conclusions and prospects. In R. DeRidder & R. C. Tripathi (Eds.), *Norm violation and intergroup relations* (pp. 173–186). Oxford: Clarendon Press.

DeRidder, R., Schruijer, S. G. L., & Tripathi, R. C. (1992b). Norm violation as a precipitating factor of negative intergroup relations. In R. DeRidder & R. C. Tripathi (Eds.), *Norm violation and intergroup relations* (pp. 3–37). Oxford, England: Clarendon Press.

DeRidder, R., & Tripathi, R. C. (Eds.) (1992). *Norm violation and intergroup relations*. Oxford: Clarendon Press.

Diamond, J. (1994). Spacious skies and tilted axes. *Natural History, 103*(5), 16, 18–23.

Diaz-Guerrero, R. (1993). Mexican ethnopsychology. In U. Kim & J. W. Berry (Eds.), *Indigenous psychologies* (pp. 44–55). Newbury Park, CA: Sage.

Durkheim, E. (1915). *The elementary forms of the religious life*. London: Allen & Unwin.

Eagly, A. H. (1995). The science and politics of comparing women and men. *American Psychologist, 50,* 145–158.

Edwards, C. P. (1981). The comparative study of the development of moral judgment and reasoning. In R. H. Munroe, R. L. Munroe, & B. B. Whiting (Eds.), *Handbook of cross- cultural human development* (pp. 501–528). New York: Garland.

Ehrlich, P. R. (1995, February 5). Whose problem is it anyway? [Review of the book *Critical masses*]. *Los Angeles Times, Book Review*, 3, 9.

Ellsworth, P. C. (1977). From abstract ideas to concrete instances: Some guidelines for choosing natural research settings. *American Psychologist, 32,* 604–615.

Ember, C. R., & Ember, M. (1988). *Guide to cross-cultural research using the HRAF archive*. New Haven, CT: HRAF Press.

Ember, C. R., & Ember, M. (1993). *Cultural anthropology* (7th ed.). Englewood Cliffs, NJ: Prentice-Hall.

Ember, C. R., & Levinson, D. (1991). The substantive contributions of worldwide cross-cultural studies using secondary data. *Behavior Science Research, 25,* 79–140.

Fallers, L. A., & Levy, M. J. Jr. (1959). The family:

Some comparative considerations. *American Anthropologist, 61,* 647–651.

Fletcher, D. J. C., & Michener, C. D. (Eds.). (1987). *Kin recognition in animals.* New York: Wiley-Interscience.

Flinn, M. V., & England, B. (1991). Childhood stress as measured by radioimmunoassay of cortisol levels in saliva. *American Journal of Physical Anthropology supplement, 12,* 73.

Ford, C. S. (1939). Society, culture, and the human organism. *Journal of General Psychology, 20,* 135–179.

Fortes, M. (1969). *Kinship and the social order.* Chicago: Aldine.

Fortescue, M., & Lennert Olsen, L. (1992). The acquisition of West Greenlandic. In D. I. Slobin (Ed.), *The crosslinguistic study of language acquisition* (Vol. 3, pp. 111–219). Hillsdale, NJ: Erlbaum.

Fortune, R. (1939). Arapesh warfare. *American Anthropologist, 41,* 22–41.

Frake, C. O. (1994). Cognitive anthropology: An origin story. In M. M. Suárez-Orozco, G. Spindler, & L. Spindler (Eds.), *The making of psychological anthropology II* (pp. 244–253). Fort Worth, TX: Harcourt Brace.

Freud, S. (1918). *Totem and taboo.* New York: Moffat, Yard.

Gauvain, M. (1995). Thinking in niches: Sociocultural influences on cognitive development. *Human Development, 38,* 25–45.

Geertz, C. (1966). Religion as a cultural system. In M. Banton (Ed.), *Anthropological approaches to the study of religion* (pp. 1–26). London: Tavistock.

Geertz, C. (1984). Comment, in Preview: A colloquy of culture theorists. In R. A. Shweder & R. A. LeVine (Eds.), *Culture theory* (pp. 1–24). Cambridge: Cambridge University Press.

Georgas, J., & Berry, J. W. (1995). An ecocultural taxonomy for cross-cultural psychology. *Cross- Cultural Research, 29,* 121–157.

Gergen, K. J. (1980). The emerging crisis in life-span developmental theory. In P. B. Baltes & O. G. Brim, Jr. (Eds.), *Life-span development and behavior* (pp. 32–65). New York: Academic Press.

Gewertz, D. (1981). A historical reconsideration of female dominance among the Chambri of Papua New Guinea. *American Ethnologist, 8,* 94–106.

Glionna, J. M. (1995, May 22). Inmates demanding their rites. *Los Angeles Times,* pp. A1, A8.

Goldschmidt, W. (1965). Theory and strategy in the study of cultural adaptability. *American Anthropologist, 67,* 402–408.

Goldschmidt, W. (1966). *Comparative functionalism.* Berkeley: University of California Press.

Goodenough, W. H. (1970). *Description and comparison in cultural anthropology.* Chicago: Aldine.

Goody, J., & Watt, I. (1968). The consequences of literacy. In J. Goody (Ed.), *Literacy in traditional societies* (pp. 27–68). New York: Cambridge University Press.

Gouldner, A. W. (1960). The norm of reciprocity: A preliminary statement. *American Sociological Review, 25,* 161–178.

Greenberg, J. H. (1966). Some universals of grammar with particular reference to the order of meaningful elements. In J. H. Greenberg (Ed.), *Universals of language* (2nd ed., pp. 73–113). Cambridge, MA: MIT Press

Greenfield, P. M., & Savage-Rumbaugh, E. S. (1990). Grammatical combination in *Pan paniscus:* Processes of learning and invention in the evolution and development of language. In S. T. Parker & K. R. Gibson (Eds.), *Language and intelligence in monkeys and apes* (pp. 540– 578). Cambridge: Cambridge University Press.

Greenfield, P. M., & Smith, J. H. (1976). *The structure of communication in early language development.* New York: Academic Press.

Haddon, A. C. (Ed). (1901, 1903). *Reports of the Cambridge Anthropological Expedition to Torres Straits* (Vol. II). Cambridge: Cambridge University Press.

Halberg, F. (1960). Temporal coordination of physiologic function. In *Cold Spring Harbor symposia on quantitative biology* (pp. 229–310). New York: Long Island Biological Association.

Hall, E. T. (1966). *The hidden dimension.* Garden City, NY: Doubleday.

Harris, M. (1968). *The rise of anthropological theory.* New York: Thomas Y. Crowell.

Heider, K. G. (1976). Dani sexuality: A low energy system. *Man* (New Series), *11,* 188–201.

Hendrix, L. (1993). Illegitimacy and other purported family universals. *Cross-Cultural Research, 27,* 212–231.

Herdt, G. (1987). *The Sambia.* New York: Holt, Rinehart and Winston.

Hewlett, B. S. (1991). *Intimate fathers: The nature and context of Aka Pygmy paternal infant care.* Ann Arbor: University of Michigan Press.

Holmberg, A. R. (1950/1969). *Nomads of the long bow.* Garden City, NY: Natural History Press.

Horowitz, D. L. (1985). *Ethnic groups in conflict.* Berkeley: University of California Press.

Hull, D. L. (1988). *Science as a process.* Chicago: University of Chicago Press.

Hyde, J. S. (1991). *Half the human experience: The psychology of women* (4th ed.). Lexington, MA: D. C. Heath.

Jackendoff, R. (1994). *Patterns in the mind.* New York: Basic Books.

Jahoda, G. (1982). *Psychology and anthropology.* London: Academic Press.

Jahoda, G. (1992). *Crossroads between culture and mind.* London: Harvester Wheatsheaf.

Jakobson, R., Fant, C., Gunnar, M., & Halle, M. (1963). *Preliminaries to speech analysis: The distinctive features and their correlates.* Cambridge, MA: MIT Press.

Johnson, A. (1991). Regional comparative field research. *Behavior Science Research, 25,* 3–22.

Johnson, A., & Johnson, O. R. (1987). *Time allocation among the Machiguenga of Shimaa.* New Haven, CT: HRAF Press.

Kagitçibasi, C. (1995). Is psychology relevant to global human development issues? Experience from Turkey. *American Psychologist, 50,* 293–300.

Kay, P., Berlin, B., & Merrifield, W. (1991). Biocultural implications of systems of color naming. *Journal of Linguistic Anthropology, 1,* 12–25.

Kaye, A. S. (1994). An interview with Kenneth Pike. *Current Anthropology, 35,* 291–298.

Kidder, A. V. (1940). Looking backward. *Proceedings of the American Philosophical Society, 83,* 527–537.

Kim, U., & Berry, J. W. (Eds.). (1993). *Indigenous psychologies.* Newbury Park, CA: Sage.

Knorosov, Y. V. (1952). Drevniaia pis'mennost' Tsentral'noi Ameriki. *Sovietskaya Etnografiya, 3,* 100–118.

Kroeber, A. L. (1948). *Anthropology.* New York: Harcourt, Brace.

Kroeber, A. L., & Kluckhohn, C. (1952). *Culture: A critical review of concepts and definitions.* Cambridge, MA: Papers of the Peabody Museum of American Archaeology and Ethnology, Vol. 47.

Kroger, R. O., Cheng, K., & Leong, I. (1979). Are the rules of address universal? A test of Chinese usage. *Journal of Cross-Cultural Psychology, 10,* 395–414.

Kroger, R. O., Wood, L. A., & Beam, T. (1984). Are the rules of address universal? II: Greek usage. *Journal of Cross-Cultural Psychology, 15,* 259–272.

Kroger, R. O., Wood, L. A., & Kim, U. (1984). Are the rules of address universal? III: Comparison of Chinese, Greek, and Korean usage. *Journal of Cross-Cultural Psychology, 15,* 273–284.

Lambert, W. W., Triandis, L. M., & Wolf, M. (1959). Some correlates of beliefs in the malevolence and benevolence of supernatural beings: A cross-cultural study. *Journal of Abnormal and Social Psychology, 58,* 162–169.

Lamm, H., & Myers, D. G. (1978). Group-induced polarization of attitudes and behavior. In L. Berkowitz (Ed.), *Advances in experimental social psychology* (Vol. 11, pp. 145–195). New York: Academic Press.

Laughlin, C. D., McManus, J., & d'Aquili, E. G. (1992). *Brain, symbol and experience.* New York: Columbia University Press.

Leary, T. (1957). *Interpersonal diagnosis of personality.* New York: Ronald Press.

Lenneberg, E. H. (1967). *Biological foundations of language.* New York: Wiley.

Levenson, R. W., Ekman P., Heider, K., & Friesen, W. V. (1992). Emotion and autonomic nervous system activity in the Minangkabau of West Sumatra. *Journal of Personality and Social Psychology, 62,* 972–998.

Levinson, D., & Malone, M. J. (1980). *Toward explaining human culture.* New Haven, CT: HRAF Press.

Lévi-Strauss, C. (1969). *The elementary structures of kinship* (Rev. ed.) Boston: Beacon Press.

Lindholm, C. (1982). *Generosity and jealousy.* New York: Columbia University Press.

Longabaugh, R. (1980). The systematic observation of behavior in naturalistic settings. In H. C. Triandis & J. W. Berry (Eds.), *Handbook of cross-cultural psychology* (Vol. 2, pp. 57–126). Boston: Allyn and Bacon.

Lonner, W. J. (1980). The search for psychological universals. In H. C. Triandis & W. W. Lambert (Eds.). *Handbook of cross-cultural psychology* (Vol. 1, pp. 143–204). Boston: Allyn and Bacon.

Lonner, W. J., & Berry, J. W. (Eds.). (1986). *Field methods in cross-cultural research.* Newbury Park, CA: Sage.

Lounsbury, F. G. (1969). The structural analysis of kinship semantics. In S. A. Tyler (Ed.), *Cognitive anthropology* (pp. 193–212). Holt, Rinehart and Winston.

Lucy, John A. (1992). *Language diversity and thought.* Cambridge: Cambridge University Press.

Luhrmann, T. M. (1994). Psychological anthropology as the naturalist's art. In M. M. Suárez-Orozco, G. Spindler, & L. Spindler (Eds.), *The making of psychological anthropology II* (pp. 60–79). Fort Worth, TX: Harcourt Brace.

Maccoby, E. E. (1990a). Children are "ruthless stereotypers." Excerpts from keynote speech, meeting of American Psychological Society. *APS Observer, 3*(4), 5-7.

Maccoby, E. E. (1990b). Gender and relationships: A developmental account. *American Psychologist, 45,* 513–520.

Malpass, R. S. (1990). An excursion into utilitarian analysis. *Behavior Science Research, 24,* 1–15.

Malpass, R. S., & Poortinga, Y. H. (1986). Strategies for design and analysis. In W. J. Lonner & J. W. Berry (Eds.), *Field methods in cross-cultural research* (pp. 47– 83). Beverly Hills, CA: Sage.

Marsella, A. J. (1980). Depressive experience and disorder across cultures. In H. C. Triandis & J. G. Draguns (Eds.), *Handbook of cross-cultural psychology* (Vol. 6, pp. 37–289). Boston: Allyn and Bacon.

Mauss, M. (1924/1954). *The gift.* Glencoe, IL: Free Press.

McGrew, W. C. (1992). *Chimpanzee material culture.* Cambridge: Cambridge University Press.

Mead, M. (1935). *Sex and temperament in three primitive societies.* New York: Morrow.

Mead, M. (1955). *Male and female.* New York: New American Library.

Medin, D. L. (1989). Concepts and conceptual structure *American Psychologist, 44,* 1469–1481.

Mencher, J., & Okongwu, A. (Eds.). (1993). *Where did all the men go?* Boulder, CO: Westview.

Minderhout, D. J. (1986). Introductory texts and social sciences stereotypes. *Anthropology Newsletter, 27*(3), 20, 14–15.

Moscovici, S., & Zavalloni, M. (1969). The group as a polarizer of attitudes. *Journal of Personality and Social Psychology, 12,* 125–135.

Mueller, L. D. (1988). Evolution of competitive ability in *Drosophila* by density-dependent natural selection. *National Academy of Sciences U.S.A., Proceedings, 85,* 4383–4386.

Mummendey, A., & Schreiber, H-J. (1984). Different just means better: Some obvious and some hidden pathways to ingroup favouritism. *British Journal of Social Psychology, 23,* 363–368.

Munroe, R. H., & Munroe, R. L. (1994a). Behavior across cultures: Results from observational studies. In W. J. Lonner & R. Malpass (Eds.), *Psychology and culture* (pp. 107–111). Boston: Allyn and Bacon.

Munroe, R. H., & Munroe, R. L. (1994b). Field observations of behavior as a cross-cultural method. In P. K. Bock (Ed.), *Handbook of psychological anthropology* (pp. 255–277). Westport, CT: Greenwood.

Munroe, R.L. (1992). Commentary on nature-culture parallelisms. *Behavior Science Research, 26,* 137–162.

Munroe, R. L., & Munroe, R. H. (1980). Perspectives suggested by anthropological data. In H. C. Triandis & W. W. Lambert (Eds.), *Handbook of cross-cultural psychology* (Vol. 1, pp. 253–317). Boston: Allyn and Bacon.

Munroe, R. L, & Munroe, R. H. (1991). Results of comparative field studies. *Behavior Science Research, 25,* 23–54.

Munroe, R. L., & Munroe, R. H. (1992). Fathers in children's environments: A four culture study. In B. S. Hewlett (Ed.), *Father–child relations* (pp. 213–229). New York: Aldine de Gruyter.

Munroe, R. L., Munroe, R. H., Suppe, A., & Muhm, A. (1993). Effects of early father absence on attentional behavior: A follow-up analysis in four cultures. *Journal of Social Psychology, 133,* 863–864.

Munroe, R. L., Munroe, R. H., & Whiting, J. W. M. (1981). Male sex-role resolutions. In R. H. Munroe, R. L. Munroe, & B. B. Whiting (Eds.), *Handbook of cross-cultural human development* (pp. 611–632). New York: Garland.

Murdock, G. P. (1945). The common denominator of cultures. In R. Linton (Ed.), *The science of man in the world crisis* (pp. 123–142). New York: Columbia University Press.

Murdock, G. P. (1949). *Social structure.* New York: Macmillan.

Murdock, G. P. (1959). Evolution in social organization. In B. J. Meggers (Ed.), *Evolution and anthropology* (pp. 126–145). Washington, DC: Anthropological Society of Washington.

Murdock, G. P. (1967). *Ethnographic atlas.* Pittsburgh: University of Pittsburgh Press.

Murdock, G. P., & White, D. R. (1969). Standard cross-cultural sample. *Ethnology, 8,* 329–369.

Nelson, J. A. (1987). *Postmodern meeting of politics.* Paper presented at the meeting of the American Political Science Association, Washington, DC.

Nerlove, S. B., & Romney, A. K. (1967). Sibling terminology and cross-sex behavior. *American Anthropologist, 69,* 179–187.

Newman, P. (1991). An interview with Joseph Greenberg. *Current Anthropology, 32,* 453–467.

Nowak, R. (1994). Chronologists out of sync over light therapy patents. *Science, 263,* 1217–1218.

Ochs, E. (1988). *Culture and language development.* Cambridge: Cambridge University Press.

Ochs, E., & Schieffelin, B. B. (1983). *Acquiring conversational competence.* London: Routledge & Kegan Paul.

Osgood, C. E., May, W. H., & Miron, M. S. (1975). *Cross- cultural universals of affective meaning.* Urbana: University of Illinois Press.

Pepperberg, I. M. (1990). An investigation into the cognitive capacities of an African Grey parrot *(Psittacus erithacus).* In J. R. Rosenblatt, C. Beer, & P. J. B. Slater (Eds.), *Advances in the study of behavior* (pp. 357–409). New York: Academic Press.

Pianka, E. R. (1978). *Evolutionary ecology* (2nd ed.). New York: Harper & Row.

Pike, K. L. (1943). *Phonetics.* Ann Arbor: University of Michigan Press.

Pinker, S. (1994). *The language instinct.* New York: Morrow.

Poortinga, Y. H., & Malpass, R. S. (1986). Making inferences from cross-cultural data. In W. J. Lonner & J. W. Berry (Eds.), *Field methods in cross-cultural research* (pp. 17–46). Beverly Hills, CA: Sage.

Poortinga, Y. H., & Van de Vijver, F. J. R. (1994). IACCP or IACP? *Cross-Cultural Psychology Bulletin, 28*(2), 3–4.

Pratto, F., Sidanius, J., Stallworth, L. M., & Malle, B. F. (1994). Social dominance orientation: A personality variable predicting social and political attitudes. *Journal of Personality and Social Psychology, 67,* 741–763.

Prowitt, D., & Daly, P. (1972). (Producers), *Mind of man.* New York: National Educational Television. (Film).

Pryor, F. L. (1986). The adoption of agriculture. *American Anthropologist, 88,* 879–897.

Quine, W. V. O. (1960). *Word and object.* Cambridge, MA: MIT Press.

Rogoff, B. (1981). Schooling and the development of cognitive skills. In H. C. Triandis & A. Heron (Eds.), *Handbook of cross-cultural psychology* (Vol. 4, pp. 233–294). Boston: Allyn and Bacon.

Rogoff, B. (1990). *Apprenticeship in thinking.* New York: Oxford University Press.

Romney, A. K. (1994). Cultural knowledge and cognitive structure. In M. M. Suárez-Orozco, G. Spindler, & L. Spindler (Eds.), *The making of psychological anthropology II* (pp. 254–283). Fort Worth, TX: Harcourt Brace.

Romney, A. K., & D'Andrade, R. G. (1964). Cognitive aspects of English kin terms. *American Anthropologist, 66,* 146–170.

Romney, A. K., & Weller, S. C. (1984). Predicting informant accuracy from patterns of recall among individuals. *Social Networks, 4,* 59–77.

Romney, A. K., Weller, S. C., & Batchelder, W. H. (1986). Culture as consensus: A theory of cultural and informant accuracy. *American Anthropologist, 88,* 313–338.

Roosens, E. E. (1989). *Creating ethnicity.* Newbury Park, CA: Sage.

Rosch, E. O. (1973). On the internal structure of perceptual and semantic categories. In T. E. Moore (Ed.), *Cognitive development and the acquisition of language* (pp. 111– 144). New York: Academic Press.

Rosen, L. N., Targum, S. D., Terman, M., Bryant, M. J., Hoffman, H., Kasper, S. F., Hamovit, J. R., Docherty, J. P., Welch, B., & Rosenthal, N. E. (1990). Prevalence of seasonal affective disorder at four latitudes. *Psychiatry Research, 31,* 131–144.

Rosenau, P. M. (1992). *Post-modernism and the social sciences.* Princeton, NJ: Princeton University Press.

Rosenberg, M. (1990). Evolutionary theory and the origins of agriculture. *American Anthropologist, 92,* 399–415.

Rosenblatt, P. C., Walsh, R. P., & Jackson, D. A. (1976). *Grief and mourning in cross-cultural perspective.* New Haven, CT: HRAF Press.

Rowe, J. H. (1946). Inca culture at the time of the Spanish Conquest. In J. H. Steward (Ed.), *Handbook of South American Indians* (Vol. II, pp. 183-330). Washington, DC: U.S. Government Printing Office.

Rymer, R. (1993). *Genie: An abused child's flight from silence.* New York: HarperCollins.

Sahlins, M. D. (1972). *Stone age economics.* Chicago: Aldine.

Sahlins, M. D. (1976). *The use and abuse of biology.* Ann Arbor: University of Michigan Press.

Sampson, E. E. (1994). Identity politics: Challenges to psychology's understanding. *American Psychologist, 48,* 1219–1230.

Sanjek, R. (1990). Urban anthropology in the 1980s: A world view. *Annual Review of Anthropology, 19,* 151–186.

Sapir, E. (1951). The unconscious patterning of behavior in society. In D. G. Mandelbaum (Ed.), *Selected writings of Edward Sapir* (pp. 544–559). Berkeley: University of California Press.

Scheper-Hughes, N. (1995). The primacy of the ethical: Propositions for a militant anthropology. *Current Anthropology, 36,* 409–420.

Schlegel, A. (1989). Gender issues and cross-cultural research. *Behavior Science Research, 23,* 265–280.

Schlegel, A. (1994). Cross-cultural comparisons in psychological anthropology. In P. K. Bock (Ed.), *Handbook of psychological anthropology* (pp. 19–39). Westport, CT: Greenwood.

Schneider, D. M. (1984). *A critique of the study of kinship.* Ann Arbor: University of Michigan Press.

Scribner, S. (1979). Modes of thinking and ways of speaking: Culture and logic reconsidered. In R. O. Freedle (Ed.), *New directions in discourse processing* (pp. 223–243). Norwood, NJ: Ablex.

Scribner, S., & Cole, M. (1973). Cognitive consequences of formal and informal education. *Science, 182,* 553–559.

Scribner, S., & Cole, M. (1981). *The psychology of literacy.* Cambridge, MA: Harvard University Press.

Sears, R. (1961). Transcultural variables and conceptual equivalence. In B. Kaplan (Ed.), *Studying personality cross-culturally* (pp. 445–455). New York: Harper & Row.

Segal, D. A. (1988). Nationalism, comparatively speaking. *Journal of Historical Sociology, 1,* 301-321.

Segall, M. H. (1983). On the search for the independent variable in cross-cultural psychology. In S. H. Irvine & J. W. Berry (Eds.), *Human assessment and cultural factors* (pp. 127–138). New York: Plenum.

Segall, M. H., Dasen, P. R., Berry, J. W., & Poortinga, Y. H. (1990). *Human behavior in global perspective.* New York: Pergamon.

Seligman, M. E. P., & Hager, J. L. (Eds.). (1972). *Biological boundaries of learning.* New York: Appleton-Century-Crofts.

Shaw, R. P., & Wong, Y. (1989). *Genetic seeds of warfare.* London: Unwin Hyman.

Shinn, M. (1978). Father absence and children's cognitive development. *Psychological Bulletin, 85,* 295–324.

Shweder, R. A., & Sullivan, M. A. (1993). Cultural psychology: Who needs it? *Annual Review of Psychology, 44,* 497–523.

Sidanius, J., Pratto, F., & Bobo, L. (1994). Social dominance orientation and the political psychology of gender: A case of invariance? *Journal of Personality and Social Psychology, 67,* 998–1011.

Slobin, D. I. (1972). Children and language: They learn the same way all around the world. *Psychology Today, 6*(2), 71–74, 82.

Slobin, D. I. (1973). Cognitive prerequisites for the development of grammar. In C. A. Ferguson & D. I. Slobin (Eds.), *Studies of child language development* (pp. 175–208). New York: Holt, Rinehart and Winston.

Slobin, D. I. (1982). Universal and particular in the acquisition of language. In E. Wanner & L. R. Gleitman (Eds.), *Language acquisition* (pp. 128–170). Cambridge: Cambridge University Press.

Slobin, D. I. (1992). Introduction. In D. I. Slobin (Ed.), *The crosslinguistic study of language acquisition* (Vol. 3, pp. 1–13). Hillsdale, NJ: Lawrence Erlbaum.

Slobodkin, L. B. (1992). *Simplicity and complexity in games of the intellect.* Cambridge, MA: Harvard University Press.

Snarey, J. R. (1985). Cross-cultural universality of social-moral development: A critical review of Kohlbergian research. *Psychological Bulletin, 97,* 202–232.

Spence, J. T., Deaux, K., & Helmreich, R. L. (1985). Sex roles in contemporary American society. In G. Lindzey & E. Aronson (Eds.), *The handbook of social psychology* (3rd ed.) (Vol.2, pp. 149–178). New York: Random House.

Spiro, M. E. (1993, November). *What is new about "postmodern subjectivity?"* Paper presented at the meeting of the American Anthropological Association, Washington, DC.

Sprecher, S., Sullivan, Q., & Hatfield, E. (1994). Mate selection preferences. *Journal of Personality and Social Psychology, 66,* 1074–1080.

Stevenson, H. W. (1982). Influences of schooling on cognitive development. In D. A. Wagner & H. W. Stevenson (Eds.), *Cultural perspectives on child development* (pp. 208–224). San Francisco: W. H. Freeman.

Stevenson, H. W., & Stigler, J. W. (1992). *The learning gap.* New York: Summit Books.

Stevenson, M. R., & Black, K. N. (1988). Paternal absence and sex-role development: A meta-analysis. *Child Development, 59,* 793–814.

Suárez-Orozco, M. M., Spindler, G., & Spindler, L. (Eds.). (1994). *The making of psychological anthropology II.* Fort Worth, TX: Harcourt Brace.

Tajfel, H. (1981). *Human groups and social categories.* Cambridge: Cambridge University Press.

Talmy, L. (1987). Lexicalization patterns: Typologies and universals. Cognitive Science Report, No. 47. Berkeley, CA: Cognitive Science Program.

Talmy, L. (1995). The cognitive culture system. *The Monist, 78,* 80–114.

Tobias, M. (1994). *World War III: Population and the biosphere at the end of the millenium.* Santa Fe, NM: Bear & Co.

Traweek, S. (1988). *Beamtimes and lifetimes: The world of high energy physicists.* Cambridge, MA: Harvard University Press.

Triandis, H. C. (1980). Introduction to *Handbook of cross-cultural psychology.* In H. C. Triandis & W. W. Lambert Eds.), *Handbook of cross-cultural psychology* (Vol. 1, pp. 1–14). Boston: Allyn and Bacon.

Triandis, H. C. (1993). EcoPsychology: A response to Roszak. *Population and Environmental Psychology News, 19* (No. 3), 4-6.

Tronick, E. Z., Thomas, R. B., & Daltabuit, M. (1994). The Quechua manta pouch: A caretaking practice for buffering the Peruvian infant against the multiple stressors of high altitude. *Child Development, 65,* 1005–1013.

Turnbull, C. M. (1962). *The forest people.* Garden City, NY: Doubleday.

Turner, J. (1978). Social categorization and social discrimination in the minimal group paradigm. In H. Tajfel (Ed.), *Differentiation between social groups* (pp. 101–140). London: Academic Press.

Tuzin, D. F. (1977). *The Ilahita Arapesh.* Berkeley: University of California Press.

Van IJzendoorn, M. H., & Kroonenberg, P. M. (1988). Cross-cultural patterns of attachment: A meta-analysis of the strange situation. *Child Development, 59,* 147-156.

Wagner, D. A. (1981). Culture and memory development. In H. C. Triandis & A. Heron (Eds.), *Handbook of cross-cultural psychology* (Vol. 4, pp. 187–232). Boston: Allyn and Bacon.

Wallace, A. F. C. (1966). *Religion: An anthropological view.* New York: Random House.

Ward, C. A. (Ed.). (1989). *Altered states of consciousness and mental health.* Newbury Park, CA: Sage.

Weinreich, U. (1966). On the semantic structure of language. In J. H. Greenberg (Ed.), *Universals of language* (2nd ed., pp. 142–216). Cambridge, MA: MIT Press.

Weisner, T. S., Bausano, M., & Kornfein, M. (1983). Putting family ideals into practice: Pronaturalism in conventional and nonconventional California families. *Ethos, 11*, 278–304.

Weisner, T. S., & Gallimore, R. (1977). My brother's keeper: Child and sibling caretaking. *Current Anthropology, 18,* 169–190.

Weller, S. C. (1987). Shared knowledge, intracultural variation and knowledge aggregation. *American Behavioral Scientist, 31,* 178–193.

Weller, S. C., & Romney, A. K. (1988). *Systematic data collection.* Newbury Park, CA: Sage.

Weller, S. C., & Romney, A. K. (1990). *Metric scaling: Correspondence analysis.* Newbury Park, CA: Sage.

Wetterberg, L. (Ed.). (1994). *Light and biological rhythms in man.* Tarrytown, NY: Pergamon.

White, G. M. (1980). Conceptual universals in interpersonal language. *American Anthropologist, 82,* 759–781.

Whiting, B. B., & Edwards, C. P. (1988). *Children of different worlds.* Cambridge, MA: Harvard University Press.

Whiting, J. W. M., Sodergren, J. A., & Stigler, S. M. (1982). Winter temperature as a constraint to the migration of preindustrial peoples. *American Anthropologist, 84,* 279–298.

Williams, J. E., & Best, D. L. (1982). *Measuring sex stereotypes.* Beverly Hills, CA: Sage.

Wilson, P. J. (1983). *Man, the promising primate.* New Haven, CT: Yale University Press.

Wittkower, E. D. (1969). Perspectives in transcultural psychiatry. *International Journal of Psychiatry, 8,* 811–824.

Wrangham, R. W. (1995, Spring). Ape cultures and missing links. *Symbols,* 2–9, 20.

Zajonc, R. B. (1968). Attitudinal effects of mere exposure. *Journal of Personality and Social Psychology Monographs* 9(2, Pt. 2).

6

EVOLUTIONARY APPROACHES[1]

HEIDI KELLER
University of Osnabrück
Germany

Contents

Introduction

The acknowledgment of a biological perspective is common in almost all hand-books and textbooks, regardless of psychological subdiscipline. W. R. Thompson contributed to the first edition of this handbook (1980) a chapter on "Cross-cul-tural uses of biological data and perspectives." Statements refer to the basic bio-logical nature of human beings, in the sense that behavior and experience in in-teraction with the social and physical environment are rooted in an organismic ground. There is a neuro-endocrinological system, there is a physiological appa-ratus, there are anatomical features, and there are certain inborn behavioral char-acteristics, such as reflexes and basic drives like hunger, thirst, sexuality, func-tioning according to homeostatic principles. And there is, of course, the brain with multiple functions for behavioral regulation. This chapter is not about the multiple interrelationships between basic organismic or cerebral features and behavioral characteristics. Rather, it applies a meta-perspective that is not so com-mon in mainstream psychology, namely an evolutionary view. Psychological analy-sis by nature is proximate, but evolutionary considerations introduce an addi-tional dimension, providing an ultimate perspective on human behaviors and actions as strategies to maximize reproductive success. The key concept of repro-ductive success refers to the optimal representation of an organism's own genes in future generations.

The evolutionary perspective implies a radical shift from classical thinking, which in essence is static, to a functional goal-directed treatment of psychological processes. It will be demonstrated that this approach offers a conceptual integra-tion in which theories of selection pressures serve to generate hypotheses about the design features of the human mind. In this respect, the approach is consid-ered crucial for the discovery of new knowledge. It stimulates the formulation of questions in one discipline and their application to the body of knowledge in an-other discipline, as well as the use of knowledge developed in one discipline to solve problems of other disciplines. As such it goes beyond multidisciplinarity towards an interdisciplinary sight (cf. also Barkow, Cosmides, & Tooby, 1992). Two common orientations are significant for biological approaches, especially when applied to cross-cultural psychology: (a.) the centrality of the comparative method, and (b.) an emphasis on naturalistic observation in the sense of taking whole individuals (animals and/or humans) as units of research (cf. Thompson, 1980). Applying a meta-perspective to structure cross-cultural knowledge and findings seems to be desirable also from the perspective that cross-cultural psy-chology has no tight theories, but merely an abundance of frameworks (cf. Triandis, 1980; Lonner & Adamapoulos, this volume), often leading to theoretical eclecticism.

The multiplicity of underlying cultural and biological influences on behav-ioral acts has been conceptualized for a long time as following the equation $B = G + E + GE$, defining *Behavior* as a function of the additive influence of *Genes, Envi-ronment* and the *Interaction* of the two. The general interaction term is ambiguous; although widely accepted, it is in reality nothing more than a preliminary descriptive statement that does not give direction to empirical research. And despite the public acceptance of an interactionist view, the underlying general ideas are still "... either to demonstrate the effect of culture or to demonstrate that culture does not matter" (Strodtbeck, 1964, p. 284).

A more refined conceptualization proposed by Reese and Overton (1970) does not transcend this dichotomy. These authors portray two major philosophical models that provide the basis for assumptions about human development. The two models have been introduced as *organicism* and *mechanicism*. Organicism refers to an active organism that develops through processes of qualitative change. Approaches as different as those of Piaget and Freud can be subsumed under this theoretical heading. Mechanicism stresses quantitative change and the major, even active role of processes outside the primary control of the individual. This view refers to the external stimulus environment as the primary source of developmental change. Behavioral or learning theorists like Bijou (1976; Bijou & Baer, 1961) are examples of this approach.

From the conception of a biological or evolutionary perspective as promoted in this chapter, the genetic endowment can no longer be misunderstood as expressing fixed, deterministic relationships between genes and behaviors (cf. Plomin, 1994). Instead, "genetic preparedness" conveys the idea that behavioral acquisition (learning) is being framed according to time windows for the low-cost acquisition of specific skills and information that have to be contextualistic in order to be adaptive. Boyd and Richerson (1985; see also Draper & Harpending, 1982) refer to "easy learning" in this sense. Plasticity, that is, the capacity to be molded in different ways by different environments, is a main feature of the human architecture. Unfortunately, the plasticity of human beings is often misunderstood as defeating biological influences, as argued by Thompson (1980) in the first edition of this *Handbook*.

The following sections develop an argument along these lines to demonstrate the unique contribution that might be derived from an evolutionary perspective. The foundation of this thinking is laid in the seminal work of Charles Darwin, which will be introduced first. In order to clarify the discussion of genetic influences in evolutionary theory, the behavioral genetic approach will briefly be presented. Later, human ethology marked the beginning of a tremendous impact of biological thinking in psychology. It became especially fruitful for cross-cultural research, because its major endeavor consists in identifying behavioral universals across cultures. Two kinds of universals are discussed: "behavior universals" and "universal contexts of development." Eye contact between caregiver and infant during early socialization is introduced as an example of behavior universality. Universal contexts of development are discussed in terms of attachment theory and research that has led to the introduction of a differential perspective. Gaze aversion is then presented as such a differential developmental pattern. It is concluded that the ethological approach includes a definition of adaptation in normative terms.

This view can be questioned from the perspective of evolutionary or sociobiological thinking, presented in the next section of the chapter. Two conceptions that are crucial for the understanding of the sociobiological approach are discussed: the role of adaptation and the conception of culture. Since reproductive success is central to evolutionary conceptions, the parameters of reproductive decisions are elaborated. The two main reproductive strategies, r- and K-strategy, are introduced. The differences between evolutionary thinking and classical ethology become apparent when, in the next subsection, attachment quality is related to different reproductive strategies.

In a separate section, an example of the application of evolutionary thinking to cross-cultural psychology is given, namely a reconsideration of ethnotheories in evolutionary terms. Finally, the prospects for an evolutionary perspective for cross-cultural psychology are evaluated.

The Evolution Theory of Charles Darwin

The basic ideas of evolution originated in 19th century thinking and have been expressed also by those other than Darwin (e.g., Ruse, 1979). However, the publication of "On the Origin of Species by Means of Natural Selection. Or the Preservation of Favoured Races in the Struggle for Life" by Charles Darwin (1859) has had and still has a tremendous impact on scientific conceptualizations. The key concept of this theory is the process of *natural selection* (cf. also Mayr, 1977) that provides the frame for understanding species-specific appearances as *adaptations* to demands that are imposed on the members of the species by the environment.

The basic assumption is that genes or genetic programs are distributed in a population dependent upon the successful reproduction of their "vehicles of survival," when these vehicles of survival are individual organisms (Dawkins, 1982; Voland, 1993). The quest for survival implies competition between organisms on the basis of their individual's variability. These ideas are expressed by Charles Darwin (1859) as "natural selection." The limitations on theoretical reproduction are based on the restricted availability of resources like food, sexual partners, and parental investment. Natural selection favors those individuals who are able to maximize availability of resources for reproductive endeavors. In this way evolutionary change reflects genetic differences in reproductive success. Genetic information with better selection traits produces a higher number of adaptive anatomical, physiological, and behavioral aspects of its phenotypes (survival of the "fittest"). It is evident that adaptation towards physical and social environmental demands is crucial for reproductive success (cf. Voland, 1993).

This general principle can be applied equally to all species; there is no distinction between humans and other species. This conclusion is still highly controversial in as much as it centrally refers to humans as cultural beings. After all, it bears directly on many conceptions, explicit or implicit, of humans as ethical and moral beings (cf. also Eckensberger & Burgard, 1983). However, it is not fruitful to draw direct parallels between animal species and human societies. As Hinde (1987) has pointed out, ". . . since there are about two hundred different species of non-human primates, and an even larger number of recognizable distinct human societies, it is not difficult to find parallels to prove whatever one wishes." (p. 413). More fertile directions may be proposed from other perspectives. On the other hand, structural analysis of socialization tasks and adaptational processes allow for meaningful comparison between different species. For example, the understanding of early bonding and attachment processes has profited tremendously from Harlow´s experiments about the role of body contact in chimpanzees (contact comfort, Harlow & Zimmermann, 1959).

The ideas to be outlined here concern the organism–environment interaction in terms of functional relationships. Functionality is defined with reference to adaptive value (Gould & Vrba, 1982). Not only morphological or anatomical structures may be functional, but also ethological structures, such as behavior (Darwin, 1872). Anatomy, physiology, pathology, psychology as well as the behavioral repertoire should be considered as products of the same developmental chain nested in phylogeny.

Inherent in Darwin's conceptions is the assumption of continuity between the species, but also between the child and the adult stage of a given species. This basic developmental approach (Dixon & Lerner, 1988) conceptualizes the present form of a species or an individual as having developed from a succession of earlier forms and being open for further development in the future. Referring to those ideas, George Stanley Hall (1883), one of the most influential and prominent psychologists at the turn of the century, synthesized Darwin's ideas with those of Ernst Haeckel's (1866) recapitulation law. This law proposed that embryonic ontogenetic progression mirrors the phylogenetic history, that is, the evolution of the species. Hall applied this idea from prenatal embryonic development to postnatal life, also viewing ontogeny in terms of recapitulating phylogeny. The applicability of these ideas is to be questioned on the basis of life history approaches (Alexander, 1988; Krebs & Davies, 1978). They evaluate any developmental stage as important in itself for reproductive success. Infancy, for example, is not just a quick recapitulation of aspects of the phylogenetic past, but lays the ground for a relationship pattern that affects mating behavior (see following discussion). It is also apparent that ontogenetic development reflects the history of *adaptive,* successful achievements during phylogeny and not the "errors" or "detours" which did not survive.

Evolution represents the process of manipulation of the total gene pool of a population. The level of the individual is addressed in direct efforts to link genetic endowment to behavioral traits on the basis of quantitative estimations. Without genetic differences between individuals, evolution is precluded. Despite this, research on behavioral genetics is rarely incorporated in evolutionary thinking. Evolutionary theory focuses on broad conceptions like species and family. However, as Plomin (1987, p. 364) states "Even though the foundation for natural selection is genetic variability among individuals in a population, evolutionary theory and predictions emanating from the theory can rarely be brought to bear upon the behavior of individual members of a species." Before going into details of the biology of social behavior, we want to introduce modern conceptions of quantitative behavioral genetics.

Behavior Genetics

The theory of quantitative behavior genetics is founded in evolutionary theory. It accepts that Mendel´s mechanisms of discrete inheritance are also valid for complex characteristics normally distributed in a population. It is implied that many genes with small effects together are responsible for interindividual differences in a population. Genetic theory explains a pattern of observable resemblance based on different family (genetic) relationships, without denying the effect of environmental influences (Plomin, 1987).

Genetic differences are defined as those aspects of the human genome that are not the same for two individuals. The genome of a person is the entity of information represented in the DNA. The genotype is expressed in the individual's genome and constitutes the entity of all genes in the nucleus (Plomin, 1987). The unproductive questions of "which" (genes or environment) and "how much," differentiating genetic and environmental influences according to specifiable percentages (e.g., 40 percent vs. 60 percent), was already evaluated as not fruitful by Anastasi (1958) in her classical formulation of the "question how." She proposed an interesting modus operandi how environmental influences and genetic endowment feed into the phenotype through two continuous variables, width (from narrow to wide) and directness (from direct to indirect). As research tools, she explicitly referred to cross-cultural comparisons.

Genetic influences in behavior patterns depend on the existence of environmental differences to which various members of a given cultural population are exposed, as well as on the existence of genetic differences between members of that population. Under homogenous environmental conditions, the genetic influences on a personality trait may be more pertinent than in heterogeneous environmental conditions. Equally, in genetically homogenous societies, environmental influences are likely to be more significant. In this discussion, the link between acknowledging proximate relationships (the question how) with evolutionary based ultimate considerations (see below) becomes apparent in the "question why," thus, introducing functional considerations (Eckensberger, 1995, personal communication).

Another factor which is often misunderstood is the age dependency of genetic influences (Plomin, 1986). Although the genome does not change over the life span, gene expression varies considerably depending on age or developmental status. Triggering of the activity of specific genes depends in part on environmental factors. Genetic "determination" means that genes synthesize certain proteins in the course of development, but they do not produce fixed behavioral forms. These considerations have influenced the recent discussions on the concept of canalization (Holt, 1931; Bertenthal, 1991) where psychobiological and behavioral genetic approaches are integrated. Canalization describes the form of interaction or co-action between genetic and environmental influences as imposing various constraints; this view is supplemented by the concept of malleability (adaptability) that also forms part of development (Gottlieb, 1991), ". . . Individual experience alters gene expressions during ontogenetic development . . ." (Gottlieb, 1991, p. 10).

The field of quantitative genetics is as useful for the study of environmental influences as it is for studying heredity (Plomin, 1987). The similarity of two related persons socialized in the same surrounding, mostly family environment, may be due to genetic influences, but also due to the shared environment. Phenotypic variability that cannot be explained by these two factors is due to non-shared environmental influences. In earlier personality research it has often been assumed that siblings raised in the same family experience the same environment and consequently are shaped by the same influences. The extensive body of research concerning the development of relationships in infancy (e.g. Lewis, 1987; Parke & Tinsley, 1987) has clearly demonstrated that each individual experiences a unique environment, even when the same caretakers are involved. Infants form different attachments with their mothers and with their fathers (Lamb, 1986), while mothers and fathers form different relationships with their first- and later-born children. Behavior genetics extends this view by claiming that more than one child per family needs to be studied in order to explore possible environmental sources of differences between children within the same family. Rowe and Plomin (1981) proposed different categories of non-shared environmental influences, including unsystematic influences, such as accidents and illnesses, as well as systematic differences, for example, in parental behavior, and in peer orientation. Especially with respect to the latter variables, it is astonishing that scientific approaches have only discovered recently the obvious differential treatment of siblings in the same family that has been documented so vibrantly in novels and poems over the centuries. "The interest in non-shared environmental influences is so new that there is not yet much research on the topic. . ." (Plomin, 1987, p. 368).

Another aspect of behavior genetics is the genetic mediation of relationships between environmental measures and measures of infant development. Environmental measures often reflect actions and attitudes of the parents, and can accordingly be conceived of as indirect measures of parental behavior. Parents create developmental niches for the infants with environmental challenges and stimulation that they believe to be important for their children's socialization and education. The conception of a developmental niche has been introduced in the cross-cultural literature by Super and Harkness (1986; see also their chapter in volume 2, this *Handbook*), thus, translating the conception of the ecological niche into socialization terms by structuring environmental influences due to their physical, social, and symbolic properties (cf. also Nsamenang, 1992). Recent cross-cultural studies try to analyze these different socialization contexts (Lamb, 1986; Leyendecker, Schölmerich, & Larson, 1994), for example, by recording complete days of infants' experiences in different contexts. Following this line of argument, it can be concluded that the parents' personality constitutes a genetic link to the environment, which has an influence on the infant. Note that this view is based on developmental models, which stress the role of parental influences in shaping infants' development. Although this view is questioned by theorists proposing systemic developmental pathways, it is in line with evolutionary thinking that ascribes to parents the role of preparing their infants for adaptive reproductive strategies (Cairns, 1991; Keller, 1991).

Plomin, DeFries, and Loehlin (1977) have proposed three types of genotype environment correlation: passive, reactive, and active. Genotype-environment *correlation* is different from genotype-environment *interaction*. Correlation refers to the extent to which individuals are exposed to environments correlated with their genetic endowment, that is, children experience family environments correlated with their hereditary propensities. Interaction denotes the differential response of genotypes to the same environment (Plomin, 1987, p. 371). Passive correlation follows from a fit between the child and a supportive environment that family members create on the basis of their genetic resemblance. Reactive correlation implies a reaction of the environment, whether genetically related or not, to specific genetic behavioral traits; for example, teachers as well as parents react to specific talents of a child through supportive or suppressive endeavors. Active correlation refers to the active construction of a fitting and supporting environment by the individual organism, such as by actively pursuing specific interests.

Scarr and McCartney (1983) have added to these conceptions a differential developmental perspective indicating that the influence of the passive correlation declines from infancy to adolescence and the importance of the active correlation increases over the same period. They conclude that "... the genotype determines the organism's responsiveness to environmental opportunities" (p. 424). This view basically expresses the notion that the genetic influence on personality traits increases over the life span, since environmental variables are controlled through active covariation.

The notion of genotype–environment correlation points to the crucial function of learning. There is a common belief in the human capacity to learn everything at every moment (cf. Lerner, 1984). This is a serious misinterpretation of human plasticity. In fact, learning is an species-, age- and developmental-level-dependent mechanism. It is interconnected with maturation. Maturation is not only an increase in material, knowledge, or capacities (Thomae, 1959), but also a decrease in the range of possibilities, as research results from environmental genetics and neurophysiology have demonstrated (Crnic, 1984; Greenough & Schwartz, 1984). It has been reported that the number of synapses in one- to two-year-old children is about 50 percent higher than in adults. This reduction is most likely an effect of experiences: those synaptic relationships survive that are stimulated by sensory and motor experiences. At the same time, the lifelong generating of novel synaptic connections constitutes a different mechanism that may reflect the enduring necessity for adaptation to environmental features of novelty and surprise.

The conception that environmental influences are not continuously effective throughout development is the core of the assumption of sensitive periods (Suomi, 1979; Immelmann & Keller, 1988). Imprinting toward a moving stimulus in the greyleg gosling directly after hatching is the classical example (Lorenz, 1969), where specific environmental influences are only effective during a specific time window. Although strict parallels cannot be found in human development, critical phases exist, for example, with respect to the easiness of learning (Draper & Harpending, 1982). General learning principles have to be psychobiologically reformulated, because it obviously does not make sense to learn just any stimulus–reaction sequence that happens to take place according to the laws of contiguity; in that case far too much irrelevant information would be acquired. Differential learning rates for certain categories of stimulus–response contiguities have been reported in different species (Garcia, McGown, & Green, 1972). The preference for the human face and the ease of learning personal characteristics of the primary social partners in the human infant illustrate the specificity of general learning dispositions (Fantz, 1963; Keller, 1992). It can be assumed that social learning is easier than learning outside the social context.

It seems obvious that the development of phenotypic behavior is much more intricate than suggested by the $B = G + E + GE$ formula. Neither a fixed conception of genes, nor of environment, is adequate. The interplay between them has to be specified according to contextual demands, developmental malleability, and constraints, focusing on a systemic organization. The important question "why" expands the proximate view of behavioral genetics to functional and, therefore, ultimate considerations. Conversely, evolutionary thinking should be specified for the individual level by including behavioral genetic approaches more explicitly.

Human Ethology

A major shift in conceptualizing behavior and development has taken place with the introduction of ethological conceptions and methods in psychology. Developmental psychology, in particular, has been substantially affected by this line of thinking that focuses on content specific aspects like imprinting or attachment formation instead of "mere" structural considerations, such as learning principles. The theoretical approach of ethology can be characterized as "descriptive constructivism," although this term may sound out of place in this observational empirical context. Based on an inherited structure, a behavior repertoire emerges in interaction with environmental demands. Through extensive field observations the behavior repertoire can be described and its function reconstructed. Ethograms constitute comprehensive lists of behaviors of a species in different domains. Functionality is evaluated in terms of the adaptive value for the survival of the species. Observation is the primary method of ethology, although experiments help to understand specific functions (e.g., testing reactions towards sounds and movements for imprinting processes—e.g., Eibl-Eibesfeldt, 1989).

Basically, the quest is for the identification of the nature of human beings. Research efforts concentrate on the description of universals that are usually vague, however. Universals can be characterized following two different conceptions. One conception refers to universal contexts of behavior development as reflecting the fundamental biological and psychological nature of human beings. Another way to define universals concerns decontexualized universal patterns of behavior that allow basic social exchanges (cf. also Lonner, 1980; Brown, 1991; Poortinga, 1975). Behavior universals will be presented first.

Behavior Universals

Behavior universals constitute the grammar of social interactions (Eibl-Eibesfeldt, 1989) or the "biogrammar" (Tiger & Fox, 1971). They consist of those aspects of human behavior that form the lexicon of social action. The greeting face, coyness, the baby schema, and so forth, are examples of behavior patterns found all over the world. The early work of Hess (1973) and especially Ekman and collaborators (Ekman, 1972, 1982; Ekman, Friesen, & Ellsworth, 1972; see also Izard, 1971) has helped identifying basic emotion displays that are correctly interpreted by members of vastly different cultures. These research strategies basically constitute *human ethology,* a term that was introduced by Eibl-Eibesfeldt in 1967. The definition of the universals is dependent upon the unit of analysis; but in itself this is insufficient and has to be complemented by functional considerations.

Papousek and Papousek (1987, 1991) have contributed detailed empirical evidence to the identification of universals, leading to an integrated systemic view of human functioning. The focus of their observation is the parent–child unit, and they describe behavioral regulations as forming an interdependent and complementary set based on behavioral predispositions that occur across sexes, ages, and cultures. They consider human infants as being equipped with a behavior repertoire—including smiling, vocalizing, looking, to name just a few of the most prominent infant behaviors—in order to engage in social interactions with significant social partners. Potential caretakers, human adults, but also children of only two to three years of age are equipped with a complementary behavioral program that matches the developmental needs of human infants.

Papousek and Papousek (1987, 1991) consider these inborn behavioral predispositions as "intuitive," because they occur within a time span from 200 to 800 milliseconds contingent upon infants´ signals. This time span is longer than that of reflexes, but shorter than cognitively mediated behaviors. The short time span between action and reaction allows the infant to relate the parental behavior to its own, thus, experiencing causality and effectance (cf. White, 1959). It has been observed that early experiences with that quality are accompanied by expressions of pleasure. They constitute basic units of the developing locus of control or control beliefs (Piaget, 1977; Perrez, 1989; Keller, 1989). The most prominent of the relevant parental behaviors include the "greeting face" (a quick flexion of the eye brows and slightly open mouth), and "baby talk" (a specific mode of verbal vocal behavior towards infants characterized by high pitch, slow tempo, many repetitions, gazing behavior and eye contact, and mimical mirroring of infant's signals). The occurrence of the temporal structure of baby talk as well as the specific displays like the greeting face has been observed in a wide range of cultural surroundings (Eibl-Eibesfeldt, 1989; Fernald et al., 1989; Keller, Schölmerich, & Eibl-Eibesfeldt, 1988). The structure and function of this intuitive repertoire is exemplified in the following paragraph that discusses early eye contact between infant and caregiver as a universal behavior pattern.

Mutual gazing is one of the most visible behavioral channels in early parent–child interactions. Infants master the developmental task of intended eye contact that is answered by an equal parental desire to establish eye contact them-selves. Thus, eye contact has been regarded as a frame for interactional exchange (D. N. Stern, 1985; Keller, Schölmerich, Miranda, & Gauda, 1987). This framing quality is inferred from the temporal structure since during the early months parents accompany their infants constantly with their gaze. Accordingly, mutual gaze is mostly the result of the infants´ gazing activity. This phenomenon seems to occur irrespective of social–cultural background (Keller & Eibl-Eibesfeldt, 1989).

Although large cultural differences could be demonstrated between German, Greeks, Yanomami-Indians, and Trobriand-Islanders in the duration of these gaz-ing episodes, the structure is similar. Parents, as well as adults without their own children and even small children, explicitly attempt to establish eye contact with babies by attracting the visual attention and turning the babies to face them. They even regulate the eye-to-eye distance to the optimal viewing capacity of infants in about 20 to 25 cm. The distance regulation is part of the intuitive accommoda-tion, because parents do this even though they may be convinced that the infants cannot yet see (Schoetzau & Papousek, 1977; Papousek & Papousek, 1987; Keller, 1989). With increased mimical variation and increased behavioral tempo parents support their efforts to attract their infant's attention. Parents contour their ver-bal/vocal behavior rhythmically and also express verbally the desire for mutual gaze (Keller, Loewer, & Runde, 1990). After having established eye contact, par-ents adapt their behavior again toward the new situation in characteristic ways: they perform the "greeting face" (cf. Eibl-Eibesfeldt, 1989; Papousek & Papousek, 1987; Keller, Chasiotis, & Runde, 1992), they decrease the behavioral tempo, and they display an exaggerated mimical and gestural reaction.

To understand the interactional meaning of eye contact behavior, the infant's part must also be taken into consideration. Visual information processing is ap-parent from birth on. During the first three months of life, the visual system ma-tures until binocular perception and accommodation are developed. The neuro-logical maturation includes postural control at that time, which allows the infant through intended head movements to control the visual input during dyadic com-munication processes. From a developmental theoretical point of view this three-month period can be regarded as a "focal time" (cf. Keller, 1989) for the develop-mental task of establishing eye contact. In a longitudinal study we could confirm an inverted U-shaped function of infants´ gazing behavior during the first half year of life, peaking at about three months, which is in accordance with Anglo-American studies (D. N. Stern, 1977; Sylvester-Bradley & Trevarthen, 1978).

At the same time, interindividual differences are pronounced, suggesting the possibility of cross-cultural differences. It can cautiously be inferred that this de-velopmental course describes the eye contact development of the Western child. It is assumed that this developmental task will be similar in non-Western cultures as well, but that different timing may be expected due to developmental contex-tual differences. As indicated earlier, especially the prevalence of dyadic facial interactional situations during routine daily experiences may be typical for the Western socialization pattern, whereas babies in other parts of the world have more body experiences by being carried around routinely (MacDonald, 1992; Keller & Chasiotis, 1994).

The socialization context of early gaze dialogues can serve different proximate functions. First, parents reflect the infant's behavior as a biological "mirror," thus enhancing the development of a sense of self in the infant (Papousek & Papousek, 1987). Second, parental facial behaviors mediate relevant messages for behavioral decisions of the infant. As has been convincingly demonstrated, infants only crawl across a simulated visual cliff (cf. Gibson, 1979) if the caretaker signals positive and encouraging affect (social referencing, e.g., Campos et al., 1978). Third, parents teach their infants by means of their facial expressions how to form sounds in order to acquire speech (Papousek & Papousek, 1987, 1991). This discussion suggests that even in the case of those clearly identifiable universals, the cultural independence is only relative (cf. Chasiotis & Keller, 1994). Probably variability itself—within the limits provided by biology of course—should be considered to be the most strong universal feature of human behavior. An understanding of universals from such a structural perspective could constitute an interesting approach.

Reciprocity could be considered another candidate in this respect. First, social exchange has been evaluated on the basis of reciprocity during the evolution of man. Second, socio-emotional reciprocity during ontogeny is universally acknowledged. Finally, the major social–emotional categories are based on the perception of reciprocity (Trivers, 1985; cf. also Chasiotis, 1995).

Universal Contexts of Development

The organization of the individual life span as a series of "developmental tasks" that have to be mastered is an idea that has been expressed in various theories in psychology. It is basic to stage theories such as Erikson's (1968) model of personality development. The wide acceptance of the term dates back to the 1948 book *Developmental tasks and education* by Havighurst who introduced developmental tasks as interfaces of biological, social, and cultural demands. A psychobiological reconceptualization of developmental tasks focuses on a new aspect, i.e. hierarchical structuring. The life span is considered to be organized in basic developmental challenges that have to be mastered; the developmental result in terms of the quality of this process determines subsequent developmental tasks. This approach is, thus, more far-reaching than the perspective of human ethology discussed so far, because differences between groups of people are inherent in this conception. Although this line of thinking is applicable across the whole life span, so far only very early developmental tasks have been analyzed empirically. The earliest developmental task is the formation of a relationship quality. The most prominent conception is attachment theory (Bowlby, 1969; Ainsworth et al., 1978). John Bowlby integrated ethological and psychoanalytical notions with his clinical experiences and formulated a conception that is based in the phylogenetic preparedness of infants for attachment to a caregiving person. Acquiring emotional bonds is regarded as equal in importance to the satisfaction of primary physiological needs like hunger and temperature regulation (cf. also Harlow & Zimmerman, 1959). He proposed a sequence of phases that the infant undergoes in order to develop a specific attachment quality. This conception relies on the inborn equipment of the infant with attachment behaviors like smiling, vocalizing, gazing, and the like, that are displayed in the presence of social partners. In this way universals are given a functional perspective, because these behaviors elicit a readiness to care and to respond to the infants´ signals in parents. Responsivity or sensitivity are broader conceptual translations of intuitive parenting described in the previous section. The fact that emotional bonds have to be actively acquired during early ontogeny on the basis of inborn behavioral tendencies highlights the plasticity of the human organism, and is in accordance with the remarks about learning and behavior acquisition made earlier. A fixed attachment program would certainly prevent infants from adapting to contextual demands.

Bowlby (1969) describes four phases in the infant's development of attachment: The first phase covers the first month and is named *preattachment*. Infants react on the basis of inborn cognitive capacities for information intake and the processing of features of the caretakers who regularly spend time with them. They prefer human faces and voices over other kinds of stimulus input and learn the characteristics of their social surroundings (Fernald, 1992). The second phase, *attachment in the making*, is marked by an emphasis on behaviors promoting contact. It reaches into the second half of the first year and culminates in the selective social smile signaling the familiarity of the social partners. The third phase, *the clear-cut attachment*, covers the second half of the first year and becomes evident with the infant's development of locomotor abilities. The infant is capable of actively seeking proximity or keeping close body contact. The fourth phase spans the second and third year of life and is named *goal-corrected attachment* or *partnership*. At this stage the infant begins to adopt the perspective of the social other, which can only occur when the infant has developed a basic sense of self. Infants start to make inferences about the effects of their behaviors and are able to manipulate the behaviors of others in these terms. At that time the infant acquires an internal working model of a relationship which presumably will influence later relationship formations.

Ainsworth (1977; Ainsworth et al., 1978) has extended the attachment theory as formulated by Bowlby with two novel aspects, one theoretical (the attachment–exploration balance) and one methodological (the "Strange Situation Procedure"). She stresses the interrelatedness of attachment with exploration. She proposes the concept of the attachment–exploration balance and the secure base phenomenon indicating that the primary attachment figure, mostly the mother, constitutes a secure base for the infant to explore the outside world.

The second aspect introduced by Ainsworth et al. (1978) is the "Strange Situation Procedure," a laboratory sequence of situations of mother–child interaction with separation, confrontation with a stranger, and reunification. The quality of the attachment relationship is evaluated mainly in terms of the ethological conception of proximity seeking in the second reunion phase. Originally three modes of attachment security were differentiated. Secure attachment (B-classification) indicates that the mother is used as a base from which to explore; after separation the infant appreciates the return of the mother positively and tries to establish close proximity in terms of physical contact. About 70 percent of American children scored as securely attached at one year of age. Anxious avoidant (A-classification) attachment is indicated by ignoring the mother when she returns or actively avoiding her; about 20 percent of the American children score as anxious avoidingly attached. The ambivalent (C-classification) attachment indicates that infants are upset during separation and often angry when the mothers return. Signs of proximity seeking and avoidance occur during reunification; about 10 percent of American one-year-old children perform this attachment classification. A fourth classificatory system was introduced by Main (cf. Main & Solomon, 1986) as the D-type of attachment, indicating a disorganized pattern consisting of bizarre components like staring or body freezing. The quality of attachment is related to later social behavior and cognitive functioning in a predictable way (Sroufe, 1983). Securely attached children are socially more competent and perform better in vocational abilities.

The attachment theory and the strange situation procedure have become very popular in the scientific community and have been applied worldwide. Significant meta-theoretical and methodological concerns have been formulated (Lamb et al., 1984). Differential distributions of the attachment qualities across different cultures have seriously questioned the validity of the assessment. For example, different classifications of attachment groups in a Northern and a Southern German sample have been reported by Grossman et al. (1981). The study of Japanese mother–infant pairs, especially, has led to differential assumptions concerning the cultural specific expression of emotional states as well as social regulatory behaviors. However, as meta-analyses have documented (Van IJzendoorn & Kroonenberg, 1990; Sagi, Van IJzendoorn, & Koren-Karie, 1991), the organization of the individual attachment qualities in different samples varies intraculturally even more than interculturally, so that the cross-cultural application of this standard procedure seems to obscure more than it clarifies cultural specific ways of relationship formation in terms of more functionally equivalent patterns within the universal task.

The early interactional contexts form the nucleus of cultural transmission, because the home environment might mirror the cultural values in terms of beliefs and customs (Benedict, 1938; Mead, 1935; Valsiner, 1987). It has been acknowledged that fathers play important roles not only in supporting the family's financial basis or disciplining older children, but also in direct care of small children (cf. e.g. Lamb, 1986). Lamb et al. (1984) classified three types of activities that fathers spend with their small children based on a literature review: *Engagement* or interaction covers direct time spent in communicative exchange; *accessibility* involves less direct interaction but signals readiness to interact; *responsibility* involves the father directly in the daily life management of the child. It is, however, evident that mothers and fathers engage in different activities with the child (Lamb, 1981). Mothers, as the primary caretakers, spend more time with the children and consequently become more sensitive to the children's needs and more intimate with their offspring. Marked differences between mothers and fathers are resulting in the course of development (Lamb, 1986).

We presented eye contact between infants and their caregivers earlier as an example of behavior universals within a normative framework, because it establishes and defines a relevant socialization situation. We concluded that differential qualities of parent–infant relationships are established not at the end of the first year as attachment theory proposes, but at a much earlier age, that is, at about three months of age. Our procedure is less intrusive, because it focuses on observations in more or less natural surroundings without imposing separation stress or stranger anxiety on the infant. However, there are babies whose behavior is dysfunctional from that perspective, because they avoid looking at their parents in close range interactional situations (Sylvester-Bradley & Trevarthen, 1978; Keller & Gauda, 1987). Having excluded difficult birth conditions and cognitive immaturity (Miranda & Fantz, 1974; Field, 1987) as possible reasons for poor looking, most authors explain gaze aversion in terms of the baby's reaction to caretakers who are generally overstimulating (Field, 1979), intrusively controlling (D. N. Stern, 1977), or unresponsive and insensitive (Keller & Gauda, 1987).

Most researchers interpret the "cut off" of the function of gaze aversion as modulating arousal or reducing tension; this interpretation is supported by the association between gaze aversion and elevated tonic heart rate in the baby (Field, 1979; Eibl-Eibesfeldt, 1989). Visual cut-off behavior has been observed as an interaction regulation process in different cultures (Eibl-Eibesfeldt, 1989). In our own longitudinal analysis (cf. Keller & Zach, 1993), we demonstrated that the eye contact status during the first months of life reflects a relationship condition that has consequences for further behavioral development. Gaze averting children at the age of three months had less harmonious play interactions with their mothers in a laboratory situation when two years old. Gaze-averting children at that early age developed a psychobiological organization at the age of four and five years with low manipulation of novel objects and increased developmental delays or disorders (Keller & Gauda, 1987).

Conclusion

The ethological shift in psychology constitutes without doubt a major progress in the understanding of human behavioral similarities as well as variations. Besides the conceptual and methodological problems of the different approaches with implicit meta-theoretical commitments, they refer to a basic human nature that should fit optimally to environmental demands. The securely attached infant represents a developmental model of health and happiness. Insecure attachment relationships are considered to be dysfunctional, because they might lead to developmental psychopathology, poor social adjustment, and even decreased intellectual performances. The normal pattern constitutes the adaptive variant.

This view implies the existence of species-specific meaningful behavior adaptation systems. The systems can be distorted due to the peculiarity of active acquisition of behavior concepts in humans; variability and plasticity may lead to "wrong" learning and to misfits or misadaptations that can be attributed to primary or proximate psychological reasons. The modern industrialized world has often been held responsible for causing those distortions. Conversely, "natural" or "primitive" societies are idealized as allowing the growth of predisposed, "natural" behaviors. In the meantime, such romantic searching for simple truths has been identified as a naturalistic fallacy that itself may distort the understanding of behavioral development. Because behaviors can only be regarded as meaningful with respect to specific contexts, transferring those natural behaviors to the context of industrialized societies seems to be inappropriate. It will be shown later that sociobiological formulations especially question those assumptions by referring to reproduction strategy calculations. This line of thinking represents a shift from group selectionist to individual selectionist approaches.

The Sociobiological Conception

As has been outlined so far, the psychobiological approach stresses the biological preparedness of human life in terms of developmental tasks that are prewired in the hardware of human architecture, the individual phenotype being molded according to contextual demands. The general validity of this assumption is evaluated on the basis of species specific peculiarities. In 1975, E. O. Wilson's book *Sociobiology: The new synthesis* marked a completely new orientation that integrated the human species into the animal world by applying the same general rules to all species, including men. Thus, the most challenging shift which has been proposed by sociobiologists´ thinking is the radical change from species-specific concerns to individual selfishness. This line of thinking was already pursued by Darwin, but there was a dilemma between (selfish) Darwinian fitness and (altruistic) group selection. Wilson made clear that it is not the phenotypic individual that forms the unit of analysis, but the genes. The successful transfer of genes to the next generation forms the meta-theoretical formulation of the meaning of life from an evolutionary biological perspective. This idea is expressed in Dawkins´ famous and often misunderstood notion that the human phenotype can be regarded as the vehicle of his or her genes (cf. Dawkins, 1976, 1982).

The analysis of altruistic behaviors that have been interpreted as supporting group selectionist´ views (survival of the species) can also be interpreted as supporting the striving for increased replication of own genes (Hamilton, 1964a, b; Voland, 1993). This means that the decision not to reproduce oneself, but to invest in genetically related individuals defines an aspect of the principle of kin selection (Maynard Smith, 1964). This is what differentiates fitness as personal reproductive success (Darwinian fitness) from *inclusive* fitness (Hamilton, 1964a, b), that is, personal (direct) fitness *plus* the reproductive success of genetic relatives (indirect fitness). The relative increase of genetic replica in a population is the basis of genetic cost–benefit-calculations for decisions of investment in direct or indirect fitness. What looks like altruistic behavior may in the long run serve genetic egoism when expressed as investment in genetically related offspring. Since the seventies, there is an expanding literature on reintroducing group selection views (cf. Wilson & Sober, 1994). It is argued that social groups can act as "vehicles" of selection, thus forming a higher structure of kin selection. Social groups may constitute adaptive units that cannot be reduced to individual interactions. Consequently, group level adaptations are regarded as the outcome of a process of natural selection on a group level. Classical evolution biologists such as Dawkins (1994) argue that the evidence presented by Wilson and Sober (1994) can be explained fully by kin selection and, thus, be traced back to the level of the genes.

Obviously, humans operate or demonstrate altruistic behavior with non-relatives as well. However, this contradicts the logic of genetic selfishness only seemingly. The conception of reciprocal altruism (Trivers, 1971) exemplifies cost–benefit calculations similar to those that have been simulated in computer programs based on game theory. The result is simple: the true egoist cooperates. "Tit for tat" was the most successful computer program designed by Rapoport (cf. Axelrod, 1984); the best strategy is to be cooperative in the first instance, thereafter imitating exactly what the other player has done before. Altruism is not understood as a basic feature of the "cultural" human, but as a strategy in being successful as an egoist.

If we consider a genetic cost–benefit calculation as determining a specific reproduction strategy, we imply that an individual's behavior is determined as if ultimate causes would be pursued. It is important to state the "as–if" character of these calculations, because they are predominantly not conscious. Ultimate causes (the question "why"; Alexander, 1987; Daly & Wilson, 1983; Mayr, 1982, 1988) refer to the selection advantage of a behavioral trait in terms of genetic reproduction. Proximate causes (the question "how") refer to reasons for the emergence of specific behaviors. In this sense, the acquisition of a certain attachment quality can be analyzed in the context of interactional experiences stressing, for example, parental responsiveness. The ultimate cause lies then in the relationship of this attachment quality to a specific reproductive strategy rooted in the prevalent resource situation. The formulation of psychological research questions obviously can gain from adopting a functionalistic ultimate view. It becomes also apparent that "bio-psychological benefits" or psychological well-being (happiness, joy) are insufficient to explain human motivation; pleasure as well as pain (Thornhill & Thornhill, 1989) are only the proximate mechanisms that lead us to approach or avoid acts that in the "environment of evolutionary adaptedness" increase or decrease reproductive success (cf. Chasiotis & Keller, 1994). The crucial role of adaptation for evolutionary thinking will be outlined in more detail next.

The Role of Adaptation

Already the early protagonists of developmental psychology have formulated their ideas of the "goodness of fit" between organisms and environment (e.g., Preyer, 1882). William Stern (1923) has condensed this principle in his "convergence theory." He stressed that mental development is neither just the appearance of inborn traits, nor the reception of external influences but the *convergence* of ". . . internal matters with external developmental conditions." (W. Stern, 1923 (translated by the author); cf. also Kreppner, 1992; Lerner, 1984; Haan, Aerts, & Cooper, 1985). It is interesting that the importance of differential aspects of the environment was also already acknowledged in the earlier psychobiological literature. Von Uexküll and Krizat (1983; Von Uexküll, 1921) have published an appealing illustration of the different "tones" that the same room might have for a fly, a dog, and a human being. Whereas the fly focuses on the light and the leftovers of the meal, every other aspect of the room remains undifferentiated; the dog focuses on possible places to sit or lay on, like chairs, sofa, and of course the leftovers of the meal; the human also notices the bookshelves and the desk as meaningful elements of the surroundings. In the context of cultural ecology, these ideas have been developed further in terms of the relatedness of selected features of the environment and a given population's subsistence ("cognized environment," Steward, 1955).

Nonhuman primates and other animal species obviously live, to a large extent, in environments that are not too different from those of their ancestors. This implies that reproductive, successfully behavioral traits can be identified with at least some validity. The environment of human beings, especially that of urban industrialized man, is defined by a complexity of variables that emerge from historical development dimensions that cannot be related directly to behavioral adaptations as a result of selection processes. The decoding of human behaviors with regard to their adaptational value in industrialized societies is extremely problematic. Barkow, Cosmides, and Tooby (1992) argue that the achievements of human history such as agriculture, government, medical care, education, and the like are all products of only the last few thousand years. The environmental conditions to which the mind was adapted, however, is represented by the pleistocene environment, because the evolution of design features of the human mind is a very slow process compared to historical time. In other words, it is not likely that the basic human design has evolved in the relatively short after-pleistocene era. As cross-cultural research has demonstrated, there is a panhuman design, stemming from our existence as hunter and gatherers (Berry, Poortinga, Segall & Dasen, 1992; Tooby & Cosmides, 1990a, b; Barkow, 1989, 1990).

It is not possible to infer a developmental sequence from so-called primitive or natural societies to modern industrialized societies. As Voland (1993) has pointed out, two approaches have to be differentiated (cf. Table 6–1). Adaptedness relies on the evolutionary chain in terms of natural selection, without referring to actual reproductive success. Adaptation, on the other hand, refers to Alexander's (1990) proposal of relying on concrete fitness consequences, describing reasons and consequences of differences in reproduction strategies (assumptions concerning behavioral evolution are not necessary).

Genetically identical individuals can develop differently in different environments, just as genetically different individuals can appear similar in the same environment. The environment is obviously not a category that can be observed or described as a unit apart from the individual. Tooby and Cosmides (1990a) have pointed to the fact that the environmental window, which is important for the development of an organism, is also part of the evolutionary inheritance,

TABLE 6–1   Two human sociobiological research approaches: Adaptation versus adaptedness in human behavior

Features	Adaptation ("selection in progress")	Adaptedness ("past adaptation")
Definition	A behavior is biologically adaptive when it results in the highest possible net fitness for the actor under the existing conditions, and compared to all possible alternatives.	A behavior is biologically adapted if it is evolved under the conditions of natural selection.
Research object	Behavior	Psyche (behavior guiding mechanisms)
Method	Comparison of reproductive consequences of alternative behaviors.	Description of the functioning of the psyche through inter- and intrapersonal comparisons.
Conclusion	No specific assumptions about behavioral evolution necessary.	No primary interest in actual reproductive success of an individual.

In E. Voland (1993), *Grundriß der Soziobiologie*, p. 16. Stuttgart/Jena: Fischer. (translated by the author).

because no organism reacts to just "any" aspect of its environment. The genetic development programs are only sensitive for specific aspects of the milieu.

> . . . *every time one gene is selected over another, one design for a developmental program is selected over another as well; by virtue of its structure this developmental program interacts with some aspect of the environment rather than others, rendering certain environmental features causally relevant to development. So, step by step, as natural selection constructs the species–gene set (chosen from the available mutations) it constructs in tandem the species developmentally relevant environment. . . . thus, both, the gene and the developmentally relevant environment are the product of evolution."* (Tooby & Cosmides, 1992, p. 84).

The Concept of Culture in Sociobiology

Evolutionary approaches have developed different models showing the relationship between nature and culture. The most simple, but also the most common view, has been already discussed as the nature–nurture debate. Nature is characterized as inherited and genetically fixed, whereas culture is regarded as the product of the human mind. Culture has developed in parallel, but independent from the natural biological development of the human being, the only difference being that culture changes faster. It may be noted that the relative independence of culture from the human mind is not questioned by sociobiologists. Even Lumsden and Wilson (1981) who offer a very strict view in this respect, do not see a direct genetic control over behavior; so called epigenetic rules relate behavior to the genes.

The more far-reaching perspective from our point of view is not captured in the question of what culture is, but *how* culture emerged and especially *why* it developed as mentioned before. The question of "why" requires an answer to the question "how" and, thus, leads to a homologous approach indicating that nature and culture can only be understood against the background of the same evolutionary context. The emergence of culture is intrinsically related to a functioning mind, that is, intelligence, because

> *(Culture) . . . is generated in rich and intricate ways by information-processing mechanisms situated in human minds. These mechanisms are in turn the elaboratory sculpted product of the evolutionary process. Therefore, to understand the relationship between biology and culture, one must first understand the architecture of our evolved psychology (Cosmides, Tooby, & Barkow, 1992, p. 3).*

Especially competencies like means–end and cause–effect relationships and a memory to store successful behavioral strategies form the adaptive cognitive apparatus. Although single competencies of these kinds may be present in different species, only primates are able to combine these in order to acquire knowledge. Acquiring knowledge and intergenerational transmission of information built the ground for establishing traditions that are actively acquired in the next generation by means of imitation. The potato and wheat washing of the Japanese redface macaques has often been cited as a proof of "animal culture"; but at present it is no longer considered an example of imitative acquisition (and, thus, as being a part of a cultural tradition), but rather an act of training (cf. Galef, 1990; Lethmate, 1994). Cultural traditions have only developed in primate societies. For example, East African chimpanzees use medicinal herbs selectively. Food traditions, for example, acquisition of food habits, are generally acknowledged as the source of cultural competence (cf. Casimir, 1994). Being close to a nursing mother for a substantial time span during early ontogeny offers opportunities to observe her nutritional intake and to imitate it. This is especially important for species relying on a variety of staples, because species relying on only one kind of staples, carnivore or herbivore, recognize their nutrition on a hereditary basis from birth on. Omniphagous offspring, on the contrary, is exposed to certain dangers like poisonous plants. Selecting an appropriate diet is necessary for survival. Trial and error learning would not represent an adaptive strategy in this respect (cf. Lawick-Goodall, 1968; Boesch & Boesch, 1990).

Also in the context of food habits, the use of tools has been developed. Chimpanzees use *one* tool for different purposes, they use *different* tools for the same purpose, and they adapt tools (e.g. sticks) for *specific* purposes. In East–West and Central Africa, special tool use zones have emerged. Even in neighboring groups of one species differing tool use customs, food preferences and even greeting ceremonies have been observed (Lethmate, 1994). McGrew (1992) introduced the term "chimpanzee ethnology" in this context.

Living in social groups imposes the problem of competing for access to resources. It can be argued that, especially, the need to deceive others in order to maximize access to resources has led to the evolution of being able to take the perspective of others. Complex social units imply benefits to be gained for each individual member both from preserving the overall structure of the group and from exploiting and outmaneuvering others within it (Humphrey, 1976). Sommer (1989) has reported numerous examples of deception in a variety of species. The interaction of two chimpanzees became especially famous (cf. Byrne & Whiten, 1988; Sommer, 1989). A chimpanzee expected a banana meal that was stored in a metal box, when a second chimpanzee approached; the first one closed the box immediately, left the place, sat down in a short distance and looked around casually. The second chimpanzee left the food place, hid behind a tree, and observed the first chimpanzee. When the first one felt unobserved, he returned to the box and opened it. Then the second chimpanzee surprised the first one by attacking him; he was successful and ate the bananas.

Social situations are characterized by change and ambiguity due to the ad hoc interactional structure and require "social skills" in order to control them. Social skills can be considered as being equivalent to intelligence because the mere accumulation of knowledge does not in itself lead to a modification of the behavior of an actor (cf. Humphrey, 1983). In order to regulate social interactions to achieve maximal individual benefit, it seems efficient to take into account and to predict the behavior of the social other. Intelligent animals constitute a social environment to one another by observing others and reacting accordingly (Van den Berghe, 1994). This implies not only the need to understand others in their behavioral strategies, but also eventually to deceive them about one's own behavior intentions. Understanding others seems to be easier, if it is possible to take the perspective of others and empathize with them. This can only be achieved if self-awareness and self-consciousness co-evolved. In order to deceive others successfully, it may be helpful not to demonstrate signs of deception that could be perceived by others (Trivers, 1985). This may have led to the development of self-deception; thus, the primary adaptive function of self-deception is to make individuals better deceivers (Alexander, 1979; Trivers, 1972, 1985). Taking this perspective, self-deception is considered an important aspect of self-conception (cf. Sommer, 1992).

The evolution of human intelligence can be understood as adaptation in the sense that ". . . mechanisms or systems of properties [are] crafted by natural selection to solve the specific problems posed by the regularities of the physical, chemical, developmental, ecological, geographical, social, and informational environments encountered by ancestral populations during the course of a species' or population's evolution . . ." (Tooby & Cosmides, 1992, p. 62). Such arguments have already been presented from an "ecocontextual" point of view (Berry, 1976), linking perceptual and cognitive styles of field-dependence–field-independence (Witkin & Berry, 1975) to ecological and cultural features of a social group. In this line of thinking, however, they are not linked to reproductive success.

The evaluation of adaptiveness of human and, thus, cultural forces, is very difficult because the evolutionary process not only produces functionally adaptive patterns, but also other outcomes like concomitants or by-products of adaptation ("spandrels"; Gould & Lewontin, 1979), and random effects (cf. Gould, 1994). Alexander (1990) has pointed out that spandrels and random effect can only be identified if adaptations are recognized. The argument that adaptive processes can only be reconstructed (i.e., successful adaptation can only be stated post hoc) is also not valid, because evolutionary approaches allow the prediction of behaviors that can be tested empirically. A major shortcoming, however, is that only central tendencies (i.e., group-level predictions) can be achieved. A challenge for future theory development would be the formulation of models, which might be applicable to the individual case.

The Parameters of Reproductive Decisions

The evolution of social living forms offers advantages such as decreased exposure to attacks from predators, possibilities of more efficient food acquisition, more successful defense of limited resources, and avoidance of high dispersion costs (Voland, 1993). Voland also discusses disadvantages of living in social groups: increased infection risk of contagious diseases and parasites, increased competition for resources like food and breeding-places and the like, and increased reproductive competition. It is obvious that for reproductive decisions the resource situation is critical.

Resources are mostly understood in an economical sense. These parameters can be assessed with at least some accuracy for many animal species. The concept of resources for the human species is difficult to operationalize. In his ecocultural model, Berry (1976) has specified ecological components that are compatible with the evolutionary idea of resources. He proposes an ecological component rooted in the interaction between features of the physical environment such as temperature or soil quality, and a motive to satisfy habitat-related needs of humans such as accessibility of food and shelter. The consequences are described as economic in terms of subsistence patterns, especially specifying the degree of food accumulation, and demographic in terms of settlement patterns. In essence, societies can be grouped and indexed according to the components of subsistence patterns, settlement patterns, and size of social community.

In empirical studies, individual resources are mostly understood as income or education (cf. Draper, & Harpending, 1982). However, it is evident that the psychological perception of a defined resource situation constitutes the really significant factor, in terms of satisfaction or even acquiring the accessible. Resources are limited and, as has been outlined, the subject of competition. Competition constitutes the social side of selfishness. The organismic or even social equivalent of resources is investment. Investments are costs that are spent for the offspring's developmental opportunities in order to maximize their reproductive capacity. They have energy, physical, and psychological components. The extreme helplessness of the human infant and its dependence on parental care, as well as prolonged periods of childhood and youth, have as a consequence the necessity of investment from both parents. Mothers and fathers, however, pursue different interests. Those differences are rooted in evident sex differences. Notably, women bear children until birth, and men can almost never be certain about fatherhood.

Mothers and fathers do not only invest unequally in their offspring for these reasons, but they also calculate their investment specifically for each individual child. Generally, the investment in one child should not exclude the upbringing of other children. The child's interest is, of course, to get as much investment as possible. This basic conflict is discussed as parent–offspring conflict (Trivers, 1974). Depending on the resources, it can be more meaningful in terms of the reproductive value to invest in daughters or in sons, and to invest in first-born or in later born children (Trivers & Willard, 1973; Hrdy, 1987).

Voland (1992; Voland, Siegelkow, & Engel, 1991) has analyzed infant mortality statistics in different Northern German communities using old church chronicles, and tax lists containing entries on land ownership. He described interrelationships between the economic situation, population growth parameters, and infant mortality as an indicator of parental investment efforts. Differential infant mortality for boys and girls was found in two neighboring communities, but in the opposite direction. In one, infant mortality of daughters of landlords was lower than that of farmers' daughters or landless people's daughters. The mortality risk of landlords' daughters was also significantly lower than that of their brothers. Older children's mortality rates reflect the same tendency. The live-born daughter of a landlord reached her 15th birthday with a probability of 83.8 percent which was significantly higher than that of daughters of farmers and landless people, but also than that of her brothers. In the other community the lowest rate of male infant mortality and the highest rate of female infant mortality occured among the highest social class, the land-owning farmers. The differences could be explained by taking population growth parameters into consideration. "Other things being equal, sons appear to fulfill the reproductive expectations of high ranking parents more often in expanding systems than daughters do, whereas in stagnating populations an over-production of sons soon becomes too costly" (Voland, 1993, p. 155). The analysis confirms the assumptions formulated by Trivers and Willard (1973) indicating that sex preferences are dependent upon the resource situation. Increasing populations indicate exploitation of resources in an increasingly efficient manner, leading to expansion competition. Demographic stagnation ". . . cause genetic displacement with a high level of local resource competition" (Voland, 1993, p. 154). The influence of local resource competition on parental sex allocation decisions in terms of sex-biased parental investment is true for humans.

The r- and K-strategy

Two different reproduction strategies can be identified. When physical conditions and, accordingly, population density are variable and poorly predictable, habitat use is opportunistic. Populations then produce high numbers of offspring to maximally exploit their reproductive potential. With the symbol "r" for growth rate, this strategy is called "r-selection" (Pianka, 1970). If the unlimited growth comes to its natural limits in terms of the capacity of a habitat, a stabilization phase will follow with the consequence of selecting individuals who are able to efficiently exploit the limited resources. High numbers of offspring do not represent a selection advantage, but rather the breeding of successful offspring by increased parental investment. This strategy is called K for the carrying capacity of a habitat (K-selection). The main differences are summarized in Table 6–2. R-strategy refers to fast maturation, a short life-span with an early onset of reproduction, high reproduction rate and low parental investment, whereas K symbolizes a long life-span, late onset of reproduction, a low reproduction rate, and high parental investment.

It should be clear that both types do not represent discrete categories, but symbolize extremes on a continuum. Individuals and species are only relatively r and K. As Rushton (1987) points out, ". . . rabbits are K-strategists compared to fish, but r-strategists compared to humans" (p. 542). He claims that primates in general are relative K-strategists and humans are the most K of all. Rushton (1985) extends this view and proposes ". . . that some people are genetically more K than others, and that K-behavior is associated with a constellation of attributes, all deeply embedded in evolutionary history." (p. 543). Regarding the life span perspective, he argues that older people would benefit more from caring for grandchildren than producing additional offspring themselves. A strong K-selection would, thus, imply to live longer in order to care for the grandchildren's generation, because reproduction is delayed to later ages. Selection pressure should have produced for this purpose good health, longevity, intelligence, internal locus of control, and social and sexual restraints (Lovejoy, 1981; Rushton, 1985,

TABLE 6–2   r- and K-selection

	r-strategy	K-strategy
Individual development	advanced	delayed
Height	reduced	increased
Life span	short	long
Reproductive rate	high	low
Onset of reproduction	early	late
Spacing of births	short	long
Litter size	high	low
Parental investment	low	high
Brain size	small	large

In E. Voland (1993), *Grundriß der Soziobiologie,* p. 203. (from Voland & Winkler, 1990). Stuttgart/Jena: Fischer (translation by the author).

1987). Weaker K-selection should foster earlier sexual maturation and a decreased tendency to nurture intensively and care for the offsprings´ gene replica.

Attachment Quality and Reproduction Strategy

Based on evolutionary considerations, Belsky, Steinberg, and Draper (1991a, b) formulated a socialization model that specifies proximate psychological factors like family context, childhood experiences, and somatic development, and combine these with reproductive strategies. In relating components of proximate psychological functioning to somatic development, specifying reproductive strategies in terms of ultimate considerations, it exceeds models that have been developed in cross-cultural psychology (see for example Berry et al., 1992) by stressing equally the interrelatedness of family context, childrearing, and psychological/behavioral development. The model is presented in Figure 6–1.

Type 1 indicates that low and inadequate resources are correlated with high stress and marital discord in the family of origin; the situation is accompanied by low parental investment in terms of the emotional climate in the family with rejecting and insensitive parenting. These background conditions result in the

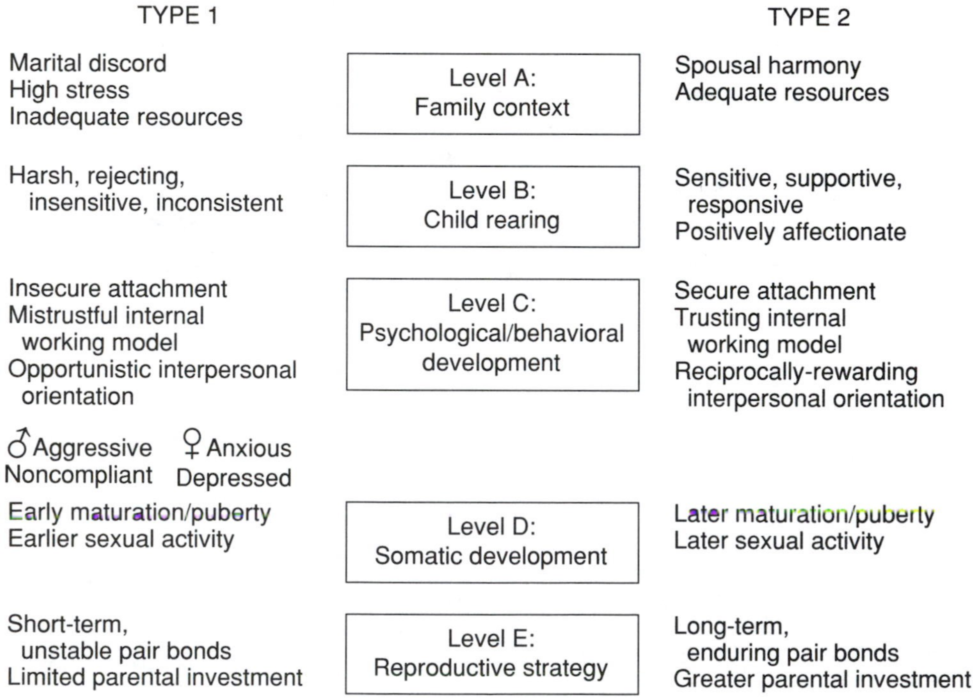

TYPE 1		TYPE 2
Marital discord High stress Inadequate resources	Level A: Family context	Spousal harmony Adequate resources

Harsh, rejecting,
  insensitive, inconsistent
	Level B:
	Child rearing
		Sensitive, supportive,
		  responsive
		Positively affectionate

Insecure attachment
Mistrustful internal
  working model
Opportunistic interpersonal
  orientation
	Level C:
	Psychological/behavioral
	development
		Secure attachment
		Trusting internal
		  working model
		Reciprocally-rewarding
		  interpersonal orientation

♂ Aggressive ♀ Anxious Noncompliant Depressed		
Early maturation/puberty Earlier sexual activity	Level D: Somatic development	Later maturation/puberty Later sexual activity

Short-term,
  unstable pair bonds
Limited parental investment
	Level E:
	Reproductive strategy
		Long-term,
		  enduring pair bonds
		Greater parental investment

FIGURE 6–1   Developmental pathways of different reproductive strategies

development of insecure attachment relationships and an internal working model that leads to subsequent development of sex-specific behavioral problems. Girls tend to develop internalizing disorders, boys tend to develop externalizing disorders. This emotional state causes an early onset of puberty, reflected in beginning of menarche in girls and beginning of the growth spurt in boys, which then represents an early beginning of sexual activity, unstable pair bonding, and early parenthood with limited parental investment, thus constituting an intergenerationally continuous pattern. Type II describes a family background of spousal harmony and adequate resources in the family of origin. Sensitive and supporting parenting leads to a secure attachment relationship and subsequently to a later onset of puberty, later sexual activity, stable pair bonding, and greater parental investment.

Empirical evidence indeed supports a view that the onset of puberty can be related to childhood experiences. Conflictuous family contexts (spousal disharmony, unemployment), unsupportive, even hostile parenting behavior, father absence (Surbey, 1990; Moffit, Caspi, Belsky, & Silva, 1992), family conflicts during childhood (Steinberg, 1988), stressful childhood experiences (Silbereisen & Schwarz, 1992) relate to early onset of puberty. In our own longitudinal research, we have tested several assumptions concerning the socialization model (cf. Chasiotis, Keller, & Restemeier, 1992) and found confirmation for the hypothesized relationships (cf. Chasiotis et al., 1995). The model links an ecocontextual perspective with ultimate considerations and, thus, offers a perspective for cross-cultural psychology where personality or behavioral differences are not the outcome variable of ecocultural influences, but one link in a chain specifying reproductive success.

An Evolutionary Reconsideration of Parental Ethnotheories

In this last section, we would like to present an example of the integration of cross-cultural psychology with evolutionary thinking:

> *The evolution of folk psychology was probably an interaction of genetic and cultural evolution (. . .), a disposition to respond to any large moving thing by "asking oneself" what does it want? would probably have surviving value (Dennett, 1983, p. 380).*

Ethnotheories about parenting and child development shape the environments of infancy and early childhood through cultural values. Ethnotheories can be understood as prescriptions for resource maximization of contextual knowledge and, thus, hold a mediating function between context and development. This view comes close to Eckensberger's (1993) when he discusses, from a different theoretical point of view, the existence of shared meanings of events and objects in terms of collective representations. He introduces culture operating as a selective pressure mechanism or canalizing force; the collective representations—that is, value systems—force individuals to act in specific terms (cf. also Valsiner, 1987). Translated into a psychobiological vocabulary one could argue that individuals share reconstructions of their environmental demands. As we have outlined in previous sections, developing attachment to the primary caregivers is the first important integrated developmental task which infants have to master (Keller, 1991). The possible sources of variation in mastering this task have been outlined in the evolutionary socialization model (Belsky et al., 1991a, b). In fact, mothers hold different perceptions of patterns of attachment behavior that are derived from their cultural values (cf. Harwood & Miller, 1991; Harwood, 1992). As a general universal adaptation strategy, the concept of intuitive parenting has been introduced earlier. More recent approaches to parental responsiveness take evolutionary aspects into closer consideration (e.g. MacDonald, 1992) and differentiate the general parenting repertoire into two different domains. One can be labeled as parental sensitivity in contingent and prompt responses to infant cues; the other can be described as warmth or affectionate climate (cf. also Hofer, 1987). These two dimensions have already been identified as powerful in earlier studies on child rearing strategies, such as Becker's (1964) circumflex model with warmth and control as orthogonal factors of parental childrearing attitudes.

The behavioral formulation of these dimensions should express implicit views on the small child, which represent adaptive frames for child development in a specific context or ecology. Parental ethnotheories thus constitute shared meaning systems that enable individuals to rely on proven socialization strategies. It reduces the costs of parenting, because adaptations need not be invented individually. They represent frames that help organize behaviors adapted to general eco- contextual demands (see Berry et al., 1992) that should have some stability over several generations. These factors cover the dangers of the immediate rearing surroundings (e.g. infants should not be in contact with the floor before one year of age in Indonesia, the evil eye taboo in different parts of the world). They also cover representations of central tendencies that are biologically motivated, such as social definitions of mating choices, of the optimal reproductive time span, and of spacing and the number of offspring.

This view also expresses a unique human experience, although learning and transfer of knowledge through imitation can be observed in animal species as well. Defined behavioral conceptions or environmental aspects are acquired individually (culture gene, Lumsden & Wilson, 1981; Dawkins, 1976). These approaches have led to the formulation of evolutionary epistemology (e.g., Plotkin, 1988; Campbell, 1974; Plotkin & Odling-Smee, 1979, 1982). It says that the capacity for knowing has not merely evolved, but individual knowledge is the product of a process identical to that which has led evolution.

Individual variations in implicit ethnotheories are shaped during early ontogeny and specify the factors outlined in the socialization model of Belsky et al. (1991a, b) described earlier. This view of ethnotheories extends the more narrow psychological conceptions presented so far. Trommsdorff (1993) argues, that child rearing goals, naive development theories and behaviors differ with cultural values (cf. also Befu, 1986; Bril, 1989). Culture specific developmental trajectories are mediated by cultural values. The relativistic view that cultural values are "external to the individual" (Durkheim, 1895/1962), is rather descriptive; it is criticized thoroughly by Tooby and Cosmides (1992) because of its low explanatory value. The position outlined so far partly favors a different direction. Although it is not questioned that the influence between ethnotheories and cultural values is bi- directional, we will focus on the impact of separate ethnotheories on socialization and enculturation patterns mirrored in cultural values. Central to this argument is the assumption that naive developmental theories reflect resource-dependent demands for optimal reproduction strategies that are translated into cultural values in order to maximize their effective impact through social control. Note that with this assumption, disagreements between cultural and individual values are also predicted, for example, if the cultural values concerning reproductive decisions are outdated because of socioecological changes (revolution), or if individuals are required to act in a way that favors other (high-ranking) individuals (polygamy). Thus, with this assumption it is anticipated that even predictive hypotheses can be formulated and tested.

Cultural diversities in naive developmental theories have been clearly confirmed in the literature (e.g., McGillicuddy-deLisi, 1982; Sigel; 1985; Goodnow, 1984; Goodnow & Collins, 1990). In addition to the physical and social aspect of the environment, parental ideas constitute a third factor of the developmental niche (Super & Harkness, 1986). The sociobiological view presented here basically postulates that a context-specific resource situation shapes specific types of early experiences that lead to a specific type of personality, pursuing a specific reproductive strategy which will be followed by individuals in later life (Draper & Harpending, 1982). Ethnotheories constrain personality development and, consequently, parenting behavior in ways that support the most adequate parenting strategy. In this way, ethnotheory is a consequence of the reproductive strategy. On the basis of this theorizing it can be predicted that ethnotheories should vary not only over different cultures in terms of developmental niches, but also according to socioeconomic status and sex, which has been confirmed in the literature (Sonuga-Barke, Thompson, & Balding, 1993; Costello & Janiszewski, 1990).

The current body of evidence in the cross-cultural literature is compatible with these notions. It has been demonstrated that desirable personality characteristics are part of ethnotheories leading to differential socialization strategies (cf. Trommsdorff, 1993). Berry (1976) has explicitly referred to socialization practices (assertion vs. compliance) to operationalize the cultural adaptation component of the ecocultural model (cf. Barry, Child, & Bacon, 1959).

Dasen (1984, 1988; Dasen et al., 1985) has analyzed the concept of intelligence among the Baoulé in West Africa and has concluded that it differs substantially from the conception of intelligence in the West. Berry and Bennett (1992) have done similar analyses with the Cree in Canada with comparable results. Basically there is a distinction describing the competent adult in terms of social responsibility and social competence as opposed to a personality pattern of independence with much emphasis on a worldview based on analytical reasoning. Accordingly, substantial cross-cultural differences have been reported in parental socialization goals promoting affectedness and dependency as opposed to independence and autonomy (Barry et al., 1959; Caudill, 1973; Caudill & Weinstein, 1969; Bornstein et al., 1992; Conroy et al., 1980, Sinha, 1985).

The Western type of mothering has been portrayed consistently as promoting early independence as a desirable socialization goal, mirroring an implicit personhood concept of an individual whose competencies and capacities are directed to autonomous functioning (Bornstein et al., 1992; Dixon et al., 1981). This view is reflected in the expectation of cognitive competencies (seeing, understanding words, recognizing pictures) earlier than among non-Western mothers and in the stimulation of cognitive development at an earlier age (e.g. Keller, Miranda, & Gauda, 1984), and in the promotion of dialogue experiences (Richman, Miller, & LeVine, 1992). Non-Western societies, like the Japanese, Indian, and Balinese, stimulate dependency in seeing the infant as an extension of the mother (cf. Bornstein et al., 1992), and promoting affective tuning and close bodily contact (Trommsdorff, 1983, 1989; Kornadt & Trommsdorff, 1990). This behavioral frame reflects an underlying personality picture of a social definition of the self (cf. also Markus & Kitayama, 1991).

One obvious factor leading to difference patterns reported so far seems to be constituted by formal schooling. Richman et al. (1992) demonstrated with Mexican mother–child pairs that formal education is correlated with more distal interactional modes such as talking and looking. Talking to the prelinguistic child, in particular, is a matter of controversial cross-cultural discussion. Richman et al. (1992) expresses a widely held opinion when they formulate, ". . . older Gusii mothers tend to ridicule the idea of talking to children before they are capable of speech." (p. 617). Whether this strict view is part of Western stereotypic perception or reflects implicit cultural models is open to discussion (cf. Nsamenang, 1992). However, there are differences in the amount of language used in interactional situations with children at least in the second part of the first year, as Konner (1977) has demonstrated with Kalahari San, Guatemalans, and American working and middle-class mothers. Even within the Western context, language differences in quantity and quality of speech directed to small children can reliably be found. Differential input strategies of maternal speech comparing U.S.–American and German mothers of two-year-old children have been reported in a study by Grimm and Shatz (1989; cf. also Keller, Chasiotis, & Runde, 1992). In conclusion, one could summarize the scattered findings as follows: cultures can be tentatively grouped according to interactional strategies relying on distal forms of behavior or more proximal behavioral exchanges. The more distal forms of behaviors are correlated with promoting a dialogue structure, where distinctive individual responsibilities are rehearsed and language plays a central role. The proximal behavioral regulation expresses possibly co-occurring affective states where social unity is fostered.

Bringing together the perspectives presented so far, the different parenting modes can be interpreted as adaptations to contextual demands. Differences in the personality organization should be a consequence. Undoubtedly ethnographic and sociolinguistic evidence suggests that varying normative contexts in terms of cultural scripts define conventions of conversational interaction between mother and the prelinguistic child (Ochs & Schieffelin, 1984; Richman et al., 1992). The reinterpretation of those relationships should be based on considerations about adaptive reproductive strategies. To shed further light in this emerging field, it is necessary to undertake cross-cultural studies. Notably, the comparison of Western and African behavioral patterns seems to be very fruitful in this respect. The cultural practice of mothers' carrying their babies on their backs would differentiate between felt (bodily) warmth and face-to-face contingency promoting interactions. Returning to the Belsky et al. model, this would imply that we need information on differing styles of mating behavior, physical developmental parameters, ethnotheories specifying socialization paths, and interactive behavioral modes from at least two generations in order to develop a functional view of behavioral contextual adaptations (as opposed to adaptedness in Table 6–1).

Conclusion

In this chapter, the development beyond general psychobiological orientations toward the application of an evolutionary logic has been elaborated. Based on the seminal work of Charles Darwin, the introduction of psychobiological (ethological) thinking in psychology, especially developmental psychology, has been outlined. Above all, the functionalistic perspective, that is, the interpretation of behaviors in terms of the adaptational value, has led to the recognition of phylogenetic roots. A differential developmental approach seems crucial in understanding behavioral organization. Although knowledge about behavior genetics is essential for psychobiological conceptions, this line of thinking has not penetrated to the most central problems. One perspective for future developmental progress consists certainly in bringing together these different lines of research.

The evolutionary approach constitutes a paradigm shift, because it affects basic metatheoretical positions connected with the very nature of human beings. From the ultimate goal of optimal genetic reproduction, the following assumptions can be derived:

1. Humans are primarily egoistic, following selfish interests. This implies that altruism and cooperation are the results of cost–benefit calculations. These principles do not only govern social interactions between strangers, but also constitute the essence of social exchange between relatives and find their most vital expression in the parent–offspring conflict.

2. Based on this differential interest management, social interactions are not primarily intended to mirror equality and justice, but to support those social others who contribute to their own fitness. These are, of course, genetic relatives. Thus, nepotism is not an aberration of the irresponsible members of a society, but a reflection of natural endowment. Relationships with non-related individuals

are based on considerations of reciprocal altruism. Individuals tend to invest in those social others who offer best reward value.

3.   In order to pursue the selfish interests, humans deceive others. In order not to be recognized and detected as a deceiver, it can be advantageous to deceive oneself. Self-deception is an argument for a powerful unconscious. Humans are usually not aware of their selfish intentions; still, they behave *as if* they follow the principles outlined here.

4.   The necessity of regulating social interactions in terms of fitness calculations is regarded as the reason behind the evolution of intelligence. The social origin of cognitive abilities is the basis for "easy learning," that is, information can be acquired faster and easier when it is related to a social context instead of being presented in an abstract way.

5.   Interindividual differences always have to be examined if human behavior is to be understood. Due to central tendencies that complement individual competition, biological marker variables like sex or age have to be taken into account, because they favor differential reproduction strategies.

6.   Reproductive strategies are developed within specific resource situations prevalent in specific environments. Context is thus not an external concept that imposes external influences on the individual, but is an inherent part of behavior development.

7.   Culture constitutes the environmental knowledge that has to be passed from one generation to the next. It can be understood as an attempt to avoid unnecessary individual constructions that would delay ontogenetic development, because it summarizes and conceptualizes the more stable or even invariant contextual features. The active acquisition of cultural concepts leaves, on the other hand, room for ". . . what biological evolution is all about, . . . not constancy but change." (Dobzhansky, 1973; p. 106). Cultural conceptions are an integral part of understanding human behavior. ". . . people are innately, genetically, and therefore irremediably diverse and unlike." (Dobzhansky, 1973; p. 4). This basic statement is often confused with discussions on equality. Equality pertains to the rights of human beings, thus constituting an ethical principle, which has nothing to do with similarity or diversity of individuals. Equality as well as inequality are socially imposed categories and go far beyond genetic or behavioral diversity. This is an important distinction with potentially political consequences. Recognizing diversity but acknowledging equality possibly can form a more powerful platform to defeat aggression or hostility to foreigners than stressing undifferentiated similarities.

Evolutionary theory poses a tremendous challenge, because it offers a scope for integration of different and, so far, separated fields. It can integrate psychoanalytical thinking of the unconscious with information processing research, emotional development with psychology of group processes. It synthesizes approaches not only from biology and psychology, but also anthropology, sociology, criminology, philosophy and other disciplines. It constitutes a truly interdisciplinary approach.

Endnote

1. I am gratefully indebted to valuable comments by Athanasios Chasiotis, and Lutz H. Eckensberger on earlier drafts of this chapter.

References

Ainsworth, M. D. S. (1977). Attachment theory and its utility in cross-cultural research. In P.H. Leiderman, S.R. Tulkin, & A. Rosenfeld (Eds.), *Culture and infancy. Variations in the human experience* (pp. 49–67). New York: Academic Press.

Ainsworth, M. D. S., Blehar, M. C., Waters, E., & Wall, S. (1978*). Patterns of attachment. A psychological study of the strange situation.* Hillsdale, NJ: Erlbaum.

Alexander, R. D. (1979). *Darwinism and human affairs.* Seattle, WA: University of Washington Press.

Alexander, R. D. (1987). *The biology of moral systems.* New York: Aldine de Gruyter.

Alexander, R. D. (1988). Evolutionary approaches to human behavior: What does the future hold? In L. Betzig, M. Bogerhoff-Mulder, & P. Turke (Eds.), *Human reproductive behaviour. A Darwinian perspective* (pp. 317–341). Cambridge: Cambridge University Press.

Alexander, R. D. (1990). Epigenetic rules and Darwinian algorithms—The adaptive study of learning and development. *Ethology and Sociobiology, 11,* 241–303.

Anastasi, A. (1958). Heredity, environment, and the question "how." *Psychological Review, 65,* 197– 208.

Axelrod, R. (1984). *The evolution of cooperation.* New York: Basic Books.

Barkow, J. H. (1989). *Darwin, sex, and status: Biological approaches to mind and culture.* Toronto: University of Toronto Press.

Barkow, J. H. (1990). Beyond the DP/DSS controvery. *Ethology and Sociobiology, 11,* 341–351.

Barkow, J. H., Cosmides, L., & Tooby, J. (1992). *The adapted mind: Evolutionary psychology and the generation of culture.* New York: Oxford University Press.

Barry, H., Child, I., & Bacon, M. (1959). Relations of child training to subsistence economy. *American Anthropologist, 61,* 51–63.

Becker, W. C. (1964). Consequences of different kinds of parental discipline. In M. L. Hoffman & L. W. Hoffman (Eds.), *Review of child development research,* (Vol. 1, pp. 169–208). New York: Russell Sage Foundation.

Befu, H. (1986). The social and cultural background of child development in Japan and the United States. In W. H. Stevenson, H. Azuma, & K. Hakuta (Eds.), *Child development and education in Japan* (pp. 13–27). New York: Freeman.

Belsky, J., Steinberg, L., & Draper, P. (1991a). Childhood experience, interpersonal development, and reproductive strategy: An evolutionary theory of socialization. *Child Development, 62,* 647–670.

Belsky, J, Steinberg, L., & Draper, P. (1991b). Further reflections on an evolutionary theory of socialization. *Child Development, 62,* 682–685.

Benedict, R. (1938). Continuities and discontinuities in cultural conditioning. *Psychiatry, 1,* 161–167.

Berry, J. W. (1976). *Human ecology and cognitive style: Comparative studies in cultural and psychological adaptation.* New York: Sage/Halsted.

Berry, J. W. & Bennett, J. A. (1992). Cree conceptions of cognitive competence. *International Journal of Psychology, 27,* 73–88.

Berry, J. W., Poortinga, Y. H., Segall, M. H., & Dasen, P. R. (1992). *Cross-cultural psychology: Research and applications.* New York: Cambridge University Press.

Bertenthal, B. I. (1991). A systems view of behavioral canalization: Theory and commentary. *Developmental Psychology, 27,* 3.

Bijou, S. W. (1976). *Child development: The basic stage of early childhood.* New York: Prentice Hall.

Bijou, S. W., & Baer, D. M. (1961). *Child development: A systematic and empirical theory, (Vol. I)*. New York: Appleton Century Crofts.

Boesch, C. & Boesch, H. (1990). Tool use and tool making in wild Chimpanzees. *Folia Primatologica, 54*, 86–99.

Bornstein, M. H., Tamis-LeMonda, C. S., Tal, J., Ludermann, P., Toda, S., Rahn, C. W., Pecheux, M.-G., Azuma, H., & Vardi, D. (1992). Maternal responsiveness to infants in three societies: The United States, France, and Japan. *Child Development, 63*, 808–821.

Bowlby, J. (1969). *Attachment and loss. Vol. I: Attachment*. New York: Basic Books.

Boyd, R. & Richerson, P. J. (1985). *Culture and the evolutionary process*. Chicago: University of Chicago Press.

Bril, B. (1989). Die kulturvergleichende Perspektive: Entwicklung und Kultur. In H. Keller (Ed.), *Handbuch der Kleinkindforschung* (pp. 71–88). Heidelberg: Springer.

Brown, D. E. (1991). *Human universals*. Philadelphia: Temple University Press.

Byrne, R. W., & Whiten, A. (1988). *Machiavellian intelligence. Social expertise and the evolution of intellect in monkeys, apes and humans*. Oxford: Oxford University Press.

Cairns, R. B. (1991). Multiple metaphors for a singular idea. *Developmental Psychology, 27*, 23–26.

Campbell, D. T. (1974). Evolutionary epistemology. In P. A. Schilpp (Ed.), *The philosophy of Karl Popper*. Chicago: Open Court Publishing.

Campos, J., Hiatt, S., Ramsay, D., Henderson, C., & Svejda, M. (1978). The emergence of fear on the visual cliff. In M. Lewis & L. Rosenblum (Eds.), *The development of affect* (pp. 149–182). New York: Plenum.

Casimir, M. J. (1994). Die Evolution der Kulturfähigkeit. In W. Schiefenhövel, C. Vogel, G. Vollmer, & U. Opolka (Eds.), *Vom Affen zum Halbgott. Der Weg des Menschen aus der Natur* (pp.43-58). Stuttgart: TRIAS Thieme Hippocrates Enke.

Caudill, W. (1973). The influence of social structure and culture on human behavior in modern Japan. *Journal of Nervous and Mental Disease, 157*, 240–257.

Caudill, W., & Weinstein, H. (1969). Maternal care and infant behavior in Japan and America. *Psychiatry, 32*, 12–43.

Chasiotis, A. (1995). Die Mystifikation der Homöostase. Das sozioemotionale Gegenseitigkeitsempfinden als grundlegende psychische Dimension. *Gestalt Theory, 17*, 88–129.

Chasiotis, A., & Keller, H. (1994). Evolutionary psychology and developmental cross-cultural psychology. In A.-M. Bouvy, F. J. R van de Vijver, P. Boski, & P. Schmitz (Eds.), *Journeys into cross-cultural psychology* (pp. 68–82). Lisse: Swets & Zeitlinger.

Chasiotis, A., Keller, H., & Restemeier, R. (1992). Childhood experience, parental attitudes and family development: A longitudinal test of evolutionary assumptions. Paper read at the "10th Conference of the European Sociobiological Society (ESS)," Augsburg, Germany.

Chasiotis, A., Riemenschneider, U., Restemeier, R., Cappenberg, M., Völker, S., Keller, H., & Lohaus, A. (1995). Early infancy and the evolutionary theory of socialization. Paper presented at the conference, "Early mother-child interaction and attachment; old and new approaches" at the Koninklijke Nederlandse Akademie van Wetenschappen, NL, March 30th–June 2nd, 1995.

Conroy, M., Hess, R. D., Azuma, H., & Kashiwai, K. (1980). Maternal strategies for regulating children's behavior: Japanese and American families. *Journal of Cross-Cultural Psychology, 2*, 153–173.

Cosmides, L., Tooby, J., & Barkow, J. H. (1992). Introduction: Evolutionary psychology and conceptual integration. In J. H. Barkow, L. Cosmides, & J. Tooby (Eds.), *The adapted mind: Evolutionary psychology and the generation of culture* (pp. 3–15). New York: Oxford University Press.

Costello, E. J., & Janiszewski, S. (1990). Who gets treated? Factors associated with referral in children with psychiatric disorders. *Acta Psychiatrica Scandinavia, 81*, 523–529.

Crnic, L. S. (1984). Early experience effects. In R. N. Emde & R. J. Harmon (Eds.), *Continuities an discontinuities in development* (pp. 355–368). New York: Plenum Press.

Daly, M. & Wilson, M. (1983). *Sex, evolution and behavior* (2nd ed.). Boston: PWS Publishers.

Darwin, C. (1859). *On the origin of species by means of natural selection, Or the preservation of favoured races in the struggle for life.* London: John Murray.

Darwin, C. (1872). *The expression of emotions in man and animals.* London: John Murray.

Dasen, P. (1984). The cross-cultural study of intelligence: Piaget and the Baoulé. *International Journal of Psychology, 19,* 407–434.

Dasen, P. (1988). Développement psychologique et activités quotidiennes chez des enfants africains. *Enfance, 41,* 3–24.

Dasen, P., Barthélémy, D., Kan, E., Kouamé, K., Daouda, K., Kouakou Adjéli, K., & Assandé, N. (1985). N´Glouelé, l´intelligence chez les Baoulé. *Archives de Psychologie, 53,* 293–324.

Dawkins, R. (1976). *The selfish gene.* New York: Oxford University Press.

Dawkins, R. (1982). *The extended phenotype—The gene as the unit of selection.* Oxford: Freeman.

Dawkins, R. (1994). *Das egoistische Gen. Aktualisierte und ergänzte Neuauflage.* Berlin: Spektrum Akademischer Verlag.

Dennett, D. C. (1983). Intentional systems in cognitive ethology: The "Panglossian paradigm" defended. *Behavioral and Brain Sciences, 6,* 343–390.

Dixon, R. A., & Lerner, R. M. (1988). A history of systems in developmental psychology. In M. H. Bornstein & M. E. Lamb (Eds.), *Developmental psychology: An advanced textbook* (pp. 3– 50). Hillsdale, NJ: Erlbaum.

Dixon, S., Tronick, E., Keefer, C., & Brazelton, T. B. (1981). Mother–infant interaction among the Gusii of Kenya. In F. M. Field, A. M. Sostek, P. Vietze, & P. H. Leiderman (Eds.), *Culture and early interactions* (pp. 149–168). Hillsdale, NJ: Erlbaum.

Dobzhansky, T. (1973). *Genetic diversity and human equality.* New York: Basic Books.

Draper, P., & Harpending, H. (1982). Father absence and reproductive strategy. An evolutionary perspective. *Journal of Anthropological Research, 38,* 255–273.

Durkheim, E. (1895/1962). *The rules of the sociological method.* Glencoe, Ill.: Free Press.

Eckensberger, L. H. (1993). Moralische Urteile als handlungsleitende normative Regelsysteme im Spiegel der kulturvergleichenden Forschung. In A. Thomas (Ed.), *Kulturvergleichende Psychologie* (pp. 259–295). Göttingen: Hogrefe.

Eckensberger, L. H., & Burgard, P. (1983). The cross-cultural assessment of normative concepts: Some considerations on the affinity between methodological approaches and preferred theories. In S. H. Irvine & J. W. Berry (Eds.), *Human assessment and cultural factors* (pp. 459–480). New York: Plenum Press.

Eibl-Eibesfeldt, I. (1967). Concepts of ethology and their significance for the study of human behavior. In H. W. Stevenson (Ed.), *Early behavior, comparative and developmental approaches* (pp. 127–146). New York: Wiley.

Eibl-Eibesfeldt, I. (1989). *Human ethology.* New York: Aldine de Gruyter.

Ekman, P. (1972). Universals and cultural differences in facial expressions of emotion. In J. K. Cole (Ed.), *Nebraska Symposium on Motivation* (pp. 207–283). Lincoln: University of Nebraska Press.

Ekman, P. (Ed.). (1982). *Emotion in the human face.* Cambridge: Cambridge University Press.

Ekman, P., Friesen, W. V., & Ellsworth, P. (1972). *Emotions in the human face: Guidelines for research and an integration of findings.* New York: Pergamon.

Erikson, E. H. (1968). *Identity, youth, and crisis.* New York: Norton.

Fantz, R. L. (1963). Pattern vision in newborn infants. *Science, 140,* 296–297.

Fernald, A. (1992). Meaningful melodies in mothers´ speech to infants. In H. Papousek, U. Jürgens, & M. Papousek (Eds.), *Nonverbal vocal communication: Comparative and developmental approaches* (pp. 262–282). Cambridge: Cambridge University Press.

Fernald, A., Taeschner, T., Dunn, J., Papousek, M., Boysson-Bardies, B., & Fukui, I. (1989). A cross-language study of prosodic modifications in mothers´ and fathers´ speech to preverbal infants. *Journal of Child Language, 16,* 977–1001.

Field, T. M. (1979). Interaction patterns of preterm and term infants. In T.M. Field, A. Sostek, S.

Goldberg, & H. H. Shuman (Eds.), *Infants born at risk* (pp. 333–356). New York: Spektrum.

Field, T. M. (1987). Affective and interactive disturbances in infants . In J. D. Osofsky (Ed.), *Handbook of infant development*, (2nd ed., pp. 972–1005). New York: Wiley.

Galef, B. G. (1990). Tradition in animals: Field observations and laboratory analyses. In M. Bekoff & D. Jamieson (Eds.), *Interpretation and explanation in the study of animal behavior* (pp. 74–95). Boulder, CO: Boulder University Press.

Garcia, J., McGown, B., & Green, K. (1972). Biological constraints on conditioning. In A. Black & W. Prokarsky (Eds.), *Classical conditioning. Volume III: Current research and theory.* New York: Appleton-Century Crofts.

Gibson, J. J. (1979). *The ecological approach to visual perception.* Boston: Houghton Mifflin.

Goodnow, J. J. (1984). Parents´ ideas about parenting and development: A review of issues and recent work. In M. E. Lamb, A. Brown, & B. Rogoff (Eds.), *Advances in developmental psychology,* (Vol. 3, pp. 193–242). Hillsdale, NJ: Erlbaum.

Goodnow, J. J. & Collins, W. A. (1990). *Development according to parents. The nature, sources and consequences of parents´ ideas.* Hillsdale, NJ: Erlbaum.

Gottlieb, G. (1991). Experiential canalization of behavioral development: Theory. *Developmental Psychology, 27,* 4–13.

Gould, S. J. (1994). *How can evolutionary theory best offer insights into human development?* Invited lecture at the "XIIIth Biennial ISSBD Meetings," Amsterdam, June 30.

Gould, S. J., & Lewontin, R. C. (1979). The spandrels of San Marco and the Panglossian program: A critique of the adaptationist programme. *Proceedings of the Royal Society of London, 250,* 281–288.

Gould, S. J., & Vrba, E. (1982). Exaptation: A missing term in the science of form. *Paleobiology, 8,* 4–15.

Greenough, W. T., & Schwartz, H. D. (1984). Age-related aspects of experience effects upon brain structure. In R. N. Emde & R. J. Harmon (Eds.), *Continuities and discontinuities in de-velopment* (pp. 69–94). New York: Plenum Press.

Grimm, H., & Shatz, M. (1989). *"Muß man können wollen?" Vermittlung und Erwerb von Modalitäten in deutschen und amerikanischen Mutter-Kind-Dyaden.* Paper presented at the 9th Conference of German-speaking Developmental Psychologists, München, September.

Grossmann, K., Grossmann, K. E., Huber, F., & Wartner, U. (1981). German children´s behavior towards their mothers at 12 months and their fathers at 18 months in Ainsworth´s Strange Situation. *International Journal of Behavioral Development, 4,* 157–182.

Haan, N., Aerts, E., & Cooper, B. (1985). *On moral grounds: The search for practical morality.* New York: New York University Press.

Haeckel, E. (1866). *Generelle Morphologie der Organismen.* Berlin: Reimer.

Hall, G. S. (1883). The contents of children´s minds. *Princeton Review, 11,* 249–272.

Hamilton, W. D. (1964a). The genetical evolution of social behaviour, I. *Journal of Theoretical Biology, 7,* 1–16.

Hamilton, W. D. (1964b). The genetical evolution of social behaviour, II. *Journal of Theoretical Biology, 7,* 17–52.

Harlow, H. F., & Zimmerman, R. (1959). Affectional responses in the infant monkey. *Science, 130,* 421–432.

Harwood, R. L. (1992). The influence of culturally derived values on Anglo and Puerto Rican mothers´ perceptions of attachment behavior. *Child Development, 63,* 822–839.

Harwood, R. L. & Miller, J. G. (1991). Perceptions of attachment behavior: A comparison of Anglo and Puerto Rican mothers. *Merrill-Palmer Quarterly, 37,* 583–599.

Havighurst, R. J. (1948/1972). *Developmental tasks and education, 3rd ed.* New York: Basic Books.

Hess, R. D. (1973). *Imprinting: Early experience and the developmental psychology of attachment.* New York: Van Nostrand.

Hinde, R. A. (1987). Can nonhuman primates help us understand human behavior?. In B. B. Smith, D. L. Cheney, R. M. Seyfarth, R. M. Wrangham, & T. T. Struhsaker (Eds.), *Primate societies* (pp. 413–420). Chicago: University of Chicago Press.

Hofer, M. A. (1987). Early social relationships: A psychobiologist's view. *Child Development, 58,* 633–647.

Holt, E. B. (1931). *Animal drive and the learning process (Vol. 1).* New York: Holt.

Hrdy, S. B. (1987). Sex biased parental investment among primates and other mammals: A critical evalutation of the Trivers-Willard Hypothesis. In R. J. Gelles & J. B. Lancaster (Eds.), *Child abuse and neglect—Biosocial dimensions* (pp. 97–147). New York: Aldine.

Humphrey, N. K. (1976). The social function of intelligence. In P. P. G. Bateson & R. A. Hinde (Eds.), *Growing points in ethology* (pp. 303–317). Cambridge: Cambridge University Press.

Humphrey, N. K. (1983). The adaptiveness of mentalism. *Behavioral and Brain Sciences, 6,* 343–390.

Immelmann, K. & Keller, H. (1988). Die Frühe Entwicklung. In K. Immelmann, K. R. Scherer, C. Vogel & P. Schmoock (Eds.), *Psychobiologie—Grundlagen des Verhaltens* (pp. 133–180). München: Psychologie Verlags Union.

Izard, C. E. (1971). *The face of emotion.* New York: Appleton-Century Crofts.

Keller, H. (1989). Entwicklungspsychopathologie: Das Entstehen von Verhaltensauffälligkeiten in der Frühesten Kindheit. In H. Keller (Ed.), *Handbuch der Kleinkindforschung* (pp. 529–543). Heidelberg: Springer.

Keller, H. (1991). A perspective on continuity in infant development. In M. E. Lamb & H. Keller (Eds.), *Infant development: Perspectives from German-speaking countries* (pp. 135–150). Hillsdale, NJ: Erlbaum.

Keller, H. (1992). The development of exploratory behavior. *The German Journal of Psychology, 16,* 120–140.

Keller, H., & Chasiotis, A. (1994). A psychobiological conceptualization of ethnotheories. Invited lecture at the International Congress "Education, famille et développement en Afrique," Abidjan, Ivory Coast, April 5–8.

Keller, H., Chasiotis, A., & Runde, B. (1992). The existence of intuitive parenting programs in German, U.S.-American and Greek parents of three months old infants. *Journal of Cross-Cultural Psychology, 23, 510–520.*

Keller, H. & Eibl-Eibesfeldt, I. (1989). Concepts of parenting: The role of eye-contact in early parent-child interactions. In D.M. Keats, D. Munro, & L. Mann (Eds.), *Heterogeneity in cross-cultural psychology* (pp. 468–476). Lisse: Swets & Zeitlinger.

Keller, H., & Gauda, G. (1987). Eye contact in the first months of life and its developmental consequences. In H. Rauh & H. C. Steinhausen (Eds.), *Psychobiology and early development* (pp. 129–143). Amsterdam: Elsevier.

Keller, H., Loewer, M., & Runde, B. (1990). Analyse spontaner Sprache von Eltern in Interaktionssituationen mit ihren Säuglingen und Kleinkindern: Entwicklungsveränderungen und kulturspezifische Aspekte. *Zeitschrift für Entwicklungspsychologie und Pädagogische Psychologie, 22,* 341–353.

Keller, H., Miranda, D., & Gauda, G. (1984). The naive theory of the infant and some maternal attitudes. A two-country study. *Journal of Cross-Cultural Psychology, 15,* 165–179.

Keller, H., Schölmerich, A., & Eibl-Eibesfeldt, I. (1988). Communication patterns in adult–infant interactions in Western and non-Western cultures. *Journal of Cross-Cultural Psychology, 19,* 427–445.

Keller, H., Schölmerich, A., Miranda, D., & Gauda, G. (1987). Exploratory behavior development in the first four years. In D. Görlitz & J. F. Wohlwill (Eds.), *Curiosity, imagination, and play* (pp. 127–150). Hillsdale, NJ: Erlbaum.

Keller, H., & Zach, U. (1993). Developmental consequences of early eye contact behaviour. *Acta Paedopsychiatrica, 56,* 31–36.

Konner, M. J. (1977). Infancy among the Kalahari Desert San. In P. H. Leiderman, S. R. Tulkin, & A. Rosenfeld (Eds.), *Culture and infancy. Variations in the human experience* (pp. 287–328). New York: Academic Press.

Kornadt, H.-J., & Trommsdorff, G. (1990). Naive Erziehungstheorien japanischer Mütter—deutsch-japanischer Kulturvergleich. *Zeitschrift für Sozialisationsforschung und Erziehungssoziologie, 2,* 357–376.

Krebs, J., & Davies, N. (1978). *Behavioural ecology—An evolutionary approach.* Oxford: Blackwell.

Kreppner, K. (1992). William L. Stern, 1871–1938: A neglected founder of developmental psychology. *Developmental Psychology, 28,* 539–547.

Lamb, M.E. (1981). The development of father–infant relationships. In M. E. Lamb (Ed.), *The role of father in child development.* New York: Wiley.

Lamb, M. E. (1986). The changing roles of fathers. In M. Lamb (Ed.), *The father's role. Applied perspectives* (pp. 3–27). New York: Wiley.

Lamb, M. E., Thompson, R. A., Gardner, W., Charnov, E. L., & Estes, D. (1984). Security of infantile attachment as assessed in the Strange Situation: Its study and biological interpretation. *Behavioral and Brain Sciences, 7,* 127–147.

Lawick-Goodall, J. (1968). The behaviour of free-living chimpanzees in the Gombe Stream Reserve. *Animal Behavior, 22,* 161–311.

Lerner, R. M. (1984). *On the nature of human plasticity.* New York: Cambridge University Press.

Lethmate, J. (1994). Die Besonderheiten des Menschen. In W. Schiefenhövel, C. Vogel, G. Vollmer, & U. Opolka (Eds.), *Vom Affen zum Halbgott. Der Weg des Menschen aus der Natur* (pp.13–41). Stuttgart: TRIAS Thieme Hippocrates Enke.

Lewis, M. (1987). Social development in infancy and early childhood. In J. D. Osofsky (Ed.), *Handbook of infant development*, (2nd ed., pp. 419–493). New York: Wiley.

Leyendecker, B., Schölmerich, A., & Larson, C. (1994). Microbehavioral analysis of maternal responsiveness during play- and teach-interactions in two developmental niches. Paper read a the IXth Biennial Meeting of the International Society for Infant Studies, Paris, July.

Lonner, W. J. (1980). The search for psychological universals. In H. C. Triandis & W. W. Lambert (Eds.), *Handbook of cross-cultural psychology,* (Vol. 1, pp. 143–204). Boston: Allyn and Bacon.

Lorenz, K. (1969). Innate bases of learning. In K. H. Pribram (Ed.), *On the biology of learning* (pp. 13–93). New York: Harcourt.

Lovejoy, C. O. (1981). The origin of man. *Science, 211,* 341–350.

Lumsden, C. J., & Wilson, E. O. (1981). *Genes, mind and culture: The coevolutionary process.* Cambridge, MA: Harvard University Press.

MacDonald, K. (1992). Warmth as a developmental construct: An evolutionary analysis. *Child Development, 63,* 753–773.

Main, M., & Solomon, J. (1986). Discovery of an insecure-disorganized/disoriented attachment pattern. In T. B. Brazelton & M. Yogman (Eds.), *Affective development in infancy.* Norwood, NJ: Ablex.

Markus, H., & Kitayama, S. (1991). Culture and the self: Implications for cognition, emotion and motivation. *Psychological Review, 98,* 224–253.

Maynard Smith, J. (1964). Group selection and kin selection. *Nature, 201,* 1145–1147.

Mayr, E. (1977). Darwin and natural selection. *American Scientist, 321–327*

Mayr, E. (1982). *The growth of biological thought.* Cambridge, MA: Harvard University Press.

Mayr, E. (1988). *Towards a new philosophy of biology.* Cambridge, MA: Harvard University Press.

McGillicuddy-deLisi, A. V. (1982).Parental beliefs about developmental processes. *Human Development, 25,* 192–200.

McGrew, W. C. (1992). *Chimpanzee material culture: Implications for human evolution.* Cambridge: Cambridge University Press.

Mead, M. (1935). *Sex and temperament in three primitive societies.* New York: Morrow.

Miranda, S. B., & Fantz, R. L. (1974). Recognition memory in Down's Syndrome and normal infants. *Child Development, 45,* 651–660.

Moffit, T. E., Caspi, A., Belsky, J., & Silva, P. A. (1992). Childhood experience and the onset of menarche: A test of a sociobiological model. *Child Development, 63,* 47–58.

Nsamenang, A. B. (1992). *Human development in cultural context. A third world perspective.* Newbury Park, CA: Sage.

Ochs, E., & Schieffelin, B. (1984). Language acquisition and socialization. Three developmental stories and their implications. In R. Shweder & R. LeVine (Eds.), *Culture theory: Essays on mind, self and emotion* (pp. 276-322). Cambridge: Cambridge University Press.

Papousek, H., & Papousek, M. (1987). Intuitive

parenting: A dialectic counterpart to the infant´s integrative competence. In J. D. Osofsky (Ed.), *Handbook of infant development, 2nd ed.* (pp. 669–720). New York: Wiley.

Papousek, M., & Papousek, H. (1991). Early verbalizations as precursors of language development. In M. E. Lamb & H. Keller (Eds.), *Infant development. Perspectives from German-speaking countries* (pp. 299–328). Hillsdale, NJ: Erlbaum.

Parke, R. D., & Tinsley, B. J. (1987). Family interaction in infancy. In J. D. Osofsky (Ed.), *Handbook of infant development*, (2nd ed., pp. 579–641). New York: Wiley.

Perrez, M. (1989). Diagnostik von Kontingenzerfahrungen in der frühen Kindheit. In G. Krampen (Ed.), *Diagnostik von Attributionen und Kontrollüberzeugungen* (pp. 172–185). Göttingen: Hogrefe.

Piaget, J. (1977). *Understanding causality.* New York: Norton.

Pianka, E. R. (1970). On r- and K-selection. *American Naturalist, 104*, 592–597.

Plomin, R. (1986). *Development, genetics, and psychology.* Hillsdale, NJ: Erlbaum

Plomin, R. (1987). Developmental behavioral genetics and infancy. In J. D. Osofsky (Ed.), *Handbook of infant development*, (2nd ed., pp. 363–414). New York: Wiley.

Plomin, R. (1994). Nature, nurture, and social development: Response. *Social Development, 3*, 71–76.

Plomin, R., DeFries, J. C., & Loehlin, J. C. (1977). Genotype-environment interaction and correlation in the analysis of human behavior. *Psychological Bulletin, 84*, 309–322.

Plotkin, H. C. (1988). An evolutionary epistemological approach to the evolution of intelligence. In H. J. Jerison & I. Jerison (Eds.), *Intelligence and evolutionary biology* (pp. 73–91). Berlin/Heidelberg: Springer.

Plotkin, H. C., & Odling-Smee, F. J. (1979). Learning, change and evolution. *Advances in the Study of Behaviour, 10*, 1–41.

Plotkin, H. C., & Odling-Smee, F. J. (1982). Learning in the context of a hierarchy of knowledge processes. In H. C. Plotkin (Ed.), *Learning development and culture: Essays in evolutionary epistemology.* Chichester: Wiley.

Poortinga, Y. H. (1975). Limitations on intercultural comparison of psychological data. *Nederlands Tijdschrift voor de Psychologie, 30*, 23–39.

Preyer, W. T. (1882). *Die Seele des Kindes.* Leipzig: Fernau.

Reese, H. W., & Overton, W. F. (1970). Models of development and theories of development. In L. R. Goulet & P. B. Baltes (Eds.), *Life-span development psychology: Research and theory.* New York: Academic Press.

Richman, A. L., Miller, P. M., & LeVine, R. A. (1992). Cultural and educational variations in maternal responsiveness. *Developmental Psychology, 28*, 614–621.

Rowe, D. C. & Plomin, R. (1981). The importance of nonshared environmental influences in behavioral development. *Developmental Psychology, 17*, 517–531.

Ruse, M. (1979). *Sociobiology: Sense or nonsense.* Dordrecht, NL: Reidel.

Rushton, J. P. (1985). Differential K theory: The sociobiology of individual and group differences. *Personality and Individual Differences, 6*, 441–452.

Rushton, J. P. (1987). Differential K theory of human multiple birthing: Sociobiology and r/K reproductive strategies. *Acta Geneticae Medicae et Genellologiae, 36, 289–296.

Sagi, A., Van IJzendoorn, M. H.., & Koren-Karie, N. (1991). Primary appraisal of the Strange Situation: A cross-cultural analysis of preseparation episodes. *Developmental Psychology, 27*, 587–596.

Scarr, S., & McCartney, K. (1983). How people make their own environments: A theory of genotype-environment effects. *Child Development, 54*, 424–435.

Schoetzau, A., & Papousek, H. (1977). Mütterliches Verhalten bei der Aufnahme von Blickkontakt mit Neugeborenen. *Zeitschrift für Entwicklungspsychologie und Pädagogische Psychologie, 9*, 231–239.

Sigel, I. E. (Ed.) (1985). *Parental belief systems: The psychological consequences for children.* Hillsdale, NJ: Erlbaum.

Silbereisen, R. K., & Schwarz, B. (1992). Frühe Belastungen und Unterschiede im Zeitpunkt psychozioler Übrgänge. In J. Zinnecker (Ed.),

Im Spiegel der Wissenschaften, Band 2 von Jugend '92: Lebenslagen, Orientierungen und Entwicklungsperspektiven im vereinigten Deutschland (pp. 197–220). Opladen: Leske & Budrich.

Sinha, S. R. (1985). Maternal strategies for regulating children´s behavior. *Journal of Cross-Cultural Psychology, 16,* 27–40.

Sommer, V. (1989). *Die Affen. Unsere wilde Verwandtschaft.* Hamburg: Gruner & Jahr.

Sommer, V. (1992). *Lob der Lüge Täuschung und Selbstbetrug bei Tier und Mensch.* München: C. H. Beck.

Sonuga-Barke, E. J. S., Thompson, M., & Balding, J. (1993). Everyday beliefs about sources of advice for the parents of difficult children. *Child Care, Health and Development, 19,* 251– 260.

Sroufe, L. A. (1983).Infant-caregiver attachment and adaptation in the preschool: The roots of competence and maladaptation. In M. Perlmutter (Eds.), *Minnesota Symposium in Child Psychology, Vol. 16.* Hillsdale, NJ: Erlbaum.

Steinberg, L. (1988). Reciprocal relation between parent-child distance and pubertal maturation. *Developmental Psychology, 24,* 122–128.

Stern, D. N. (1977). *The first relationship: Infant and mother.* Cambridge, MA: Harward University Press.

Stern, D. N. (1985). *The interpersonal world of the infant: A view from psychoanalysis and developmental psychology.* New York: Basic Books.

Stern, W. (1914/1923). *Psychologie der frühen Kindheit.* Leipzig: Quelle & Meyer.

Steward, J. (1955). *The concept and method of cultural ecology. Theory of culture change.* Urbana: University of Illinois Press.

Strodtbeck, F. L. (1964). Considerations of metamethod in cross-cultural studies. *American Anthropologist, 66,* 223–229.

Suomi, S. J. (1979). Differential developmental various social relationships by Rhesus monkey infants. In M. Lewis & L. A. Rosenblum (Eds.), *The social network of the child.* New York: Plenum Press.

Super, C. M., & Harkness, S. (1986). The developmental niche: A conceptualization at the interface of child and culture. *International Journal of Behavioral Development, 9,* 545-569.

Surbey, M. (1990). Family composition, stress, and human menarche. In F. Bercovitch & T. Zeigler (Eds.), *The socioendocrinology of primate reproduction* (pp. 71–97). New York: Lisse.

Sylvester-Bradley, B., & Trevarthen, C. (1978). Baby talk as an adaptation to the infant´s communication. In N. Waters & C. Snow (Eds.), *The development of communication* (pp. 75–92). New York: Wiley.

Thomae, H. (1959). Entwicklungsbegriff und Entwicklungstheorie. In H. Thomae (Ed.), *Handbuch der Psychologie: Entwicklungspsychologie* (pp. 3–20). Göttingen: Hogrefe.

Thompson, W. R. (1980). Cross-cultural uses of biological data and perspectives. In H. C. Triandis & W. W. Lambert (Eds.), *Handbook of cross-cultural psychology,* (Vol. 1, pp. 205–252). Boston: Allyn and Bacon.

Thornhill, R. & Thornhill, N. W. (1989). The evolution of psychological pain. In R. W. Bell & N. J. Bell (Eds.), *Sociology and the social sciences* (pp. 73–104). Lubbock, TX: Texas University Press.

Tiger, L., & Fox, R. (1971). *The imperial animal.* New York: Holt, Rinehart & Winston.

Tooby, J., & Cosmides, L. (1990a). On the universality of human nature and the uniqueness of the individual: The role of genetics and adaptation. *Journal of Personality, 58,* 17–67.

Tooby, J., & Cosmides, L. (1990b). The past explains the present: Emotional adaptations and the structure of ancestral environments. *Ethology and Sociobiology, 11,* 375–424.

Tooby, J., & Cosmides, L. (1992). The psychological foundations of culture. In J. H. Barkow, L. Cosmides, & J. Tooby (Eds.), *The adapted mind* (pp. 19–136). New York: Oxford University Press.

Triandis, H. C. (Ed.). (1980). *Handbook of cross-cultural psychology.* Boston: Allyn and Bacon.

Trivers, R. L. (1971). The evolution of reciprocal altruism. *Quarterly Review of Biology, 46,* 35–57.

Trivers, R. L. (1972). Parental investment and sexual selection. In B.G. Campbell (Ed.), *Sexual selection and the descent of man: 1871-- 1971* (pp. 136–179). Chicago: Aldine de Gruyter.

Trivers, R. L. (1974). Parent-offspring conflict. *American Zoologist, 14*, 249–264.

Trivers, R. L. (1985). *Social evolution.* Menlo Park, CA: Benjamin/Cummings.

Trivers, R. L., & Willard, D. E. (1973). Natural selection of parental ability to vary the sex ratio of offspring. *Science, 179*, 90–92.

Trommsdorff, G. (1983). Value change in Japan. *International Journal of Intercultural Relations, 7*, 337–360.

Trommsdorff, G. (Ed.) (1989). *Sozialisation im Kulturvergleich.* Stuttgart: Enke Verlag.

Trommsdorff, G. (1993). Entwicklung im Kulturvergleich. In A. Thomas (Ed.), *Kulturvergleichende Psychologie* (pp. 103–143). Göttingen: Hogrefe.

Valsiner, J. (1987). *Culture and the development of children's action.* Chichester: Wiley.

Van den Berghe, P. L. (1994). *Biological determinants of society.* Paper read at the Zif-Conference "The formative Process of society. The transition from natural to cultural history," November 17–19.

Van Ijzendoorn, M. H. , & Kroonenberg, P. (1990). Cross-cultural consistency of coding the Strange Situation. *Infant Behavior and Development, 13*, 469–485.

Voland, E. (1992). Reproduktive Konsequenzen sozialer Strategien. Das Beispiel der Krummhörner Bevölkerung im 18. und 19. Jahrhundert. In E. Voland (Ed.), *Fortpflanzung: Natur und Kultur im Wechselspiel* (pp. 290–305). Frankfurt/M.: Suhrkamp.

Voland, E. (1993). *Grundriß der Soziobiologie.* Stuttgart, Jena: Fischer.

Voland, E., Siegelkow, E., & C. Engel (1991). Cost/benefit oriented parental investment by high status families: The Krummhörn case. *Ethology and Sociobiology, 12*, 105–118.

Von Uexküll, J. (1921). *Umwelt und Innenwelt der Tiere,* (2nd ed.). Berlin: Springer.

Von Uexküll, J., & Krizat, G. (1983). *Streifzüge durch die Umwelten von Tieren und Menschen.* Frankfurt/M.: Fischer.

White, R. W. (1959). Motivation reconsidered: The concept of competence. *Psychological Review, 66*, 297–333.

Wilson, D. S., & Sober, E. (1994). Reintroducing group selection to the human behavioral sciences. *Behavioral and Brain Sciences, 17*, 585–654.

Wilson, E. O. (1975). *Sociobiology: The new synthesis.* Cambridge, MA: Belknap Press.

Witkin, H., & Berry, J. W. (1975). Psychological differentiation in cross-cultural perspective. *Journal of Cross-Cultural Psychology, 6*, 4–87.

7

METHODS AND DATA ANALYSIS
OF COMPARATIVE RESEARCH

FONS VAN DE VIJVER
Tilburg University
The Netherlands

KWOK LEUNG
Chinese University of Hong Kong
Hong Kong

Contents

Introduction

The major goal of this chapter is to provide a comprehensive overview of the methodological issues encountered in cross-cultural research. Since the reviews in the first edition of the *Handbook* on testing and assessment by Irvine and Carroll (1980) and on experimentation by Brown and Sechrest (1980), many developments have taken place. In our presentation, we focus on data sets that are comparative in nature. Most studies of this type involve data from at least two cultural groups, but some studies are monocultural. In such studies, previous work must provide data and results before meaningful cross-cultural comparisons to be made. Monocultural studies commonly conducted by ethnographers and anthropologists that do not touch upon cross-cultural comparison will fall outside of the scope of our review.

We see the process of conducting cross-cultural research as composed of three important steps. First, the research questions must be explicitly stated. Second, a method that is appropriate to the research questions raised should be selected. Method is defined here as the design, sampling, administration, and instrumentation involved in the collection of data. Finally, the appropriate data analysis should be chosen in light of the research questions raised and the method chosen. We consider these three steps as intertwined, and they should be considered simultaneously prior to data collection. This three-step framework is used in organizing the materials that follow.

The first section of the chapter describes specific issues of cross-cultural research, such as quasi-experimentation. The second section describes in more detail the methodological aspects of cross-cultural studies. The third section deals with the analysis of cross-cultural data. The fourth section reviews the main issues in the methodology and analysis of four common types of cross-cultural studies. Conclusions are drawn in the final section.

Specific Issues in Comparative Methodology and Data Analysis

Before the methods and analyses of cross-cultural studies can be discussed, the applicability of "true experiments" (Campbell & Stanley, 1966) and the associated statistical framework to these studies—the Neyman–Pearson theory—should be explored in order to highlight their special characteristics.

The classical Neyman–Pearson theory provides the most commonly applied statistical framework in testing intergroup differences in psychology. The framework is appropriate for analyzing data from experiments with experimental and control groups. The two groups are considered to be equal, except for the manipulation that is present in the experimental group and absent in the control group ("all other things being equal," as it is often called). The theoretical question the researcher wants to examine concerns the presence of a difference in the dependent measures between the experimental and control groups. This is tested by a *t* test or analysis of variance. The researcher chooses *a priori* a probability that is considered appropriate, usually .05 or .01, for concluding whether or not there are differences between the experimental and control groups. The framework has been developed as a tool to analyze data collected in experimental settings and to reduce the risk of making false inferences.

The framework has turned out to work well mainly in so-called true experiments (Campbell & Stanley, 1966), in which subjects are randomly assigned to different experimental conditions. The "all other things being equal" argument in general does not apply to studies in which subjects are not assigned randomly to experimental treatments. Group membership, a major experimental treatment in cross-cultural studies, is predetermined and cannot be randomly assigned. When the cultural differences between the groups of subjects involved in a cross-cultural study are extensive, it does not make much sense to assume the validity of the "all other things being equal" argument and to compare the groups as if the data were collected in a true experiment. In cross-cultural studies, the application of the Neyman–Pearson framework can yield misleading results (Poortinga & Malpass, 1986). For instance, when cognitive tests are presented to Western literate and non-Western illiterate subjects, the educational and cultural differences between the two groups tend to be so massive that a test of the null hypothesis of no intergroup differences in performance is inadequate. Quite likely, every item will show a significant difference between the two groups.

Furthermore, the interpretation of such a test is equivocal. In the experimental paradigm the interpretation of the difference in the dependent measures is simple. The treatment, typically well defined, such as a drug that has been administered, has produced the score difference between the experimental and control groups. In a similar vein, the differences in the cognitive tests between the literates and illiterates can be attributed to the treatment "culture." However, the attribution does not convey much meaning and dodges the question of a proper interpretation of the score differences. Culture is too global a concept to be used as a meaningful independent variable in the interpretation. In comparison to the experimental branches of psychology, cross-cultural psychology should be much more sensitive to the interpretability of findings. Whereas the task often ends for the experimental psychologist with the observation of a significant difference because the observation will typically confirm or falsify a hypothesis, the task of the cross-cultural psychologist is certainly not complete with the observation of significant intergroup differences.

A crucial problem in quasi-experiments (in which there is no random assignment of subjects) is the ruling out of rival hypotheses. This issue has been extensively discussed, and the consensus is that culture must be "unpackaged" (e.g., Whiting, 1976; Poortinga, Van de Vijver, Joe, & Van de Koppel, 1989). The use of culture as an explanatory variable is not satisfactory, and culture must be decomposed into a set of psychologically meaningful constructs, which are then used to explain the cultural differences observed (e.g., Leung, 1989; Poortinga & Van de Vijver, 1987). When cultural differences on a dependent variable are documented, it is almost impossible to pin down which aspect of culture is responsible for the observed differences, in the absence of additional data. A feasible strategy is to identify the most likely variables that may account for the expected cultural differences and measure these variables in the study. A number of analytical procedures, which will be described later, can be employed to identify which aspect is indeed the most plausible explanation for the cultural differences observed. An adequate cross-cultural study must have built-in elements in its design to rule out plausible rival hypotheses (cf. Cook & Campbell, 1979).

Equivalence

Equivalence is a major concern in cross-cultural research; meaningful cross-cultural comparisons can only be made if the data from different cultures are comparable. Equivalence has been discussed extensively, and several types have been identified (e.g., Berry, 1969; Poortinga, 1971, 1989; Van de Vijver & Poortinga, 1982). Because terms used in the literature to describe equivalence are often unclear and confusing, we propose that three types of equivalence be distinguished: *structural, measurement unit,* and *scalar.* Cross-cultural researchers are often interested in *structural equivalence,* which refers to the similarity of psychometric properties of data sets from different cultures. Specifically, psychometric properties are often taken to refer to correlations of the items of an instrument (*instrument* is used in this chapter for any measurement device such as tests, questionnaires, and observational scales) or to correlations of an instrument with external measures. Multidimensional scaling, factor analysis, and the analysis of covariance structures (structural equations) are commonly employed to study structural equivalence. Thus, if equal factor structures are obtained in various cultural groups, it can be concluded that the psychological constructs underlying the instrument are identical. However, structural equivalence does not imply that both the origin and the measurement unit of the instrument are identical. Structural equivalence is primarily based on similarity in correlations across a variety of cultures and correlations are not affected by linear transformations of the variables. For example, if the scores of all persons in one cultural group are multiplied by a positive constant, the correlations remain unaffected and the factor loadings will also remain the same. Therefore, similar factor loadings can arise from scales with different origin and measurement units.

The second and third types of equivalence are concerned with measurement equivalence. When the scores of two cultural groups are compared, it is possible that the unit of measurement is identical, but that the scales do not have a common origin. This will be called *measurement unit equivalence.* Temperature scales in degrees of Celsius and Kelvin show this kind of equivalence. It has been argued that some intelligence tests can be validly applied within but not across cultural groups due to different origins of the scale in the cultural groups. In the case of measurement unit equivalence, differences between two scores (e.g., the scores between two classmates or the scores of an individual at two measurement occasions) can be compared both within and across cultures, while the scores themselves can only be compared within cultures.

If it can be ascertained that scores show not only an identical unit of measurement, but also a common origin, *scalar equivalence* or *full score comparability* is said to have been obtained. Scalar equivalence allows the comparison of the scores obtained, both within and across cultural groups. Examples are such variables as weight and height. For psychological measurements it is often difficult to establish scalar equivalence. In general it is easier to disprove than to prove scalar equivalence.

In the cross-cultural literature, the term *metric equivalence* has often been introduced to refer to the case when two or more data sets from different cultures exhibit similar psychometric properties (Berry, 1969). Within this framework, *subsystem validation* refers to the case when independent and dependent variables show the same relationship within cultures and across cultures (e.g., Roberts & Sutton-Smith, 1962). *Scalar equivalence* refers to the case in which scores from different cultures have a similar origin and unit of measurement (e.g., Poortinga, 1971).

We find some of this terminology imprecise. The term *metric* in metric equivalence denotes the unit of measurement in common usage in the psychometric literature, and does not denote structural equivalence nor a common origin of the scores, both of which are implied in the current usage of the term. Thus, we propose that this term be abandoned.

The first subtype of metric equivalence, subsystem validation, is actually a special case of structural equivalence, and can be subsumed under structural equivalence. The second subtype, scalar equivalence, is defined in the same way as in our scheme, and should be retained.

Methods

Sampling of Cultures

The selection of cultures in a cross-cultural study is often central to its scope for evaluating the hypotheses proposed. Three types of sampling procedures for the selection of cultures are commonly found in the literature. First, *convenience sampling* is often adopted in cross-cultural studies. Researchers select a culture simply because they may be from that culture, are acquainted with collaborators from that culture, or happen to be spending a sabbatical leave in that culture. The choice of culture is haphazard, driven by convenience, and not related to the theoretical questions raised. Very often, these studies adopt a "let's look and see" approach and do not develop any *a priori* predictions about cultural differences. When cultural differences are found, post hoc explanations are often developed to explain the differences.

The second approach is *systematic sampling*, in which cultures are selected in a systematic, theory-guided fashion. Usually, cultures are selected because they represent different values on a theoretical continuum. The classic study by Berry (1967) provides an excellent example of this approach. Two groups were studied, one agricultural and one hunting. It was hypothesized that agricultural societies impose stronger pressure on conformity, and hence will lead to field dependence. Hunting societies encourage their members to be autonomous and hence are conducive to field independence. These two groups were selected systematically to evaluate this hypothesis. Another example of this approach is provided by Leung, Au, Fernandez-Dols, and Iwawaki (1992). In their study, four cultures were selected, namely, Spain, Japan, Canada, and the Netherlands. Japan and Spain tend to collectivistic, whereas Canada and the Netherlands tend to be individualistic (Hofstede, 1980). The comparison of these two groups will reveal the impact of individualism–collectivism. On the other hand, Spain and the Netherlands tend to be feminine, whereas Japan and Canada tend to be masculine (Hofstede, 1980). The comparison of Spain and the Netherlands with Japan and Canada will reveal the effects of cultural masculinity and femininity. An interesting feature of this study is that in both types of comparison, each group is composed of a Western and an Eastern culture. If differences are found between the two groups, the possibility that the differences are due to East–West differences can be ruled out.

We believe that in the systematic approach, bicultural comparisons are adequate only if there is a compelling theoretical framework in which the results can be interpreted, as is the case in Berry's (1967) study. When a study is exploratory, or when the theoretical framework guiding the study is rudimentary, the number of cultures in a study should be preferably larger than two. Campbell (1986) argued that the number of rival explanations is greatly reduced when the number of cultures involved in evaluating a hypothesis increases (cf. Leung et al.'s, 1992, study mentioned above).

In order to maximize the effectiveness of the systematic approach, cultures that are far apart on the theoretical dimension upon which they vary should be selected. This approach will maximize the chance to detect cultural differences. However, if only two cultures are selected that are highly dissimilar, they are likely to vary in other dimensions as well, and numerous alternative interpretations have to be ruled out. The problem does not arise when more than two cultures are studied; the larger the number of cultures selected, the fewer the alternative interpretations will be possible.

The third approach is *random sampling.* In this approach, a large number of cultures are randomly sampled, usually for evaluating a universal structure or a pan-cultural theory. Truly random samples are basically nonexistent in the literature, as no one has the resources to select a large number of cultures on a random basis for a single study. However, several studies have tried to follow this approach, and their sample may eventually begin to approximate a random sample (usually not of all groups but of all literate groups). For instance, Schwartz (1992, 1994) has sampled 36 cultures to evaluate the structure of human values. He basically included any cultural group in which he could find a collaborator to participate in the project. Buss et al. (1990) also followed a similar approach in sampling 37 cultures in their study of mate selection. Peterson et al. (1995) have surveyed managers from more than 20 countries on event management issues.

Sampling of Subjects

In order to make valid cross-cultural comparisons, the subjects from different cultural groups must be similar in terms of relevant background characteristics. Otherwise, it is hard to conclude whether the cultural differences observed are due to cultural differences or sample-specific differences. If we compare a group of illiterate subjects from one culture to a group of highly educated subjects from another culture, the differences observed are likely to be explainable in terms of educational differences rather than differences in some other aspect of their cultures. One approach to overcome this problem is to match the samples in terms of demographic characteristics so that sample differences can be ruled out as alternative explanations for observed cultural differences. For instance, college students from different cultures are often compared, and it is usually assumed that college students from different cultures are similar in their demographical characteristics. In a similar vein, Hofstede (1980, 1983) reduced the influence of unwanted intergroup differences by studying subjects from a single multinational organization from 53 countries. Schwartz (1992, 1994) sampled secondary school teachers from various countries to maximize the comparability of his subjects.

It is sometimes impossible to match samples from different cultures because of practical reasons, or because there are sharp cross-cultural differences in the demographic background of subjects. An adequate approach is then to measure the major demographic variables and treat them as covariates in the subsequent data analysis. For instance, in a study comparing the delinquent behaviors of adolescents in the United States, Australia, and Hong Kong, it was found that there were substantial differences in the father's educational standing in the three cultures (Feldman, Rosenthal, Mont-Reynaud, Leung, & Lau, 1991). The educational standing of the fathers of the Hong Kong subjects was significantly lower than that of the fathers of the Australian and American subjects. To overcome this problem, an analysis of covariance was used to compare cultural means partialling out the influence of father's educational standing.

It is unfortunate that many cross-cultural studies tend to ignore sample differences and fail to assess the impact of such differences. As the results are confounded by sample differences, it is difficult to provide an unambiguous interpretation.

Procedure

In this section we will review issues related to the procedural aspects of a cross-cultural study: the selection and evaluation of the adequacy of a measurement instrument, its translation, and its administration.

In an early stage of a project the question has to be raised whether the same instrument can be applied in all cultural groups. In the case of an already existing measurement instrument, its appropriateness in an intercultural context has to be judged. This amounts to answering the question whether the operationalizations chosen in the instrument will be adequate in all cultural groups studied. Are the measurement operations specified in the instrument an adequate representation of the psychological domain that is to be covered? Embretson (1983) has introduced the concept of construct representation. The concept refers to the coverage of the psychological domain. Do the measurement operations specified in the instrument represent an adequate and sufficient sample of the behavioral manifestations of the psychological construct that is measured by the instrument? Any answer to this question requires knowledge of the cultural context in which the instrument will be applied.

The outcome of the decision process can take three forms: to *apply* the instrument, to *adapt* it, or to *assemble* a new version. In the first alternative the instrument or a translated version will be used without any modification. If the construct is not fully covered in the new group, the instrument can be adapted by rephrasing, adding, or replacing items that measure the missing aspects. If the researcher finds the original instrument entirely inadequate, a new instrument has to be assembled.

The decision whether to apply or adapt an existing instrument or to assemble a new one has both theoretical and practical implications. We propose to make the application of the same instrument the default choice. The advantages of this choice are (1.) the possibility to compare research results with other results reported in the literature, (2.) the possibility to maintain scalar equivalence (which is not achievable if results of newly assembled instruments are compared), and (3.) the small amount of money and effort that is required to administer an existing instrument as compared to the development and establishment of the psychometric properties of a new or adapted instrument. However, the direct application of an existing instrument may not always be the best choice. If an instrument does not cover important aspects of the psychological construct under study or if it shows a clear ethnocentric bias, adaptation or the assemblage of a new instrument would be a better choice. The decision may be seen as involving a cost–benefit analysis, with time and money as the costs and construct representation as the benefit.

There are numerous examples of *application* in the literature. For instance, Hofstede's (1980, 1983) classic study involves a value questionnaire that was administered in over 10 languages in 53 countries. The use of the Minnesota Multiphasic Personality Inventory (MMPI) in China provides a good example to illustrate the process of *adaptation.* When the items of the MMPI were tested in China, it was found that some items were meaningless in the Chinese context, and these items had to be modified (Cheung, 1989). However, most of the original items in the MMPI were retained, and it was actually possible to interpret the Chinese results in light of the American norms. The case of *assembling* a new instrument is rare in the literature, but two examples can be cited. Church (1987) argued that Western personality instruments are unable to capture many of the indigenous personality constructs of the Filipino culture. In light of these difficulties, he proposed a number of directions for the construction of a new personality instrument for the Filipino culture. In a similar vein, Cheung et al. (1996) have argued that adaptation of Western personality instruments is inadequate in capturing all the major dimensions of personality in the Chinese culture. They started from scratch and created a personality instrument, called the Chinese Personality Assessment Inventory (CPAI), for the Chinese people. This instrument contains several indigenous personality dimensions, such as "face" and "harmony," as well as many items that are particularly meaningful in the Chinese context.

Instrument Translation

In the case of the *application* and the *adaptation* the instrument has to be translated. The translation–backtranslation method is probably the best known method for instrument translations (e.g., Brislin, 1980; Hambleton, 1993, 1994). An instrument is translated from one language to another and then backtranslated to the original language by an independent translator. This method often provides adequate results, but sometimes it produces a stilted language that reproduces the original language version well, but is not easily readable and comprehensible. This is particularly the case when test items contain local idioms that, almost by definition, are difficult to translate. Backtranslations can provide researchers who lack proficiency in the target language control of the adequacy of the translation. However, it is noteworthy that in the field of professional translations the procedure is almost never utilized (Wilss, 1982). Professional translations are commonly produced and checked by teams of competent bilinguals; hence, instead of relying on backtranslations, these teams utilize judgmental methods to assess the accuracy of the translation.

Werner and Campbell (1970) have proposed to decenter instruments that are used in a cross-cultural context—to adjust both the original and the translated versions simultaneously. The aim in decentering is not the verbatim reproduction of the original text but the enhancement of the naturalness and readability of the original and translated version.

Brislin, Lonner, and Thorndike (1973) have generated a useful set of guidelines to ensure good translatability (cf. Brislin, 1980, p. 432):

1. Use short, simple sentences in order to minimize the cognitive load of the instrument; a simple item-per-item check whether the phrasing can be simplified can lead to considerable improvement in translatability.
2. Employ the active rather than the passive voice.
3. Repeat nouns instead of using pronouns (which in some languages may be difficult to translate).
4. Do not use metaphors and colloquialisms, which are usually not well translatable.
5. Avoid the subjunctive mood (e.g., verb forms with "could" and "would").
6. Add sentences when key concepts are communicated. Reword these phrases to provide redundancy.
7. Avoid adverbs and prepositions telling "where" and "when," such as beyond and upper.

8. Avoid possessive forms where possible.
9. Use specific words, such as chickens and pigs, rather than general terms, such as livestock.
10. Avoid words indicating vagueness, such as probably and frequently.
11. Use wording familiar to translators where possible.
12. Avoid sentences with two different verbs that suggest different actions.

Various techniques have been proposed to check the accuracy of translations. An overview has been presented by Hambleton (1993, 1994). A distinction can be made between judgmental and empirical methods. Judgmental evidence of translation equivalence usually amounts to the application of a translation–backtranslation design. An assessment of the accuracy of the translation by a set of competent bilinguals is an alternative way to assess accuracy. Hambleton proposes three designs to study the accuracy of translations: (1.) bilinguals take the source and target versions of the test; (2.) source language monolinguals take the original and backtranslated versions, and (3.) monolinguals in both languages take the test. The latter is by far the most frequently applied design. Various psychometric techniques are available to evaluate the equivalence of the items in the source and target languages. These are known as item bias or *differential item functioning* techniques and will be discussed later.

Administration

Four areas will be distinguished in the following overview of issues related to a proper administration of instruments in a cross-cultural study (cf. Van de Vijver & Poortinga, 1991, 1992): the personal characteristics of the tester (or interviewer), interactions between the tester and the examinees, response procedures, and the stimuli of the instrument. In general, it will be difficult or even impossible to generate an exhaustive list of the problems that may arise in the administrative aspects of cross-cultural research. However, an overview of the common problems may sensitize the reader to the kinds of problems that can be encountered.

The presence of a tester, experimenter, or interviewer can be a threat to the validity of the results, particularly when this person has a different cultural background from the subjects in the sample. The potential influence has been recognized in observational studies of mother–child interactions (Super, 1981). In intelligence testing, the influence of racial differences between the tester and the examinee has been studied systematically (Jensen, 1980). Overall, the influence tends to be small, though the results are not consistent. In many cross-cultural studies the cultural distance between the tester or interviewer and the subjects will be considerably larger than in the American studies reviewed by Jensen. No systematic study has been undertaken of tester effects in settings more representative of cross-cultural settings.

A second area to be considered is the interaction between the tester and the respondent. In many research designs there is verbal communication between the two, and various problems may occur as a result of such communication. In some cases the choice of the language used may be problematic. For instance, when Reuning and Wortley (1973) administered a variety of cognitive tests to the Bushmen, Kalahari desert dwellers, they faced the problem that their subjects had a highly heterogeneous linguistic background. Because it would have been difficult to hire and train an interpreter for each vernacular, they chose to minimize the verbal exchange in the testing procedure.

The reduction of verbal communication is not always possible because verbal exchange is essential in surveys and psychological testing. If the researcher decides to administer the instruments with the help of one or more interpreters, the potential influence of the interpreters should be evaluated, even when they are carefully trained. An assessment of the interpreter's influence usually requires that a group of respondents be interviewed by two interpreters. The results obtained by these interviewers are then compared with the help of an index of agreement. The choice of this index depends, among other things, on the nature of the data gathered. Cohen's kappa or its weighted version can be used in the case of nominal or ordinal data (Cicchetti, Showalter, & McCarthy, 1990; Cohen, 1960), and an intraclass correlation (Shrout & Fleiss, 1979) or Cronbach's alpha (e.g., Winer, 1971) in the case of interval data.

The third area involves response procedures. Subjects may be unfamiliar with a certain response procedure. For instance, the Porteus' Maze Test, a paper-and-pencil test, has been administered to groups of subjects who had never used a pencil before. Not surprisingly, their scores were very low (cf. Van de Vijver & Poortinga, 1991). If subjects are unfamiliar with a response procedure, it is important to reserve time for familiarizing the subjects with the procedure as part of the test introduction. In the area of personality and social psychology, Likert scales are often applied. Particularly among groups having little experience with this response format, the use of verbal descriptions of the response alternatives instead of numbers might be preferred.

A good example of the impact of response procedures can be found in the work of Serpell (1979). He administered a pattern-copying task to children in the United Kingdom and Zambia. The children's copying skills were assessed using two response media: pencil-drawing and iron-wire modelling, a popular pastime among Zambian boys. It was found that the British children scored higher than the Zambian children on the pencil-drawing task while the Zambian children reached higher scores on the iron-wire modelling task.

In some cases no empirical evidence may be available to judge the accuracy of a response procedure. A pilot study could then be carried out in which potentially useful response procedures are compared in a monotrait–multimethod matrix, in which several response procedures for measuring the same construct are examined. The correspondence of the results across the response procedures indicates the validity of the procedures.

Stimulus-related aspects are by far the most extensively studied area of procedural problems in cross-cultural research. Stimulus familiarity is the most often mentioned source of invalid intergroup score differences in the literature (e.g., Irvine & Carroll, 1980). A study by Deregowski and Serpell (1971) illustrates the importance of stimulus familiarity. Scottish and Zambian children were asked to sort miniature models of animals and motor vehicles in one experimental condition and their photographs in another one. No intergroup differences were found for the actual models whereas in the sorting of photographs, the Scottish children obtained higher scores than the Zambian children.

In the past, various attempts have been made to adapt the stimuli of cognitive tests in such a way that intergroup differences caused by stimulus familiarity would be eliminated. Both the culture-free and culture-fair test movements were intended to serve this purpose. Even though the original ideas of the movements have been long abandoned and it is widely acknowledged that such tests cannot be constructed (Frijda & Jahoda, 1966), the concern for stimulus familiarity is still widely shared. Stimuli differ in terms of their cultural entrenchment. Simple geometrical stimuli such as squares, circles, and triangles are often used as stimuli in cognitive tests because their cultural loading is assumed to be limited though certainly not absent.

In the area of personality and social psychology, stimulus familiarity also plays an important role. Items of personality scales frequently use complex words or expressions. Effort should be made to use simple, unambiguous stimuli and to avoid the undesirable introduction of verbal abilities, such as vocabulary and text comprehension skills, as sources of individual differences.

Design

A distinction will be made between the design of structure-oriented and level-oriented studies in cross-cultural psychology. Structure-oriented studies examine relationships among variables and attempt to identity similarities and differences in these relationships across cultures. For example, is the structure of intelligence universal? Level-oriented studies, on the other hand, focus on differences in the magnitude of variables across cultures. For example, are members of culture A more individualistic than members of culture B?

The design of structure-oriented studies is often straightforward: it replicates the design of the original study. The design of level-oriented studies tends to be more complicated, and an adequate choice of research variables and design is needed to enhance the interpretability of the findings obtained. There is at least one important issue common to all level studies: Which covariates should be included? It was argued before that the Neyman–Pearson framework assumes a random assignment of individuals to treatments and that cross-cultural studies can never adopt a truly experimental design. Cultural groups differ in many respects, only some of which are of interest in a particular study. All these group differences can in principle explain observed score differences. An important aid in the reduction of the number of rival explanations are covariates. Covariates can be helpful in the interpretation of cross-cultural score differences in two ways. First, they can be used to validate the interpretation of the cross-cultural differences as hypothesized by the experimenter. For instance, if individualism–collectivism is assumed to be related to a psychological phenomenon, say intergroup hostility, individuals from individualistic and collectivistic countries could be included in the study. In addition to an intergroup hostility measure, a test of individualism–collectivism should be administered to all individuals. These scores could then be used in an analysis of covariance, in which cultural groups are the independent variable, the hostility measure the dependent measure, and the individualism–collectivism score the covariate. The covariate is used to validate the cross-cultural differences postulated by the theory. Earley (1989) has evaluated the effect of individualism–collectivism on social loafing with this approach.

Second, covariates can also be used to check the effects of nuisance variables. The inclusion of such covariates will control for cultural differences that influence the behavior in question, but that are not specified by the theory. For instance, if men and women differ in the level of hostility and if the student groups in the two cultures in the previous example have a different male–female ratio, gender could be used as a covariate, because the observed cross-cultural differences could be due to the difference of gender composition of the two groups as well as to cross-cultural differences in intergroup hostility. The covariate is not meant here to provide an explanation of the cross-cultural differences, but to control for nuisance variables. Covariance analysis as discussed in textbooks is almost always exclusively concerned with the elimination of the impact of nuisance variables. The conclusions of an analysis of covariance can be misleading if the assumption of parallel regression lines within each cultural group is violated (cf. Lord, 1967). A simple statistical test of the equality of regression coefficients in two cultural groups is described in Cohen and Cohen (1983: chapters 10 and 12) and Pedhazur (1982, chapter 12).

Covariates can be based on aggregate rather than individual measures as the previous examples could suggest. In a study of intergroup differences in some cognitive test, educational quality could be assessed. Such a measure located at the class or even cultural level can be used as a covariate at the individual level, meaning that all subjects of a class or school will get the same score on the variable.

We strongly encourage the use of covariates because they provide an effective way to confirm a particular interpretation of intergroup differences and to falsify alternative interpretations. Yet, the limitations of methodological and statistical procedures should be acknowledged. Statistical techniques can help to evaluate the impact of contextual variables, but will not provide information on which covariates to choose. For example, intergroup differences in cognitive test performance might be assumed to be related to educational quality or to Westernization, to mention a few possibilities. Methodological and statistical considerations cannot dictate the choice. All that can be asked from methodology and statistics is a set of tools to enable the evaluation of the accuracy of the choice, or, in case both sets of variables have been measured, the evaluation of their relative importance.

Leung and Zhang (1995) have concluded that many studies have been exported from the West to non-Western countries, and some of the issues examined in these studies are of little relevance to the local culture. It is entirely possible that results obtained in many of these studies are shaped by the cultural background of the researchers, and that different results may be obtained if a different cultural vantage point is taken in the design of these studies. Two approaches may be adopted to design a culturally balanced study, in which no single culture will dominate the research questions explored and bias the results obtained. First, a *decentered* approach can be adopted, in which a culturally diverse perspective is taken in the conceptualization and design of a study. For instance, when Schwartz (1992) tested his pan-cultural model of value structure, he encouraged researchers from different cultures to add culture-specific value items to his pan-cultural set. Smith and Peterson (1988) have taken into account the influence of culture in their formulation of a theory of leadership behavior and their empirical test of the theory (Peterson et al., 1995).

The second approach is the *convergence* approach. The basic idea is to design a study that is as culturally distant as possible from existing studies and to see if the results obtained overlap with existing results. If the new results overlap with existing results, it can be concluded that the cultural origin of existing studies have not biased the results obtained. If different results are obtained, however, the possibility that the cultural origin of existing studies has biased the results must be further investigated. The best examples to illustrate this approach are provided by Bond and his colleagues. The Chinese Culture Connection (1987) designed a value survey based entirely on Chinese values and administered it in 22 countries. It was found that three factors showed overlap with factors identified by Hofstede (1980), whose results were based on a Western instrument. A new factor emerged, termed Confucian work dynamism, which correlated highly with economic growth. In the realm of person perception, Yang and Bond (1990) administered a set of emic Chinese descriptors together with a set of imported American descriptors to a group of Taiwanese subjects. Of the five Chinese factors identified, only four were adequately explained by the American factors, and one factor was uniquely Chinese.

Data Analysis

In this section we will first describe bias, followed by a description of psychometric techniques to detect differential item functioning as a special case of bias. In the last part of the section we will describe the most common statistical techniques for analyzing cross-cultural data sets.

Preliminary Analyses

Prior to the data analysis that addresses the central research question or hypothesis, preliminary analyses will often be required. If a psychological instrument is used, its psychometric properties should be established, in particular its reliability. In most cross-cultural studies this seems to be routine practice. It is surprising that tests of intergroup differences in reliability are almost never carried out even though the observation of dissimilar reliability coefficients can provide valuable clues about measurement accuracy and hence, the appropriateness of an instrument for cross-cultural comparison. Procedures to test the equality of independent alpha coefficients have been described by Kraemer (1981) and Hakstian and Whalen (1976).

The interpretation of intergroup differences can be seen as an attribution process. Two kinds of attributions can be envisaged. Observed intergroup differences may be valid, and members of group A have on average more of a particular propensity such as anxiety, intelligence, or collectivism than members of group B. The observed differences may also be due to bias (measurement problems). For instance, the items used may be affected by intergroup differences in stimulus familiarity or social desirability, which have produced the cultural differences observed.

A distinction can be made between three types of bias. The first is called *construct bias*. This kind of bias occurs when the psychological construct is not identical across cultural groups. Construct bias implies that the theoretical construct is not or is inadequately represented in the instrument. In Embretson's (1983) terms, construct bias refers to a poor construct representation. An example can be found in the area of intelligence. Everyday conceptions of intelligence, mainly in non-Western cultures, have been found to differ from the conception underlying intelligence tests (Serpell, 1993; Sternberg, 1985; Super, 1983). Everyday conceptions of intelligence tend to be broader than scientific theories. In addition to reasoning and factual knowledge that are shared in both conceptions, "social intelligence" is also included in everyday conceptions. "Social intelligence" involves social skills, obedience, and knowing one's role in the family, class, and peer group. A Western intelligence test will therefore show construct bias in many non-Western contexts. Culture-bound syndromes, such as amok, that are studied in ethnopsychiatry provide another example (Draguns, 1989; Harkness & Super, 1990). In the area of personality the Chinese concept of "filial piety" can be mentioned; filial piety refers to taking care of one's parents, conforming to their requests, and treating them well. The Chinese concept is much broader than the Western concept of being a good son or daughter (Ho, in press). A direct comparison of these two will result in construct bias.

It was argued before that a cross-cultural researcher may choose to apply or adapt an existing instrument, or assemble a new one. In the terminology of this section, the decision should be based on whether construct bias is present in the instrument. The assessment of construct bias should be based on knowledge about the cultural groups. If an instrument has been applied in several cultural groups with the same instrument and no additional data are available, statistical tests alone will not lead to a full understanding of the nature of the construct bias present. A proper assessment of construct bias should be based on research conducted in each cultural group, exploring whether the implicit definitions of the concept of the test are consistent across the cultural groups. Examples of this approach can be found in the work of Serpell (1993), Sternberg (1985), and Super (1983).

The second kind of bias is called *method bias*. If method bias occurs, the psychological construct is well represented by the instrument but the assessment procedure introduces unwanted intergroup differences. Empirical studies that reveal method bias are Deregowski and Serpell's (1971) sorting task of miniature models and pictures of animals and motor vehicles, described earlier and Serpell's (1979) study of pattern copying using a paper-and-pencil format and iron-wire models.

Method bias can be examined by monotrait–multimethod matrices or triangulation. In this approach, a psychological construct is investigated using a systematic variation of methods. If the cross-cultural differences observed are similar across methods, method bias is unlikely. Method bias is said to occur if the intergroup differences vary across the methods. An analysis of covariance structures is often used in this situation, as will be illustrated later on.

A specific way to study method bias involves the repeated administration of the same instrument. Test–retest studies of cognitive tests have often shown score increases that are larger in non-Western groups than in Western groups (Kendall, Verster, & Von Mollendorf, 1988; Van de Vijver, Daal, & Van Zonneveld, 1986). A significant improvement in one group at the second occasion, or a gain pattern that is differential across groups, undermines the validity of the first test administration.

The third kind of bias is the most investigated. It was originally called *item bias* and is now better known as *differential item functioning*. Whereas construct bias and method bias involve the appropriateness of the whole instrument, differential item functioning occurs at the item level. Item bias refers to anomalies in the instrument at the item level caused by poor translation or inappropriate items in a particular context. A widely accepted definition of differential functioning has been proposed in the area of ability testing. An item is said to show item bias if persons from different cultural groups with an equal ability do not have the same probability of giving a correct answer. Individuals with an equal ability or attitude from different cultural groups should, apart from chance fluctuations, show the same average score for items of an unbiased instrument. From a psychometric point of view, the assessment of this kind of bias is best developed. A multitude of psychometric techniques have been proposed to test the presence of item bias. We will not describe them in detail. Rather, we shall briefly describe and illustrate two of them, followed by the presentation of a taxonomy of the techniques.

Historically speaking, analysis of variance was probably the first technique that has been applied to study differential item functioning (Cleary & Hilton, 1968). We shall discuss here a slightly modified procedure. Suppose that a test for authoritarianism of 30 five-point Likert-scale items has been administered in two cultural groups of 200 persons each. If we are interested in the presence of differential item functioning, the first step is to divide the subjects into score level groups. Individuals with an equal score are assumed to have an equal level of authoritarianism, and subjects with the same score are grouped together. Because the scores on the Likert scale range from one to five, the total score can vary from a minimum of 30 to a maximum of 150. The split of the score distribution into score levels should be based on the score of all cultural groups together; the same cutoff scores should be applied to all cultural groups. Theoretically speaking, there can be 121 score level groups in this case (from 30 to 150, including both ends). In practice, a much smaller number will be used as the number of subjects will be unevenly distributed across the score levels (Clauser, Mazor, & Hambleton, 1994). Quite often, an attempt is made to choose the cutoff scores in such a way that the number of subjects in each group is approximately the same. Score level will be one of the independent variables in our data analysis; the other one will be the cultural group. Differential item functioning is tested in a set of analyses of variance, one per item, with culture and score level as independent variables and the item score as dependent variable.

Following Mellenbergh (1982), we shall make a distinction between two types of item bias: uniform and nonuniform. Figure 7–1 presents the curves which depict the average score of two groups on a particular item, technically called empirical item characteristic curves (Allen & Yen, 1979). When the curves more or less coincide, there is no bias (Figure 7–1a). When the curves are more or less parallel without coinciding, there is uniform bias (Figure 7–1b). When the curves are not parallel, the items are said to show a nonuniform bias (Figure 7–1c). In this case, the difference in the average test score will depend on the score level. For instance, for low authoritarian subjects, the item is endorsed more strongly in one culture, while for high authoritarian subjects, the item is endorsed more strongly in the other culture. A combination of both types of bias is presented in Figure 7–1d. In terms of the analysis of variance, an item is said to be uniformly biased when the main effect of culture is significant. In this case subjects from one cultural group have a consistently higher score than individuals with the same underlying propensity from another cultural group. A significant interaction of level and culture indicates the presence of nonuniform bias.

Item bias analyses can be carried out in an iterative or a noniterative way. In the latter case the analyses of variance are carried out for all items and the presumably biased items (i.e., all items with a significant main effect for culture and/or a significant interaction between culture and level) are removed simultaneously. Intergroup score comparisons are carried out on the reduced item set. In an iterative procedure the elimination proceeds on an item-by-item basis. In the first step, all items are considered. The item with the largest bias component (i.e., the smallest probability in the computer output) is then removed if the component is significant. The whole procedure is then repeated for the reduced set of items until no more bias components are significant. An attractive feature of iterative procedures is that the total score is updated in each iterative step, which allows for a finer detection of bias. It might well be that after the removal of a few items the meaning of the total score changes somewhat and this change can result in the removal of different items than in the case of a noniterative procedure. However, iterative procedures are cumbersome because after the removal of an item new cutoff scores for the score levels have to be calculated.

The removal of biased items does not inevitably lead to the elimination of intergroup differences in the average scores (Poortinga & Van der Flier, 1988). Items can be biased or unbiased, irrespective of the presence (or absence) of inter-

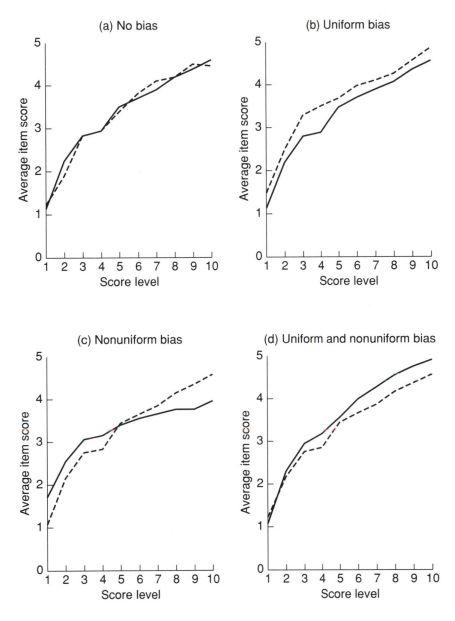

FIGURE 7–1 The average performance of the two cultural groups on an item that shows (a) no bias (b) uniform bias (c) non-uniform bias, and (d) both uniform and nonuniform bias (hypothetical example).

group differences. After all, item bias analysis does not test whether there are overall intergroup differences in total score, that is, whether individuals of group A would have a higher propensity on X than individuals of group B. Rather, item bias analyses test whether there are intergroup differences per score level, that is, whether individuals from group A with a particular attitude level have the same average score on a particular item as people from group B with the same attitude level. The item bias analysis uses an analysis of variance with level and cultural group as independent variables and a particular item score as dependent variable. In contrast, an analysis of variance testing the presence of overall intergroup differences treats culture as the independent variable and the item or total test score as the dependent variable.

The most popular technique to test differential item functioning today is the Mantel–Haenszel statistic (Holland & Thayer, 1988). The statistic is closely related to item response theory (e.g., Hambleton & Swaminathan, 1985). More specifically, the Mantel–Haenszel statistic tests whether a single Rasch model, a model from item response theory, fits the data in each group. The rationale behind the Mantel–Haenszel statistic and the analysis of variance approach explained earlier is similar. The major difference is that the Mantel–Haenszel procedure works with dichotomous data whereas the analysis of variance is based on interval data.

Item response theory represents a more general approach for assessing differential item functioning (e.g., Hambleton & Swaminathan, 1985; Hulin, 1987). This model assumes that an unbiased item evokes a similar response from respondents that are similar in their standing on a latent trait regardless of their cultural backgrounds. In the general form, this model links item responses to latent traits by means of a logistic curve specified by three parameters. The first parameter is concerned with the discrimination capability of the item; the second parameter is concerned with the difficulty level of the item; and the third is concerned with the extent to which guessing is involved in responding to the item. In specific applications, two-parameter models, which exclude the guessing parameter, are often employed for modelling attitudinal data. To detect biased items, item characteristic curves, which relate the probability of making a certain response to standing on a latent trait, are examined. Items are equivalent across two cultures if their item characteristic curves are similar across these cultures. Differential item functioning is present when parameters differ significantly across cultural groups. Item response theory has been applied in cross-cultural research on self-concept (Leung & Drasgow, 1985), job satisfaction (Candell & Hulin, 1987), intelligence (Ellis, 1989; Van de Vijver, 1988), and attitudes toward mental health (Ellis & Kimmel, 1992).

The standard procedure for the application of item response theory is as follows:

1. Item response theory assumes that a scale is unidimensional, and the unidimensionality of the scale must be checked. If the scale is multidimensional, each unidimensional subscale must be examined separately.
2. An item response theory model with the appropriate number of parameters is selected to fit the data in each culture.

3. The parameters identified for each cultural group are equated on the same metric through an iterative linking procedure.
4. Biased items are detected and eliminated with the aid of item characteristic curves and a chi-square test. The parameters are equated again with the linking procedure with unbiased items only, and this procedure stops when no biased items are detected.
5. The biased items identified are eliminated from the scale before cross-cultural comparisons are made.

Item response theory has characteristics that make it appropriate for cross-cultural applications. First, the estimates of item parameters do not depend on the propensity level of the group studied. This is not the case in classical test theory in which the difficulty of an item, operationalized as item average, depends on the average ability level of the group. Similarly, the estimates of person parameters in item response theory are independent of the items of the instrument. Second, most models in item response theory allow for a fit test. The extent to which the empirical data can be taken to obey the theoretical model can be examined (e.g., Hambleton & Swaminathan, 1985; Lord, 1980; Van den Wollenberg, 1988).

The most important limitations of item response theory are twofold. The applicability of item response models may be reduced by the strict assumptions that have to be met, particularly in the Rasch model. Furthermore, large sample sizes are required to obtain stable estimates, particularly in the three-parameter model.

TABLE 7–1   Schematic overview of differential item functioning techniques (after Van de Vijver, 1994)

Sampling distribution	Model equation	
	Linear	Nonlinear
Unconditional procedures		
Unknown	Partial correlation index (Stricker, 1982)	Delta plots (Angoff, 1982)
Known	Analysis of variance (Cleary & Hilton, 1968)	
Conditional procedures		
Unknown	Standardized p-difference (Dorans & Kulick, 1986)	Item response theory (McCauley & Mendoza, 1985)
Known	Analysis of variance with score level as one of the variables	Mantel-Haenszel procedure (Holland & Thayer, 1988)

Three questions are relevant in the choice of a particular item bias statistic, First, what kind of measurement model should be used? Some techniques are based on a linear model such as an analysis of variance, while others, such as the Mantel–Haenszel statistic, are based on a nonlinear model. In general, interval-level data tend to be analyzed using linear models, while dichotomous data are often analyzed by item response theory, a nonlinear model. Second, is the technique conditional or unconditional? Most modern techniques are so-called conditional procedures. These techniques compare the scores of individuals across cultural groups per score level. Both of the previous examples are conditional. Until the eighties, unconditional procedures were more common, such as the comparison of item averages. It has been shown several times (e.g., Lord, 1977, 1980) that unconditional procedures can underestimate the number of biased items. Therefore, conditional procedures are to be preferred. The third question refers to the sampling distribution of the item bias statistic. In both our examples, the sampling distributions are known. This allows for a statistically rigorous test of the null hypothesis of no bias. Yet, various bias statistics that have been proposed have unknown sampling distributions, which makes a statistical evaluation of item bias questionable, whatever the intuitive appeal of the statistic (e.g., Stricker's, 1982, partial correlation index). A taxonomy of basis statistics on the basis of these three questions is presented in Table 7–1.

A perusal of the cross-cultural literature shows that differential item functioning techniques are infrequently applied in cross-cultural psychology. We find this disappointing; in many cases it should be standard practice to carry out an item bias analysis prior to the actual data analysis. Item bias techniques have been mostly applied to cognitive test scores, and much less so in the area of personality and social psychology. There is no good reason for the uneven distribution of the application of item bias techniques, unless one would want to maintain that items in personality questionnaires are of a much higher quality and less open to bias than are cognitive test items.

Two general findings emerge from the application of differential item functioning techniques in cross-cultural psychology. First, item bias may be psychometrically well defined and operationalized, but it may be difficult to grasp its psychological meaning. In current applications, it is not uncommon to find that item bias is reported but no sensible explanation can be provided for the bias (Scheuneman, 1987; Van de Vijver, 1994). Furthermore, item bias indices are not stable in cross-validation studies. Retests with the same instrument may show other items to be biased. The common difficulties encountered in empirical applications of item bias techniques, such as inadequate stability and interpretability, may reduce the attractiveness of these procedures. Still, if we start to routinely apply item bias techniques to cross-cultural data, we may build up a body of knowledge about item quality from a cross-cultural perspective.

Second, some item bias studies have shown a substantial proportion of items to be biased, sometimes more than half of the items. In such a case the item bias analysis seems to point to a serious lack of validity of the instrument. A prudent approach would then be to refrain from intergroup comparisons.

Establishing Scalar Equivalence

Techniques based on correlations such as factor analysis have been proposed and used to test scalar equivalence. For instance, Eysenck and his coworkers concluded that scalar equivalence can be assumed when the factor structures obtained with a measurement instrument in various cultural groups are similar. A similar argument has been put forward by Berry (1980). However, as argued before, similarity of correlations matrices or factor structures across cultural groups can only demonstrate structural equivalence, and does not speak to scalar equivalence. Structural equivalence imposes fewer restrictions on the data than scalar equivalence.

At least three approaches have been proposed to establish full score comparability in the literature. First, various authors assume but do not test full score comparability. If a test is administered in two cultural groups and the test scores are compared without any concern for comparability, full score comparability is implicitly assumed. An example comes from the literature on culture-free and culture-fair intelligence testing. Reports involving these somewhat obsolete instruments hardly involve statistical tests of full score comparability (e.g., Anastasi, 1976; Cattell, 1940; Cattell & Cattell, 1963). In our view, researchers should attempt to provide evidence for full score comparability of their instruments.

The second and third approaches are internal validation procedures. The procedures are called internal because the data used to validate equivalence are derived from the instrument itself. The second approach involves intra-cultural techniques in which empirical data are compared to theoretical expectations for each culture. It is possible to formulate hypotheses about the order of difficulty or endorsement rate of items in some instruments. For instance, items of tests of arithmetic abilities can often be ordered by the complexity of the arithmetical operation required. Operations requiring the manipulation of one-digit numbers will be easier than operations requiring two-digit numbers; additions and subtractions will be easier than multiplications and divisions. Strong evidence against scalar equivalence is obtained if theoretical expectations are not borne out. As a second example, the use of fit tests in applications of item response theory can be mentioned (e.g., Hambleton & Swaminathan, 1985; Lord, 1980; Van den Wollenberg, 1988). A good fit within each group provides initial evidence for scalar equivalence. Intracultural validation techniques provide necessary though insufficient evidence for the presence of scalar equivalence.

The third approach can be called *cross-cultural validation*. The best known example is the work on item bias, or differential item functioning (Berk, 1982; Holland & Wainer, 1993). Various psychometric techniques have been developed which scrutinize consequences of the lack of bias at the item level (cf. the description of item bias before).

A special case of the monotrait–multimethod approach, described earlier for the examination of method bias, is the use of multiple measures to capture the same construct. Triangulation, as this procedure is often called, can provide some insight in scalar equivalence, especially when the statistical techniques described in the previous section do not apply, such as in the case of single- item measures (e.g., measures in Piagetian psychology, social behavior). Triangulation amounts to utilizing multiple measures, as diverse as possible, to measure the construct. If convergent results are obtained with different measures, bias is not likely to have produced the results. For instance, Hess, Chang, and McDevitt (1987) found that in comparison with American mothers, Chinese mothers were more likely to attribute the academic performance of their children to effort. Consistent with this result, Chinese children were also more likely to attribute their academic performance to their own effort than were American children. The convergence between the children and mothers has strengthened the validity of the cultural difference observed. In contrast, Serpell's (1979) study of Zambian and Scottish children's copying skills using iron-wire models and pencil-drawing is an example of nonconvergent operations. It should be pointed out that although multiple measures can assess the confounding influence of bias, it does not guarantee scalar equivalence even when convergence is obtained. The equality of the origin and the unit of the measurement scale is not directly assessed in triangulation.

Statistical Tests of Cross-Cultural Differences: Introduction

The statistical techniques described in the previous section examine the cross-cultural applicability of research instruments and the validity of the use of these instruments in cross-cultural comparisons. In this section, we will describe statistical tests that are applied after the adequacy of the psychometric characteristics and the absence of bias have been established. A distinction between structure- and level-oriented techniques will be made in our presentation. Because of space limitation, we will only provide a brief overview of the statistical techniques.

Prior to any statistical analyses, it should be decided whether the data need to be standardized, and if so, which standardization procedure is to be used (e.g., Hofstede, 1980; Leung & Bond, 1989). Culture-level analyses can yield strikingly dissimilar results for standardized and nonstandardized data sets. Standardization is usually defined as the computation of z scores ($z = (X - M)/S$, in which X is the score to be standardized, M is the mean and S is the standard deviation). Standardization is defined here more generally and refers both to z scores and to transformations to other deviance scores such as X/S and $X - M$. The aim of standardization is the reduction or elimination of unwanted intergroup differences such as those due to response sets. If scores are standardized per cultural group, intergroup differences in means, standard deviations, or both are eliminated. Such a procedure requires justification, because intergroup differences in average scores may not be exclusively due to response sets or other unwanted sources but may reflect valid differences. The justification is usually based on the presumed equality of averages across cultures. For instance, Schwartz (1992), who has transformed raw scores to deviations from the mean in his value survey, argues that the average importance score that people give to all the value items in his inventory should be similar across individuals, because his instrument represents a comprehensive set of human values. If such a reasoning cannot be justified, analyses based on the original as well as the standardized data should be conducted and the results obtained compared.

Statistical Tests of Cross-Cultural Differences: Level-Oriented Techniques

The most frequently reported statistical tests of *level* differences are the *t* test and analysis of variance (e.g., Glass & Hopkins, 1984; Hays, 1994). The most commonly tested null hypothesis specifies that there are no intergroup differences. In a *t* test, the cultural group is the independent variable and the score on a psychological instrument is the dependent variable. The popularity of the *t* test, in cross-cultural psychology as well as elsewhere, is undoubtedly attributed to its simplicity, availability (in computer packages), and robustness against violations of assumptions. The same holds for the analysis of variance, which is carried out when data of more than two cultural groups are studied. The major interest tends to be in the main effect for culture, which, assuming that the effect is significant, indicates that at least one culture has an average on the dependent variable different from the other cultures. More complex designs, so-called factorial designs, are often reported in cross-cultural research. These are designs in which, in addition to culture, one or more independent variables, such as gender or age, are included. The inclusion of such additional variables, say gender, is particularly relevant when the reaction patterns of men and women are expected to differ across the cultures studied (e.g., the male–female differences on the dependent variable are more pronounced in one culture). These differences in reaction patterns will come out in an analysis of variance as a significant interaction of culture and gender.

Regression analysis is often used in level-oriented studies. Regression analysis evaluates the influence of one or more independent variables on a dependent variable in terms of the amount of variance in the dependent variable that the independent variables can explain. Regression coefficients express the degree of relationship between the independent and the dependent variables. The squared multiple correlation, another relevant statistic of the regression analysis, is the amount of variance explained by the independent variables, which gives an overall evaluation of the success of the independent variables in predicting variation in the dependent variable. In cross-cultural studies, level-oriented hypotheses involve a test of whether the intercept of a regression equation is similar across different cultural groups (Cohen & Cohen, 1983; Pedhazur, 1982).

Regression analysis can be carried out on raw or standardized scores (mean of zero and unit variance). Standardization affects the size of the coefficients, but leaves the significance level unaffected. In practice it has become more common to report standardized regression coefficients because they are independent of the measurement units of the independent variables.

The choice between an analysis of variance (or *t* test or *z* test) and a regression analysis mainly depends on the measurement level of the independent variables. Nominal and ordinal data are often analyzed in an analysis of variance, whereas predictors based on interval data are usually analyzed with a regression model. Yet, the choice is more a matter of convenience than of principle, given the close link between the two. Cohen and Cohen (1983) and Pedhazur (1982) describe how an analysis of variance can be seen as a regression analysis; the independent variables of an analysis of variance are the predictors of a regression analysis. The significance tests of the regression coefficients in the regression analysis (which are t tests) yield similar results as the significance tests of the analysis of variance (F test). Specifically, the squared t values of the regression statistics are equal to the F ratios of the analysis of variance.

Regression analyses can be used to identify relationships that hold both within and across cultures, which are actually structure-oriented issues. This approach is illustrated with two variables (X and Y). The first step in this technique is to obtain a pan-cultural regression equation of Y on X, in which data from all cultures are included. In the second step, culture is added as a dummy variable, and another regression analysis including X, the dummy variable, and the interaction of X and the dummy variables as predictors, is carried out. The multiple correlations of the two equations are then tested for equality. If there is no significant difference between these two multiple correlations, it is concluded that the relationship holds within each culture and across all cultures. In other words, the regression weights and the intercepts of the equation are similar in all cultures. A significant difference of the two multiple correlations points to the presence of intergroup differences on the dependent variable not explained by X. For an elaboration of this approach, see Leung (1987) and Poortinga and Van de Vijver (1987).

When more than one dependent variable is involved, covariance structure analysis employing models such as LISREL and EQS becomes appropriate. The basic idea is to test whether the interrelationships of the variables are similar in different cultures. For instance, confirmatory factor analysis involving two or more cultures is frequently conducted to see if a factor structure is similar in different cultures (e.g., De Groot, Koot, & Verhulst, 1994; Leung et al., 1992; Marsh & Byrne, 1993; Sachs, 1992; Watkins, 1989). The reader is referred to Poon, Chan, Lee, and Leung (1993) for a method to compare the equivalence of a covariance structure in a large number of cultures.

Multilevel analysis is another procedure that can be used to address both level- and structure-oriented issues (Bock, 1989; Bryk & Raudenbush, 1992; Goldstein, 1987; Lee, 1990). Even though these procedures have not been applied in cross-cultural research, their potential value is obvious. At least two levels of analysis are possible in cross-cultural research (e.g., Leung, 1989; Leung & Bond, 1989). In the culture-level approach, culture is the unit of analysis, and the results obtained are characterizations of cultures, but not individuals. The classic study on values by Hofstede (1980) is based on this approach. There is no assumption with regard to whether relationships found across cultures will hold within each of the cultures included in the analysis. Culture-level analyses can guard against the ecological fallacy, the incorrect application of culture-level characteristics to individuals. When a culture is known to be individualistic, the mean score on a scale of individualism will be higher than in a collectivistic culture, but it does not mean that each person has a high score on individualism. Furthermore, cross-level inferences can be fallacious because of a difference in meaning of constructs at individual and cultural levels. Gender at the individual level can have two values, male and female; an aggregated gender score at the cultural level refers to the proportion of males and females in a group, which is quite a different concept.

In the individual-level approach, the individual is the unit of analysis, and this is the dominant approach in cross-cultural psychology. The relationships between variables at individual and cultural levels need not be equal (cf. Ostroff, 1993). Yet, it is more elegant theoretically to demonstrate their equality. An example can be found in "subsystem validation," in which "hypotheses are examined both intraculturally and cross-culturally, so that explanatory variables may be tested at two levels" (Berry & Dasen, 1974, p. 19). The objective of this approach is to establish that the relationships among a set of variables hold within a culture as well as across cultures. For instance, in the classic study by Segall, Campbell, and Herskovits (1966), it was found that when a culture is associated with a more "carpentered" environment (more corners formed of intersecting planes perpendicular to each other), people from this culture are more susceptible to geometric illusions. This finding explains why one cultural group is more susceptible to geometric illusions than another cultural group. Their findings also imply that if a person is exposed to a more carpentered environment, he or she is more susceptible to geometric illusions. Thus, their findings are able to explain cultural differences as well as individual differences in susceptibility to geometric illusions.

Statistical Tests of Cross-Cultural Differences: Structure-Oriented Techniques

Cross-cultural psychologists are often interested in a comparison of the *structure* underlying the data rather than a direct comparison of the observed variables as discussed in the previous section. For instance, much research has been devoted to the question of whether the structure of intelligence is universal. Do the same cognitive processes contribute to test performance in different cultural groups? These questions have probably their intellectual roots in the notion of the psychic unity of humankind (Tylor, 1871), which can be interpreted as the idea that the structure behind human behavior is universal.

While multivariate statistical techniques are often applied in structure-oriented analysis, ANOVA or *t* tests are commonly applied when the independent variables are discrete. The focus is here to evaluate whether the differences of the dependent variable across the various levels of the independent variable are similar or different in each culture. For instance, Buss (1989) applied *t* tests to examine mate preferences of males and females in 33 cultures. He confirmed hypothesized gender differences in mate preferences in the cultures studied.

The similarity of psychological structure has been studied mostly by means of factor analysis (Harman, 1976; McDonald, 1985). Like regression analysis, factor analysis postulates that an observed score is a weighted sum of a usually limited set of contributing factors. Unlike in regression analysis, however, the contributing factors are not observable in factor analysis. An observed score, for example, an intelligence test score of a person, is a weighted sum of unobservable factor scores, such as reasoning ability, perceptual speed, and memory, which in turn are determined by subtests of the intelligent test. Based on the intercorrelations of the subtests, factor analysis determines the score of each person on the factors and the correlations of the subtests with the factors, the so-called factor loadings. We will not dwell upon the classical problems of factor analysis here, which include the determination of the number of factors and the rotation problem, because these problems are inherent to factor analysis and not unique to its cross-cultural applications.

When factor analysis is applied to cross-cultural data, one major question to be considered is the (lack of) similarity of the factor analytic solution across the groups. The question amounts to a check on the equality of the factor loadings. Do the instruments (tests, items, and observational measures) have the same correlations with the factors in each cultural group? The equality of the factor loadings is sometimes visually checked, which is a questionable practice as more powerful procedures exist.

Such a procedure starts with a so-called target rotation (e.g., McDonald, 1985). Factor analytic solutions can be freely rotated (the rotation problem). This subjectivity is usually "solved" by applying a rotation procedure such as Varimax. However, independently obtained factor loadings (no matter whether they are rotated by Varimax or any other rotation procedure) may be more similar than a visual inspection may suggest. The factor loading matrices may be rotated to each other in order to maximize their agreement. This is a legitimate procedure because of the arbitrariness of factor analytic solutions. In a target rotation the axes are rotated in such a way that the agreement between the sets of factor loadings is optimized. One of the groups is arbitrarily chosen as the target to which the factor loading matrices of the other groups will be rotated.

After having rotated the factor loadings, their similarity can be evaluated in a factor by factor comparison by means of a coefficient of agreement. The most often used coefficient of agreement has been developed by Tucker (1951); it has become known as *Tucker's coefficient of agreement* and also as proportionality coefficient (Zegers & Ten Berge, 1985). The coefficient is comparable to a correlation coefficient, the only difference is that, unlike a correlation coefficient, the coefficient of agreement is sensitive to a constant that is added to one of the variables. As an alternative to the coefficient of agreement, the identity coefficient can be proposed that is sensitive to any linear transformation (Zegers & Ten Berge, 1985). The coefficient is defined as

$$e_{xy} = \frac{2 \sum x_i y_i}{\sum x_i^2 + \sum y_i^2},$$

in which x_i and y_i represent the factor loadings in the two groups. As a rule of thumb, values of the identity coefficient lower than .90 are taken to point to a lack of agreement and values higher than .95 are seen as evidence for the similarity of the factor matrices.

Other procedures have also been developed to evaluate the agreement of factor analytic solutions across groups. Thus, equivalence of the Eysenck personality scales (e.g., Eaves, Eysenck, & Martin, 1989; Eysenck & Eysenck, 1983) has often been studied employing a procedure proposed by Kaiser, Hunka, and Bianchini (1971). There has been some debate as to whether procedures such as those proposed by Kaiser et al. (1971) or by Tucker (1951) are sufficiently powerful to detect item bias. Using simulated data, the critics (e.g., Bijnen, Van der Net, & Poortinga, 1986; Van de Vijver & Poortinga, 1994) have shown that values well over .90 can be obtained when in fact there are items with dissimilar loadings across groups. So, caution is required because these agreement indices sometimes do not reflect the influence of nonequivalent items.

Multidimensional scaling procedures have also been employed to compare the structure of cross-cultural data sets. An example can be found in the work of Schwartz (e.g., Schwartz, 1992, 1994; see also Endler, Lobel, Parker, & Schmitz, 1991; Russell, Lewicka, & Niit, 1989). Multidimensional scaling attempts to reproduce the distances between stimuli (such as test or item scores or behavioral measures) in a small number of dimensions. To compare multidimensional scaling solutions obtained in different groups, the technique has the same rotational problem as factor analysis. Distances between stimuli are not affected by (orthogonal) rotations of the axes. Consequently, configurations of such analyses as obtained in different cultural groups have an arbitrary spatial orientation. Target rotations have to be applied prior to an evaluation of the agreement of the solutions; when such rotations are not carried out, the agreement will be underestimated. The procedure of carrying out target rotations and computing an index of agreement of the solutions described above for factor analysis also applies here. No empirical applications of target rotations following a multidimensional scaling procedure are known to the authors.

Cluster analysis is another technique that aims to reduce a large set of correlations or distances to a smaller number of dimensions or factors. However, although this technique is suitable for cross-cultural research, it has not been used much in the cross-cultural literature.

The final techniques to be discussed here have also been mentioned in the discussion of level-oriented techniques, namely the analysis of covariance structures or linear structure models, which analyzes the covariance matrix of a set of measures (Bollen, 1989; Byrne, 1989). Two common computer packages for covariance modelling, namely LISREL (Byrne, 1989; Jöreskog & Sörbom, 1993) and EQS (Bentler, 1992; Byrne, 1994), can be used to analyze multigroup data. Several applications of linear structure models in cross-cultural research can be envisaged, including confirmatory factor analysis and the analysis of multitrait–multimethod (or monotrait–multitrait) matrices for assessing method bias. Confirmatory factor analysis is a versatile tool for testing cross-cultural differences in covariance structures. Compared to the classical factor analytic procedures described above, confirmatory factor analysis allows for the test of a large set of hierarchically linked hypotheses of cross-cultural invariance. The analyses usually consist of two series. The first analysis tests whether the covariance matrix of the measures is the same for all cultural groups. Fit tests play an essential role in covariance structure analysis. Unfortunately, fit tests in LISREL and EQS are not easy to interpret. The overall goodness-of-fit index is a chi-square distributed variable that is known to be sensitive to sample size; in large samples small inter-group differences in the covariance matrix will yield a significant value. Various fit measures have been developed that are less dependent on sample size (Bollen & Long, 1993).

If the null hypothesis is not rejected, it is highly likely that the psychological structure underlying the performance is identical across cultural groups. If the hypothesis of equal covariance matrices has to be rejected (which is usually the case), the second series of hypothesis testing will start. The second series consists of a set of hierarchically nested models that successively increase the number of equality constraints across groups. The choice of the models is free, but the order specified here (as well as in various other sources; e.g., Jöreskog & Sörbom, 1993; Vandenberg & Self, 1993; Van de Vijver & Harsveld, 1994) usually follows a theoretically relevant sequence. The first analysis of the second series specifies an equal number of factors in each group. The specification of the number of factors should be based on preliminary analyses or on earlier research findings. If the hypothesis of an equal number of factors has to be rejected, an exploratory factor analysis can be carried out to investigate the reason for the lack of fit; for instance, factors may have split up or merged in various cultural groups. If this is the case, the analyses may proceed with different numbers of factors across groups. A total lack of correspondence of the factors, after the possibilities of split and merged factors have been explored, would point to a small overlap in the psychological meaning of the instrument across the groups. Such a lack of correspondence can be expected for statistical reasons when many correlations in one or more groups are close to zero. The input variables of the factor analysis (item scores, test scores, etc.) are then largely independent of each other and the use of any multivariate technique should be strongly questioned.

The second step of the second series will test whether the matrix of factor loadings can be considered equal across the cultural groups. A set of factor loadings have to be left free in the first group; the values in the other groups are constrained to have the same values as the factor loadings in the first group. This will again yield various fit indices, among which are incremental fit indices. Because this model is subsumed in the previous model (stating an equal number of factors), the difference in the chi-square fit indices of the two models can be interpreted meaningfully: the difference in chi-square values follows a chi-square distribution with a number of degrees of freedom that is equal to the difference of the number of degrees of freedom of the two models. Acceptance of the hypothesis points to the equality of the composition of the latent factors across the groups. Rejection of the hypothesis provides evidence that the psychological structure underlying the data is dissimilar across the cultural groups. A better fit may be found when only a subset of the factor loadings are set equal to each other across cultural groups. If this is the case, subtle differences in the psychological structure have been observed. If an acceptable fit of a model specifying equal factor loadings is found, constraints can be added, such as equality of the covariance matrices of the latent factors in all groups. The study of the fit of hierarchically nested models provides a flexible tool to analyze covariance structures. It can be used to detect smaller or larger differences in psychological meaning of measurement instruments across cultural groups. For an example of confirmatory factor analysis in cross-cultural psychology, the reader is referred to Watkins (1989).

Covariance structure analysis can also be employed for causal modelling. A set of variables, either consisting of observed variables or of a combination of observed and latent (i.e., unobservable) variables, are assumed to have *a priori* specified antecedent–consequence relationships. The model can be based on theoretical expectations or an earlier exploratory study. In some cases the exploratory study and the test of the causal model are derived from random splits of the same sample; the model is then developed on half of the data and cross-validated in the other half. An example of a cross-cultural application of a causal model can be found in Van Haaften and Van de Vijver (in press). The number of applications of causal modelling in the cross-cultural literature is limited (cf., however, Little, Oettingen, & Baltes, 1995; Little, Oettingen, Stetsenko, & Baltes, 1995), but given its flexibility and usefulness, its use is recommended.

Covariance structure analysis can also be used to assess method bias, either in a test–retest design or in a monotrait–multimethod approach. In the latter case all methods that are employed (observed variables) load on the same latent factor(s). LISREL and EQS allow for a test of the similarity of the loadings of the methods across the two groups.

Finally, it should be pointed out that the distinction between level- and structure-oriented techniques is not strict in some statistical techniques. In regression, multilevel, and covariance modelling techniques, the differentiation between level- and structure-oriented questions is quite subtle. For instance, suppose that educational achievement is predicted on the basis of a set of aptitude tests in two different cultures and equality of regression lines is tested. Similarity of regression coefficients involves structural relationships whereas equality of the intercept would refer to level-oriented relationships. The same applies to multi-level models that can tackle both level- and structure-oriented questions. In empirical applications of covariance modelling there tends to be an emphasis on structural relationships. However, the models are sufficiently flexible to deal with inter-group differences in averages as well. In sum, the designation of regression and multilevel models as level-oriented and covariance modelling as structure-oriented is more inspired by their common usage than by theoretical characteristics of these models. They could as well be seen as hybrid models.

Four Common Types of Comparative Studies

In the remainder of the chapter we shall make a distinction between four types of cross-cultural studies, depending on whether the orientation is exploratory or hypothesis testing, and on whether or not contextual factors are considered (see Table 7–2).

TABLE 7–2   **Common types of comparative studies**

Consideration of contextual factors	Orientation	
	Hypothesis testing	Exploration
No	Generalizability	Psychological differences
Yes	Theory-driven	External validation

The first two types emphasize hypothesis testing. The first kind of studies, *generalizability studies*, attempts to establish the generalizability of research findings obtained in one, typically Western, group to other Western or non-Western groups. In general, these studies make little or no reference to local cultural elements.

In the second type, called *theory-driven studies*, cultural factors are part of the theoretical framework. Cultural variation is deliberately sought as a validation of the model, and specific *a priori* predictions are proposed and tested. The framework is tested by sampling various cultures that differ on some focal dimension. Theory-driven studies test a theory about a particular relationship between cultural variables and a psychological outcome. Contextual elements are crucial in this type of studies.

Hypothesis testing receives little emphasis in the following two types of cross-cultural research. The first type, *psychological differences* studies, is probably most common in the literature. A measurement instrument is applied in at least two cultures and the researcher is interested in whether there are any differences in averages, standard deviations, reliabilities, or other psychometric properties of the instrument across the cultural groups. Usually, the original instrument has been applied before in a Western context, and an application of the instrument in another cultural group is thought to provide an interesting extension. There is often no compelling theory about the nature of the cross-cultural differences to be expected. Contextual factors are typically not included in the design, and post hoc explanations are invoked to interpret the cross-cultural differences observed.

The last type of cross-cultural research refers to what has been called *external validation,* which attempts to explore the meaning and causes of cross-cultural differences with the aid of contextual factors. In this type of studies, specific *a priori* hypotheses are absent and usually a large set of contextual variables are included in an exploratory manner. Only a few statistical techniques have been applied in external validation studies. Regression analysis is the most frequently applied technique, which assesses the effectiveness of independent variables in explaining cross-cultural variations in the dependent variable. This kind of validation does not address structural or scalar equivalence, but aims at providing evidence for a particular interpretation of cross-cultural differences.

Poortinga and Van de Vijver (1987) have outlined a general procedure for external validation with the inclusion of covariates. The procedure presupposes that data (tests, observational instruments, interviews, surveys, etc.) are collected in at least two cultural groups. Data should also be collected on additional variables, termed *context variables*, that are likely to be able to explain cross-cultural differences that may be obtained. The data analysis starts with an analysis of variance to test the null hypothesis of no cultural differences. In the next analysis context variables are introduced; they are used as covariates in an analysis of covariance or as predictors in a regression analysis. In terms of an analysis of variance, the main effect of culture is tested twice; the first analysis tests group differences before correction for context variables; the second analysis tests intergroup differences in residual scores after orrection. Let us call the corresponding F ratios F_1 and F_2, respectively. Significant F values point to intergroup differences. A comparison of the significance of F_1 and F_2 can yield various possibilities. If F_1 is not significant, there are no intergroup differences to be explained (even though there is still a remote possibility that the introduction of context variables could reveal significant intergroup differences). Context variables will play a central role when F_1 is significant. Introduction of context variables can give rise to three possibilities. First, context variables may be unrelated to the dependent variable, in which case intergroup differences cannot be accounted for by these context variables. Second, context variables can be related to the dependent variable and intergroup differences on the dependent variable become smaller after correction, but they are still significant. In this case context variables provide a partial explanation of intergroup differences. Third, when F_2 is not significant, intergroup differences can be accounted for entirely by the context variables.

It should be pointed out that internal and external validation procedures have different goals. Internal validation aims at establishing the cross-cultural equivalence of the data. The key question is to ascertain whether the scores of individuals in all cultural groups can be directly compared. In external validation procedures, scalar equivalence is assumed, and the research goal is to shed light on the meaning and interpretation of the cross-cultural differences. In other words, internal validation procedures attempt to detect and remove culturally biased items, whereas external validation procedures attempt to explore the causes of cross-cultural differences observed.

Methods and Analysis of Four Common Types of Comparative Studies

In this section, the four types of cross-cultural studies—generalizability, theory-driven, psychological differences, and external validation—are examined with regard to the following issues: sampling of cultures and of subjects, procedure, design, analysis, and major strengths and weaknesses. See Table 7–3 for a summary. Examples from the literature will be described.

In *generalizability studies* a theory, a correlational or causal relationship, or an instrument derived from a theory is tested in another cultural context. The goal of the study is to establish the generalizability of the theory, the relationship, or

TABLE 7-3 Methods and analysis for the four common types of comparative studies

Type of study	Sampling of cultures	Design	Major analysis	Major strength	Major weakness
Generalizability	convenience	replication of original study or new study	structure techniques (e.g., correlations, factor analysis, analysis of co-variance structures)	study of equivalence	no contextual variables included
Psychological differences	systematic or convenience sampling	replication of original study or new study	both level (e.g., t test and ANOVA) and structure techniques	"openmindedness" about cross-cultural differences	ambiguous interpretation
Theory-driven	systematic (maximize contrast on focal variable)	new study; covariates may be included	both level and structure techniques	study of relationship of cultural factors and behavior	lack of attention to alternative interpretations
External validation	systematic	measures at different levels of aggregation; co-variates included	level techniques	focus on interpretation of cross-cultural differences	choice of covariate variables may be meaningless

the instrument. The cultures are often chosen on the basis of convenience sampling. Two different subject sampling schemes can be applied: random or matched sampling. Generalizability will be high when the original results are replicated and the subjects are sampled randomly. However, a lack of replicability cannot be interpreted unambiguously in random sampling. Negative findings could be due to cultural differences or to a lack of equivalence of the samples. A new data set using matched samples is then required to establish a more unambiguous interpretation. The procedure of the study usually follows the procedure of the original one; in some cases stimuli may be added to enhance the appropriateness of the instrument for the local context. The design, too, is a replication of the original one.

For replications, data analysis will consist of two parts: the first part will be identical to the analysis of the original study. Second, because the establishment of generalizability is the aim of the study, an assessment of the similarity of the original and new results is required. Factor analyses, followed by target rotation and the computation of an index of agreement or multigroup analyses of covariance structures, are to be preferred over a more informal evaluation of the similarity of the outcome. Compared to studies in which results can be constrasted with those obtained in previous studies conducted in other cultures, studies that are conducted simultaneously in a number of cultures will employ more exploratory data analyses for identifying cultural similarities and differences in the results.

The major strength of generalizability studies is their ability to test the equivalence of the results across cultures. As prior data are available with which new data sets can be compared, various hypotheses about cross-cultural differences and similarities can be investigated. A weakness of generalizability studies is that they often fail to include contextual variables. If cultural differences are found, it is often not at all clear how these should be interpreted. Furthermore, bias analyses are infrequently carried out in these studies. Thus, it is too common to take unexpected differences in item scores at face value (instead of carrying out an item bias analysis).

Most examples of generalizability studies in the literature involve studies of applications of an instrument, derived from a theory. Schwartz (1992) has collected data from various countries on the universality of the structure of human values. Irvine (1979) and Vernon (1969, 1979) have compared the structure of intelligence across cultures. A study of the choice of conflict resolution procedures (Leung, 1987) is an example of a cross-cultural study of a causal relationship. Amir and Sharon's (1987) replication of Western social–psychological studies in Israel among high school and university students is another good example of a generalizability study. Finally, there are many attempts recently to validate the big-five personality factors in a variety of cultures (e.g., McCrae & Costa, 1985; McCrae & John, 1992).

In *theory-driven studies*, cultures are often systematically sampled in order to maximize their contrast on some focal variable. The sampling of subjects requires scrutiny. The cultures in the sample will often differ in many more respects than those intended and of interest to the researcher. As the matching of the groups on all relevant ambient variables cannot be achieved, contextual measures should be added to enhance the interpretability of the findings. The measurement instruments should assess various other variables on which the cultures differ and which could obscure the cross-cultural differences being studied. The experimental procedure used is often similar across cultures. Because theory-driven studies are usually level-oriented studies, data analysis usually involves analysis of variance or covariance. In the latter case the context variables are the covariates.

The most important strength of theory-driven studies is the explicit postulation of the relationship between cultural factors and the focal behavior, which is often considered the main goal of cross-cultural psychology (e.g., Berry, Poortinga, Segall, & Dasen, 1992). The major weakness of theory-driven studies is their lack of attention to item bias and alternative explanations for the cross-cultural differences observed.

An example of a theory-driven study without covariates is Berry's (1976; Berry et al., 1986) study of the cognitive styles of hunters and food gatherers. Cultural variations in perceptual styles, educational patterns, and societal structures are all hypothesized to be interrelated and to be functionally related to the food gathering patterns of a cultural group. An example with a covariate is Earley's (1989) study in which American subjects were found to show more social loafing (the phenomenon that people work less when they are in a group than when they have to do the same task individually) than Chinese subjects. In the study, subjects' individualism–collectivism score was measured as a covariate. After controlling for cross-cultural differences in individualism–collectivism in an analysis of covariance, the cross-cultural differences in social loafing disappeared. The covariance analysis provided strong evidence for the role of individualism–collectivism in explaining cross-cultural differences in social loafing.

Studies of *psychological differences* involve the application of a measurement instrument such as a test, an interview scheme, or an observation scale, in a new cultural context. The purpose is to explore cross-cultural differences either in the magnitude recorded by the instrument or in the structure underlying the instrument. Many articles in the *Journal of Cross–Cultural Psychology* fall into this category. For instance, Guida and Ludlow (1989) compared the test anxiety of American and Chilean school children and found that for upper and middle-class subjects, American subjects reported a lower level of test anxiety than Chilean subjects. Two post hoc explanations were then given to explain this finding, none of which was tested in the study.

Two schemes for sampling cultures are employed: systematic and convenience sampling. The subjects can be chosen freely, and as usual, a choice has to be made between matched or random sampling. The procedure will typically amount to the administration of a translated instrument in a new culture. If the instrument has been applied before, the design of the previous study will usually be replicated. Covariates are typically not included in this type of study. The statistical analysis can be based on either level- or structure-oriented techniques. Quite often both aspects are combined; evidence is first provided for the similarity of psychometric properties (e.g., reliability analysis, factor analysis and target rotations, or analysis of covariance structures), followed by an analysis of variance or *t* test at the item level.

The strength of psychological differences studies is their "open-mindedness" about the presence or absence of cross-cultural differences, a useful strategy to explore cross-cultural differences. When no cross-cultural differences are observed, it is quite likely that neither bias nor intergroup differences exist. The weaknesses of the studies are rather severe. The occurrence of bias is usually not explored. Also, because of the absence of context variables in these studies, the interpretation of the cross-cultural differences observed is not self-evident. It is often difficult to evaluate post hoc interpretations put forward to explain the observed cross-cultural differences. Finally, "fishing" may occur (Cook & Campbell, 1979). It is common that a large number of statistical tests are conducted to test the null hypothesis of no cultural differences. Such multiple testing procedures ("fishing" for significance) can easily lead to the false rejection of the null hypothesis, and hence to incorrect conclusions about the occurrence of cross-cultural differences. Various simple remedies have been proposed in the literature, such as post hoc procedures in analysis of variance or Bonferroni procedures (e.g., Glass & Hopkins, 1984; Hays, 1994). These procedures control for Type I errors when a large number of statistical tests are performed.

External validation studies start from observed cross-cultural differences. These studies aim to identify an appropriate interpretation of the differences. In some cases, external validation is based on previous studies (either generalizability or psychological differences studies) in which cross-cultural differences are reported, while in other cases the observation of cross-cultural differences and external validation are combined in one study. In both cases the choice of cultures, subjects, procedure, and design are straightforward. External validation studies usually involve survey data or secondary data (i.e., data derived from other sources, such as information on national income). External validation studies may be based on various aggregation levels (cf. the section on multilevel modelling). Most frequently reported are the individual level (e.g., when a test of individualism–collectivism is administered and is used as a covariate), an intermediate level (e.g., family and school), and the cultural level (e.g., gross national product, population density). Culture-level data can be derived from various sources such as the Human Relations Area Files (HRAF files; Barry, 1980), other cross-cultural research, and yearbooks of national and international organizations such as OECD, WHO, and UNICEF.

External validation studies are either exploratory in clarifying sources of cross-cultural differences. Analysis of covariance, regression, and causal modelling are the major statistical techniques for studying external validation.

The strength of this approach is its focus on the interpretation of cross-cultural differences, an often neglected issue in cross-cultural psychology. In principle, external validation provides a refutable framework for interpretation. However, the choice of variables and the level of analysis may be arbitrary or meaningless from a psychological point of view. As an example, the distance from a country's capital to the equator has been found to be a good predictor of various psychological test scores, for example, of cognitive tests. It is obvious that the statistical result does not convey much information about the psychological variables underlying the performance differences.

Examples of this approach can be found in the work of Bond (1991) and Williams and Best (1982). These authors first demonstrated cross-cultural differences (in health measures in Bond's study and in gender stereotypes in Williams and Best's studies). They then related the differences to a wide variety of culture-level measures, such as values, GNP, and per capita expenditure on education and health. The results obtained allow them to interpret the cross-cultural differences observed in terms of these external variables.

Conclusion

The research question or hypothesis, method, and data analysis of cross-cultural studies are closely related. Only properly chosen methods and data analytical procedures will permit an unbiased evaluation of proposed theoretical formulations. In cross-cultural psychology, the interpretation of the meaning of research findings is crucial but evasive. Many interpretations can usually be generated to explain a cross-cultural difference, and it is often difficult to assess their validity. The best approach is to formulate a number of rival hypotheses on an *a priori* basis and design studies that are able to rule out inappropriate explanations. In our opinion, knowledge in cross-cultural psychology accumulates at an unnecessarily slow pace primarily because many cross-cultural researchers rely heavily on post hoc theorizing. This chapter is meant to encourage cross-cultural researchers to place more emphasis on methods and data analysis to improve the effectiveness of their studies. It is also hoped that the chapter will dispel the myth that methodological and statistical sophistication is an obstacle or a distraction in the research enterprise. Quite the contrary, proper methods and data analytical procedures can help clarify conceptual ambiguities, disentangle the influence of confounding variables, and rule out invalid interpretations of cross-cultural differences. Berry (1980) has stated clearly that "Cross-cultural psychology is defined primarily by its *method*" (p. 1, italic in original). Researchers who are committed to cross-cultural research should take methodological issues seriously. This chapter may facilitate cross-cultural researchers to take full advantage of the methodological and statistical procedures available for shaping their work and contributing to the advancement of the field.

References

Allen, M. A., & Yen, W. M. (1979). *Introduction to measurement theory.* Monterey, CA : Brooks/ Cole.

Amir, Y., & Sharon, I. (1987). Are social psycho-

logical laws cross-culturally valid? *Journal of Cross-Cultural Psychology, 18,* 383–470.

Anastasi, A. (1976). *Psychological testing* (4th ed.). New York: Macmillan.

Angoff, W. H. (1982). Use of difficulty and discrimination indices for detecting item bias. In R. A. Berk (Ed.), *Handbook of methods for detecting bias* (pp. 96–116). Baltimore, MD: Johns Hopkins University Press.

Barry, H. (1980). Descriptions and uses of the Human Relations Area Files. In H. C. Triandis & J. W. Berry (Eds.), *Handbook of cross-cultural psychology* (Vol. 2, pp. 445–478). Boston: Allyn and Bacon.

Bentler, P. M. (1992). *EQS structural equation program manual.* Los Angeles: BMDP Statistical Software.

Berk, R. A. (Ed.). (1982). *Handbook of methods for detecting item bias.* Baltimore: Johns Hopkins University Press.

Berry, J. W. (1967). Independence and conformity in subsistence-level societies. *Journal of Personality and Social Psychology, 7,* 415–418.

Berry, J. W. (1969). On cross-cultural comparability. *International Journal of Psychology, 4,* 119–128.

Berry, J. W. (1976). *Human ecology and cognitive style: Comparative studies in cultural and psychological adaptation.* Beverly Hills, CA: Sage.

Berry, J. W. (1980). Introduction to methodology. In H. C. Triandis & J. W. Berry (Eds.), *Handbook of cross-cultural psychology* (Vol. 1, pp. 1–28). Boston: Allyn and Bacon.

Berry, J. W., & Dasen, P. R. (Eds.) (1974). *Culture and cognition: Readings in cross-cultural psychology.* London: Methuen.

Berry, J. W., Poortinga, Y. H., Segall, M. H., & Dasen, P. R., (1992). *Cross-cultural psychology. Research and applications.* Cambridge: Cambridge University Press.

Berry, J. W., Van de Koppel, J. M. H., Sénéchal, C., Annis, R. C., Bahuchet, S., Cavalli-Sforza, L. L., & Witkin, H. A. (1986). *On the edge of the forest: Cultural adaptation and cognitive development in Central Africa.* Lisse: Swets & Zeitlinger.

Bijnen, E. J., Van der Net, T. Z. J., & Poortinga, Y. H. (1986). On cross-cultural comparative studies with the Eysenck Personality Questionnaire. *Journal of Cross-Cultural Psychology, 17,* 3–16.

Bock, D. (1989). *Multilevel analysis of educational data.* New York: Academic Press.

Bollen, K. J. (1989). *Structural equations with latent variables.* New York: Wiley.

Bollen, K. J., & Long, J. S. (Eds.). (1993). *Testing structural equation models.* Newbury Park, CA: Sage.

Bond, M. H. (1991). Chinese values and health: A cross-cultural examination. *Psychology and Health, 5,* 137–152.

Brislin, R. W. (1980). Translation and content analysis of oral and written material. In H. C. Triandis & J. W. Berry (Eds.), *Handbook of cross-cultural psychology* (Vol. 1, pp. 389–444). Boston: Allyn and Bacon.

Brislin, R. W., Lonner, W. J., & Thorndike, R. (1973). *Cross-cultural research methods.* New York: Wiley.

Brown, E. D., & Sechrest, L. (1980). Experiments in cross-cultural research. In H. C. Triandis & J. W. Berry (Eds.), *Handbook of cross-cultural psychology* (Vol. 2, pp. 297–318). Boston: Allyn and Bacon.

Bryk, A. S. & Raudenbush, W. (1992). *Hierarchical linear models: Applications and data analysis methods.* Newbury Park, CA: Sage.

Buss, D. (1989). Sex differences in human mate preferences: Evolutionary hypotheses tested in 37 cultures. *Behavioral and Brain Sciences, 12,* 1–49.

Buss, D. M., Abbott, M., Angleitner, A., Asherian, A., Biaggio, A., Blanco-Villasenor, A., Bruchon-Schweitzer, M., Ch'u, H., Czapinski, J., De Raad, B., Ekehammar, B., El Lohamy, N., Fioravanti, M., Georgas, J., Gerde, P., Guttman, R., Hazan, F., Iwawaki, S., Janakiramaiah, N., Khosrokhani, F., Kreitner, S., Lachenicht, L., Lee, M., Liik, M., Little, B., Mika, S., Moadel-Shadid, M., Moane, G., Montero, M., Mundy-Castle, A. C., Niit, T., Nsenduluka, E., Pienkowski, R., Pirttila-Blackman, A-M., Ponce de Leon, J., Rousseau, J., Runco, M. A., Safir, M. P., Samuels, C. Sanitioso, R., Serpell, R., Smid, N., Spencer, C., Tadinac, M., Todorova, E. N., Troland, K., Van den Brande, L., Van Heck, G., Van Langenhove, L., & Yang, K-S. (1990). International preferences in selecting mates. A study of 37 cultures. *Journal of Cross-Cultural Psychology, 21,* 5–47.

Byrne, B. M. (1989). *A primer of LISREL: Basic ap-*

plications and programming for confirmatory factor analytic models. New York: Springer.

Byrne, B. M. (1994). *Structural equation modelling with EQS and EQS/Windows: Basic concepts, applications, and programming*. Thousand Oaks, CA: Sage.

Campbell, D. T. (1986). Science's social system of validity-enhancing collective believe change and the problems of the social sciences. In D. W. Fiske & R. A. Shweder (Eds.), *Metatheory in social science* (pp. 108–135). Chicago: University of Chicago Press.

Campbell, D. T., & Stanley, J. C. (1966). *Experimental and quasi-experimental designs for research*. Chicago: Rand McNally.

Candell, G. L., & Hulin, C. L. (1987). Cross-language and cross-cultural comparisons in scale translations: Independent sources of information about item nonequivalence. *Journal of Cross-Cultural Psychology, 17*, 417–440.

Cattell, R. B. (1940). A culture-free intelligence test, I. *Journal of Educational Psychology, 31*, 176–199.

Cattell, R. B., & Cattell, A. K. S. (1963). *Culture Fair Intelligence Test*. Champaign, IL: Institute for Personality and Ability Testing.

Cheung, F. M. (1989). A review on the clinical applications of the Chinese MMPI. *Psychological Assessment, 3*, 230–237.

Cheung, F. M., Leung, K., Fan, R. M., Song, W. Z., Zhang, J. X., & Chang, J. P. (1996). Development of the Chinese Personality Assessment Inventory (CPAI). *Journal of Cross- Cultural Psychology, 27*, 181–199.

Chinese Culture Connection (1987). Chinese values and the search for culture-free dimensions of culture. *Journal of Cross-Cultural Psychology, 18*, 143–164.

Church, T. A. (1987). Personality research in a non-Western setting: The Philippines. *Psychological Bulletin, 102*, 272–292.

Cicchetti, D. V., Showalter, D., & McCarthy, P. (1990). A computer program for calculating subject-by-subject kappa or weighted kappa coefficients. *Educational and Psychological Measurement, 50*, 153–158.

Clauser, B. E., Mazor, K. M., & Hambleton, R. K. (1994). The effects of score group width on the Mantel-Haenszel procedure. *Journal of Educational Measurement, 31*, 67–78.

Cleary, T. A., & Hilton, T. L. (1968). An investigation of item bias. *Educational and Psychological Measurement, 28*, 61–75.

Cohen, J. (1960). A coefficient of agreement for nominal scales. *Educational and Psychological Measurement, 20*, 37–46.

Cohen, J., & Cohen, P. (1983). *Applied multiple regression/correlation analysis* (2nd ed.). Hillsdale, NJ: Erlbaum.

Cook, T. D., & Campbell, D. T. (1979). *Quasi-experimentation: Design and analysis issues for field settings*. Chicago: Rand McNally.

De Groot, A., Koot, H. M., & Verhulst, F. C. (1994). Cross-cultural generalizability of the Child Behavior Checklist cross-informant syndromes. *Psychological Assessment, 6*, 225–230.

Deregowski, J. B., & Serpell, R. (1971). Performance on a sorting task: A cross-cultural experiment. *International Journal of Psychology, 6*, 273–281.

Dorans, N. J., & Kulick, E. (1986). Demonstrating the utility of the standardization approach to assessing unexpected differential item performance on the scholastic aptitude test. *Journal of Educational Measurement, 23*, 355–368.

Draguns, J. (1989). Normal and abnormal behavior in cross-cultural perspective: Specifying the nature of their relationship. *Nebraska Symposium on Motivation, 37*, 235–277. Lincoln, NE: University of Nebraska Press.

Earley, C. (1989). Social loafing and collectivism: A comparison of the United States and the People's Republic of China. *Administrative Science Quarterly, 34*, 565–581.

Eaves, L. J., Eysenck, H. J., & Martin, N. G. (1989). *Genes, culture and personality: An empirical approach.* London: Academic Press.

Ellis, B. B. (1989). Differential item functioning: Implications for test translations. *Journal of Applied Psychology, 74*, 912–921.

Ellis, B. B., & Kimmel, H. D. (1992). Identification of unique cultural response patterns by means of item response theory. *Journal of Applied Psychology, 77*, 177–184.

Embretson, S. E. (1983). Construct validity: Construct representation versus nomothetic span. *Psychological Bulletin, 93*, 179-197.

Endler, N. S., Lobel, T., Parker, J. D., & Schmitz, P. (1991). Multidimensionality of state and trait anxiety: A cross-cultural study comparing American, Canadian, Israeli and German young adults. *Anxiety Research, 3,* 257–272.

Eysenck, H. J., & Eysenck, S. B. J. (1983). Recent advances in the cross-cultural study of personality. In J. N. Butcher & C. D. Spielberger (Eds.), *Advances in personality assessment* (Vol. 2, pp. 41–69). Hillsdale, NJ: Erlbaum.

Feldman, S. S., Rosenthal, D. A., Mont-Reynaud, R., Leung, K., & Lau, S. (1991). Ain't misbehavin': Adolescent values and family environments as correlates of misconduct in Australia, Hong Kong, and the United States. *Journal of Research on Adolescence, 1,* 109–134.

Frijda, N., & Jahoda, G. (1966). On the scope and methods of cross-cultural research. *International Journal of Psychology, 1,* 109–127.

Glass, G. V., & Hopkins, K. D. (1984). *Statistical methods in education and psychology* (2nd ed.). Englewood Cliffs, NJ: Prentice-Hall.

Goldstein, H. (1987). *Multilevel models in educational and social research.* New York: Oxford University Press.

Guida, F. V., & Ludlow, L. H. (1989). A cross-cultural study of test anxiety. *Journal of Cross-Cultural Psychology, 20,* 178–190.

Hakstian, A. R., & Whalen, T. E. (1976). A *k*-sample significance test for independent alpha coefficients. *Psychometrika, 41,* 219–231.

Hambleton, R. K. (1993). Translating achievement tests for use in cross-national studies. *European Journal of Psychological Assessment, 9,* 57–68.

Hambleton, R. K. (1994). Guidelines for adapting educational and psychological tests: A progress report. *European Journal of Psychological Assessment (Bulletin of the International Test Commission), 10,* 229–244.

Hambleton, R. K., & Swaminathan, H. (1985). *Item response theory: Principles and applications.* Dordrecht: Kluwer-Nijhoff.

Harkness, S., & Super, C. M. (1990). Culture and psychopathology. In M. Lewis & S.

M. Miller (Eds.), *Handbook of developmental psychopathology. Perspectives in developmental psychology* (pp. 41–52). New York: Plenum Press.

Harman, H. H. (1976). *Modern factor analysis* (3rd rev. ed.). Chicago: University of Chicago Press.

Hays, W. L. (1994). *Statistics* (5th ed.). Orlando, FL: Harcourt Brace & Company.

Hess, R. D., Chang, C. M., & McDevitt, T. M. (1987). Cultural variations in family beliefs about children's performance in mathematics: Comparisons among People's Republic of China, Chinese-American, and Caucasian-American families. *Journal of Educational Psychology, 79,* 179–188.

Ho, D. Y. F. (in press). Filial piety and its psychological consequences. In M. H. Bond (Ed.), *Handbook of Chinese Psychology.* Hong Kong: Oxford University Press.

Hofstede, G. (1980). *Culture's consequences: International differences in work-related values.* Beverly Hills, CA: Sage.

Hofstede, G. (1983). Dimensions of national cultures in fifty countries and three regions. In J. B. Deregowski, S. Dziurawiec, & R. C. Annis (Eds.), *Expiscations in cross-cultural psychology* (pp. 335–355). Lisse: Swets & Zeitlinger.

Holland, P. W., & Thayer, D. T. (1988). Differential item performance and the Mantel-Haenszel procedure. In H. Wainer & H. I. Braun (Eds.), *Test validity* (pp. 129–145). Hillsdale, NJ: Erlbaum.

Holland, P. W., & Wainer, H. (Eds.). (1993). *Differential item functioning.* Hillsdale, NJ: Erlbaum.

Hulin, C. L. (1987). Psychometric theory of item and scale translations: Equivalence across languages. *Journal of Cross-Cultural Psychology, 18,* 115–142.

Irvine, S. H. (1979). The place of factor analysis in cross-cultural methodology and its contribution to cognitive theory. In L. Eckensberger, W. Lonner, & Y. H. Poortinga (Eds.), *Cross-cultural contributions to psychology* (pp. 300–341). Lisse: Swets & Zeitlinger.

Irvine, S. H., & Carroll, W. K. (1980). Testing and assessment across cultures. In H. C. Triandis & J. W. Berry (Eds.), *Handbook of cross-cultural psychology* (Vol. 2, pp. 181–244). Boston: Allyn and Bacon.

Jensen, A. R. (1980). *Bias in mental testing.* New York: Free Press.

Jöreskog, K. G., & Sörbom, D. (1993) *LISREL 8.* Chicago: Scientific Software International.

Kaiser, H. F., Hunka, S., & Bianchini, J. (1971). Relating factors between studies based upon different individuals. *Multivariate Behavioral Research, 6,* 409–422.

Kendall, I. M., Verster, M. A., & Von Mollendorf, J. W. (1988). Test performance of blacks in South Africa. In S. H. Irvine & J. W. Berry (Eds.), *Human abilities in cultural context* (pp. 299–339). Cambridge: Cambridge University Press.

Kraemer, H. C. (1981). Extension of Feldt's approach to testing homogeneity of coefficients of reliability. *Psychometrika, 46,* 41–45.

Lee, S. Y. (1990). Multilevel analysis of structural equation models. *Biometrika, 77,* 763–772.

Leung, K. (1987). Some determinants of reactions to procedural models for conflict resolution. *Journal of Personality and Social Psychology, 53,* 898–908.

Leung, K. (1989). Cross-cultural differences: Individual-level vs. culture-level analysis. *International Journal of Psychology, 24,* 703-719.

Leung, K., Au, Y., Fernandez-Dols, J. M., & Iwawaki, S. (1992). Preference for methods of conflict processing in two collectivist cultures. *International Journal of Psychology, 27,* 195-209.

Leung, K., & Bond, M. H. (1989). On the empirical identification of dimensions for cross-cultural comparison. *Journal of Cross-Cultural Psychology, 20,* 133-151.

Leung, K., & Drasgow, F. (1985). Relation between self-esteem and delinquent behavior in three ethnic groups: An application of item response theory. *Journal of Cross-Cultural Psychology, 17,* 151–167.

Leung, K., & Zhang, J. X. (1995). Systemic consideration: Factors facilitating and impeding the development of psychology in developing countries. *International Journal of Psychology, 30,* 693–706.

Little, T. D., Oettingen, G., & Baltes, P. B. (1995). *The revised Control, Agency, and Means- Ends Interview (CAMI).* Berlin: Max-Planck-Institut für Bildungsforschung.

Little, T. D., Oettingen, G., Stetsenko, A., & Baltes, P. B. (1995). Children's action-control beliefs and school performance: How do American children compare with German and Russian children? *Journal of Personality and Social Psychology, 69,* 686–700.

Lord, F. M. (1967). A paradox in the interpretation of group comparisons. *Psychological Bulletin, 68,* 304–305.

Lord, F. M. (1977). A study of item bias, using Item Characteristic Curve Theory. In Y. H. Poortinga (Ed.), *Basic problems in cross-cultural psychology* (pp. 19–29). Lisse: Swets & Zeitlinger.

Lord, F. M. (1980). *Applications of item response theory to practical testing problems.* Hillsdale, NJ: Erlbaum.

Marsh, H. W., & Byrne, B. M. (1993). Confirmatory factor analysis of multigroup-multimethod self-concept data: Between-group and within-group invariance constraints. *Multivariate Behavioral Research, 28,* 313–349.

McCrae, R. R., & Costa, P. T. (1985). Updating Norman's "adequacy taxonomy": Intelligence and personality dimensions in natural language and in questionnaires. *Journal of Personality and Social Psychology, 49,* 710–721.

McCrae, R. R., & John, O. P. (1992). An introduction to the five-factor model and its applications. *Journal of Personality, 60,* 175–215.

McCauley, C. D., & Mendoza, J. (1985). A simulation study of item bias using a two-parameter item response model. *Applied Psychological Measurement, 9,* 389–400.

McDonald, R. P. (1985). *Factor analysis and related methods.* Hillsdale, NJ: Erlbaum.

Mellenbergh, G. J. (1982). Contingency table models for assessing item bias. *Journal of Educational Statistics, 7,* 105–118.

Ostroff, C. (1993). Comparing correlations based on individual-level and aggregated data. *Journal of Applied Psychology, 78,* 569–582.

Pedhazur, E. J. (1982). *Multiple regression in behavioral research* (2nd ed.). New York: Holt, Rinehart, & Winston.

Peterson M. F., Smith, P. B., Akande, A., Ayestaran, S., Bochner, S., Callan, V., Cho, N. G., Jesuino, J. C., D'Amorim, M., Francois, P., Hofmann, K., Koopman, P. L., Leung, K., Lim, T. K., Mortazavi, S., Munene, J., Radford, M., Ropo, A., Savage, G., Setiadi, B., Sinha, T. N., Sorenson, R., & Viedge, C. (1995). Role conflict, ambiguity, and overload: A 21-nation study. *Academy of Management Journal, 38,* 429–452.

Poon, W. Y., Chan, W., Lee, S. Y., & Leung, K. (1993). Preliminary analysis of multiple group structural equation modelling via cluster analysis. *Proceedings of the American Statistical Association 1993 Convention, Social Statistics Section,* 368–373.

Poortinga, Y. H. (1971). Cross-cultural comparison of maximum performance tests: Some methodological aspects and some experiments with simple auditory and visual stimuli. *Psychologia Africana,* Monograph Supplement, No. 6.

Poortinga, Y. H. (1989). Equivalence of cross-cultural data: An overview of basic issues. *International Journal of Psychology, 24,* 737–756.

Poortinga, Y. H., & Malpass, R. S. (1986). Making inferences from cross-cultural data. In W. J. Lonner & J. W. Berry (Eds.), *Field methods in cross-cultural psychology* (pp. 17–46). Beverly Hills, CA: Sage.

Poortinga, Y. H., & Van de Vijver, F. J. R. (1987). Explaining cross-cultural differences: Bias analysis and beyond. *Journal of Cross-Cultural Psychology, 18,* 259–282.

Poortinga, Y.H., Van de Vijver, F. J. R., Joe, R. C., & Van de Koppel, J. M. H. (1987). Peeling the onion called culture: A synopsis. In C. Kagitcibasi (Ed.), *Growth and progress in cross-cultural psychology* (pp. 22–34). Lisse: Swets & Zeitlinger.

Poortinga, Y. H., & Van der Flier, H. (1988). The meaning of item bias in ability tests. In S. H. Irvine & J. W. Berry (Eds.), *Human abilities in cultural context* (pp. 166–183). Cambridge: Cambridge University Press.

Reuning, H., & Wortley, W. (1973). Psychological studies of the Bushmen. *Psychologia Africana,* Monograph Supplement, 7.

Roberts, J., & Sutton-Smith, B. (1962). Child training and game involvement. *Ethology, 1,* 166–185.

Russell, J. A., Lewicka, M., & Niit, T. (1989). A cross-cultural study of a circumplex model of affect. *Journal of Personality and Social Psychology, 57,* 848–856.

Sachs, J. (1992). Covariance structure analysis of a test of moral orientation and moral judgment. *Educational and Psychological Measurement, 52,* 825–833.

Scheuneman, J. D. (1987). An experimental, exploratory study of causes of bias in test items. *Journal of Educational Measurement, 24,* 97–118.

Schwartz, S. H. (1992). Universals in the content and structure of values: Theoretical advances and empirical tests in 20 countries. In M. Zanna (Ed.), *Advances in experimental social psychology* (Vol. 25, pp. 1–65). Orlando, FL: Academic Press.

Schwartz, S. H. (1994). Studying human values. In A. Bouvy, F. J. R. Van de Vijver, P. Boski, & P. Schmitz (Eds.), *Journeys into cross-cultural psychology* (pp. 239–254). Lisse: Swets & Zeitlinger.

Segall, M. H., Campbell, D. T., & Herskovits, M. J. (1966). *The influence of culture on visual perception.* Indianapolis, IN: Bobbs-Merrill.

Serpell, R. (1979). How specific are perceptual skills? *British Journal of Psychology, 70,* 365-380.

Serpell, R. (1993). *The significance of schooling. Life-journeys in an African society.* Cambridge: Cambridge University Press.

Shrout, P. E., & Fleiss, J. L. (1979). Intraclass correlations: Uses in assessing rater reliability. *Psychological Bulletin, 86,* 420–428.

Smith, P. B., & Peterson, M. F. (1988). *Leadership, organizations and culture.* Beverly Hills, CA: Sage.

Sternberg, R. J. (1985). Implicit theories of intelligence, creativity, and wisdom. *Journal of Personality and Social Psychology, 49,* 607–627.

Stricker, L. J. (1982). Identifying test items that perform differentially in population subgroups: A partial correlation index. *Applied Psychological Measurement, 6,* 261–273.

Super, C. M. (1981). Behavior development in infancy. In R. H. Munroe, R. L. Munroe, & B. B. Whiting (Eds.), *Handbook of cross-cultural human development* (pp. 181–270). New York: Garland SPTM Press.

Super, C. M. (1983). Cultural variation in the meaning and uses of children's "intelligence." In J. B. Deregowski, S. Dziurawiec, & R. C. Annis (Eds.), *Expiscations in cross-cultural psychology* (pp. 199–212). Lisse: Swets & Zeitlinger.

Tucker, L. R. (1951). *A method for synthesis of factor analysis studies* (Personnel Research Section Report No. 984). Washington, DC: Department of the Army.

Tylor, E. B. (1871). *Primitive culture* (2 vols.). London: Murray.

Van de Vijver, F. J. R. (1988). Systematizing item content in test design. In R. Langeheine & J. Rost (Eds.), *Latent trait and latent class models* (pp. 291–307). New York: Plenum.

Van de Vijver, F. J. R. (1994). Item bias: Where psychology and methodology meet. In A. Bouvy, F. J. R. Van de Vijver, P. Boski, & P. Schmitz (Eds.), *Journeys into cross-cultural psychology* (pp. 111–126). Lisse: Swets & Zeitlinger.

Van de Vijver, F. J. R., Daal, M., & Van Zonneveld, R. (1986). The trainability of abstract reasoning: A cross-cultural comparison. *International Journal of Psychology, 21,* 589–615.

Van de Vijver, F. J. R., & Harsveld, M. (1994). The incomplete equivalence of the paper-and-pencil and computerized version of the General Aptitude Test Battery. *Journal of Applied Psychology, 79,* 852–859.

Van de Vijver, F. J. R., & Poortinga, Y. H. (1982). Cross-cultural generalization and universality. *Journal of Cross-Cultural Psychology, 13,* 387–408.

Van de Vijver, F. J. R., & Poortinga, Y. H. (1991). Testing across cultures. In R. K. Hambleton & J. Zaal (Eds.), *Advances in educational and psychological testing* (pp. 277–308). Dordrecht: Kluwer.

Van de Vijver, F. J. R. & Poortinga, Y. H. (1992). Testing in culturally heterogeneous populations: When are cultural loadings undesirable? *European Journal of Psychological Assessment, 8,* 17–24.

Van de Vijver, F. J. R., & Poortinga, Y. H. (1994). Methodological issues in cross-cultural studies on parental rearing behavior and psychopathology. In C. Perris, W. A. Arrindell, M. Eisemann (Eds.), *Parental rearing and psychopathology* (pp. 173–197). Chicester: Wiley.

Van den Wollenberg, A. L. (1988). Testing a latent trait model. In R. Langeheine & J. Rost (Eds.), *Latent trait and latent class models* (pp. 31–50). New York: Plenum.

Van Haaften, E. H., & Van de Vijver, F. J. R. (in press). Psychological consequences of environmental degradation, *Journal of Health Psychology.*

Vandenberg, R. J., & Self, R. M. (1993). Assessing newcomers' changing commitments to the organization during the first 6 months of work. *Journal of Applied Psychology, 78,* 557–568.

Vernon, P. E. (1969). *Intelligence and cultural environment.* London: Methuen.

Vernon, P. E. (1979). *Intelligence: Heredity and environment.* San Francisco: Freeman.

Watkins, D. (1989). The role of confirmatory factor analysis in cross-cultural research. *International Journal of Psychology, 24,* 685–702.

Werner, O., & Campbell, D. T. (1970). Translating, working through interpreters, and the problem of decentering. In R. Naroll & R. Cohen (Eds.), *A handbook of cultural anthropology* (pp. 398–419). New York: American Museum of Natural History.

Whiting, B. B. (1976). The problem of the packaged variable. In K. Riegel & J. Meacham (Eds.), *The developing individual in a changing world* (Vol. 1, pp. 303–309). The Hague: Mouton.

Williams, J. E., & Best, D. L. (1982). *Measuring sex stereotypes: A thirty-nation study.* Beverly Hills, CA: Sage.

Wilss, W. (1982). *The science of translation: Problems and methods.* Tuebingen: Narr.

Winer, B. J. (1971). *Statistical principles in experimental design* (2nd ed.). New York: McGraw Hill.

Yang, K. S., & Bond, M. H. (1990). Exploring implicit personality theories with indigenous or imported constructs: The Chinese case. *Journal of Personality and Social Psychology, 58,* 1087–1095.

Zegers, F. E., & Ten Berge, J. M. F. (1985). A family of association coefficients for metric scales. *Psychometrika, 50,* 17–24.

8

CULTURE AS PROCESS: EMPIRICAL METHODS FOR CULTURAL PSYCHOLOGY

PATRICIA M. GREENFIELD[1]
University of California, Los Angeles
United States

Contents

Introduction

This chapter links concepts and methodology for the study of culture as psychological process. Methods must be based on a conceptual framework. In this chapter, the framework is the notion of culture as psychological process (Cole, 1995; Valsiner, 1989). This framework leads to particular kinds of research questions, which, in turn, implicate particular kinds of methods that are capable of addressing the original research questions. Because of the tight link between theory and method, methods are not theoretically neutral, but contain an implicit theory (e.g., Ochs, 1979). Beginning with a contrast between cultural and cross-cultural psychology, we lay claim to a series of methodological principles and practices that can guide research on cultural action and interaction, while revealing the ontogenetic, sociohistorical, and phylogenetic origins of human cultural processes. Where possible, sample studies that serve as models for a particular research method will be presented or cited.

Conceptual Framework

As a species, humans are biologically primed to create, acquire, and transmit culture. The creation, acquisition, transmission, and use of culture are psychological and interpsychological processes. It is the study of these processes that is the paradigmatic subject of cultural psychology. This chapter asks what methods and what methodology are suitable to the study of culture as psychological and interpsychological process.

The social interaction among beings biologically primed for culture creates culture for the group and for the individuals in it. Culture is therefore viewed as a socially interactive process with two main component processes: the creation of shared activity (cultural practices) and the creation of shared meaning (cultural interpretation). Empirical methodology must be adequate to study both shared meaning and shared activity, the two major embodiments of shared cultural knowledge.

Culture as shared activity is an important focus of methods for the study of everyday life. However, it is the human capacity to create shared meaning that produces the distinctive methodological contribution of cultural psychology. Indeed, the centrality of creating meaning in cultural processes and human life has profound methodological consequences. This is because not only subjects but also researchers are engaged in a meaning-making process.

How to do research that minimizes the researcher's projection of meaning onto the subject and sheds maximum light on the subject's creation of cultural meanings is a major methodological issue in cultural psychology. This issue leads to a number of specific topics in this chapter: the importance of researcher perspective, research as a communication process, and the methodological role of anthropology in cultural psychology.

Both components of cultural process, shared meaning and shared activity, are cumulative in nature. This is because culture is created by processes that occur between, as well as within, generations. Meanings and activities not only accumulate but also transform over historical time. This cumulative and temporal characteristic of culture creates the necessity for developmental methods for studying the transmission and socialization of culture from the older to the newer generation. It also creates the necessity for historical methods of studying culture as psychological process. Developmental as well as historical methodologies for cultural psychology (as well as their various combinations) will therefore be major topics of this chapter.

Because of the sociohistorical specificity of each group's cultural meanings and shared activities, a case is made for the use of culture-specific procedures. An important (and somewhat unusual) claim is that culture-specific procedures are compatible with the discovery of generalizations about the psychology of culture that transcend particular cultural settings. Such discoveries require the field to transcend methodological behaviorism (Hatano, personal communication, 1996). Methodological behaviorism requires researchers to equate procedures on the level of the smallest unit of experimenter behavior and subject response. In so far as cultural psychology engages in the comparative enterprise, its methodological goal must be to equate procedures at the deeper level of cultural meaning. (See also discussion by Sinha, this volume, of the compatibility of indigenous and universal psychologies.)

In order to provide a context for the methodological perspective that will be developed, the chapter begins by first providing an extended example of cultural process and then discussing the relationship between cultural and cross-cultural psychology. Major sections on metamethodology and methodology for the study of cultural processes follow. In the final section, the substantive consequences of this methodology are discussed.

An Example of Cultural Process

Both shared activities and shared meanings are intrinsic to the human mode of adaptation for survival. They are two facets of shared cultural knowledge. An example will elucidate this theoretical formulation of cultural processes. At the same time the example indicates the subject matter for which we must specify our methods and methodology.

During the Los Angeles earthquake of 1994, many of the ecocultural supports of everyday survival and life, such as water, electricity, and roads, were destroyed. In small groups and through the media, people developed new shared knowledge concerning survival activities, such as where to get water, how to circumvent damaged roads to get from point A to point B, and methods for detecting leaking gas. Expertise was shared with novices, as when a contractor showed his neighbors how to turn off their gas, or a ham radio operator provided news of the location and magnitude of the earthquake in the absence of electricity. The nature of culture as a tool for organizing everyday life (Weisner, 1994) was quite apparent.

Symbolic communication, through both language and visual media, is a critical means by which social sharing takes place; communication processes were quite intense during this period of adapting to the physical conditions created by the earthquake. As a result, new shared activities that enhanced physical survival were created through cultural processes of social interaction.

Simultaneously, though, shared meanings were also created to rationalize and understand the events that had taken place. Like shared activities, shared meanings arose through communication processes. One shared meaning that developed was the custom of asking people how they fared in the earthquake, the normative reply was, "I was fortunate." The search to create shared meaning for a stunning physical event was particularly apparent when, a few days after the earthquake, a local public affairs radio show host convened clergy from many religions to ask them about the larger meaning of the earthquake. His question was, "Did God send the earthquake to punish Los Angeles?" Clearly, adaptation to the aftermath of the earthquake could not be reduced to a process of adapting to physical conditions; the interpretation of these conditions, that is, processes of creating meaning were part and parcel of the shared culture that developed in response to the earthquake.

This example provides a model of processes that are assumed to occur whenever a new member of society is born: the creation of shared knowledge, activities, conventions, and meanings through communication and social interaction. This microdevelopmental example of culture recreation by adults occurs in each generation in the macrodevelopmental processes of children. The example is also a model and metaphor of culture change provoked by new ecological conditions. Finally, this example illustrates the potential for cultural variability as a response to different ecological conditions (Berry, 1976).

If this is the nature of culture as process, the question at hand is what empirical methods will be useful for its empirical study. It is necessary to have an array of techniques that can address the development of shared activities, the development of shared meanings, and the communicative processes through which they are acquired. Cultural psychology has (and continues to develop) empirical methods that can systematically document processes of cultural creation such as these.

The Relationship between Cultural and Cross-Cultural Psychology

The terms cultural psychology and cross-cultural psychology are each fuzzy concepts with partially overlapping sets of exemplars. There are focal (Rosch, 1973) or paradigmatic instances of the two approaches that are sharply distinctive, but there are also many research exemplars that combine attributes of each approach. This is because the methods are more complementary than competing. However, paradigmatic definitions will be used to illustrate the methodological consequences of each.

In cross-cultural psychology, culture is generally operationalized as an antecedent variable (Berry, 1976). This is the perspective offered by Van de Vijver and

Leung in this volume of the *Handbook*. In the paradigmatic instances of such an approach, culture is implicitly viewed as outside of and apart from the individual. Culture and human activity are seen as distinguishable. In cultural psychology (Price-Williams, 1980; Cole, 1990; Shweder, 1990), in contrast, culture is not seen as outside the individual, but as inside in an important way (Jahoda, 1992). Culture is "a way of knowing, of construing the world and others" (Bruner, 1993, p. 516). Thus, culture and behavior, culture and mind, are viewed as indistinguishable (Jahoda, 1992).

Cultural psychology has grown out of dissatisfaction with cross-cultural psychology (Cole, 1995; Eckensberger, 1995), on the one hand. On the other hand, it has also grown out of anthropology's wish to understand the person (Shweder & Bourne, 1982; Shweder & Miller, 1985; Shweder & Sullivan, 1990), not merely the supra individual envelope (Cole, 1995). As such, the methodology of cultural psychology reflects integration of psychology and anthropology, as well as active dialogue between the two fields.

Methodological Differences between Cultural and Cross-Cultural Psychology

The methodological ideal of the paradigmatic cross-cultural psychologist is to carry a procedure established in one culture, with known psychometric properties, to one or more other cultures in order to make a cross-cultural comparison (Berry, Poortinga, Segall & Dasen, 1992). In contrast, the methodological ideal of the paradigmatic cultural psychologist is to derive procedures for each culture from the lifeways and modes of communication of that culture. Any cross-cultural comparison is secondary to such culturally differentiated procedures.

There is a second, closely related difference. Whereas cross-cultural psychology tends to derive its problems and procedures from established psychological methodology, cultural psychology derives its problems and procedures from an analysis of the nature of culture (e.g., Scribner & Cole, 1981; Scribner, 1984, 1985). In other words, the ideal in cultural psychology is for problems and procedures to flow from the nature of culture, both in general and in specific terms. Cross-cultural psychology's reliance on the methodological armoire of psychology, rather than on the nature and practice of culture, probably explains why Poortinga and Malpass (1986) can conclude that "culture as a product of human action has not received much attention in cross-cultural psychology" (p. 20).

Variables versus Processes

Insofar as cross-cultural psychology operationalizes culture as an antecedent or independent variable, it is being studied as an *index* rather than a *process*. B. Whiting (1976) has talked about how each independent variable of a sociocultural nature must be "unpackaged" into its component processes. This is clear for ethnic labels; such a label creates a package for distinctive cultural processes such as values and behaviors. The label serves simultaneously as an index for a variety of behaviors and as an independent variable that facilitates cross-cultural comparison. Cultural psychologists, in contrast, study cultural processes directly; they rely much less on "packaged" or indexical variables in their research designs.

Just as cross-cultural psychology "packages" culture in independent variables, it also "packages" the individual subject in dependent variables. In the same way that independent variables are stand-ins for complex cultural processes, so too dependent variables generally function as indices of individual cultural processes, rather than constituting the processes themselves. A dependent variable is something that can be measured; it often functions to summarize a process. Again, cultural psychology attempts to study the process itself.

An example of this distinction between dependent variable and individual cultural process is the contrast between *qualitative process* analysis and a *continuous quantitative scale*. This point will be illustrated with a particular study. Greenfield, Raeff, & Quiroz (in press) developed scenarios that are based on real-life value conflicts experienced by Latino families who immigrate to Los Angeles. One scenario is the following:

> *Anna and Christina both got ten dollars from their uncle. Christina buys a blouse. A week later Anna wants to wear Christina's blouse, and Christina says, "This is my blouse, and I bought it with my own money." Anna says, "But you're not using it now." Christina tells their mother.*

The subject is then asked: What do you think the mother should do?

Immigrant mothers (who were given the scenarios in Spanish) were frequently collectivistic in their responses (Let Anna borrow the blouse). In contrast, their children were most often struggling to resolve and harmonize the collectivistic orientation of their families with the individualistic orientation of their school in particular and the dominant society in general. For example, one fourth grade girl answered that the mother should tell Anna to pay Christina for the blouse and then Christina can buy another blouse for herself. According to a *qualitative process analysis,* this is a response that integrates the individualistic concept of personal property with the collectivistic concept of sharing with extended family members. If, in a contrasting *quantitative* approach to the data, we were to place this response midway on an *interval scale* going from collectivism to individualism, we would miss the dynamics of the psychological process of cross-cultural value integration that this child has accomplished. Individualism/collectivism as a continuous dependent variable would become a packaged *index* of a cultural process; the package would hide the process itself.

Cultural Process or Cross-Cultural Comparison

Cross-cultural comparison is the method of choice for cross-cultural psychology (Triandis, 1980, p. 1). Comparisons are at the heart of quantitative methodology in psychology. Through statistical analysis, psychology uses comparison to pinpoint differences. Cross-cultural psychology is based on a comparative methodology in which statistics are used to identify different frequencies in different cultural groups of a phenomenon of interest (cf. Van de Vijver & Leung, this volume). To do this, it is necessary to assume that what is being measured is the same across groups, that only the frequencies vary. However, this is often not the case. Different adaptations and different systems of meaning, in response to a history of different conditions, imply that phenomena are qualitatively, not merely quantitatively different in different cultural groups. Whereas much discussion in cross-cultural methodology has focused on the best techniques for gaining comparable measurement (Berry, et al., 1992), the notion in indigenous psychology (Kim & Berry, 1993; Sinha, this volume), as in cultural psychology (Stigler & Shweder, 1990), is that the very phenomena are different. An important methodological conclusion flows from this idea: there can not be comparable measurement of incomparable phenomena. The measuring instruments themselves must change.

Cross-cultural comparison is not eschewed in cultural psychology (see, for example, Miller, Bersoff, & Harwood, 1990). For example, Shweder and Sullivan (1993) speak of cultural psychology as "a designation for the comparative study of the way culture and psyche make each other up" (p. 498). However, comparison is not central in the methodology of cultural psychology. Indeed, cross-cultural comparison tends to be done both cautiously and differently: distinctive procedures are often used for each culture being compared (e.g., Morelli, Rogoff, Oppenheim, & Goldsmith, 1992). This is also true of the cross-indigenous approach advocated by Kim and Berry (1993).

The methodology of cultural psychology is therefore distinct from the *psychometric approach* to cross-cultural psychology (see chapter by Van de Vijver & Leung, this volume). There, methods used in each culture should, ideally, be *formally equivalent*. Psychometrics assume that if a questionnaire is used in one culture, the questionnaire format must be used in all others being compared; and that each item must have a corresponding item in all versions/translations. In practice, though, cross-culturalists have frequently accepted variations in questionnaire content, in order to take local cultural meanings into account. In contrast, the position of cultural psychology is that one must communicate with subjects in each culture in a way that is comfortable and appropriate to that culture. This will lead to the use of very different methods to study the same issues in different cultures. Comparison and the testing of universals will come at the more abstract conceptual and theoretical levels, not on the level of concrete methods and specific behaviors generated by formally equivalent procedures. The use of *parallel procedures* across cultures, the hallmark of cross-cultural psychology, works best when cultures are not too different—for example, when all of the samples have had formal education (e.g., Hofstede's 1980 cross-national study of individualism and collectivism). The use of *qualitatively different procedures* across cultures works best when the cultures are very different, and when they have different epistemological and communicative presuppositions, topics discussed later in this chapter. As Triandis (1995) points out, cross-cultural psychology provides a methodology for comparing similar cultures, whereas cultural psychology provides a methodology for comparing dissimilar cultures.

An important facet of both cross-cultural comparison and the study of cultural process is the selection of cultures to be studied. The ideal in cross-cultural psychology is to select the cultures to be compared, based on theoretical analysis of the independent variables (Berry et al., 1992). In contrast, cultural psychology, like cultural anthropology, puts a premium on deriving procedures and problems from each culture (Wassman, 1995); this requires in-depth knowledge of the culture. Therefore, in cultural psychology, cultures are often chosen because the researcher knows the language or otherwise has a good entree into the culture. Because of this requirement of in-depth cultural knowledge, including language skill, cultural psychologists most often research a single culture. Indeed, they often research their own cultures (e.g., Lave, Murtaugh, & de la Rocha, 1984; Valsiner & Hill, 1989).

When cultural psychologists make cross-cultural comparisons, they often deal with different cultures or social groups within a single country (e.g., Greenfield, 1966; Greenfield, Reich, & Olver, 1966; Wagner, 1984; Wassman & Dasen, 1994; Scribner & Cole, 1981; Serpell, 1993). This type of research design provides better control than a simple comparison between groups in two different countries; it also lies in that overlapping or border area between cross-cultural and cultural psychology.

Because of the labor-intensive methods used within each culture, cultural psychologists are often dependent on other researchers to collect data when they wish to compare cultures across national borders (e.g., Greenfield & Childs, 1978; last chapter of LeVine et al., 1994; Saxe, 1981). However, because comparison is on an abstract theoretical level and because the procedures for each distinctive culture are derived from that culture, the need for exact replication does not come into play.

Removing Unconstructive Stereotypes of Cultural Psychology

To define culture as process and to look for appropriate methods of studying cultural processes removes the present approach from some common misconceptions in the field about cultural psychology and its differences from cross-cultural psychology:

1. This chapter will *not* assume the absence of universal psychological processes. The view of this chapter is that universal psychological processes clearly exist and therefore need to be incorporated into methodology and theory. From the theoretical perspective, this is clearly implicit in the idea, expressed earlier, that humans are biologically primed for culture, as well as for cultures. Indeed, there is a psychic unity of humankind.

Shweder's formulation is the notion of "one mind, many mentalities" (LeVine & Shweder, 1995; cf. Shweder, 1995). In this chapter, one mind is viewed as the human capacity for cultural learning (Tomasello, Kruger, & Ratner, 1993), and many mentalities as the result of cultural variability in the conditions presented by different cultures, each with its own distinctive ecology and economy.[2]

2. This chapter rejects a dichotomous choice between understanding behavior in its cultural context (stereotypical of cultural psychology) and understanding behavior as indices of universally shared psychological processes (stereotypical

of cross-cultural psychology). Cultural does not mean context-bound, as opposed to universal. All behavior is both relative to a context and representative of universal principles or laws. In other words, to act in a cultural context is in itself a major universal principle of behavior. To place a particular conclusion from research in one cultural context into a universal framework is to move to a more general level of conceptualization; it is not to reject the notion of contextualized behavior. Methodology that permits the transfer of contextualized research to general principles of psychology will be one of the foci of this chapter.

Metamethodology

Objectivity versus Perspective

Modern psychology was born from the methodological ideology of objectivity, the erasure of perspective, generally known as bias. In sharp contrast to this tradition, an important tenet of cultural psychology (also voiced by Miller in her theoretical chapter in this volume) is the logical impossibility of an observer–independent or objective perspective. In cultural anthropology, the notion that results are relative to the position (cultural, class, gender) of the observer has led to self-flagellation and the total rejection of empiricism (Patai, 1994). Cultural psychology, in contrast, is developing methods and concepts suitable to the inclusion of observer perspective in research.

When studying behavior in one's own culture (as most psychologists do), one has an insider's cultural perspective. Partly because this fact runs counter to the very ideological assumptions of psychological science, the insider's perspective almost always goes unacknowledged (cf. Rogoff & Morelli, 1989). Yet this perspective is crucial. With reference to one's own group, the insider understands the meanings and motives behind in-group behaviors, meanings and motives that may be misinterpreted or devalued by outsiders looking through the lenses of their own cultural values (Berry, 1979).

An example of the unacknowledged insider perspective is the topic of self-esteem in U.S. psychology. Not until the work of Markus and Kitayama (1991) did it become apparent that self-esteem is not a universal quality, but a culture-specific ideal. In sharp cultural contrast, Markus and Kitayama noted the importance of self-effacement, rather than self-esteem, in the development of a Japanese person. Note too that this bicultural team of researchers reflects both an insider and an outsider perspective on both cultures they have studied. This is probably an important reason why they were able to remove the cultural blinders informing self-esteem research in the United States.

In essence, the insider 's role is to safeguard the perspective of the subjects, so that it will be represented in the problem definition, methods, and interpretation of results of the research. (See Serpell, 1993, p. 66, for an example of the conscious use of the insider in actual research.) However, in recent years, there have come to be even more direct methods of investigating and therefore safeguarding this perspective have been developed. [The reader is referred to the discussion of Tobin, Wu, and Davidson's (1989; Tobin, 1989) work in the section on video technology and to the section on methods for the study of cultural meaning later in this chapter.]

At the same time, however, a knowledgeable outsider has an important perspective as well. An out-group member can see, and therefore study, aspects of the dominant culture that insiders have taken for granted or even repressed. The outsider can also serve as a cultural intermediary in making one culture more understandable to another.

Perhaps even more important to the methodology of cultural psychology is the role of the culturally marginal person, a particular type of outsider. In 1987 a panel of five leading cross-cultural psychologists assembled at the IACCP meeting in Newcastle, Australia to present their intellectual autobiographies. Every one of them had had the experience of being culturally marginal (in the sense of being between two cultures) at some early point in development. Because of their positions *between* cultures, they had ceased to take culture for granted; it was no longer the air they breathed. The contrast between cultures that they had experienced had made them personally aware of culture per se. In crossing over cultures in their personal lives, they had arrived at cross-cultural psychology in their professional lives.

There are a number of examples of researchers who have moved permanently into a new culture as adults, who have seen aspects of cultural psychology in their adoptive culture that had been missed by indigenous social scientists. A notable one is John Ogbu, an immigrant from Nigeria to the United States. Upon arriving he became interested in the paradox of explanations for low African-American school achievement. Factors such as poverty and level of parental schooling were being cited as causal explanations for this psychoeducational phenomenon. Yet, having come from Africa where poverty and lack of parental schooling are everyday phenomena, he knew these explanations could not be right, for school achievement was not problematical at all in Africa. At the same time, having lived as a member of the dominant majority in Nigeria, he saw a social phenomenon that Americans had been blind to: caste. This became his explanatory construct for African-American underachievement in *Minority Education and Caste* (Ogbu, 1978). Ogbu used his outsider's perspective to gain an important insight into the cultural psychology of Americans. At the same time, as a permanent resident in the United States and a product of its university system, he was also very knowledgeable about his adoptive culture. Because of firsthand knowledge of two cultures, he could use the perspective of one to raise to consciousness an important aspect of the other, one that insiders had heretofore been unconscious of.

Cross-cultural psychology has accepted the desirability and possibility of objectivity, while acknowledging ethnocentrism as a barrier to it (Berry et al., 1992). Campbell (1970) has proposed a research design whereby each of two cultures, to be compared, is studied by an insider and an outsider. By replicating the same study twice in each culture, one is supposed to be able to separate ethnocentrism from "real" cultural differences. This view provides a good foundation for cultural psychology, but the proposed methodology does not go nearly far enough. Meanings are considered only at the level of data interpretation; Campbell assumes that the same procedure will be understood in the same way and will be equally meaningful to subjects in both cultures. However, this is not necessarily the case. Therefore, we still have no idea of what the differences mean. In addition, there is no provision in Campbell's design for both insider and outsider to *design* their own study. Comparison of insider and outsider research design can go much further in assessing the effect of cross-cultural differences in the construction of meaning on comparative research itself. In fact, there are many procedures in cross-cultural psychology (see Berry et al.; 1992, chapter 9) that seek evidence for such variations in meaning (e.g., item bias indicators), and efforts are made to control them.

Research as a Communication Process

Data collection is a process of communication between subjects and researchers. Although human communication is based on universal capacities, the default assumptions about knowledge and communication are culturally variable. The implication of this cultural variability is that data collection must be based on familiar modes of communication in each culture, rather than formally identical modes and means of communication. This is the cultural psychology approach to dealing with a problem noted in cross-cultural psychology—that particular instrument formats may not be meaningful in all cultures (Berry et al., 1992). However, cross-cultural psychology tries to adjust a single instrument to multiple cultures, whereas cultural psychology paradigmatically adopts the notion of using different procedures in different cultures to study comparable issues. But for the reader to understand how this might work, it is first necessary to be more specific about the nature of cultural variability in presuppositions about the communication process itself.

Cognitive Realism or Cognitive Relativism?: Cultural Variability in the Theory of Mind

A radical departure from the assumption that there is a separation of the knowing subject from the known object can wreak havoc with many psychological procedures. An example follows.

Greenfield (1966; Greenfield & Bruner, 1966 [1969]) brought tests of conservation of quantity to Senegal in order to study the Piagetian stage of concrete operations. After transferring water from a shorter, fatter beaker into a longer, thinner one, unschooled Wolof children were asked (in their native language of Wolof) if the quantity of water was the same, more, or less. After their response, the interview procedure used in Cambridge, Massachusetts (Bruner, Greenfield, Olver, *et al.*, 1966) was continued, and they were asked to justify their quantity judgment: "Why do you think it is the same (or more, or lesser) amount of water?" This question format met with no response. Even when the wording was changed to "Why do you *say* it is the same (or more, or lesser) amount of water?", the question elicited only uncomprehending silence.

Not until the question was changed to "Why *is* the water the same (or more or less)?" were justifications for the original quantity judgment successfully elicited. At that point, the unschooled children gave reasons for their judgments that were as articulate as those given to Piaget and his colleagues in Geneva.

These children had an epistemology of mental realism. According to their implicit theory of mind, they were not making a distinction between the nature of reality and their knowledge of it. Consequently, the idea of explaining a statement was meaningless; only the external event could be meaningfully explained (Greenfield & Bruner, 1966 [1969]). Implicit in this theory of mind was an assumption that there was only a single way to perceive the event of water transfer and its results.

Had an exact translation of the Cambridge conservation procedure been used, it would have been erroneously concluded that the unschooled Wolof children were not able to explain the reasoning behind their quantity judgments. Their theory of mind would have been confounded with their reasoning about the world. The research publication would have incorrectly concluded that unschooled Wolof children had a major cognitive lack in reasoning skill. Instead, the conclusion from pilot testing was that unschooled Wolof children had a different epistemology and therefore required a different interview procedure. When tested with an epistemologically appropriate procedure, the cognitive deficit in reasoning about the world disappeared.

In contrast to the unschooled children, the Wolof children who attended school responded well to a question form that made no sense to the unschooled children: "Why do you *say* the water is the same (or more, or less)?" They produced articulate reasons indistinguishable from the reasons of children in Switzerland and the United States. Apparently, the process of schooling had changed their epistemological presuppositions to accord with those of the psychological experiment. Our conclusion was that it was the introduction by the school of the written word into an oral culture that had made the difference (Greenfield, 1972): In the medium of writing, thoughts about the world are visibly distinct (on the printed page) from the world itself (Greenfield & Bruner, 1966 [1969]). It seemed likely that the written word had transformed an epistemology of cognitive realism into one of cognitive relativism, an epistemology in which a given person can have a variety of thoughts about the same thing, or different people can have different thoughts about the same thing.

This difference between schooled and unschooled children has important implications for the kinds of populations to whom one can validly transfer procedures: It implicates formal education as a potentially important variable in developing the implicit epistemology required by the communication process common to many psychological procedures and instruments.

Notions of the Nature of Knowledge

An example is the difference between individualistic and collectivistic notions of the nature of knowledge. Many societies think of knowledge as a group, not an individual, process. Co-construction of knowledge, as it normally occurs in the course of conversation, is the norm. Interviewing Zinacantecan Maya girls and their mothers about learning, experience, and technique in textile production, the author envisioned each girl and each mother as an individual subject with an individual interview protocol. But that is not how Zinacantecans saw it. The notion that a girl would have an independent viewpoint, piece of knowledge, or perspective was not within the world view of this Maya group from Highland Chiapas. Instead, they expected more knowledgeable mothers to answer for young girls and for members of the family grouping to answer questions cooperatively. Their perspective seemed to be that the overall information would be as accurate as possible, because it was the product of a group effort. The partitioning of this information individual by individual was at odds with their world view. A similar phenomenon has been described for the A-Chewa people in Zambia (Serpell, 1993, p. 230).

The Zinacantecans and A-Chewa illustrate an assumption that is common to many collectivistic societies. However, this is not just a substantive finding about cultural variability in communication processes. It is also a methodological finding that impacts procedures that can be meaningfully used to collect data. The procedure used to collect information in such a society must permit the cooperative construction of knowledge. For example, the author allowed anyone who was knowledgeable to provide information about a subject's weaving experience. Usually this knowledgeable person was the girl's mother.

Although the procedure involves the co-construction of knowledge, the individual subject can still function as the unit of analysis. Thus, in the textile interview example, the author emerged with information about each girl and her mother as distinct individuals. What was different from the nature of research communication in the United States was that the information on each subject was co-constructed by more than one person.

Cultural Variability in the Right to Opinions

Closely related are cultural differences regarding who has the right to have opinions (Lonner & Berry, 1986). In the United States and other industrialized countries, it is assumed that everyone has the right to have an individual opinion on any subject whatsoever. That is why opinion polls work in these countries. However, in many societies, opinions are formed on the group level, not by individuals. In such societies, the group's leaders and elders are given the right to an opinion. Others are not encouraged to express an individual perspective. In such a society, polling ordinary individuals on their opinions or attitudes is not an effective way to communicate with subjects (cf. Lerner, 1958).

Independent Questions or Connected Discourse?

Another epistemological surprise that relates to the use of surveys or questionnaires is the assumption of independent questions. Surveys are often constructed so that successive questions do not follow the conventions of connected discourse. Instead, they are conceived as a series of independent items. However, this convention flies in the face of conversational conventions, in which each turn is a response to the preceding turn as well as a stimulus to the next. A questionnaire or structured interview, with its independent "turns," can therefore seem strange. For example, Zinacantecans seemed very malcontent when a later question seemed to ignore a previous answer. The genre of the structured interview or questionnaire was foreign to their culture. As a result, so was the convention of independent questions specific to this genre.

Culture Specificity of Ignorant or Out-of-Context Questions
The absence of such a convention particularly interferes with a common system of internal validity checks in psychological instruments; such a system is based on redundancy, that is, asking for the same information in two different ways. Far from enhancing validity, redundancy could destroy validity in communities unused to the independent "turns" of the psychological instrument genre. For example, Zinacantecan subjects could barely tolerate redundant questions. The attitude transmitted to the author was "Why are you so stupid as to ask the same question twice?"

Closely related was the Zinacantecans lack of tolerance for ignorant questions. It is likely that the Zinacantecos are similar to many other groups in this. The point is that a rigid questionnaire cannot be used to interview on a topic of great unfamiliarity to the researcher. As a prior step, ethnographic field work or focus groups must be used to figure out what the intelligent questions are. (Such prior steps as these will be discussed later in the chapter.)

Another assumption of the interview or questionnaire is that questions can be successfully asked out of context. Not all groups share this assumption. L. Devereaux (personal communication, 1992) developed a methodology based on her perception that Zinacantecans would not provide meaningful responses to questions asked out of the context of an ongoing activity. She developed a technique of interviewing around ongoing activities. For example, she would interview about weaving when weaving was taking place, about child development when children were present, and so forth. Greenfield adapted this technique to a structured interview. She was having a hard time eliciting information about the activities of play weaving and play embroidery until she started using a play weaving and a play embroidery as stimuli to ask if subjects had ever made such items when they were little. The recognition and comprehension were instantaneous. Meaningfulness was evident in the enthusiasm and spontaneity with which subjects responded. This spontaneity and enthusiasm contrasted strongly with the ennui and lack of comprehension that greeted questions about absent objects and events.

Communicating Across Cultures or Age Levels
This same point, that variability in the epistemology of communication between subject and researcher can undermine research communication and invalidate results, has been made with respect to young children (Schubauer-Leoni, Perret-Clermont, & Grossen, 1993; Siegal 1991a, 1991b, in press) Siegal points out that, in a data collection procedure, the violation of communication conventions—

e.g., failing to minimize redundancy—can cause children to perform at lower levels because of communication failure between researcher and child.

Thus, cross-cultural and cross-age communication hold exactly the same methodological dangers of eliciting invalid information because of systematic but unrealized communication failure. The conclusion is that methods of eliciting data from subjects must be adapted to the presuppositions about communication that are held by each cultural group. This is yet another reason why the most valid cross-cultural comparisons will often be based on radically different procedures used in each culture.

The final point relates to the methodological significance of a researcher's intersubjectivity. Intersubjectivity, the sharing of a perspective, is the foundation of all communication (Trevarthen, 1980). Applying this idea to the notion of research as a communication process with subjects, we must conclude that the validity of data depends on the researcher's achievement of intersubjectivity with his or her subjects. This is because cooperative conversation depends on the sharing of conversational goals (Grice, 1975). If such goals are not shared, the subject may be answering a different question than the researcher had in mind. It follows, then, that the more the researcher can share the perspective of a subject, regardless of the culture of that subject, the more valid the data that will be gathered and the more valid the interpretation of the data. This conclusion is very different from the received wisdom in psychology: The most valid perspective is an objective or detached perspective.

Validity

The methodology of cultural psychology impels the field to go beyond traditional psychological concepts of validity. A new type of validity - Maxwell's (1992) notion of *interpretive validity*—is most relevant to the metamethodological discussion of perspective and communication just discussed. Interpretive validity involves a concern with what "objects, events, and behaviors mean to the people engaged in and with them" (Wells, Hirshberg, Lipton, & Oakes, 1995, p. 288). If we expand this concept to include what questions and other conversational moves mean to the people engaged in them, then interpretive validity will include (1.) understanding the basic communicational and epistemological presuppositions of our subjects, and (2.) making sure that all data collection procedures conform to these presuppositions. Much work remains to be done to establish methods for ensuring interpretive validity.

A second type of validity that is particularly relevant to the methodology of cultural psychology is *ecological validity*. This, a more well-known type of validity in psychology, involves the extent to which a procedure elicits data that is representative of behavior outside the research context. Many of the methods for studying adaptive behaviors in everyday contexts that we will describe have ecological validity built into them. In studying naturally-occurring rather than laboratory behavior, ecological validity is insured. In deriving research problems and methods from the cultural context, rather than from the science of psychology, ecological validity is automatically enhanced. In basing experiments on ethnographic observations, a topic to be discussed later, ecological validity is maximized. Thus, ecological validity is implicit in the very foundations of cultural psychology.

When a researcher directly studies a phenomenon of interest, rather than measuring it indirectly through items in an instrument, traditional types of validity checks, such as assessment of content validity, become superfluous. This is because these traditional types of validity concerns are based on using some measurement as an *index* of the phenomenon of interest. However, when a behavioral phenomenon is studied directly, rather than indexed indirectly, the necessity to check representativeness through a content validity check becomes unnecessary; it is ensured *ipso facto.* This point applies to the important cultural psychology method (elaborated later in this chapter) of studying behavior in its natural context.

Another relevant type of validity is *theoretical validity* (Maxwell, 1992). This involves "the presence of a more abstract explanation of described actions and interpreted meanings" (Miles & Huberman, 1994, p. 279). Theoretical validity is particularly important because it gives culture-specific research its generalizability (Miles & Huberman, 1994).

The Necessity of Methods for Studying Cultural History

A key aspect of human culture is its cumulative quality: culture is both transmitted and transformed between and within generations. If cultural psychology is to be grounded in the nature of culture, then a key aspect of empirical methodology will be the development of methods for studying the role of cultural history in the current psychological functioning of individual members of a cultural group. As part of this effort, it will be necessary to have methods that can relate the interactive processes of intergenerational transmission to the cumulative nature of cultural knowledge. At the same time, the other side of cultural accumulation, cultural transformation and change, must also be a focus of empirical methodology. It is particularly important that the methods of cultural psychology be able to study the ways in which historical roots and cultural change combine to affect the enculturation of individuals in a cultural group at a given point in time (Greenfield & Cocking, 1994a).

Developmental Methods

A theoretically important process in cultural psychology is the expert–novice relationship in which someone with greater cultural knowledge in a meaningful domain of activity interacts with someone with lesser knowledge in that domain, enhancing shared knowledge in a way that moves the novice toward expertise (Rogoff, 1990). The repetition of this process across generations leads to the cumulative nature of cultural knowledge and the importance of cultural history in cultural psychology (Scribner, 1985). The capacity of the novice to respond to different kinds of input provided by the expert is influenced partly by chronologically based maturity. In addition, the movement from cultural novice to cultural expert does not occur all at once; it is a step-by-step process. Hence, the importance of *developmental methodology* to cultural psychology (cf. Eckensberger, 1979).

As Valsiner (1989) notes, an important goal of cultural psychology is to understand how the process of development takes place within a culture. (See also chapter by Valsiner and Lawrence, in Volume 2 of this *Handbook*). This "entails development of empirical methodologies that document the process of interaction between the child and his/her environment . . . a research paradigm that is primarily directed towards explaining how culture organizes the conditions for children's development, and how children assimilate these conditions, and simultaneously accommodate to them" (Valsiner, 1989, pp. 4–5). Methods for the study of developmental processes are a methodological keystone for the study of culture as psychological process.

The Relevance of Cross-Species and Neuroscience Methodologies

Bruner (1972) discussed the evolutionary foundations of culture and culture learning. More recently Cole (1992) has spoken of the necessity to integrate universal biological factors into a general theory of cultural psychology. The biological priming of culture includes what have been termed cognitive constraints (Carey & Gelman, 1991; Hirschfeld & Gelman, 1994) or, more accurately, learning biases (Gallistel, Brown, Carey, Gelman, & Keil, 1991). For example, humans are "biased" to learn language (e.g., Pinker, 1994), an important component of cultural processes. The methodological implications of the universal human propensity to culture include investigations of the evolutionary foundation of culture through cross-species comparisons in domains relevant to the learning, use, and transmission of culture such as tools (e.g., Goodall, 1986; Greenfield, 1991; Matsuzawa, 1991; McGrew, 1992), symbolic communication (e.g., Plooij, 1978; Greenfield & Savage-Rumbaugh, 1991), cultural variability (Nishida, 1987) and observational learning (e.g., Tomasello, Davis-Dasilva, Camak, & Bard, 1987). (See also chapter by Keller, this volume.)

Tomasello, Kruger, and Ratner's (1993) formulation of three levels of culture learning—emulation, imitation, and collaboration—relevant to the evolution of culture stems from and suggest cross-species comparison of culture learning mechanisms. This methodology can provide insights (and has already done so) into the evolutionary (and therefore biological) foundations for culture learning. An outstanding example is Boesch's (1991) naturalistic study establishing that chimpanzee mothers in the Tai forest of the Ivory Coast use intentional teaching techniques to transmit the hammer/ anvil technique of nut cracking to their young. This technique is cultural not only in the sense of involving social transmission, but also in the sense of being a technique that is distinctive to chimpanzees in a particular geographical region.

The human propensity for culture also implies investigations of the biological, especially the neural foundations of various cultural skills such as language and tools (e.g., Greenfield, 1991; Deacon, in press). Perusse (1993) has done a behavior genetics study establishing the heritability of parental teaching style, an important process in cultural transmission. Segal (1993) has used twin methodology to explore the importance of genetic relatedness in stimulating important cultural behavior such as helpfulness and cooperation. Her studies indicate that methods addressing not just the biology of individuals but the genetic relationships between individuals will be important to understanding cultural behavior.

Methodological Role of Anthropology

It is clear from the inclusion of anthropological approaches in this and other handbooks (Goodenough, 1980; Munroe & Munroe, 1986; see also chapter by Munroe & Munroe, this volume) that anthropology has a role to play in cross-cultural psychology. However, this role is particularly important in cultural psychology where culture is considered a process rather than an independent variable.

First, and probably most important, is the anthropological notion of ethnography as a methodological concept. Weisner proposes a central role for ethnography because "it brings the importance of lived experience in a cultural place to the center of attention, transforming it from ground to figure" (Weisner, in press, ms. p. 3). This method is crucially important as the first stage of any cultural psychological research in a new, unfamiliar setting. Ethnography, according to Goodenough (1980), "describes what people must have learned in order to participate acceptably in most of the activities of that society" (p. 29). This is a broad anthropological notion that assumes that it is possible to master most activities of a society.

For the purposes of studying the psychological processes of culture, a more limited ethnographic goal seems more appropriate. As Packer (1995) puts it, ethnography involves firsthand experience of the settings in which the human activity of research interest occurs. The classical method of experiencing settings is by participant observation. Goodenough (1980) and others have described how to keep systematic records of participant observation. In the course of becoming a participant–observer, the researcher establishes an identity in the setting (Rizzo, Corsaro, & Bates, 1992). An important aspect of ethnography is to be able to communicate with the people of the study community in their own language.

Sometimes, as Packer (1995) notes, firsthand experience can be approximated by open-ended conversations and interviews. Unstructured focus groups can provide another approximation to firsthand experience.

Even when researching in one's own culture, any new setting can be an unknown cultural niche. Packer (1995) relates his experience with the ethnographic phase of a study of a kindergarten class: "I spent two years hanging out with the children in a pre-school kindergarten class, and that experience was invaluable; it helped me interpret and analyze the video-recordings I made. First it gave me a sense of the tone and climate of the school, and the style and manner of the children. . . . In addition to the affective level, practical engagement with the artifacts of a context is quite different from the detached, objective observation of these artifacts. . . . To understand the common-sense that the participants in a context employ—and, as Clifford Geertz has insisted, this common-sense is a cultural system—we need to encounter it first hand" (pp. 3–4).

This statement stresses ethnography as a way to uncover and discover the subjects' own perspective. But, as Weisner, a psychological anthropologist, points out, "ethnography is not limited to understanding meaning and the construction of experience by culture members. It is also central in understanding social institutions and social structure, demographic trends, economic exchanges, power and influence, and other, presumably more formal, distal or etic influences on development in a cultural place" (Weisner, in press, ms. p. 8).

Weisner (in press) also stresses the complementarily of ethnography with other methods. Combinations of ethnography with other methods often permit the researcher to integrate data concerning different levels of the sociocultural system. This is a methodological concept that Rogoff has explicated in speaking of the complementary "lenses" through which the researcher can see the developing child on a variety of planes: as individual, as member of a dyad, as part of a community setting (Rogoff, Baker-Sennett, Lacasa, & Goldsmith, 1995).

Wells, Hirshberg, Lipton, & Oakes (1995) point out that sociocultural planes are not themselves static units that can be defined in advance. Instead, the planes are co-constructions between researchers and subjects. Researchers must learn through interacting with subjects and observing their activities which relationships and community institutions are relevant to the focal subjects. This approach is quite different from the notion of random sampling that cross-cultural psychology (Lonner & Berry, 1986; Berry et al., 1992) has adopted from traditional psychology.

Another type of complementarily between anthropology and psychology is that of ethnography and experimentation. A wonderful example of a study in which full-blown ethnographic study was the basis for experimental research is Beach's study of the role of external memory cues in learning to become a bartender. In the ethnographic phase of his research, Beach (1984, 1992) enrolled in and went through a bartending school's two-week course. Based on his ethnography, Beach then designed experimental studies to verify and extend the ethnographic findings. His experimental procedure was based directly on an existing school practice, the speed drill for mixing drinks. However, in the experimental phase, he could vary stimuli systematically (e.g., glass shape) in order to pinpoint the cognitive issue of interest, microdevelopmental change in the use of external memory cues with increasing expertise.

Another excellent example of this methodology lies in the work of the Brazilian team of Nunes, Schliemann, Carraher, and colleagues (e.g., 1993; see also chapter by Schliemann, Carraher & Ceci, Volume 2, this *Handbook*). For example, in one study, (Schliemann, 1984), naturalistic observation of carpenters at work and of a carpentry school yielded realistic mathematical problems that carpenters must solve in their everyday work. These problems were then the basis for using experiments to compare professional carpenters and apprentices at different levels in order to find out the nature of the development of cognitive strategies for solving the mathematical problems required in this particular ecological context. In other studies, experimental problems are based on interviews with experts in a particular activity context rather than observation (e.g, Grando, 1988). (See also chapter by Schliemann, Carraher & Ceci in Volume 2 of this *Handbook*.)

In cross-cultural psychology, prior ethnographies are recognized as a valuable foundation for research (Berry et al., 1992). However, whereas cross-cultural psychologists generally rely on anthropologists or their local colleagues to learn the language and the culture ethnographically, cultural psychologists more often make learning the language and participating in the culture an important part of their own research. This is because the procedures and methods of cultural psychology arise from the culture itself, not from the methodological cupboard of psychology. As a consequence, the ethnographic stage of research is indispensable. The prior examples make clear the potentially close, and even isomorphic, relationship between ethnography and psychological experimentation.

The integration of anthropological and psychological methods can be facilitated by interdisciplinary teams consisting of a psychologist and an anthropologist. Recently Jurg Wassman (anthropologist) and Pierre Dasen (psychologist) have developed a methodology for integrating the two disciplinary perspectives. They "advocate the following general research strategy in three steps: (1.) interviews with a few key informants and "jpfs" [just plain folks]; (2.) behaviour observations in everyday settings to get at the application of knowledge in daily life; and (3.) setting tasks, to induce behaviour that is not observable in everyday situations" (Wassmann & Dasen, 1994, p. 23). The first two steps draw primarily on anthropological methodology, whereas the last step draws on psychological methodology.

The research strategy of Wassman and Dasen was developed partly as a way of addressing the sampling problem that stemmed from the anthropological reliance on "key informants." Reliance on "key informants" was based on the conception of culture as a homogenous entity, ignoring its internal structural diversity and the individual differences so important to the field of psychology. Interviewing "just plain folks" expands the researchers' sample beyond "key informants" and allows comparison of various viewpoints within a culture. Others in psychology have also argued for sampling as an important way of modifying classical ethnography:

> *Newman and Saxe both develop the argument that careful sampling can be crucial for ethnographic work. Newman samples particular groups for generational identity differences, and Saxe compares Brazilian street sellers who are adepts and others who are novices in folk math tasks (Weisner, in press, ms. pp. 12–13).*

In essence, sampling is a way of dealing with the problem of perspective in ethnography. Miles and Huberman (1984) point out that qualitative field research typically involves purposive rather than random sampling, both within and between subjects: "These may be, for example, samples of actors, settings, events, time periods, and processes" (Miles & Huberman, 1984, p. 25). This is something that has been strongly debated in recent years:

*Critical and feminist theories alike question the historical bases of gender, power,
or control from which ethnographies and ethnographers come (di Leonardo, 1991;
Marcus & Fischer, 1986; Weisner, in press, ms. p. 5).*

Yet it must be noted that methods for reducing and evaluating bias, as well as
methods for enhancing and evaluating validity and reliability in ethnographic
data do exist. Validity was discussed earlier, so the examples presented here will
concern bias and reliability. Procedures suggested by Miles and Huberman (1994)
to avoid the biasing influence of researcher effects include staying as long on-site
as possible; spending some time simply hanging around, fitting into the landscape, taking a lower profile; and using unobtrusive measures where possible
(Miles & Huberman, 1994, p. 266). In order to evaluate bias, the authors suggest
a number of relevant queries, including:

- Can we follow the actual sequence of how data were collected, processed,
  condensed/transformed, and displayed for specific conclusion drawing?
- Has the researcher been explicit and self-aware as possible about personal
  assumptions, values and biases, and affective states—and how they may have
  come into play during the study?
- Were competing hypotheses or rival conclusions really considered? If so, at
  what point in the study? Do other rival hypotheses seem possible (Miles &
  Huberman, 1994, p. 278)?

For ethnographic research, reliability involves processes of "quality control"
(Miles & Huberman, 1994). Some suggested queries to evaluate reliability include:

- Is the researcher's role and status within the site explicitly described?
- Were data quality checks made (e.g., for bias, deceit, informant knowl-
  edgeability?) (Miles & Huberman, 1994, p. 278).

Another way in which anthropological methods can be integrated into cultural psychology is through training in anthropology for psychologists and through
training in psychology for anthropologists. Many researchers in cultural psychology have had this type of cross-disciplinary training. Such training enhances interdisciplinary collaboration, as well as the integration of cross-disciplinary methodology by a single researcher.

Methodology

Qualitative Methods are Primary in the Understanding of Process

The conversational analyst, Schegloff (1993) wrote:

In examining large amounts of data, we are studying multiples or aggregates
of single instances. *Quantitative analysis is, in this sense, not an alternative to
single case analysis, but rather is built on its back (p. 102).*

Schegloff's point is that it is necessary to understand the phenomenon under study before being able to aggregate multiples of them in a quantitative test of their frequency or typicality. Indeed, it is necessary to *discover* the phenomenon under study before being able to aggregate multiple instances; in such a case the N of 1 functions as an important existence proof (T. Au, personal communication). Qualitative methods (the study of single instances, that is, data are not aggregated) are particularly crucial when it is important to stay in touch with the structural unity of a process (Fisher, 1994). Here is an example from attachment research of the danger of aggregating data without understanding each individual case, with its structurally unified process.

A baby in the United States participated in Ainsworth's Strange Situation Procedure; the baby was classified as "resistant," not "securely" attached to his mother, because he played alone quietly and contentedly (rather than resisting) when left alone with a stranger. As his mother watched this behavior through a one-way mirror, she "proudly commented to the researchers, "Look how independent he is! See how he can play by himself? This is what I have been working for by having him be with other kids and families while I am working' " (Weisner, in press, ms. p. 11). Weisner (in press) continues:

> *This mother was a single parent by choice. She had told us about her cultural goals for independence for herself and her child, her commitment to feminism, her struggles to sustain work and parenting, and many other values. Her construction of her child's behavior came from this framework of beliefs and practices. The knowledge gleaned through such informal conversations with the mother about her ideas about her child, done along with ongoing ethnographic observations of what she is doing in her everyday world to operationalize those ideas, is surely a powerful tool in understanding trust and attachment in cultural context"* (ms. p. 11).

Does it make sense to aggregate this baby with other infants showing the same behavior for completely different cultural reasons? This is the sort of question raised by Schegloff's discussion.

Schegloff goes on to say that "We need to know what the phenomena are, how they are organized, and how they are related to each other as a precondition for cogently bringing methods of quantitative analysis to bear on them" (p. 114) (cf., Hatano, 1995). In other words, qualitative analysis must precede and inform quantitative analysis. This principle is illustrated by the following example involving eye contact as a communication and socialization process for infants:

Based on an analysis of mother-infant eye contact, LeVine and colleagues (LeVine, Dixon, LeVine, Richman, Leiderman, Keefer, & Brazelton, 1994) concluded that infants receive less maternal eye contact in Africa than in the United States. However, unlike the norm for European-derived cultures, siblings are important caregivers in African families (LeVine et al., 1994; Weisner & Gallimore, 1977; Zukow, 1989). Based on this qualitative analysis of the social organization of child care in a particular ecological context, Sigman et al. (1994) measured the aggregate amount of eye contact Emba babies in Kenya received from *all* of their caregivers, including siblings. The results were very different: the amount of eye contact, rather than being less than Euro-American norms, was, if anything, greater. The earlier conclusion that East African babies were "deprived" of eye contact was changed to the conclusion that they were "enriched" in this regard. A different qualitative analysis of *what* to count, the nature of the phenomenon, led to a different quantitative analysis and, eventually, to different conclusions. The point is that (1.) quantitative results are strongly affected by qualitative analysis of the phenomenon under study; and (2.) the qualitative nature of a given phenomenon (e.g., infant caregiving) varies from culture to culture.

Cultural Adaptation, Practice, and Naturalistic Methodology

If behavioral adaptations to ecological conditions are central psychological processes in cultural psychology, this point has methodological implications: the study of natural behavior *in situ* (in contrast to controlled experimentation) becomes critical to answering questions concerning conventionalized (i.e., cultural) behavioral adaptations under varying ecological conditions. Skills must be studied in practice (Lave, 1988) before they are studied in the laboratory. *In situ* observation is important because it highlights dynamic processes in contrast to static products of cultural adaptation. The freer the behavior, the less the adaptive processes are likely to have been distorted by the research procedure. Insofar as cross-cultural psychology has been wedded to the index (item, stimulus) rather than to the process, it can deal only indirectly with behavioral adaptation to ecological contexts. However, cross-cultural psychology has recognized the importance of ecological adaptation, and the need to employ ethnographic and observational methods to study it prior to the development of psychological instruments (Berry, 1980; Berry et al, 1992).

Everyday activities reflect cultural adaptation to ecological conditions. An excellent example of the study of everyday activity in context is Rogoff's (in press) analysis of developmental transitions in children's participation in sociocultural activities. That analysis is based on *in situ* observations of preschool children in their interaction with one-year olds in two communities, a Mayan town in the Highlands of Guatemala and a city in the United States. But behavioral observations *in situ* are not sufficient, as Rogoff argues. In order to understand the *meaning* of the observed *in situ* behavioral differences in the two cultures, it was necessary to also investigate "the social organization of family roles and cultural expectations of childhood in each community" (ms. p. 18, Rogoff, in press).

Methods for the Study of Cultural Meaning

Although interpretive processes of meaning construction and practical activities of materialistic adaptation are always intertwined in any real-world situation of cultural processes (as in Rogoff's example above), cultural psychology highlights the interindividual construction of meaning. It follows that this is also the distinctive methodological contribution of cultural psychology. Therefore, this chapter now turns to a discussion of concepts and methods for the psychological study of cultural meaning. As Feldman, Bruner, Kalmar, and Renderer (1993) point out, it has not been easy to see what form empirical research would take within a cultural cognitive psychology focused on meaning-making processes. Nonetheless, considerable steps have been taken, and will be outlined in the following sections.

Intersubjectivity and Shared Meaning

The sharing of meaning transforms individual meaning into cultural meaning. Methods that explore the conventionalization of meaning between two partners are relevant to the growth of shared meaning as the basis of culture (Bruner, 1990). The foundation for shared meaning is the same intersubjectivity that makes communication possible. Trevarthen (1980) sees intersubjectivity as the foundation of human culture. Appreciation of other individual minds creates intersubjectivity and therefore culture. According to him, human beings have from infancy an intrinsic motivation to gain knowledge from others, thereby showing themselves to be intrinsically social and cultural. In this view, social sharing, the basis of culture, is as natural as any other human activity. Hence, methods for exploring the development of shared understandings and information exchange in the communication process (e.g., Ochs & Schieffelin, 1983) are basic methods in cultural psychology.

Cross-cultural psychology has recognized the problem of meaning in designing comparative studies. It is conceptualized as a problem of comparability (Berry, et al., 1992) or equivalence (Poortinga, 1989; Poortinga & Malpass, 1986).[3] However, for cross-cultural psychology, variability in cultural meanings is looked upon as a barrier to cross-cultural equivalence and comparability. Diversity in cultural meaning is seen as something to eliminate in the interest of finding universals; it is not viewed as something to be studied in its own right. Cultural psychology goes deeper in identifying the nature of the problem and develops methods for the direct study of meaning. In cultural psychology, cultural meanings are not a barrier to research; they are the central topic of investigation. A discussion of some methods for studying the construction of cultural meanings follows.

Meaning can be communicated and shared through reciprocal social interaction. This process requires a theory of other minds. Hence, the cross-cultural study of theory of mind is central to the study of shared meaning in cultural psychology.

The developmentally earliest paradigm for social reciprocity and sharing is what Marcel Mauss (1954) called *le don*, the gift. When an infant gives a gift, he/she is applying social reciprocity to the world of objects. Studies of the development of forms of reciprocity in different cultures (e.g., Rabain, 1979) are therefore relevant to investigating the ontogeny of cultural meaning.

Many studies document the transmission of and development of cultural values through everyday processes of interaction and communication (e.g., Blake, 1994; Choi, 1992; Greenfield, Brazelton, & Childs, 1989; Greenfield, Raeff, & Quiroz, in press; Heath, 1983; Ochs, 1982; Rabain-Jamin, 1994; Schieffelin, 1983; Schneider, Hieshima, Lee, & Plank, 1994; Shweder & Much, 1987). Greenfield, Raeff, and Quiroz (1995) use discourse analysis to document cooperative and conflicting cultural constructions of the child; their study illustrates the use of discourse analysis to study dynamic cultural processes in everyday processes of communication and interaction.

All of these studies use microanalytic methods for analyzing interactive processes. These range from discourse to semantics, grammar, and nonverbal communication. Methodological sources for discourse analysis are found in Sinclair and Coulthard (1975) and Edwards and Lampert (1993). The latter focuses on transcription and coding.

The study of social ethnotheories is another important method for the study of shared cultural meanings and their acquisition (see also chapter by Super and Harkness in volume 2 of this *Handbook*) . A social ethnotheory expresses human qualities that are valued by a particular group. Ethnotheories of intelligence (Berry & Bennett, 1992; Dasen, 1984; Serpell, 1993; Wober, 1974) and of parenting (e.g., Harkness & Super, 1995; Zukow, 1984) have been of particular interest. Let us look more closely at the latter. A parental ethnotheory is a culture-specific conception of the goals of child development. Probably the most seminal paper for cultural psychology was the "three developmental stories" paper by Ochs and Schieffelin (1984). This paper was important for two reasons. First, it depicted the theoretical stance of developmental psycholinguistics as a culture-specific ethnotheory, rather than a universal truth. Second, it linked everyday interaction to the cultural value systems beneath it.

Other studies have used interview methodology to study parental ethnotheories (e.g., Goodnow, 1985). Another technique is the use of scenarios in which different child development goals lead to different resolutions of the scenario (e.g., Greenfield, Raeff, & Quiroz, in press). By analyzing open-ended responses and letting the categories emerge from the data themselves, this technique enables researchers to study the social construction of the child both intraculturally and cross-culturally. An important extension of methods for studying ethnotheories of child development and cultural socialization is the "multivocal ethnography" pioneered by Tobin, Wu, and Davidson (1989). It is discussed in detail as a use for video technology in a later section. A social psychological version of multivocal ethnography has been pioneered by Kitayama, Markus, Matsumoto and Norasakkunkit (in press).

Note that methods for studying the construction of meaning all have as their goal to reveal the nature of the research subject's perspective or subjectivity. Jones and Thorne (1987) point out that the perspective of the subject can also be a methodological tool to evaluate the meanings of assessment procedures, particularly useful in exploring intercultural clinical assessment.

Narrative Methods
Bruner (1986, 1990) proposes narrative as an intrinsically cultural mode of thinking (Lucariello, 1995). Narrative thought involves structuring the world in terms

of characters with intentions who perform actions in settings, using particular means. Narrative therefore highlights the human interpretive understanding of other human beings and their activity as central to culture. At the same time, narrative as a cultural category emphasizes the making of meaning rather than the performing of behavior. Narrative is a dynamic process because it involves interpreting sequences of ongoing events. As a cultural mode, it is also dynamic and process-oriented in that it permits the study of human generative creativity: there are infinite combinations of characters, intentions, actions, settings, and means that may produced in a narrative construction.

Labov and Waletsky (1967) provide a basic source on the methodology of narrative analysis. *Narratives from the crib* (Nelson, 1989) presents further examples of narrative analysis; at the same time it illustrates how cultural psychology centers on the developmental acquisition of cultural modes of activity, in this case, the production of narrative. Another example of narrative analysis as a technique is provided by Ochs and Taylor (1992) their analysis of dinner table narratives.

Combining the Study of Materialistic and Symbolic Culture: Constraints and Preferences

The fact that cultural processes are both shared activities adapted to ecological conditions and shared meanings for these activities implicates methods that assess both constraints (based on material conditions) and preferences (based on values or cultural meanings) (Shweder, Jensen, & Goldstein, 1995). Shweder and colleagues' study of sleeping arrangements in India and the United States was innovative in distinguishing constraints based on material ecological conditions (e.g., size of family, gender composition of family, number of beds available) from preferences that were based on culturally meaningful values (e.g., caring for the young, incest avoidance, chastity anxiety). The authors distinguished constraints from preferences by asking subjects (in India) about sleeping arrangements of a hypothetical seven-person family under varying resource conditions. Such a method allows one to specify both the shared cultural meanings that generate preferences (e.g., care of the young in India, autonomy in the United States) and the shared cultural responses to limited resource conditions (the number of beds). The methodology of this study points out the limitations of simple behavioral observation: Observing who sleeps with whom would not permit the analytical distinction between constraints and preferences to be made (Shweder, Jensen, & Goldstein, 1995). Simple behavioral observation, no matter how thorough, would confound cultural preferences (symbolic or idealist meaning) with cultural responses to ecological constraint (materialist adaptation).

Methods for the Study of Cultural History

All of the empirical methods discussed so far assume that the study of the psychology of culture takes place at one point in time. However, an important tenet of cultural psychology is that the present psychology of culture reflects residues of past cultural history (Scribner, 1985). What methods are appropriate for examining this past residue? One method suggested by Vygotsky was to study the influence of cultural tools and artifacts, because each artifact is itself the product of cultural history (Cole, 1995). Cole writes, "human beings live in an environment transformed by the artifacts of prior generations, extending back to the beginning of the species (Geertz, 1973; Ilyenkov, 1977; Sahlins, 1976; Wartofsky, 1979). The basic function of these artifacts is to coordinate human beings with the physical world and each other" (Cole, 1992, p. 9). Thus, when Scribner and Cole (1981) studied the cognitive effects of three different literacies used by the Vai in Liberia, they were in essence studying the effects of a complex cultural history that had produced the three writing systems and the practices with which each is associated. Saxe (1982a, 1982b) has studied number systems and their use as the product of cultural history.

Another important methodological approach to the study of cultural history is the comparison of psychological processes of the same ethnic group in different societal contexts. Sometimes this is done directly by a single researcher (e.g., Ho, 1989). Other times, it is done indirectly by comparing the findings of different researchers (e.g., Greenfield & Cocking, 1994a). The commonalities in psychological phenomena of the same ethnic group in different societal contexts point to the effect of ancestral cultural influences that predate the divergence of the ethnic group into different societal contexts. On the other hand, differences between ethnic group members residing in different cultural contexts reflect a different sort of history, the history of intergroup contact under varying societal conditions. The development of methodology for studying the impact of different patterns of intergroup contact on the same ethnic group has been pioneered by Ogbu (e.g., 1978, 1994).

Such differences reflect the dynamic, changing quality of cultural history. There have been a number of attempts to capture the psychological nature of cultural change indirectly by synchronic or cross-sectional methods. Perhaps the first was Vygotsky' and Luria's attempt to assess the cognitive impact of the post-revolutionary process of farm collectivization in the Soviet Union by comparing cognitive processes in peasants living on traditional farms with those who had been collectivized on a number of cognitive tasks (Luria, 1976). Recent examples of this research strategy include Saxe's (1982a, b) studies in New Guinea comparing the mathematical cognition of Oksamin people who have been more touched by the recent introduction of commerce and money with those who have been less touched. Draper and Cashden (1988) have explored the impact of sedentarization on sex role socialization among the Efe by comparing Efe still living as hunter/ gatherers with those living as agriculturalists. (See also chapter by Berry & Sam, in Volume 3 of this *Handbook*, on the psychological consequences of culture contact and change.)

Perhaps the most direct of all of the synchronic approaches to diachronic change is the study of families who have immigrated from the same country in different generations. An example of this strategy is Delgado-Gaitan's (1993, 1994) comparison of immigrant and first-generation Mexican–American families' intrafamilial interaction patterns and values. What differs at one point in time between the immigrant and first-generation families is used to model the cultural assimilation process over time in a single family. In all of these research designs, the logic of the method is to take advantage of current variability in the diffusion of a cultural change to reconstruct the impact of that cultural change over historical time.

This indirect methodological strategy has the potential problem of making assumptions about unidirectional cultural evolution (cf. Eckensberger, Krewer, & Kasper, 1984). Consequently, the simulation of cultural change by comparative research must be based on specific knowledge of actual cultural change, not general theories of cultural evolution. In addition, there is the methodological problem of assuring group comparability in factors other than those connected with social change.

A more direct way of assessing the impact of cultural change is through diachronic methods, termed *longitudinal* in psychology. Longitudinal studies of historical change are a recent addition to cultural psychology. Three examples of this new method can be cited:

1. Through the comparison of two generations of children from the same families, Greenfield (1993) has studied the impact of economic development on interactional processes of informal education and individual processes of cognitive representation in a Mayan community in Chiapas, Mexico.[4]
2. Through longitudinal study in both Puerto Rico and the United States of Puerto Rican families before and after immigrating to the New York area, Laosa (in progress) has been able to trace the impact of cultural change on psychological and family interaction processes.
3. Through the longitudinal observation of dairy workers adapting to computerization of their jobs, Scribner, Sachs, Di Bello, and Kindred (1991), studied the cognitive adaptation to a major change in the technological side of culture.

Because longitudinal or diachronic methods are intrinsically historical, they are more direct than cross-sectional or synchronic ones. Therefore, they should take on increasing importance in the study of the psychological impact of cultural history. However, the two types of method are mutually complementary. Sometimes, for example, massive historical change may make it impossible to delineate exactly what factors caused what psychological changes. Synchronic variability in a range of factors can then be used to model the historical change process with more precision. This strategy is currently being used by Greenfield, Childs, and Maynard to delineate precisely what aspects of the Zinacantecos' historical economic movement from agriculture to commerce are the proximal and distal causes of the associated changes in learning, teaching, and cognition.

The analysis of cultural change, whether the change be historical or evolutionary, requires particular attention to an aspect of data that is often ignored in psychology: its variability. The nature of evolutionary change is that, in response to environmental change, natural selection takes adaptive characteristics that are less frequent and makes them more frequent over long periods of time. In cultural change as well, minority trends at one time may expand into dominant trends under new conditions. Therefore, infrequent behavioral phenomena may often furnish more clues as to historical or evolutionary cultural change than do normative trends. The methodological implication holds that it is necessary to recognize the theoretical significance of infrequent as well as frequent behavioral phenomena in understanding the psychological dimensions of cultural change. Central tendency may often lead one astray in the study of social change.

The Unique Methodological Role of Video Technology

Video is uniquely suited for the study of processes of *in situ* cultural adaptation and for the study of the construction of cultural meaning. Examples of research that have drawn upon video for the former purpose are Childs and Greenfield's (1980) study of weaving apprenticeship and Stigler's study of U.S., Chinese, and Japanese classrooms (Stigler & Perry, 1990). Video also solves certain problems of reliability and validity, posed but not solved by classical psychology. It provides a permanent record by which other researchers can check the basis for interpretations and conclusions. Whereas the classic criterion of replicability of findings has been called into question (Valsiner, 1989) because of the possibility of change over time (either developmental or cultural), video freezes data in time, thus allowing the analysis to be replicated without repeating the observation.

Whereas video furnishes the *data* for the study of *in situ* processes of cultural adaptation, video can also furnish *stimuli* for studying the construction of cultural meaning (Jacobs et al., 1996; Tobin, Wu, & Davidson, 1989; Tobin, 1989). In this latter method, members of different cultures are given the task of evaluating everyday practices on video from the same range of cultures. In the study of Tobin et al. and of Jacobs, they focus on the evaluation of classroom practices in China, Japan, and the United States. The design is cross-cultural at two levels, the level of the stimuli and the level of the subjects. For example, in Jacobs' (in press) study, Japanese and American teachers are given an opportunity to evaluate videos of Japanese and American classroom lessons. The notion of multiple perspectives is built right into the design of the study itself.

An important point is the difference between this empirical approach to multiple perspectives and the post-structuralist approach which simply decries the researchers' ethnocentric perspective without trying to do anything about it (cf. Patai, 1994). Tobin (1989) describes the thought behind the Tobin et al. (1989) study in this way: "We have sought to develop a method for doing research and a narrative stance for our writing that would *decenter* as well as *deprivilege* the author–anthropologist. Rather than replacing the persona of the omniscient, positivistic, confident, gentleman–scholar with the persona of the apologetic, soul-searching, self-centered, reflexive anthropologist, we strive to shift narrative attention and the authority to define meaning away from the author. We strive to give voice—the power to name, interpret, and analyze—to the teachers, students, parents, and children who have traditionally been objects rather than partners in investigation" (Tobin, 1989, p. 174).

Tobin et al. accomplished exactly that in their innovative study. They first videotaped a preschool in each of three cultures, China, Japan, and the United States. They then showed the tapes to preschool staff, parents, and child development experts in each country, asking them to evaluate their own and each other's schools. This method led to "a multicultural discussion of such issues as freedom, conformity, creativity, and discipline" (Tobin et al., 1989, dust jacket). This method leads the authors beyond cultural differences in educational practices to the values and child development goals that lie beneath the practices.

Some of the most interesting discussion took place when the video sequences from one country violated norms of another. Nothing is as effective in revealing cultural norms and values as the reactions people have when the norms are broken. In many cases, the norms of one culture, shown on video, violated the norms of the "outsider" observing the video. The cross-cultural showing of videos provides a systematic opportunity to comment on norm violation, thus revealing the very existence of normative values.

Video technology involves a host of other methodological fine points, including transcription, coding, and interobserver reliability. The focus here will be on a new method developed by J. Stigler. In the course of a cross-cultural study of classroom practices, he and his colleagues have developed software that allows coding to be done on or next to the video frames, for instant retrieval and statistical access. After a tape has been digitized onto CD-ROM, the software allows instant access to any of the codes or video frames. This system has the potential to speed up video coding tremendously. For one reason, it will no longer be necessary to transcribe simply to keep a record of what was going on at the time a code was made; the original video clip is stored with the code. At the same time, the advances in video and computer technology enable frames to be captured on computer and, ultimately, paper, to illustrate results and to constitute a visual part of discourse transcription (e.g., Goodwin, in press).

Quantitative Methods for the Study of Behavior as Part of a Cultural System

Once qualitative understanding has been achieved, quantitative methods involving issues of frequency are useful and appropriate (Gaskins, 1994). However, not all statistical techniques are equally suitable for answering cultural questions. Insofar as cultural psychologists are interested in the varying levels and layers of culture from the most macro to the most micro, particular kinds of statistical techniques are often more appropriate. One major problem with traditional techniques such as analysis of variance and regression, is the division into independent and dependent variables. Although cross-cultural psychology generally interprets culture as an independent variable or even a set of independent variables (Jahoda, 1990), this approach has major problems.

First, culture is a system with interrelated, not independent parts (Berry, 1983). An excellent statistical technique to capture these interrelations is structural equation modeling (e.g., Bentler, 1989). This technique permits a model with multiple interacting variables. Any variable can have links with any or all of the other variables. Analyses of covariance structures are another example of a statistical technique that has these characteristics. These methods are discussed by Van de Vijver and Leung, this volume.

Second, variables cannot be neatly divided into cause and effect. Most variables function both as causes of some things and effects of others. For example, Greenfield and Childs (Greenfield, 1993) have proposed a causal model in which it is hypothesized that historical factors influence economic activity , which in turn, influences how weaving is transmitted intergenerationally. In this model, economic activity is treated as the effect of historical era and the cause of style of informal education. Given data on each of these levels, such a model can then be tested by structural equation modeling.

Third, in cultural systems, variables often function as both cause and effect. An example is the influence of symbolic cultural tools such as video games on individual development, and the effect of individual differences on the use of these tools. Such reciprocal two-way relationships can also be tested by structural equation modeling (e.g., Greenfield, Brannon, & Lohr, 1994). In general, structural equation modeling is consistent with the concept of culture as a system that is not apart from the individual. It allows the testing of models involving a whole web of social, cultural, and personal factors over time in a single model. However, the very same flexibility that is an asset of these models can also be a disadvantage. If a researcher is using them in an exploratory fashion, as a rule, some structure will emerge. However, the post hoc interpretation of such an outcome is open to question. In such a case, the validity of a given model depends on testing and ruling out theoretically plausible alternatives.

Cultural Adaptation of Procedures and Measures

A cogent example of the conceptual and theoretical problems that arise when measuring instruments are transported across cultures without adaptation comes from the study of attachment (LeVine & Miller, 1990; Takahashi, 1990). Attachment is a topic particularly suitable for cultural and cross-cultural investigation because adult–infant attachment is a key foundation for cultural transmission and for the social relations upon which human culture is based. (See also chapter by Keller, this volume.)

LeVine and Miller (1990) recount how a procedure, the Strange Situation, that had been devised by Ainsworth as a culture-specific adaptation to measure attachment in the United States came to be used universally in the interest of cross-cultural comparison. In moving her study of attachment from Uganda (Ainsworth, 1967) to the United States, Ainsworth had changed her attachment measuring instrument to accord with the greater autonomy and independence encouraged in U. S. infants. Nonetheless, the deceptive standardization of the Strange Situation subsequently sent it all over the world, with no thought as to its cross-cultural validity and dubious comparative results (see Takahashi's critique, 1990). LeVine and Miller (1990) point out that in 1978 Ainsworth and colleagues wrote, "It seems entirely likely that Ainsworth's (1967) Ganda infants and Konner's (1972) Bushmen babies could not have tolerated the strange situation" (Ainsworth,

Blehar, Waters, & Wall, 1978, p. iv). Recently, Takahashi (1986, 1990) announced that the Japanese mothers of her sample would not consent to leaving their babies alone in an unfamiliar situation.

Clearly, the same situation had totally different meanings for babies and mothers in these different cultures. Mindful of this critique, Harwood (1992) did a cross-cultural study of the interpretive meaning of the Strange Situation and the behaviors that occur in it for Puerto Rican and Euro-American mothers. Indeed, she found that the meaning of responses to this situation was different in the two cultural groups: In keeping with their more individualistic orientation, Euro-American mothers "describe an active yet related infant as most desirable and a clingy, distressed infant as most undesirable" (Harwood, 1992, p. 831). Puerto Rican mothers, in keeping with their more sociocentric or collectivistic orientation, "describe as most desirable a quiet, responsive infant whose behavior is tipped more toward proximity maintenance than toward active exploration" (Harwood, 1992, p. 831). If the culturally desired response to the Strange Situation is culturally variable, then it is not possible to standardize behavioral categories and the interpretations of these categories across different cultures. In line with the earlier discussion of single case analysis as applied to the Strange Situation, cross-cultural quantitative comparisons also become problematic.

Going one step further, note that the Strange Situation measures attachment through response to separation. Given that the ability to cope with separation is normative in only a minority of cultures (often termed individualistic), one might also want to measure attachment as proximity maintenance behavior, in line with the Puerto Rican (and other collectivistic societies') ideal of attachment behavior. In other words, this analysis of attachment reveals how culture-specific a measuring instrument can be. To use the Strange Situation in both an individualistic and collectivistic culture is to have a biased comparison. The infants in one society will be tested by the same measure that their upbringing has utilized; the infants in the other society will be tested on how well they can do in a culturally-foreign situation. If only one single testing situation is to be used in cross-cultural comparison, it should be one that provides room for a range of ideals to be actualized. A procedure for measuring attachment that allowed *both* proximity maintenance and tolerance for separation to be manifest as normative attachment would provide this range. Such a situation would be culturally fairer than the classical Strange Situation that forces mother-child separation on all babies, whether or not they have ever experienced it in their everyday lives (Takahashi, 1990).

Substantive Consequences of Empirical Methodology for Cultural Psychology

Cultural Adaptation of Procedures Leads to Generalizable Processes of Cognition and Culture Acquisition

Generalizations concerning universal processes must be a part of cultural psychology, insofar as the culture-making capacities of the human species are being

considered. However, cross-cultural generalizations must arise from a more abstract level than the level of similar or identical measuring tools. An example
illustrating this point is taken from a study of the development of kinship terminology carried out by Greenfield and Childs (1978) in Zinacantan, a Mayan community in Chiapas, Mexico. Children of different ages were asked about various
sibling relations in their own households, using the complex sibling terminology
of their Tzotzil language in which there are separate terms for older and younger
siblings, as well as for the sibling of a boy and the sibling of a girl. Samples of the
type of question asked are, "What is the name of your older sister?" and "as for
older sister, Shunka, what is the name of her younger brother?" From anthropology, linguistics, and developmental psychology, Greenfield and Childs extracted
theories that might have explained the results. The theories from anthropology
and linguistics were *relativistic*, emphasizing the role of culture-specific values
(the importance of the older–younger relationship) and language-specific structure (the complexity and organization of the sib terminology system). The theories from psychology, Piagetian and information processing, were *universalistic*,
emphasizing common responses as a function of chronological age (Piaget) and
memory load (information processing).

Piaget (1928) had done a study in the same domain with Swiss children. Greenfield
and Childs' procedure, however, was quite different from his. Whereas he asked
quantitative questions ("How many brothers do you have?"), Greenfield and Childs
asked qualitative ones ("What is the name of your older brother?). (To have been
required to answer quantitative questions would have demanded an unfamiliar skill
for Zinacanteco children.) Whereas Piaget asked simply about the two terms, brother
and sister, Greenfield and Childs asked about the six different Tzotzil sibling terms.
(Note that comparability would have dictated aggregating sets of sibling terms, such
as older sister, girl's younger sister, and boy's younger sister. Yet, to do this would
have violated the organization of Tzotzil sibling organization.)

A maxim of the use of "comparable" instruments for cross-cultural comparison is that comparable instruments are necessary in order to elucidate universal
processes. A corollary would be that the lack of comparable instruments will lead
only to culture-specific conclusions. This maxim, with its corollary, was belied by
Greenfield and Childs' results. Whereas their culture-specific procedure should,
according to this way of thinking, have led to the verification of culture-specific
processes (triggered, in this case, by cultural values or linguistic terminology),
the results showed no evidence of any such culture-specific processes. Instead,
all of the results led to the validation of putatively universal developmental and
cognitive processes. For example, Piaget had posited the development of a stage
of concrete operations in middle childhood, a stage where children can symboli-
cally represent the transformations of concrete objects. In Greenfield and Childs'
data, there was evidence of concrete operational development, from egocentrism
to understanding of reciprocity to understanding of reversible relations (e.g., I
am my older brother's younger brother), occurring in the same age range described by Piaget for Swiss children. Greenfield and Childs also found evidence
of memory development and the influence of category size on memory retrieval,
theorized to be universal processes.

The methodological point of this example is that maximum adaptation of methods to each particular culture in which a phenomenon is studied maximizes the possibility of uncovering nomothetic, even universal, processes at the same time as it obviates the possibility of direct, quantitative cross-cultural comparison (cf., Enriquez, 1977). Ironically, the comparable methods required for direct comparison in this example would probably have reduced, if not eliminated, the manifestation of universal processes. For example, unfamiliar quantitative questions would not have been answered so well by Zinacantecos, and cognitive competencies in kinship terminology would have been masked. Similarly, the use of unfamiliar aggregates of siblings to conform to the French sibling terms used by Piaget would have been confusing and would have hidden the Zinacanteco child's mastery of a more complex sibling system. The paradox is that universal processes are revealed more by *noncomparable methods* and *theoretical comparison* than by *comparable methods* and *quantitative comparison* across cultures.

However, this study was not explicitly comparative. Is it possible to use noncomparable methods in an explicitly comparative study? Morelli, Rogoff, Oppenheim, and Goldsmith (1992) did exactly that in a comparative study of sleeping arrangements in Utah and in a Maya community in Guatemala. In each place, "the interview was tailored in ways appropriate to each community" (p. 606). The tailoring did not preclude basic quantitative comparisons, although the emphasis was on qualitative results. Of great pragmatic interest to those advocating noncomparable methods as a way of drawing conclusions both about cultural variability and possible universals is the fact that this article was published by a mainstream journal.

Cultural Generation of Procedures Leads to Generalizable Processes of Cognition and Culture Acquisition

This important point will be illustrated with the example of the cognitive appropriation of cultural tools. Processes of transforming cultural tools into mental tools (Bruner, 1964; Vygotsky, 1978.; Saxe, 1991) are part of universal cognitive equipment and operations. The exploration of these processes demands the identification of particular cultural tools, an understanding of how they function in cultural practices, and experimental methods by which the transformation and use of the tools can be studied. The important point is that, although a particular tool is rarely universal, its learning and use will draw upon and reveal universal processes in the cognitive appropriation of cultural tools (Saxe, 1991).

An outstanding example is the exploration of the "mental abacus" begun by Hatano, Miyake, and Binks (1977) and continued by Stigler and colleagues (Stigler, 1984; Stigler, Chalip, & Miller, 1986). The research begins with an analysis of the abacus as a calculation tool. Clearly, an understanding of the cultural tool in question is an important part of the methodology. This understanding must be gained either by being a cultural insider who has been exposed to and trained in the use of the tool, by ethnographic exploration, or by collaboration with a cultural insider.

A number of different methodological strategies have been used to explore the transformation of the physical abacus into a mental tool and the operation of the "mental abacus." One strategy (Stigler, 1984) is based on identifying steps in the arithmetic problem-solving process that were specific to abacus use (i.e., would not be used in standard numerically-based calculations). When shown photographs of an abacus with its beads in various positions, experts were extremely accurate at distinguishing abacus states that were intermediate steps to the solution of particular problems from states that were not part of the problem's solution. In addition, response time was slower if the depicted abacus state occurred later in the problem-solving sequence.

A second methodological strategy was to do an error analysis to see if the nature of abacus user errors reflected a mental representation specific to abacus use (Stigler, 1984). Because the abacus has upper beads that represent the quantity five, errors that deviate by exactly five would reveal the use of an internal abacus representation in mental calculation. Abacus operators made significantly more mistakes that were off by exactly five, both in using the abacus and in mental calculation, than did American students.

Consequently, it could be concluded that (1.) abacus experts had internalized a representation of an abacus that they could operate upon mentally, (2.) they carried out operations on the mental abacus in the same sequence as would be done on the physical abacus, and (3.) their errors bore the trace of the mental abacus. The point is that the conclusions from this research are not specific to the abacus, a cultural tool particular to certain cultures. The point is not whether subjects could generalize their skills to other tools. In essence, the conclusions are about potentially universal processes of transforming cultural tools into mental tools (Gauvain, 1995).

By studying the effects on representation and problem-solving of activities using other culture-specific tools, further conclusions about the scope and nature of these cognitive processes of cultural appropriation (Saxe, 1991) can be drawn. For example, in the domain of math, the influence of money denominations on the representation of math problems was demonstrated by Saxe (1982a, 1982b) in New Guinea. Note that these findings about the representational impact of money generalize the conclusions of Stigler and colleagues about the representational impact of the abacus, even though Saxe used different procedures to study the effects of a different tool in a different society. Indeed, the cognitive consequences of using a range of cultural tools in a variety of activities have been studied (Greenfield & Lave, 1982; Guberman & Greenfield, 1991): tailoring (Lave, 1977), pottery making (Price-Williams, Gordon, & Ramirez, 1969), video games (Greenfield, 1993; Greenfield & Cocking, 1994b), candy selling (Saxe, 1991), money (Saxe, 1982a, 1982b; Guberman, in press a, b), weaving (Greenfield & Childs, 1977), and bartending (Beach, 1984, 1992). In each case the structure of the artifact is internalized as a partially isomorphic representation.

The method of using cultural tools embedded in cultural activities as a methodological strategy not only reveals information about how cognitive enculturation *varies* from culture to culture, depending on the tools available in a particular cultural niche. The method also reveals information about the *universal* role of tools in developing processes of mental representation. Only by generating particular studies out of the specific tool-using activities that occur in a given cultural niche can the general question of the relation between cultural tools and cognitive processes be addressed. The ability to generalize cannot be based on using formally equivalent procedures across cultures. Instead, generalization is based on using common conceptual questions about situated cognition to generate a multiplicity of procedures that are appropriate to diverse cultural niches.

Conclusion

The methodology for studying culture as process must elucidate the ontogenetic, sociohistorical, and phylogenetic origins of psychological functioning in the enculturated adult human being (Vygotsky & Luria, 1993). But methodology must go farther. It must be adequate to deal with socially shared cognition (Resnick, Levine, & Teasley, 1991) and with the participation of the individual in social relations and in a cultural community (Rogoff, in press). The development of research methodology adequate to these requirements is an extremely demanding task. The suggestions in this chapter should be of practical utility to researchers and students who wish to study culture as psychological process.

Endnotes

1. The author wishes to thank Jennifer Jacobs, Shinobu Kitayama, Ashley Maynard, Joan Miller, Richard Shweder, and James Stigler for helpful comments on an earlier draft of this chapter.

2. Along with Jahoda, 1977, this chapter rejects the etic/emic distinction as a useful way to talk about methods for studying universal and culture-specific patterns of thinking.

3. Often the problem of variable cultural interpretations is dealt with as a statistical issue internal to a particular instrument (e.g., Berry et al., 1992; Van de Vijver & Poortinga, 1991). Statistical problems then find statistical solutions. One example of such a solution is the measurement of bias ("all unwanted factors that unequally affect scores in different cultural groups" [p. 225]). Even when insider judgments of the cultural appropriateness of individual stimuli are used, the possibility that the very method (e.g., opinion survey) on which a particular instrument is based may have different meanings in different cultures is not dealt with.

4. An unanticipated methodological insight from this historical study was that more open-ended, naturalistic methods are more sensitive to sociohistorical change than are more controlled experimental procedures. The latter provide too much constraint on subject responses to be sensitive to future cultural change, unknown at the time of the historical baseline observations.

References

Ainsworth, M. D. S. (1967) *Infancy in Uganda: Infant care and the growth of attachment.* Baltimore: John Hopkins University Press.

Ainsworth, M. D. S., Blehar, M. C., Waters, E., & Wall, S. (1978). *Patterns of attachment.* Hillsdale NJ: Erlbaum.

Beach, K. (1984). The role of external memory cues in learning to become a bartender. *The Quarterly Newsletter of the Laboratory of Comparative Human Cognition, 6* (1 & 2), 42–43.

Beach, K. (1993). Becoming a bartender: The role of external memory cues in a work-directed educational activity. *Applied Cognitive Psychology, 7,* 191–204.

Bentler, P. (1989). *EQS structural equations manual.* Los Angeles: BMDP Statistical Software, Inc.

Berry, J. W., (1976). *Human ecology and cognitive style: Comparative studies in cultural and psychological adaptation.* New York: Sage/Halsted.

Berry, J. W. (1979). Unobtrusive measures in cross-cultural research. In L. Sechrest (Ed.), *New directions in methodology of behavioral science, 1,* 47–57.

Berry, J. W. (1980). Ecological analyses for cross-cultural psychology. In N. Warren (Ed.), *Studies in cross-cultural psychology,* (Vol. 2, pp. 157–189). London: Academic Press.

Berry, J. W. (1983). Textured contexts: Systems and situations in cross-cultural psychology. In S.H. Irvine & J.W. Berry (Eds.), *Human assessment and cultural factors* (pp. 117–125). New York: Plenum.

Berry, J. W., & Bennett, J. A. (1992). Cree conceptions of cognitive competence. *International Journal of Psychology, 27,* 73–88.

Berry, J. W., Poortinga, Y. H., Segall, M. H., & Dasen, P. R. (1992). *Cross-cultural psychology: Research and Applications.* Cambridge: Cambridge Univerisity Press.

Blake, I. K. (1994). Language development and socialization in young African-American children. In P. M. Greenfield & R. R. Cocking (Eds.), *Cross-cultural roots of minority child development* (pp. 167–195). Hillsdale, NJ: Erlbaum.

Boesch, C. (1991). Teaching among wild chimpanzees. *Animal Behavior, 41,* 530–532.

Bruner, J. S. (1964). The course of cognitive growth. *American Psychologist, 19,* 1–15.

Bruner, J. S. (1972). The nature and uses of immaturity. *American Psychologist, 27,* 1–22.

Bruner, J. (1986). *Actual minds, possible worlds.* Cambridge, MA: Harvard University Press.

Bruner, J. (1990). *Acts of meaning.* Cambridge, MA: Harvard University Press.

Bruner, J. (1993). Do we "acquire" culture or vice versa? *Behavioral and Brain Sciences, 16,* 515–516.

Bruner, J. S., Greenfield, P. M., Olver, R. R., et al. (1996). *Studies in cognitive growth.* New York: Wiley.

Campbell, D. T. (1970). Natural selection as an epistemological model. In R. Naroll & R. Cohen (Eds.), *A handbook of method in cultural anthropology* (pp. 51–85). New York: Natural History Press.

Carey, S., & Gelman, R. (Eds.). (1991). *The epigenesis of mind: Essays on biology and cognition.* Hillsdale, NJ: Erlbaum.

Childs, C. P. & Greenfield, P. M. (1980). Informal modes of learning and teaching: The case of Zinacanteco weaving. In N. Warren (Ed.), *Studies in cross-cultural psychology,* (Vol. 2, pp. 269–316). London: Academic Press.

Choi, S.H. (1992). Communicative socialization processes: Korea and Canada. In S. Iwawaki, Y. Kashima & K. Leung (Eds.), *Innovations in cross-cultural psychology,* (pp. 103–122). Lisse, Holland: Swets & Zeitlinger.

Cole, M. (1990). Cultural psychology: a once and future discipline? In J.J. Bergman (Ed.), *Nebraska symposium on motivation, 1989: Cross-cultural perspectives.* (Vol. 37, pp. 279–336). Lincoln: University of Nebraska Press.

Cole, M. (1992). Context, modularity, and the cultural constitution of development. In L. T. Winegar, & J. Valsiner (Eds.), *Children's development within social context.* Hillsdale, (pp. 5–31) NJ: Lawrence Erlbaum Associates.

Cole, M. (1995). Culture and cognitive development: From cross-cultural research to creating systems of cultural mediation. *Culture and Psychology, 1,* 25–54.

Dasen, P. R. (1984). The cross-cultural study of intelligence: Piaget and the Baoule. In P. S. Fry (Ed.), *Changing conceptions of intelligence and intellectual functioning: Current theory and research* (pp. 107–134). Amsterdam: North-Holland.

Deacon, T. (in press). *The idea that changed the brain: The coevolution of language and brain.* New York: W. W. Norton.

Delgado-Gaitan, C. (1993). Parenting in two generations of Mexican American families. *International Journal of Behavioral Develpment, 16,* 409–427.

Delgado-Gaitan, C. (1994). Socializing young children in Mexican–American families: An intergenerational perspective. In P.M. Greenfield & R.R. Cocking (Eds.), *Cross-cultural roots of minority child development* (pp. 55–86). Hillsdale, NJ: Erllbaum.

Draper, P., & Cashden, E. (1988). Technological change and child behavior among the !Kung. *Ethnology, 27,* 339–365.

Eckensberger, L. H. (1979). A metamethodological evaluation of psychological theories from a cross-cultural perspective. In L. H. Eckensberger, W. J. Lonner, & Y. H. Poortinga (Eds.), *Cross-cultural contributions to psychology.* (pp. 255–275), Amsterdam: Swets & Zeitlinger.

Eckensberger, L. H. (1995). Activity or action: Two different roads towards an integration of culture into psychology? *Culture and Psychology, 1,* 67–80.

Eckensberger, L. H., Krewer, B., & Kasper, E. (1984). Simulation of cultural change by cross-cultural research: Some metamethodological considerations. In K. A. McCluskey & H. W. Reese (Eds.), *Life-span developmental psychology: Historical and generational effects* (pp. 73–107). Orlando, FL: Academic Press.

Edwards, J. A., & Lampert, M. D. (Eds.). (1993). *Talking data: Transcription and coding in discourse research.* Hilsdale, NJ: Erlbaum.

Enriquez, V. G. (1977). Toward cross-cultural knowledge through cross-indegenous methods and perspectives. *Philippine Journal of Psychology, 12,* 9–16.

Feldman, C., Bruner, J., Kalmar, D., & Renderer, B. (1993). Plot, plight, and dramatism: interpretations at three ages. *Human Development, 36,* 327–342.

Fisher, C. (1994). Qualitative and quantitative empirical methods: Their relative power. Paper presented at the American Psychological Association, Los Angeles.

Gallistel, C. R., Brown, A. L., Carey, S., Gelman, R., & Keil, F. C. (1991). Lessons from animal learning for the study of cognitive development. In S. Carey & R. Gelman (Eds.), *The epigenesis of mind: Essays in biology and knowledge* (pp. 3–36). Hillsdale, NJ: Erlbaum.

Gaskins, S. (1994). Integrating interpretive and quantitative methods in socialization research. *Merrill-Palmer Quarterly, 40,* 313–333.

Gauvain, M. (1995). Thinking in niches: Sociocultural influences on cognitive development. *Human Development, 38,* 25–45.

Geertz, C. (1973). *The interpretation of cultures.* New York: Basic Books.

Goodall, J. (1986). *The chimpanzees of Gombe: Patterns of behavior.* Cambridge, MA: Harvard University Press.

Goodenough, W. H. (1980). Ethnographic field techniques. In H. C. Triandis, & J. W. Berry (Eds.), *Handbook of cross-cultural psychology: methodology.* (Vol. 2, pp. 29–55). Boston: Allyn and Bacon.

Goodnow, J. J. (1985a). Change and variation in parents' ideas about childhood and parenting. In I. E. Sigel (Ed.), *Parental belief systems* (pp. 1235–1270). Hillsdale, NJ: Erlbaum.

Goodwin, C. (1994) Professional vision. *American Anthropologist, 96,* 606–633.

Grando, N. I. (1988). A matematica na agricultura e na escola [Mathematics in agriculture and school.] Unpublished master's thesis, Universidade Federal de Pernambuco, Recife.

Greenfield, P. M. (1966). On culture and conservation. In J. S. Bruner, R. R. Olver, P. M. Greenfield, et al., *Studies in cognitive growth,* (pp. 225–256). New York: Wiley.

Greenfield, P. M. (1972). Oral or written language: The consequences for cognitive development in Africa, the United States, and England. *Language and Speech, 15,* 169–178. Reprinted in M. Maer & W. M. Stallings (Eds.), *Culture, child, and school: Socio-cultural influences on learning.* Monterey: Brooks/Cole Publishing, 1975.

Greenfield, P. M. (1984). A theory of the teacher in everyday life. In B. Rogoff & J. Lave (Eds.), *Everyday cognition: Its development in social context* (pp. 117–138). Cambridge, MA: Harvard University Press.

Greenfield, P. M. (1991). Language, tools, and brain: The ontogeny and phylogeny of hierarchically organized sequential behavior. *Behavioral and Brain Sciences, 14,* 531–551.

Greenfield, P. (1993). Historical change and cognitive change: A two-decade follow-up study in Zinacantan, a Mayan community of Southern Mexico. Paper presented in P. Greenfield (Chair), Sylvia Scribner Memorial Symposium: Culture, Activity, and Development, Society for Research in Child Development, New Orleans.

Greenfield, P. M. (1994). Independence and interdependence as developmental scripts: Implications for theory, research, and practice. In P. M. Greenfield & R. R. Cocking (Eds.). *Cross cultural roots of minority child development*, (pp. 1–37). Hillsdale, NJ: Erlbaum.

Greenfield, P. M. (1995). Review of *The Significance of Schooling* by Robert Serpell. *Mind, Culture, and Activity: An International Journal, 2*, 54–58.

Greenfield, P. M., Brannon, C., & Lohr, D. (1994). Two-dimensional representation of movement through three-dimensional space: The role of video game expertise. *Journal of Applied Developmental Psychology, 15*, 87–103.

Greenfield, P. M., Brazelton, T. B., & Childs, C. (1989). From birth to maturity in Zinacantan: Ontogenesis in cultural context. In V. Bricker & G. Gossen (Eds.), *Ethnographic encounters in Southern Mesoamerica: Celebratory essays in honor of Evon Z. Vogt* (pp. 177–216). Albany: Institute of Mesoamerican Studies, State University of New York.

Greenfield, P. M., & Bruner, J. S. (1966). Culture and cognitive growth. *International Journal of Psychology, 1*, 89–107. (A revised version appears in D. Goslin (Ed.), *Handbook of socialization theory*. Chicago: Rand McNally, 1969, pp. 653–657).

Greenfield, P. M., & Childs, C. P. (1977). Weaving, color terms and pattern representation: Cultural influences and cognitive development among the Zinacantecos of Southern Mexico. *Inter-American Journal of Psychology, 11*, 23–48.

Greenfield, P. M., & Childs, C. P. (1978). Understanding sibling concepts: A developmental study of kin terms in Zinacantan. In P. R. Dasen (Ed.), *Piagetian psychology* (pp. 335–358). New York: Gardner Press.

Greenfield, P. M., Childs, C. P., & Maynard, A. (unpublished data).

Greenfield, P. M., & Cocking, R. R. (1994a). *Cross cultural roots of minority child development*. Hillsdale, NJ: Erlbaum.

Greenfield, P. M., & Cocking, R. R. (Ed.). (1994b). Effects of interactive entertainment technologies on development. *Journal of Applied Developmental Psychology, 15(1)*, 1–39.

Greenfield, P. M., & Lave, J. (1982). Cognitive aspects of informal education. In D. Wagner & H. Stevenson (Eds.), *Cultural perspectives on child development* (pp. 181–207). San Francisco: Freeman.

Greenfield, P. M., Raeff, C., & Quiroz, B. (in press). Cross-cultural conflict in the social construction of the child. In S. Harkness, C. Raeff, & C. Super (Eds.), *New directions for child development*. San Francisco: Jossey-Bass.

Greenfield, P. M., Reich, L. C., & Olver, R. R. (1966). On culture and equivalence-II. In J. S. Bruner, R. R. Olver, P. M. Greenfield, et al., *Studies in cognitive growth* (pp. 270–318). New York: Wiley.

Greenfield, P. M. & Savage-Rumbaugh, E. S. (1991). Imitation, grammatical development, and the invention of protogrammar. In N. Krasnegor, D. Rumbaugh, M. Studdert-Kennedy, & R. Schiefelbusch (Eds.), *Biological and behaviorial determinants of language development* (pp. 235–258). Hillsdale, NJ: Erlbaum.

Grice, H. P. (1975). Logic and conversation. In P. Cole & J. L. Morgan (Eds.), *Syntax and semantics* (*Vol. 3, Speech acts*, pp. 41–58). New York: Academic Press.

Guberman, S. (in press a). The development of everyday mathematics in Brazilian children with limited formal education. *Child Development*.

Guberman, S. (in press b). Children's mathematical activities and achievements: A comparative study of Latino and Korean American children. *SRCD Monographs*

Guberman, S., & Greenfield, P. M. (1991). Learning and transfer in everyday cognition. *Cognitive Development, 6*, 223–260.

Harkness, S. & Super, C. H. (Eds.). (1995). *Parents' cultural belief systems: Their origins, expressions, and consequences*. New York: Guilford Press.

Harwood, R. D. (1992). The influence of culturally derived values on Anglo and Puerto Rican mothers' perceptions of attachment behavior. *Child Development, 63*, 822–840.

Hatano, G. (1995). Cultural psychology of conceptual development: The need for numbers and narratives. In F. S. Kessel & M. Cole (Chairs), Towards a cultural psychology of development: I. Methodological matters. Symposium at the biennial meeting of the Society for Research in Child Development, Indianapolis.

Hatano, G., Miyake, Y., & Binks, M. G. (1977). Performance of expert abacus operators. *Cognition, 5*, 57–71.

Heath, S. B. (1983). *Ways with words: Language, life, and work in communities and classrooms.* Cambridge, MA: Cambridge University Press.

Hirschfeld, L. & Gelman, S. (Eds.). (1994). *Mapping the mind: Domains, culture and cognition.* New York: Cambridge University Press.

Ho, D. (1989). Continuity and variation in Chinese patterns of socialization. *Journal of Marriage and the Family, 51*, 149–163.

Hofstede, G. (1980). *Culture's consequences: International differences in work-related values.* London: Sage.

Illyenkov, E. V. (1977). The problem of the ideal. In *Philosophy in the USSR: Problems of dialectical materialism.* Moscow: Progess.

Jacobs, J. (in press).

Jacobs, J. K., Yoshida, M., & Fernandez, C. (1996). Teachers' beliefs: Japanese and American teachers' evaluations of fifth grade mathematics lessons. Unpublished manuscript, Department of Psychology, University of California, Los Angeles.

Jahoda, G. (1977). In pursuit of the emic-etic distinction: Can we ever capture it? In Y.H. Poortinga (Ed.), *Basic problems in cross-cultural psychology* (pp. 55–63). Lisse: Swets and Zeitlinger.

Jahoda, G. (1990). Variables, systems and the problem of explanation. In F. J. R. van de Vijver & G. J. M. Hutschemaekers (Eds.), *The investigation of culture: Current issues in cultural psychology* (pp. 115–130). Tilburg: Tilburg University Press.

Jahoda, G. (1992). Foreword. In J. W. Berry, Y. H. Poortinga, M.H. Segall, & P.R. Dasen, *Cross-cultural psychology: Research and Applications* (pp. x–xii). Cambridge: Cambridge University Press.

Jones, E. E. & Thorne, A. (1987). Rediscovery of the subject: Intercultural approaches to clinical assessment. *Journal of Consulting and Clinical Psychology, 55*, 488–495.

Kim, U., & Berry, J. W. (Eds.) (1993) *Indigenous psychologies: Research and experience in cultural context.* Newbury Park: Sage Publications.

Kitayama, S., Markus, H. R., Matsumoto, H., & Norasakkunkit (in press). Individual and collective processes of self-esteem management: Self-enhancement in the United States and self-depreciation in Japan. *Journal of Personality and Social Psychology.*

Konner, M. J. (1972). Aspects of the developmental ethology of a foraging people. In N. Blurton Jones (Ed.), *Ethological studies of child behaviour.* Cambridge: Cambridge University Press.

Labov, W. & Waletsky, J. (1967). Narrative analysis. In J. Holm (Ed.), *Essay on the verbal and visual arts* (pp. 12–44). Seattle: University of Washington Press.

Lave, J. (1977). Cognitive consequences of traditional apprenticeship training in West Africa. *Anthropology and Education Quarterly, 8*, 177–180.

Lave, J. (1988). *Cognition in practice.* New York: Cambridge University Press.

Lave, J. , Murtaugh, M., & de la Rocha, O. (1984). The dialectic of arithmetic in grocery shopping. In B. Rogoff & J. Lave (Eds.), *Everyday cognition: Its development in social context* (pp. 67–94). Cambridge, MA: Harvard University Press.

Lerner, D. (1958). *The passing of traditional society: Modernizing the Middle East.* Glencoe: Free Press.

LeVine, R., Dixon, S., LeVine, S., Richman, A., Leiderman, P. H., Keefer, C. H., & Brazelton, T. B. (1994). *Child care and culture: Lessons from Africa.* New York: Cambridge University Press.

LeVine, R. A. & Miller, P.M. (1990). Commentary. *Human Development, 33*, 73–80.

LeVine, R. A. & Shweder, R. A. (1995). Culture, psychic pluralism, and the nature-nurture problem. In F. S. Kessel & R. A. Shweder (Chairs), Towards a cultural psychology of development: I. Theoretical themes. Symposium at the biennial meeting of the Society for Research in Child Development, Indianapolis.

Lonner, W. J., & Berry, J. W. (1986). Sampling and surveying. In Lonner, W. J. & Berry, J. W. (Eds.), *Field methods in cross-cultural research* (pp. 85–110). London: Sage.

Lucariello, J. (1995). Mind, culture, person: Elements in a cultural psychology. *Human Development, 38,* 2–18.

Luria, A. R. (1976). *Cognitive development: Its cultural and social foundations.* Cambridge: Harvard University Press.

Marcus, G. E., & Fischer, M. M. J. (1986). *Anthropology as cultural critique: An experimental moment in the human sciences.* Chicago: University of Chicago Press.

Markus, H. R., & Kitayama, S. (1991). Culture and the self: Implications for cognition, emotion, and motivation. *Psychological Review, 98,* 224–253.

Matsuzawa, T. (1991). Nesting cups and metatools in chimpanzees. *Behavioral and Brain Sciences, 14,* 570–571.

Mauss, M. (1954). *The gift: Forms and functions of exchange in archaic societies.* Glencoe, IL: Free Press.

Maxwell, J. A. (1992). Understanding and validity in qualitative research. *Harvard Educational Review, 62,* 279–300.

McGrew, W. C. (1992). *Chimpanzee material culture: Implications for human evolution.* Cambridge: Cambridge University Press.

Miles, M., & Huberman, A. M. (1984). Drawing valid meaning from qualitative data: Toward a shared craft. *Educational Researcher, 13* (5), 20–30.

Miles, M., & Huberman, A. M. (1994). *Qualitative data analysis. An expanded sourcebook.* (4th ed.). Thousand Oaks, CA: Sage.

Miller, J. G., Bersoff, D. M. & Harwood, R. L. (1990). Perceptions of social responsibilities in India and in the United States: Moral imperatives or personal decisions? *Journal of Personality and Social Psychology, 58,* 33–47.

Morelli, G. A., Rogoff, B., Oppenheim, D., & Goldsmith, D. (1992). Cultural variation in infants' sleeping arrangements: Questions of independence. *Developmental Psychology, 28,* 604–613.

Munroe, R. L., & Munroe, R. H. (1986). Field work in cross-cultural psychology. In W. J. Lonner & J. W. Berry (Eds.), *Field methods in cross-cultural research* (pp. 111–136). London: Sage.

Nelson, K. (1989). *Narratives from the crib.* Cambridge: Harvard University Press.

Nishida, T. (1987). Local traditions and cultural transmission. In B. Smuts, D. Cheney, R. Seyfarth, R. Wrangham, & T. Struhsaker (Eds.), *Primate societies.* Chicago: University of Chicago Press.

Nunes, T., Schliemann, A. D., & Carraher, D. W. (Eds.). (1993). *Street mathematics and school mathematics.* Cambridge: Cambridge University Press.

Ochs, E. (1979). Transciption as theory. In E. Ochs & B. B. Schieffelin (Eds.), *Developmental pragmatics* (pp. 43–72). New York: Academic Press.

Ochs, E. (1982). Talking to children in Western Samoa. *Language in Society, 11,* 77–104.

Ochs, E., & Schieffelin, B. B. (1983). *Acquiring Conversational Competence.* Boston: Routledge & Kegan Paul.

Ochs, E., & Schieffelin, B. B. (1984). Language acquistition and socialization: Three developmental stories and their implications. In R. A. Shweder & R. A. LeVine, (Eds.), *Culture theory: Essays on mind, self, and emotion,* (pp. 276–320). New York: Cambridge University Press.

Ochs, E., & Taylor, C. (1992). Science at dinner. In C. Kramsch (Ed.), *Text and context: Cross-disciplinary perspectives on language study* (pp. 29–45). Lexington, MA: D.C. Heath.

Ogbu, J. (1978). *Minority education and caste: The American system in cross-cultural perspective.* New York: Academic Press.

Ogbu, J. (1994). From cultural differences to differences in cultural frame of reference. In P. M. Greenfield & R. R. Cocking (Eds.), *Cross-cultural roots of minority child development* (pp. 365–391). Hillsdale, NJ: Erlbaum.

Packer, M. (1995). The logic of interpretive inquiry. In F. S. Kessel & M. Cole (Chairs), Towards a cultural psychology of development: I. Methodological matters. Symposium at the biennial meeting of the Society for Research in Child Development, Indianapolis.

Patai, D. (1994). Sick and tired of scholars'

nouveau solipsism. *The Chronicle of Higher Education,* Feb. 23, A52.

Perusse, D. (1993). Human parental behavior: Nurture as nature? In P. Hefner & W. Irons (Chairs), *Models of biocultural evolution: Understanding human social and moral development.* American Association for the Advancement of Science, Boston.

Piaget, J. (1928). *Judgment and reasoning in the child.* New York: Harcourt, Brace.

Piaget, J. (1965). *The child's conception of number.* New York: W. W. Norton.

Pinker, S. (1994). *The language instinct.* NY: William Morrow.

Plooij, F. X. (1978). Some basic traits of language in wild chimpanzees. In A. Lock (Ed.), *Action, gesture, and symbol: The emergence of language* (pp. 111–131). New York: Academic Press.

Poortinga, Y. H. (1989). Equivalence of cross-cultural data: An overview of basic issues. *International Journal of Psychology, 24,* 737–756.

Poortinga, Y. H., & Malpass, R. S. (1986). Making inferences from cross-cultural data. In W. J. Lonner & J. W. Berry (Eds.), *Field methods in cross-cultural research* (pp. 17–46). Beverly Hills, CA: Sage.

Price-Williams, D. (1980). Toward the idea of cultural psychology: A superordinate theme for study. *Journal of Cross-Cultural Psychology, 11,* 75–88.

Price-Williams, D. R., Gordon, W., & Ramirez, M. (1969). Skill and conservation: A study of pottery-making children. *Developmental Psychology, 1,* 769.

Rabain, J. (1979). *L'enfant du lignage. Du sevrage à la classe d'âge chez les Wolof du Sénégal* [Child of the lineage. From weaning to age-graded peer group among the Wolof of Senegal]. Paris: Payot.

Rabain-Jamin, J. (1994). Language and socialization of the child in African families living in France. In P. M. Greenfield & R. R. Cocking (Eds.), *Cross-cultural roots of minority child development* (pp. 147–166). Hillsdale, NJ: Erlbaum.

Resnick, L. B., Levine, J. M., & Teasley, S. D. (Eds.). (1991). *Perspectives on socially shared cognition.* Washington, DC: American Psychological Association.

Rizzo, T. A., Corsaro, W. A., & Bates, J. E. (1992). Ethnographic methods and interpretive analysis: Expanding the methodological options of psychologists. *Developmental Review, 12,* 101–123.

Rogoff, B. (1990). *Apprenticeship in thinking: Cognitive development in social context.* New York: Oxford University Press.

Rogoff, B. (in press). Developmental transitions in children's participation in sociocultural activities. In A. Sameroff & M. Haith (Eds.), *Reason and responsibility: The passage through childhood.* Chicago: University of Chicago Press.

Rogoff, B., Baker-Sennett, J. Lacasa, P., & Goldsmith, D. (1995). Development through participation in sociocultural activity. In J. Goodnow, P. Miller, & F. Kessel (Eds.), *Cultural practices as contexts for development* (pp. 45–65). San Francisco: Jossey-Bass.

Rogoff, B., & Morelli, G. A. (1989). Perspectives on children's development from cultural psychology. *American Psychologist, 44,* 343–348.

Rosch, E. (1973). On the internal structure of perceptual and semantic categories. In T. Moore (Ed.), *Cognitive development and the acquisition of language* (pp. 111–144). New York: Academic Press.

Sahlins, M. (1976). *Culture and practical reason.* Chicago: Chicago University Press.

Saxe, G. B. (1981). When fourth can precede second. *Journal of Cross-Cultural Psychology, 12,* 37–50.

Saxe, G. B. (1982a). Developing forms of arithmetical thought among the Oksapmin of Papua New Guinea. *Developmental Psychology, 18,* 583–594.

Saxe, G. B. (1982b). Culture and the development of numerical cognition: Studies among the Oskapmin of Papua New Guinea. In C. J. Brainerd (Ed.), *Children's logical and math-*

ematical cognition (pp. 157–176). New York: Springer-Verlag.

Saxe, G. B. (1991). *Culture and cognitive development: Studies in mathematical understanding.* Hillsdale, NJ: Erlbaum.

Schegloff, E. (1993). Reflections on quantification in the study of conversation. *Research on Language and Social Interaction, 26,* 99–128.

Schieffelin, B. B. (1983). Talking like birds: Sound play in a cultural perspective. In E. Ochs & B. B. Schieffelin, *Acquiring conversational competence,* (pp. 177–184). London: Routledge & Kegan Paul.

Schliemann, A. D. (1984). Mathematics among carpenters and apprentices. In P. Damerow, M. W. Dunckley, B. F. Nebres, & B. Werry (Eds.), *Mathematics for all* (pp. 92–95). Paris: UNESCO.

Schneider, B., Hieshima, J. A., Lee, S., & Plank, S. (1994). East-Asian academic success in the United States: Family, school, and community explanations. In P. M. Greenfield & R. R. Cocking (Eds.), *Cross-cultural roots of minority child development* (pp. 323–350). Hillsdale, NJ: Erlbaum.

Schubauer-Leoni, M. L., Perret-Clermont, A., & Grossen, M. (1993). The construction of the adult-child intersubjectivity in psychological research and in school. In M. von Cranach, W. Doise, & G. Mugny (Eds.), *Social representation and the social bases of knowledge.* Bern: Hans Huber Verlag.

Scribner, S. (1984). Studying working intelligence. In B. Rogoff & J. Lave (Eds.), *Everyday cognition: Its development in social context* (pp. 9–40). Cambridge, MA: Harvard University Press.

Scribner, S. (1984). Cognitive studies of work. *Quarterly Newsletter of the Laboratory of Comparative Human Cognition, 6* (1&2).

Scribner, S. (1985). Vygotsky's uses of history. In J. V. Wertsch (Ed.), *Culture, communication, and cognition: Vygotskian perspectives* (pp. 119–145). Cambridge: Cambridge University Press.

Scribner, S., & Cole, M. (1981). *The psychology of literacy.* Cambridge, MA: Harvard University Press.

Scribner, S., Sachs, P., Di Bello, L. & Kindred J.

(1991). *Knowledge acquisition at work* (Tech. Rep. No. 22). New York: Center City University of New York, The Graduate School and University.

Segal, N. L. (1993). Twin, sibling, and adoption methods: Tests of evolutionary hypotheses. *American Psychologist, 48,* 943–956.

Serpell, R. (1993). *The significance of schooling: Life journeys in an African society.* Cambridge: Cambridge University Press.

Shweder, R. A. (1990). Cultural psychology: What is it? In J. W. Stigler, R. A. Shweder, & G. Herdt (Eds.), *Cultural psychology: Essays on comparative human development* (pp. 1–4). Cambridge: Cambridge University Press.

Shweder, R. (1995). The confessions of a methodological individualist. *Culture and Psychology, 1* (1), 115–122.

Shweder, R. A., & Bourne, E. J. (1982). Does the concept of the person vary cross-culturally? In R. A. Shweder & R. A. LeVine (Eds.), *Culture theory: Essays on mind, self, and emotion* (pp. 158–199). New York: Cambridge University Press.

Shweder, R., Jensen, L., & Goldstein, W. (1995). Who sleeps by whom revisited: A method for extracting the moral goods implicit in practice. In J. J. Goodnow, P. Miller, & F. Kessel (Eds.), *Cultural practices as contexts for development* (pp. 21–39). San Francisco: Jossey-Bass.

Shweder, R. A., & Miller, J. G. (1985). The social construction of the person: How is it possible? In K. J. Gergen & K. E. Davis (Eds.), *The social construction of the person* (pp. 1–22). New York: Springer-Verlag.

Shweder, R. A., & Much, N. C. (1987). Determinations of meaning: Discourse and moral socialization. In W. M. Kurtines & J. L. Gewirtz (Eds.), *Moral development through social interaction* (pp. 197–244). New York: Wiley.

Shweder, R. A., & Sullivan, M. (1990). The semiotic person of cultural psychology. In L. Pervin (Ed.). *Handbook of Personality,* (pp. 399–416). New York: Guilford.

Shweder, R. A., & Sullivan, M. A. (1993). Cultural psychology: Who needs it? *Annual Review of Psychology, 44,* 497–523.

Siegal, M. (1991a). A clash of conversational

worlds: Interpreting cognitive development through communication. In L. B. Resnick, J. M. Levine, & S. Behrens (Eds.), *Perspectives on socially shared cognition* (pp. 23–40). Washington, DC: American Psychological Association.

Siegal, M. (1991b). *Knowing children: Experiments in conversation and cognition.* Hove, UK: Erlbaum.

Siegal, M. (in press). Conversation and cognition. In R. Gelman & T. Au (Eds.), E. C. Carterette & M. Friedman (Gen. Eds.), *Handbook of perception and cognition: Vol. 13. Perceptual and cognitive development.* San Diego, CA: Academic Press.

Sigman, M., Beckwith, L., & Cohen, S. E. (1994). Caregiver–infant interactions in rural Kenya and the United States. Paper presented at the International Conference on Infant Studies, Paris.

Sinclair, J., & Coulthard, R. M. (1975). *Towards an analysis of discourse: The English used by teachers and pupils.* London: Oxford University Press.

Stigler, J. W. (1984). "Mental abacus": The effect of abacus training on Chinese children's mental calculation. *Cognitive Psychology, 16,* 145–176.

Stigler, J. W., Chalip, L., & Miller, K. F. (1986). Consequences of skill: the case of abacus training in Taiwan. *American Journal of Education, 94,* 447–479.

Stigler, J. W., & Perry, M. (1990). Mathematics learning in Japanese, Chinese, and American classrooms. In J. W. Stigler, R. A. Shweder, & G. Herdt (Eds.), *Cultural psychology* (pp. 328–353). Cambridge: Cambridge University Press.

Stigler, J. W., Shweder, R. A., & G. Herdt (Eds.) (1990). *Cultural psychology: Essays on comparative human development.* Cambridge: Cambridge University Press.

Takahashi, K. (1986). Examining the strange situation procedure with Japanese mother and 12-month-old infants. *Developmental Psychology, 22,* 265–270.

Takahashi, K. (1990). Are the key assumptions of the 'strange situation' procedure universal? A view from Japanese research. *Human Development, 33,* 23–30.

Tobin, J. J. (1989). Visual anthropology and multivocal ethnography: A dialogical approach to Japanese preschool class size. *Dialectical Anthropology, 13,* 173–187.

Tobin, J. J., Wu, D. Y. H., & Davidson, D. H. (1989). *Preschool in three cultures: Japan, China, and the United States.* New Haven: Yale University Press.

Tomasello, M., Davis-Dasilva, M., Camak, L., & Bard, K. (1987). Observational learning of tool use by young chimpanzees. *Human Evolution, 2,* 175–183.

Tomasello, M., Kruger, A. C., & Ratner, H. H. (1993). Cultural learning. *Behavioral and Brain Sciences, 16,* 495–552.

Trevarthen, C. (1980). The foundations of intersubjectivity: Development of interpersonal and cooperative understanding in infants. In D. R. Olson (Ed.), *The social foundations of language and thought* (pp. 316–342). NY: Wiley.

Triandis, H. C. (1980). Introduction to Handbook. In H. C. Triandis & W. W. Lambert (Eds.), *Handbook of Cross-Cultural Psychology* (Vol. 1, pp. 1–14). Boston: Allyn and Bacon.

Triandis, H. C. (1995, July). Discussion. In J. Adamopoulos (Chair), Psychology and culture: The search for appropriate paradigms. Symposium presented at the European Congress of Psychology, Athens.

Valsiner, J. (1989). How can developmental psychology become "culture-inclusive"? In J. Valsiner (Ed.), *Child development in cultural context* (pp. 1–8). Toronto: Hogrefe & Huber.

Valsiner, J., & Hill, P. E. (1989). Socialization of American toddlers for social courtesy. In J. Valsiner (Ed.), *Child development in cultural context* (pp. 163–179). Toronto: Hogrefe & Huber.

Van de Vijver, F. J. R., & Poortinga, Y. H. (1991). Testing across cultures. In R.K. Hambleton & J. N. Zaal (Eds.), *Advances in educational and psychological testing: Theory and applications* (pp. 277–309). Dordrecht: Kluwer.

Vygotsky, L. S. (1978). *Mind in society: The development of higher psychological processes* (pp. 52–57). Cambridge, MA: Harvard University Press.

Vygotsky, L. S., & Luria, A. R. (1993). *Studies on the history of behavior: Ape, primitive, and child.* V. I. Golod & J. E. Knox (Trans.). Hillsdale, NJ: Erlbaum.

Wagner, D. (1984). Ontogeny in the study of culture and cognition. In D. A. Wagner & H. W. Stevenson (Eds.), *Cultural perspectives on child development.* (pp. 105–123). San Francisco: W. H. Freeman.

Wartofsky, M. (1979). *Models: Representations and and Scientific Understanding.* Dordrecht, Netherlands: Reidel.

Wassmann, J. (1995). The final requiem for the omniscient informant? An interdisciplinary approach to everyday cognition. *Culture and Psychology, 1,* 167–201.

Wassmann, J., & Dasen, P. R. (1994). "Hot" and "cold": classification and sorting among Yupno of Papua New Guinea. *International Journal of Psychology, 29,* 19–38.

Weisner, T. S. (in press). Why ethnography should be the most important method in the study of human development. In A. Colby, R. Jessor, & R. Shweder (Eds.), *Ethnography and human development.* Chicago: University of Chicago Press.

Weisner, T. S. (1994). What is culture? Seminar on culture and human development. Los Angeles, UCLA.

Weisner, T., & Gallimore, R. (1977). My brother's keeper: Child and sibling caretaking. *Current Anthropology, 18,* 169–190.

Wells, A. S., Hirshberg, D., Lipton, M., & Oakes, J. (1995). Bounding the case within its context: A constructivist approach to studying detracking reform. *Educational Researcher, 24,* 18–24.

Whiting, B. B. (1976). Unpackaging variables. In K. F. Riegel & J. A. Meacham (Eds.), *The changing individual in a changing world* (Vol. 1, pp. 303–309). Chicago: Aldine.

Wober, M. (1974). Towards and understanding of the Kiganda concept of intelligence. In J. W. Berry & P. R. Dasen (Eds.), *Culture and cognition,* (pp. 261–280). London:: Methuen.

Zukow, P.G. (Ed.). (1989). *Sibling interaction across cultures: Theoretical and methodological issues.* New York: Springer-Verlag.

Zukow, P.G. (1984). Folk theories of comprehension and caregiver style in a rural-born population in Central Mexico. *Quarterly Newsletter of the Laboratory of Comparative Human Cognition, 6,* 62–67.

9

TOWARDS CONVERGENCE?

YPE H. POORTINGA
Tilburg University, The Netherlands
University of Leuven, Belgium[1]

Contents

Introduction

Diversity is the spice of life. Applied here to cross-cultural psychology this saying argues against a reduction of the variation in approaches and topics covered by the authors of this *Handbook,* and no such plea will be made in this chapter. Convergence has been chosen as a theme not with a view to resolve differences in outlook, but to explore them in relationship to each other. The various orientations on culture–behavior relationships are often seen to be in conflict with each other. Researchers rarely transgress self-imposed paradigmatic boundaries except to denounce those in another camp. They are apt to limit the range of phenomena they investigate or to overextend the reach of their preferred scientific traditions rather than to give these up. It is obvious that there are conflicting interpretations of the same phenomena that cannot be simultaneously valid. However, in many instances different approaches, if not actually compatible, are complementary to each other; they are largely dealing with different aspects of a phenomenon, emphasizing different concerns.

The intention of this chapter is to bring together some of the major themes and controversies, to discuss inherent limitations, and to point in directions that may be conducive to bridge divergent positions. In the first section culture-comparative, cultural, and indigenous research are described as complementary efforts, each with its own difficulties. The second section discusses the controversy between biological and social orientations on behavior. The third section presents some frameworks that try to overarch current incompatibilities. A brief final section moves from formal scientific arguments to the issue of the justification of cross-cultural research, namely whether and how this enterprise can be of significance for the citizens of the contemporary world.

Cross-Cultural and Cultural Research

The conceptualization of the relationship between culture and behavior is the most important theoretical theme in this edition of this *Handbook* and certainly of this volume. The shifts between relativism and universalism are central in the historical review of Jahoda and Krewer. The chapters by Miller and by Greenfield take a more relativistic perspective. Other chapters such as those by Lonner and Adamopoulos, by L. H. and R. H. Munroe, and by Van de Vijver and Leung reflect a universalistic orientation. In these chapters the authors give an overview of the topics and traditions they have been asked to describe. In this section some of the basic concerns and inherent problems of the two major orientations are juxtaposed.

Of course, a dichotomy cannot do justice to the varied positions that a closer scrutiny would reveal. There are arguments for a more diversified nomenclature (Krewer & Jahoda, 1993), and for a further differentiation with ethnic psychology or intercultural psychology (i.e., the study of culture contacts) as a separate field (Berry, 1994; Bouvy, Van de Vijver, Boski, Schmitz & Krewer, 1994). Still, two perspectives are distinguished in most of this *Handbook*, namely cultural psychology and cross-cultural or culture comparative psychology. It is important to note that the term *cross-cultural* has a double meaning: it is used to indicate the entire field covered in this *Handbook*, but also refers to the approach that is focused on the comparison of data gathered in different cultural populations. The view taken here is that cross-culturalists have a legitimate claim to a "culture inclusive" psychology (cf. Segall, 1993). At the same time, it is acknowledged that cultural psychologists are also concerned with differences in psychological functioning between cultures, even if they tend to avoid direct comparison of data.

Culture-Comparative Approaches

In the first of the two perspectives, emphasis is on comparison of behavior across populations defined in cultural terms. As reviewed by Lonner and Adamopoulos (this volume), there is a tendency to take the cultural context, including ecological as well as sociocultural variables, as a set of antecedent conditions, while behavior phenomena, including attitudes and meanings as well as observed behaviors, are seen as the outcomes or consequents of these antecedent influences. In line with the canons of psychological science the focus is on systematic variation of the antecedent conditions to explore or test a priori specified hypotheses and the use of methods that allow measurements to be made in a manner that, in essence, is the same for all persons for which the outcomes are to be compared. The aim is the understanding and explanation of differences and similarities in behavior of human populations defined in cultural terms. The findings that have emerged from this enterprise are varied. For example, there is substantial evidence that social perceptions of the characteristics of men and women are widely shared across societies (Williams & Best, 1982; cf. Best & Williams, Volume 3 of this *Handbook*) and that there is a universal tendency to evaluate one's own group more positively than any other group (Brewer & Campbell, 1976; cf. Gudykunst & Bond, Volume 3 of this *Handbook*). But it has also been found that there are differences in the susceptibility to simple visual illusions as a function of certain ecological factors (Segall, Campbell & Herskovits, 1966; Deregowski, 1989) and that the desire for more children differs according to economic needs of parents (Kagitçibasi, 1982). Massive regularities in empirical data reviewed throughout this *Handbook* suggest (1.) that there are common psychological processes and mechanisms, (2.) that identifiable factors in the social and natural environment are antecedent to consistent differences in behavior patterns between populations, and (3.) that an individual person is formed by the ecological and sociocultural context to a far greater extent than he or she has a formative influence on this environment.

Through the testing of emerging notions in a broader range of cultural contexts cross-cultural psychology is meant to contribute to psychological science. The "extension of the range of variation" has been recognized as the essential characteristic of the field (Whiting, 1954, p. 524). The conceptual basis for comparison lies in the compelling observation of similarities in behavior patterns

across the entire range of human societies and the impression that we can understand the motives and values of members of other cultures when we gain information about them, even if we may not share their beliefs and priorities. The
evidence does not come only from psychology. A book by Brown (1991) entitled
Human universals and the chapter in this volume by L. H. Munroe and R. H.
Munroe review findings from cultural anthropology. On the biological side of
psychology, ethology and sociobiology provide a theoretical basis for the invariances in human behavior (Keller, this volume).

For the present discussion two points may be noted. The first is that subjective culture theory, with Triandis (e.g., 1972) as a major representative, traditionally is part of the cross-cultural enterprise. It is a misperception that subjective
data, such as reports on own experiences, would be inadmissable in comparative
studies. For the experimental approach as such it is not so important what kind
of data a researcher is dealing with; the question is, rather, whether there is some
common aspect or dimension across cultural populations on which a meaningful
comparison can be made.

This leads to the second point, namely that the comparative approach is rooted
in the idea of universality of psychic functioning. This notion has several meanings that can be distinguished conceptually as well as psychometrically (cf. Berry,
Poortinga, Segall & Dasen, 1992; Van de Vijver & Poortinga, 1982). In the broad-
est sense universality refers to formulations of *functional concerns* of the human
species, such as hunger and thirst, or the need for some kind of social organization (Malinowski, 1944). Psychological universals that are the consequences of
such functions have been discussed by Lonner (1980) in the previous edition of
this *Handbook*. More precise similarity in human psychological functioning is presumed when universality is defined at the level of *explanatory concepts* as they are
found in psychological theories on cognition, personality, or social interaction.
The assumption is that any theoretically meaningful personality trait, cognitive
ability, emotion, or value dimension should have universal validity. A major part
of cross-cultural studies is looking for such evidence. Universality as meant here
does not require identity of actual behavior in every culture. The same motive,
ability, or value may find expression cross-culturally in quite different behavior
patterns. There is a third level of universality characterized by cross-cultural similarity of actual *behavior manifestations.* Universals at this level are found in the
domains of psychophysiology, early development, and certain areas of sensation
and perception. In other domains such as emotions, or non-verbal communication, universality of expression is often debated (cf. Mesquita, Frijda & Scherer,
Volume 2 of this *Handbook*; Kendon, 1984).

Comparative studies are modeled on the methodology of the natural sciences,
with a preference for standard instruments and with a priori formulated hypotheses being tested in an experimental or quasi-experimental fashion (cf. Lonner &
Adamopoulos, this volume). There are serious difficulties with this approach (cf.
Van de Vijver & Leung, this volume) that can be summarized in three (to some
extent related) points. First, for the results of an experiment to be interpretable
unambiguously, some basic assumptions have to be met. In essence, the experi-

ment presumes that the researcher can manipulate the variable of interest to create different treatments for randomly selected subjects from a single population. This is a prerequisite not only for a proper laboratory experiment where subjects are allocated in a random manner to conditions, but also for a field study with a quasi-experimental design and data collected on existing groups. In addition, the (quasi-) experiment presumes that the researcher has control over, or at least a good insight into, what constitutes the treatment and to what extent there are differences in treatment between groups. In particular, Donald Campbell (cf. Overman, 1988) has made clear that a cultural context constitutes a highly complex set of variables with multiple effects. In fact, a frequently heard complaint is that comparative analysis pays only token tribute to cultural context and is little concerned with the substance of culture (e.g. Boski, 1996; Georgas & Berry, 1995; Jahoda, 1992; L. H. Munroe & R. H. Munroe, this volume). As a consequence, observed differences between groups tend to be open to a range of alternative interpretations.

The second difficulty lies in the fact that measurements—whether based on standard tests, interviews, or observation schedules—tend to produce scores that are not culturally equivalent. That is, a certain score cannot be interpreted in the same way for subjects belonging to different cultural populations. Psychometric issues of inequivalence, or bias, are discussed by Van de Vijver and Leung (this volume).

The third difficulty has to do with the statistical analysis of data. The testing of hypotheses is geared towards the identification of differences; a successful prediction is achieved when the null-hypothesis can be rejected.

The combined effect of negligence of the last two points is likely to lead to an overestimation of cross-cultural differences; the long-term effect in a large body of research is that too much is made of human behavioral diversity (cf. Malpass & Poortinga, 1986). At the same time, it has to be recognized that the less than optimal research practices that lead to such systematic error are related to a conceptual problem that has proved difficult to handle. This problem is the culture-embeddedness or culture-specificity, not only of behavior-as-observed, but also of theoretical formulations. There are various ways to identify this problem, one is the emic-etic distinction, another the notion of construct bias.

The emic–etic distinction was introduced by Pike (1967) and elaborated for cross-cultural psychology by Berry (1969, 1989) and Triandis (Triandis, Malpass & Davidson, 1972). It refers to a research orientation as well as to a quality of the behavior studied by researchers. Behavior is *emic*, or culture-specific, to the extent that it can only be understood within the cultural context in which it occurs; it is *etic* or universal, in as much as it is common to human beings independent of their culture. The distinction reflects a sharp awareness that researchers start with ideas about what is etic and that these may not be valid; they are then dealing with "imposed etics." True etics can be approximated through an iterative research procedure, gradually leading to an unraveling of what is culture-specific and what is culture-common. Berry's viewpoint that such a procedure is feasible is reflected in his use of the term "derived etics," that is, aspects of behavior that emerge as common, at least to the range of populations investigated. Also, Triandis is of the opinion that the distinction between emic and etic can be resolved empirically. An example of how this should be realized in practice can be found in Davidson, Jaccard, Triandis, Morales & Diaz-Guerrero (1976). However, at the same time it should be recognized that opinions differ on the success of emic–etic scheme (Jahoda, 1983). Berry's iterative procedure is a research agenda, more than a method that leads to unambiguous evidence; and in the study by Davidson et al. the criteria for psychometric equivalence across cultures are not clearly formulated (cf. Berry et al., 1992, p. 235).

Construct bias or concept bias implies that theoretical notions are not independent of the cultural context within which they were initially formulated. Context effects also enter into formal definitions and operationalizations (Poortinga & Malpass, 1986; Van de Vijver & Leung, this volume). As a rule there are no clear criteria for this form of bias; lack of success in establishing equivalent or unbiased methods is the main reason to question the cross-cultural validity of theoretical formulations. This issue will be raised again in the next subsection. Here it may be noted that taking construct bias seriously leads to the acceptance of culture-specificity in the formulation of theories. According to Price-Williams (1980, p. 82) "contexts are not necessarily unique; they can be compared. But the methodology involved is probably more complicated than is usually the case with our traditional investigations."

The criticisms raised concern the practice of comparative research more than its epistemological foundations; if a researcher starts with a well-defined theory, if a proper analysis is made of antecedent differences between cultural populations (the "cultural treatment"), and if inferences are protected against alternative interpretations using the numerous tools that are available, it can be argued that the comparative method is less vulnerable to invalid findings than the more interpretative approaches to be discussed later. At the same time, both the emic-etic distinction and the notion of concept bias are a reflection of difficulties with the comparative perspective that have not been solved and presumably can only be solved partly within an experimental paradigm.

Cultural Approaches

Cultural psychology encompasses a broad range of approaches (cf. Miller, this volume). In the most general terms the cultural approaches represent a revival of phenomenology in reaction to the dominant positivistic paradigm of the mid twentieth century. There are strong influences from Marxist philosophy, especially through the work of Vygotsky. Cultural research tends to be presented as a new paradigm, pointing to issues that have not been solved satisfactorily by the dominant traditions in psychology, but Krewer and Jahoda (this volume) make clear that it has long roots in history. The most direct precursor to its recent growth may well be the shift in cultural anthropology from culture as external context to "culture in the mind of the people" (Geertz, 1973).

In the opinion of most cultural psychologists, culture and behavior are essentially inseparable. This is most evident in the rejection by many of the universalistic notion of a "psychic unity of mankind" (Jahoda, 1992; Miller, this volume). Psychological functioning tends to be described in terms of the understanding of behavior and experience by the members of a cultural group themselves. The cultural approach is relativistic; it emphasizes the study of unique events or unique constellations of events (Boesch, 1991; cf. Lonner & Adamopoulos, this volume). Thus, the domain of research of the culturalist schools tends to differ from that of the comparativists; there is less emphasis on behavior as observed by experts and more on the meaning that behavior has for the behaving person and the intentions this person has with an act of behavior.

Although the differences in emphasis between cultural and cross-cultural psychology can be defined in many ways, perhaps the two most distinguishing features are intentionality (purposeful action) and historicity. In the words of Shweder (1991, p. 97) " . . . the life of the psyche is the life of intentional persons, responding to, and directing their action at, their own mental objects or representations and undergoing transformation through participation in an evolving intentional world that is the product of the mental representations that make it up." Thus, "cultural psychology is the study of intentional worlds. It is the study of personal functioning in particular intentional worlds" (Shweder, 1990, p. 3). Shweder is quite emphatic in the rejection of objective inferences about a real world; "[i]ntentional things have no "natural" reality or identity separate from human understandings and activities" (1990, p. 2). In this viewpoint the natural world tends to disappear beyond the horizon and is inaccessible for critical empirical examination. Not all authors who subscribe to cultural psychology go so far. Related to intentionality (but without the denial of the natural world as knowable) is the concept of action, as put forward by, for example, Eckensberger (1996). He sees actions as "future-oriented, goal directed activities of a potentially self-reflecting agency." To understand the full meaning of this statement it is necessary to place it in the context of Eckensberger's metatheoretical analyses, which will be discussed later in this chapter.

The emphasis on historicity, the second characteristic of the cultural approaches, reflects first and foremost the principle that behavior is context-dependent. Whereas comparative approaches are concerned with differences and similarities *between* cultural populations (thus decontextualizing behavior, at least to some extent), historical approaches tend to focus on continuity and change in behavior and understanding over time, usually *within* a single society (cf. Peeters, in press). Historicity is also prominent in social constructionism, a school of thinking that can be said to represent postmodernism in psychology (Gergen, 1982, 1994; Miller, this volume). In social constructionism behavior is considered as grounded in social interaction and communication, particularly linguistic communication. "The terms in which the world is understood are social artifacts, products of historically-situated interactions between people" (Peeters, 1996). Analyses of rhetoric in arguments (Billig, 1987) or the use of expertise as power in social relationships (Parker & Shotter, 1990) can be revealing and informative. However, for the theme of convergence, which is the focus of this chapter, strong historicism such as Gergen's social constructionism, or for that matter strong intentionality as advocated in some of the writings of Shweder, has little to offer. The majority of psychologists, certainly those outside the field of social psychology, do not seem to be prepared to negotiate about the axiom that there are observable regularities in human behavior going beyond time-and-location-bound accounts of actors and that these regularities are the subject of study for psychology. The rationale for this majority position is argued, among others, by Jahoda (1986), by Smith (1994) and by L. H. Munroe and R. H. Munroe (this volume).

The historical and contextual nature of behavior is also a major concern in sociocultural theory which goes back to Vygotsky (cf. Miller, this volume). He saw the development of the so-called higher mental functions as a historical process both at the level of societies and the individual level. In individual ontogeny these functions appear on the social level as interpsychological categories before they can occur within the individual person as intrapsychological categories (Vygotsky, 1978). The sociohistorical character of mental functions follows from Marxist dialectical materialism, where the human organism is determined by material circumstances, but intervenes in these circumstances through dialectical process (Peeters, 1996). The axiomatic *a priori* of sociocultural development has led to the assumption of cultural inequalities in psychological operations (Luria & Vygotsky, 1992). The pervasiveness of this conviction seems evident in the famous study of Luria (1976) on syllogistic thinking in Central Asia. When illiterate subjects were unable to provide the logically correct answers to simple syllogistic problems while subjects with relatively little schooling performed much better, Luria drew far-reaching conclusions concerning the absence or presence of mental functions in cultural populations (cf. also Luria, 1971; and chapter by Mishra, Volume 2, this *Handbook*). In later studies evidence showed that not a faculty for logical thinking but the acceptance by the subject of the logical nature of the problem was the most crucial variable (e.g., Scribner, 1979).

This points to cultural mediation of complex cognitive processes at the level of specific skills and metacognitions, rather than at the level of mental functions that manifest themselves in broad domains of behavior. The resulting perspective on behavior as context-specific and modular is characteristic of the work of Cole, the main representative of the sociocultural school (e.g., Laboratory of Comparative Human Cognition, 1983). The historical and natural context leads to the development of context specific competencies. In many respects the research by Cole and his colleagues can be seen as complementary to the comparative tradition, making context more explicit and more readily adapting methods to context (Cole, Gay, Glick & Sharp, 1971; Scribner & Cole, 1981). In more recent work of Cole, to be discussed later in this chapter, a further shift can be discerned from behavior as a reflection of internal process to an emphasis on cultural–historical context. This seems to indicate a rapprochement between the symbolic interaction theory of Boesch and Eckensberger and the sociocultural school, rather than to a convergence with the comparative approach.

Related to historicity is a focus on development (cf. Cole, 1990). Developmental cross-cultural psychology is treated extensively in Volume 2 of this *Handbook*, but it may be noted here that the importance of a developmental perspective has long been recognized also in comparative research (Heron & Kroeger, 1980). Most cross-cultural studies are static; in a sense this is also the case for the large majority of developmental studies where differences in development are inferred from differences in the patterns of scores across age cohorts. Still, because most cultural variables are fairly stable over time, this kind of design can lead to valid findings. Of course, longitudinal comparative studies are to be preferred, but these are extremely rare because of the effort involved (exceptions are e.g., Bornstein, Pêcheux & Lécuyer, 1988; Logan, Snarey & Schrader, 1988; McDevitt et al., 1987). In cultural psychology more attention is paid to development as a dynamic process that can be observed (Greenfield, this volume), or retrospectively gauged from personal accounts from subjects (Valsiner & Lawrence, Volume 2 of this *Handbook*). However, the emphasis is on studies within a single culture, implying less usage of the explanatory power that comes with the broader range of variation in culture-comparative studies, and on unique events with inherent problems of interpretation, as will be argued now.

As with the comparative tradition, there are in the cultural traditions connections between theory and methodology. The overall wider range of theoretical approaches in itself already leads to more variation in methods. In addition, the choice of a particular method is often based more on pragmatic considerations than on traditional canons of science (cf. Miller, this volume; Greenfield this volume). This makes it more difficult to assess the strong and weak points of cultural approaches as has been done earlier in this section for comparative cross-cultural research.

The main methodological issue in non-positivistic social science, including cultural psychology, is the analysis of qualitative data. There are two aspects of the quantitative–qualitative dichotomy: a measurement aspect and an interpretation aspect. The term qualitative often is used when research procedures do not result in scores on an interval or ratio scale. For example, in Asendorpf and Valsiner (1992) pleas for qualitative research argue for the viability of measurement on ordinal, and particularly on nominal scales. A number of the chapters in their edited book are on analysis techniques for nominal data. It is true that there has been a strong focus on interval scales in psychology, stressing a level of measurement that is difficult to reach and is not required for many cultural and cross-cultural studies. It appears that there is no major controversy here; the choice of a scale level should be dependent on the questions asked in a study.

The qualitative–quantitative distinction is often a matter of interpretation rather than of measurement. This becomes evident when one takes into consideration the connotations of the distinction that include exploratory data analysis, the interpretation of *ad hoc* findings, and ultimately the idiographic–nomothetic contrast. This latter contrast revolves mainly around two points: the scientific status of the unique event or the unique constellation of events, and the status of the researcher in the process of data collection and interpretation. As argued before, in the culture-comparative orientation replicability and objectivity, in the sense of inter-observer agreement, are seen as necessary requirements for achieving validity of data. Research procedures are aimed at minimizing the influence of the researcher as person on the process of data collection and interpretation. Behavioral events that are manipulated in the laboratory meet these conditions best; in field studies this ideal should be approximated as closely as possible.

In cultural orientations the emphasis is more on the detailed description of behavioral actions (or interactions) and/or their meaning in the eyes of the actors. It can be said that the aim is to reconstruct past events, either in an objective sense, as in traditional ethnography that describes a "reality-out-there," or in a subjective sense, when cultural meaning is emphasized, or both. As mentioned, self-reports of subjects, including expressions of meaning, are quite acceptible as data, also in a positivistic framework. The critical issue lies in the uniqueness of the events that are the subject of study, and the status of the observer, which in many cultural methods becomes confounded with the measurement procedure, thus ruling out replicability.

In broad analyses, not guided by a specific theory, like ethnographic descriptions of the system characteristics of a culture, the range of phenomena included and the range of interpretations can be extended virtually *ad infinitum*. There are few if any agreed upon a priori procedures how to deal with the limitations of the subjective insights of the researcher and how to evaluate evidence. Examples are claims of high specificity in emotions, such as the presence of emotions unknown in the United States among the Ifaluk in the Pacific (Lutz, 1988; cf. also Mesquita, Frijda & Scherer, Volume 2 of this *Handbook*). The account by Mesquita et al. shows that the evidence for specificity in emotions tends to come from anthropological descriptions of remote groups; as a rule these are not easily accessible to cross-validation. In a broader sense this problem pertains to much of ethnography. In an analysis of six pairs of ethnographies, each pair dealing with the same population, Kloos (1988) found so many discrepancies that sometimes the name of the population was the clearest evidence that the same culture was being dealt with. His relativistic stance on the nature of anthropological knowledge and his empirically unsupported claim that later ethographies are of better quality, are unlikely to convince the sceptics.

It is not the veridicality of a unique event per se that is the point of discussion. In a good reconstruction the transparency (Lincoln & Guba, 1985) or the plausibility (Van de Vijver & Poortinga, 1990) is maximized by collecting as much pertinent information as possible, and one can even make predictions about this additional information before it is gathered. The resulting account can be very convincing, as illustrated, for example, by judicial trials where reconstruction of a specific event (i.e., a crime) is accepted, by judge or jury, as having been demonstrated "beyond reasonable doubt," and in science by the status of evolution theory that is widely acclaimed, though largely a reconstruction of past events. However, such a degree of certainty requires that the quality of the evidence, (i.e., the validity), can be assumed to be high.

A questionable point in many cultural approaches is the relative absence of formal procedures for establishing the validity of findings. There is no parallel in relativism for procedures that either are open to independent scrutiny by virtue of replicability (like the experiment), or for establishing validity by means of statistical procedures (like the standardized instrument). These problems are even more serious when the aim of study is not the description of a state of affairs, but the reconstruction of meaning beyond the direct self-reports of subjects (here better named "informants"). In such cases the researcher is not the recorder, as in ethnography, but explicitly takes the role of interpreter. These analyses tend to be characterized by a strong search for convergent evidence (the authors have to make their viewpoint plausible), but with neglect of discriminant validation (Campbell & Fiske, 1959) and, thus, a lack of serious consideration of alternative interpretations.

Of course, these criticisms are not pertinent to all research from a cultural perspective; an example that easily matches any comparative study in methodological sophistication is the work on the cognitive effects of literacy among the Vai, reported by Scribner and M. Cole (1981). In addition, the criticisms mentioned here may not be unsurmountable. In her chapter on methodology for cultural psychology, Greenfield (this volume) modifies the notion of objectivity as a condition for validity. This condition traditionally refers to an agreement between "experts" (objectivity as intersubjectivity); in cross-cultural psychology the experts include local colleagues. Greenfield replaces objectivity by a condition of agreement between a researcher and the local participants in the study. On the issue of validation she emphasizes the communication of the meaning of questions and ecological validity (cf. also, Reuning and Wortley's, 1973, work with the Bushmen). Most significant in Greenfield's writing on validity is the emphasis on behavior as ongoing process. The use of observation and video recording techniques allows a direct route to the study of change and development that has not been fully utilized in traditional more static approaches, while providing a permanent record that is open to reanalysis and reinterpretation.

In summary, just as for the comparative approach, the cultural orientations are not without problems. Both perspectives struggle with finding a balance between the culture-general and the culture-specific. It can be said that comparativists stress similarities in behavior, while the cultural approaches tend to ignore these, especially in the denial of the psychic unity of mankind. This relativism leads to differences in orientation as far as the subject matter of scientific analysis is concerned, especially in the emphasis on the meaning and interpretation given by actors to their own behavior. The more relativistic orientations are also reflected in the methods employed in cultural studies; these are varied and tend to accept, more explicitly than culture comparative studies, evidence as it presents itself to the researcher.

Indigenous Psychologies

A review of indigenous psychologies is given by D. Sinha (this volume). This newly emerging literature contains a heterogeneous set of ideas, but with some focal themes. Most clearly is the criticism of traditional psychology, including cross-cultural psychology, because of its incompleteness. Authors differ on what this entails: it can be defined politically (Mehryar, 1984); or the emphasis can be on the insufficient recognition of non-euroamerican research and findings (D. Sinha, this volume). However, the most salient aspect of incompleteness is that the issues addressed by Western researchers are only relevant to Western societies. By and large the problems particularly of developing countries are given short shrift in the literature. This ethnocentrism is often acknowledged (e.g. Berry et al., 1992), but western psychologists who seriously try to overcome it are few. In fact, the growth in the cross-cultural literature is far more in studies of national differences between industrialized countries (including Japan) and of ethnic issues within western societies, than in studies of those countries, that are aptly called the "majority world" (cf. e.g., Kagitçibasi, 1995 for this term).

The next most frequent argument is that the extant psychology is culture-bound, and that each cultural population needs to develop its own psychology; hence, the preference for the plural (indigenous psycholog*ies*). It should be obvious that such a relativistic viewpoint tends to be closer to the cultural than to the comparative perspective.

The theme of the relative emphasis on the culture-general and the culture-specific is prominent in the indigenization movement, with frequent references to Wundt's Völkerpsychologie as a fundamental source. Jahoda and Krewer (this volume) make clear that Wundt's inquiry was directed at the development of higher mental processes, the evidence for which was to be found in culture–historical analysis. Wundt sought to deal with the question of the "lawfulness of the mental development" of humanity (1913, p. iii). The subtitle of the twelve volume "Völkerpsychologie" reads, "An investigation of the developmental laws of language, myth and customs" (Wundt, (1911/1975). For Wundt, development amounts to a process of evolution from primitive man, via an era of totemism, and one of heroes and gods, to an era of humanity. Historical and prehistorical developments of language, mythology, and law are discussed in their interaction with and consequences for psychological functioning, but often also in their own right. Apart from reflecting a social-evolutionary viewpoint with mental development seen as progressive over time, Wundt's analysis appears from these quotations as distinctly universalistic. Psychological processes and mechanisms (once they have emerged) are seen as invariant across cultural populations, with differences in their manifestations depending on context (cf. Berry et al., 1992, chapter 10, for an elaboration of such a form of universalism).

Another notable point is the range of phenomena included by Wundt. Perhaps the lack of attention in mainstream psychology for the cultural aspects of Wundt's work in part reflects a discomfort about the tremendously broad definition of the discipline that is implied. Kim and Berry (1993a) even go further, defining a position for "cultural science" that overarches and incorporates all sciences, including the natural sciences. Apart from the question whether such inclusiveness (which may look like imperialism to outsiders) is the best way to achieve interdisciplinarity, it raises unanswerable questions about the formulation of researchable theories and methods.

D. Sinha (this volume) makes clear that the relationship between indigenous approaches and the contemporary mainstream should be seen as complementary rather than antagonistic. Indigenous approaches are a recent development; Sinha's chapter consequently is more a contribution to their definition and justification than a summary of achievements. Nevertheless, from a viewpoint of convergence the question has to be asked how the findings of indigenous approaches relate to a broader psychology (Kagitçibasi, 1992). For this purpose three types of studies can be distinguished. First, and closest to the current mainstream, are extensions of method. For example, Puhan (1982; Kulkarni & Puhan, 1988) has developed a "projective-inventory" technique in which the projective reactions of a subject are given in the form of answers on inventory type response scales (agree-disagree). The actual test was developed for an Indian population, but could be adapted for use elsewhere maintaining the theory and principles of test construction.

More difficult to transfer to other populations is a second kind of study, namely those based on indigenous psychological concepts. An example is the work by Naidu and Pande (Naidu, 1983; Pande & Naidu, 1992) on *anasakti* (non-detachment), a concept prominent in Hindu religion and ancient writings. The methods followed to operationalize and validate this concept are much the same as used elsewhere, but the notion of anasakti is seen as part of a worldview in which identification with the material world is considered an impediment to self-realisation. Other examples include *amae* in Japan (Doi, 1993) and the "nurturant task leadership" style in India (J. B. P. Sinha, 1980). Studies of this kind in which indigenous notions are formally conceptualized as personality traits, social norms, values, or therapeutic principles, appear to be the empirical mainstay of indigenous research (cf. D. Sinha, this volume; Kim & Berry, 1993b). It can be argued that they are also the most fruitful, in that they most obviously extend the range of behavioral phenomena considered in cross-cultural psychology. From a relativistic perspective such studies provide further evidence for the necessity of culture-bound interpretation. In a comparative approach it is less evident how such findings are to be integrated (cf. the earlier remarks on construct bias). When Naidu introduces *detachment*, is he simply adding a trait that has been overlooked so far, is he redefining some aspect of personality, or is he cutting the pie of personality differently with consequences for the entire constellation of traits that makes up personality? In a universalistic perspective the last alternative will hardly be considered; in a relativistic approach it is likely to be emphasized. By relating *anasakti* to a particular worldview, Pande and Naidu appear to choose the latter option. At the same time, one of the aims of their study was "to demonstrate the possibility of conceptual bridges between disparate paradigms" (Pande & Naidu, 1992, p. 99).

The third kind of study moves beyond specific methods or concepts by trying to develop an entire psychology on the basis of the body of knowledge available in a cultural population. The initial steps towards such a psychology have been set most clearly in the Philippines, where attempts have been made to develop a local psychology on the basis of indigenous concepts through the use of indigenous methods (Enriquez, 1990). Important concepts as they are expressed in local language have been listed and methods (*pagtatanung-tanong*, asking around) combining elements of surveying and interviewing of informants has been identified (Church, 1987; Pe-Pua, 1990; cf. also the reference by Greenfield, this volume, to work by Deveraux). It is not clear how far further research will lead to a psychology that epistemologically differs from current Western theories. Enriquez (1993) leaves no doubt that he sees indigenous psychologies as an intermediate, although necessary, step towards a universal psychology. In his view cross-indigenous comparisons can lead to universals. However, it remains an open question in his writings, as well as with other authors (Kim & Berry, 1993a; D. Sinha, this volume), how such an integration of knowledge derived in different cultural systems actually can be realized.

In summary, the main rationale for the development of indigenous psychological knowledge in non-Western countries appears to lie in the ethnocentrism of Western psychological research. There may be disagreement on the question of whether or not such ethnocentrism is inescapable because of the contextual nature of scientific knowledge, but it cannot be denied that psychological research caters predominantly for the needs and fashions of the wealthy nations of the world. Indigenous psychologies are a welcome development to counteract this tendency. Although the problem of how to integrate other bodies of knowledge with Western (indigenous) psychology needs more attention, the increase in the range of viewpoints as well as the widening of the body of data that comes with it ultimately should enrich not only cross-cultural psychology, but also psychology in general.

Divergent Interpretations of Evidence

In paradigmatic controversies of the scientific world, those advocating new approaches tend to concentrate their criticisms on the weak points of the establishment. In his well-known treatise on the nature of scientific revolutions, Kuhn (1962) addressed the shortcomings in the position of Popper (1959) and other positivists, not their strong points. But does this mean that the epistemological notion of refutation propagated by Popper has no merits? From the position taken in this chapter the answer to this question is negative. Kuhn has not so much demonstrated that Popper was wrong, but that his principles of the logic of scientific discovery in practice tend to be limited by historical realities of a subjective and individual nature residing in scientists as persons with private convictions and interests. This subjectivity affects the selection and interpretation of empirical evidence in many ways. There are numerous incidental examples and these presumably will be corrected over time. This subsection is meant to illustrate that there are also lasting controversies that lead to systematic and incompatible differences in the design of studies and the interpretation of a mutually known body of evidence.

Selectivity of design can be illustrated by contrasting the two following projects. Shweder, Mahapatra and Miller (1990), studying moral understanding of certain groups living in India and the United States, worked with a set of items many of which refer to religious norms and practices, such as a widow not being allowed to eat fish. It is not surprising that little cross-cultural agreement was found on the importance of observing such norms. In a comparative study of intergroup norm violations in India and The Netherlands, DeRidder and Tripathi (1992) found that about half of the items written either by Dutch or Indian psychologists had so much correspondence in meaning that they could be used in the other country after literal translation. For other items this was not the case; jumping a queue seemed less of a norm violation in India than in The Netherlands, the teasing of a boy by a girl more so. But no item was encountered that was not readily understandable as a norm violation by members of the other society as where it was formulated. Perhaps it is also not surprising that in this study, which looked at interactions between groups, much similarity was found in patterns of results from the two countries. Of course, these are only two projects, but the seriousness of the problem hardly needs further argument if indeed the prior orientation of a research team determines the outcome of a study to a significant extent.

Selectivity is easy to show too in the interpretation of available evidence. Reference was made earlier to the discussion on the cross-cultural study of emotions that past anthropological research resulted in differences more than did psychological studies. (cf. Mesquita et al., Volume 2 of this *Handbook*). Another example, also mentioned before, are controversies on the sociocultural origin of higher mental processes. While some authors acknowledge the universal presence of abstract thinking (cf. Segall, Dasen, Berry & Poortinga, 1990), others continue to emphasize language and education-mediated differences (e.g. Tulviste, 1991). Even the old debate on the universality of color perception (a major issue in linguistic relativity) that seemed to be resolved after the work of Berlin and Kay (1969) and of Rosch (1972) is still alive.

Saunders (1992) has challenged not only the (culturally) evolutionary sequence in the emergence of words in various languages for basic colors, but also the neurophysiological base of the color space that is presumed to underlie classifications such as the Munsell color scheme. In her opinion, the physiological capacity to distinguish colors does not make color a universal perceptual category. Saunders provides numerous cases where, in her opinion, terms have not been assigned correctly by Berlin and Kay. She also criticizes the work of Rosch on color recognition and better memory for focal (as opposed to non-focal) colors. She argues, for example, that Rosch failed to find positive evidence among the New Guinea Dani for the salience of the (Western) focal colors. A major argument is that Rosch's experiments must have been quite meaningless to the Dani subjects. In the end Saunders dismisses all universalistic arguments, because the neurophysiological processes involved in color naming and color perception remain essentially unknown, and she concludes that there is little hard evidence on which to build the elaborate structure of the color-naming paradigm. She offers an alternative view based on interviews with members of the Kwakiutl group on the Pacific coast in Canada. The absence of "color" words in their language for some hues that have functional salience in the culture and a reinterpretation of anthropological records leads Saunders to suggest that current color terms among the Kwakiutl originally were not based on hue, but reflected other modes of understanding.

Saunders' analysis undoubtedly exposes weaknesses in the arguments for universality, for example, when she points to the necessity to distinguish sharply between color perception and color naming. On the other hand, she seems to neglect or dismiss too lightly evidence incompatible with her viewpoint, particularly findings on the physiological basis for color categories, as reported for example by Bornstein and colleagues in experiments with young babies (Bornstein, Kessen & Weiskopf, 1976).

Saunders' study has been mentioned here because it can be seen as a penetrating criticism of the universalist perspective.[2] However, accepting her objection that universalists are skating on thin ice, the question looms how strong the evidence is for her alternative that color terms are (merely) cultural inventions. Unless some common ground is found, such discussions can only end in a deadlock.

A Suggestion for Demarcation

Contrary to what has been suggested by Shweder (1991), psychic unity perhaps does not refer so much to a preference among comparativists for the philosophical traditions of rationality and romanticism, as to a pragmatic recognition of an empirical reality of similarities in behavior across the human species. For a productive coexistence between culture comparativists and culturalists it seems important to find formulations that do justice to the concerns raised in each of the two perspectives, while curtailing suggestions of (over)inclusiveness. In this section one such formulation is being attempted. For the juxtaposition of the positivistic or (nomothetic) and the phenomenological (or idiographic) orientations that seems to be at the heart of the main controversy, a pair of terms will be used that have been suggested by Eckensberger (e.g., 1995, 1996). He distinguishes between "psychological laws" and "cultural rules." On the one hand there are regularities in behavior that reflect natural propensities (laws); on the other hand there are regularities that follow from cultural norms and practices (rules). The comparative perspective can be qualified as a search for laws, the cultural perspective as a reflection on rules. Using this terminology the following three propositions are put forward as one possible way to reach compatibility:

1. *There are aspects of behavior that lend themselves to explanation in terms of psychological laws and there are aspects that can be interpreted more readily in terms of cultural rules.* This proposition has relevance for various requirements of theory and methodology, the status of context, and the interpretation of data; these requirements have been discussed extensively in this volume and in this chapter, and are summarized in Table 9–1.

With respect to theory, the focus on universality is contrasted with the conventional character of meaning (where a convention is an agreed upon practice or belief in a cultural population). The main methodological distinction is in terms of comparison. Comparative research requires a comparison standard, i.e., some common procedure of measurement or observation; in cultural approaches the

TABLE 9–1   Distinctions between culture-comparative and cultural approaches

Culture-comparative	Cultural
Theory Criterion of universality; cc differences are explained within a common framework. Behavior manifestations are signs of universal processes which are defined by the researcher as expert.	Criterion of conventionality; behavior manifestations are sui generis (they have an existence of their own). Meaning is determined by the actor.
Methodology Standard of comparison defined in operational terms; validity of comparisons has to be tested experimentally or psychometrically.	Standard of comparison defined as context dependent; criteria for sound explanation are plausibility and coherence of argument.
Culture Culture is conceptualized as (a set of) antecedent factors; they take the form of indepndent variables in a (quasi-) experimental approach.	Culture and behavior are defined as interwoven tightly.
Generalization Interpretation mostly in terms of (presumed) basic or superordinate categories with a tendency towards high levels of inclusiveness (over-generalization).	Interpretations vary in terms of the range of phenomena included as well as in "depth."

contextuality of behavior is given precedence. The third contrast in the table refers to the question how culture is conceptualized for the purposes of research, in terms of antecedent–consequent relationships, or as context, quite inextricably interwoven with behavior. The last entry in the table is on generalization. It refers primarily to the level of inclusiveness of interpretations of data (Poortinga & Malpass, 1986). Following Rosch (1978), Pettigrew and Van de Vijver (1990) have made a distinction between between basic categories of psychological functioning (such as traditional personality traits and cognitive abilities), subordinate categories (for example, Cole's context– dependent cognitions; cultural conventions), and superordinate categories, (e.g., the notion of intelligence and conceptualizations of self). Another dimension, mentioned earlier on, is between generalizations that are more descriptive or observational (e.g., ethnographic categorization of kin relationships) and those that infer more about deep levels of the psyche (e.g., symbolic meaning). It is suggested in the table that on both dimensions, generalizations in cultural research vary more widely than those in cross-cultural studies, with the latter tending to high levels of inclusiveness (cf. the discussion of Lonner and Adamopoulos, this volume, on current theories).

2. *The imposition of an interpretation (in terms of "laws" or "rules") to which data do not lend themselves leads to a less than optimal account of the phenomena under investigation.* An explanation of a cultural custom or convention that is rooted in a specific historical event in terms of presumed regularities in psychological functioning is misleading, but so is the interpretation of lawful aspects of behavior in culture-specific terms. As noted earlier, the unique event falls outside the domain of things that can be meaningfully analyzed in an experiment. Equally, a phenomenological analysis that seeks the understanding of a single (constellation of) events is at most a tentative route to establish what is invariant in human psychological functioning.

3. *Psychological laws confine the range of viable cultural rules, rather than the other way around.*

This statement is primarily meant to limit the scope of the argument that a particular scientific paradigm itself is merely a product of culture, not only as a form of action but also in its findings. This is not the place to argue the merits of the philosophical implications; let an example suffice to illustrate that there are at least grades of contextuality in human activity. The designing and construction of a molecule by applying principles derived from chemistry does not lead to an outcome that is culture-specific in the same way as the application of rules for greeting or of rules for artistic expression. The principles of chemistry transcend cultural boundaries; cross-cultural comparative research tries to reach for such transcendence by mapping out psychological functions and processes underlying observed culture–behavior relationships.

There are three more formal arguments which appear to justify the search for psychological laws. The first is based on the principle of parsimony: a more general, culture-transcending, explanation is to be preferred over a less general explanation that is restricted to a single cultural population. The second argument is that laws expressing causal relationships (propter hoc) are logically more compelling than rules describing relationships (post hoc). The third and most important reason to which we shall turn in the next section lies in the importance of biological functions in phylogenetic and ontogenetic development.

Incorporating Biological Thinking

The chapter in this volume that addresses biological issues first and foremost is that by Keller. But other authors touch on biological aspects of behavior by drawing attention to cross-cultural similarities or biologically oriented research (e.g., Lonner & Adamopoulos, this volume). This is especially so in the chapter by L. H. Munroe and R. H. Munroe that refers to cross-cultural invariances in perception and cognition and in social interactions, as well as to invariances in somatic functioning. In part the argument is based on a reflection of what the maximum range of variation for a phenomenon could have been if any imaginable pattern of behavior would indeed be found. They mention, for example, that "a system with stronger affective ties between more remote relatives and weaker ties among primary relatives would go against all expectations" (p. 195). In addition to cultural anthropology there are other areas from which empirical findings pertinent to cross-cultural psychology can be drawn, including human ethology (Eibl-Eibesfeldt, 1989), psychobiology (Immelman, Scherer, Vogel & Schmoock, 1988), psychiatry (Simons & Hughes, 1985), behavior genetics (Plomin & McClearn, 1993), and developmental psychology (Cole & Cole, 1993). Keller's chapter primarily deals with theoretical approaches to the relationship between behavior and its biological underpinnings. In line with current thinking the chapter focusses on evolutionary approaches to human behavior. The direction taken is that of evolutionary psychology, a school of thought closely related to sociobiology and human ethology.

Two questions are prominent in this section. The first is *how far* cross-cultural similarities in behavior are to be explained in terms of species-wide uniformities in human genetic make-up, i.e., how "close" or "tight" are gene-behavior relationships. An extension of this question is how far cross-cultural differences in behavior patterns can be explained as due to differences in demands of the environment to which humans react in a genetically predetermined fashion (i.e., gene–environment interactions). The opposite of this first question is to what extent differences in behavior patterns point to biological indeterminacy. The second question is *how* gene-behavior relationships are best conceptualized.

These formulations, particularly that of the first question, suggest an opposition of "nature" and "nurture." Although any such opposition between the two tends to be vehemently denied (e.g., Boyd & Richerson, 1985), their relative importance continues to form a major focus of research. For example, the National Advisory Mental Health Council (1995, p. 489) of the United States argues in a report on a national plan for behavioral research that ". . . cross-cultural studies of humans can indicate which behavioral patterns represent biological imperatives and which represent cultural options."

The Empirical Record

Universality of a behavior pattern is difficult to demonstrate in a formal sense. Even if clear empirical data on all currently existing cultural populations were available, we still would have no information on past and future populations. However, in practice the notion of universality tends to be upheld if there are findings from a wide range of cultures none of which forms a too obvious exception to the general rule. In this sense there are numerous examples of universals. At the level of concrete behaviors these include the kiss, the display of coyness (Eibl-Eibesfeldt, 1989), and the shrug (Argyle, 1988). At a somewhat more general level there are, for example, universals in language as identified by Greenberg (cf. L. H. Munroe & R. H. Munroe, this volume), and in "intuitive parenting" (e.g., Papousek & Bornstein, 1992), especially talking in a particular tone of voice (called "motherese") to babies.

Controversies arise in the case of more complex patterns of interactions and communication for which there are obvious cross-cultural differences in manifestation. Eibl-Eibesfeldt (1979, 1989) readily admits that there is rich variation, but places great weight on common elements in behavior processes that have similar functions. An example is his analysis of greeting rituals in which he invariably perceives elements of both (aggressive) display and appeasement. In his view, the gun salute and the flowers offered by a little girl to the visiting head of state in Western societies correspond with the greeting ceremony of a war dance by a Yanomami Indian accompanied by a child waving palm flowers. Even the common handshake has an aggressive and an appeasing aspect according to Eibl-Eibesfeldt. He infers from the available evidence that there is a universal grammar of human social behavior. Similar considerations in the domain of language have led to the postulate of a universal grammar for human languages, notably by Chomsky (1965, 1980). Empirical cross-cultural evidence questioning the status of this latter theory is discussed in Mohanty and Perregaux (Volume 2 of this *Handbook*).

The examples mentioned come mainly from ethological or developmental research using observational methods. A quite different tradition is behavior genetics with a focus on the heritability of individual cognitive abilities and personality traits as studied in differential psychology with tests and questionnaires. Heritability (i.e., the proportion of total, or phenotypic, variance that is attributable to genetic influence) is estimated from the correspondence in test scores between genetically closely related subjects (notably monozygotic twins) compared to the correspondence between genetically less related or unrelated subjects (notably adopted children). The basic equation is given in the chapter by Keller (this volume). Over the years designs have become more sophisticated, extending the research to interactions of heredity and environment. Environment is no longer seen as gene-independent, but as a factor that will be acted on differently by individuals who are different in genetic constitution (e.g., Plomin & Daniels, 1987; Plomin & Bergeman, 1991; Plomin & McClearn, 1993). Although there are variations between separate studies, the thrust of the findings is that individual differences in most personality traits and cognitive abilities have a major genetic component.

Thus, the main strength of the behavior genetics tradition lies in the empirical research that time and again gives results that are seen by behavior geneticists as demonstrating the genetic basis of interindividual differences. As argued by Keller (this volume), the main weakness is that there is a model, but hardly any theory which specifies how observed relationships between genes and observable behavior should be explained. In fact, the a priori likelihood that a linear additive model (as used by behavior geneticists) is the best representation of gene action is very small (e.g., Bock & Zimowski, 1987). Moreover, behavior genetics research has tended to study variation between individuals in similar settings, thus limiting the range of environmental variation and, consequently, the variation in behavior that is to be explained in environmental terms (e.g., Bronfenbrenner & Ceci, 1994).

Another source of evidence on the biological basis of social behavior is the comparative ethological study of primate species. The chimpanzee, presumably a very close relative of the human species, has been studied intensively as a source of information, not only on learning and other basic psychological functions, but also on social behavior. Authors like Kortlandt (1962) and Goodall (1986) have assembled an impressive record of similarities between chimpanzees and humans. These similarities tend to be explained in terms of homologies, i.e., behaviors that have been genetically transmitted from common ancestors. Recent findings on the bonobo (pygmy chimpanzee) have illustrated that such interpretations are not flawless. The genetic divergence between chimpanzee and bonobo occurred later in history than that between these two species and humans, so there is no reason to assume that there are more genetic differences of humans with bonobos than with chimpanzees. However, compared to the male-dominated chimpanzee bands, bonobos are female-centered and egalitarian, with frequent and "promiscuous" sexual activities and little aggressiveness (De Waal, 1988, 1995).

Among the more important ethological findings for the study of culture–behavior relationships are those that point to culture as a not uniquely human phenomenon. Regional differences between bands of macaques, and especially chimpanzees, in the use (versus non-use) of certain available foods and in customs of social interactions suggest that these species satisfy common criteria of human culture (McGrew, 1992). Of course, it is always possible to define culture in such a way that it is unique to the human species, as McGrew points out, but it is not clear what can be gained from such an anthropocentric viewpoint.

Traditionally the main stronghold of an environmentalistic perspective is variation that has *not* been explained, postulating biological indeterminedness or plasticity of human behavior patterns on the basis of observable cross-cultural variation (Sahlins, 1977; Warren, 1980). The problem with this argument is that it tends to equate the presently unexplained with the unexplainable. On the other hand, a biological perspective, in which plasticity is the capacity of humans to develop context specific solutions in response to ecological and sociocultural demands (Eibl-Eibesfeldt, 1989), faces the danger of looking at cross-cultural differences merely as variance yet to be explained in biological terms. In the terminology of Van de Vijver and Leung (this volume), many studies in the ethological tradition are of the exploratory type, be it that similarities rather than differences in behavior are emphasized. They are exposed to an important weakness of this kind of study, namely the limited control on alternative interpretations.

As repeatedly indicated, the illustrations in this section are not uncontested, but together they point to the importance of biological approaches for psychology. Although some texts pay attention to issues of biology (e.g., Berry et al., 1992), the field of cross-cultural psychology can be said to recognize two parent disciplines, psychology and cultural anthropology. Such an orientation appears to be shortsighted, despite the many criticisms that can be raised against specific results and interpretations of biologically oriented studies. From a perspective of convergence, a culture-inclusive psychology should not restrict itself to the analysis of context, but also incorporate a view of culture as a biological property of the human species.

Evolutionary Theory and Beyond

The second question posed in the beginning of this section was *how* gene-behavior relationships are to be conceptualized. To answer this question relevant theory will have to be considered. An integrative approach has been proposed in ethology in which (1.) the mechanisms or causes of behavior, (2.) its evolutionary history, (3.) its ontogenetic development and (4.) the function it supposedly serves, are brought together. Tinbergen (1963, p. 430) has stated "that behaviour is part and parcel of the adaptive equipment of animals; that, as such, its short-term causation can be studied in fundamentally the same way as that of other life processes; that its survival value can be studied just as systematically as its causation; that the study of its ontogeny is similar to the study of the ontogeny of structure; and that the study of its evolution likewise follows the same lines as that of the evolution of form." The application of this program of functional analysis to human behavior gained considerable ground after the development of sociobiology (Wilson, 1975) and subsequently of evolutionary psychology, the perspective that Keller emphasizes in her chapter.

This perspective has to its credit a number of theoretically derived predictions for which supportive empirical evidence has been found. One example is the study by Buss (1989) on cross-culturally consistent sex differences in certain parameters of mate preference (cf. Lonner & Adampoulos, this volume). Another example is the research by Kenrick and Keefe (1992) on differences between men and women in the preferred age of a partner, and the changes in this preference over the life span. Both examples were inspired by theoretical analyses of differences between men and women in parental investment strategies (Daly & Wilson, 1983; cf. Keller, this volume). However, the claims of evolutionary psychology reach much further. It is axiomatic in this theory that behavior in all its aspects has to be considered in function of reproductive fitness. Ethnocentrism (Reynolds, Falger & Vine, 1987) and individual development (MacDonald, 1988), as well as aesthetics (Dissanayake, 1992), have been explained in evolutionary terms.

In evolutionary psychology, functions refer to design features of the human mind that have been shaped by evolution. The separate features are linked together in the reproduction of the human organism and this leads to a coherent overall design. In the process of selection those variations are retained that are functional (as opposed to dysfunctional, i.e., reproductively less successful). This leads to outcomes that are called adaptations (Tooby & Cosmides, 1992). However, the reconstruction of adaptations is *post hoc* and is notoriously difficult, according to biologists such as Gould and Lewontin (1979; Lewontin, 1978). Because any single gene as a rule has a range of effects on the phenotype, a specific genetic change in reaction to environmental demands is also not limited to a single (functional) effect; there are concomitant changes that can be seen as by-products (or "pleiotropic" effects) of adaptations. According to Tooby and Cosmides (1992) it is characteristic of these by-products that, though part of the overall design, they are not functionally organized.

Thus, in an examination of evolutionary studies a major question is whether sufficient evidence exists for validity or plausibility of a suggested functional explanation. Findings like those of Buss and Kenrick that were mentioned earlier are not immune to alternative culture-based interpretations. Moreover, even when cross-cultural regularities are accepted as evidence of genetic effects, the amount of variance attributable to these effects (male–female differences) tends to be smaller than the environmental (cross-cultural) variance, a tendency that has not gone unnoticed (Smith & Bond, 1993; Buss et al., 1990; cf. also the discussions in Buss, 1989 and Kenrick & Keefe, 1992). Again, the status of these (remaining) cross-cultural differences is disputable; from a strictly biological viewpoint they reflect differences in reactions solicited by specific environments, but for many social scientists they are the outcome of cultural and historical processes.

The theoretical question whether complex human behavior can be dissected in "functions" as meant by Tinbergen is at the core of discussions about the level of behavioral organization at which genetic effects are to be postulated. Content-specific genetic mechanisms are suggested, for example, by Tooby and Cosmides (1992). At the other extreme are notions of learning as propagated by classical behaviorism, where biologically based learning mechanisms are seen as entirely neutral with respect to content and the human brain is conceived of as a central processor for environmental (including social) stimuli. This latter viewpoint, implying that any stimulus–response contingency would be equally easy to learn, had to be abandoned in view of the domain-specificity of stimulus–response connections already in the sixties (Garcia & Koelling, 1966).

In addition to uniform theories, there are other ways in which researchers have sought to the resolve the dilemma that continues to be posed by biological versus environmentalistic thinking. Especially in cognitive psychology the discussion is on "modules," i.e., genetically determined and largely independent special-purpose functions (Fodor, 1985). The biological givenness of modular or functional entities as they appear in the behavior repertoire is questioned by authors such as Greenfield (1991) and Karmiloff-Smith (1994). They see modules in part as the outcome of developmental processes that are influenced by the organism's interaction with the environment.

Frequently the resolution of the dilemma is sought in the distinction of levels of functioning, where a higher level in the hierarchy presupposes the lower levels, but cannot be reduced to these in a meaningful way. Boyd and Richerson (1985) have proposed a dual inheritance model in which they distinguish two principles of information transmission, the genetic inheritance system and the cultural inheritance system. The latter is based on learning; the propensity for learning is acquired through genetic inheritance, but learning operates through cultural inheritance. The two systems have different properties. For example, parenthood is not the same in the two systems. An individual may have many cultural parents (e.g., teachers) beyond the two biological parents who determine biological inheritance. More diversified are Plotkin and Odling-Smee's (1981) postulates of (1.) development, (2.) individual learning and (3.) socioculture as levels additional to genetic selection. The most diversified conceptualization of organism–environment relationships is that of Campbell (1974; cf. Overman, 1988) in whose evolutionary epistemology a range of discrete levels is distinguished, including among others, genetic adaptation, observational learning and imitation, cultural cumulation, and science.[3]

Another hierarchical model is that of Hinde (1987). Although it is based in ethology and individual development, levels of varying social complexity are also part of it. Hinde mentions that interindividual interactions evolve into relationships when there is a series of such interactions extending over time. In turn these relationships are located within larger networks of groups, and ultimately in society. According to Hinde (1987, p. 25), each of these levels of social complexity has properties that are not found at the lower levels. The relationships between the levels are dialectical; they mutually influence each other. Moreover, for each of the levels there are relationships with the physical and socio-cultural context. An example mentioned by Hinde (1992) is fear of snakes, a propensity that is part of the human biological heritage, is influenced by social experience, and plays a role at the cultural level through symbolic qualities attached to snakes.

Hierarchical models often have a strong developmental component. Differences due to environmental influences start early in the developmental trajectory and affect all higher levels. Even with phylogenetically early species the expression of genes is not only a maturational (autonomously biochemical) event, but is also influenced by interactions between organism and environment (e.g., Raven & Johnson, 1989). Another feature of hierarchical models is their compatibility with the observation that the extent of cross-cultural variation is not the same for all forms of behavior. Little variation is found for aspects of behavior that are closely linked to the physical survival of the organism, such as psychophysiological indices of arousal and properties of elementary stimulus processing. On the other hand, there is much cultural variation in the domain of cognition and in social interaction patterns (Poortinga, Kop & Van de Vijver, 1990). This suggests a variation in the strictness of gene-behavior relationships that can be expressed as a variation in "constraints" (e.g., Hinde, 1987), a notion that will be taken up in the next section.

The most obvious weakness of hierarchical models is that they lack the theoretical strength of evolutionary psychology. The specification of relations between levels at the higher end tends to be vague and based on exemplary rather than experimental evidence; a notion like Hinde's dialectical relationships is theoretically unspecific.

In summary, recent perspectives on the interrelationship between cultural and biological aspects of human behavior have seriously challenged the traditional contrast between nature and nurture. Most of the relevant theoretical developments have come from ethology, but there is a rapidly growing audience in psychology. Ethology with its traditional emphasis on invariant aspects of human behavioral functioning provides, as it were, a lower bound estimate of the effects of cultural conditions. Cross-cultural psychology, in which variations in behavior patterns across groups are a traditional focus of research, tends to lead to upper bound estimates. Genes and environment have become attuned to each other in the development of the human species (cf. Keller, this volume). Their interactions are difficult to trace, but more so in monocultural than in cross-cultural approaches.

Bridging the Gaps?

The starting point also of this section is the assumption that a comprehensive psychological conceptualization of culture–behavior relationships has to acknowledge at the same time psychological invariances and cross-cultural differences as empirical realities. In the most general sense there seems to be no dispute; the possibility of meaningful communication across cultural boundaries is taken for granted by all researchers. Whatever the basis for explanation and/or understanding, communication between researcher and informant (whether subject or participant) apparently can transcend cultural restrictions (cf. Greenfield, this volume).

When it comes to a more precise delineation of how culture and behavior are related viewpoints rapidly diverge. To begin with, there are three scientific disciplines: cultural anthropology, with its emphasis on institutional level phenomena; psychology, with the behaving human individual as the main focus; and ethology, the study of behaving organisms and the evolutionary roots of behavior. A second dimension of diversification lies in the unit of study that ranges from simple S-R connections via actions, plans, conventions, personality traits and cognitive abilities, to systems of symbols and meanings. There are two aspects to this dimension, namely the level of generality in the presumed antecedent conditions (or the culture side of the co-constructed reality) and the level of generality in the behavior consequents of these antecedents (the person side). For both aspects variations are found not only in the culture-comparative literature with predominantly linear additive models, but also in cultural psychology where the relationships between context and person tend to be more complex and less formalized. A third dimension is that of static versus dynamic approaches with acculturation, culture change, and development as central concerns. In development, again, several levels can be distinguished at which the phenomena under study can be specified, with time or periodicity as the main parameter.

The best way to overcome the limitations inherent in any one discipline is the combination of academic resources, i.e., interdisciplinary cooperation. This is not an easy enterprise, because researchers need to be mutually aware of the metatheoretical and paradigmatic assumptions that are implied in their theories and methods. An example of a cooperative study in which an anthropological and a psychological researcher pooled their methods has been reported by Wassmann and Dasen (1994a, 1994b). They analyzed the number system and classification and sorting among the Yupno in New Guinea, not only as a cultural phenomenon that was revealed through the collective representations of informants, but also as a cognitive ability in respect of which there were substantial interindividual differences that could be related to demographic and educational variables (cf. Greenfield, this volume).

The choice for a particular level and for a static or dynamic approach is determined mostly by the questions that researchers seek to answer. The specification of aspects of psychological outcomes that are included in a study and the postulated nature of person–context relationships primarily depends on the underlying theoretical notions. As noted in the first section of this chapter, it is much easier to evaluate the validity or plausibility of inferences with limited generality than that of inferences encompassing broader psychological processes; the assessment of skills usually gives fewer problems than that of intellectual aptitudes, and the same holds for attitudes vis à vis value dimensions. Similarly, the description of cultural practices and customs tends to be less problematic than that of cultural system parameters derived from these descriptions, and the biological basis of coyness is less controversial than that of a "universal grammar of social behavior."

There have been numerous attempts to create some order in the multitude of approaches and topics and to deal systematically with the controversies discussed in this volume. There seem to be three possible routes. The first of these is the concentration on a single level of the phenomena of interest. Examples are social constructionism with analysis focused on the historicity of behavior, and evolutionary psychology that gives primacy to biological principles. In the following sections two other routes will be explored. One of these is the integration of concerns from different levels, transcending these levels as it were by defining overarching approaches; the other route is through a more precise delineation of the domain of applicability (the range of convenience) of various approaches.

Integrative Perspectives

Several authors have tried to define integrative positions. In this volume Lonner and Adamopoulos and Miller pay some attention to these efforts. Other recent examples include Bornstein (1995) who presents a scheme to bring together formal and substantive aspects of behavior and Kashima and Kashima (1995) who argue for connectionism as providing a scope for the integration of both culture and behavior as dynamic processes.

Among attempts at integration that have been worked out in more detail, the paradigmatic analysis of Eckensberger (1979) is perhaps the most complete. He has distinguished no less than five "world views" in psychology that are organized in a hierarchical order. The first of these models applies the language of mathematics to theory construction and tries to grasp reality in terms of "multitude and extent." Purely statistically-defined relations fall in this category, but they are considered meaningless by Eckensberger, unless there is a theory in terms of which these relationships can be explained. The second model is based on a mechanistic metaphor of the person. S-R relations as postulated by traditional learning theory fall in this category. Eckensberger criticizes this kind of theory for assuming only causal relationships between organism and environment, and for being adevelopmental. The majority of culture–comparative studies falls within this paradigm. The third model is based on an organismic conception. It tends to include development, but with its origin in the person, as in the theory of Piaget. The relationship between the individual and the environment is assumed to be functional, with environmental variables not as causes but as incitement conditions, which can but need not facilitate development. However, there is no explanation possible of specific changes that take place at the cultural level and at the individual level. The relationships required for such explanations are partly incorporated in the fourth model, that of the organism/environment system. Here the relationship of organisms with each other and with the natural environment is considered. A central concept is the ecosystem, conceived of as a dynamic network. The notion of behavior setting (Barker, 1968) is mentioned as an example. Shortcomings that Eckensberger finds with this model are that development can be explained at the phylogenetic level—as in sociobiological theory—but not at the individual level, and that there is no place for unique meanings and events.

The last model is that of the reflexive person who in principle is capable of acting consciously and in a future-oriented (i.e., intentional) way. The relationship between person and environment in this paradigm is neither causal nor functional, but dialectic. This dialectical relationship between person and environment takes place via actions of the person, making the action the appropriate unit of analysis. Persons can construct their reality, and choose between actions to reach a goal. In Eckensberger's opinion this last statement meets three important concerns. First, both cultural variables and individual variables can be interpreted as results from actions and as presuppositions for actions. Second, it incorporates development at three levels: the development of a single action towards a goal, ontogenetic development, and historical processes of social and cultural change. Third, it allows for general laws and concepts, as well as for unique events.

Each model in this series incorporates the previous one, thus successively extending the domain of phenomena that are accessible to investigation. Each is seen by Eckensberger as fruitful for answering particular questions. In addition, methodological difficulties in cross-cultural psychology can be understood better if the underlying papradigms of researchers are recognized (Eckensberger & Burgard, 1983). However, for the full understanding of human behavior Eckensberger only accepts the last, most inclusive paradigm.

The more comprehensive paradigms in this hierarchy allow progressively less procedural control on validity and on the exclusion of alternative interpretations. Thus, this sophisticated attempt at integration falls short on the question how to justify one's interpretations. Another objection to Eckensberger is that biological aspects of behavior, although they are incorporated in earlier paradigms of the hierarchy, hardly have a place in the one that he prefers.

Also in the ecocultural framework developed by Berry (cf. Berry et al., 1992) a broad range of variables is included at the population level as well as at the individual level. A presentation of the main features of this model is given in the chapter Lonner and Adamopulos (this volume) and this framework will not be discussed further here. The main objections this time will come from the cultural psychology perspective. Culture takes the form of a set of antecedent variables in the positivistic sense and in most of his writings Berry (e.g. 1994) sees a universal psychology as the ultimate goal; indigenous theories are intermediate steps that are needed to overcome the ethnocentrism of existing ones. In addition, development does not receive the emphasis it has in Eckensberger's synthesis. From a more biological perspective the position of biological adaptation which appears to be seen as consequential rather than as antecedent to socio-political context (cf. Figure 2 in Lonner & Adamoulos, this volume) seems questionable.

Another attempt at integration can be found in the work of Cole (1992a, 1992b; cf. also Miller, this chapter). The basic framework consists of three components of development, namely, biological, environmental, and cultural. Cole notes that there has been a long debate on the relative importance of nature and nurture in human behavior, with sometimes the one and sometimes the other given more prominence. In his view this debate is misguided and has to be transcended by postulating a third entity, namely culture in the sense of historically specific features of the environment. To allow for this he reduces "environment" in the traditional sense to "universal features of the environment." Cole (1992a, p. 735) writes: "According to this cultural context view, the two factors *biology* and *the environment* or *the individual* and the *society* . . . do not interact directly. Rather their interaction is mediated through a third factor, culture" (italics in orginal). The co-evolution of the human brain and the cultural environment is emphasized, with as a focal point the use of artifacts, both material and symbolic. To incorporate different levels Cole makes use of various time scales—physical, phylogenetic, culture-historical, ontogenetic, and microgenetic. In a long-time perspective, causal relationships between biology and culture are not unidirectional but bidirectional. His conception of culture incorporates historical time; culture as social context (with system properties) is also the medium in which ontogenetic development takes place. Although Cole remains somewhat vague on this, his text and the figure he uses to depict his ideas suggest that ontologically culture has an existence "sui generis" (of its own); culture is definitely not merely the outcome of interaction processes between biological and environmental factors.

A difficulty with Cole's framework is the postulate of culture as a third entity. Apart from its ontological status, it makes the framework less parsimonious than most other schemes in which there is only one major distinction, between organism and environment. For example, in Berry's framework co-evolution, both in phylogenetic and in historical (sociocultural) time, can be described as population-mediated adaptation. Cole takes the somewhat unusual position of restricting "environment" to universal features of the environment, to create a niche for culture as a medium for behavioral development.

For each of the three frameworks mentioned a few basic questions were raised to illustrate problems that come with the integration of a wide range of phenomena. Perhaps such difficulties are most evident in the writings of Eckensberger because his explicit distinctions between paradigms bring these to light. As he

moves from one paradigm to the next, solutions to some difficulties gain prominence, but other problems tend to be lost. Therefore, one may ask whether integration is the most viable route for the further development of cross-cultural
psychology.

Culture-Behavior Relationships Reconsidered

Quite a different route can be taken when full weight is given to the consideration
that scientific analysis offers only a very partial and biased representation of reality. Different disciplines, and even different paradigms and theories within a discipline, all offer particular viewpoints with respect to sets of only partly overlapping phenomena. Each can be seen as having legitimate concerns that drive the
theorizing, while at the same time separately and combined they fall (far) short
of a correct and full account of whatever they seek to describe or explain. In
psychology this inadequacy finds expression in the proportion of unexplained
variance in data, which more often than not is considerably higher than the proportion of variance accounted for, unless, of course, the researcher provides an
"explanation" *post hoc*, a practice that is suspect for the very reason of the discrepancies between prediction and postdiction.

In this connection Berry et al. (1992) have argued that in current theories
perhaps too close systematic relationships between culture and behavior are assumed. It appears from the literature as if for any difference in the behavior repertoire of two cultural populations there has to be a psychological reason systematically related to some cultural difference (subjectively or objectively defined).
A new scope for theorizing arises when this assumption is relaxed and when the
finding is taken seriously that also in most cross-cultural studies the larger part
of the variance remains unexplained.

This lead has been taken up by Poortinga (1990/1992). He proposes for psychology that "culture becomes manifest in shared constraints that limit the behavior repertoire available to members of a certain group in a way different from
individuals belonging to some other group" (1992, p. 10). Constraints can be classified as internal to the organism, due to either biological or cultural inheritance,
or as external due to context. They also can be defined at various levels. For
example, at the biological and physiological level genetic transmission leads to
universal propensies of the human species. The ecological context with factors
of climate and soil imposes limits on economic subsistence for the population
and on individual behavior patterns (e.g., socialization patterns, Barry, Child &
Bacon, 1959; susceptibility to visual illusions, Segall et al., 1966). The socioeconomic and historical context implies limits on a wide variety of aspects, including educational opportunities and patterns of values, norms, and beliefs that come
about in a given socialization process. The final level of constraints is that of the
concrete situation in which the range of choices of the person is limited by factors
at each of the levels mentioned.

Constraints curtail the range of behaviors available to a person, but within
the limits set by various constraints there is a range of behavior alternatives (i.e.,

affordances or opportunities). Within this range the choice of a specific action is not predictable or explainable in a lawful manner.[4] In as much as constraints are the same for members of a single population and not the same across populations, consistent differences between these populations may arise. Proposed explanations for such differences should be open to quasi-experimental analysis and prediction. In as much as there is freedom from constraints the search for systematic antecedent–consequent relationships will be fruitless; within the range of behavioral choice, description and reconstruction of events are the appropriate forms of analysis.

As mentioned, the distinction between what is constrained, and thus subject to bounded regularity, and what is free from constraints is dependent on the level at which phenomena are studied. The realization of the human chin appears to be a fluke in phylogenetic history (Lewontin, 1978), but it has lawful implications for human speech. The decision of a person whether or not to go to university may depend on trivial factors, but the outcome is likely to have life-long consequences (cf. Valsiner & Lawrence, Volume 2 of this *Handbook*). Similarly, some technical invention that has come about by accident can have far-reaching consequences for a cultural population; the same invention in some other population may have quite different consequences. But at another level of analysis such effects by and large are "pleiotropic"; they can be seen as accidental by-products.

Obvious examples of phenomena at the level of cultural populations that do not lend themselves to psychologically lawful analysis are conventions, in the sense of more or less arbitrary agreements within a society about how to act in a certain situation (Van de Koppel & Schoots, 1986). One can perhaps trace a convention's historical origin, and find a perfectly plausible reason why it has arisen, but there is no psychological lawfulness in the specific form of its manifestation. Thus, one finds at the cultural level cultural rules that cannot be related to broader domains of norms or values; the rule of right-hand or left-hand traffic is probably the ultimate example (Poortinga, 1993). More generally, the subjective meanings—symbols and intentions that make a culture or person unique—can be seen as constructions within a realm of opportunities.

Probably the major problem with this conceptualization is that the boundaries between constraints and affordances are very fuzzy. Poortinga refers to chaos theory, which is meant to describe the behavior of systems that are unstable within given boundaries, as the best analog of the relationship between the constrained and the unconstrained. The most famous example of a chaotic system is the weather. Just like the weather, behavior is difficult to predict at a medium term, and just like the weather has highly regular seasonal fluctuations, there are regularities in behavior patterns and trajectories of development, both for individuals and cultures. Moreover, chaos theory may lead to an understanding how through chaotic change a higher level of organization is reached by an organism (e.g. Barton, 1994; Robertson, 1995), thus providing a kind of relationship between levels that has aspects of randomness in concrete situations, but simultaneously is deterministic in a longer time perspective.

It may be pointed out that the notion of constraints has been mentioned by other authors in this volume (see Lonner and Adamopoulos, and L. H. Munroe and R. H. Munroe) and that it takes an important position in the work of authors refered to in this chapter, (Hinde and Cole). The theoretical underpinnings in chaos or, more broadly, nonlinear dynamics, represent a way of thinking that is rapidly gaining attention in psychology (cf. Robertson & Combs, 1995) and especially in developmental psychology (e.g., Thelen, 1995; Van Geert, 1994).

In summary, the proposed definition of culture illustrates one possible way in which seemingly incompatible orientations to behavior–culture relationships can be defined as compatible and complementary. It is a minimal definition, but it encompasses the domains of psychological laws and cultural rules (cf. Table 9–1). Both methodologically and theoretically such a complementary perspective should take much of the sting out of current controversies. Methodologically the so-called qualitative and quantitative methods are suited to the unconstrained and the constrained respectively. Theoretically the perspective can encompass the biological basis of behavior as well as its crystallization in culture-specific norms and customs.

Applications of Cross-Cultural Psychology

The mind-set of the reader of this chapter is most likely oriented toward an environment in which books like this one are being written and used. However, a cross-cultural psychologist has to realize that the modal citizen of the world is a child, woman, or man with a low cash income and little or no formal schooling, who is engaged in domestic work or agriculture, has limited or no access to health facilities and modern media, is impressed with the economic wealth of the urban industrial nations and shocked with their moral and religious depravity. Closer to all cross-cultural psychologists are minorities, belonging to underprivileged ethnic groups or to socially disadvantaged groups within the majority population of their societies. What is the relevance of the theoretical discussions in this volume for these clients of the cross-cultural researcher?

It is a cherished belief among researchers that the knowledge and insights they accumulate have a bearing on the application of their science. For psychology this belief can be challenged, as shown by Schönpflug (1993). He argues that applied psychology as practiced in clinics and organizations does not originate from basic psychology but from other sources. Applied psychology has had an autonomous development and has not benefited substantially from academic research. Although counter examples can be mentioned, such as behavior therapy which is based in learning theory to a considerable extent, Schönpflug's thesis has sufficient merit to demand attention.

The ethical codes of national psychologists' associations state invariably that the professional activities of psychologists in their interaction with clients are justified on the basis of their competence in psychology.[5] In turn, competence is founded on education in psychology, professional training, and sometimes experience; scientific knowledge is the first and foremost requirement. However, this is only a meaningful basis if there exists indeed a fund of knowledge that has sufficient empirical validity to warrant application. In as much as such knowledge is lacking in contemporary psychology (e.g., Dawes, 1994), the suspicion can be raised that the main function of academic psychology for practitioners lies in the scientific respectibility it lends to the profession (Schönpflug, 1994).

All this begs the question of how far there is a worthwhile body of basic knowledge in cross-cultural psychology. The chapter by D. Sinha on indigenization points to the irrelevance of much of Western psychology for clients in the majority world. In one workshop on health and cross-cultural psychology in which the organizers had the courage to raise the question of applicability explicitly, the participants were asked to list items of knowledge in three categories (Berry, Dasen & Sartorius, 1988, p. 298–299):

> *"(a)* *a contribution to general knowledge without specific possibility of application,*
> *(b)* *conducive to being "translated" into behavioral or other intervention; and*
> *(c)* *already applicable."*

According to the authors this was found to be a mind-stretching exercise. There were very few facts that were "already applicable." In explanation, the authors elaborate on the difficulties of cross-cultural psychology and the context-bound nature of psychological knowledge, but in a sense this only seems to confirm the difficulties.

Perhaps a quite modest view of the relevance of cross-cultural research is the most realistic and ultimately the most fruitful. It can be argued that in many instances there is relevant academic knowledge exists, but that this knowledge is partial. The available fund of research findings merely may allow a better definition of the range of alternative answers to a problem. It is also possible that information is available allowing the judgment, that for some suggested solution to a problem, this would form a "wrong" or "unpromising" course of action. In this way, even if existing knowledge is quite inadequate, less viable solutions may be avoided. In other words, there can be constraints based in scientific knowledge which limit the range of viable solution alternatives.

Some examples arising from this volume about how general knowledge can be helpful in influencing the course of interventions are the following:

- There is now more sophistication in the thinking about behavior–culture relationships than a few decades ago. These theoretical views should influence the range of possible actions that are considered; early childhood education is a case in point (e.g., Eldering & Leseman, 1993).
- Although the interface between "nature" and "nurture" remains extremely problematic, the acknowledgment that biological influences play a significant role in behavior as studied by psychologists and social scientists is now virtually beyond dispute, providing constraints on the variability in psychological functioning of cultural populations.

- Methodologically the pitfalls and limitations of quantitative comparison can be mapped out much more clearly than in the past, and the need to specify cultural context and study behavior in context is more widely acknowledged (though admittedly this knowledge is often not sufficiently used even in research projects).
- Perhaps most important, it is recognized that psychology as it exists today is a Western enterprise. The indigenization of psychology is an important strategy for reducing erroneous and invalid applications.

Examples of knowledge conducive to application (the second of the three categories distinguished earlier) include the Standards for the Adaptation and Translation of Tests of the International Test Commission (cf. Van de Vijver & Leung, this volume) and the emphasis on methods allowing the study of behavior processes (cf. Greenfield, this volume). Also, there are shifts in research topics, for example, from perception to social behavior. Although there are multiple reasons, of which trends and fashions are undoubtedly the most important, it can be argued that some issues have been resolved through research. Thus, studies in the sixties and seventies on the perception of depth in two-dimensional representations have shown that as far as common depth cues are concerned, pictures in school books will create few problems in any society (cf. Deregowski, 1980).

It is not so surprising that cross-culturally readily applicable knowledge is rare, and that the third of the three abovementioned categories remained largely empty. In many respects this is in accordance with the thesis of contemporary cross-cultural psychology that at the level of concrete actions behavior is contextualized. It also fits the relative independence between academic research and application noted by Schönpflug, and it is in line with the suggestion made in the previous section that culture–behavior relationships are to a certain extent arbitrary in terms of psychological laws.

The argument in this section is limited to the relationship between basic research and application. In Volumes 2 and 3 of this *Handbook* there are several chapters that reflect more directly relevant empirical knowledge, making more visible the scope for application. However, one further consideration may upset any careful argument about the ideal relationship between theory and practice, namely the need for action. In the present *Handbook* this is most dramatically demonstrated by Aptekar and Stöcklin (Volume 2 of this *Handbook*) in their analysis of children growing up in difficult circumstances. In the end there is always a dilemma between scientific restraint, only applying knowledge that has been tested in order to avoid ideologically- and fashion- driven applications, and the acceptance of risks because existing needs have to be addressed now.

Conclusion

The field of cross-cultural psychology continues to expand. International communication and contacts are ever increasing and there is more attention to cultural diversity as societies become more multiethnic. In addition, there is a new interest in the relationship between the biological basis of behavior and its cultural expression. The multiple perspectives that are characteristic of the field of cross-cultural psychology will probably continue to be developed in parallel. Human behavior can be investigated as the product of gene–environment interactions; it can also be studied as the outcome of creative and historical processes. In this chapter the complementarity of various perspectives has been stressed. An attempt has been made to do justice to a wide range of concerns, but with one restriction. The onus is on researchers to make plausible that the inferences they draw from their data are valid, and to use methods that allow others to scrutinize these inferences. This is a general requirement that presumably will continue to form the core of scientific enquiry in psychology. In cross-cultural psychology, where so many theories and perspectives already exist, the critical and demythologizing role of science seems particularly needed. It is this role that has been emphasized in this chapter.

Endnotes

1. Lutz Eckensberger, Heidi Keller, and Fons van de Vijver read an earlier draft of this chapter. Their comments are greatly appreciated.

2. From the perspective of this chapter Saunders' argument is relativistic. It may be noted that she herself (personal communication) sees her approach as transcending the universalism–relativism contrast (cf. also Saunders & Van Brakel, in press).

3. Campbell sees a selective retention process operating at each level that leads to elimination of error and increasing organization. In this chapter it should be noted what he has to say about science: "What is characteristic of science is that the selective system which weeds out among the variety of conjectures involves deliberate contact with the environment through experiment and quantified prediction, designed so that outcomes quite independent of the investigator are possible" (Campbell, 1988, p. 416; reprinted from Campbell, 1974).

4. More precisely, in a given instance the prediction of an event can be (much) better than chance, but not better than the a priori probability that this event will take place.

5. What is being said holds at least for the ethical codes of the national associations in Austria, Canada, Germany, Netherlands, Spain, the Scandinavian countries and the United States. I am not aware of any exception in other national codes.

References

Argyle, M. (1988). *Bodily communication* (2nd ed.). London: Methuen.

Asendorpf, J. B., & Valsiner, J. (Eds.). (1992). *Stability and change in development: A study of methodological reasoning.* Newbury Park, CA: Sage.

Barker, R. G. (1968). *Ecological psychology.* Stanford: Stanford University Press.

Barry, H., Child, I., & Bacon, M. (1959). Relation of child training to subsistence economy. *American Anthropologist, 61,* 51–63.

Barton, S. (1994). Chaos, self-organization, and psychology. *American Psychologist, 49,* 5–14.

Berlin, B., & Kay, P. (1969). *Basic color terms: Their universality and evolution.* Berkeley, CA: University of California Press.

Berry, J. W. (1969). On cross-cultural comparability. *International Journal of Psychology, 4,* 119–128.

Berry, J. W. (1989). Imposed etics-emics-derived etics: The operationalization of a compelling idea. *International Journal of Psychology, 24,* 721–735.

Berry, J. W. (1994, July). *On the unity of the field: Variations and communalities in understanding human behavior in cultural context.* Paper presented at the 23rd congress of the International Association of Applied Psychology, Madrid.

Berry, J. W., Dasen, P. R., & Sartorius, N. (1988). Conclusions. In P. R. Dasen, J. W. Berry, & N. Sartorius (Eds.), *Health and cross-cultural psychology,* (pp. 298–314). Newbury Park, CA: Sage.

Berry, J. W., Poortinga, Y. H., Segall, M. H., & Dasen, P. R. (1992). *Cross-cultural psychology: Research and applications.* Cambridge: Cambridge University Press.

Billig, M. (1987). *Arguing and thinking: A rhetorical approach to social psychology.* Cambridge: Cambridge University Press/Paris: Editions de la Maison des Sciences de l'Homme.

Bock, R. D., Zimowski, M. F. (1987). Contributions of the biomedical approach to individual differences in personality measures. *Behavioral and Brain Sciences, 10,* 17–18.

Boesch, E. E. (1991). *Symbolic action theory and cultural psychology.* Berlin: Springer Verlag.

Bornstein, M. H. (1995). Form and function: Implications for studies of culture and human development. *Culture and Psychology, 1,* 123–137.

Bornstein, M. H., Kessen, W. H., & Weiskopf, S. (1976). The categories of hue in infancy. *Science, 191,* 201–202.

Bornstein, M. H. Pêcheux, M-G, & Lécuyer, R. (1988). Visual habituation in human infants: Development and rearing circumstances. *Psychological Research, 50,* 130–133.

Boski, P. (1996). Cross-cultural psychology at the crossroads. In H. Grad, A. Blanco & J. Georgas (Eds.), *Key issues in cross-cultural psychology* (pp. 25–41). Lisse: Swets and Zeitlinger.

Bouvy, A-M., Van de Vijver, F. J. R., Boski, P.,

Schmitz, P., & Krewer, B. (1994). Introduction. In A-M Bouvy, F. J. R. Van de Vijver, P. Boski & P. Schmitz (Eds.), *Journeys into cross- cultural psychology* (pp. 1–6). Lisse: Swets and Zeitlinger.

Boyd, R., & Richerson, P. J. (1985). *Culture and the evolutionary process.* Chicago: University of Chicago Press.

Brewer, M., & Campbell, D. T. (1976). *Ethnocentrism and intergroup attitudes: East African evidence.* London: Sage.

Bronfenbrenner, U., & Ceci, S. J. (1994). Nature-nurture-reconceptualized in developmental perspective: A bioecological model. *Psychological Review, 101,* 568–586.

Brown, D. E. (1991). *Human universals.* Philadelphia: Temple University Press.

Buss, D. M. (1989). Sex differences in human mate preferences: Evolutionary hypotheses tested in 37 cultures. *Behavioral and Brain Sciences, 12,* 1–49.

Buss, D. M. et al. (1990). International preferences in selecting mates: A study of 37 cultures. *Journal of Cross-Cultural Psychology, 21,* 5–47.

Campbell, D. T. (1974). Evolutionary epistemology. In P. A. Schilpp (Ed.), *The philosophy of Karl Popper* (pp. 413–463). La Salle, IL: Open Court Publishers.

Campbell, D. T. (1988). Evolutionary epistemology. In E. S. Overman (Ed.), *Methodology and epistomology for social science: Selected papers of Donald T. Campbell* (pp. 393–434). Chicago: University of Chicago Press.

Campbell, D. T., & Fiske D. W. (1959). Convergent and discriminant validation by the multitrait–multimethod matrix. *Psychological Bulletin, 56,* 81–105.

Chomsky, N. (1965). *Aspects of a theory of syntax.* Cambridge, MA: MIT Press.

Chomsky, N. (1980). *Rules and representations.* Oxford: Blackwell.

Church, A. T. (1987). Personality research in a non-western culture: The Philippines. *Psychological Bulletin, 102,* 272–292.

Cole, M. (1990). Cultural psychology: A once and future discipline. In J. J. Berman (Ed.), *Nebraska symposium on motivation 1989: Cross-cultural perspectives* (pp. 279–335.).

Cole, M. (1992a). Culture in development. In M.

H. Bornstein & M. Lamb (Eds.), *Developmental psychology: An advanced textbook* (3rd ed., pp. 731–789). Hillsdale, NJ: Erlbaum.

Cole, M. (1992b). Context, modularity, and the cultural constitution of development. In L. T. Winegar & J. Valsiner (Eds.), *Children's development within social context* (Vol. 2, pp. 5–31). Hillsdale, NJ: Erlbaum.

Cole, M., & Cole, S. R. (1993). *The development of children* (2nd ed.). New York: Freeman.

Cole, M., Gay, J., Glick, J., & Sharp, D. (1971). *The cultural context of learning and thinking.* New York: Basic Books.

Daly, M., & Wilson, M. (1983). *Evolution and behavior* (2nd ed.). Boston: Willard Grant Press.

Davidson, A. R., Jaccard, J. J., Triandis, H. C., Morales, M. L., & Diaz-Guerrero, R. L. (1976). Cross-cultural model testing: Toward a solution of the etic-emic dilemma. *International Journal of Psychology, 11,* 1–14.

Dawes, R. M. (1994). *House of cards: Psychology and psychotherapy built on myth.* New York: Free Press.

Deregowski, J. B. (1980). *Illusions, patterns and pictures: A cross-cultural perspective.* London: Academic Press.

Deregowski, J. B. (1989). Real space and represented space: Cross-cultural perspectives. *Behavioral and Brain Sciences, 12,* 51–119.

De Waal, F. B. M. (1988). The communicative repertoire of captive bonobos (pan paniscus) compared to that of chimpanzees. *Behaviour, 106,* 183–251.

De Waal, F. B. M. (1995). Bonobo sex and society. *Scientific American, 272(3),* 58–64.

DeRidder, R., & Tripathi, R. C. (Eds.). (1992). *Norm violations and intergroup relations.* Oxford: Clarendon Press.

Dissanayake, E. (1992). *Homo aestheticus: Where art comes from and why.* New York: Free Press.

Doi, T. (1973). *The anatomy of dependence.* Tokyo: Kodansha International.

Eckensberger, L. H. (1979). A metamethodological evaluation of psychological theories from a cross-cultural perspective. In L. Eckensberger, W. Lonner, & Y. H. Poortinga (Eds.), *Cross-cultural contributions to psychology* (pp. 255–275). Lisse: Swets & Zeitlinger.

Eckensberger, L. H. (1995). Activity or action: Two different routes towards an integration of culture into psychology. *Culture and Psychology, 1,* 67–80.

Eckensberger, L. H. (1996). Agency, action, and culture: Three basic concepts for psychology in general and for cross-cultural psychology in specific. In J. Pandey, D. Sinha & D. P. S. Bhawuk. *Asian contributions to cross-cultural psychology* (pp. 72–102). New Delhi: Sage.

Eckensberger, L. H., & Burgard, P. (1983). The cross-cultural assessment of normative concepts. In S. H. Irvine & J. W. Berry (Eds.), *Human assessment and cultural factors* (pp. 459–480). New York: Plenum Press.

Eibl-Eibesfeldt, I. (1979). Human ethology: Concepts and and implications for the sciences of man. *Behavioral and Brain Sciences, 2,* 1–57.

Eibl-Eibesfeldt, I. (1989). *Human Ethology.* New York: Aldine de Gruyter.

Eldering, L., & Leseman, P. (1993). *Early intervention and culture: Preparation for literacy.* UNESCO Publishing.

Enriquez, V. G. (Ed.). (1990). *Indigenous psychologies.* Quezon City: Psychology Research and Training House.

Enriquez, V. G. (1993). Developing a Filipino psychology. In U. Kim & J. W. Berry (Eds.), *Indigenous psychologies: Research and experience in cultural context* (pp. 152–169). Newbury Park, CA: Sage.

Fodor, J. (1985). Précis of The modularity of mind. *Behavioral and Brain Sciences, 8,* 1–46.

Garcia, J, & Koelling, R. A. (1966). Relation of cue to consequence in avoidance learning. *Psychonomic Science, 4,* 123–124.

Geertz, C. (1973). *The interpretation of cultures.* New York: Basic Books.

Gergen, K. (1982). *Towards transformation in social knowledge.* New York: Springer.

Gergen, K. (1994). Exploring the postmodern: Perils or potentials? *American Psychologist, 49,* 412–416.

Georgas, J., & Berry, J. W. (1995). An ecocultural taxonomy for cross-cultural psychology. *Cross- Cultural Research 29,* 121–157.

Goodall, J. (1986). *The chimpanzees of Gombe.* Cambridge, MA: Harvard University Press.

Gould, S. J., & Lewontin, R. C. (1979). The spandrels of San Marco and the Panglossian paradigm: A critique of the adaptationist programme. *Proceedings of the Royal Society, B205,* 581–598.

Greenfield, P. M. (1991). Language, tools and brain: The ontogeny and phylogeny of hierarchically organized sequential behavior. *Behavioral and Brain Sciences, 14,* 531–595.

Heron, A., & Kroeger, E. (1980). Introduction to developmental psychology. In H. C. Triandis, A. Heron, & E. Kroeger (Eds.), *Handbook of cross-cultural psychology* (Vol. 4, pp. 1–15). Boston: Allyn and Bacon.

Hinde, R. (1987). *Individuals, relationships and culture.* Cambridge: Cambridge University Press.

Hinde, R. A. (1992). Developmental psychology in the context of other behavioral sciences. *Developmental Psychology, 28,* 1018–1029.

Jahoda, G. (1983). The cross-cultural emperor's conceptual clothes: The emic-etic issue revisited. In J. B. Deregowski, S. Dziurawiec & R. C. Annis (Eds.), *Expiscations in cross-cultural psychology* (pp. 19–37). Lisse: Swets and Zeitlinger.

Jahoda, G. (1986). Nature, culture and social psychology. *European Journal of Social Psychology, 16,* 17–30.

Jahoda, G. (1992). *Crossroads between culture and mind.* New York: Harvester Wheatsheaf.

Immelman, K., Scherer, K. R., Vogel, C., & Schmoock, P. (Eds.). (1988). *Psychobiologie: Grundlagen des Verhaltens* [Psychobiology: Foundations of behavior]. Stuttgart: Fischer Verlag.

Kagitçibasi, C. (1982). Old-age security value of children: Cross-national economic evidence. *Journal of Cross-Cultural Psychology, 13,* 29–42.

Kagitçibasi, C. (1992). Linking the indigenous and universalist orientations. In S. Iwawaki, Y. Kashima & K. Leung (Eds.), *Innovations in cross-cultural psychology* (pp. 29–37). Lisse: Swets and Zeitlinger.

Kagitcibasi, C. (1995). *Family and human development across countries: A view from the other side.* Hillsdale, NJ: Erlbaum.

Karmiloff-Smith, A. (1994). Précis of Beyond modularity: A developmental perspective on cognitive science. *Behavioral and Brain Sciences, 17,* 693–745.

Kashima, Y., & Kashima, E. S. (1995, July). *Culture,* situated practice, and connectionism. Paper presented at the 4th European Congress of Psychology, Athens.

Kendon, A. (1984). Did gestures have the happiness to escape the curse at the confusion of Babel? In A. Wolfgang (Ed.), *Non-verbal behavior: Perspectives, applications, intercultural insights* (pp. 75–114). Lewiston: Hogrefe.

Kenrick, D. T., & Keefe, R. C. (1992). Age preferences reflect sex differences in human reproductive strategies. *Behavioral and Brain Sciences, 15,* 75–133.

Kim, U., & Berry, J. W. (1993a). Introduction. In U. Kim & J. W. Berry (Eds.), *Indigenous psychologies: Research and experience in cultural context* (pp. 1–29). Newbury Park, CA: Sage.

Kim, U., & Berry, J. W. (Eds.). (1993b). *Indigenous psychologies: Research and experience in cultural context.* Newbury Park, CA: Sage.

Kloos, P. (1988). *Door het oog van de anthropoloog* [Through the eye of the anthropologist]. Muiderberg: Coutinho.

Kortlandt, A. (1962). Chimpanzees in the wild. *Scientific American, 206,* 128-138

Krewer, B., & Jahoda, G. (1993). Psychologie et culture: vers une solution du "Babel" [Psychology and culture: Towards a solution of "Babel"]. *International Journal of Psychology, 28,* 367–375.

Kuhn, T. S. (1962). *The structure of scientific revolutions.* Chicago: University of Chicago Press.

Kulkarni, S. S., & Puhan, B. N. (1988). Psychological assesssment: Its present and future trends. In J. Pandey (Ed.), *Psychology in India: The state of the art* (Vol. 1, 19–91). New Delhi: Sage.

Laboratory of Comparative Human Cognition (1983). Culture and cognitive development. In P. H. Mussen & W. Kessen (Eds.), *Handbook of child psychology* (Vol. 1, pp. 295–356). New York: Wiley.

Lewontin, R. C. (1978). Adaptation. *Scientific American, 239,* 156–169.

Lincoln, Y. S., & Guba, E. G. (1985). *Naturalistic inquiry.* Beverly Hills: Sage.

Logan, R., Snarey, J., & Schrader, D. (1990). Autonomous versus heteronomous moral judgment types. *Journal of Cross-Cultural Psychology, 21,* 71–89.

Lonner, W. J. (1980). The search for psychological universals. In H. C. Triandis & W. W. Lambert (Eds.), *Handbook of cross-cultural psychology* (Vol. 1, Perspectives, pp. 143–204). Boston: Allyn and Bacon.

Luria, A. R. (1971). Towards the problem of the historical nature of psychological processes. *International Journal of Psychology, 6,* 259–272.

Luria, A. R. (1976). *Cognitive development: Its cultural and social foundations.* Cambridge, MA: Harvard University Press.

Luria, A. R., & Vygotsky, L. S. (1992). *Ape, primitive man and child: Essays in the history of behavior.* New York: Harvester Wheatsheaf.

Lutz, C. (1988). *Unnatural emotions.* Chicago: University of Chicago Press.

Malinowski, B. (1944). *A scientific theory of culture.* Chapel Hill, NC: University of North Carolina Press.

Malpass, R. S., & Poortinga, Y. H. (1986). Strategies for design and analysis. In W. J. Lonner & J. W. Berry (Eds.), *Field methods in cross-cultural research* (pp. 47–84). Beverly Hills, CA: Sage.

McDevitt, T. M., Hess, R. D., Kashiwagi, K., Dickson, W. P., Miyake, N., & Azuma, H. (1987). Referential communication accuracy of mother-child pairs and children's later scholastic achievement: A follow-up study. *Merrill-Palmer Quarterly, 33,* 171–185.

MacDonald, K. B. (Ed.). (1988). *Sociobiological perspectives on human development.* New York: Springer Verlag.

McGrew, W. C. (1992). *Chimpanzee material culture.* Cambridge: Cambridge University Press.

Mehryar, A. (1984). The role of psychology in national development: Wishful thinking and reality. *International Journal of Psychology, 19,* 159–167.

Naidu, R. K. (1983, December). *A developing program of stress research.* Paper presented at the seminar on Stress, Anxiety and Mental Health, Allahabad.

National Advisory Mental Health Council (1995). Basic behavioral science research for mental health. *American Psychologist, 50,* 485–495.

Overman, E. S. (Ed.). (1988). *Methodology and epistomology for social science: Selected papers of Donald T. Campbell.* Chicago: University of Chicago Press.

Pande, N., & Naidu, R. K. (1992). Anasakti and health: A study of non-attachment. *Psychology and Developing Societies, 4,* 91–104.

Papousek, H., & Bornstein, M. H. (1992). Didactic interactions: Intuitive parental support of vocal and verbal development in human infants. In H. Papousek, U. Jürgens & M. Papousek (Eds.), *Non-verbal communication: Comparative and developmental approaches* (pp. 209–229). Cambridge: Cambridge University Press/Paris: Editions de la Maison des Sciences de l'Homme.

Parker, I., & Shotter, J. (Eds.). (1990). *Deconstructing social psychology.* London: Routledge.

Pe-Pua, R. (1990). Pagtatanung-tanong: A method for cross-cultural research. In V. G. Enriquez (Ed.), *Indigenous psychologies* (pp. 231–249). Quezon City: Psychology Research and Training House.

Peeters, H. F. M. (1996). *Psychology: The historical dimension.* Tilburg: Tilburg University Press.

Pettigrew, T. F., & Van de Vijver, F. J. R. (1990). Thinking both bigger and smaller: Finding the basic level for cross-cultural psychology. In P. J. D. Drenth, J. A. Sergeant & R. J. Takens (Eds.), *European perspectives in psychology* (Vol. 3, pp. 339–353). Chichester: Wiley.

Pike, K. L. (1967). *Language in relation to a unified theory of the structures of human behavior.* (2nd ed.). The Hague: Mouton.

Plomin, R., & Bergeman, S. C. (1991). The nature of nurture: Genetic influence on "environmental" measures. *Behavioral and Brain Sciences, 14,* 373–427.

Plomin, R., & Daniels, D. (1987). Why are children of the same family so different from one another? *Behavioral and Brain Sciences, 10,* 1–16.

Plomin, R., & McClearn, G. E. (Eds.). (1993). *Nature, nurture, and psychology.* Washington DC: American Psychological Association.

Plotkin, H. C., & Odling-Smee, T. J. (1981). A multiple-level model of evolution and its implications for sociobiology. *Behavioral and Brain Sciences, 4,* 225–268.

Poortinga, Y. H. (1990/1992). Towards a conceptualization of culture for psychology. *Cross-

Cultural Psychology Bulletin, 24(3), 2–10 [reprinted in S. Iwawaki, Y. Kashima & K. Leung (Eds.), *Innovations in cross-cultural psychology* (pp. 3–17)].

Poortinga, Y. H. (1993). Cross-culturally invariant personality variables: A study in India and The Netherlands. In G. L. Van Heck, P. Bonaiuto, I. J. Deary & W. Novack (Eds.), *Personality psychology in Europe* (Vol. 4, pp. 105–153). Tilburg: Tilburg University Press.

Poortinga, Y. H., Kop, P. F. M., & Van de Vijver, F. J. R. (1990). In P. J. D. Drenth, J. A. Sergeant & R. J. Takens (Eds.), *European perspectives in psychology* (Vol. 3, pp. 355–376). Chichester: Wiley.

Poortinga, Y. H., & Malpass, R. S. (1986). Making inferences from cross-cultural data. In W. J. Lonner & J. W. Berry (Eds.), *Field methods in cross-cultural research* (pp. 17–46). Beverly Hills, CA: Sage.

Popper, K. R. (1959). *The logic of scientific discovery.* New York: Basic Books.

Price-Williams, D. (1980). Toward the idea of a cultural psychology: A superordinate theme for study. *Journal of Cross-Cultural Psychology, 11,* 75–88.

Puhan, B. N. (1982). *Issues in psychological measurement.* Agra: National Psychological Corporation.

Raven, P. H., & Johnson, G. B. (1989). *Biology* (2nd ed.). St. Louis, MO: Times Mirror / Mosby College Publishers.

Reuning, H., & Wortley, W. (1973). Psychological studies of the Bushmen. *Psychologia Africana,* Monograph Supplement No. 7.

Reynolds, V., Falger, V., & Vine, I. (Eds.) (1987). *The sociobiology of ethnocentrism.* London: Croom Helm.

Robertson, R. (1995). Chaos theory and the relationship between psychology and science. In R. Robertson & A. Combs (Eds.), *Chaos theory and the life sciences* (pp. 3–15). Mahwah, NJ: Erlbaum.

Robertson, R., & Combs, A. (Eds.). (1995). *Chaos theory and the life sciences.* Mahwah, NJ: Erlbaum.

Rosch (Heider) E. (1972). Universals in color naming and memory. *Journal of Experimental Psychology, 93,* 10–20.

Rosch, E. (1978). Principles of categorization. In E. Rosch & B. L. Lloyd (Eds.), *Cognition and categorization* (pp. 27–48). Hillsdale, NJ: Erlbaum.

Sahlins, M. (1977). The use and abuse of biology. London: Tavistock.

Saunders, B. A. C. (1992). *The invention of basic color terms.* Utrecht: ISOR.

Saunders, B. A. C., & Van Brakel, J. (in press). Colour: A case of scientific ekphrasis. *Behavioral and Brain Sciences.*

Schönpflug, W. (1993). Applied psychology: Newcomer with a long tradition. *Applied Psychology: An International Review, 42,* 5–66.

Schönpflug, W. (1994). Professional training in psychological departments: A critical analysis. *News from EFPPA, 8(4),* 15–17.

Scribner, S. (1979). Modes of thinking and ways of speaking: Culture and logic reconsidered. In R. O. Freedle (Ed.), *New directions in discourse processing* (pp. 223–243). Norwood, NJ: Ablex.

Scribner, S., & Cole, M. (1981). *The psychology of literacy.* Cambridge: MA: Harvard University Press.

Segall, M. H. (1993). Cultural psychology: Reactions to some claims and assertions of dubious validity. *Cross-Cultural Psychology Bulletin, 27,* 2–4.

Segall, M. H., Campbell, D. T., & Herskovitz, M. J. (1966). *The influence of culture on visual perception.* Indianapolis, IN: Bobbs-Merrill.

Segall, M. H., Dasen, P. R., Berry, J. W., & Poortinga, Y. H. (1990). *Human behavior in global perspective: An introduction to cross-cultural psychology.* New York: Pergamon.

Shweder, R. A. (1990). Cultural psychology—what is it? In J. W. Stigler, R. A. Shweder, & G. Herdt (Eds.), *Cultural psychology: Essays on comparative human development* (pp. 1–43). Cambridge: Cambridge University Press.

Shweder, R. A. (1991). *Thinking through cultures: Expeditions in cultural psychology.* Cambridge, MA: Harvard University Press.

Shweder, R. A., Mahapatra, M., & Miller, J. G. (1990). Culture and moral development. In J. W. Stigler, R. A. Shweder, & G. Herdt (Eds.), *Cultural psychology: Essays on comparative human development* (pp. 130–204). New York: Cambridge University Press.

Simons, R. C., & Hughes, C. C. (Eds.). (1985). *The culture-bound syndromes.* Dordrecht: Reidel.

Sinha, J. B. P. (1980). *The nurturant task leader.* New Delhi: Concept Publishing House.

Smith, M. B. (1994). Selfhood at risk: Postmodern perils and the perils of postmodernism. *American Psychologist, 49,* 405–511.

Smith, P. B., Bond, M. H. (1993). *Social psychology across cultures: Analysis and perspectives.* New York: Harvester Wheatsheaf.

Thelen, E. (1995). Motor development: A new synthesis. *American Psychologist, 50,* 79–95.

Tinbergen, N. (1963). On aims and methods of ethology. *Zeitschrift für Tierpsychologie, 20,* 410–433.

Tooby, J., & Cosmides, L. (1992). The psychological foundations of culture. In J. Barkow, L. Cosmides & J. Tooby (Eds.), *The adapted mind: Evolutionary psychology and the generation of culture* (pp. 19–136). New York: Oxford University Press.

Triandis, H. C. (1972). *The analysis of subjective culture.* New York: Wiley.

Triandis, H. C., Malpass, R. S., Davidson, A. (1972). Cross-cultural psychology. *Annual Review of Anthropology, 1,* 1–84.

Tulviste, P. (1991). *The cultural-historical development of verbal thinking.* Commack, NY: Nova Science Publishers.

Van de Koppel, J. M. H., & Schoots, N. H. (1986). Why are all trains in Holland painted yellow? *Nederlands Tijdschrift voor de Psychologie, 14,* 189–196.

Van de Vijver, F. J. R., & Poortinga, Y. H. (1982). Cross-cultural generalization and universality. *Journal of Cross-Cultural Psychology, 13,* 387–408.

Van de Vijver, F. J. R., & Poortinga, Y. H. (1990). A taxonomy of cultural differences. In F. J. R.

Van de Vijver & G. J. M. Hutschemaekers (Eds.), *The investigaton of culture: Current issues in cultural psychology* (pp. 91–114). Tilburg: Tilburg University Press.

Van Geert, P. (1994). *Dynamic systems of development: Change between complexity and chaos.* New York: Harvester Wheatsheaf.

Vygotsky, L. S. (1978). *Mind in society: The development of higher social processes.* Cambridge, MA: Harvard University Press.

Warren, N. (1980). Universality and plasticity, ontogeny and phylogeny. The resonance between culture and development. In J. Sants (Ed.), *Developmental psychology and society* (pp. 290–326). London: Macmillan.

Wassmann, J., & Dasen, P. R. (1994a). "Hot" and "cold": Classification and sorting among the Yupno of Papua New Guinea. *International Journal of Psychology, 29,* 19–38.

Wassmann, J., & Dasen, P. R. (1994b). Yupno number system and counting. *Journal of Cross-Cultural Psychology, 25,* 78–94.

Whiting, J. W. M. (1954). The cross-cultural method. In G. Lindzey (Ed.), *The handbook of social psychology* (Vol. 1, pp. 523–531). Reading, MA: Addison-Wesley.

Williams, J. E., & Best, D. L. (1982). *Measuring sex stereotypes: A thirty nation study.* London: Sage.

Wilson, E. O. (1975). *Sociobiology: The new synthesis.* Cambridge, MA: Holt, Rinehart and Winston.

Wundt, W. (1911/1975). *Völkerpsychologie: Eine Untersuchung der Entwicklungsgesetze von Sprache, Mythus und Sitte* (3rd ed., Vol. 1, Part 1). Stuttgart: Kröner Verlag/Aalen: Scientia Verlag.

Wundt, W. (1913). *Elemente de Völkerpsychologie* (2nd ed.). Leipzig: Alfred Kroner Verlag.

NAME INDEX

SUBJECT INDEX